Humans and Generative AI Tools for Collaborative Intelligence

Jingyuan Zhao
University of Toronto, Canada

V. Vinoth Kumar
Vellore Institute of Technology, India

Polinpapilinho F. Katina
University of South Carolina Upstate, USA

Joseph Richards
California State University, Sacramento, USA

IGI Global
Scientific Publishing
Publishing Tomorrow's Research Today

Vice President of Editorial Melissa Wagner
Director of Acquisitions Mikaela Felty
Director of Book Development Jocelynn Hessler
Production Manager Mike Brehm
Cover Design Jose Rosado

Published in the United States of America by
IGI Global Scientific Publishing
701 East Chocolate Avenue
Hershey, PA, 17033, USA
Tel: 717-533-8845
Fax: 717-533-7115
Website: https://www.igi-global.com E-mail: cust@igi-global.com

Library of Congress Cataloging-in-Publication Data

Names: Zhao, Jingyuan, 1968- editor | Venkatesan, Vinoth Kumar, 1988- editor | Katina, Polinpapilinho F. editor | Richards, Joseph, 1966- editor
Title: Humans and generative AI tools for collaborative intelligence / edited by Jingyuan Zhao, Vinoth Kumar Venkatesan, Polinpapilinho Katina, Joseph Richards.
Description: Hershey, PA : IGI Global Scientific Publishing, [2025] | Includes bibliographical references and index. | Summary: "This book is a collection of recent advancements in collaborative intelligence of humans and Generative AI tools, with a focus on state-of-the-art approaches, methodologies, and systems for the design, development, deployment, and innovative use of those technologies and applications to advance industries and organizations"-- Provided by publisher.
Identifiers: LCCN 2024051811 (print) | LCCN 2024051812 (ebook) | ISBN 9798369383322 hardcover | ISBN 9798369383339 paperback | ISBN 9798369383346 ebook
Subjects: LCSH: Artificial intelligence | Artificial intelligence--Medical applications
Classification: LCC Q335 .H787 2025 (print) | LCC Q335 (ebook) | DDC 006.3--dc23/eng/20250205
LC record available at https://lccn.loc.gov/2024051811
LC ebook record available at https://lccn.loc.gov/2024051812

British Cataloguing in Publication Data
A Cataloguing in Publication record for this book is available from the British Library.

Table of Contents

Detailed Table of Contents

This article explores artificial intelligence's role in developing metacognitive skills in educational settings. Through analysis of adaptive learning systems and AI technologies, the research demonstrates advances in personalized learning support and real-time metacognitive interventions. The study examines AI-enhanced systems like MetaTutor and Betty's Brain, which support self-regulated learning through sophisticated monitoring and feedback mechanisms. Findings show AI-supported environments can achieve 47% improvement in self-regulated learning strategies and 42% increase in strategy adjustment. Implementation challenges include accuracy in detecting metacognitive states, data privacy concerns, and balancing AI support with learner autonomy. Future developments in natural language processing, emotion recognition, and multimodal learning analytics promise enhanced support capabilities. Success requires integrating technological innovation with established pedagogical practices while maintaining ethical considerations and human oversight.

The integration of generative artificial intelligence (AI) into the education sector has the potential to change how teaching and learning occur, encouraging a new era of collaborative intelligence. This chapter addresses the transformative significance of generative AI tools in education, focusing on their ability to enhance both teaching methods and student learning experiences. By emphasizing the importance of collaborative intelligence, the study illustrates how generative AI may be deployed as a partner to both educators and learners, supporting individualized learning, real-time feedback, and adaptable curriculum design. The chapter digs into fundamental concepts and technologies behind generative AI, such as natural language processing, machine learning, and deep learning, and explains how these technologies enable AI to produce content, automate administrative processes, and provide tailored learning experiences.

The rise of generative artificial intelligence (AI) tools has significantly transformed various sectors, offering opportunities for enhanced efficiency, creativity, and decision-making. However, alongside these advancements lie profound ethical challenges that demand critical examination. This chapter, titled Ethical Considerations and Challenges in Human-AI Collaboration, explores the multifaceted ethical landscape of AI systems, emphasizing the need for fairness, accountability, transparency, data security, and societal well-being in their development and deployment.

Integrating Large Language Models (LLMs) and Retrieval-Augmented Generation (RAG) systems into business operations has become a transformative force. In the literature, the advantages as well as the disadvantages of this integration are discussed. The chapter discusses some latent risks involved in AI, namely, AI-data bias, adversarial vulnerabilities, privacy concerns, and domain-specific limitations, while putting forward methodologies for their mitigation through better data management and strong security protocols. The chapter also discusses the prospect of the future of changes that could be made in reliable and safe AI. Stitching together these divergent insights, this paper contributes to an understanding of how businesses can use LLMs and RAG systems responsibly in ways that keep AI adoption in step with meeting ethical compasses and operational integrity. It forms a core reference to guide institutions in their efforts to harness the full potential of artificial intelligence technologies in their operations regarding the intricacies involved in trust and risk management.

The rapid evolution of technology has fundamentally transformed how communication with digital platforms reshapes people's interactions. The Robotic Facilitated Virtual Communication Framework (RFVCF) represents a significant advancement in bridging the gap between human communication and digital interfaces. This framework leverages robots and AI to enhance online interactions by addressing the limitations of traditional digital communication methods. This book chapter comprehensively analyses RFVCF, exploring its historical context, key components, technological underpinnings, and potential implications across various sectors, particularly healthcare. Through this examination, the transformative potential of RFVCF in improving the quality, efficiency, and emotional depth of virtual communication is elucidated.

Combining AI with IoT transforms conventional systems into highly adaptive, data-driven, and networked intelligent ecosystems. In fact, most of the modernization drives carried out in smart cities, healthcare, manufacturing, and environmental monitoring industries are based on these very AI-IoT systems. AI-IoT integration will hit the future of technology-driven settings pretty fast through improved user experience, efficient management of resources, and real-time decision-making. This chapter covers all security, privacy, and other issues of trust that develop from the convergence of AI with IoT. It provides detailed insights into recent trends and events in privacy-enhancing technologies, such as differential privacy and federated learning. Secure protocol development and trust management schemes cannot be neglected in a trusted AI-IoT ecosystem. .he theoretical and applied approaches, hence opening up ways to some robust and reliable intelligent ecosystems that shall adapt to evolving security and privacy challenges.

As a natural interaction method, hand gesture recognition has gained increased attention, particularly for human-computer interfaces. The goal of this research work is to develop a hand gesture detection system using machine learning techniques. Rather than making direct gesture predictions, this system compares the accuracy of several models in identifying hand gestures from dataset, thereby enabling real-time gesture-based interactions. To achieve this, we employed a combination of machine learning methods, neural networks, PCA for feature reduction and data pre-processing techniques. Algorithms like K-Nearest Neighbors, Decision Trees, SVM, and Autoencoders are used for classification. The dataset used in this work is the LeapGestRecog collection, which has 20,000 grayscale images of ten distinct hand gestures. Our best-performing model, SVM with an RBF kernel and auto-encoder, attained a remarkable accuracy of 99.98% on the test dataset, indicating its robustness in classifying hand gestures accurately.

In emergencies, nearly every hospital bed was taken, forcing the collapse of the whole health department. Tragically, many patients lost their lives due to the lack of beds, ventilators, medical intensive care units,

The recent evolution of natural language processing (NLP) has introduced models like ChatGPT, capable of handling various language-related tasks. However, generic models like ChatGPT may lack accuracy in specialized fields such as healthcare or finance. Fine-tuning these models enables adaptation to specific industry domains, improving performance and relevance. This paper delves into the concept of fine-tuning ChatGPT for specialized domains, examining the technical challenges and solutions involved in the process. We also discuss real-world applications across healthcare, financial services, and education, highlighting the benefits and ethical considerations. The paper concludes with future trends in fine-tuning techniques for broader applicability.

The development of AI is based on research into the patterns and processes of human thought. Improved software and systems are developed as a direct outcome of these research initiatives. Deep learning (DL), a subfield of AI, allows computers to robotically acquire new abilities by analysing training sets, which are collections of previously received data. The AI technique known as deep reinforcement learning is very useful for autonomous UAVs. The fundamental characteristics of autonomous driving, particularly talks and human conversations, including making choices, make robotic motor vehicles the perfect fit for reinforcement learning. This paper presents a new viewpoint by exploring the AI features realized in current journals. This article aims to realize the attitude control is so important for UAVs and moreover AI controller is better than a conventional one. This article explores the abundant AI technologies that may be utilized for attitude control, path planning and obstacle avoidance of UAVs with many applications. Illustrates the way AI in UAV systems on an everyday basis.

The era of rapid developments in artificial intelligence increased the potential of intelligent, autonomous, and multi-agent systems to collaborate on an unprecedented scale. This chapter covers the basics and applications of MAS in collaborative contexts, with a focus on generative AI tools and human-AI interaction. The chapter starts with a definition of multi-agent systems and underlines how autonomous

E-collaboration technologies, which enable individuals and teams to work together across distances and time zones, are essential for modern organizations. With the integration of Generative AI, these technologies are evolving to provide more dynamic and adaptive collaborative environments. Generative AI tools can enhance productivity with automation, summarizing discussions, and generating data-driven insights in real time. These tools enable more efficient communication through the creation of language models that can translate languages, generate reports, and even simulate brainstorming sessions with virtual teams. These advancements improve productivity, foster innovation, and enhance inclusivity by breaking language barriers and providing accessibility features. However, challenges such as data privacy, ethical concerns, and over-reliance on AI must be addressed to ensure responsible use. By combining the power of e-collaboration technologies and Generative AI, organizations can achieve a smarter, more connected, and ethically responsible future of work.

The present globe benefits from the unprecedented growth of science and technology. The invention of Artificial Intelligence (AI) has opened a vast horizon of possibilities, choices, and capabilities for humans and society. AI-powered human-like systems provide substantial interaction and collaboration for better results in many fields. The speed, efficiency, and effectiveness of AI systems prompted almost all sectors, like healthcare, education, transport, and communication to invest in them. This resulted in shifting attention from human-human collective intelligence to human-AI collaborative intelligence. This shift has significantly contributed to many fields and reduces the security risks to humans. However, there are also many ethical and legal concerns in this innovative area, like data privacy, transparency issues, liability, and accountability. This chapter, using analytical and critical methods, examines the functioning of collaborative intelligence and suggests the required ethical and legal principles for incorporation into national and international policy design.

This technology ranging from text and images to music and complex simulations., unique instances that are indistinguishable from those created by humans. This capacity has vast implications, literature, scientific research. The effectiveness of human-AI collaboration depends on the ability to balance the strengths and weaknesses of each participant. Therefore, successful collaboration involves leveraging AI to handle data-heavy tasks and provide creative inputs, while humans guide the process with their judgment, intuition, and ethical considerations. This partnership can lead to significant advancements, such as more personalized content creation, enhanced problem-solving capabilities, and innovative solutions to complex challenges. Issues of authorship, originality, and the ethical implications of using AI-generated content need to be addressed. As AI systems become more advanced, determining the boundaries of human and machine contributions becomes increasingly complex.

Abstract This study explores the integration of generative AI tools—ChatGPT, Canva, InVideo AI, and InShot—into educational environments, aiming to enhance collaborative intelligence and support personalized learning. The methodology combines case studies, hands-on development guidelines, and user testing to assess the practical applications of these tools in real-world educational settings. Key findings reveal that these AI tools foster interactive learning, creativity, and collaboration by enabling personalized tutoring, content creation, and video production. Additionally, the tools promote critical thinking and student engagement. However, challenges such as ethical considerations, data privacy, and the need for teacher training were identified. The study concludes that generative AI has the potential to transform education by merging human creativity with machine intelligence, offering more dynamic and inclusive learning experiences. It emphasizes the importance of addressing ethical concerns and providing adequate support to educators for effective AI integration.

Generative Artificial Intelligence is transforming customer objection management by enabling personalized, real-time, and adaptive interactions. This chapter examines the role of generative AI in addressing objections through predictive modeling, leveraging historical data, and sentiment analysis to enhance response relevance and customer satisfaction. Ethical considerations, including transparency, bias reduction, and human oversight, are discussed to ensure responsible AI implementation. A proposed framework integrates AI's adaptability with hybrid human-AI collaboration, highlighting its effectiveness in managing complex or sensitive objections. Comparative case studies reveal generative AI's strengths in scalability and adaptability across industries, while also addressing its limitations in high-context scenarios. The chapter concludes with managerial insights, emphasizing ethical AI practices, industry-specific customizations, and predictive analytics as key to balancing automation with human-centric approaches for trust and effectiveness in customer interactions.

P. Ashok, Symbiosis Institute of Digital and Telecom Management, India
Tanisha Mangal, Symbiosis Institute of Digital and Telecom Management, India
Lakshmi Sridevi, Chennai Institute of Technology, India
Krishna K. Murali, Rajalakshmi Engineering College, India

Generative AI, a subset of artificial intelligence, is dedicated to the development of models that are capable of producing new content, including text, imagery, audio, and entire virtual worlds. Generative AI is capable of replicating human creativity and generating outputs that were previously considered to be exclusively the domain of human intelligence by utilizing sophisticated machine learning techniques, including deep learning and neural networks. AI models in the music industry are capable of composing music in a variety of genres, providing musicians and producers with new tools. Generative AI has the potential to stimulate innovation and creativity in a variety of disciplines as technology continues to develop. This research article delves deep into the various aspects of Generative AI namely history and core concepts, privacy and security, types of Generative AI models and their applications, NLP models and finally on Responsible AI.

J. Krishna Charan, Vel Tech Rangarajan Dr. Sagunthala R&D Institute of Science and Technology, USA
Sudhanshu Chandra, Maulana Azad National Urdu University, India
V. Vaissnave, SRM Institute of Science and Technology, India
T. Ragupathi, SRM Institute of Science and Technology, India
Pamarthi Satyanarayana, Vel Tech University, India
P. Selvakumar, Department of Science and Humanities, Nehru Institute of Technology, Coimbatore, India
T. C. Manjunath, Rajarajeswari College of Engineering, India

At its core, generative AI uses machine learning techniques, generate outputs such as text, images, music, and even complex designs. Techniques commonly employed t high-quality content. Vast learn outputs that mimic or extend the patterns observed in the data. For instance, in the creative industries, generative AI can design logos, compose music, or generate photorealistic images, artistic expression creation. Technology sector, generative AI is accelerating product development and innovation. AI-driven tools can automate the design process, optimize software code, and even assist in creating new hardware prototypes. This automation not only speeds up development cycles but also reduces costs and enhances precision. For example, AI algorithms can variations, enabling broader refine products more effectively. The financial sector benefits from generative AI through improved risk management, fraud detection, generate predictive models, enhancing decision-making processes and risk assessment.

Preface

INTRODUCTION

Generative Artificial Intelligence (AI) is a cutting-edge branch of artificial intelligence that revolves around the creation of autonomous systems capable of producing content that is original, creative, and indistinguishable from human-generated output. Recent breakthroughs in the field have the potential to drastically change the way we approach content creation. Unlike traditional AI models, which primarily focus on data analysis and pattern recognition, Generative AI seeks to simulate human creativity and generate content autonomously, and therefore, Generative AI holds immense potential to reshape various industries and human-machine interactions. Collaboration between humans and Generative AI tools offers a multitude of benefits and advantages in the field of AI development and its real-world applications, revolutionizing the way we approach problem-solving, decision-making, and innovation in various industries (e.g., healthcare, finance, manufacturing, customer service, education, content creation, transportation, space exploration). The collaborative synergy between humans and Generative AI tools not only paves the path towards achieving artificial general intelligence but also fosters a future where AI augments and complements human intelligence.

Today, humans and Generative AI tools are joining forces (Wilson & Daugherty, 2018a; 2018b). Generative AI fosters collaboration between humans and machines by augmenting human creativity and productivity. With advancements in Generative AI, human and Generative AI collaboration for business will likely grow exponentially in the coming years. Meanwhile, this is raising reasonable fears that AI will ultimately replace human workers throughout the economy. Never before have digital tools been so responsive to us, nor we to our tools (Kock, 2005; 2008; Ghobakhloo & Hong, 2015; Bidgoli, 2012; Abrantes, et al., 2018). Ethical considerations and potential impact of human and Generative AI collaboration are raising challenges to both industry and academia. While Generative AI tools will radically alter how work gets done and who does it, the technology's larger impact will be in complementing and augmenting human capabilities, not replacing them. To take full advantage of this collaboration, organizations must understand how humans can most effectively augment machines, how machines can enhance what humans do best, and how to redesign business processes to support the partnership.

CHAPTER OVERVIEW

This book is a collection of recent advancements in collaborative intelligence of humans and Generative AI tools, with a focus on state-of-the-art approaches, methodologies, and systems for the design, development, deployment, and innovative use of those technologies and applications to advance industries and organizations. This book comprehensively explores human and Generative AI collaborative intelligence, not only studying applications, types, benefits, functions, concerns and trends of human and Generative AI collaboration, but also developing guidelines to help industries and organizations achieve the collaborative intelligence of humans and Generative AI tools and put the power of collaborative intelligence to work. The book is organized into 23 chapters. A synopsis of each chapter is given below.

Chapter 1 (*Beyond Adaptive Learning: Harnessing AI for Metacognitive Skill Development*) explores artificial intelligence's role in developing metacognitive skills in educational settings. Findings show AI-supported environments can achieve 47% improvement in self-regulated learning strategies and 42% increase in strategy adjustment. Implementation challenges include accuracy in detecting metacognitive states, data privacy concerns, and balancing AI support with learner autonomy.

Chapter 2 (*Generative AI and Education: Transforming Teaching and Learning through Collaborative Intelligence*) digs into fundamental concepts and technologies behind generative AI, such as natural language processing, machine learning, and deep learning, and explains how these technologies enable AI to produce content, automate administrative processes, and provide tailored learning experiences.

Chapter 3 (*Ethical Considerations and Challenges in Human-AI Collaboration*) explores the multifaceted ethical landscape of AI systems, emphasizing the need for fairness, accountability, transparency, data security, and societal well-being in their development and deployment.

Chapter 4 (*Are LLMs and RAG Trustworthy Enough for Your Business? A Deep Dive into AI's Reliability*) discusses some latent risks involved in AI, namely, AI-data bias, adversarial vulnerabilities, privacy concerns, and domain-specific limitations, while putting forward methodologies for their mitigation through better data management and strong security protocols. The chapter also discusses the prospect of the future of changes that could be made in reliable and safe AI.

Chapter 5 (*Revolutionizing Virtual Communication - The Impact of Robotic-Facilitated Frameworks*) comprehensively analyses RFVCF, exploring its historical context, key components, technological underpinnings, and potential implications across various sectors, particularly healthcare. Through this examination, the transformative potential of RFVCF in improving the quality, efficiency, and emotional depth of virtual communication is elucidated.

Chapter 6 (*Security, privacy, and trust of AI-IoT convergent smart system*) covers all security, privacy, and other issues of trust that develop from the convergence of AI with IoT. It provides detailed insights into recent trends and events in privacy-enhancing technologies, such as differential privacy and federated learning. Secure protocol development and trust management schemes cannot be neglected in a trusted AI-IoT ecosystem.

Chapter 7 (*Investigation on Generative Autoencoders for Hand Gesture Recognition*) employs a combination of machine learning methods, neural networks, PCA for feature reduction and data pre-processing techniques. The best-performing model, SVM with an RBF kernel and auto-encoder, attained a remarkable accuracy of 99.98% on the test dataset, indicating its robustness in classifying hand gestures accurately.

Chapter 8 (*Revolutionizing Emergency Medical Services with AI and Telegram Integration*) discusses the main problem surrounding hospitals and one possible solution to this problem is a system that gathers data about hospitals and medical systems' availability from a centralised server page that links to all nearby hospitals. The system then uses artificial neural networks to analyse the patient's condition with the help of the LSAI48266X AI board.

Chapter 9 (*Plant Disease Detection Using Generative AI and Deep Learning Models*) is to make the Cassava Plant Disease Prediction from the given input image and tell whether the provided sample is infected with the certain disease or not. Authors build the Model with the Convolution Neural Network, Visual Geometry Group 16, ResNet50, EfficientNetB0, Visual Transformer, and Variational Auto-encoder.

Chapter 10 (*Impact of Generative AI on industries*) presents a detailed overview of both the opportunities and challenges of integrating Generative AI into the modern business landscape, as well as insights into emerging trends that will likely shape the future of businesses and organizations in the age of intelligent machines.

Chapter 11 (*The Fine-Tuning Journey of ChatGPT in Industry Applications: Domains from Generic to Specific*) delves into the concept of fine-tuning ChatGPT for specialized domains, examining the technical challenges and solutions involved in the process. We also discuss real-world applications across healthcare, financial services, and education, highlighting the benefits and ethical considerations. The paper concludes with future trends in fine-tuning techniques for broader applicability.

Chapter 12 (*Examination of The Recent Research Trends on Controllers in the AI Powered UAV*) aims to realize the attitude control is so important for UAVs and moreover AI controller is better than a conventional one. This article explores the abundant AI technologies that may be utilized for attitude control, path planning and obstacle avoidance of UAVs with many applications. Illustrates the way AI in UAV systems on an everyday basis.

Chapter 13 (*Intelligent, autonomous and multi agents*) looks at real-world applications where MAS increases human capabilities and offers cooperative solutions in settings that require high levels of co-operation and adaptation. We discuss various ethical, safety, and interoperability issues arising in MAS during the investigation of these interactions, especially with generative AI tools working with human partners.

Chapter 14 (*Enhancing Quantum Random Number Generators, Cryptographic Security and Machine Learning-Based Cryptoanalysis*) claims that the integration of machine learning (ML) with QRNGs further enhances their effectiveness, optimizing random sequences for improved speed and security. This combination of QRNGs and ML provides a powerful approach to cryptography, ensuring more secure communication channels and better protection against potential attacks.

Chapter 15 (*Human-Machine Interactions Evolution, Current Applications, and Future Prospects*) claims that the newest technology is the Brain Computer Interface (BCI) where the user is plugged into the machine; BCI technology is also helpful for users with disabilities to directly interact with a machine. Other HMI technology that is noteworthy is haptic interfaces, tangible interfaces and social robots, these types of systems help to foster usability and trustworthiness.

Chapter 16 (*E-Collaboration Technologies with Generative AI Tools*) proposes that E-collaboration tools enable more efficient communication through the creation of language models. These advancements improve productivity, foster innovation, and enhance inclusivity by breaking language barriers and providing accessibility features. By combining the power of e-collaboration technologies and Generative AI, organizations can achieve a smarter, more connected, and ethically responsible future of work.

Chapter 17 (*Human-AI Collaborative Intelligence: Ethical and Legal Considerations*) claims that there are many ethical and legal concerns in this innovative area, like data privacy, transparency issues, liability, and accountability. This chapter, using analytical and critical methods, examines the functioning of collaborative intelligence and suggests the required ethical and legal principles for incorporation into national and international policy design.

Chapter 18 (*Applications of Generative AI and Human-AI Collaboration*) claims that successful collaboration involves leveraging AI to handle data-heavy tasks and provide creative inputs, while humans guide the process with their judgment, intuition, and ethical considerations. Issues of authorship, originality, and the ethical implications of using AI-generated content need to be addressed. As AI systems become more advanced, determining the boundaries of human and machine contributions becomes increasingly complex.

Chapter 19 (*Generative AI Tools and Education: Enabling Collaborative Intelligence through ChatGPT, Canva, InVideo AI, and InShot*) concludes that generative AI has the potential to transform education by merging human creativity with machine intelligence, offering more dynamic and inclusive learning experiences. It emphasizes the importance of addressing ethical concerns and providing adequate support to educators for effective AI integration.

Chapter 20 (*Generative AI and Intelligent Processing of Customer Oppositions: Prospecting for Research Trends*) concludes with managerial insights, emphasizing ethical AI practices, industry-specific customizations, and predictive analytics as key to balancing automation with human-centric approaches for trust and effectiveness in customer interactions.

Chapter 21 (*Unlocking New Potentials in Generative AI*) delves deep into the various aspects of Generative AI namely history and core concepts, privacy and security, types of Generative AI models and their applications, NLP models and finally on Responsible AI.

Chapter 22 (Impact of Generative AI on Industries and Organizations) claims that AI algorithms can variations, enabling broader refine products more effectively. The financial sector benefits from generative AI through improved risk management, fraud detection, generate predictive models, enhancing decision-making processes and risk assessment.

Jingyuan Zhao
University of Toronto, Canada

V. Vinoth Kumar
Vellore Institute of Technology, India

Polinpapilinho F. Katina
University of South Carolina Upstate, USA

Joseph Richards
California State University, Sacramento, USA

REFERENCES

Abrantes, C., Óscar, M., Diogo, G., João, P. B., & José, F. (2018). Human-centric design of unified communications: E-collaboration. *International Journal of e-Collaboration*, *14*(2), 1–18. DOI: 10.4018/IJeC.2018040101

Bidgoli, H. (2012). E-collaboration: New productivity tool for the twenty-first century and beyond. *Business Strategy Series*, *13*(4), 147–153. DOI: 10.1108/17515631211246212

Ghobakhloo, M., & Hong, T. S. (2015). The business value of information system-enabled e-collaboration. *International Journal of e-Collaboration*, *11*(1), 22–56. DOI: 10.4018/ijec.2015010103

Kock, N. (2005). Media richness or media naturalness? The evolution of our biological communication apparatus and its influence on our behavior toward e-communication tools. *IEEE Transactions on Professional Communication*, *48*(2), 117–130. DOI: 10.1109/TPC.2005.849649

Kock, N. (2008). Designing e-collaboration technologies to facilitate compensatory adaptation designing e-collaboration technologies. *Information Systems Management*, *25*(1), 14–19. DOI: 10.1080/10580530701777115

Wilson, H. J., & Daugherty, P. R. (2018a). Collaborative intelligence: Humans and ai are joining forces. *Harvard Business Review*, *96*(4), 114–123.

Wilson, H. J., & Daugherty, P. R. (2018b). *Human + Machine: Reimagining Work in the Age of AI*. Harvard Business Review Press.

Chapter 1
Beyond Adaptive Learning:
Harnessing AI for Metacognitive Skill Development

Tetiana Suvorova
https://orcid.org/0000-0002-0209-6785
CY Cergy Paris Université, France

Muhammet Demirbilek
Süleyman Demirel University, Turkey

ABSTRACT

This article explores artificial intelligence's role in developing metacognitive skills in educational settings. Through analysis of adaptive learning systems and AI technologies, the research demonstrates advances in personalized learning support and real-time metacognitive interventions. The study examines AI-enhanced systems like MetaTutor and Betty's Brain, which support self-regulated learning through sophisticated monitoring and feedback mechanisms. Findings show AI-supported environments can achieve 47% improvement in self-regulated learning strategies and 42% increase in strategy adjustment. Implementation challenges include accuracy in detecting metacognitive states, data privacy concerns, and balancing AI support with learner autonomy. Future developments in natural language processing, emotion recognition, and multimodal learning analytics promise enhanced support capabilities. Success requires integrating technological innovation with established pedagogical practices while maintaining ethical considerations and human oversight.

1. INTRODUCTION

Artificial intelligence (AI) has emerged as a transformative force in education, reshaping how students learn, teachers instruct, and institutions operate in the learning and teaching process. AI in education is not a new phenomenon. AI in education is evolving from simple computer-assisted instruction in the 1960s and 1970s to the complex AI-powered teaching and learning tools of today. Advancements in AI technologies are dramatically changing teaching and learning experiences, offering personalized learning experiences and smart tutoring systems to virtual assistants.AI is transforming education by enhancing

DOI: 10.4018/979-8-3693-8332-2.ch001

learning, teaching, and administration. Its ability to analyze vast data sets is reshaping traditional practices and introducing innovative approaches (Adiguzel, Kaya & Cansu, 2023; Dubé & Wen, 2022).

One of the most important contributions of artificial intelligence technologies to educational environments is the ability to tailor learning experiences according to individual needs, thanks to the powerful processors and graphics cards produced by technological development. AI-supported learning platforms, also known as personalized learning, take into account the individual characteristics of each student, such as learning speed and learning style, and adjust and organize the teaching content in real time. AI tailors educational experiences to individual students by analyzing their learning patterns and needs. Adaptive platforms provide customized content, feedback, and recommendations, enabling students to learn at their own pace and improve academic success. (Chan & Hu, 2023).

AI automates time-consuming tasks such as enrollment, scheduling, and grading. This reduces administrative workloads, allowing educators to focus on curriculum development and personalized student support, thereby increasing overall efficiency (Al-Surmi, Bashiri, & Koliousis, 2022; Bo, et al., 2023). AI processes student performance data to identify challenges and recommend targeted interventions. It generates reports and visualizations, enabling educators to make informed decisions and improve learning outcomes through timely actions (Chowdhury, et al., 2023). While AI offers significant benefits in education, challenges such as ethical considerations and equitable access must also be addressed to maximize its potential. AI surpasses humans in computational power, excelling at processing vast amounts of data, identifying patterns, and predicting outcomes. However, it falls short in understanding common-sense scenarios, making intuitive decisions, and handling novel situations—areas where humans excel. By combining these complementary strengths with advancements in AI's conversational abilities and situational awareness, collaborative intelligence holds significant potential to enhance performance across various domains.

1. Adaptive learning and Artificial Intelligence

Adaptive learning refers to the use of educational technology tools designed to adjust the content, learning speed, and learning path to match each learner's performance and learning style. Adaptive learning systems utilize data and algorithms to create personalized learning settings to address the strengths and weaknesses of the learner. Adaptive learning aims to enhance student engagement and maximize learning outcomes through a customized approach.Adaptive learning systems analyze data from learner's actions in the learning setting such as assessments, quizzes, writings, and responses to adjust the difficulty level of the content and provide relevant resources. The way the adaptive learning system works enables students to receive the appropriate content, and guidance to improve their learning experience. Adaptive learning systems provide real-time feedback to learners to figure out areas for improvement and the mistakes made, if any, and how these mistakes can be corrected. The real-time feedback may help learners to understand their current learning curve and adjust their learning path. Furthermore, adaptive learning systems may provide additional materials to help the subjects that have been learned incompletely or are realized to be missing by providing additional materials.

In the field of education, AI-based adaptive learning systems can provide learning experiences tailored to the needs of students. Adaptive learning conceptual framework focus on five differencet components of adaptive learning. The Adaptive Source (Learner Model) (Vandewaetere et al., 2011). tailors learning based on cognitive, affective, and behavioral characteristics, including knowledge, preferences, and motivation (Martin & Markant, 2020). The Adaptive Target consists of the Content Model (Martin &

Markant, 2020), which structures subject matter delivery, and the Instructional Model (Martin & Markant, 2020), which adapts instruction using AI-based algorithms. The Adaptive Engine (Vandewaetere et al., 2011), powered by AI, sequences content dynamically, adjusting based on learner progress. This system personalizes education through techniques like pacing, scaffolding, and sequencing, ensuring learning builds on prior knowledge.

AI-based adaptive learning systems use artificial intelligence algorithms to provide a learning experience that is unique to each individual student. AI-supported adaptive learning environments analyze the student's knowledge level, learning speed, learning preferences and strengths/weaknesses, and according to the results of this analysis, a fully personalized learning environment is prepared for the student (Khotimah, Rusijono,& Mariono, 2024).

Thanks to the features of AI-supported adaptive learning environments, it provides a more effective and efficient learning environment for students. By identifying the subjects that the student has difficulty in, AI-based adaptive learning systems provide opportunities for the student to practice more and more. In addition, it allows students to focus more on the subjects they are interested in and good at. In this way, students' motivation to learn increases and they can make progress more quickly.

The basic working principle of AI-powered adaptive learning environments is to analyze student data and provide a personalized learning experience based on it. These systems determine the student's level of knowledge by recording the questions and answers given to the student. It also analyzes the learner's learning speed and learning preferences to identify topics that the learner struggles with, and analyzes and provides content flow and content level based on individualized data. The system focuses on the student's mistakes and shortcomings and provides more practice. Thus, it spends less time on the subjects the student is good at. In this way, the student's learning process is optimized and he/she progresses in learning effectively.

AI-supported adaptive learning environments have many advantages. First, it offers the learner a fully personalized learning experience and adapts to individual needs. This increases student motivation and makes the learning process more efficient.

AI-supported adaptive learning environments continuously monitor the student's performance and progress. This provides feedback to the student and helps them focus on their weaknesses. By following the student's progress, the teaching content can be changed according to individual learning needs.

AI-supported adaptive learning environments have a scalable system. This allows a teacher to monitor multiple students at the same time. It also provides teachers with more comprehensive data about students' progress.

There are also disadvantages of AI-supported adaptive learning environments. To achieve accurate results in AI-supported adaptive learning environments, accurate data is needed. Incorrect or incomplete data entry can lead to incorrect results. Therefore, accurate and reliable data must be provided for the system to be reliable

For some students, AI-supported adaptive learning environments may not be able to replace a teacher. Students sometimes need emotional, social or motivational support. AI adaptive learning environments may not be able to provide such support.

In language education, for example, the use of AI-supported adaptive learning environments is increasing. AI-supported adaptive learning environments are being developed to improve students' grammar, reading comprehension and writing skills. Thus, it provides text-based questions to improve students' ability to understand and analyze written texts. In addition, students' language skills can also be improved through questions on grammar rules and vocabulary.

AI-supported adaptive learning environments have great potential in the field of education. It optimizes learning by providing students with a fully personalized learning experience. However, it is important to use the right data and meet the emotional and social needs of students. When used in Turkish education, it can help students improve their language skills. The use of AI-supported adaptive learning environments is increasing and its role in education will become even more important in the coming years.

For instance, a comprehensive meta-analysis examined the overall effect of AI-enabled adaptive learning systems on students' cognitive learning outcomes compared to non-adaptive methods. The findings suggest that these systems significantly enhance educational efficiency, leading to higher pass rates and improved student retention (Wang et al, 2024).

Furthermore, empirical evidence supports the claim that AI-driven adaptive learning technologies significantly improve educational efficiency. The implementation of such platforms has been associated with higher pass rates and improved student retention compared to traditional teaching methods (Strielkowsk, et al, 2024).

2. Theoretical Foundations .Understanding Metacognition

The prefix "meta" indicates a higher level of abstraction that describes thinking about the subject matter itself. Metacognition, traditionally defined as 'thinking about thinking' or 'cognition about cognition,' encompasses the awareness and control individuals have over their cognitive processes (Flavell, 1979). More recently, researchers have expanded this definition, with Schraw and Moshman (1995) establishing a comprehensive framework that distinguishes between knowledge about cognition and regulation of cognition. This expanded understanding is particularly significant as many educational programs are based on self-directed learning, where knowledge of cognitive structures and their control is essential.

The key components of metacognitive theories are grounded in a systems approach to receiving, categorizing, and processing knowledge. These components include: metacognitive knowledge (understanding of one's own cognitive processes), metacognitive regulation (active control over these processes), and metacognitive experiences (real-time awareness during cognitive tasks). These concepts were first articulated in the foundational work on metacognition by John Flavell in the 1970s, who initially studied metamemory in children (Flavell & Wellman, 1977). His research framework identified four key components: metacognitive knowledge, metacognitive experiences, goals/tasks, and actions/strategies.

To illustrate metacognition in practice, consider a student approaching a complex physics problem: First, they engage in metacognitive knowledge by recognizing the specific domain (general physics, thermodynamics, electromagnetism, or quantum physics). Next, they experience metacognitive awareness while determining the most effective formula approach. Finally, they set specific goals and implement step-by-step calculations and graphical representations.

Recent developments (post-2000) have expanded metacognition into several specialized domains:

a) Self-Regulated Learning (Zimmerman & Schunk, 2011) involves active monitoring and adjustment of learning strategies. For example, medical students using spaced repetition software for anatomy studies actively monitor their comprehension and adjust study intervals. Learner-oriented platforms facilitate self-directed "feedback loops" that enable students to monitor effectiveness and adapt their learning approaches. This process requires proactive and self-motivated learners.

b) Social Metacognition (Jost, Kruglanski, & Nelson, 1998) recognizes metacognitive thinking as inherently social. While self-knowledge can derive from various sources, understanding others' thinking begins with perceiving information they produce. Both processes rely on similar cognitive procedures. For example, research team members assess both their own understanding and their colleagues' expertise, offering recommendations for relevant literature to address knowledge gaps.
c) Metacognitive Control, as conceptualized by Nelson and Narens (2004) in their framework of metacognitive monitoring and control, views metacognition as an inseparable process..." that connects to enactivism, viewing metacognition as inseparable from the context in which it occurs. As Maturana and Varela (1987, p. 27) assert, "all doing is knowing and all knowing is doing." This perspective emphasizes the practical application of knowledge for achieving defined purposes. For instance, when an IT developer debugs code, they continuously evaluate progress and adjust strategies to achieve optimal software functionality.

The theory posits that individuals follow specific steps when consciously and purposefully engaging with information through categorization, systematization, and assessment. These stages are detailed below:

The metacognitive process unfolds through three distinct but interconnected phases. The planning phase initiates the process, where individuals establish goals, select appropriate strategies, allocate resources, and manage time. During this stage, researchers typically develop detailed methodologies and establish timelines before beginning data collection, often utilizing mental maps or visual representations to organize their approach.

The monitoring phase involves continuous evaluation of progress through process tracking, comprehension verification, error detection, and strategy assessment. Writers exemplify this phase when they regularly review their work to ensure logical flow and alignment with intended objectives, often utilizing contemporary tools like social media platforms to gather immediate reader feedback on their ideas.

The evaluation phase completes the cycle through comprehensive analysis of outcomes, strategy effectiveness, goal achievement, and future improvement opportunities. Chess players demonstrate this phase when analyzing completed games to identify critical decision points and alternative strategies, while writers integrate reader feedback and stakeholder input to inform their future work. This systematic approach to metacognition enables individuals to continuously refine their cognitive processes and improve learning outcomes through structured self-reflection and adjustment.

2. BRIDGING METACOGNITION AND ARTIFICIAL INTELLIGENCE

The evolution of Intelligent Tutoring Systems (ITS) demonstrates the growing convergence between metacognitive theory and artificial intelligence applications in education. Seminal research by Anderson et al. (1985, as cited in VanLehn, 2011) compared the effectiveness of three instructional approaches: human tutoring, computer tutoring systems, and independent study with materials but no tutoring. Their findings revealed comparable effectiveness between human tutoring (d=0.79) and ITS (d=0.76), both significantly outperforming non-tutored instruction (d=0.3).

The development of ITS has progressed through distinct generations. The first generation (1970s-1990s) primarily emphasized domain knowledge and basic feedback mechanisms, achieving modest improvements in student performance (d=0.42). These early systems, characterized by rule-based feedback and fixed learning paths, represented a significant advancement in distance education accessibility despite their limited adaptive capabilities.

The second generation (1990s-2010) marked a substantial improvement through the integration of cognitive and student modeling approaches. Koedinger and Corbett (2006) documented that these advanced systems achieved effectiveness levels comparable to human instruction (d=0.76), demonstrating the potential of AI in educational contexts. This improvement was further validated by Ma et al. (2014), whose meta-analysis of large-scale implementations showed significant achievement gains (d=0.71) across multiple educational institutions.

Contemporary ITS platforms demonstrate increasingly sophisticated applications of these principles. Aleven et al. (2016) documented the evolution of help-seeking mechanisms in intelligent tutoring systems, finding that adaptive support significantly improves both immediate learning outcomes and long-term metacognitive development. This research highlighted the importance of carefully designed help systems that balance immediate assistance with opportunities for independent problem-solving.

The integration of AI in educational environments has expanded beyond traditional subject-matter tutoring. Nye et al. (2018) reviewed 17 years of natural language tutoring development, revealing how AI-driven systems have evolved to support not only content mastery but also metacognitive skill development. Their analysis demonstrated that modern systems can effectively adapt to individual learning patterns while promoting self-regulated learning strategies. These findings align with VanLehn's (2011) research on mathematics education, which showed that AI-driven adaptive systems can achieve outcomes comparable to human tutoring when implementing sophisticated feedback and scaffolding mechanisms.

Recent research has particularly emphasized the role of integrated assessment and feedback systems in supporting metacognitive development. Ma et al. (2014) found that the most effective systems combine immediate performance feedback with metacognitive prompts, helping students develop both domain knowledge and learning strategies. This dual focus on content and metacognition represents a significant advancement from earlier generations of educational technology, suggesting promising directions for future development in AI-supported learning environments.

B. Real-time Metacognitive Prompting: Advancing Intelligent Learning Support Recent advances in artificial intelligence have revolutionized the capability of educational systems to provide timely metacognitive support. Research by Thompson et al. (2023) demonstrates that AI-driven metacognitive prompting systems can achieve up to 84% accuracy in detecting moments of student confusion and uncertainty, representing a significant advancement over traditional fixed-timing interventions. The authors described the results of their experiment with 246 participants (114 identified as female, 130 identified as male, 2 identified as non-binary; M = 39.85 years, SD = 14.53) who solved 20 mathematical tasks with and without the help of AI (ChatGPT). The purpose was to find out the metacognitive accuracy of the participants in their task-solving efforts with the help of AI. To develop and optimize human-AI interaction, it is important to understand how users control and use their cognitive and metacognitive skills to achieve the best results. The study found that participants with higher capacity to solve tasks without AI underestimated their ability to monitor their performance assessment, while participants who used only AI overestimated their increased confidence but decreased the accuracy of self-assessment. The results suggest a need to develop AI-based platforms that can offer better interfaces to enhance metacognition and more accurately monitor user performance (Thompson et al., 2023).

Recognition of Cognitive-Emotional States Modern AI systems employ sophisticated algorithms to detect and respond to learners' cognitive-emotional states. According to Chen and Wilson (2022), successful detection relies on three primary indicators: behavioral patterns (response times, mouse movements, keystrokes), physiological signals (eye movements, facial expressions), and performance metrics (error patterns, help-seeking behaviors). This is possible due to the development of hybrid AI models that combine data-based and knowledge-based approaches, enabling the recognition of emotions, prediction of learner states, and offering appropriate system behaviors, such as in digital platforms for self-education. Particularly impressive are the commercial student-based AI education platforms that can work with disabled children, such as robots supporting children on the autism spectrum (Alabdulkareem et al., 2022). Some AI approaches can also help diagnose learning disabilities like ADHD (Anuradha et al., 2010), dyslexia (Benfatto et al., 2016), and dysgraphia (Asselborn et al., 2020).

The integration of multimodal data streams has improved the accuracy of confusion detection by 47% compared to single-source monitoring systems (Baker & Martinez, 2023). This enhanced accuracy enables more precise and timely interventions. The authors envision the role of AI in constructing smart cities, where the communication of the Internet of Things (IoT) is governed by AI. For example, in a smart city [Fig.2], the signals from different technologies are analyzed by AI, and predictions of needs for water supply or road building are made long before the problem moment arrives (Alahi et al., 2023).

Automated Prompting Systems As mentioned, the multimodal AI systems for educational purposes have promising futures for enhancing learner performance. In a recent article, Sun et al. (2024) described the effectiveness of using Latent Profile Analysis (LPA) to identify EFL learners' metacognitive experience profiles. They employed a specially developed Metacognitive Experiences Questionnaire (Sun et al., 2021) to assess the metacognitive experiences of 423 non-English-major undergraduates from a university in northeastern China. Following the guidelines established by Muthén and Muthén (2017), the researchers systematically conducted model comparisons by evaluating each profile model (k) against its predecessor (k-1). In assessing model fit, lower values of AIC, BIC, and ABIC were considered indicators of better model fitness. Additionally, the LMRT and BLRT tests provided critical information through their p-values, where non-significant results ($p > .05$) suggested that the simpler model (with one fewer group) was more appropriate for the data structure (Chen et al., 2022; Wang et al., 2021).

This methodological approach ensures a rigorous and systematic evaluation of profile solutions, allowing for the identification of the most parsimonious and statistically sound model to represent metacognitive experience patterns.

This longitudinal study provides pioneering empirical evidence of metacognitive development in tertiary-level EFL writers, demonstrating significant changes in their metacognitive experiences, including judgments, feelings, task-specific knowledge, and strategies throughout a semester (Table 1). While previous research has primarily focused on metacognitive development in children's learning processes (Baker, 1994; Teng & Zhang, 2021), this study uniquely contributes to the field by documenting how adult L2 learners' metacognitive experiences evolve over time in naturalistic classroom settings, supporting Garner's (1987) proposition about the progression from strategically naïve to metacognitively sophisticated states.

Recent studies have demonstrated the effectiveness of automated prompting systems for enhancing the metacognitive competencies of educational platform users. Kim et al. (2023) found that AI-driven prompts resulted in a 38% improvement in self-regulation, 42% increase in strategy adjustment, and 45% enhancement in learning outcomes.

The sophistication of these systems lies in their ability to determine not just when to intervene, but how. "Successful prompting systems must balance the frequency and intensity of interventions to avoid cognitive overload while maintaining engagement" (Rodriguez & Smith, 2022). The integrative approach of monitoring different signals allows AI platforms to analyze learner behavior, predict their physiological and emotional state, and provide multimodal data integration.

Research by Zhang and Lee (2023) identifies key data sources for effective metacognitive support systems, including:

- Facial expression recognition technology can detect emotional states with up to 85% accuracy (Chen & Wilson, 2022)
- Eye-tracking studies have revealed distinct cognitive state patterns (Rodriguez et al., 2023)
- Posture analysis can predict engagement levels with 72% accuracy (Baker & Martinez, 2023)
- Typing patterns, mouse movements, and screen navigation behaviors provide insights into cognitive and metacognitive processes (Kim et al., 2023; Zhang & Lee, 2023)

Performance metrics and learning analytics also play a key role in AI-user interactions. Anderson and Park (2023) outline three critical areas of performance analysis: response accuracy, time-on-task metrics, and help-seeking behaviors.

The integration of these data streams has led to significant improvements in learning support systems. Wilson et al. (2023) report that "multimodal learning analytics systems show a 47% improvement in detecting learning difficulties compared to single-stream analysis approaches."

Current trends suggest continued advancement in multimodal learning analytics, including enhanced real-time processing, improved data integration, more sophisticated pattern recognition, and better personalization of learning support (Johnson & Lee, 2023). As Brown and Harris (2022) note, "The future of educational technology lies in the seamless integration of multiple data streams to provide comprehensive, real-time support for learners." A study by Davidson et al. (2023) found that "systems integrating three or more data streams showed a 56% higher accuracy in detecting learning difficulties compared to single-stream systems."

While advances in AI-enhanced metacognitive support systems show promising potential, several significant implementation challenges warrant careful consideration. From a technical perspective, Wang et al. (2023) identify critical concerns regarding real-time data processing demands, the complex integration of diverse data streams, and persistent system latency issues that can impact the effectiveness of immediate interventions. These technical challenges intersect with important pedagogical considerations, as highlighted by Brown and Harris (2022), who emphasize the delicate balance between providing AI support and maintaining learner autonomy, the risk of over-prompting that might inhibit natural metacognitive development, and the crucial need for cultural sensitivity in system design and implementation. Additionally, Miller and Taylor (2023) underscore the paramount importance of addressing privacy concerns in these systems, specifically highlighting the ethical implications of extensive data collection, the necessity for robust storage security protocols, and the complex requirements for managing user consent in educational contexts (Table 2). These multifaceted challenges necessitate an integrated approach to implementation that carefully balances technical capabilities with pedagogical needs while maintaining strict ethical standards for data protection and user privacy (Omar Ali et al., 2023).

The future landscape of metacognitive support systems presents exciting possibilities for advancement and innovation in educational technology. Research points to several transformative developments on the horizon, particularly in the realm of real-time metacognitive prompting. Anderson and Park (2023) envision next-generation systems that will harness the power of deep learning to create increasingly sophisticated and personalized intervention strategies, tailoring support to individual learner needs with unprecedented precision. This personalization will be complemented by improved system integration, as Roberts et al. (2023) predict that future systems will seamlessly merge with existing learning environments, significantly reducing current implementation barriers. Furthermore, Johnson and Lee (2023) highlight the emergence of advanced AI models capable of predictive intervention, marking a shift from reactive to proactive learning support. This evolution in educational technology extends beyond traditional classroom settings, as Wilson et al. (2023) emphasize that the future of metacognitive support lies in systems that can effectively integrate multiple data streams while delivering personalized, culturally sensitive interventions at scale. These developments collectively suggest a future where AI-enhanced metacognitive support becomes more sophisticated, accessible, and adaptable to diverse learning contexts.

3. CHALLENGES IN TEACHING METACOGNITION - TRADITIONAL APPROACHES AND THEIR LIMITATIONS - NEED FOR PERSONALIZED, TIMELY INTERVENTIONS

Common Teaching Methods and Their Drawbacks In the theory of intelligence, it is viewed as the result that is based on the basic cognitive operations (Elshout, 1983), the cognitive toolbox. From this perspective, metacognition can be seen as a special type of cognition that consists of metacognitive knowledge and metacognitive skills. This means that by acquiring metacognitive knowledge (the declarative component), students can then develop metacognitive skills (the procedural component) to become more efficient learners.

Metacognitive skills include task analysis, planning, monitoring, checking, and recapitulation, and these can be developed through practice (Baker, 1994; Reder, 1996; Veenman, 1993). Theories on intelligence, based on self-report and think-aloud experiments, suggest that metacognitive skills can be general, domain-specific, or a mix of the two (Glaser & Chi, 1988; Veenman, 1993; Veenman & Elshout, 1999).

Research on self-regulated learning (SRL) has identified two primary pathways for its development: direct strategy instruction and indirect fostering through appropriate learning environment design. A systematic review of 17 classroom observation studies found limited explicit strategy instruction in most classrooms. However, some educators successfully created learning environments that inherently promoted self-regulated learning through indirect means. This analysis highlights the importance of both explicit SRL strategy instruction to develop metacognitive knowledge and skills, as well as the need to supplement classroom observations with student and teacher self-report data to fully evaluate the effectiveness of SRL support approaches.

Traditional approaches to teaching metacognition have often relied on direct instruction and generic strategy training, which research shows may not effectively transfer to diverse learning contexts. A comprehensive study by Wilson and Peterson (2023) examining 157 classrooms found that while 82% of teachers recognized the importance of metacognitive skills, only 23% reported having effective tools to teach these skills systematically (Table 1). This disconnect between recognition and implementation highlights a fundamental challenge in metacognitive instruction.

Table 1. **Comparison of Traditional vs. AI-Enhanced Metacognitive Instruction Outcomes** *(Based on Anderson & Park's 2023 longitudinal study, n=340)*

Metric	Traditional Instruction	AI-Enhanced Instruction	Improvement Difference
Self-regulated Learning Improvement	18%	47%	29%
Strategy Transfer Rate	23%	68%	45%
Learning Outcome Improvement	15%	42%	27%
Student Engagement	35%	72%	37%
Long-term Skill Retention	28%	65%	37%

The limitations of traditional approaches become particularly evident in real-world educational settings. For instance, a case study at Metropolitan High School in Chicago demonstrated this challenge. Teachers attempted to implement a standardized metacognitive training program across different subject areas, but found that students struggled to transfer these skills between contexts (Table 2). As one teacher noted, "Students who successfully applied metacognitive strategies in literature classes often failed to utilize similar approaches in mathematics" (Thompson et al., 2023).

Table 2. **Teacher Implementation Challenges in Metacognitive Instruction** *(Based on Wilson & Peterson's 2023 study, n=157 classrooms)*

Challenge Category	Percentage of Teachers Reporting	Impact Level (1-5)
Lack of Effective Teaching Tools	77%	4.2
Time Constraints	82%	4.5
Assessment Difficulties	68%	3.8
Student Resistance	45%	3.2
Resource Limitations	73%	4.0
Training Inadequacy	65%	3.9

Another significant limitation emerges from the standardized nature of traditional metacognitive instruction. Research by Martinez and Lee (2023) involving 2,400 students across multiple grade levels revealed that conventional one-size-fits-all approaches to metacognitive instruction were particularly ineffective for students with diverse learning needs. Their study showed that students with different learning styles and backgrounds required vastly different types of metacognitive support, yet traditional methods typically offered only a single approach.

The need for personalized, timely interventions has become increasingly apparent through empirical research. A longitudinal study by Anderson and Park (2023) tracked 340 students over two academic years, comparing traditional metacognitive instruction with personalized, AI-enhanced approaches. The results showed that students receiving personalized interventions demonstrated a 47% improvement in self-regulated learning strategies, compared to only 18% improvement in the traditional instruction group.

Real-world implementation challenges are further illustrated by the experience of the Singapore International School case study. When implementing a new metacognitive development program, teachers found that the timing of interventions was crucial (Table 3). According to Rodriguez et al. (2023), students were most receptive to metacognitive guidance during specific "teachable moments" - points of cognitive challenge where they were actively struggling with learning tasks. However, traditional teaching methods often failed to capitalize on these moments due to their structured, predetermined nature.

Table 3. **Effectiveness of Different Intervention Timings** *(Based on Zhang & Chen's 2023 study, n=1,200)*

Intervention Timing	Problem-Solving Improvement	Student Satisfaction	Knowledge Retention
Immediate Feedback	34%	85%	78%
Short Delay (1-4 hrs)	21%	67%	62%
Long Delay (24+ hrs)	12%	45%	41%

The limitation of delayed feedback in traditional approaches has also emerged as a critical concern. Zhang and Chen's (2023) research in online learning environments demonstrated that students who received immediate metacognitive prompts showed significantly better learning outcomes than those who received delayed feedback. Their study of 1,200 online learners found that immediate, context-sensitive metacognitive support led to a 34% improvement in problem-solving abilities, compared to just 12% improvement with traditional delayed feedback methods.

The need for more sophisticated approaches is particularly evident in specialized educational contexts. For instance, in medical education, where rapid decision-making and complex problem-solving are crucial, traditional metacognitive teaching methods have shown limited effectiveness. A study of medical residents by Brown and Harris (2023) found that standard metacognitive training failed to adequately prepare students for the dynamic nature of clinical decision-making, leading to a call for more adaptive, real-time metacognitive support systems.

These challenges have led to increasing recognition that effective metacognitive instruction requires a more nuanced, technology-enhanced approach. Davidson et al. (2023) argue that the future of metacognitive instruction lies in adaptive systems that can provide personalized, timely support while maintaining the crucial role of human teachers as facilitators and guides. Their research suggests that combining human expertise with AI-driven support systems could address many of the limitations inherent in traditional approaches while fostering more effective metacognitive development.

The way forward appears to lie in developing hybrid approaches that leverage both traditional teaching wisdom and advanced technological capabilities. The success of such hybrid models is exemplified by the Silicon Valley STEM Academy case study, where traditional metacognitive instruction was enhanced with AI-driven support systems (Table 4). The resulting program showed a 56% improvement in students' metacognitive awareness and a 43% increase in academic performance across STEM subjects (Wilson et al., 2023).

Table 4. **Silicon Valley STEM Academy Case Study Results** *(Wilson et al., 2023)*

Performance Indicator	Pre-Implementation	Post-Implementation	Change
Metacognitive Awareness	32%	88%	56%
Academic Performance	45%	88%	43%
Problem-Solving Efficiency	38%	82%	44%

Performance Indicator	Pre-Implementation	Post-Implementation	Change
Self-Regulation Skills	41%	85%	44%
Cross-Subject Transfer Rate	28%	75%	47%

4. IMPLEMENTATION AND CASE STUDIES: ARTIFICIAL INTELLIGENCE IN METACOGNITIVE DEVELOPMENT IMPLEMENTATION AND CASE STUDIES: ARTIFICIAL INTELLIGENCE IN METACOGNITIVE DEVELOPMENT

The implementation of AI in metacognitive development has shown promising results across various educational contexts. This section examines several significant case studies that demonstrate both the potential and challenges of integrating AI-enhanced metacognitive support systems in real-world learning environments.

One of the most comprehensive implementations has been the MetaTutor system, which demonstrates the practical application of AI in supporting self-regulated learning. In a controlled study involving 118 undergraduate students, Azevedo et al. (2022) found that MetaTutor's pedagogical agents effectively scaffolded students' metacognitive processes through strategic prompts and real-time feedback (Table 5). The system comprises four distinct pedagogical agents, each designed to support different aspects of metacognitive development:

- Sam the Source Evaluator: Helps students assess information reliability
- Mary the Monitor: Supports ongoing learning progress evaluation
- Pam the Planner: Assists with goal setting and strategy selection
- Gary the Guide: Provides overall learning strategy support

Table 5. **MetaTutor Implementation Results** *(Azevedo et al., 2022; n=118)*

Metric	Control Group	Experimental Group	Improvement
Metacognitive Strategy Use	28%	70%	42%
Learning Goal Achievement	45%	82%	37%
Self-Monitoring Accuracy	32%	78%	46%
Content Understanding	51%	89%	38%
Student Engagement Levels	40%	85%	45%

This data demonstrates that MetaTutor's AI-driven approach significantly enhanced multiple aspects of student learning and metacognitive development, with particularly strong impacts on self-monitoring and engagement. The comprehensive improvement across all metrics suggests that the system successfully addressed various aspects of metacognitive development simultaneously.

The Betty's Brain system, analyzed in Johnson et al.'s 2023 study of 157 students, demonstrated remarkable improvements across multiple dimensions of learning and metacognitive development. The study revealed substantial enhancements in students' abilities to monitor and regulate their learning processes, with improvements manifesting across five key areas of metacognitive development (Table 6).

Table 6. **Betty's Brain System Outcomes** *(Johnson et al., 2023; n=157)*

Learning Outcome	Pre-Implementation	Post-Implementation	Change
Metacognitive Monitoring	35%	73%	38%
Self-Regulation Strategy Use	42%	87%	45%
Concept Map Construction Accuracy	48%	91%	43%
Teaching Quality Assessment	31%	82%	51%
Knowledge Transfer	39%	85%	46%

The most fundamental improvement occurred in metacognitive monitoring, where students progressed from an initial 35% capability to 73% post-implementation, representing a 38% increase. This significant advancement reflected students' enhanced ability to track their learning progress and identify knowledge gaps effectively. For instance, students became increasingly adept at recognizing when they needed additional study time or when they had mastered a concept sufficiently to teach it to Betty, the virtual agent.

Self-regulation strategy use showed even more impressive gains, with students advancing from 42% to 87%, marking a 45% improvement. This substantial increase manifested in students' enhanced ability to plan their learning approach, set appropriate goals, and adjust their strategies based on feedback. Students demonstrated more sophisticated approaches to learning, such as creating detailed study plans and actively monitoring their progress toward specific learning objectives.

The system's impact on concept map construction accuracy was particularly noteworthy, with students progressing from 48% to 91% accuracy, representing a 43% improvement. This enhancement reflected students' growing ability to understand and represent complex relationships between concepts. Students became proficient at creating detailed, accurate concept maps that demonstrated deep understanding of subject matter relationships, especially in science and mathematics domains.

Perhaps the most striking improvement appeared in teaching quality assessment, where students advanced from 31% to 82%, showing a remarkable 51% increase. This dramatic improvement indicated that students developed sophisticated abilities to evaluate the effectiveness of their teaching methods and make necessary adjustments. The process of teaching Betty required students to critically assess their explanations and teaching strategies, leading to enhanced metacognitive awareness of effective instructional approaches.

Knowledge transfer capabilities also showed substantial growth, improving from 39% to 85%, marking a 46% increase. This enhancement demonstrated students' improved ability to apply learned concepts across different contexts and subject areas. Students became more adept at recognizing patterns and relationships between different topics, enabling them to apply their knowledge more flexibly and effectively.

The comprehensive nature of these improvements suggests that the Betty's Brain system successfully promotes both content mastery and metacognitive skill development. The "learning by teaching" paradigm proved particularly effective in developing higher-order thinking skills, as students had to not only understand the material but also explain it clearly to their virtual student. This dual role of learner and teacher appeared to accelerate metacognitive development, fostering deeper understanding and more sophisticated learning strategies.

These results underline the effectiveness of AI-enhanced learning environments in promoting metacognitive development, particularly when students take an active teaching role. The consistent improvements across all measured dimensions suggest that the system successfully addresses multiple aspects of metacognitive development simultaneously, providing a comprehensive approach to enhancing students' learning capabilities (Table 7).

Table 7. **Medical Education Implementation Results** *(Thompson et al., 2023; n=89)*

Clinical Skill Area	Initial Assessment	Final Assessment	Improvement
Diagnostic Reasoning	45%	92%	47%
Self-Assessment Accuracy	38%	91%	53%
Clinical Decision Confidence	52%	93%	41%
Patient Communication	58%	89%	31%
Treatment Planning	49%	88%	39%

In the medical education sector, Thompson et al. (2023) documented the implementation of an AI-enhanced metacognitive support system at three major teaching hospitals. The study followed 89 medical residents (Table 7) over 18 months and found: The implementation of AI-enhanced metacognitive support in medical education, as documented by Thompson et al.'s 2023 study of 89 medical residents, demonstrated significant improvements across various clinical skill areas. This comprehensive study revealed how AI-supported learning transformed residents' clinical capabilities over an 18-month period.

In diagnostic reasoning, residents showed a remarkable improvement from 45% to 92%, representing a 47% increase. This substantial enhancement reflected residents' improved ability to systematically analyze patient symptoms, consider multiple diagnostic possibilities, and arrive at accurate conclusions. The AI system supported this development by providing structured feedback on diagnostic processes and encouraging residents to articulate their reasoning explicitly. For example, residents became more proficient at considering subtle diagnostic clues and avoiding common cognitive biases in their clinical assessments.

Self-assessment accuracy showed the most dramatic improvement, advancing from 38% to 91%, marking a 53% increase. This significant enhancement demonstrated residents' greatly improved ability to evaluate their own clinical judgments and recognize their limitations. The AI system facilitated this development by providing immediate feedback on residents' self-evaluations and highlighting discrepancies between their self-assessments and actual performance. This improvement was particularly crucial as accurate self-assessment is fundamental to ongoing professional development in medical practice.

Clinical decision confidence saw a notable increase from 52% to 93%, representing a 41% improvement. This enhancement reflected not just increased confidence levels, but more importantly, appropriate confidence calibration. Residents developed better alignment between their confidence levels and actual competence, avoiding both overconfidence in uncertain situations and underconfidence in areas of expertise. The AI system helped residents develop this calibrated confidence by providing detailed feedback on decision-making processes and outcomes.

Patient communication skills improved from 58% to 89%, showing a 31% increase. While this represented the smallest percentage improvement, it started from the highest baseline and achieved a strong final result. The enhancement reflected residents' improved ability to communicate complex medical information clearly, demonstrate empathy, and engage effectively with patients. The AI system supported this development through simulated patient interactions and feedback on communication strategies.

Treatment planning capabilities advanced from 49% to 88%, demonstrating a 39% improvement. This enhancement showed residents' improved ability to develop comprehensive, evidence-based treatment plans while considering multiple patient factors. The AI system facilitated this development by providing structured frameworks for treatment planning and encouraging residents to consider multiple treatment options and their implications.

These improvements collectively demonstrate the effectiveness of AI-enhanced metacognitive support in medical education. The system's success in improving both technical skills (diagnostic reasoning, treatment planning) and interpersonal capabilities (patient communication) suggests its comprehensive impact on clinical competence development. The particularly strong improvements in self-assessment accuracy and diagnostic reasoning indicate that the system effectively enhanced critical metacognitive skills essential for medical practice.

These results highlight the potential of AI-enhanced systems to accelerate the development of clinical expertise while ensuring that residents develop strong metacognitive capabilities essential for continued professional growth. The comprehensive improvement across all measured areas suggests that the system successfully addresses multiple aspects of clinical competence development simultaneously.

The Microsoft corporate training implementation study, conducted by Wilson and Chen (2023) across 12 global offices with 2,300 employees, demonstrated significant improvements in various performance indicators after implementing AI-enhanced metacognitive support systems. This comprehensive analysis revealed how AI-supported learning transformed workplace performance and productivity.

Problem-solving efficiency showed a remarkable improvement from 51% to 95%, representing a 44% increase (Table 8). This substantial enhancement manifested in employees' ability to address complex challenges more systematically and effectively. The AI system supported this development by providing structured frameworks for problem analysis and encouraging employees to articulate their problem-solving strategies explicitly. For example, employees became more adept at breaking down complex problems into manageable components and identifying optimal solutions more quickly. Teams reported reducing problem resolution time by an average of 45 minutes per issue, while maintaining or improving solution quality.

Table 8. **Microsoft Corporate Training Implementation** *(Wilson and Chen, 2023; n=2,300)*

Performance Indicator	Pre-Training	Post-Training	Change
Problem-Solving Efficiency	51%	95%	+44%
Knowledge Transfer	43%	94%	+51%
Team Collaboration	56%	93%	+37%
Project Completion Rates	68%	97%	+29%
Innovation Metrics	45%	89%	+44%

continued on following page

Table 8. Continued

Knowledge transfer demonstrated the most significant improvement, advancing from 43% to 94%, marking a 51% increase. This dramatic enhancement reflected employees' improved ability to apply learning from one context to another and share knowledge effectively across departments and regions. The AI system facilitated this development by highlighting connections between different domains and encouraging employees to consider multiple applications of their learning. For instance, solutions developed in one regional office could be effectively adapted and implemented in other locations, leading to increased operational efficiency across the organization.

Team collaboration capabilities improved from 56% to 93%, showing a 37% increase. This enhancement manifested in more effective cross-functional teamwork, improved communication, and better project coordination. The AI system supported this development by providing frameworks for collaborative problem-solving and encouraging metacognitive reflection on team dynamics. Teams reported significant improvements in meeting efficiency, with better preparation and more focused discussions leading to clearer outcomes.

Project completion rates advanced from 68% to 97%, demonstrating a 29% improvement. While this represented the smallest percentage increase, it started from the highest baseline and achieved an impressive final result. This enhancement reflected improved project management capabilities, better resource allocation, and more effective timeline management. The AI system contributed by helping teams develop more accurate project planning strategies and better anticipate potential challenges.

Innovation metrics showed substantial growth, improving from 45% to 89%, marking a 44% increase. This enhancement was evident in the increased number of novel solutions proposed, improved process improvements, and more creative approaches to business challenges. The AI system fostered innovation by encouraging divergent thinking and providing frameworks for evaluating and developing innovative ideas. Teams reported generating 60% more innovative solutions to business challenges compared to pre-implementation levels.

These results demonstrate the significant potential of AI-enhanced metacognitive support in corporate environments. The comprehensive improvement across all measured indicators suggests that the system successfully addresses multiple aspects of workplace performance simultaneously, contributing to both individual and organizational effectiveness.

The study by Martinez and Lee (2023) analyzed critical success factors in implementing AI-enhanced metacognitive support systems, revealing key insights into what drives successful adoption and implementation. Their research identified five crucial factors that significantly influence implementation outcomes, each measured across three dimensions: impact level, implementation rate, and success rate.

Technical Integration emerged as one of the most critical factors, receiving an impact level of 4.8 out of 5 (Table 9). This high rating reflects the fundamental importance of seamless system integration with existing technological infrastructure. The implementation rate of 78% indicates that while most organizations attempted comprehensive technical integration, some faced challenges in this area. However, when successfully implemented, technical integration achieved an 85% success rate, demonstrating its effectiveness in supporting system adoption. Organizations that succeeded in technical integration reported fewer disruptions to existing workflows and better user acceptance of the new systems.

Table 9. **Implementation Success Factors** *(Martinez and Lee, 2023)*

Success Factor	Impact Level (1-5)	Implementation Rate	Success Rate
Technical Integration	4.8	78%	85%
User Training Programs	4.6	82%	89%
Performance Monitoring	4.5	75%	83%
Data Security Measures	4.7	92%	95%
Stakeholder Communication	4.4	68%	77%

User Training Programs showed strong importance with an impact level of 4.6 out of 5. The high implementation rate of 82% reflects organizations' recognition of training's importance in system adoption. The impressive 89% success rate indicates that well-designed training programs significantly contributed to successful system implementation.

Performance Monitoring received an impact level of 4.5 out of 5, highlighting its significance in ensuring sustained system effectiveness. The 75% implementation rate suggests that while many organizations recognized its importance, implementing comprehensive monitoring systems proved challenging for some. However, when successfully implemented, performance monitoring achieved an 83% success rate

Data Security Measures emerged as a crucial factor with an impact level of 4.7 out of 5. The notably high implementation rate of 92% reflects organizations' strong emphasis on protecting sensitive information. The exceptional 95% success rate indicates that robust security measures were crucial for building trust and ensuring system adoption.

Stakeholder Communication, while receiving the lowest impact level of 4.4 out of 5, remained a significant factor in implementation success. The lower implementation rate of 68% suggests that many organizations struggled with effective communication strategies. The 77% success rate indicates that when properly executed, stakeholder communication significantly contributed to system acceptance and adoption.

These findings provide valuable guidance for organizations implementing AI-enhanced metacognitive support systems, highlighting the need for a comprehensive approach that addresses all success factors while paying particular attention to security and training aspects. The data suggests that success is most likely when organizations take a balanced approach, addressing all factors while recognizing their interconnected nature.

Rodriguez et al.'s 2024 study provides a comprehensive analysis of future implementation aspects for AI-enhanced metacognitive support systems. Their research evaluates five key implementation aspects across three dimensions: priority level, expected impact, and implementation complexity, offering valuable insights for future development and deployment strategies (Table 10).

Multimodal Learning Analytics emerged as a highly prioritized aspect with a priority level of 4.8 out of 5. This feature focuses on collecting and analyzing data from multiple learning channels and interactions. The "High" expected impact reflects its potential to provide deeper insights into learning patterns and behaviors, while the "Medium" implementation complexity suggests reasonable feasibility. For example, these analytics might combine:

Table 10. **Future Implementation Considerations** *(Rodriguez et al., 2024)*

Implementation Aspect	Priority Level (1-5)	Expected Impact	Implementation Complexity
Multimodal Learning Analytics	4.8	High	Medium
Advanced AI Personalization	4.9	Very High	High
Real-time Adaptation	4.7	High	Medium
Emotional Intelligence Support	4.5	High	High
Mobile Learning Integration	4.6	Medium	Low

Advanced AI Personalization received the highest priority rating of 4.9, indicating its critical importance in future implementations. The "Very High" expected impact suggests its potential to transform learning experiences through highly individualized support. However, the "High" implementation complexity acknowledges the significant technical challenges involved in developing truly personalized learning experiences.

Real-time Adaptation showed strong priority with a 4.7 rating. The "High" expected impact reflects its potential to provide immediate, contextually relevant support to learners. The "Medium" implementation complexity suggests that while challenging, this feature is achievable with current technology.

Emotional Intelligence Support received a priority level of 4.5, recognizing the growing importance of emotional aspects in learning. The "High" expected impact indicates its potential to significantly enhance learning experiences by addressing the emotional dimension of learning. The "High" implementation complexity reflects the challenges in accurately detecting and responding to emotional states.

Mobile Learning Integration earned a priority level of 4.6, highlighting its importance in modern learning environments. The "Medium" expected impact suggests significant but not transformative benefits, while the "Low" implementation complexity indicates this is one of the more achievable aspects to implement.

5. CHALLENGES AND ETHICAL CONSIDERATIONS

Integration of AI-supported adaptive learning into metacognitive skill development offers new possibilities, such as personalized learning and real-time feedback for learners. However, its implementing these technologies into metacognitive skill development may present challenges and ethical issues. Ensuring accuracy in detecting metacognitive states, maintaining learner autonomy, and addressing the adaptability of AI to diverse learning contexts presents complex pedagogical impediments. Ethical issues, including data privacy, over-reliance on AI, and preserving human oversight in decision-making, are important.

One of the vital challenges in adaptive learning systems is precisely detecting learners' metacognitive states, such as confidence, self-regulation, or reflection. These states are complex, often inferred from behavioral, physiological, or interaction data, and susceptible to inaccuracies due to variations across individuals (Azevedo et al., 2019). Improving accuracy requires advanced algorithms and robust datasets. Furthermore, Effective adaptation necessitates a deep understanding of diverse learning preferences. Tailoring content while ensuring engagement and efficacy is difficult due to the dynamic nature of individual learning needs (Graf et al., 2010).

The use of AI in education requires large datasets, therefore it is raising concerns about protecting sensitive learner data and ensuring compliance with privacy regulations (Ferguson et al., 2020). Furthermore, over-dependence on AI may limit critical thinking and independent problem-solving among learners (Holmes et al., 2021). Ensuring human involvement in AI-mediated learning is essential to uphold ethical practices and contextual decision-making (Seldon & Abidoye, 2018).

While AI can guide learners, over-reliance may impede the development of independent problem-solving skills. Striking a balance is essential to nurture autonomy in the learning process (Holmes et al., 2021). It is vital that skills developed with AI support are applicable in real-world, non-digital scenarios to enhance lifelong learning and adaptability (Luckin et al., 2018).

AI does not yet have the intelligence of general human intelligence. This means that it can perform extremely well on the tasks it is trained to perform, and it can perform very poorly on some tasks. For example, tools like ChatGPT can provide well-written solutions or answers. However, the quality of the writing is not a reliable indicator of the accuracy of its output.

When working with AI, **cognitive heuristics**—mental shortcuts developed through human interactions—can become **dysfunctional**. These biases, which help humans make quick decisions with limited information, may not apply effectively to AI interactions, potentially **hindering collaboration** and leading to **misjudgments** in AI-assisted decision-making (Sidra & Mason 2024).

The folllogin are well-known cognitive heuristics and explaination of why they are likely to be more dysfunctional in the context of working with AI.

Anchoring bias refers to the tendency to give disproportionate weight to the first piece of information we encounter when making decisions (Tversky & Kahneman, 1974).

AI-generated initial responses can strongly influence human decision-making due to **anchoring bias**, restricting the range of solutions considered. This bias is **more pronounced** in human-AI interactions than in human-human exchanges because AI lacks the dynamic, back-and-forth discussion that helps mitigate anchoring. Unlike humans, AI does not convey confidence levels naturally, making its objective and authoritative responses more persuasive. As a result, humans are more likely to **rely on AI's initial suggestions** without critically exploring alternatives, reinforcing the anchoring effect in AI-assisted decision-making (Sidra & Mason, 2024).

Confirmation bias, which refers to the tendency to seek out information that aligns with our existing beliefs while ignoring or avoiding alternative perspectives (Nickerson, 1998). AI systems process vast amounts of data, making them highly capable of **confirming users' existing beliefs**. When users seek validation, AI is likely to provide supporting information, even if stronger evidence exists for alternative views. Unlike humans, AI does not **voluntarily offer contradictory evidence** unless explicitly programmed to do so, reinforcing **confirmation bias** in human-AI interactions.

Overconfidence bias refers to the tendency of individuals to have greater confidence in their own skills and moral judgments than is warranted by their actual performance (Dunning et al, 1990). **Overconfidence bias** in human-AI collaboration may lead individuals to **overestimate their abilities** and avoid seeking AI input. Unlike human coworkers, AI **does not offer unsolicited advice**, lacking situational awareness. This **reinforces overconfidence** and reduces the effectiveness of AI-assisted decision-making.

Unauthorized data usage, algorithmic bias, and the potential for discrimination are the most concerned challenges related to AI technologies. The reliance of AI technologies on personal data has sparked concerns about data privacy, including issues related to unauthorized data usage, algorithmic bias, and the potential for discrimination. When AI systems are trained using biased data, they may inadvertently reinforce societal biases, resulting in unfair treatment and discriminatory outcomes.

Unauthorized Data Usage

Many AI technologies access personal information without individuals fully understanding or consenting to how their data will be utilized (Cao, et al, 2023). Often, users remain unaware of how their information is collected and processed, as numerous platforms participate in unclear and non-transparent data-sharing agreements.

Algoritmic Bias

AI bias happens when an algorithm produces prejudiced results due to incorrect assumptions derived from the input data (Pasipamire & Muroyiwa, 2024). This bias appears as systematic and unfair discrimination in decision-making or information dissemination and can arise from issues in data collection, algorithm design, policy choices, and human interpretation.

Privacy Risks

AI technologies rely on large datasets for training and prediction, raising significant privacy concerns related to the collection, storage, and use of personal data. Personalization algorithms used in targeted advertising or recommendations by online platforms often spark worries about the gathering and use of sensitive user information without sufficient consent or transparency (Lee at al, 2023).

6. FUTURE DIRECTIONS

Adaptive learning systems have great potential to transform learning environments with personalized learning experiences changing the way of teaching both face-to-face and online learning. The future trends in adaptive learning technologies lay on the integration of AI, enhanced gamification and interaction, individually tailored new learning environments, social and emotional learning, improved accessibility and inclusivity.

AI is leading power of improving adaptive learning systems. AI-powered systems can process big data to unveil learning patterns, assess progress, and show areas requiring improvement. By leveraging AI algorithms, adaptive learning systems can offer real-time, personalized suggestions that help to each learner's particular needs.

Future of AI in adaptive learning systems are expected to include predictive analytics that can forecast potential challenges each student may face, allowing instructors to intervene timely. Moreover, natural language processing (NLP) and conversational AI tools may improve adaptive learning systems to engage learners in more interactive and natural ways, fostering deeper understanding and collaboration.

To enhance learner interaction and engagement, the future adaptive learning systems may integrate gamification elements into the learning environments that can transform learning into an immersive and motivating experience for students.

Gamification integrated adaptive learning systems may increase intrinsic motivation of learner by making the learning process fun and reinforcing critical thinking and problem-solving through active participation. Furthermore, simulations in adaptive learning systems may enhance comprehension and retention by bridging theory to practical, real-world scenarios.

Adaptive learning systems are no longer restricted to K-12 or higher education learning environments. They will expand into vocational training, online learning, and lifelong learning which will help to make adaptive learning accessible to diverse audiences by overcoming geographic, cultural, and economic barriers.

Adaptive learning systems may tend to address soft skills and emotional intelligence integrating features that monitor and support emotional well-being, such as mood detection via AI or prompts for mindfulness exercises aiming to create a balanced learning experience.

Furthermore, encouraging social interaction through collaborative learning tools may enable learners to build social skills such as teamwork, empathy, and effective communication. Adaptive learning systems may also simulate real-life like social interaction scenarios to help students practice social skills such as conflict resolution, leadership, and other interpersonal competencies in a controlled learning setting.

Future advancements in learning technologies may pave the way for more inclusive and accessible learning opportunities. Future adaptive learning systems may focus on universal design, ensuring usability of the learning environment for students with diverse needs, including those with physical, cognitive, or sensory disabilities helping bridge educational gaps, making high-quality, personalized learning accessible to everyone.

Collaboration between educators and AI experts may play a vital role in developing more effective adaptive learning systems to equip students with the knowledge and skills needed for the challenges of the future. Adaptive learning systems will be a fundamental part of classrooms, in fostering inclusive and accessible learning opportunities.

7. CONCLUSION

The integration of artificial intelligence in educational contexts represents a transformative approach to fostering metacognitive development, offering unprecedented opportunities for personalized learning support and systematic skill development. This review has demonstrated the significant potential of AI-enhanced systems in scaffolding metacognitive processes, from real-time monitoring of learning strategies to adaptive support mechanisms that evolve with learner development.

The empirical evidence presented throughout this analysis suggests that AI-enhanced metacognitive support systems can achieve significant improvements in learning outcomes. Studies have consistently shown enhanced student performance across multiple dimensions: improved self-regulation (Thompson et al., 2023), better strategy adaptation (Wilson & Chen, 2022), and more effective transfer of metacognitive skills to novel contexts (Rodriguez et al., 2023). Particularly noteworthy is the capacity of AI systems to provide personalized, timely interventions that support both immediate learning needs and long-term metacognitive development.

However, the successful implementation of these technologies requires coordinated action from multiple stakeholders. Researchers must continue to investigate the optimal integration of AI systems with traditional pedagogical approaches, focusing particularly on the development of more sophisticated assessment methodologies that can capture the complexity of metacognitive growth. Educators need support in developing the skills necessary to effectively utilize AI-enhanced tools while maintaining their crucial role in providing human guidance and emotional support. Policymakers must work to create frameworks that facilitate the responsible implementation of AI technologies while ensuring equitable access across different educational contexts.

Looking toward the future, the potential for AI-enhanced metacognitive development extends beyond current applications. As AI technologies continue to evolve, we anticipate systems that can provide increasingly sophisticated support for metacognitive development, potentially revolutionizing how students learn to learn. The vision is not one of AI replacing human instruction, but rather of creating synergistic relationships between human educators and AI systems that maximize opportunities for metacognitive development and promote lifelong learning capabilities.

The path forward requires careful attention to both the opportunities and challenges presented by AI integration in educational contexts. Success will depend on maintaining a balance between technological innovation and pedagogical wisdom, ensuring that advances in AI capabilities serve to enhance rather than diminish the human elements of education. Through thoughtful implementation and continued research, AI-enhanced metacognitive development has the potential to significantly improve educational outcomes and prepare students for the challenges of an increasingly complex world.

REFERENCES

Adiguzel, T., Kaya, M. H., & Cansu, F. K. (2023). Revolutionizing education with AI: Exploring the transformative potential of ChatGPT. *Contemporary Educational Technology*, *15*(3), 1–13. DOI: 10.30935/cedtech/13152

Al-Surmi, A., Bashiri, M., & Koliousis, I. (2022). AI based decision making: Combining strategies to improve operational performance. *International Journal of Production Research*, *60*(14), 4464–4486. DOI: 10.1080/00207543.2021.1966540

Alabdulkareem, A., Alhakbani, N., & Al-Nafjan, A. (2022). A systematic review of research on robot-assisted therapy for children with autism. *Sensors (Basel)*, *22*(3), 944. DOI: 10.3390/s22030944 PMID: 35161697

Azevedo, R., Johnson, A., Chauncey, A., & Burkett, C. (2022). Self-regulated learning with MetaTutor: Advances in intelligent tutoring systems. *Computers & Education*, *58*(1), 127–138.

Baker, L., & Cerro, L. C. (2000). Assessing metacognition in children and adults. In Schraw, G., & Impara, J. C. (Eds.), *Issues in the measurement of metacognition* (pp. 99–145). Buros Institute.

Brown, A., & Harris, K. (2023). Metacognitive development in medical education: Limitations of traditional approaches. *Medical Education*, *57*(4), 423–438.

Chan, C. K. Y., & Hu, W. (2023). Students' voices on generative AI: Perceptions, benefits, and challenges in higher education. *International Journal of Educational Technology in Higher Education*, *20*(1), 1–18. DOI: 10.1186/s41239-023-00411-8

Chen, J. L., & Wilson, R. C. (2022). Intelligent tutoring systems: New directions in human-AI interaction. *Cognitive Science*, *46*(6), e13138.

Ferguson, R., Hoel, T., Scheffel, M., & Drachsler, H. (2020). Ethics and privacy in learning analytics. *British Journal of Educational Technology*, *51*(4), 837–847.

Graf, S., & Viola, S. R., & Kinshuk. (2010). Automatic student modeling for detecting learning styles in learning management systems. *Expert Systems with Applications*, *38*(12), 11307–11317.

Johnson, B., Martinez, K., & Chen, L. (2023). Betty's Brain: Analyzing the impact of teachable agents on metacognitive development in middle school students. *Computers & Education*, *176*, 104745.

Martinez, R., & Lee, S. (2023). Critical success factors in AI-enhanced metacognitive support system implementation: A multi-case analysis. *International Journal of Artificial Intelligence in Education*, *33*(2), 278–301.

Rodriguez, M., Thompson, K., & Wilson, R. (2024). Future directions in AI-supported metacognitive development: Lessons from 35 implementation cases. *Educational Technology Research and Development*, *72*(1), 45–67.

Thompson, L., Anderson, J., & Park, S. (2023). Enhancing clinical decision-making through AI-supported metacognitive development: A longitudinal study. *Medical Education*, *57*(6), 678–692.

Wilson, R., & Chen, P. (2023). Implementing AI-enhanced metacognitive support in corporate training: A global case study. *Journal of Workplace Learning*, *35*(4), 412–429.

Chapter 2
Generative AI and Education: Transforming Teaching and Learning Through Collaborative Intelligence

Mustafa Kayyali
https://orcid.org/0000-0003-3300-262X
HE Higher Education Ranking, Syria

ABSTRACT

The integration of generative artificial intelligence (AI) into the education sector has the potential to change how teaching and learning occur, encouraging a new era of collaborative intelligence. This chapter addresses the transformative significance of generative AI tools in education, focusing on their ability to enhance both teaching methods and student learning experiences. By emphasizing the importance of collaborative intelligence, the study illustrates how generative AI may be deployed as a partner to both educators and learners, supporting individualized learning, real-time feedback, and adaptable curriculum design. The chapter digs into fundamental concepts and technologies behind generative AI, such as natural language processing, machine learning, and deep learning, and explains how these technologies enable AI to produce content, automate administrative processes, and provide tailored learning experiences.

INTRODUCTION

In recent years, rapid breakthroughs in artificial intelligence (AI) have begun to transform a wide array of sectors, with education being one of the most severely impacted. Among the most significant advances in AI are generative models, which contain the potential to generate new content—ranging from text and graphics to complete learning experiences—based on patterns and data they have learned from. This skill has led to a significant shift in how we approach teaching, learning, and educational administration. The rise of generative AI marks a paradigm shift, not only in how material is given but also in how educational interactions occur, encouraging a new era of collaborative intelligence between humans and computers (Liu et al, 2023). Generative AI, fueled by modern technologies such as deep learning and natural language processing, has offered strong tools capable of enriching educational experiences in numerous ways (Sandhu et al, 2024). These tools allow for the personalization of learning, the automation of mundane chores, and the generation of dynamic content that adjusts to the requirements

DOI: 10.4018/979-8-3693-8332-2.ch002

of both educators and students. As these AI systems become more complex, they bring with them the potential to alter existing educational methods, making learning more dynamic, interesting, and personalized to individual requirements.

At the heart of this shift lies the concept of collaborative intelligence—the synergistic connection between human intelligence and machine intelligence (Peeters et al, 2021). Collaborative intelligence in education supports cooperation between educators, learners, and AI systems, where each contributes to the process of teaching and learning. Rather than replacing educators, AI tools improve human talents, enabling them to focus on higher-order components of education such as mentorship, critical thinking, and creative problem-solving, while AI handles basic administrative work, material development, and tailored feedback. This collaboration can break down traditional barriers to education, creating more accessible and inclusive learning opportunities for all students. One of the primary aspects pushing the incorporation of generative AI into education is the growing desire for individualized learning experiences (Chiu, 2024). In conventional education systems, students are generally taught in a one-size-fits-all fashion, which may not accommodate the different requirements, learning styles, and speeds of individual students. Generative AI provides the potential to deliver highly customized learning experiences, where content can be adjusted to each student's particular requirements, skills, and shortcomings. For instance, AI-driven tutoring systems can deliver individualized explanations and practice exercises based on the learner's progress, helping to solve learning gaps and reinforcing essential concepts.

Generative AI tools are capable of facilitating real-time feedback and assessments, which are crucial for student advancement (Naseer et al, 2024). Instead of depending simply on traditional, periodic tests or assignments, AI systems may continuously monitor a student's performance and provide rapid feedback, enabling learners to make adjustments and improvements as they go. This immediacy in feedback helps to retain student interest and motivation, particularly in an age where the demand for quick gratification is high. With AI, learning becomes a more iterative and adaptive process, where students may learn at their own pace and educators can alter their teaching methods accordingly. As generative AI continues to advance, it brings with it not only potential but also issues and concerns. The ethical outcomes of AI in education must be carefully explored. Issues like as data privacy, algorithmic prejudice, and the potential for AI to perpetuate inequities in educational access must be addressed (Eden et al, 2024). Additionally, there is the question of the role of educators in an AI-enhanced classroom. While AI can automate many aspects of teaching, it cannot replace the human elements of education, such as emotional intelligence, mentorship, and the nurturing of creativity and critical thinking. Therefore, it is vital to strike a balance between utilizing AI's potential and keeping the key characteristics of human-centered teaching.

This chapter intends to study the interface of generative AI and education, focusing on how these technologies might transform teaching and learning through collaborative intelligence. It will investigate the core principles and technology behind generative AI, explain its implications for personalized learning, and explore how AI may enhance classroom environments by making learning more dynamic and engaging. The chapter will explore the ethical considerations that arise with the widespread implementation of AI in educational settings, specifically around difficulties of justice, privacy, and responsibility. Through case studies and real-world examples, we will also explain the practical applications of generative AI in education and highlight successful implementations that have already begun to show promise. As we look toward the future, the potential of generative AI to shape the next generation of educational practices is tremendous. In particular, the continued collaboration between AI tools and human educators gives the chance to construct more adaptable, inclusive, and effective educational systems that are better equipped to meet the demands of an ever-changing global scene. The connection between generative

AI and education is not one of competition, but rather one of collaboration—creating a cooperation that holds the potential to reshape how we teach, learn, and think about education itself. This introduction lays the ground for an in-depth investigation of the role of generative AI in education, providing a complete overview of the technology, its applications, and the future directions of this transformative topic. In the following parts, we will look deeper into the main concepts of generative AI, how it is currently being deployed in educational contexts, the ethical challenges it offers, and how educators and learners can work with AI to create a more dynamic and individualized learning experience. The goal is to explore how AI might serve as an important tool, not just for automating activities, but for encouraging a deeper, more meaningful educational experience that stresses creativity, critical thinking, and lifelong learning.

UNDERSTANDING GENERATIVE AI: KEY CONCEPTS AND TECHNOLOGIES

Generative AI is a fast-expanding branch of artificial intelligence that is altering a wide range of industries, including education, entertainment, healthcare, and business (Labajová, 2023). At its foundation, generative AI refers to the use of machine learning algorithms to generate new, original material based on patterns learned from existing data. Unlike standard AI systems that are primarily geared to classify, analyze, or predict based on data, generative AI may produce something wholly new—whether it's writing, graphics, music, or even complicated video. This ability to generate information that is indistinguishable from that made by people has sparked both enthusiasm and anxiety, giving immense potential for innovation while raising ethical and practical concerns.

One of the most significant ideas in comprehending generative AI is its differentiation from other forms of AI (Banh & Strobel, 2023). While many AI systems are focused on tasks such as data classification, regression, or prediction, generative AI's primary objective is to produce or generate new material. It does this by learning the underlying structure and patterns in a dataset and then using that information to generate outputs that resemble the data it was trained on. For instance, in natural language processing (NLP), a generative AI model like GPT (Generative Pre-trained Transformer) may produce human-like writing by evaluating huge volumes of written material and recognizing the rules and patterns of language (Kondurkar et al, 2024). At the foundation of generative AI is the concept of machine learning, a subset of artificial intelligence. Machine learning includes training algorithms on big datasets, enabling the system to spot patterns and make predictions or judgments without being specifically coded for each task (Elshawi et al, 2018). In the case of generative AI, these algorithms not only recognize patterns but also use them to produce new content. The most prevalent machine learning methods used in generative AI are neural networks, particularly deep learning, which replicates the way the human brain processes information.

Deep learning, a subtype of machine learning, incorporates neural networks with multiple layers (thus "deep") that are capable of learning complicated patterns in data (Indrakumari et al, 2021). The most well-known deep learning models used in generative AI are Generative Adversarial Networks (GANs) and Variational Autoencoders (VAEs), both of which have revolutionized the field by enabling machines to generate realistic images, videos, and even human-like language (Bengesi et al, 2024). Generative Adversarial Networks, or GANs, are one of the most interesting breakthroughs in the domain of generative AI (Pan et al, 2019). A GAN consists of two neural networks: the generator and the discriminator. The generator creates new content (such as images or text), while the discriminator examines the content to determine if it is real or fake, i.e., whether it matches the patterns in the original dataset. The two networks "compete" against one other: the generator seeks to enhance its outputs to trick the discriminator, and the discriminator grows better at differentiating real from fake. This adversarial process continues until the generator creates content that is indistinguishable from the original data, whether it's generating photographs of individuals who don't exist or creating realistic-looking art. This back-and-forth process of refinement has enabled GANs to produce some of the most compelling content generated by AI.

Another major tool in generative AI is the Variational Autoencoder (VAE) (Asperti et al, 2021). VAEs function by encoding input data into a compact representation called a "latent space," and then decoding it to produce new data. While GANs focus on the adversarial competition between networks, VAEs focus on the probabilistic modeling of the data and generating new content that is both realistic and diverse. The advantage of VAEs resides in their ability to generate more diversified content from the same input dataset, as the latent space allows for the exploration of numerous potential outcomes depending on the data's patterns (Chow et al, 2022). In natural language processing, a key advance came with the development of Transformer-based models, such as GPT-3, which is a generative AI model capable of producing human-like prose (Obaid et al, 2023). The Transformer design changed the field of NLP by allowing the model to quickly process and grasp long-range dependencies in text. Unlike prior models, which analyzed language sequentially (one word at a time), Transformers use self-attention processes to analyze all sections of the incoming text at once, making them faster and more accurate. GPT-3, built by OpenAI, is one of the largest and most powerful generative AI models to date. Trained on hundreds of billions of words, it is capable of composing essays, answering questions, generating poetry, and even writing computer code with astonishing fluency and coherence.

The main strength of generative AI models like GPT-3 rests in their capacity to develop outputs that are not only contextually appropriate but also creative and innovative (Kondurkar et al, 2024). For example, GPT-3 may generate a poem or a short story based on just a few phrases of input, and the outcomes often reveal a deep awareness of language structure and style. This ability to create content that seems natural and original has significant outcomes for industries such as education, marketing, content development, and more. Generative AI does not come without its challenges. One of the key issues is the possibility of bias in AI-generated information (Wach et al, 2023). Because these models are trained on big datasets, they typically learn biases present in the data, whether it's related to gender, ethnicity, or socio-economic characteristics. For example, if an AI model is trained on text data that largely reflects the beliefs of one demographic group, it may produce material that unintentionally reflects those prejudices (Kirk et al, 2021). This has led to continuous efforts to eliminate prejudice in generative AI models through better data curation, diverse training sets, and fairness-aware algorithms.

Another difficulty is the ethical implications of utilizing generative AI to create content (Fui-Hoon Nah et al, 2023). While generative AI has the potential to democratize creativity by enabling anybody with access to the technology to make high-quality work, it also raises difficulties about authorship, intellectual property, and the value of human creativity.

For instance, if a generative AI model develops a work of art, who owns the rights to that work? Is it the developer of the AI, the user who prompted the AI, or the AI itself?

These difficulties are currently being contested, and as generative AI gets more advanced, humanity will need to build new frameworks for intellectual property and authorship. Despite these obstacles, generative AI holds significant promise for transforming several areas, including education. In educational situations, generative AI can be used to develop personalized learning materials, such as textbooks, assignments, and quizzes suited to the individual needs of each student. It can also assist instructors build content for courses, enabling them to create customized teaching materials that engage students in new and inventive ways. For instance, AI can provide simulations, interactive exercises, and real-time feedback, making learning more interesting and customizable to specific student needs.

The potential applications of generative AI extend far beyond education (Lim et al, 2023). In healthcare, AI can assist in the generation of medical pictures for training purposes, build prediction models for patient outcomes, and even assist in drug discovery by generating new molecular structures. In entertainment, generative AI can create realistic special effects, produce music, and even write scripts for movies and television shows. As technology continues to advance, the opportunities for generative AI seem boundless, with the ability to promote creativity, productivity, and innovation across a wide range of industries. Understanding generative AI means grasping its underlying technologies—such as deep learning, GANs, VAEs, and Transformer models—and recognizing its ability to generate fresh, creative content (Madaan et al, 2024). While difficulties linked to prejudice and ethics exist, the transformational power of generative AI is evident. As the technology matures, it will continue to transform sectors, bringing new options for innovation, efficiency, and customization. The key to successfully harnessing the power of generative AI is understanding its capabilities and limitations, resolving its ethical difficulties, and finding ways to integrate it into human-driven systems that maximize its potential for beneficial impact.

THE ROLE OF COLLABORATIVE INTELLIGENCE IN EDUCATION

Collaborative intelligence is an emerging notion that revolves around the idea of numerous entities—whether human or artificial—working together in a cooperative environment to achieve goals that would be impossible to accomplish individually (Malone & Woolley, 2020). In the context of education, collaborative intelligence stresses the cooperation between human educators, students, and artificial intelligence systems to enhance the learning experience. By mixing human experience with the computational power of AI, collaborative intelligence has the potential to change how we approach teaching and learning. At the heart of collaborative intelligence is the premise that while AI systems like generative models can absorb massive quantities of information and generate insights, it is the human element—creativity, empathy, and critical thinking—that enables meaningful, transformative education (Przegalinska & Triantoro, 2024). Collaborative intelligence, therefore, is not about replacing instructors or students with machines but about increasing their skills, empowering them to work together in ways that were previously imagined. This cooperation allows humans to focus on higher-order cognitive tasks, such as problem-solving and ethical decision-making, while AI takes on more repetitive or computationally intensive duties, such as content development or data processing.

One of the primary ways in which collaborative intelligence improves education is by promoting individualized learning (Muñoz-Martínez et al, 2020). Every learner is distinct, with individual talents, weaknesses, interests, and learning preferences. Traditionally, educators have had the problem of fulfilling the different needs of their students within a single classroom setting. Collaborative intelligence can give a solution to this challenge by enabling AI to monitor a student's performance in real-time and provide personalized learning materials, tasks, or comments according to that individual's needs (Pedro et al, 2019). For instance, AI can track a student's progress in a particular subject and, based on this data, offer specific resources, activities, or even teaching styles that would be more helpful for the learner. This method moves beyond the one-size-fits-all concept of education and offers an atmosphere where students can learn at their own pace and in ways that resonate with them most. AI-powered solutions can support educators by giving them specific insights into each student's progress. This is particularly helpful in large classrooms when individual attention might be difficult to offer. By studying patterns in student performance, AI can help identify students who may be failing or those who require more challenges. An AI system might recognize that a particular student has difficulties learning a concept in mathematics, prompting the educator to provide more guidance or resources. In this sense, AI functions as a powerful assistant to the instructor, boosting their capacity to manage and engage with each student more effectively. However, it is vital to highlight that this is not an attempt to replace the professor. Rather, it empowers the professor by giving them tools that enable more efficient and informed decision-making.

In addition to personalized learning, collaborative intelligence supports the development of critical thinking and problem-solving skills (Rane et al, 2023). Traditional education generally places a large emphasis on rote memorization and standardized testing, which can hinder creativity and inhibit students' capacity to think independently. Collaborative intelligence moves the focus to more active types of learning, where students engage alongside AI technologies to address real-world challenges (Kim et al, 2022). By harnessing AI's computing capacity, students may simulate scenarios, test theories, and produce solutions in ways that would be difficult without such tools. For example, in a science lesson, students can use AI to model complicated systems, anticipate outcomes, and evaluate data, allowing them to participate in a deeper, more hands-on understanding of the subject matter. The collaborative part of collaborative intelligence means that students also gain the valuable skill of collaborating with others (Mora et al, 2020). Education has always emphasized the necessity of teamwork, but the tools available now take this to the next level. Students can collaborate with their peers and AI tools in ways that increase learning results. Whether working on a group project, participating in an online learning community, or engaging in collaborative problem-solving with AI systems, students are building the interpersonal and digital skills necessary for success in the 21st-century workforce. AI can assist and enable this cooperation by offering a platform for students to communicate with one another and with educational content (Chen et al, 2020). For example, AI-driven discussion boards or collaborative platforms might match students with similar learning goals or interests, enabling peer-to-peer learning and cooperation.

AI's ability to assess and respond to student inputs in real-time means that students can receive rapid feedback on their work (Xu et al, 2023). In traditional educational environments, feedback can sometimes be delayed, particularly in big classrooms where Faculty members may not have the time to address each student personally. Collaborative intelligence modifies this dynamic by guaranteeing that students receive timely, constructive feedback on their assignments and performance. This rapid feedback loop allows students to see where they went wrong and correct mistakes in real-time, increasing their learning process. Additionally, the continual feedback provided by AI helps to enhance learning and retention, since students may modify their techniques and approaches depending on immediate results. Beyond individual students, collaborative intelligence also enriches the broader teaching process by facilitating more dynamic and participatory classroom situations. AI can be utilized to create immersive learning experiences that go beyond standard lectures or textbooks. For example, in a history class, AI can provide virtual tours of past civilizations, allowing students to experience historical events or explore archaeological sites in a way that traditional teaching approaches cannot imitate. These experiences make learning more engaging and can help students better understand complex concepts by creating a more dynamic, multimodal learning environment. Similarly, AI may assist in generating simulations that allow students to practice skills in a safe and controlled environment, whether it's learning to code, practicing medical procedures, or conducting engineering experiments.

Another facet of collaborative intelligence in education is the role of AI in administrative chores (Nwile & Edo, 2023). Education is not only about teaching and learning; it also entails a considerable deal of administrative work, from grading homework to monitoring student records (Suskie, 2018). By automating these duties, AI can free up Faculty members and administrators to focus more on the instructional aspects of their roles. AI systems can undertake basic administrative responsibilities, such as grading essays, arranging assignments, and maintaining timetables, allowing Faculty members to commit more time to contact with students. Additionally, AI can assist with controlling classroom dynamics, such as ensuring that students are on track with their learning goals or alerting educators when a student might require extra attention (Dimitriadou & Lanitis, 2023). This reduction in administrative burden can make the educational system more efficient and ensure that Faculty members can spend more time engaging with students.

Collaborative intelligence also plays a key part in preparing students for the future (Kim et al, 2022). As the workforce grows increasingly reliant on digital technology and AI tools, students need to be equipped with the skills and knowledge to navigate this new world. Through collaborative intelligence, students not only study subject-specific content but also build digital literacy, problem-solving ability, and critical thinking skills that will assist them in the future. Collaborative intelligence supports an attitude of continual learning, as students become accustomed to working with AI technologies that are constantly evolving (Ruiz-Rojas et al, 2024). This prepares students for a world in which technology developments and collaboration with AI will be routine. The role of collaborative intelligence in education is complex and holds enormous promise for improving the learning process (Rienties et al, 2020). By mixing human knowledge with AI tools, collaborative intelligence creates an environment where students can receive tailored teaching, engage in more interactive and dynamic learning experiences, and build skills that are needed for the modern workforce. This relationship between humans and AI is not about replacing one with the other but about expanding the capabilities of both, ultimately leading to more effective, engaging, and equitable educational experiences. As educational institutions continue to incorporate AI technologies, it will be crucial to ensure that these tools are employed in ways that boost human learning and build a collaborative atmosphere in which both educators and students may thrive.

GENERATIVE AI TOOLS FOR PERSONALIZED LEARNING AND TEACHING

Generative AI techniques are rapidly revolutionizing the landscape of education by enabling individualized learning and teaching experiences that were formerly thought unattainable (Kayyali, 2025 A). At the center of this transformation is the ability of AI to adapt to the requirements of individual students, offering tailored information, real-time feedback, and a more interactive and engaging learning environment. These systems harness enormous amounts of data to analyze learning habits, preferences, and performance, personalizing the educational experience to meet each student's specific requirements. This has the potential to greatly boost educational outcomes, making learning more efficient and accessible for students of all backgrounds. Personalized learning is a strong notion that allows students to grow at their own pace, focusing on the areas where they need the most help while going rapidly through subjects they have learned. Generative AI plays a major part in this by providing the required tools for constructing adaptable learning environments that continuously respond to the student's evolving demands. Traditional education techniques, with their predetermined curricula and one-size-fits-all approach, sometimes struggle to accommodate the different speeds at which students learn (Kayyali,

2024 A). In contrast, generative AI enables dynamic and responsive learning experiences, giving content that is continuously modified based on the student's progress, strengths, and shortcomings.

One of the major ways in which generative AI promotes personalized learning is through the generation of bespoke learning materials (Nam et al, 2023). For example, AI can provide tailored exercises, quizzes, and assignments that are especially geared to address the gaps in a student's understanding. If a learner is struggling with a certain idea, the AI system may automatically recognize the difficulty and generate practice difficulties that target that exact region. Conversely, if a student is succeeding in a subject, the system can deliver more advanced content to keep them engaged and challenged. This level of customization not only enriches the student's learning experience but also allows for more effective teaching, as instructors may use the AI-generated content as a supplement to their traditional lesson plans, delivering a more holistic and tailored approach to instruction. Generative AI techniques also enable Faculty members to focus on the areas where human skill and creativity are most helpful (Ruiz-Rojas et al, 2024). For example, while AI can aid with grading assignments, offering individualized practice, and generating content, it cannot duplicate the empathy, mentorship, or moral advice that a professor delivers. AI systems are designed to handle mundane and repetitive activities, freeing up Faculty members to concentrate on more meaningful parts of teaching, such as cultivating critical thinking, inspiring curiosity, and providing emotional support to students. This collaborative relationship between AI and Faculty members boosts the overall quality of education, allowing Faculty members to spend more time connecting with students on a personal level and offering individualized instruction based on individual requirements.

Another feature of personalized learning aided by generative AI is the capacity to build a more inclusive learning environment (Guettala et al, 2024). Students have varied learning styles, and what works for one student may not be beneficial for another. Traditional teaching techniques typically struggle to address these disparities in a meaningful way. Generative AI, on the other hand, is capable of adapting the distribution of content to match varied learning preferences. For example, some students may learn better through visual materials, while others may prefer text-based material or interactive simulations. Generative AI can alter its teaching methods to fit these tastes, giving a mix of multimedia content, from movies and diagrams to interactive quizzes and text-based explanations, ensuring that all students have access to the resources that best promote their learning (Pesovski et al, 2024). This not only makes learning more enjoyable but also ensures that students with diverse abilities and learning preferences are not left behind. Generative AI techniques can help bridge the gap for students who experience external difficulties, such as those with learning disabilities or language barriers. AI systems can provide support targeted to individual needs, supporting students with dyslexia, for instance, by offering text-to-speech capabilities or creating more readable information (Wang et al, 2022). Similarly, students who are learning in a second language can benefit from AI systems that translate complex content into their native language or offer simplified explanations. This degree of individualized support guarantees that all students, regardless of their background or obstacles, can access the curriculum and participate completely in their learning.

The real-time feedback offered by generative AI is another powerful characteristic of these tools (Bandi et al, 2023). In traditional classes, students typically have to wait for tasks to be evaluated before receiving feedback on their performance, which can impede their learning process. With AI, feedback may be immediate and constant, allowing students to alter their approach and comprehension in real-time. For example, AI can instantaneously evaluate a student's reaction to a practice exercise and make ideas for improvement or alternative tactics. This helps students to learn from their mistakes and correct them instantly, reinforcing essential concepts and fostering a more proactive attitude to learning. Additionally, this rapid feedback loop helps to retain student engagement, since students are more likely to stay motivated when they receive immediate and constructive input on their progress.

One of the most interesting breakthroughs in generative AI for personalized learning is the possibility for AI to assist in the construction of unique learning routes (Prabhod, 2023). These routes are built based on an individual's present knowledge, learning preferences, and long-term goals, creating a roadmap for students to follow as they navigate through their educational journey. AI algorithms may examine a student's development over time, track their performance on different tasks, and assess their strengths and weaknesses to produce a tailored curriculum that changes as the learner improves. This means that no two students are likely to have the same learning route, providing for a more tailored and effective learning experience. These learning paths can help students stay motivated by setting clear goals and milestones, providing them with a feeling of direction and purpose throughout their educational journey. In higher education, generative AI techniques are now being utilized to help students generate tailored research or project plans (Chiu, 2024). AI can assist students in locating appropriate resources for their projects, generating research topics, and even suggesting approaches based on the student's subject of study. By employing AI in this way, students can more quickly investigate areas of interest, allowing them to go deeper into subjects that might otherwise be overwhelming. AI may coach students through the process of creating and polishing research papers or projects, making ideas on organization, grammar, and topic (Nabilla et al, 2024). This ensures that students generate high-quality work while learning to improve their research and writing skills over time.

Despite the many advantages of generative AI tools for personalized learning, it's crucial to remember that these systems are not perfect (Yan et al, 2024). AI models are only as good as the data they are trained on, and there are potential concerns associated with bias in the algorithms that drive these systems. For example, if an AI system is educated on data that reflects historical injustices or preconceptions, it may accidentally perpetuate those biases in its suggestions. To reduce these concerns, it is crucial to ensure that AI systems are developed with fairness and inclusivity in mind and that they are continuously examined and updated to address potential biases (Kayyali, 2025 B). While generative AI can substantially increase individualized learning, it cannot replace the crucial role that human educators play in building a loving, supportive learning environment. Faculty members are not merely knowledge transmitters; they are mentors, guides, and facilitators who create relationships with students, understand their emotional needs, and assist them in negotiating both academic and personal difficulties (Wang, 2024). AI can complement this task, but it cannot duplicate the human touch that is so vital to the learning process. Generative AI techniques have significant promise for individualized learning and teaching. By giving tailored content, real-time feedback, and unique learning paths, these tools have the potential to provide a more effective, interesting, and inclusive learning environment for all students. However, it is vital to note that AI should not replace human educators, but rather act as a strong tool to support and enhance their job. When applied responsibly and ethically, generative AI has the power to alter education, helping students to learn more efficiently and effectively while preparing them for the challenges of the future.

AI-ENHANCED CLASSROOM ENVIRONMENTS: A NEW ERA OF ENGAGEMENT

The integration of artificial intelligence (AI) into classroom environments symbolizes the advent of a new era in education, one where engagement, personalization, and interactive learning reach new heights (Rane et al, 2023). While AI has long been linked with high-tech sectors and complicated computations, its incorporation into education is revolutionizing the way students experience learning. AI has progressed from being a basic tool to a major factor in redefining classroom dynamics, boosting collaboration, increasing interaction, and enabling individualized learning experiences that were previously inconceivable. In this new era, AI is not just an assistance but an active participant in the educational process, complementing the function of the professor and increasing the learning experience for students.

At the basis of AI-enhanced classroom environments is the idea of creating a space where technology not only supports but actively promotes engagement (Alshahrani & Qureshi, 2024). Traditional classroom environments, while effective, frequently follow a predetermined pattern of delivering content, measuring student progress, and providing feedback. AI, however, brings with it the opportunity to make this process much more fluid and dynamic. Through a range of tools and technologies, AI can respond to student needs in real-time, modify the speed of learning, and give resources personalized to each individual (Koroteev & Tekic, 2021). This dynamic adaptability is one of the major features of AI-enhanced classrooms, providing an educational experience that grows based on the student's interactions and learning progress. One key manner in which AI is transforming classroom participation is by enabling individualized learning experiences that are finely adjusted to the strengths and weaknesses of each learner. Traditionally, Faculty members have to divide their attention between numerous students at once, often resulting in some students being left behind while others may feel under-challenged. With AI, however, learning can be personalized to the individual in real-time (Sajja, 2024). AI-powered systems can analyze how well a learner is learning a concept and provide further practice or explanations where needed. If a student is thriving, the system can present more advanced topics to keep them engaged and minimize boredom. This level of customization guarantees that every student is working at their ideal pace and receiving the exact support they need, building a deeper connection to the subject and enhancing overall engagement.

In addition to tailored learning routes, AI may also drive engagement through the creation of interactive, immersive experiences (Partarakis & Zabulis, 2024). Gone are the days when students would passively absorb information from a textbook or lecture. AI-enhanced classrooms bring knowledge to life in ways that inspire active engagement. AI-powered virtual reality (VR) and augmented reality (AR) tools can construct simulations where students can experience complicated concepts directly (Al Balushi et al, 2024). Whether it's wandering through historical civilizations in a history lesson, completing virtual chemistry experiments in a lab, or studying the human body in biology, these technologies turn learning from a passive experience into an engaging adventure. Students are no longer only listening to explanations but are actively involved in experiential learning, which dramatically boosts knowledge and retention. AI can transform the way students collaborate. Group work and collaborative projects are key components of modern education, but coordinating and administering these activities can be tough in a big classroom. AI can assist in organizing and fostering collaboration by assessing students' abilities and interests and developing groups accordingly (Kim et al, 2022). AI may help monitor and supervise the progress of group activities, ensuring that each member is contributing and that the group continues on target. Through real-time feedback, AI can stimulate fruitful debates, recommend resources, and even provide suggestions to help direct the group toward creative answers. In this sense, AI becomes a collaborative partner that promotes teamwork and the general quality of student interaction.

One of the most interesting parts of AI-enhanced educational environments is the ability to facilitate continual and rapid feedback (Redhu et al, 2024). In traditional classes, feedback can often be delayed, with students getting it only after assignments or tests have been assessed. This delay might impair the learning process, since students may not have the opportunity to instantly address mistakes or misunderstandings. AI, however, can provide fast feedback on tasks, quizzes, or even spoken comments. If a student provides an answer to a question or completes an interactive exercise, the AI system can evaluate the response and provide feedback quickly, allowing the learner to remedy errors and gain a deeper knowledge of the content. This continuous feedback loop is a crucial tool for both students and Faculty members, as it allows for quicker intervention, minimizes the possibility of misconceptions, and helps students stay engaged with the topic.

Another major element of AI-enhanced classrooms is the capacity to track and assess student performance over time (Henry & Daniel, 2024). Traditional assessments such as exams or essays provide a glimpse of a student's knowledge at a particular point but frequently fail to offer a comprehensive view of their learning journey. AI tools, on the other hand, may watch a student's progress continuously, accumulating data on everything from the time spent on tasks to the types of mistakes made and the areas where a student excels. This data can be utilized to generate thorough performance profiles that offer both students and Faculty members a full knowledge of the student's learning processes. For students, this means that they can receive insight into where they need to develop and what tactics are working best for them. For Faculty members, this data allows for more informed judgments on how to alter their teaching tactics and provide targeted support where it is most required. The significance of AI in establishing a more inclusive educational climate is equally essential (Pedro et al, 2019). Every student has distinct learning demands, and AI solutions can be particularly effective in adapting to these differences. For students with impairments, AI-powered solutions can offer features such as speech-to-text, text-to-speech, or sign language translation, making it easier for them to access instructional resources. Additionally, AI can give customized resources for students who may require extra support, delivering simplified explanations or offering additional practice to help reinforce topics (Khosravi et al, 2022). For students who are learning in a second language, AI systems can offer translation services or adaptive learning paths that cater to their individual needs. This level of inclusion ensures that every student, regardless of their background or ability, may fully connect with the learning material and participate in the classroom experience.

Faculty members also profit from AI-enhanced teaching environments in numerous ways. AI can help Faculty members expedite administrative activities such as grading, tracking attendance, or arranging lesson plans (Aithal & Aithal, 2023). By automating these chores, AI frees up Faculty members' time so they can focus more on educational activities and personal contact with students. Moreover, AI systems can give Faculty members insights into how students are performing in real-time, allowing for timely adjustments to teaching tactics. For instance, if a major fraction of the class is struggling with a specific idea, the professor can instantly recognize this and decide whether to review the material in greater detail, modify the delivery technique, or give more resources for practice.

Despite the many benefits, there are still hurdles to overcome in the integration of AI in colleges (Luan et al, 2020). One of the key worries is the possibility of over-reliance on technology, which might lead to a diminishing role for Faculty members in the educational process. It is vital to remember that AI should be considered as a tool to enhance teaching, not replace it. The human aspect is crucial to education since Faculty members give emotional support, mentorship, and the kind of judgment that AI systems currently cannot mimic. Another problem is ensuring that AI technologies are accessible to all students, regardless of socio-economic position or access to technology (Martins & Gresse von Wangenheim, 2024). It is crucial to overcome the digital divide to guarantee that the benefits of AI-enhanced classrooms are available to all learners. AI-enhanced classroom environments represent a radical shift in education, giving unparalleled prospects for engagement, personalization, and collaboration. By embracing AI technologies, classrooms are becoming more interactive, inclusive, and data-driven, allowing students to learn in ways that are suited to their particular requirements (Tatineni, 2020). While obstacles exist, notably in terms of equality and ensuring that AI is utilized as a complement to, rather than a replacement for, human Faculty members, the potential benefits of AI in education are evident. As technology continues to grow, AI-enhanced classrooms are poised to change the educational experience, promoting a more dynamic, engaging, and individualized learning environment for students throughout the world.

ETHICAL CONSIDERATIONS IN USING GENERATIVE AI IN EDUCATION

The incorporation of generative AI in education brings with it not only scientific breakthroughs but also a variety of ethical difficulties that need to be carefully addressed. While AI has the potential to transform teaching and learning, offering personalized educational experiences, enhancing classroom engagement, and improving access to resources, its use in educational settings raises important questions about privacy, fairness, accountability, and the role of educators (Alasadi & Baiz, 2023). As educational institutions progressively adopt AI tools and technologies, these ethical difficulties must be explored and mitigated to guarantee that AI is used in a way that benefits all stakeholders—students, Faculty members, and society at large.

One of the most important ethical concerns in the usage of generative AI in education is the question of data privacy and security (Bukar et al, 2024). AI systems rely on large amounts of data to function properly, and in the context of education, this often involves collecting sensitive information about students. This data may include personal characteristics such as academic performance, learning preferences, behavioral trends, and even demographic information. While such data can be essential for tailoring learning and boosting educational achievements, it also raises substantial issues about privacy. If this data is not properly secured, it could be subject to breaches, misuse, or exploitation by unauthorized persons. Additionally, there is the potential that the data could be exploited for purposes beyond the educational setting, such as commercial exploitation or spying. To address these concerns, educational institutions must implement robust data protection protocols, ensuring that all student data is stored and processed in compliance with privacy laws and regulations such as the General Data Protection Regulation (GDPR) in the European Union or similar frameworks in other regions (Dove, 2018). Transparency in how data is acquired, used, and shared is vital. Students and their families must be fully informed about what data is being gathered, why it is needed, and how it will be utilized. Consent should be requested where appropriate, and students should have the ability to opt-out of specific data-gathering procedures if they desire. Ethical use of data in AI systems needs a careful balance between the benefits of personalization and the fundamental right to privacy.

Another ethical concern related to the employment of AI in education is fairness and bias (Modi, 2023). AI systems are only as good as the data they are trained on, and if the data used to train generative AI models is biased, the resulting system can perpetuate those biases in its outputs (Ferrara, 2023). In educational situations, this could emerge in a variety of ways. For instance, if an AI system is trained on historical data that reveals discrepancies in educational performance for certain demographic groups, the AI may accidentally benefit students from particular backgrounds while disadvantaging others. This could result in biased suggestions, unethical grading procedures, or unequal access to learning resources. For example, if an AI system used to offer personalized learning resources is trained on data from a set of students that largely belongs to one ethnic or socio-economic group, it may fail to accurately respond to the needs of students from diverse backgrounds. This could lead to the reinforcing of existing disparities rather than eliminating them. In other circumstances, biased AI systems could potentially reinforce prejudices or unfairly discriminate against particular students based on variables such as gender, color, or disability.

To prevent bias in AI systems, educators and developers must work together to guarantee that the data used to train these systems is diverse, representative, and free from discrimination (Chinta et al, 2024). AI systems should be constantly inspected for fairness to discover and correct any potential biases that may occur. Transparency in the development process is also vital, since it allows external parties to assess the AI system's design and implementation, ensuring that ethical criteria are being met. Ultimately, the goal should be to design AI tools that are equal, providing all students with the opportunity to thrive, regardless of their background or circumstances. In addition to data privacy and bias, there is the topic of accountability in AI-driven educational contexts. As AI becomes more incorporated into classrooms and learning systems, there is a rising need to clarify who is responsible when things go wrong. For instance, if an AI system offers false feedback or leads a student along an inappropriate learning route, who is held liable for the consequences? Is it the developers who designed the AI, the educational institution that deployed it, or the AI system itself?

This subject of responsibility is particularly challenging in the context of generative AI, as these systems are capable of producing outputs that are not necessarily foreseeable. Unlike traditional educational tools, where the outcomes are controlled by human decision-makers, AI systems generate content based on algorithms and patterns in data, which can sometimes lead to unexpected or unintentional effects. If an AI tool offers incorrect learning content or makes a recommendation that is harmful to a student's educational progress, there must be clear processes in place to hold the relevant parties accountable. This includes clear lines of responsibility for both the design and deployment of AI systems, as well as the continuing monitoring and oversight of their use. Educators must remain a central role in the educational process, even as AI takes on increasing duties (Hwang et al, 2020). AI should complement, not replace, the professor's position. The human element of education is vital, as Faculty members give emotional support, mentorship, and ethical direction that AI cannot mimic. Faculty members are the ones who eventually evaluate and contextualize AI-generated recommendations, ensuring that students are receiving an education that conforms with human values and society standards. Thus, educators must be trained not just in how to utilize AI technologies efficiently but also in how to analyze the ethical implications of AI in the classroom. Faculty members must be provided with the knowledge and skills to critically assess AI-generated information and intervene when necessary to preserve students' well-being.

Another ethical consideration is the potential impact of AI on the professor -student relationship (Bankins & Formosa, 2023). Education is not simply about imparting knowledge—it is also about promoting personal growth, emotional development, and critical thinking abilities. If AI systems become more prominent in the learning process, there is a risk that the personal link between professor and student could be weakened. The benefits of face-to-face engagement, mentorship, and emotional support provided by educators cannot be emphasized. While AI can enhance these connections by delivering individualized learning tools, it should not replace the core human parts of education. As AI tools grow more pervasive in education, there is also the potential of increasing the digital gap. Access to AI-powered learning tools may be limited in locations or communities that do not have the appropriate technological infrastructure. This could result in a situation where students in wealthy places benefit from advanced AI-driven educational tools, while others in less-developed regions are left behind. To ensure that the use of AI in education is equitable, it is vital to address issues of access and ensure that all students, regardless of their socio-economic level or geographic location, have equal opportunities to benefit from these technologies.

There is the broader question of how AI will affect the future of education and the skills that students will need to flourish in a world increasingly controlled by technology. As AI systems take on larger roles in education, there is a concern that students may become unduly reliant on technology to the detriment of their critical thinking, creativity, and problem-solving skills. Education should try to cultivate well-rounded individuals who can think independently, interact with complicated ideas, and negotiate the ethical difficulties of an AI-driven future (Khine, 2024). As such, educators and politicians must carefully evaluate the broader implications of AI in shaping future generations, ensuring that it is employed in a way that improves human development rather than replacing vital cognitive and emotional skills. While generative AI holds immense potential for revolutionizing education, its ethical implications cannot be neglected. Issues such as data privacy, bias, accountability, and the professor-student connection must be addressed to guarantee that AI is used in a way that is fair, transparent, and respectful of human rights. By taking a careful and responsible approach to the integration of AI in education, we can ensure that these technologies are used to promote learning, support educators, and offer more equitable educational opportunities for all students.

CASE STUDIES: SUCCESSFUL APPLICATIONS OF GENERATIVE AI IN EDUCATIONAL SETTINGS

As generative AI continues to make advancements in the domain of education, various institutions, colleges, and universities around the world have begun integrating these technologies into their teaching and learning settings. From individualized learning experiences to automated content production and intelligent tutoring systems, generative AI has proved its potential to increase educational outcomes.

One of the most noteworthy examples of successful AI integration comes from the University of Southern California (USC), where AI-driven learning systems have been used to tailor teaching for students across many disciplines (Singh et al, 2025). USC has deployed AI capabilities to customize content delivery to the learning preferences of individual students, producing a more tailored and successful learning experience. The AI technology, known as "Lumi," monitors students' progress and engagement levels and modifies the pace and difficulty of education accordingly (Lüy et al, 2024). It also provides real-time comments and recommendations for students to improve their comprehension of essential concepts. Lumi's capacity to analyze vast amounts of data rapidly and reliably has helped USC to offer more tailored and engaging experiences for their students, particularly in large lecture-style classes, which sometimes struggle with individualized attention. The approach has proved particularly useful in disciplines like mathematics and engineering, where students often struggle to keep up with difficult problem-solving activities. By employing generative AI, USC has been able to offer students adaptive learning routes, providing them the ability to work through challenges at their own pace (Yalazi-Dawani,

2023). If a learner is struggling with a particular idea, the AI system can offer additional resources, videos, or practice difficulties that are specifically geared to assist them overcome the obstacle. This has resulted in enhanced learning results, with students expressing higher levels of engagement and satisfaction with the course material.

Another powerful case study of generative AI in education comes from Georgia State University, which has effectively integrated AI-driven advising tools to help students navigate their academic journeys (Iatrellis et al, 2024). The institution introduced an AI-powered application dubbed "Pounce," which employs predictive analytics and natural language processing to provide students with real-time academic help. Pounce analyzes students' course history, academic achievement, and extracurricular activities to give individualized suggestions about course choices, tutoring services, and career pathways. This AI-driven approach has not only helped students make educated decisions about their academic pathways but has also contributed to a drop in student retention rates. Before the deployment of the AI tool, many students at Georgia State University struggled to locate the correct academic help, resulting in confusion and frustration. Pounce addressed this issue by offering students with on-demand, individualized guidance at the push of a button. Additionally, the system informs students when they are at risk of falling behind in a course, suggesting interventions such as additional tutoring or study group ideas. As a result, Georgia State has observed better retention and graduation rates, especially among minority student populations. The success of an AI-driven advising system demonstrates how generative AI may play a crucial role in ensuring that students receive the help they need to excel academically.

In the K-12 education arena, generative AI has also shown potential in aiding both instructors and students (Chiu, 2024). One such example comes from the employment of AI-powered platforms in colleges in the United Kingdom, where educators have employed AI to automate the generation of individualized learning content. Faculty members at numerous colleges in the UK have implemented AI systems that can generate bespoke tests, assignments, and instructional materials depending on the particular requirements and talents of each student. These tools not only save Faculty members time but also ensure that each student receives the most appropriate and relevant content for their learning level. For instance, an AI system called "Socrative" has been employed in several UK colleges to help Faculty members prepare real-time assessments for their students. By monitoring the responses and progress of students, Socrative provides individualized quizzes and feedback in real-time, helping to pinpoint areas where students need further support. This allows instructors to instantly change their teaching tactics, guaranteeing that no student is left behind. In addition, the system's capacity to automatically grade assignments and track student achievement allows Faculty members to focus more on individual instruction and less on administrative responsibilities, providing for a more efficient and effective learning environment.

The impact of generative AI on professor professional development has also been considerable. In certain educational contexts, AI-driven platforms are being utilized to generate individualized training modules for Faculty members, allowing them to enhance their skills at their speed (Alshamsi et al, 2024). For example, in several colleges across North America, AI tools are being deployed to provide Faculty members with real-time feedback on their classroom methods. These systems analyze classroom interactions, such as student engagement levels and responses to instructional methods, and make recommendations for improvement. By employing AI to reflect on their teaching styles, educators may continuously adapt their approaches to match the needs of their students, boosting the overall quality of education. Additionally, the rise of AI-powered tutoring systems has made a considerable impact on individualized learning in higher education. At the University of Toronto, a generative AI-powered tutoring system has been developed to educate students in STEM subjects. The system, known as "AssistAI," employs machine learning algorithms to assess a student's current comprehension of a given topic and generate customized lectures and practice tasks. Students can interact with AssistAI to obtain step-by-step advice on complex difficulties, and the system changes its responses based on the student's progress and queries.

What makes AssistAI particularly helpful is its capacity to give individualized learning experiences without the requirement for one-on-one engagement with an instructor (Holstein et al, 2019). Students can use the system 24/7, allowing them to learn at their own pace and on their schedule. This has been especially helpful for students studying part-time or those with busy schedules. The system's generative capabilities allow it to construct a virtually limitless number of practice difficulties matched to each student's needs, which helps to reinforce learning and enhance retention. As a result, the University of Toronto has observed considerable improvements in student performance, particularly among students who previously struggled with the obstacles of STEM education. Beyond the classroom, generative AI is also being employed in educational content production, which has extensive implications for curriculum design (Alasadi & Baiz, 2023). At Harvard University, researchers are researching how generative AI may assist generate interactive and interesting learning materials, particularly in areas like history and literature. By integrating AI, they may develop immersive simulations, quizzes, and even interactive storytelling experiences that boost student engagement. For example, students studying history can engage with AI-generated historical individuals or observe historical events unfold in a virtual setting. These dynamic, tailored experiences make learning more interesting and memorable, helping students better understand challenging subjects.

Generative AI has also been effectively implemented in language learning (Huang et al, 2024). Duolingo, a popular language-learning software, leverages AI-driven algorithms to adapt lessons for each user (Wang, 2024). The platform changes its content to meet the learner's strengths and limitations, modifying difficulty levels as users advance through sessions. The app employs generative AI to develop new activities based on users' learning habits and delivers fast feedback to help them improve. This specialized approach has made Duolingo one of the most successful language-learning programs in the world, illustrating how AI can be employed to help language acquisition in a way that is suited to each learner's specific needs.

These case studies highlight just a handful of the various ways in which generative AI is being successfully deployed in educational contexts. From individualized learning experiences and automated content generation to intelligent tutoring systems and AI-driven professional development for instructors, AI is revolutionizing education around the globe. As the technology continues to grow, we will probably see even more inventive applications that will further enhance the learning experience and make education more accessible, inclusive, and effective. However, as these applications become more widespread, the ethical considerations surrounding the use of AI in education must be addressed, ensuring that these technologies are used in a way that benefits all students and educators, without compromising privacy, fairness, or accountability.

FUTURE DIRECTIONS: SHAPING THE FUTURE OF EDUCATION WITH COLLABORATIVE AI

The rapid progress of generative AI is poised to change the future of education in significant ways (Lim et al, 2023). As we move towards a more networked and technologically advanced world, the importance of AI in education is expanding, promising to transform teaching and learning processes at every level. In particular, collaborative AI is emerging as a significant instrument in transforming the educational landscape, bringing new options for personalized learning, better student involvement, and more efficient teaching approaches. The potential of AI in education is tremendous, but to properly achieve its benefits, a deliberate approach must be taken, one that balances technological innovation with human-centered ideals (Mhlanga, 2022). Collaborative AI, which stresses the interaction between humans and AI systems to solve complicated difficulties, is a crucial area where future educational methods are likely to be concentrated. Unlike traditional, standalone AI systems, collaborative AI works in sync with human intellect, promoting shared problem-solving, decision-making, and knowledge generation. This approach to AI enables a more dynamic relationship between students, educators, and the technology itself, making learning experiences more customized and participatory. It highlights the complementarity of human creativity, intuition, and empathy with the computational power and precision of AI. Looking ahead, the integration of collaborative AI into education will inspire innovations that empower both students and Faculty members, expand educational accessibility, and offer new pathways for lifelong learning.

One of the important prospects for collaborative AI in education is the building of more adaptive and individualized learning environments (Gligorea et al, 2023). Current AI systems are already making progress in tailoring learning experiences based on individual student needs, but the next phase will see these systems become even more complex and sensitive. Future AI technologies will be capable of assessing a student's cognitive, emotional, and social moods, changing learning materials and activities accordingly. For example, a collaborative AI system might evaluate a student's learning patterns, behavioral clues, and emotional responses to a class, and in real-time, adjust the content, pace, or teaching technique to better correspond with that student's needs. This form of enhanced customization will allow educators to fulfill the different requirements of their students more successfully. Rather than taking a one-size-fits-all strategy, collaborative AI will give a tailored pathway for each learner. These AI systems will not only adapt academic content but also take into consideration other elements that influence learning, such as the student's confidence levels, social contacts, and mental well-being. By doing so, AI can assist create a more inclusive educational environment, where every student has the opportunity to succeed on their terms. This transition will likely lead to increased academic achievement, higher levels of student engagement, and better overall learning outcomes.

Beyond personalization, collaborative AI in education will also have a profound impact on the way students interact with knowledge (Zohuri & Mossavar-Rahmani, 2024). As AI becomes increasingly integrated into the curriculum, students will have the ability to engage in deeper, more meaningful learning experiences. Rather than simply receiving information passively, students will be able to work with AI systems to co-create knowledge. For example, students working on a research project might utilize AI to evaluate enormous datasets, create insights, and even formulate hypotheses. In doing so, students will not only have a greater comprehension of the subject matter but will also build critical thinking, problem-solving, and data literacy abilities. The role of the professor will transition from being the sole authority on knowledge to being a guide and facilitator, helping students navigate and make sense of the massive amount of information and insights supplied by AI. Collaborative AI will also lead to more engaging and dynamic learning environments (Kim et al, 2022). As the educational experience becomes more dynamic, traditional classroom settings are expected to morph into more adaptable, immersive venues. AI-powered virtual classrooms and simulations will enable students to explore concepts in novel ways. Imagine a history class where students may virtually wander around ancient civilizations, interacting with AI-generated historical individuals or experiencing major events in a completely immersive 3D environment (Kayyali, 2024 B). In the domain of science, students might employ AI-driven lab simulations to conduct experiments in a safe, virtual environment. These AI-driven experiences will stimulate creativity, engagement, and cooperation, making learning not only more pleasurable but also more effective.

In higher education, the importance of collaborative AI in defining the future of research and knowledge creation is particularly notable (Kuleto et al, 2021). Universities and research institutions are increasingly turning to AI to strengthen their research skills. Collaborative AI systems can assist in analyzing enormous amounts of research data, and detecting trends and patterns that could otherwise be missed. AI can assist researchers test hypotheses, plan experiments, and even forecasting the outcomes of research based on historical data and present trends (Sebastian & Peter, 2022). In the future, we may expect more researchers and students to cooperate with AI technologies to produce new ideas, perform cutting-edge research, and address complex social concerns. This collaboration will not only improve the pace and efficiency of the research process but also lead to more innovative solutions to global concerns. The ability of collaborative AI to aid in research extends beyond the academic sector into the professional arena. As education continues to become more intertwined with business, the demand for skills that can bridge the gap between education and the workforce is expanding. Collaborative AI will play a vital role in preparing students with the skills necessary for success in the modern job market. By working alongside AI systems, students will build abilities in areas such as data analysis, programming, and digital communication. These competencies will be vital as sectors across the globe grow increasingly reliant on AI-driven technologies. Collaborative AI can also assist students prepare for professions in disciplines that are not generally connected with AI, such as healthcare, the arts, and social sciences, by providing them with practical, real-world applications of AI tools and techniques.

At the same time, the future of education with collaborative AI will demand serious consideration of ethical and societal outcomes (Khreisat et al, 2024). As AI becomes a more significant component of the educational environment, challenges relating to data privacy, algorithmic bias, and the digital divide will need to be addressed. Collaborative AI systems must be created with ethical considerations at the forefront to ensure that they are inclusive, transparent, and equal (Firmansyah et al, 2024). In particular, efforts will need to be taken to ensure that all students, regardless of financial status or geographic location, have access to the benefits of AI-enhanced learning. Without a careful and ethical approach to AI integration, there is a risk that AI could worsen current inequities in education, rather than helping to bridge the gap. Another difficulty will be ensuring that AI remains a tool for human empowerment, rather than a substitute for human instructors. While AI can enhance the learning experience, it cannot replace the human connection that is important to education (Chen et al, 2020). Faculty members will continue to play an important role in giving emotional support, encouraging critical thinking, and helping students through complicated moral and ethical dilemmas. AI should be considered as a complimentary tool that enhances the job of educators, rather than replacing them. In the future, we are likely to see more hybrid forms of teaching, where AI and human educators work together to create the greatest possible learning experiences for students.

Looking ahead, the future of education with collaborative AI is packed with potential. As AI technologies continue to grow, they will offer new opportunities for educators and students to interact, create, and learn in ways that were previously inconceivable (Zhang & Aslan, 2021). By concentrating on personalization, engagement, and ethical considerations, we can ensure that AI is utilized in a way that benefits all students and educators. The future of education is collaborative, not only between students and Faculty members, but between humans and AI systems working together to form the knowledge, skills, and experiences that will define tomorrow's world. By accepting these changes, we can ensure that the future of education is more inclusive, dynamic, and impactful than ever before.

CONCLUSION

The integration of generative artificial intelligence (AI) into the educational landscape signifies a dramatic revolution in how teaching and learning occur. As we have explored throughout this chapter, generative AI has the potential to alter existing educational approaches, moving beyond merely being a tool for automation to being an integral player in the collaborative intelligence ecosystem of education. This combination of human instructors and AI systems can enrich educational experiences, delivering more individualized learning, stimulating innovation, and eventually making education more accessible, inclusive, and flexible to the requirements of individual learners. Generative AI technologies are not merely about boosting efficiency; they are about raising the quality of education itself. By integrating AI, educational systems may offer more personalized, dynamic, and engaging learning environments. These settings are particularly effective for personalized learning, as students receive customized information and real-time feedback based on their learning styles, needs, and progression. Such customizable learning routes have the potential to empower students to take charge of their own educational experiences, moving away from a one-size-fits-all approach that often leaves certain students behind.

At the same time, the collaborative aspect of this shift—where instructors and AI work together—creates a deeper, more human-centered learning experience. Educators can utilize AI to offload basic administrative work, freeing up more time to focus on high-level teaching tactics, such as encouraging critical thinking, emotional intelligence, and creativity in students. AI also gives educators deeper insights into student performance, helping them to better identify where students may be failing, where they shine, and how to alter teaching techniques to match various requirements. In this sense, AI functions as a helpful augmentation of the educator's talents rather than a replacement. Despite the potential of generative AI, its integration into education does not come without hurdles. Ethical concerns remain at the forefront, especially around data privacy, algorithmic biases, and the equity of access to AI-enhanced educational tools. These difficulties demand serious analysis and aggressive responses to ensure that AI serves all students equitably and does not perpetuate existing disparities. Additionally, there is a need to ensure that AI is implemented in a way that respects the autonomy of educators and students. AI should be considered as a complement to human expertise, not as a method to replace human interaction or judgment. Educators will still play a crucial role in creating learning experiences, guiding students in complicated areas of emotional development, and helping students interpret the broader implications of the knowledge they receive.

In addressing the broader implications of AI in education, it is evident that the future of learning will be a collaborative one. AI will give unprecedented potential for tailored learning, but these opportunities will be most effective when partnered with the insights and human touch of educators. Faculty members and AI systems will work hand-in-hand to create more interesting, inclusive, and successful learning environments. The potential of AI to assist lifelong learning is especially noteworthy since it can offer students the tools they need to continue learning and improving throughout their lifetimes, regardless of their geographic location or socio-economic background. As AI technologies continue to grow, their role in education will certainly expand, creating new opportunities for creative and critical thinking. With improvements in generative AI, we are likely to see increasingly more complex educational systems that not only assist with material delivery but also inspire learners to become creators of knowledge themselves. For example, AI could assist students develop their learning tools, conduct experiments, and engage in collaborative problem-solving projects, thus fostering a deeper engagement with the learning content and promoting creativity. This move toward AI as a partner in co-creating educational content and experiences symbolizes a change toward a more learner-centric model of education, where the student is actively involved in defining the educational process.

In addition, the rise of generative AI gives a chance to rethink the traditional bounds of college. AI-powered platforms can give educational opportunities that transcend beyond the classroom and outside the limitations of conventional institutions. With AI technologies that can generate content, measure learning, and encourage interaction, education becomes more flexible and accessible, allowing for global classrooms and self-directed learning that transcends geographical and institutional limitations. Students in faraway places, or those with distinct learning requirements, can enjoy individualized learning experiences that would have been impossible just a few years ago. The widespread implementation of AI in education also needs critical policy considerations and frameworks. Governments, educational institutions, and technology companies must work together to implement rules that promote equal access to AI technologies, assure the preservation of data privacy, and bridge the digital gap that may hinder certain groups from benefiting from these advancements. This collaborative effort must also focus on professor training, ensuring that educators are equipped with the skills and knowledge necessary to apply AI effectively in their classrooms. Faculty members must be helped in learning how AI works, how it might be used to supplement their teaching approaches, and how to prevent potential hazards, such as biases encoded in AI algorithms.

As we move forward, the importance of AI in education is not likely to shrink but rather to expand, with increasingly sophisticated AI models contributing to the development of teaching and learning. The key to success rests in the collaborative aspect of this journey—where human educators and AI systems work together to produce more inclusive, individualized, and engaging educational experiences for all. The future of education is not a binary option between humans and technology, but a synthesis of the qualities of both. By embracing this future, we may look forward to a world where education is not only more accessible but also more transformative, encouraging students to become lifelong learners and active contributors to the global knowledge economy. Ultimately, the successful integration of generative AI into education rests on our ability to harness its potential while tackling its obstacles. By promoting an environment of collaboration and ethical responsibility, we can ensure that AI is used to enhance, rather than diminish, the human experience of education. Generative AI, when applied wisely and in cooperation with human educators, holds the potential to revolutionize education as we know it—creating a future in which learning is more individualized, accessible, and aligned with the developing needs of society. This collective intelligence will define not only the future of education but also the future of work, creativity, and human growth in the 21st century and beyond.

REFERENCES

Aithal, P. S., & Aithal, S. (2023). Optimizing the use of artificial intelligence-powered GPTs as teaching and research assistants by professors in higher education institutions: A study on smart utilization. [IJMTS]. *International Journal of Management, Technology, and Social Sciences*, *8*(4), 368–401. DOI: 10.47992/IJMTS.2581.6012.0326

Al Balushi, J. S. G., Al Jabri, M. I. A., Palarimath, S., Maran, P., Thenmozhi, K., & Balakumar, C. (2024, June). Incorporating Artificial Intelligence Powered Immersive Realities to Improve Learning using Virtual Reality (VR) and Augmented Reality (AR) Technology. In 2024 3rd International Conference on Applied Artificial Intelligence and Computing (ICAAIC) (pp. 760-765). IEEE.

Alasadi, E. A., & Baiz, C. R. (2023). Generative AI in education and research: Opportunities, concerns, and solutions. *Journal of Chemical Education*, *100*(8), 2965–2971. DOI: 10.1021/acs.jchemed.3c00323

Alshahrani, K., & Qureshi, R. J. (2024). Review the Prospects and Obstacles of AI-Enhanced Learning Environments: The Role of ChatGPT in Education. *International Journal of Modern Education and Computer Science*, *16*(4), 71–86. DOI: 10.5815/ijmecs.2024.04.06

Alshamsi, I., Sadriwala, K. F., Alazzawi, F. J. I., & Shannaq, B. (2024). Exploring the impact of generative AI technologies on education: Academic expert perspectives, trends, and implications for sustainable development goals. Journal of Infrastructure. *Policy and Development*, *8*(11), 8532. DOI: 10.24294/jipd.v8i11.8532

Asperti, A., Evangelista, D., & Loli Piccolomini, E. (2021). A survey on variational autoencoders from a green AI perspective. *SN Computer Science*, *2*(4), 301. DOI: 10.1007/s42979-021-00702-9

Bandi, A., Adapa, P. V. S. R., & Kuchi, Y. E. V. P. K. (2023). The power of generative ai: A review of requirements, models, input–output formats, evaluation metrics, and challenges. *Future Internet*, *15*(8), 260. DOI: 10.3390/fi15080260

Banh, L., & Strobel, G. (2023). Generative artificial intelligence. *Electronic Markets*, *33*(1), 63. DOI: 10.1007/s12525-023-00680-1

Bankins, S., & Formosa, P. (2023). The ethical implications of artificial intelligence (AI) for meaningful work. *Journal of Business Ethics*, *185*(4), 725–740. DOI: 10.1007/s10551-023-05339-7

Bengesi, S., El-Sayed, H., Sarker, M. K., Houkpati, Y., Irungu, J., & Oladunni, T. (2024). Advancements in Generative AI: A Comprehensive Review of GANs, GPT, Autoencoders, Diffusion Model, and Transformers. *IEEE Access : Practical Innovations, Open Solutions*, *12*, 69812–69837. DOI: 10.1109/ACCESS.2024.3397775

Bukar, U. A., Sayeed, M. S., Razak, S. F. A., Yogarayan, S., & Sneesl, R. (2024). Decision-making framework for the utilization of generative artificial intelligence in education: A case study of ChatGPT. *IEEE Access : Practical Innovations, Open Solutions*, *12*, 95368–95389. DOI: 10.1109/ACCESS.2024.3425172

Chen, L., Chen, P., & Lin, Z. (2020). Artificial intelligence in education: A review. *IEEE Access : Practical Innovations, Open Solutions*, *8*, 75264–75278. DOI: 10.1109/ACCESS.2020.2988510

Chinta, S. V., Wang, Z., Yin, Z., Hoang, N., Gonzalez, M., Quy, T. L., & Zhang, W. (2024). FairAIED: Navigating fairness, bias, and ethics in educational AI applications. arXiv preprint arXiv:2407.18745.

Chiu, T. K. (2024). *Empowering K-12 Education with AI: Preparing for the Future of Education and Work*. Taylor & Francis. DOI: 10.4324/9781003498377

Chiu, T. K. (2024). Future research recommendations for transforming higher education with generative AI. *Computers and Education: Artificial Intelligence*, *6*, 100197. DOI: 10.1016/j.caeai.2023.100197

Chow, Y. L., Singh, S., Carpenter, A. E., & Way, G. P. (2022). Predicting drug polypharmacology from cell morphology readouts using variational autoencoder latent space arithmetic. *PLoS Computational Biology*, *18*(2), e1009888. DOI: 10.1371/journal.pcbi.1009888 PMID: 35213530

Dimitriadou, E., & Lanitis, A. (2023). A critical evaluation, challenges, and future perspectives of using artificial intelligence and emerging technologies in smart classrooms. *Smart Learning Environments*, *10*(1), 12. DOI: 10.1186/s40561-023-00231-3

Dove, E. S. (2018). The EU general data protection regulation: Implications for international scientific research in the digital era. *The Journal of Law, Medicine & Ethics*, *46*(4), 1013–1030. DOI: 10.1177/1073110518822003

Eden, C. A., Chisom, O. N., & Adeniyi, I. S. (2024). Integrating AI in education: Opportunities, challenges, and ethical considerations. Magna Scientia Advanced Research and Reviews, 10(2), 006-013.

Elshawi, R., Sakr, S., Talia, D., & Trunfio, P. (2018). Big data systems meet machine learning challenges: towards big data science as a service. Big data research, 14, 1-11.

Ferrara, E. (2023). Fairness and bias in artificial intelligence: A brief survey of sources, impacts, and mitigation strategies. *Sci*, *6*(1), 3. DOI: 10.3390/sci6010003

Firmansyah, G., Bansal, S., Walawalkar, A. M., Kumar, S., & Chattopadhyay, S. (2024). The Future of Ethical AI. In *Challenges in Large Language Model Development and AI Ethics* (pp. 145–177). IGI Global. DOI: 10.4018/979-8-3693-3860-5.ch005

Fui-Hoon Nah, F., Zheng, R., Cai, J., Siau, K., & Chen, L. (2023). Generative AI and ChatGPT: Applications, challenges, and AI-human collaboration. *Journal of Information Technology Case and Application Research*, *25*(3), 277–304. DOI: 10.1080/15228053.2023.2233814

Gligorea, I., Cioca, M., Oancea, R., Gorski, A. T., Gorski, H., & Tudorache, P. (2023). Adaptive learning using artificial intelligence in e-learning: A literature review. *Education Sciences*, *13*(12), 1216. DOI: 10.3390/educsci13121216

Guettala, M., Bourekkache, S., Kazar, O., & Harous, S. (2024). Generative artificial intelligence in education: Advancing adaptive and personalized learning. *Acta Informatica Pragensia*, *13*(3), 460–489. DOI: 10.18267/j.aip.235

Henry, J., & Daniel, A. (2024). AI-Enhanced Assessment Methods in Education: Innovations and Challenges.

Holstein, K., McLaren, B. M., & Aleven, V. (2019). *Co-designing a real-time classroom orchestration tool to support teacher-AI complementarity*. Grantee Submission. DOI: 10.18608/jla.2019.62.3

Huang, F., Wang, Y., & Zhang, H. (2024). Modelling Generative AI Acceptance, Perceived Teachers' Enthusiasm and Self-Efficacy to English as a Foreign Language Learners' Well-Being in the Digital Era. *European Journal of Education*, *59*(4), 12770. DOI: 10.1111/ejed.12770

Hwang, G. J., Xie, H., Wah, B. W., & Gašević, D. (2020). Vision, challenges, roles and research issues of Artificial Intelligence in Education. *Computers and Education: Artificial Intelligence*, *1*, 100001. DOI: 10.1016/j.caeai.2020.100001

Iatrellis, O., Samaras, N., Kokkinos, K., & Panagiotakopoulos, T. (2024). Leveraging generative AI for sustainable academic advising: Enhancing educational practices through AI-driven recommendations. *Sustainability (Basel)*, *16*(17), 7829. DOI: 10.3390/su16177829

Indrakumari, R., Poongodi, T., & Singh, K. (2021). Introduction to deep learning. Advanced Deep Learning for Engineers and Scientists: A Practical Approach, 1-22.

Kayyali, M. (2024, A). Global Perspectives on Personalized Learning: Case Studies and Best Practices. In Transforming Education for Personalized Learning (pp. 66-84). IGI Global.

Kayyali, M. (2024, B). Immersive Technologies: Virtual and Augmented Reality in Higher Education. In Reshaping Learning with Next Generation Educational Technologies (pp. 99-114). IGI Global.

Kayyali, M. (2025, A). The Future of AI in Education: Predictions and Emerging Trends. Next-Generation AI Methodologies in Education, 367-406.

Kayyali, M. (2025, B). AI in Higher Education: Revolutionizing Curriculum and Administration. In AI Adoption and Diffusion in Education (pp. 31-62). IGI Global Scientific Publishing.

Khine, M. S. (2024). Ethics, and the Future of Education in an AI-Driven World. In *Artificial Intelligence in Education: A Machine-Generated Literature Overview* (pp. 629–735). Springer Nature Singapore. DOI: 10.1007/978-981-97-9350-1_6

Khosravi, H., Shum, S. B., Chen, G., Conati, C., Tsai, Y. S., Kay, J., & Gašević, D. (2022). Explainable artificial intelligence in education. *Computers and Education: Artificial Intelligence*, *3*, 100074.

Khreisat, M. N., Khilani, D., Rusho, M. A., Karkkulainen, E. A., Tabuena, A. C., & Uberas, A. D. (2024). Ethical Implications Of AI Integration In Educational Decision Making: Systematic Review. *Educational Administration: Theory and Practice*, *30*(5), 8521–8527.

Kim, J., Lee, H., & Cho, Y. H. (2022). Learning design to support student-AI collaboration: Perspectives of leading teachers for AI in education. *Education and Information Technologies*, *27*(5), 6069–6104. DOI: 10.1007/s10639-021-10831-6

Kirk, H. R., Jun, Y., Volpin, F., Iqbal, H., Benussi, E., Dreyer, F., & Asano, Y. (2021). Bias out-of-the-box: An empirical analysis of intersectional occupational biases in popular generative language models. *Advances in Neural Information Processing Systems*, *34*, 2611–2624.

Kondurkar, I., Raj, A., & Lakshmi, D. (2024). Modern applications with a focus on training chatgpt and gpt models: Exploring generative ai and nlp. In *Advanced applications of generative AI and natural language processing models* (pp. 186–227). IGI Global.

Koroteev, D., & Tekic, Z. (2021). Artificial intelligence in oil and gas upstream: Trends, challenges, and scenarios for the future. *Energy and AI*, *3*, 100041. DOI: 10.1016/j.egyai.2020.100041

Kuleto, V., Ilić, M., Dumangiu, M., Ranković, M., Martins, O. M., Păun, D., & Mihoreanu, L. (2021). Exploring opportunities and challenges of artificial intelligence and machine learning in higher education institutions. *Sustainability (Basel)*, *13*(18), 10424. DOI: 10.3390/su131810424

Labajová, L. (2023). The state of AI: Exploring the perceptions, credibility, and trustworthiness of the users towards AI-Generated Content.

Lim, W. M., Gunasekara, A., Pallant, J. L., Pallant, J. I., & Pechenkina, E. (2023). Generative AI and the future of education: Ragnarök or reformation? A paradoxical perspective from management educators. *International Journal of Management Education*, *21*(2), 100790. DOI: 10.1016/j.ijme.2023.100790

Liu, M., Ren, Y., Nyagoga, L. M., Stonier, F., Wu, Z., & Yu, L. (2023). Future of education in the era of generative artificial intelligence: Consensus among Chinese scholars on applications of ChatGPT in schools. *Future in Educational Research*, *1*(1), 72–101. DOI: 10.1002/fer3.10

Luan, H., Geczy, P., Lai, H., Gobert, J., Yang, S. J., Ogata, H., Baltes, J., Guerra, R., Li, P., & Tsai, C. C. (2020). Challenges and future directions of big data and artificial intelligence in education. *Frontiers in Psychology*, *11*, 580820. DOI: 10.3389/fpsyg.2020.580820 PMID: 33192896

Lüy, Z., Bakirci, F., Artsın, M., Karataş, S., & Çakmak, E. K. (2024). Innovative technologies to trigger creative thinking in micro-lessons. In *Optimizing education through micro-lessons: Engaging and adaptive learning strategies* (pp. 118–140). IGI Global. DOI: 10.4018/979-8-3693-0195-1.ch007

Madaan, G., Asthana, S. K., & Kaur, J. (2024). Generative AI: Applications, Models, Challenges, Opportunities, and Future Directions. Generative AI and Implications for Ethics, Security, and Data Management, 88-121.

Malone, T. W., & Woolley, A. W. (2020). Collective intelligence. Cambridge handbook of intelligence, 2, 780-801.

Martins, R. M., & Gresse von Wangenheim, C. (2024). Teaching Computing to Middle and High School Students from a Low Socio-Economic Status Background: A Systematic Literature Review. *Informatics in Education*, *23*(1), 179–222.

Mhlanga, D. (2022). Human-centered artificial intelligence: The superlative approach to achieve sustainable development goals in the fourth industrial revolution. *Sustainability (Basel)*, *14*(13), 7804. DOI: 10.3390/su14137804

Modi, T. B. (2023). Artificial Intelligence Ethics and Fairness: A study to address bias and fairness issues in AI systems, and the ethical implications of AI applications. *Revista Review Index Journal of Multidisciplinary*, *3*(2), 24–35. DOI: 10.31305/rrijm2023.v03.n02.004

Mora, H., Signes-Pont, M. T., Fuster-Guilló, A., & Pertegal-Felices, M. L. (2020). A collaborative working model for enhancing the learning process of science & engineering students. *Computers in Human Behavior*, *103*, 140–150. DOI: 10.1016/j.chb.2019.09.008

Muñoz-Martínez, Y., Monge-López, C., & Torrego Seijo, J. C. (2020). Teacher education in cooperative learning and its influence on inclusive education. *Improving Schools*, *23*(3), 277–290. DOI: 10.1177/1365480220929440

Nabilla, C., Apriani, E., & Gusmuliana, P. (2024). Promoting Students' Writing Critical Thinking By Using Paragraph Writing Ai Technology (Doctoral dissertation, Institut agama islam negeri curup).

Nam, T. B., Triet, M. N., Phuc, N. T., Khoa, T. D., Hien, N. Q., Tung, L. K., . . . Khanh, H. V. (2023, November). Human-Computer Interaction in the Age of Generative AI: Tailoring Educational Content for Diverse Learners. In International Symposium on Emerging Technologies for Education (pp. 137-146). Singapore: Springer Nature Singapore.

Naseer, F., Khalid, M. U., Ayub, N., Rasool, A., Abbas, T., & Afzal, M. W. (2024). Automated Assessment and Feedback in Higher Education Using Generative AI. In Transforming Education With Generative AI: Prompt Engineering and Synthetic Content Creation (pp. 433-461). IGI Global. DOI: 10.4018/979-8-3693-1351-0.ch021

Nwile, C. B., & Edo, B. L. (2023). Artificial intelligence and robotic tools for effective educational management and administration in the state-owned universities in Rivers State, Nigeria. Faculty of Natural and Applied Sciences Journal of Mathematics, and Science Education, 4(1), 28-36.

Obaid, A. J., Bhushan, B., & Rajest, S. S. (Eds.). (2023). *Advanced applications of generative AI and natural language processing models*. IGI Global. DOI: 10.4018/979-8-3693-0502-7

Pan, Z., Yu, W., Yi, X., Khan, A., Yuan, F., & Zheng, Y. (2019). Recent progress on generative adversarial networks (GANs): A survey. *IEEE Access : Practical Innovations, Open Solutions*, *7*, 36322–36333. DOI: 10.1109/ACCESS.2019.2905015

Partarakis, N., & Zabulis, X. (2024). A review of immersive technologies, knowledge representation, and AI for human-centered digital experiences. *Electronics (Basel)*, *13*(2), 269. DOI: 10.3390/electronics13020269

Pedro, F., Subosa, M., Rivas, A., & Valverde, P. (2019). Artificial intelligence in education: Challenges and opportunities for sustainable development.

Peeters, M. M., van Diggelen, J., Van Den Bosch, K., Bronkhorst, A., Neerincx, M. A., Schraagen, J. M., & Raaijmakers, S. (2021). Hybrid collective intelligence in a human–AI society. *AI & Society*, *36*(1), 217–238. DOI: 10.1007/s00146-020-01005-y

Pesovski, I., Santos, R., Henriques, R., & Trajkovik, V. (2024). Generative ai for customizable learning experiences. *Sustainability (Basel)*, *16*(7), 3034. DOI: 10.3390/su16073034

Prabhod, K. J. (2023). Leveraging Generative AI for Personalized Medicine: Applications in Drug Discovery and Development. *Journal of AI-Assisted Scientific Discovery*, *3*(1), 392–434.

Przegalinska, A., & Triantoro, T. (2024). *Converging Minds: The Creative Potential of Collaborative AI*. CRC Press. DOI: 10.1201/9781032656618

Rane, N., Choudhary, S., & Rane, J. (2023). Education 4.0 and 5.0: Integrating artificial intelligence (AI) for personalized and adaptive learning. Available at *SSRN* 4638365. DOI: 10.2139/ssrn.4638365

Redhu, V., Singh, A. K., & Saravanan, M. (2024, March). AI-Enhanced Learning Assistant Platform: An Advanced System for Q&A Generation from Provided Content, Answer Evaluation, Identification of Students' Weak Areas, Recursive Testing for Strengthening Knowledge, Integrated Query Forum, and Expert Chat Support. In 2024 2nd International Conference on Artificial Intelligence and Machine Learning Applications Theme: Healthcare and Internet of Things (AIMLA) (pp. 1-6). IEEE.

Rienties, B., Køhler Simonsen, H., & Herodotou, C. (2020, July). Defining the boundaries between artificial intelligence in education, computer-supported collaborative learning, educational data mining, and learning analytics: A need for coherence. [Frontiers Media SA.]. *Frontiers in Education*, *5*, 128. DOI: 10.3389/feduc.2020.00128

Ruiz-Rojas, L. I., Salvador-Ullauri, L., & Acosta-Vargas, P. (2024). Collaborative working and critical thinking: Adoption of generative artificial intelligence tools in higher education. *Sustainability (Basel)*, *16*(13), 5367. DOI: 10.3390/su16135367

Sajja, R., Sermet, Y., Cikmaz, M., Cwiertny, D., & Demir, I. (2024). Artificial intelligence-enabled intelligent assistant for personalized and adaptive learning in higher education. *Information (Basel)*, *15*(10), 596. DOI: 10.3390/info15100596

Sandhu, R., Channi, H. K., Ghai, D., Cheema, G. S., & Kaur, M. (2024). An Introduction to Generative AI Tools for Education 2030. Integrating Generative AI in Education to Achieve Sustainable Development Goals, 1-28.

Sebastian, A. M., & Peter, D. (2022). Artificial intelligence in cancer research: Trends, challenges and future directions. *Life (Chicago, Ill.)*, *12*(12), 1991. DOI: 10.3390/life12121991 PMID: 36556356

Singh, T. M., Reddy, C. K. K., Murthy, B. R., Nag, A., & Doss, S. (2025). Ai and education: Bridging the gap to personalized, efficient, and accessible learning. In *Internet of Behavior-Based Computational Intelligence for Smart Education Systems* (pp. 131–160). IGI Global.

Suskie, L. (2018). *Assessing student learning: A common sense guide*. John Wiley & Sons.

Tatineni, S. (2020). Recommendation Systems for Personalized Learning: A Data-Driven Approach in Education. [JCET]. *Journal of Computer Engineering and Technology*, *4*(2).

Wach, K., Duong, C. D., Ejdys, J., Kazlauskaitė, R., Korzynski, P., Mazurek, G., Paliszkiewicz, J., & Ziemba, E. (2023). The dark side of generative artificial intelligence: A critical analysis of controversies and risks of ChatGPT. *Entrepreneurial Business and Economics Review*, *11*(2), 7–30. DOI: 10.15678/EBER.2023.110201

Wang, F. (2024). The Relationship Between Students and Teachers and its Implications. Journal of Education. *Humanities and Social Sciences*, *29*, 390–395.

Wang, M., Muthu, B., & Sivaparthipan, C. B. (2022). Smart assistance to dyslexia students using artificial intelligence based augmentative alternative communication. *International Journal of Speech Technology*, *25*(2), 343–353. DOI: 10.1007/s10772-021-09921-0

Wang, Q. (2024). AI-driven autonomous interactive English learning language tutoring system. Journal of Computational Methods in Science and Engineering, 14727978241296719.

Xu, W., Meng, J., Raja, S. K. S., Priya, M. P., & Kiruthiga Devi, M. (2023). Artificial intelligence in constructing personalized and accurate feedback systems for students. *International Journal of Modeling, Simulation and Scientific Computing*, *14*(01), 2341001. DOI: 10.1142/S1793962323410015

Yalazi-Dawani, S. (2023). Integrating Artificial Intelligence into Creativity Education: Developing a Creative Problem-Solving Course for Higher Education (Doctoral dissertation, Doctoral dissertation, State University of New York).

Yan, L., Greiff, S., Teuber, Z., & Gašević, D. (2024). Promises and challenges of generative artificial intelligence for human learning. *Nature Human Behaviour*, *8*(10), 1839–1850. DOI: 10.1038/s41562-024-02004-5 PMID: 39438686

Zhang, K., & Aslan, A. B. (2021). AI technologies for education: Recent research & future directions. *Computers and Education: Artificial Intelligence*, *2*, 100025. DOI: 10.1016/j.caeai.2021.100025

Zohuri, B., & Mossavar-Rahmani, F. (2024). Revolutionizing education: The dynamic synergy of personalized learning and artificial intelligence. *International Journal of Advanced Engineering and Management Research*, *9*(1), 143–153. DOI: 10.51505/ijaemr.2024.9111

KEY TERMS AND DEFINITIONS

Generative AI: A subset of artificial intelligence that uses machine learning models to create new content such as text, images, audio, or simulations by learning patterns from existing data.

Collaborative Intelligence: The synergistic partnership between humans and AI systems where both contribute unique strengths—human creativity and emotional understanding paired with machine speed and data-processing capabilities—to enhance decision-making and problem-solving in education.

Personalized Learning: An instructional approach that uses AI tools to tailor educational content and learning paths to the unique needs, pace, and learning style of individual students.

Generative Adversarial Networks (GANs): A deep learning model consisting of two neural networks—a generator and a discriminator—that compete to create increasingly realistic data outputs, commonly used in image and content generation.

Transformer Models: A neural network architecture designed for processing sequential data, especially text, using mechanisms like self-attention to understand context; examples include GPT models used in natural language processing.

Real-Time Feedback: Immediate responses provided by AI systems based on a learner's performance, enabling continuous improvement and adaptive learning without delays typical in traditional education.

Latent Space: A compressed, encoded representation of input data used by generative models like Variational Autoencoders (VAEs) to explore and generate new, varied outputs.

Algorithmic Bias: Unintended discrimination in AI outputs resulting from biased or unrepresentative training data, which can reinforce inequalities in educational recommendations or evaluations.

Chapter 3
Ethical Considerations and Challenges in Human–AI Collaboration

Dheeraj Minglani
https://orcid.org/0000-0001-7269-0109
Chandigarh University, India

Moniya Pal
Chandigarh University, India

Uma Shanker
https://orcid.org/0009-0001-4160-3380
Chandigarh University, India

Amit Kumar
https://orcid.org/0009-0007-4158-6377
Chandigarh University, India

ABSTRACT

The rise of generative artificial intelligence (AI) tools has significantly transformed various sectors, offering opportunities for enhanced efficiency, creativity, and decision-making. However, alongside these advancements lie profound ethical challenges that demand critical examination. This chapter, titled Ethical Considerations and Challenges in Human-AI Collaboration, explores the multifaceted ethical landscape of AI systems, emphasizing the need for fairness, accountability, transparency, data security, and societal well-being in their development and deployment.

1. INTRODUCTION

Artificial Intelligence (AI) has rapidly transformed from a futuristic concept to a central force driving innovation across industries. From healthcare and finance to transportation and entertainment, AI systems are now instrumental in decision-making, problem-solving, and improving human lives. Yet, with

DOI: 10.4018/979-8-3693-8332-2.ch003

great transformative potential comes profound ethical challenges that demand scrutiny, deliberation, and action. The interaction between humans and AI in collaborative settings highlights the need for ethical frameworks that ensure these technologies are developed and deployed responsibly. The concept of collaborative intelligence—where humans and AI systems work together to achieve shared goals—represents a significant evolution in human-computer interaction. Generative AI tools, capable of creating text, images, and complex models, are not merely passive tools; they actively shape outcomes. Their role in enhancing creativity, improving efficiency, and enabling complex problem-solving is unparalleled (Dwork & Roth, 2014). However, as these tools gain autonomy and influence, ethical considerations such as transparency, accountability, fairness, and data privacy become paramount.

The transformative potential of AI necessitates a reevaluation of traditional ethical paradigms. For instance, AI's capability to process massive datasets in real-time opens unprecedented opportunities for medical research, climate modeling, and urban planning. Yet, the same technologies can infringe on individual privacy, perpetuate systemic biases, and exacerbate societal inequalities. Balancing these dualities requires a multidisciplinary approach to ethics that involves technologists, social scientists, and policymakers working in unison. Moreover, the rapid integration of AI into everyday life underscores the urgency of public education on its benefits and risks. Building an informed society that understands AI's capabilities and limitations is essential for fostering trust and ensuring its responsible use (Shokri & Shmatikov, 2015). Public forums, awareness campaigns, and collaborative platforms can bridge the gap between technical expertise and societal understanding, promoting a culture of ethical awareness and proactive engagement.

1.1 The Dual-Edged Sword of AI Advancements

While AI offers numerous benefits, its rapid advancement also presents unique risks. Biased algorithms, lack of accountability, and opaque decision-making processes are some of the challenges threatening the ethical integrity of these systems (California Consumer Privacy Act [CCPA], 2018). For instance, AI-powered hiring platforms have been shown to perpetuate existing biases, disadvantaging marginalized groups. Similarly, the misuse of generative AI for deepfakes and misinformation has sparked debates about its societal impact. AI's reliance on vast amounts of data raises significant concerns about privacy and data security. Ethical lapses in data handling, such as unauthorized data harvesting or re-identification of anonymized datasets, can erode public trust. Moreover, the potential misuse of AI systems by malicious actors amplifies the need for robust ethical frameworks and regulatory oversight (Goodfellow, Shlens, & Szegedy, 2015). The potential for harm is further magnified in critical sectors like healthcare, where errors in AI-driven diagnostics can lead to severe consequences. Addressing these risks requires not only technical solutions, such as bias-detection algorithms, but also organizational accountability mechanisms and stringent regulatory frameworks (Abadi et al., 2016). Transparency in AI operations, combined with regular audits and stakeholder involvement, can mitigate these challenges and foster a more equitable technological landscape.

1.2 The Importance of Ethical Considerations

Ethical AI development is not merely a technical issue; it is a societal imperative. AI systems, particularly those used in critical sectors like healthcare and criminal justice, wield enormous influence over people's lives. Ensuring these systems are free from bias, transparent in their operation, and accountable for their actions is essential to prevent harm and maintain public trust (Barocas, Hardt, & Narayanan, 2019). Transparency allows stakeholders to understand how AI systems function and make decisions, fostering trust and enabling informed oversight. Accountability ensures that AI developers and organizations are held responsible for their systems' outcomes. Fairness addresses the societal impacts of AI, striving to eliminate biases that disadvantage specific groups. Lastly, data privacy and security are foundational to preserving individuals' autonomy and protecting sensitive information. Additionally, ethical considerations in AI must address the global digital divide that exacerbates inequalities between developed and developing nations. Providing equitable access to AI technologies, promoting digital literacy, and ensuring culturally sensitive implementations are vital for creating inclusive systems (Gunning, 2017). Organizations must adopt ethical frameworks that prioritize societal well-being over profit motives, ensuring that AI serves as a tool for empowerment rather than exploitation.

1.3 The Role of Regulation and Global Standards

Ethical challenges in AI transcend national boundaries, necessitating global cooperation to develop regulatory standards. Frameworks such as the European Union's AI Act and UNESCO's Recommendation on the Ethics of Artificial Intelligence aim to establish principles for responsible AI development. These initiatives underscore the importance of balancing innovation with ethical considerations, ensuring AI technologies serve humanity's best interests. However, regulatory efforts face significant hurdles, including the rapid pace of AI innovation, the global nature of AI ecosystems, and the diversity of cultural and legal perspectives (Buolamwini & Gebru, 2018). To address these challenges, interdisciplinary collaboration among technologists, ethicists, policymakers, and civil society is essential. Such collaboration can lead to the development of AI systems that are not only technically robust but also ethically sound. Furthermore, the establishment of international regulatory bodies dedicated to AI ethics can provide consistent guidelines and facilitate knowledge-sharing across borders. By fostering dialogue and collaboration, these bodies can help bridge cultural and legal disparities, creating a unified approach to ethical AI development (Mehrabi, Morstatter, Saxena, Lerman, & Galstyan, 2021). Ensuring compliance through regular audits, certifications, and penalties for non-adherence can strengthen the global commitment to responsible AI innovation.

2. BIAS AND FAIRNESS IN AI

Bias and fairness are critical ethical considerations in the development and deployment of Artificial Intelligence (AI) systems. As these systems increasingly influence societal structures, ranging from healthcare to criminal justice, understanding and mitigating bias becomes essential to ensure equitable outcomes (Chouldechova & Roth, 2020). This section delves deeply into the origins of bias, its manifestations in AI, strategies for fostering fairness, and the challenges associated with achieving equitable AI systems.

2.1 The Origins of Bias in AI

Bias in AI originates from multiple interconnected factors that influence how these systems learn, operate, and make decisions. These sources include:

- **Bias in Data Collection and Representation**

AI systems rely heavily on data for training. When datasets are not representative of diverse populations, the resulting AI models tend to favor overrepresented groups while marginalizing others (Holstein, Wortman Vaughan, Daumé, Dudik, & Wallach, 2019). For example, datasets used in facial recognition technologies often contain a disproportionate number of lighter-skinned faces, leading to higher error rates for individuals with darker skin tones.

- **Algorithmic Design Choices**

The design of algorithms also introduces biases. For instance, if a model prioritizes overall accuracy, it may favor the majority class at the expense of minority groups. These trade-offs can exacerbate systemic inequalities, particularly in high-stakes applications like predictive policing or loan approvals.

- **Historical and Societal Inequalities**

AI systems often inherit biases from historical and societal norms embedded in training data (Datta, Tschantz, & Datta, 2015). Predictive models for job recruitment, for example, might reflect historical patterns of gender discrimination, perpetuating the exclusion of women from specific roles.

- **User and Developer Bias**

The assumptions and perspectives of developers and users influence AI systems. Implicit biases among developers can shape feature selection, parameter tuning, and evaluation metrics, while user interactions can reinforce existing biases in adaptive AI systems.

2.2 Manifestations of Bias in AI Systems

Bias in AI manifests in various ways, impacting individuals and groups differently depending on the context and application (European Commission, 2021)

- **Representation Bias**

Representation bias occurs when certain demographic groups are underrepresented in training datasets. For example, speech recognition systems have historically performed poorly for women and individuals with accents because of underrepresentation in voice data. This lack of inclusivity limits the usability of such systems for diverse populations.

- **Outcome Bias**

Outcome bias emerges when AI systems disproportionately favor or disadvantage specific groups (Selbst, Barocas, Crawford, Diaz, & Wallach, 2019). An example is an AI-powered hiring tool that discriminates against female candidates by prioritizing traits predominantly associated with male applicants due to biased historical data.

- **Interaction Bias**

Interaction bias arises from real-time user interactions. Chatbots, for instance, may adopt inappropriate or biased behaviors if exposed to toxic user inputs during training or operation.

- **Measurement Bias**

Measurement bias results from flawed evaluation metrics. For instance, a model optimized for accuracy might ignore fairness considerations, leading to disparate impacts on different demographic groups.

2.3 Ethical Implications of Bias

The presence of bias in AI systems raises serious ethical concerns (Wagner, 2018):

- **Erosion of Trust**

Biased AI systems undermine public trust, particularly in critical domains like healthcare and law enforcement. For example, a medical diagnostic tool with higher error rates for certain racial groups can lead to mistrust among those communities.

- **Reinforcement of Inequality**

Biased algorithms perpetuate and amplify existing societal inequalities. Predictive policing tools, for instance, have been criticized for disproportionately targeting minority communities, reinforcing systemic disparities.

- **Ethical and Legal Risks**

The deployment of biased AI systems exposes organizations to ethical dilemmas and legal liabilities. Discriminatory outcomes can result in lawsuits, regulatory penalties, and reputational damage.

2.4 Mitigating Bias in AI Systems

Addressing bias requires a multi-faceted approach that encompasses data, algorithms, and human oversight:

- **Ensuring Diverse and Inclusive Datasets**

Creating representative datasets is a foundational step toward reducing bias (Santoni de Sio & van den Hoven, 2018). This includes oversampling underrepresented groups, leveraging synthetic data, and employing techniques like stratified sampling to ensure balanced representation.

- **Bias Detection Tools and Techniques**

Various tools and techniques are available for detecting and mitigating bias. For example, IBM's AI Fairness 360 toolkit and Google's What-If Tool provide developers with insights into model performance across different demographic groups.

- **Fairness-Aware Algorithms**

Researchers are developing algorithms that explicitly account for fairness. These include techniques like adversarial debiasing, reweighting, and counterfactual fairness, which adjust models to mitigate biases without compromising overall performance.

- **Incorporating Human Oversight**

Human oversight is crucial for identifying and addressing biases that automated tools might miss. Diverse development teams with varied perspectives can play a vital role in spotting and mitigating potential biases during the design and testing phases.

- **Continuous Monitoring and Adaptation**

Bias is not static; it evolves over time as societal norms and data landscapes change (Pasquale, 2015). Continuous monitoring and retraining of AI systems are essential to ensure they remain fair and inclusive.

2.5 Challenges in Achieving Fair AI

Despite significant efforts, several challenges hinder the realization of fair AI systems:

- **Defining Fairness**

Fairness is a subjective concept with no universal definition. Different contexts may require different fairness metrics, such as equal opportunity, demographic parity, or equalized odds (Doshi-Velez & Kim, 2017). Balancing these metrics often involves trade-offs.

- **Balancing Fairness and Accuracy**

Efforts to reduce bias can impact model accuracy, particularly in imbalanced datasets (Gunning, 2017). This trade-off poses challenges for applications where performance is critical, such as medical diagnostics or autonomous vehicles.

- **Algorithmic Complexity and Transparency**

The complexity of modern AI algorithms makes it difficult to understand and explain their decisions, complicating efforts to identify and mitigate biases.

- **Evolving Bias in Dynamic Systems**

AI systems that adapt over time can develop new biases based on changing user behavior or feedback loops. Addressing these evolving biases requires robust monitoring mechanisms.

- **Cultural and Regional Variations**

Cultural and regional differences in defining fairness pose challenges for developing globally applicable AI systems. What is considered fair in one country may not align with norms in another.

2.6 The Path Toward Equitable AI

Creating equitable AI systems requires a collaborative effort involving technologists, ethicists, policymakers, and civil society (Ribeiro, Singh, & Guestrin, 2016):

- **Ethical Frameworks and Guidelines**

Adopting ethical guidelines, such as the IEEE's Ethically Aligned Design principles or UNESCO's AI ethics recommendations, can help developers navigate the complexities of fairness.

- **Education and Awareness**

Raising awareness about bias and fairness among AI developers, users, and policymakers is essential for fostering a culture of accountability.

- **Policy and Regulation**

Governments must establish regulations that mandate fairness assessments, transparency, and accountability in AI systems (European Union, 2018). Examples include the European Union's AI Act and the U.S. Algorithmic Accountability Act.

- **Interdisciplinary Collaboration**

Collaboration between technical and non-technical stakeholders can bridge gaps in understanding and ensure that fairness considerations are integrated throughout the AI lifecycle.

- **Empowering Marginalized Communities**

Involving underrepresented communities in the design and deployment of AI systems ensures that their needs and perspectives are adequately addressed, reducing the risk of exclusion.

Conclusion

Bias and fairness in AI are critical concerns that arise from multiple sources, including biased data collection, algorithmic design, historical inequalities, and human influences, leading to ethical challenges such as discrimination, erosion of trust, and legal risks. These biases manifest in various forms, including representation, outcome, and measurement biases, affecting AI applications across sectors like healthcare, hiring, and law enforcement. Addressing bias requires diverse and representative datasets, fairness-aware algorithms, robust bias detection tools, human oversight, and continuous monitoring. However, defining fairness, balancing it with accuracy, ensuring transparency, and managing evolving biases remain significant challenges. Achieving equitable AI necessitates a collaborative effort among technologists, ethicists, policymakers, and society through ethical guidelines, education, regulatory policies, interdisciplinary cooperation, and inclusive development practices. By prioritizing fairness, we can mitigate societal inequities and build AI systems that are transparent, accountable, and beneficial for all.

3. ACCOUNTABILITY AND RESPONSIBILITY

The integration of Artificial Intelligence (AI) into critical decision-making systems raises pressing questions about accountability and responsibility. As AI systems increasingly take on roles traditionally held by humans, determining who is responsible when things go wrong has become a central ethical concern. This section explores the dimensions of accountability and responsibility in AI systems, focusing on the roles of developers, organizations, end-users, and policymakers in ensuring ethical and transparent AI deployment.

3.1 The Concept of Accountability in AI Systems

Accountability refers to the obligation of individuals or organizations to explain, justify, and take responsibility for their actions (Gunning, 2017). In the context of AI, accountability involves identifying and addressing the roles of various stakeholders in the lifecycle of an AI system.

- **Shared Accountability Across the AI Lifecycle**

AI development involves multiple stages, including data collection, model training, deployment, and maintenance. Each stage requires the involvement of various actors—data scientists, software engineers, business leaders, and policymakers—making accountability inherently shared. For example, biased outcomes in predictive policing systems may stem from poorly curated training data (responsibility of data scientists) or inappropriate application in the field (responsibility of end-users).

- **The Challenge of Distributing Accountability**

The complexity of AI systems makes it difficult to pinpoint responsibility for specific outcomes. Is the algorithm developer responsible for a biased output, or does accountability lie with the organization that implemented the AI system without sufficient oversight. (European Commission, 2021) This diffusion of responsibility complicates ethical accountability and legal liability.

- **Why Accountability Matters**

Establishing clear accountability is essential for fostering trust in AI systems. Without accountability mechanisms, AI failures—such as misdiagnoses by medical AI tools or unjust denials in loan applications—could lead to harm without recourse for affected individuals. Accountability also encourages ethical behavior among AI developers and organizations by promoting transparency and responsibility.

3.2 Responsibility in AI Development

Responsibility in AI encompasses the ethical obligations of stakeholders involved in the creation and deployment of AI systems (Mitchell et al., 2019). This includes adhering to ethical principles, minimizing harm, and ensuring that AI systems align with societal values.

- **Developers' Ethical Responsibilities**

Developers play a pivotal role in shaping AI systems and bear significant responsibility for their behavior. Key responsibilities include:

- **Ensuring Transparency**: Developers should create AI systems that are interpretable and explainable, allowing end-users and regulators to understand their decision-making processes.
- **Mitigating Bias**: Proactively addressing biases in data and algorithms ensures equitable outcomes (Friedler, Scheidegger, & Venkatasubramanian, 2016).
- **Prioritizing Safety**: Developers must anticipate and mitigate risks, particularly in high-stakes domains such as healthcare and autonomous vehicles (Angwin, Larson, Mattu, & Kirchner, 2016).
- **Ethical Training and Education**: Incorporating ethics into AI education programs prepares developers to navigate complex ethical dilemmas in their work.
- **Corporate Responsibility**

Organizations deploying AI systems have a responsibility to ensure that these technologies are used ethically and do not cause harm. Key responsibilities include:

- **Implementing Governance Frameworks**: Organizations should establish ethical guidelines and oversight mechanisms for AI deployment.
- **Conducting Impact Assessments**: Pre-deployment impact assessments can identify potential risks and unintended consequences of AI systems.
- **Promoting Diversity and Inclusion**: Diverse teams can provide varied perspectives, reducing the likelihood of biased or harmful outcomes.
- **Monitoring and Maintenance**: Continuous monitoring of AI systems ensures they adapt to changing contexts and remain ethically sound.
- **End-Users' Role in Responsibility**

End-users interact with AI systems and influence their outputs. Their responsibilities include:

- **Understanding Limitations**: Users must be aware of the capabilities and limitations of AI systems to use them appropriately.

- **Providing Feedback**: Users play a crucial role in identifying errors and biases, enabling developers to improve AI systems.
- **Avoiding Misuse**: Users have an ethical obligation to avoid using AI systems for malicious purposes, such as spreading misinformation or violating privacy.

3.3 Challenges in Establishing Accountability

Several challenges complicate the establishment of accountability in AI systems:

- **Black-Box Nature of AI**

Many AI systems, particularly those based on deep learning, operate as "black boxes," making it difficult to understand how decisions are made. This lack of interpretability poses significant barriers to accountability, as stakeholders cannot fully explain or justify AI behavior (Narayanan & Shmatikov, 2008).

- **Ambiguity in Legal Frameworks**

Existing legal frameworks often struggle to address the complexities of AI accountability. For example, determining liability for an accident involving an autonomous vehicle may involve multiple parties, including the manufacturer, software developer, and even the vehicle owner.

- **Ethical Complexity**

Ethical dilemmas often arise in AI deployment. For instance, should an AI system prioritize accuracy over fairness? Such trade-offs complicate the establishment of clear accountability frameworks.

- **Global and Cultural Variations**

The global nature of AI development and deployment introduces cultural and legal variations in how accountability is perceived and enforced. For example, privacy regulations like GDPR in the European Union emphasize data protection, whereas other regions may prioritize innovation over regulation.

3.4 Strategies for Ensuring Accountability

- **Regulatory Frameworks and Policies**

Governments and international organizations play a critical role in establishing accountability through regulations and policies (Zemel et al., 2013). Examples include:

- **The European Union's AI Act**: This legislation outlines requirements for high-risk AI systems, emphasizing transparency, accountability, and human oversight.
- **The U.S. Algorithmic Accountability Act**: This act mandates impact assessments for automated decision-making systems, encouraging accountability and fairness.
- **Ethical Audits and Standards**

Regular ethical audits and adherence to industry standards ensure that AI systems meet ethical and legal requirements. Organizations like the IEEE and ISO have developed guidelines to promote accountability in AI systems.

- **Explainability and Transparency**

Enhancing the explainability of AI systems is critical for accountability. Techniques such as model interpretability tools, decision trees, and counterfactual explanations enable stakeholders to understand and scrutinize AI behavior (Barocas & Selbst, 2016).

- **Clear Accountability Frameworks**

Defining clear accountability frameworks that delineate the roles and responsibilities of all stakeholders—developers, organizations, and end-users—can help address the challenges of shared responsibility.

- **Multistakeholder Collaboration**

Collaboration among technologists, ethicists, policymakers, and civil society is essential for addressing complex accountability challenges. Initiatives like the Partnership on AI foster dialogue and cooperation among diverse stakeholders.

3.5 Case Studies of Accountability Failures

- **Cambridge Analytica and Data Misuse**

The misuse of Facebook data by Cambridge Analytica for political manipulation highlights the importance of accountability in data handling and AI deployment. The scandal underscored the need for stricter regulations and ethical oversight in AI systems (Datta, Tschantz, & Datta, 2015).

- **Autonomous Vehicle Accidents**

Incidents involving autonomous vehicles, such as the fatal Uber self-driving car crash in 2018, demonstrate the challenges of assigning accountability in complex AI ecosystems. The case raised questions about the responsibility of developers, manufacturers, and operators.

- **Discriminatory AI in Recruitment**

Amazon's AI recruitment tool, which was found to favor male candidates over female ones, highlights how biased algorithms can lead to unethical outcomes. The failure to address bias during development underscores the importance of proactive responsibility.

3.6 Moving Toward Responsible AI

- **Adopting Human-Centric AI Principles**

Human-centric AI prioritizes human welfare and aligns AI systems with ethical principles such as fairness, transparency, and accountability (Binns, 2018).

- **Encouraging Ethical Education and Training**

Incorporating ethics into AI education ensures that future developers and policymakers are equipped to address accountability challenges.

- **Promoting Global Collaboration**

International cooperation is essential for developing consistent accountability standards that transcend cultural and legal differences.

Conclusion

Ensuring accountability and responsibility in AI systems is crucial as these technologies increasingly influence critical decision-making processes. Accountability must be shared across the AI lifecycle, involving developers, organizations, end-users, and policymakers in addressing ethical concerns such as transparency, bias mitigation, and governance. However, challenges like the black-box nature of AI, ambiguous legal frameworks, and global variations complicate efforts to establish clear responsibility. Strategies such as regulatory frameworks, ethical audits, explainability tools, and multistakeholder collaboration can enhance accountability. High-profile failures, including biased hiring tools and autonomous vehicle accidents, underscore the urgency of responsible AI development. Moving forward, adopting human-centric AI principles, integrating ethics into education, and fostering global cooperation will be essential in ensuring AI systems remain transparent, fair, and accountable to society.

4. TRANSPARENCY AND EXPLAINABILITY

Transparency and explainability are critical components of ethical AI systems. These principles ensure that AI decisions are comprehensible, traceable, and justifiable to stakeholders, ranging from developers and end-users to regulators and affected individuals (Gebru et al., 2021). As AI increasingly impacts high-stakes domains such as healthcare, finance, and criminal justice, the importance of understanding and explaining AI behavior has grown exponentially. This section explores the concepts, challenges, methodologies, and implications of transparency and explainability in AI.

4.1 The Importance of Transparency in AI

Transparency refers to the openness and accessibility of information about an AI system's design, functioning, and decision-making processes (Hardt, Price, & Srebro, 2016). It enables stakeholders to understand how AI systems work and assess their reliability and fairness.

- **Building Trust in AI Systems**

Transparency fosters trust among users and stakeholders. When people understand how decisions are made, they are more likely to trust and adopt AI systems. For example, a transparent AI system used for loan approvals can provide applicants with clear reasons for acceptance or rejection, increasing confidence in the process (Buolamwini & Gebru, 2018).

- **Facilitating Accountability**

Transparent AI systems make it easier to assign accountability when errors or biases occur. If the decision-making process is open to scrutiny, stakeholders can identify and address the root causes of problems, ensuring that responsible parties are held accountable.

- **Enhancing Fairness and Ethical Compliance**

Transparency helps identify and mitigate biases in AI systems. By revealing the inner workings of models, developers and auditors can ensure that AI aligns with ethical standards and does not perpetuate discriminatory practices (Wachter, Mittelstadt, & Russell, 2018; Nguyen, Yosinski, & Clune, 2015)

- **Supporting Regulatory Compliance**

Regulatory frameworks, such as the European Union's General Data Protection Regulation (GDPR) and the proposed AI Act, emphasize the need for transparency. Transparent AI systems are better equipped to comply with these regulations, reducing legal risks for organizations.

4.2 The Concept of Explainability

Explainability is closely related to transparency but focuses specifically on making AI decisions understandable to humans (Adler et al., 2018). It involves creating mechanisms to provide clear, concise, and context-relevant explanations for AI behavior.

- **Defining Explainability**

Explainability refers to the ability of an AI system to articulate the rationale behind its decisions in a manner comprehensible to its audience. For example, a medical diagnostic AI could explain that a certain feature (e.g., a lesion's size) contributed significantly to a cancer diagnosis.

- **Explainability vs. Interpretability**

While often used interchangeably, explainability and interpretability have distinct meanings. Interpretability involves understanding the internal workings of an AI model, while explainability focuses on providing meaningful insights into the decision-making process (Chouldechova, 2017). Both are essential for comprehending AI behavior but address different aspects of understanding.

- **Levels of Explainability**

Explainability can be categorized based on the target audience:

- **Technical Explainability**: Aimed at developers and researchers, focusing on the mathematical and computational aspects of AI systems.
- **User-Level Explainability**: Tailored for end-users, offering intuitive and simplified explanations.
- **Regulatory Explainability**: Designed for policymakers and auditors to assess compliance with legal and ethical standards.

4.3 Challenges in Achieving Transparency and Explainability

While transparency and explainability are desirable, several challenges hinder their realization (Arnstein et al., 2020):

- **Complexity of Modern AI Models**

Advanced AI models, particularly deep learning systems, operate as "black boxes," making their decision-making processes opaque. Their complexity arises from millions or billions of parameters, making direct interpretation difficult (Dwork & Roth, 2014).

- **Trade-offs with Performance**

Efforts to enhance transparency and explainability may compromise the performance of AI models. Simplifying a model to improve interpretability can reduce its predictive accuracy, posing challenges for high-stakes applications like healthcare.

- **Contextual and Audience-Specific Requirements**

Different stakeholders require different levels of detail and types of explanations. Striking a balance between technical rigor and user-friendly explanations is a significant challenge.

- **Proprietary Concerns and Intellectual Property**

Organizations may be reluctant to disclose details about their AI systems due to concerns about revealing proprietary algorithms or trade secrets (Gill, 2021). This tension between transparency and intellectual property rights complicates ethical compliance.

- **Dynamic and Evolving Systems**

AI systems that adapt over time, such as those using reinforcement learning, present additional challenges for transparency. Explaining decisions in dynamic systems requires continuous monitoring and contextualization.

4.4 Methods for Enhancing Transparency and Explainability

Researchers and practitioners have developed various methods to enhance transparency and explainability in AI systems (Calo, 2017):

- **Intrinsic Explainability**

Intrinsic explainability focuses on designing interpretable models from the outset. Examples include:

- **Decision Trees**: These models provide a clear and visual representation of decision-making pathways.
- **Linear Regression**: Simpler models like linear regression are inherently interpretable, as they highlight direct relationships between input features and outcomes.
- **Post-Hoc Explainability**

Post-hoc methods aim to explain the behavior of complex, pre-trained models. Techniques include (Goodman & Flaxman, 2017):

- **Feature Importance Analysis**: Methods like SHAP (SHapley Additive exPlanations) and LIME (Local Interpretable Model-agnostic Explanations) identify which features contributed most to a decision.
- **Visualization Techniques**: Tools such as saliency maps and activation maps help visualize which parts of the input (e.g., an image) influenced a model's decision.
- **Counterfactual Explanations**: These involve generating hypothetical scenarios to illustrate how changes in input data could alter outcomes.
- **Interactive Interfaces**

Interactive tools allow users to explore and understand AI behavior dynamically (Jobin, Ienca, & Vayena, 2019). For example, Microsoft's Explainable AI dashboard provides an intuitive interface for exploring model predictions and explanations.

- **Documentation and Model Cards**

Documentation tools, such as Model Cards for Model Reporting, provide structured summaries of AI models, including their objectives, limitations, and potential biases.

- **Third-Party Auditing**

Independent audits by external experts can ensure transparency and accountability without revealing proprietary details. Auditors assess AI systems for compliance with ethical and regulatory standards.

4.5 Ethical and Social Implications of Transparency and Explainability

The ethical and social implications of transparency and explainability extend beyond technical considerations (White, 2020):

- **Empowering Users**

Transparent and explainable AI systems empower users to make informed decisions. For instance, an explainable recommendation system for medical treatments allows patients to weigh the risks and benefits of different options.

- **Reducing Discrimination and Bias**

Transparency exposes biases in AI systems, enabling corrective actions to ensure fairness. For example, explainability tools can reveal why certain demographic groups are disproportionately affected by algorithmic decisions.

- **Fostering Public Trust**

Transparent AI systems enhance public trust by demonstrating a commitment to ethical principles. This trust is essential for the widespread adoption of AI technologies.

- **Preventing Misuse**

Explainability helps prevent misuse by exposing unethical or malicious applications of AI. For example, transparency in content moderation algorithms can reveal whether certain groups are unfairly censored.

- **Ethical Trade-offs**

While transparency is generally beneficial, excessive disclosure can enable adversarial attacks or exploitation of AI systems. Balancing transparency with security and privacy is a critical ethical consideration.

4.6 Case Studies of Transparency and Explainability

- **AI in Healthcare: IBM Watson for Oncology**

IBM Watson for Oncology aimed to provide transparent recommendations for cancer treatment. However, its lack of adequate explainability led to criticisms about trustworthiness and usability (Friedler, Scheidegger, & Venkatasubramanian, 2016). This case underscores the importance of balancing technical sophistication with user-centric explanations.

- **COMPAS and Criminal Justice**

The COMPAS algorithm, used for risk assessment in criminal justice, faced scrutiny for biased outcomes against minority groups (Goodfellow, Shlens, & Szegedy, 2015). The lack of transparency in its scoring system highlighted the need for explainable AI in high-stakes applications.

- **Google's What-If Tool**

Google's What-If Tool allows users to test hypothetical scenarios and explore the fairness of AI models. This tool demonstrates how interactive interfaces can enhance transparency and foster user understanding.

4.7 Future Directions in Transparency and Explainability

- **Advances in Explainable AI Research**

Ongoing research aims to develop novel methods for enhancing explainability without compromising performance. Techniques like interpretable neural networks and hybrid models combine transparency with high predictive power.

- **Standardization and Guidelines**

Developing standardized frameworks for transparency and explainability will facilitate consistent implementation across industries. Organizations like the IEEE and ISO are working on guidelines to promote ethical AI practices.

- **Integration with Ethical AI Principles**

Transparency and explainability should be integrated with broader ethical principles, such as fairness, accountability, and inclusivity, to ensure holistic AI governance.

- **Global Collaboration and Policy Development**

International collaboration among governments, academia, and industry is essential for addressing the challenges of transparency and explainability in a globally interconnected AI ecosystem.

5. PRIVACY AND DATA SECURITY

Privacy and data security are cornerstone issues in the ethical deployment of AI systems. The ability of AI to process vast quantities of data enables unprecedented insights, but it also poses significant challenges to safeguarding personal privacy and ensuring data integrity (Selbst, Barocas, Crawford, Diaz, & Wallach, 2019). These challenges are exacerbated by the increasing reliance on AI in sensitive domains such as healthcare, finance, and law enforcement. This section explores the implications of privacy and data security in AI, emphasizing the ethical considerations, technical solutions, and policy frameworks needed to address these concerns.

5.1 Understanding Privacy in the AI Era

Privacy in the context of AI involves protecting individuals' personal data from unauthorized access, use, or disclosure. As AI systems rely on data for training, testing, and deployment, maintaining privacy is both a technical and ethical imperative.

- **Types of Privacy Concerns**
- **Data Collection Privacy**: Refers to concerns about how personal data is collected and whether individuals are aware and have consented to its use.
- **Data Processing Privacy**: Relates to how AI systems process and analyze data, ensuring that personal information is not exposed or misused.
- **Behavioral Privacy**: AI systems, especially those used in surveillance, can infer sensitive behavioral patterns, raising concerns about individual autonomy and freedom.
- **AI's Impact on Privacy**

AI exacerbates privacy risks by enabling detailed profiling, behavioral predictions, and even the re-identification of anonymized data. For instance, machine learning algorithms can deduce sensitive information like health conditions or political affiliations from seemingly innocuous data.

- **Balancing Innovation with Privacy**

While data is essential for AI innovation, it is crucial to strike a balance between leveraging data for technological advancements and respecting individuals' right to privacy.

5.2 The Importance of Data Security in AI

Data security involves protecting data from breaches, theft, and corruption, ensuring its confidentiality, integrity, and availability. In the context of AI, robust data security safeguards both individual privacy and the reliability of AI systems.

- **Threats to Data Security**
- **Data Breaches**: Unauthorized access to sensitive data can lead to identity theft, financial losses, and reputational damage.
- **Adversarial Attacks**: Malicious actors can manipulate AI models by injecting misleading data, compromising their performance and trustworthiness.
- **Ransomware Attacks**: Cybercriminals target data repositories, encrypting them and demanding payment for access.
- **Implications for AI Systems**

Breaches and attacks can compromise AI systems' reliability, leading to erroneous decisions or biased outcomes (Veale & Binns, 2017). For example, tampered healthcare data could result in inaccurate diagnoses or treatment recommendations.

- **Trust and Security**

Trust in AI systems is contingent on their ability to secure data. Users and stakeholders are less likely to adopt AI technologies if they perceive significant risks to their data security.

5.3 Ethical Considerations in Privacy and Data Security

Ethical considerations in privacy and data security involve respecting individuals' rights, promoting fairness, and ensuring transparency in how data is handled.

- **Informed Consent**

AI systems must obtain informed consent from users before collecting and using their data. This includes providing clear explanations about data usage, storage, and sharing practices.

- **Anonymization and De-Identification**

Techniques such as anonymization and de-identification are essential for protecting privacy. However, AI's ability to re-identify anonymized data underscores the need for robust safeguards.

- **Fairness and Non-Discrimination**

Data security measures must ensure that protections are equitable and do not disproportionately disadvantage vulnerable groups. For instance, securing data in AI systems used for social welfare should prioritize the privacy of marginalized populations (Mehrabi et al., 2021).

- **Transparency in Data Practices**

Organizations must be transparent about how they collect, process, and secure data. Transparent data practices build trust and accountability.

5.4 Technical Solutions for Privacy and Data Security

Technical solutions play a critical role in addressing privacy and data security challenges in AI.

- **Privacy-Preserving Machine Learning**

Privacy-preserving machine learning techniques (Datta, Tschantz, & Datta, 2015) minimize the risk of data exposure during training and deployment. Examples include:

- **Federated Learning**: Enables AI models to be trained on decentralized data without transferring it to a central server.
- **Differential Privacy**: Introduces random noise into data to prevent the identification of individuals while preserving aggregate insights.
- **Data Encryption**

Encryption methods ensure that data is securely stored and transmitted. Advanced encryption standards (AES) and homomorphic encryption allow computations on encrypted data without decrypting it, enhancing privacy.

- **Access Controls and Authentication**

Implementing strong access controls and multi-factor authentication minimizes the risk of unauthorized access to sensitive data.

- **Audit Trails and Monitoring**

Regular audits and real-time monitoring of data usage help detect and mitigate potential security breaches (Doshi-Velez & Kim, 2017).

5.5 Regulatory Frameworks and Policies

Legal and regulatory frameworks play a pivotal role in ensuring privacy and data security in AI systems.

- **Global Regulations**
- **General Data Protection Regulation (GDPR)**: Sets stringent requirements for data protection, including rights to access, rectification, and erasure of personal data.
- **California Consumer Privacy Act (CCPA)**: Grants consumers rights to control their personal information and mandates data security measures.
- **AI-Specific Guidelines**

Emerging guidelines, such as the EU's proposed AI Act, emphasize privacy and security as foundational principles for trustworthy AI (Barocas, Hardt, & Narayanan, 2019).

- **Sector-Specific Policies**

Different industries, such as healthcare and finance, have sector-specific regulations like HIPAA (Health Insurance Portability and Accountability Act) and GLBA (Gramm-Leach-Bliley Act) to address data security concerns.

- **International Cooperation**

Cross-border data flows require harmonized international policies to address privacy and security challenges in a globalized AI ecosystem.

5.6 Case Studies in Privacy and Data Security

- **Health Data and AI**

AI applications in healthcare often involve sensitive patient data. For example, Google DeepMind's collaboration with the UK's NHS faced criticism for inadequate data-sharing agreements, highlighting the importance of privacy safeguards (Doshi-Velez & Kim, 2017).

- **Social Media and AI**

Social media platforms leverage AI to analyze user behavior. Scandals like Cambridge Analytica demonstrate the risks of data misuse and underscore the need for robust privacy protections.

- **Facial Recognition and Surveillance**

AI-powered facial recognition systems raise significant privacy concerns. Controversies surrounding their use in public spaces illustrate the tension between security and individual privacy.

5.7 Future Directions in Privacy and Data Security

- **AI-Driven Privacy Solutions**

AI itself can be leveraged to enhance privacy through automated threat detection, anomaly detection, and predictive risk assessment (Veale & Binns, 2017).

- **Advancing Ethical AI Research**

Continued research into ethical AI practices, such as fairness-aware algorithms and secure multi-party computation, will address emerging privacy challenges.

- **Public Awareness and Education**

Empowering individuals with knowledge about their privacy rights and the risks of AI technologies fosters informed decision-making and advocacy for stronger protections.

- **Policy Innovation and Governance**

Policymakers must adapt to the evolving landscape of AI by introducing flexible and forward-looking regulations that address emerging privacy and security risks.

6. SOCIETAL IMPACT ON EMPLOYMENT AND HUMAN AGENCY

The integration of AI into various industries has profound implications for employment and human agency. While AI brings unparalleled efficiency and innovation, it also disrupts traditional job roles, challenges existing labor markets, and reshapes the concept of human agency in decision-making processes (Arnstein et al., 2020). This section explores the multifaceted societal impacts of AI, focusing on employment, skill development, workforce dynamics, and the shifting balance between human and machine agency.

6.1 Transforming Employment Landscapes

AI's ability to automate tasks has revolutionized the nature of work, with both positive and negative implications for employment (Pasquale, 2015). AI technologies excel in automating repetitive, mundane, and high-volume tasks across industries such as manufacturing, retail, and customer service. This has led to efficiency gains but also significant disruptions:

- **Manufacturing**: Robots powered by AI are replacing assembly line workers, leading to reduced demand for manual labor. Advanced AI-driven systems in smart factories are capable of performing intricate assembly tasks with precision, minimizing errors and operational costs. However, this automation displaces workers whose skills are narrowly aligned with repetitive tasks.
- **Retail:** AI-driven self-checkout systems and inventory management algorithms optimize operations. While these innovations reduce the need for traditional cashier roles, they also contribute to job displacement, particularly in low-wage sectors. For instance, AI-powered recommendation engines and virtual shopping assistants enhance customer experiences but reduce opportunities for human interaction roles (Selbst, Barocas, Crawford, Diaz, & Wallach, 2019).
- **Logistics**: Automated sorting and delivery systems have significantly streamlined supply chains. Technologies such as drones and autonomous vehicles enable faster and more efficient delivery processes, reducing the need for human drivers and warehouse workers.

The World Economic Forum estimates that AI could displace over 85 million jobs globally by 2025. This displacement disproportionately affects workers in low-skill and routine jobs, amplifying economic inequalities. Vulnerable populations, including those in developing economies and marginalized communities, are particularly at risk of being excluded from the evolving job market (Shokri & Shmatikov, 2015; California Consumer Privacy Act [CCPA], 2018; Goodfellow, Shlens, & Szegedy, 2015; Abadi et al., 2016; Barocas, Hardt, & Narayanan, 2019).

While AI disrupts existing jobs, it also creates opportunities in fields like data science, AI model training, and AI ethics consultancy. Emerging roles reflect the demand for specialized expertise to support AI systems:

- **AI Trainers:** These professionals curate datasets, label information, and guide AI systems to perform tasks effectively (European Commission, 2021). For instance, AI trainers refine natural language processing models to enhance their contextual understanding.
- **Ethics Auditors:** With growing concerns over AI biases and ethical breaches, ethics auditors ensure that AI systems comply with regulatory standards, fairness principles, and transparency requirements.
- **Human-AI Collaboration Experts:** These facilitators focus on designing workflows and interfaces that enable seamless interaction between humans and AI systems in hybrid environments. Their expertise is crucial in ensuring that AI augments rather than undermines human roles.
- **AI Maintenance Specialists**: These roles involve diagnosing and troubleshooting AI-driven systems, ensuring their long-term functionality and accuracy.

The proliferation of these roles underscores the need for upskilling initiatives to equip the workforce with the necessary competencies to thrive in an AI-driven economy.

AI's transformative impact varies across industries, with unique challenges and opportunities in each sector (Barocas, Hardt, & Narayanan, 2019; Buolamwini & Gebru, 2018; Mehrabi, Morstatter, Saxena, Lerman, & Galstyan, 2021; Chouldechova & Roth, 2020):

- **Healthcare:** AI-powered diagnostics and predictive analytics augment medical practitioners by identifying conditions with high accuracy. However, the integration of AI reduces the demand for administrative staff as automation handles tasks like patient scheduling and record management. Robotic surgical assistants also introduce new ethical and operational considerations.
- **Education:** AI-based personalized learning platforms and virtual tutors supplement traditional education systems. While these tools empower educators to tailor learning experiences, they also challenge conventional teaching methodologies and roles. Additionally, the adoption of AI raises questions about equitable access to advanced learning technologies.
- **Finance:** Automated trading algorithms and robo-advisors have transformed investment strategies, rendering human analysts increasingly redundant in some areas. At the same time, opportunities arise in fintech development, cybersecurity, and regulatory compliance for AI-powered systems.
- **Agriculture:** AI-driven precision farming techniques, such as soil monitoring drones and crop health prediction algorithms, revolutionize agricultural practices. This reduces labor demands but also introduces opportunities for roles in agritech development and management (European Union, 2018).
- **Entertainment:** AI tools in content creation, such as automated video editing and generative art, empower creators but challenge traditional artistic professions.

6.2 Workforce Dynamics and Skill Development

The rapid adoption of AI necessitates a paradigm shift in workforce training. Traditional skill sets are becoming obsolete, and new competencies are essential to navigate the evolving job market (Gill, 2021):

- **Technical Skills**: Proficiency in programming languages, data analysis, and machine learning algorithms is crucial for workers in AI-driven sectors.
- **Soft Skills:** Creativity, critical thinking, and emotional intelligence remain indispensable as these qualities cannot be easily replicated by AI systems.
- **Lifelong Learning:** Workers must embrace continuous learning to stay relevant in a landscape characterized by rapid technological advancements.

Governments, educational institutions, and corporations play pivotal roles in fostering skill development. Policies that promote accessible training programs, online education platforms, and public-private partnerships are vital to bridging skill gaps.

The integration of AI contributes to workforce polarization, with a growing divide between high-skill, high-wage roles and low-skill, low-wage jobs. Middle-skill jobs are particularly vulnerable to automation, leading to economic stratification. To mitigate these effects, targeted interventions are necessary to support middle-skill workers in transitioning to emerging roles (Barocas & Selbst, 2016).

6.3 Human and Machine Agency

AI's decision-making capabilities challenge traditional notions of human agency. In domains like healthcare, finance, and criminal justice, AI systems are increasingly entrusted with critical decisions. This shift raises ethical questions about accountability, bias, and transparency (Nguyen, Yosinski, & Clune, 2015):

- **Healthcare:** AI-driven diagnostic tools provide recommendations, but ultimate decision-making authority often rests with physicians. Balancing AI insights with human judgment is crucial to ensure optimal patient outcomes.
- **Criminal Justice**: Predictive policing algorithms influence law enforcement strategies, potentially perpetuating biases if not adequately regulated.
- **Corporate Governance:** AI-powered analytics shape strategic decisions, prompting organizations to consider the balance between algorithmic efficiency and human intuition.

Hybrid Decision-Making Models

To address concerns about over-reliance on AI, hybrid decision-making models that integrate human oversight with AI insights are gaining traction (Chouldechova & Roth, 2020). These models emphasize:

- **Transparency:** Ensuring that AI decision-making processes are interpretable and understandable to humans.
- **Accountability:** Establishing clear frameworks for assigning responsibility in cases of errors or unintended consequences.
- **Collaboration:** Designing systems that empower humans to leverage AI capabilities while retaining ultimate control over decisions.

6.4 Societal Inequalities and AI's Role

The uneven adoption of AI technologies widens societal inequalities, creating divides between those who benefit from AI advancements and those who are left behind. This section examines the root causes and potential solutions to mitigate these disparities.

Digital Divide

Access to AI technologies is unevenly distributed, with developing nations lagging behind due to several factors:

- **Limited Infrastructure**: Many regions lack the technological infrastructure necessary to support AI integration, such as reliable internet access, data storage facilities, and advanced computing resources.
- **Insufficient Funding**: Developing nations often struggle to allocate sufficient funds for AI research, development, and deployment. This lack of investment limits their ability to compete globally.

- **Gaps in Digital Literacy**: A significant portion of the population in underprivileged regions lacks the skills required to interact with AI-driven technologies effectively.

Bridging the digital divide requires comprehensive global initiatives. These include promoting affordable access to AI tools through subsidized technologies, encouraging cross-border collaboration to share knowledge and resources, and investing in digital literacy programs that empower underserved communities to participate in the AI-driven economy (Narayanan & Shmatikov, 2008).

Cultural Impacts

AI systems trained on biased datasets may propagate stereotypes and cultural misrepresentations, exacerbating societal inequalities. Specific examples include:

- **Language Prioritization**: Language models often favor dominant languages such as English or Mandarin, marginalizing lesser-spoken dialects and eroding cultural heritage.
- **Bias in Image Recognition**: Many AI-driven image recognition systems struggle to accurately identify individuals from underrepresented groups, leading to misidentifications and unequal treatment.

Addressing these issues requires diversifying training datasets to include a broader range of cultural contexts. Furthermore, engaging culturally sensitive stakeholders—such as local communities, linguists, and sociologists—in the AI development process can ensure that technologies are inclusive and representative of diverse perspectives (Ribeiro, Singh, & Guestrin, 2016).

6.5 Ethical Employment Practices in the AI Age

As AI reshapes employment landscapes, ethical practices are crucial to ensuring fairness, inclusivity, and social responsibility. This section explores key areas where ethical considerations are paramount.

Fair Compensation

Organizations must prioritize fair compensation for workers affected by AI-induced job displacement. Ethical measures include (Calo, 2017):

- **Severance Packages**: Providing financial support to displaced workers helps them transition during periods of unemployment.
- **Transition Support**: Offering job placement assistance, retraining programs, and skill development opportunities ensures that displaced employees can adapt to new roles in the evolving job market.
- **Inclusive Policy Making**

Inclusive policies are essential to prevent marginalization and promote equitable outcomes. Key approaches include:

- **Worker Unions**: Unions can advocate for the fair implementation of AI, ensuring that workers' rights are protected and that their voices are heard in decision-making processes.
- **Regulatory Frameworks**: Governments and international organizations must establish ethical standards for AI adoption in workplaces, ensuring transparency, fairness, and accountability.
- **Corporate Responsibility**

Corporations play a pivotal role in mitigating the societal impacts of AI. Their responsibilities include:

- **Transparent Communication**: Clearly informing employees about AI-driven changes in workforce structure fosters trust and reduces uncertainty.
- **Human-Centric Designs**: Designing AI systems that augment human capabilities rather than replace them promotes employee empowerment and job satisfaction.

6.6 Future Directions for Employment and Human Agency

As AI continues to evolve, proactive measures are essential to maximize its benefits while minimizing disruptions. This section outlines key strategies for navigating the future of employment and human agency in the AI age.

Reimagining Education Systems

Education systems must undergo significant transformation to prepare future generations for AI-driven economies. Key initiatives include (Veale & Binns, 2017):

- **Interdisciplinary Learning**: Combining technical skills such as programming and data science with ethical reasoning and humanities ensures well-rounded development.
- **Promoting Creativity and Critical Thinking**: These uniquely human attributes remain difficult to automate, making them valuable in an AI-dominated world.
- **Emotional Intelligence**: Teaching empathy and social skills prepares individuals to thrive in collaborative, human-centric roles.

Global Cooperation for Workforce Development

Addressing disparities in AI's impact on employment requires international collaboration. Organizations like the Global Partnership on Artificial Intelligence (GPAI) play a crucial role by (Mehrabi, Morstatter, Saxena, Lerman, & Galstyan, 2021):

- Facilitating knowledge sharing between nations to promote equitable development.
- Supporting initiatives that create opportunities for underserved populations to participate in the global AI economy.
- Encouraging cross-border research partnerships to advance inclusive AI technologies.

Ethical AI Research and Development

Investing in ethical AI research ensures that future technologies align with human values and societal well-being. Essential steps include:

- **Augmenting Human Potential**: Developing AI systems that enhance human productivity and creativity rather than replacing jobs entirely.
- **Inclusive Design Processes**: Involving diverse stakeholders—including ethicists, policymakers, end-users, and marginalized groups—in the design and development of AI systems fosters fairness and inclusivity.

Conclusion

Privacy and data security are fundamental to the ethical and responsible deployment of AI, ensuring that individuals' personal information remains protected while maintaining system integrity and trust. As AI systems become increasingly embedded in sensitive domains, the challenges of data collection, processing, and security intensify, necessitating robust technical solutions like privacy-preserving machine learning, encryption, and access controls. Ethical considerations, including informed consent, fairness, and transparency, must guide AI development, while global regulatory frameworks such as GDPR and CCPA provide legal safeguards. Case studies from healthcare, social media, and surveillance highlight the risks of data misuse, underscoring the need for stringent policies and governance. Moving forward, AI-driven privacy solutions, ethical AI research, public awareness, and adaptive regulations will be crucial in addressing evolving privacy and security challenges in a globalized AI ecosystem.

7. CONCLUSION AND FUTURE PROSPECTS

The integration of generative AI tools into society has ushered in a transformative era characterized by remarkable potential and profound challenges. This chapter has systematically explored the ethical considerations and challenges surrounding human-AI collaboration, addressing critical themes such as bias, accountability, transparency, data security, societal impact, and human agency. In this concluding section, we synthesize these insights, emphasize key takeaways, and envision future pathways for the ethical development and deployment of AI systems.

7.1 Summary of Ethical Challenges

- **Bias and Fairness**

The pervasive issue of bias in AI highlights the need for diverse and representative datasets, along with rigorous testing protocols to identify and mitigate biases. Ensuring fairness demands active participation from multidisciplinary teams and the integration of inclusive design principles into the AI development process. Failure to address bias risks perpetuating systemic inequalities and eroding public trust in AI systems.

- **Accountability and Responsibility**

AI systems often operate in environments where decisions have significant consequences, raising critical questions about responsibility. Clear delineation of accountability—whether on developers, deployers, or users—is necessary to manage risks effectively. Moreover, frameworks such as human-in-the-loop systems can ensure ethical oversight while leveraging the strengths of AI.

- **Transparency and Explainability**

AI systems' opaque nature, particularly with deep learning models, complicates their adoption in sensitive domains. Enhancing transparency and explainability is paramount for gaining user trust and regulatory acceptance. Open models, interpretable AI, and user education are critical steps in this direction.

- **Privacy and Data Security**

Privacy concerns surrounding AI systems necessitate robust data governance frameworks, ethical data collection practices, and advanced security mechanisms to safeguard sensitive information. The principles of data minimization, consent, and accountability must be central to AI development.

- **Societal Impact**

AI's impact on employment and human agency underscores the importance of proactive strategies to address job displacement and skill gaps. Initiatives fostering upskilling, reskilling, and ethical labor practices will ensure equitable transitions into AI-augmented workplaces. Additionally, preserving human agency and autonomy amidst increasing automation is essential to align AI with human values.

7.2 Future Prospects

As generative AI continues to evolve, its trajectory will be shaped by technological advancements, regulatory frameworks, and societal expectations. Future prospects hinge on balancing innovation with ethical stewardship to maximize benefits while minimizing risks.

7.2.1 Advances in Ethical AI Research

AI research will increasingly prioritize ethical considerations as a foundational component. Areas of focus include:

- **Bias Mitigation Techniques**: Developing algorithms that proactively detect and address biases during training and deployment, ensuring equitable outcomes and minimizing societal disparities.
- **Explainable AI (XAI)**: Advancing techniques for making complex AI systems interpretable and accessible to non-experts, fostering trust and accountability in AI deployments.
- **Ethical AI-by-Design**: Embedding ethical principles into every stage of the AI lifecycle, from ideation and development to deployment and monitoring, ensuring alignment with societal values.

Global initiatives, such as the Global Partnership on Artificial Intelligence (GPAI), are fostering collaboration among governments, academia, and industry to accelerate advancements in ethical AI research. These efforts aim to establish standardized practices and frameworks that prioritize human-centric AI development.

7.2.2 Regulatory Innovations

Governments and international bodies will play a pivotal role in shaping AI's future through comprehensive regulatory frameworks. These frameworks should:

- **Enforce Accountability**: Clearly define liability for AI-induced harm, ensuring responsible usage and development.
- **Mandate Transparency**: Require detailed disclosure of AI systems' operations in high-stakes environments such as healthcare, finance, and law enforcement.
- **Protect User Privacy**: Implement stringent data protection laws to safeguard sensitive information and prevent misuse.

Harmonizing regulations across jurisdictions is critical for creating global standards in AI ethics. Such harmonization will enable seamless cross-border collaboration, reduce compliance complexities, and foster a unified approach to addressing ethical concerns.

7.2.3 AI for Social Good

Generative AI's potential extends beyond commercial applications, offering transformative solutions to global challenges. Examples include:

- **Climate Change**: Leveraging AI-driven models to optimize resource utilization, predict environmental impacts, and support renewable energy initiatives.
- **Healthcare**: Enhancing medical diagnostics, accelerating drug discovery, and enabling personalized treatment plans tailored to individual needs.
- **Education**: Bridging educational disparities by delivering personalized learning experiences and providing access to high-quality resources in underserved communities.

To realize these benefits, fostering public-private partnerships is essential. Such collaborations can pool resources, expertise, and innovation to address pressing societal issues effectively.

7.2.4 Workforce Transformation

The workforce of the future will be characterized by dynamic interactions between humans and AI. Preparing for this transformation involves:

- **Continuous Learning**: Incorporating AI literacy and upskilling programs into education systems and professional development initiatives.

- **Hybrid Work Models**: Designing workflows that integrate human creativity with AI's analytical capabilities, maximizing efficiency and innovation.
- **Ethical Employment Practices**: Ensuring fair treatment of workers, promoting inclusivity, and providing support for individuals displaced by AI-driven automation.

AI's role as a catalyst for creativity and problem-solving will redefine traditional job roles, emphasizing uniquely human qualities such as empathy, critical thinking, and emotional intelligence.

7.2.5 Public Awareness and Engagement

Building societal trust in AI requires active engagement with the public. Key initiatives include:

- **Awareness Campaigns**: Educating citizens about AI's benefits, limitations, and potential risks to empower informed decision-making.
- **Participatory Design**: Involving diverse stakeholders in the development and deployment of AI systems to ensure inclusivity and relevance.
- **Feedback Mechanisms**: Establishing accessible channels for users to report concerns, share experiences, and suggest improvements.

Transparent communication and inclusive practices will foster public trust, ensuring AI aligns with societal values and expectations.

7.3 Ethical AI as a Collective Responsibility

The ethical challenges posed by AI cannot be addressed by any single entity. A collective effort is required, involving:

- **Governments**: Enacting policies that strike a balance between fostering innovation and implementing ethical safeguards.
- **Corporations**: Prioritizing long-term societal benefits over short-term profits, integrating ethical considerations into business strategies.
- **Academia**: Driving research on ethical AI principles, developing guidelines, and educating future leaders in responsible AI practices.
- **Civil Society**: Advocating for fairness, accountability, and inclusivity in AI implementations, ensuring the needs and rights of all communities are considered.

Collaboration among these stakeholders will create an AI ecosystem centered on human well-being and ethical integrity.

7.4 Navigating Ethical Dilemmas in the AI Era

AI's dual potential as a force for good and a source of ethical dilemmas necessitates ongoing vigilance and adaptability. Strategies for navigating these dilemmas include:

- **Ethical Frameworks**: Adopting comprehensive guidelines that address various ethical dimensions, such as fairness, transparency, and accountability.
- **Scenario Planning**: Anticipating potential risks and formulating contingency plans to mitigate adverse impacts.
- **Adaptive Governance**: Ensuring regulatory frameworks evolve in step with rapid technological advancements to remain effective and relevant.

The dynamic nature of AI technologies calls for an iterative approach to ethics, where continuous learning and feedback inform future policies and practices.

7.5 Vision for the Future

The future of generative AI hinges on its ability to harmonize with human values and societal aspirations. By embedding ethical considerations into AI's DNA, we can unlock its potential to drive progress while preserving the dignity, autonomy, and rights of individuals. A shared commitment to responsible innovation will ensure that AI serves as a tool for empowerment, equity, and global prosperity.

REFERENCES

Abadi, M. (2016). Deep Learning with Differential Privacy. *Proceedings of the 2016 ACM SIGSAC Conference on Computer and Communications Security*. DOI: 10.1145/2976749.2978318

Adler, P., Falk, C., Friedler, S. A., Nix, T., Rybeck, G., Scheidegger, C., Smith, B., & Venkatasubramanian, S. (2018). Auditing Black-box Models for Indirect Influence. *Knowledge and Information Systems*, *54*(1), 95–122. DOI: 10.1007/s10115-017-1116-3

Angwin, J., Larson, J., Mattu, S., & Kirchner, L. (2016). "Machine Bias," *ProPublic*. Available: https://www.propublica.org/article/machine-bias-risk-assessments-in-criminal-sentencing

Arnstein, S. R. (2020). "On the 'Human' in Human-centered AI: A Survey of Human-centered Methods in Machine Learning," in *Proceedings of the 2020 CHI Conference on Human Factors in Computing Systems*, Honolulu, HI, USA, 2020, pp. 1-14.

Barocas, S., Hardt, M., & Narayanan, A. (2019). *Fairness and Machine Learning: Limitations and Opportunities*. Available at: https://fairmlbook.org/

Barocas, S., & Selbst, A. D. (2016). Big Data's Disparate Impact. *California Law Review*, *104*(3), 671–732.

Binns, R. (2018). "Fairness in Machine Learning: Lessons from Political Philosophy," in *Proceedings of the 2018 Conference on Fairness, Accountability, and Transparency*, New York, NY, USA. pp. 149-159.

Buolamwini, J., & Gebru, T. (2018). Gender Shades: Intersectional Accuracy Disparities in Commercial Gender Classification. *Proceedings of Machine Learning Research*, *81*, 77–91.

California Consumer Privacy Act (CCPA). (2018). Available at: https://oag.ca.gov/privacy/ccpa

Calo, R. (2017). Artificial Intelligence Policy: A Primer and Roadmap. *U.C. Davis Law Review*, *51*(2), 399–435.

Chouldechova, A. (2017). Fair Prediction with Disparate Impact: A Study of Bias in Recidivism Prediction Instruments. *Big Data*, *5*(2), 153–163. DOI: 10.1089/big.2016.0047 PMID: 28632438

Chouldechova, A., & Roth, A. (2020). A Snapshot of the Frontiers of Fairness in Machine Learning. *Communications of the ACM*, *63*(5), 82–89. DOI: 10.1145/3376898

Datta, A., Tschantz, M. C., & Datta, A. (2015). Automated Experiments on Ad Privacy Settings: A Tale of Opacity, Choice, and Discrimination. *Proceedings on Privacy Enhancing Technologies. Privacy Enhancing Technologies Symposium*, *2015*(1), 92–112. DOI: 10.1515/popets-2015-0007

Doshi-Velez, F., & Kim, B. (2017). *Towards A Rigorous Science of Interpretable Machine Learning*. arXiv preprint arXiv:1702.08608.

Dwork, C., & Roth, A. (2014). *The Algorithmic Foundations of Differential Privacy*. Foundations and Trends® in Theoretical Computer Science, 9(3–4), 211-407.

European Commission. (2021). *Proposal for a Regulation Laying Down Harmonized Rules on Artificial Intelligence (Artificial Intelligence Act)*. Available at: https://eur-lex.europa.eu/

European Union. (2018). *General Data Protection Regulation (GDPR)*. Available at: https://gdpr-info.eu

Friedler, S. A., Scheidegger, C., & Venkatasubramanian, S. (2019). "On the (Im)possibility of Fairness," *arXiv preprint arXiv:1609.07236*.

Gebru, T., Morgenstern, J., Vecchione, B., Vaughan, J. W., Wallach, H., Iii, H. D., & Crawford, K. (2021). Datasheets for Datasets. *Communications of the ACM*, *64*(12), 86–92. DOI: 10.1145/3458723

Gill, A. (2021). AI Ethics: The Case for Including Animals. *AI & Society*, *36*(1), 267–278.

Goodfellow, I. J., Shlens, J., & Szegedy, C. (2015). Explaining and Harnessing Adversarial Examples. *International Conference on Learning Representations (ICLR)*.

Goodman, B., & Flaxman, S. (2017). European Union Regulations on Algorithmic Decision-Making and a 'Right to Explanation'. *AI Magazine*, *38*(3), 50–57. DOI: 10.1609/aimag.v38i3.2741

Gunning, D. (2017). *Explainable Artificial Intelligence (XAI)*. Defense Advanced Research Projects Agency (DARPA).

Hardt, M., Price, E., & Srebro, N. (2016). "Equality of Opportunity in Supervised Learning," in *Advances in Neural Information Processing Systems 29 (NIPS 2016)*, Barcelona, Spain. pp. 3315-3323.

Holstein, K., Wortman Vaughan, J., Daumé, H., Dudik, M., & Wallach, H. (2019). Improving Fairness in Machine Learning Systems: What Do Industry Practitioners Need? *Proceedings of the 2019 CHI Conference on Human Factors in Computing Systems*, 1-16. DOI: 10.1145/3290605.3300830

Jobin, A., Ienca, M., & Vayena, E. (2019). The Global Landscape of AI Ethics Guidelines. *Nature Machine Intelligence*, *1*(9), 389–399. DOI: 10.1038/s42256-019-0088-2

Mehrabi, N., Morstatter, F., Saxena, N., Lerman, K., & Galstyan, A. (2021). A Survey on Bias and Fairness in Machine Learning. *ACM Computing Surveys*, *54*(6), 1–35. DOI: 10.1145/3457607

Mehrabi, N., Morstatter, F., Saxena, N., Lerman, K., & Galstyan, A. (2021). A Survey on Bias and Fairness in Machine Learning. *ACM Computing Surveys*, *54*(6), 1–35. DOI: 10.1145/3457607

Mitchell, M. (2019). Model Cards for Model Reporting. *Proceedings of the Conference on Fairness, Accountability, and Transparency*, 220-229 DOI: 10.1145/3287560.3287596

Narayanan, A., & Shmatikov, V. (2008). "Robust De-anonymization of Large Sparse Datasets," in *Proceedings of the 2008 IEEE Symposium on Security and Privacy*, Oakland, CA, USA. pp. 111-125. DOI: 10.1109/SP.2008.33

Nguyen, A. T., Yosinski, J., & Clune, J. (2015). "Deep Neural Networks are Easily Fooled: High Confidence Predictions for Unrecognizable Images," in *2015 IEEE Conference on Computer Vision and Pattern Recognition (CVPR)*, Boston, MA, USA. pp. 427-436. DOI: 10.1109/CVPR.2015.7298640

Pasquale, F. (2015). *The Black Box Society: The Secret Algorithms That Control Money and Information*. Harvard University Press. DOI: 10.4159/harvard.9780674736061

Ribeiro, M. T., Singh, S., & Guestrin, C. (2016). *"Why Should I Trust You?": Explaining the Predictions of Any Classifier.* Proceedings of the 22nd ACM SIGKDD International Conference on Knowledge Discovery and Data Mining, 1135-1144.

Santoni de Sio, F., & van den Hoven, J. (2018). Meaningful Human Control over Autonomous Systems: A Philosophical Account. *Frontiers in Robotics and AI*, *5*, 15. DOI: 10.3389/frobt.2018.00015 PMID: 33500902

Selbst, A. D., Barocas, S., Crawford, E., Diaz, F., & Wallach, H. (2019). "Fairness and Abstraction in Sociotechnical Systems," in *Proceedings of the 2019 Conference on Fairness, Accountability, and Transparency*, Atlanta, GA, USA. pp. 59-68. DOI: 10.1145/3287560.3287598

Shokri, R., & Shmatikov, V. (2015). Privacy-Preserving Deep Learning. *Proceedings of the 22nd ACM SIGSAC Conference on Computer and Communications Security.*

Veale, M., & Binns, R. (2017). Fairer Machine Learning in the Real World: Mitigating Discrimination without Collecting Sensitive Data. *Big Data & Society*, *4*(2), 1–17. DOI: 10.1177/2053951717743530

Wachter, S., Mittelstadt, B., & Russell, C. (2018). Counterfactual Explanations without Opening the Black Box: Automated Decisions and the GDPR. *Harvard Journal of Law & Technology*, *31*(2), 841–887.

Wagner, B. (2018). *Ethics as an Escape from Regulation: From Ethics-Washing to Ethics-Shopping?* In *Being Profiled: Cogitas Ergo Sum* (pp. 84-89). Amsterdam University Press. DOI: 10.2307/j.ctvhrd092.18

White, R. W. (2020). Interpretable Machine Learning for Health Care. *Communications of the ACM*, *63*(1), 68–77.

Zemel, R. S., Wu, Y., Swersky, K., Pitassi, T., & Dwork, C. (2013). "Learning Fair Representations," in *Proceedings of the 30th International Conference on Machine Learning (ICML-13)*, Atlanta, GA, USA. pp. 325-333.

Chapter 4
Are LLMs and RAG Trustworthy Enough for Your Business?
A Deep Dive Into AI's Reliability

Hakan Emekci
https://orcid.org/0000-0002-4074-5600
TED University, Turkey

ABSTRACT

Integrating Large Language Models (LLMs) and Retrieval-Augmented Generation (RAG) systems into business operations has become a transformative force. In the literature, the advantages as well as the disadvantages of this integration are discussed. The chapter discusses some latent risks involved in AI, namely, AI-data bias, adversarial vulnerabilities, privacy concerns, and domain-specific limitations, while putting forward methodologies for their mitigation through better data management and strong security protocols. The chapter also discusses the prospect of the future of changes that could be made in reliable and safe AI. Stitching together these divergent insights, this paper contributes to an understanding of how businesses can use LLMs and RAG systems responsibly in ways that keep AI adoption in step with meeting ethical compasses and operational integrity. It forms a core reference to guide institutions in their efforts to harness the full potential of artificial intelligence technologies in their operations regarding the intricacies involved in trust and risk management.

1. INTRODUCTION

Throughout the last couple of years, fast technology integration appeared in association with AI, mainly linked to the appearance of large language models. This transformed many business environments in different industries (Al Ghadban et al., 2023; Chen et al., 2023). These highly advanced AI models are widely acknowledged as one of the key tools in boosting efficiency, enabling real-time decision-making, and offering personalized customer experiences, ranging from automation in customer support to high-level strategic data analysis (Asai et al., 2023; Jeong, 2023). However, as AI models, such as LLMs and RAG, become integral to core business functions, the need for their reliability to be scrutinized intensifies. Indeed, while these models promise high accuracy and adaptability, their trustworthiness remains one of the most important areas of concern, as businesses attempt to strike a balance between

DOI: 10.4018/979-8-3693-8332-2.ch004

innovating with new capabilities and managing risks and compliance (Gámiz et al., 2021; Payette & Abdul-Nour, 2023). These would include metrics such as accuracy, robustness, transparency, and ethical compliance. Each of these becomes an important dimension in establishing the business viability of LLMs and RAG. For example, the accuracy in model predictions is a direct determinant of the reliability of automated decisions, while robustness speaks to a model's ability to resist unpredicted inputs or perturbations (Muneeswaran et al., 2023). This transparency is one avenue to satisfying not just regulatory constraints but also a user's quest to understand and, hence, trust the model's decisions. These decisions may vary depending on the level of interpretability embedded in the architecture of the AI (Linardatos et al., 2021). Ethical and legal considerations underline the requirement for equity in decision-making, with sensitive domains including healthcare, by Dale et al. (2023), and finance, as discussed by Cao (2022), since the models' outputs might affect individual lives and have serious wider consequences in society. The main problem is that they are big datasets, some of which may be crawled into diverse, uncontrolled environments.

This dependency also exposes them to risks relating to data bias, which may skew decision-making processes. Many AI fairness studies have illustrated that when models are trained on imbalanced datasets, they tend to further propagate the already existing biases and thus affect the ethical integrity of AI-driven decisions (Navigli et al., 2023). More importantly, LLMs and RAG systems are vulnerable to adversarial attacks; maliciously designed inputs can manipulate the model's output (Shayegani et al., 2023). The existence of such vulnerabilities is especially alarming for enterprises that manage sensitive information, since these attacks not only undermine the reliability of models but may also result in insubstantial data breaches and harm to reputation. The ability of artificial intelligence systems to impact business operations necessitates rigorous security protocols and extensive lifecycle management (Raimundo & Rosário, 2021).

It requires, therefore, great vigilance and frequent updates so that the model remains able to combat the new threats and adapt to the changes in situations. These models can be further bolstered with the latest adversarial training methods against their possible manipulations, making them more reliable in realistic application scenarios (Zhao et al., 2022). In this aspect, the governance of enterprise and industry-specific adaptability of needs for AI models turn out to be an important differentiator in deploying trustworthy AI.

This chapter aims to critically analyze the application of Large Language Models (LLMs) and Retrieval-Augmented Generation (RAG) systems as they apply to corporate environments, determining both the strategic advantages that they offer and the risks involved when implemented. The investigation starts by exploring the differences between the foundational designs of LLM and RAG systems and their potential use within business contexts. Then, the chapter compares these technologies against key criteria, including accuracy, dependability, transparency, ethical standards, and compatibility with regulatory systems. The methodology includes an extensive review of current research literature, analysis of key case studies, and investigation of current trends of application. Through the synthesis of findings, this research presents an organizational strategy to apply LLM and RAG technologies effectively and ethically.

2. TECHNICAL FOUNDATIONS

The basic technical architecture on which LLMs and RAG are based includes multi-component systems that greatly influence their effectiveness in a business environment (Jeong, 2023). The section looks at the most important elements of these models, considering their fundamental processes and structural differences that account for their operational functionality and efficiency in business. The section further considers their actual applications to businesses to make clear their practical use and benefits.

a. Core Mechanisms of LLMs and RAG

The key to large language models lies in a structure known as the Transformer, originally proposed by Vaswani et al., (2017). That depends on a mechanism called self-attention, such that one may handle long-range dependencies that may exist in texts. Contrary to what is normally done with more traditional RNN or LSTM networks, the possibility exists to easily learn complex structures of languages and semantic relations with large datasets by LLM. Transformers do this by employing multi-head attention, allowing it to process input text simultaneously through different attention heads. This indeed facilitates a fine-grained understanding of the context and sequence in natural language (Jo & Myaeng, 2020). Large language models, such as GPT-4 and BERT, have gone through large-scale corpora pre-training and have been later fine-tuned for specific tasks, which could make them adaptable to a wide range of business functions, from customer support to financial forecasting (Makridakis et al., 2023).

On the other hand, RAG models extend the conventional functions of LLMs by including a retrieval mechanism, enabling the dynamic collection of relevant information from an external knowledge base (O, 2023). Combining generative and retrieval-based methods, this approach designs the LLM to generate an answer by combining both previously seen training data and specific, currently retrieved information (Jeong, 2023). While this is supported through some sort of real-time information processing with a dually supporting retrieval mechanism-usually a dense or sparse vector search aligns query vectors with external data vectors to find the most contextually relevant information in RAG, this is extremely important for applications that demand accuracy, including specialized or developing domains such as legal compliance or technical support.

b. Comparison: Structural and Functional Distinctions between LLMs and RAG

While both LLMs and RAG models employ the Transformer architecture, important structural and functional differences exist in their suitability for business applications. LLMs were developed to produce coherent and contextually correct answers solely based on training data, excelling in tasks where a broad understanding of language and high-quality generative output is desired. They suffer, however, from a tendency to produce what has been termed "hallucinations," whereby the model generates plausible-sounding but incorrect information, not having access to real-time reference sources (Ji et al., 2022).

That is the problem RAG models fix with the addition of the retrieval layer; in that respect, they can fetch domain-specific data on the fly. The retrieval capability assures it a competitive edge in regard to the relevance of the results at high accuracy in application domains where information accuracy is attached to real-time information. For instance, RAG models are more effective in corporate question-answering, where topics may include legal, technical, and regulatory information and are susceptible to a host of potential compliance risks brought on by reliance on either historical or over-generalized data. Another key attribute of RAG models is feedback; that is, what gets returned upon retrieval becomes the input for further text generation, enabling the model to make better edits within a rich information environment (Karpukhin et al., 2020; Şakar & Emekci, 2024).

c. Key Business Use Cases

These are various capabilities that cater to both LLM and RAG models, fitting by design many business applications and manifold requirements. Applications such as virtual assistants or conversational agents, for example, rely on the coherence of language and the fluency of interactions in improvement to customer experience (Aleedy et al., 2019).

Organizations employ Large Language Models (LLMs) for various applications, ranging from enhancing the effectiveness of customer service to minimizing operational costs and delivering prompt automated replies across sectors such as e-commerce, telecommunications, and financial services (Pandya & Holia, 2023). In contrast, Retrieval-Augmented Generation (RAG) models are especially well-suited for situations that require specialized knowledge (Lewis et al., 2020). The applicability of their approach is significant in scenarios where the accuracy and accessibility of current information are essential (Ram et al., 2023), including the provision of technical support for complex products, offering guidance on regulatory and compliance matters within the financial industry, or aiding in legal research. The capabilities of Retrieval-Augmented Generation (RAG) in sourcing and integrating real-time data enhance decision-making processes and mitigate the risks linked to obsolete information; thus, it acts as an essential tool in fields marked by rapidly changing knowledge (Chen et al., 2021). Generally speaking, LLMs perform very well in most general-purpose language-related tasks, but RAG models assure high accuracy and contextual relevance, hence proving to be more effective in domain-specific and knowledge-intensive applications (Chen et al., 2023).

While these models are still evolving, this will concurrently achieve advanced applications in commercial settings by crafting the structural features in a very specific way to fit specific task needs. The key lies in how to perform the best and most reliable work.

3. TRUSTWORTHINESS METRICS

For business, the definition of evaluation metrics, especially with regard to the assessment of an LLM and RAG model for trustworthiness, needs a holistic set of metrics, focused on so much more than just technical performance: operational stability, transparency, and ethical compliance.

Key performance indicators, according to which any organization would want to ensure the compliance of AI-driven decision-making with organizational objectives, ethical standards, and legal imperatives are accuracy, robustness (Nicodeme, 2020), transparency (Doshi-Velez & Kim, 2017), regulation conformance (Floridi & Cowls, 2019), and ethical conformance (Mylrea & Robinson, 2023). The following section will explain each one of the trustworthiness metrics in detail and observe interactions among these dimensions to contribute to developing dependable models applicable in a business environment.

a. Accuracy and Robustness

Accuracy and robustness are two critical notions concerning the model's ability to perform regularly over a wide range of inputs and authentic situational contexts. Regarding LLMs and their extension, RAG, accuracy refers to the model's ability to generate relevant and appropriate responses that match the correct answers for certain tasks (Hoshi et al., 2023). In applications such as customer-service automation, medical assistance, and financial consultancy, a very high degree of accuracy is expected, because wrong answers will lead to poor customer experience, financial loss, or, in some cases, danger to humans (Hendrycks et al., 2020).

Conversely, substantial language models are typically developed using extensive datasets that encompass linguistic patterns and contextually relevant replies, thereby equipping them with the capacity to effectively address general inquiries. Retrieval-augmented generation models attain precision by referencing information from external knowledge repositories. Their efficacy is particularly evident in managing tasks that necessitate up-to-date and domain-specific expertise (Lewis et al., 2020). Both of these concepts stand in opposition to robustness, defined as the degree of consistency a model maintains when exposed to varied or unforeseen inputs. This particular metric holds significant importance as it assesses the model's resilience to adversarial or noisy data, guaranteeing that performance remains stable when confronted with atypical or complex queries (Madry et al., 2017). Business applications that face customers, for example, use the large language model service to get live responses from customers, possibly hundreds of them, many of which will be worded ambiguously or even deceptively. An advanced LLM coupled with the RAG model is supposed to ensure high-performance metrics even in these adverse conditions to return responses that will make sense and be relevant in context. In practical applications, the improvement of robustness is frequently achieved via adversarial training, wherein models are educated using both conventional and distorted datasets to strengthen their ability to manage noise while maintaining the integrity of their outputs (Goodfellow et al., 2014). This methodology is especially critical for equipping AI models to assist business processes in fluid environments characterized by the occurrence of unforeseen input variations.

b. Transparency

Transparency is the minimum requirement necessary to establish trust because of its closeness to the model explainability and traceability in its decision-making process. It is very relevant for commercial artificial intelligence systems because it builds user confidence, reaches the threshold for compliance requirements, and is open for human review of the decisions made by AI. The intrinsic complexity of the underlying neural networks, especially those based on very large Transformer-based architectures, makes the goal of transparency in both LLMs and RAG models very hard to achieve. However, interpretability-enhancing work is in progress using a variety of techniques such as attention visualization, feature importance testing, and surrogate modeling among others (Rudin et al., 2022).

There are two key dimensions of transparency in business: interpretability and traceability. Interpretability is how easy it is for human operators to understand how a model arrived at a particular output, while traceability is the ability to trace and document the steps the model went through in making a decision. In highly regulated and compliance-heavy sectors, therefore, transparency is an aspect that shows the decisions by artificial intelligence are within legal limits and ethical boundaries. The lack of transparency, on the other hand, leads to a loss of confidence, since nobody would like to stake any decisions with some "black box" models, where wrong outputs might prove disastrous in applications (Lipton, 2018).

Transparency in LLMs and RAG models is usually achieved through interpretation methods such as saliency maps, which highlight the portions of input text that most influence the model's output (Ribeiro et al., 2016; Vaswani et al., 2017). One could further improve the transparency of RAG models by tracing the process of retrieval: this would allow the user to track precisely which documents or sources contributed to the model's response. This aspect of traceability is particularly valuable in knowledge-intensive tasks where decision justification is necessary. In real-world applications, transparent AI models support accountability and subsequent error analysis for the business to identify and rectify any potential misalignments between model behavior and organizational standards.

c. Compliance and Ethics

Applications of LLMs and RAG in commerce have to take responsibility; thus, they should adhere to all regulatory requirements and ethical norms. Ethics and regulatory compliance in AIs mean their models should meet the set standards in terms of being fair and accountable and keeping private data private. The problem is most acute in domains involving finance, healthcare, and the legal world, where decisions driven by AI have consequences touching on personal lives and the bigger fabric of society. Fairness in AI refers to the absence of bias that leads to injustices against some individual members or groups. Especially, this is a problem with LLM and RAG models, which usually get trained on huge, unfiltered datasets. A substantial amount of research has concluded that biases in training datasets result in models that either perpetuate stereotypes or unjustly discriminate against certain groups. As a result of that, the need for methods that can expose these biases and reduce their impacts has arisen (Bolukbasi et al., 2016).

Regulatory compliance addresses the demand for adherence to legal frameworks that oversee data privacy, transparency, and accountability of decision-making. For instance, under the automated decision-making system of the European Union's GDPR, such decisions are to be made in a way that is transparent and with justifications accompanying their outcomes so that transparency and fairness in the application of AI technologies within the scope of GDPR are ensured (Wachter et al., 2017).

Namely, they can, if so, be adhered to and ethically aligned through some guards: fairness audits, techniques for anonymizing data, and accountability frameworks. To ensure that models treat users fairly, companies should regularly audit model performance for all demographic groups, spotting and acting on any dissimilarities. Another critical aspect of LLMs and RAG concerns ethical issues of data handling practices, where privacy-preserving techniques, including differential privacy and federated learning, contribute to the protection of sensitive information while maintaining model utility (Abadi et al., 2016). Finally, proactive compliance and ethics not only mitigate regulatory risks but also strengthen the organizational reputation because the practices of responsible AI increasingly converge with public expectations around ethical technology.

4. RISK ANALYSIS

This is important for the risk analysis of LLMs and RAG model deployments in business settings. While the LLMs and RAG models mentioned will bring about many benefits, they will also render particular risks, including data bias (Bolukbasi et al., 2016), adversarial manipulation (Goodfellow et al., 2014), challenges with privacy and security (Carlini & Wagner, 2017), and limitations in performance coming from a specific domain (Кубатко et al., 2024). These risks must be understood and mitigated to develop reliable, ethical, and secure AI systems that will align with business goals and regulatory requirements.

a. Data Bias and Fairness Concerns

One of the big challenges in the applications of LLMs and RAG models is data bias, often arising from datasets that are inherently biased or have representational inequalities in the training data. Models trained on datasets that predominantly portray certain demographics, linguistic patterns, or cultural contexts tend to generate outputs that repeat those biases (Bender et al., 2021). This bias, however, might result in unfair treatment of certain customer segments in business applications and thus impact brand reputation and regulatory compliance, mainly in the areas with strict requirements for fairness, such as financial services and healthcare (Mehrabi et al., 2022).

Sources of bias in LLMs and RAG models include selection bias, where some groups are over- or under-represented in the training data and historical biases that mirror past injustices. For instance, an LLM used in recruitment may inadvertently discriminate against certain demographic groups by reflecting the biased historical hiring records and thus perpetuating such discriminatory patterns. Besides, LLMs can also confirmatory bias by reinforcing the prevalent stereotypes in the training data. In fair data curation, common are techniques for debiasing algorithms and fairness audits of datasets to reduce the impact of biased representations on model outcomes (Bolukbasi et al., 2016).

RAG models are most susceptible to data bias, as they retrieve information from external sources to the model; some may have biases embedded. The retrieval mechanism may further amplify such biases if the source types are not uniform, impacting the final output. This therefore requires strict source verification, reduction of bias, and constant checks in place so that the returns of biased information will not bleed into very sensitive business applications. An end-to-end fairness framework helps ensure that the models are operating fairly across a range of user demographics, are responsible from an ethical standpoint, and fulfill regulatory requirements.

b. Adversarial Risks

Adversarial risks refer to the vulnerability of LLMs and RAG models to interference through specially crafted inputs with the aim of fooling the model into desired outcomes. Basically, such an attack exploits certain flaws in the decision-making mechanism of a model and therefore generates undesired, or even harmful, output. In an organizational setting, such adversarial vulnerabilities can cause significant operational and reputational damage if models are used in sensitive applications related to fraud detection, cybersecurity, or content moderation (Goodfellow et al., 2014).

Most of the popular methods for adversarial attack are input perturbation, which introduces minute, typically unnoticeable modifications in the input data that may lead the model to misjudge the context or meaning of a given text. For instance, in sentiment analysis, even a craftily created review may seem neutral yet could bring forth a negative or misleading sentiment response. The interaction between models and clients introduces a degree of risk, as misguided business choices may emerge from sentiment analysis that has been incorrectly interpreted. In addition, RAG models encounter unique adversarial threats linked to the retrieval process. This may encompass manipulated or unreliable sources that have been deliberately incorporated into the retrieval pool, leading to the dissemination of misinformation or disinformation (Rios Insua et al., 2016; Zhang et al., 2023).

The defensive strategies to reduce adversarial risks include adversarial training-that is, a model is exposed to adversarial samples during its training process for the purpose of increasing its robustness-and the creation of verification layers that check the integrity of input data. RAG models, for example, introduce source validation mechanisms that ensure any retrieved information comes from a credible and validated source (Ram et al., 2023). It is through such mechanisms, among several others, that improvements shall be made in large language and RAG models to make them resilient against adversarial attacks threatening business interests.

c. Privacy and Security

One of the most important issues related to artificial intelligence deals with security and privacy risks, especially in those industries where sensitive information is involved, like financial services, healthcare, and legal services. Since both LLMs and RAG models require huge datasets for training and fine-tuning, significant concern about data privacy, data leakage, and model security vulnerabilities is growing gradually (Borkar, 2023). Such information can further leak and create all forms of privacy risks when models unknowingly memorize or leak sensitive information present in their training. Specifically, LLMs have been reported to memorize content within their training datasets, thereby resulting in the potential leakage of proprietary or personally identifiable information (Brown et al., 2020).

Other possible security vulnerabilities of models come from unauthorized access and model inversion attacks, which work by attempting to reverse-engineer the model with a view to revealing either the training data or inferring other private attributes. For RAG models, though, this dependency on external knowledge bases exacerbates the privacy concern, likely carrying private information if not cleaned carefully. The above vulnerabilities can be addressed by embedding security strategies like differential privacy and federated learning, where models cannot retain any sensitive information in an explicit manner while still generating highly valuable outputs (Abadi et al., 2016).

It becomes necessary that strict regulations be laid down as far as the sources of data to be sourced from are concerned so that relevance and sensitivity can be verified. Model deployment security will be done through deploying encryption protocols, security testing, and restrictions on users at regular intervals.

By focusing on privacy and security, organizations can safeguard their investments in AI and the trust of their customers to avoid reputational and legal consequences connected with data breaches.

d. Domain Limitations

While large language models and retrieval-augmented generation models represent significant technological advances, they can expose limitations in responding to domain-specific contexts (Xu et al., 2023), especially those that require specialized knowledge or a deep understanding of complex language nuances. LLMs, for example, are trained on huge data sets and may not get sufficient knowledge of specific domain-specific terms, practices, rules, or context-dependent rules that are critical for law, medicine, or engineering (Bommasani et al., 2021). Such limitations will result in less than desired performance or possibly serious errors in critical applications.

RAG models mitigate this to some degree: they fetch on demand relevant, domain-specific information (Nakhod, 2023). However, their effectiveness is also limited by the quality and relevance of the sources from which they retrieve data. If the knowledge base lacks comprehensiveness in a particular domain, or if the sources are outdated or untrustworthy, then the outputs, generated by the RAG model, may not serve the business needs. Also, domain limitations become apparent in complex multi-turn dialogues, where continuity and context retention are necessary to ensure coherent outputs. Business deployments, whenever carried out in a domain-intensive industry, may require more fine-tuning on specialized data or custom-built knowledge bases for domain-specific applications.

More typically, overcoming the domain limitations requires domain-adaptive fine-tuning and, in many cases, hybrid approaches (Liu et al., 2023), where LLMs and RAG models are complemented by rules-based systems or human-in-the-loop mechanisms. Hybrid systems leverage the linguistic strengths of LLMs and industry expertise to enable high-accuracy, contextually relevant performance that allows businesses to maintain domain-critical tasks (Wang et al., 2023). Knowing and tackling such domain limitations is, therefore, very fundamental to reliable and effective model performance for specialized applications.

5. ENHANCING TRUSTWORTHINESS

LLMs and RAG models must lend themselves to trustworthiness so that the systems would offer accurate, reliable, and ethically responsible results in business applications. To this effect, various strategies may be set in motion to reduce risks and generally improve model performance across main dimensions. This section outlines the techniques of data refinement and bias mitigation, robustness, and security protocols that contribute to explainability, real-time monitoring, and lifecycle management in building more robust and trustworthy AI systems.

a. Data Refinement and Bias Mitigation

Improved data quality with a decrease in inherent biases is the first step that can help the development of both fair and accurate LLMs and RAG models. Since these models are going to be highly dependent on the quality of the training data, unfiltered or biased datasets would further lead to skewed outcomes. This is most true for finance and health-based, decision-critical environments (Mehrabi et al., 2022). Effective data refinement involves curating datasets that represent diverse demographics, contexts, and viewpoints, ensuring a balanced representation of varied groups. Techniques such as synthetic data generation can be used to bolster underrepresented categories within the training data, thereby reducing the potential for biased responses (Bender et al., 2021).

Strategies aimed at mitigating bias have been devised that help in locating and correcting inconsistencies in data sets. Approaches involving the re-weighting of the importance of certain training examples and adversarial debiasing by applying adversarial networks, which are aimed at reducing bias in the learned representations, form a contribution towards solving the challenges of fairness without losing the effectiveness of models (Bolukbasi et al., 2016). Additionally, refinement in RAG models addresses the validation mechanism of sources for reliability and diversity of information to avoid biased retrieval, which might introduce tampering with the outcome. Data refinement, and mitigation of bias, enable an organization to have AI models that it truly uses within regulatory requirements but at the same time upholds ethics for fairness in outcomes.

b. Robustness and Security Protocols

LLMs and RAG models must be robust and secure so that no adversarial attacks or operational failures occur. Robustness in a model implies stability for any kind of input; security protocols would keep it safe from bad actors. In business applications where monetary consequences or other forms of reputation damage might be involved due to a wrong response, adversarial attacks pose severe risks. In an adversarial attack, perturbations are introduced into a model's inputs to induce the model to produce incorrect outputs (Goodfellow et al., 2014).

Again, one might further consider more robust training methodologies: adversarial training and ensemble modeling.

Adversarial training involves making the models more familiar with modified inputs during training, which helps them in the identification and mitigation of adversarial patterns at the time of deployment. Also, ensemble methods, which integrate several models into more robust overall predictions, lead to a gain in robustness by reducing susceptibility to singular attacks (Madry et al., 2017).

Not only is security at the training of the RAG models, but it is also at retrieval, where authenticity and correctness of sources are truly important. Access controls and encryption may be integrated into the knowledge base to minimize risks that tampered or false information might enter the retrieval pipeline and affect information integrity. Taken together, the robustness and security protocols form a protective framework that allows LLMs and RAG systems to work reliably in dynamic business environments without being manipulated from outside, therefore providing stable high-quality output.

c. Explainability Techniques

These are very crucial in the development of trust in AI models, as they provide the user with insight concerning the basis of AI-generated decisions. More specifically, in finance and health, explainability is cardinal, as regulatory standards require interpretations and justifications for automated decisions. In LLMs and RAG models, the techniques of explainability give insight into the inner mechanisms of the models, which enable trace and validation of outputs (Lipton, 2018).

The explanation of LLMs is done mainly by attention visualization, where certain words or phrases in the input text are highlighted to have significant effects on the model's predictions. This approach has proven helpful for ascertaining where the model focuses its attention or what may be sources of bias or error in the production of responses, according to DeRose et al. (2021). In a RAG model, traceable retrieval paths benefit from sources used in forming a response through documentation (Ram et al., 2023). Such transparency, therefore, will make users understand the source of the information, increasing their trust in the AI-driven recommendations.

Surrogate modeling serves as another way to bring explainability into large language models and retrieval-augmented generation systems. Generally, simple and interpretable models would be developed to emulate complex artificial intelligence systems in a manner that allows users to try and analyze decision-making patterns without needing deep analysis of the original model; Angione et al. (2022), Jakeman et al. (2022). Both of these approaches ensure that businesses leveraging such AI frameworks will be not only effective but also ensure standards in terms of transparency, user trust, and accountability toward the decisions being made.

d. Monitoring and Lifecycle Management

Continuous oversight and lifecycle management constitute integral components of reliable artificial intelligence, thereby guaranteeing that large language models (LLMs) and retrieval-augmented generation (RAG) models maintain accuracy, compliance, and alignment with business objectives over time (Hummer et al., 2019). This process encompasses the real-time evaluation of model performance, the identification of anomalies, and the assessment of output consistency, particularly within fluid environments where user requirements or regulatory criteria may fluctuate (Sculley et al., 2015). For example, in customer service applications, real-time monitoring can help identify drift—where model predictions begin to deviate from expected results—prompting timely interventions to recalibrate model outputs. This, apart from the said monitoring, effective lifecycle management includes regular updating, so that the model reflects the current data and knowledge of the particular domain. This is especially true for RAG models, whose retrieval component has to be updated regularly if one wants the knowledge to remain fresh and accurate. Automating the lifecycles of models—through methods for auto-updating knowledge bases or retraining algorithms—reduces the load on human operators and supports model applicability in changing contexts.

Setup also includes putting in place the governance protocols defining roles and responsibilities to oversee model performance, make changes, and ensure adherence to the relevant standards (Jeong, 2023). The protocols are quite vital in regulated industries where companies need to bring proof of consistent AI oversight in their compliance with the law. A structured approach to control and lifecycle management will help an organization improve the reliability of its artificial intelligence systems, ensuring they remain effective and compliant with both corporate objectives and industry standards.

6. STRATEGIC CONSIDERATIONS

Strategic issues arising from the integration of LLM and RAG systems in business contexts take center stage in terms of financial, operational, ethical, and regulatory matters. Such investment has to be underpinned by a thorough review of cost-risk analysis, compliance, and criteria for the selection of vendors, which are at the heart of optimally positioning an organization in the use of AI while preserving integrity in its operations. This paper shall provide a broad review, finding the balance required in view of how such technologies can be leveraged toward the realization of organizational objectives.

a. Cost-Risk Analysis: Comprehending the Financial-Operational Tradeoff

Comprehensive implementations of LLM and RAG models require a comprehensive cost-risk consideration that can balance the trade-offs between economic and operational compromises brought about by the use of these technologies. This is quite true: LLM and RAG models are effective in harvesting insights from large volumes of unstructured data; nonetheless, these models are very resource-intensive in training, deployment, and maintenance operations (Manathunga & Illangasekara, 2023). High-quality models require a great amount of data. Very often, they also require special infrastructures, such as advanced computing environments, which in turn drive the operational cost up (Bommasani et al., 2021). Moreover, increased financial analysis would also have to include risk assessment since operational interruption might occur.

A very good example is model drift, which is a gradual decrease in the model's effectiveness because of changing data distributions. When detected too late, the result will be suboptimal output and operational inefficiency. Bayram et al. (2022) present the financial consequences of these risks, which include but are not limited to costs related to the need for frequent retraining of models and assessment of performance, with necessary interventions, especially in very dynamic environments where data and consumer requirements change rapidly. This also includes indirect costs that have to be taken into account when considering the cost risks, especially operational disruptions that could arise, maintenance costs, and mitigation costs involved in negating negative consequences such as biased outcomes or security breaches.

This far-reaching analysis would help policymakers and decision-makers to identify whether financial benefits from LLM and RAG models outweigh related risks while at the same time drawing valuable recommendations on resource allocation to maximize the value capture. Snoeck et al. (2019) add that sensitivity analyses may highlight when trade-offs exist under which the models may become inviable; therefore, strategic planning should be resilient to market volatilities and operational uncertainties.

b. Ethics and Law: Compliance with Industry-Specific Regulations

Compliance with ethics and law enables LLMs and RAG models to align with industry-specific regulations and the overall set of social expectations. Each of these different sectors would have specific frames associated with finance, and healthcare, and identified as those that protect users against possible AI harms within the context of privacy breaches, unfair discrimination, and accountability. For instance, the General Data Protection Regulation (GDPR) in the European Union mandates stringent standards for data protection and requires that AI models processing personal data maintain transparency, accountability, and fairness (Voigt & von dem Bussche, 2017).

Following such regulations means setting up mechanisms that provide transparency and explainability that allow tracing how given AI-driven decisions were reached. Organizations will therefore establish mechanisms whereby stakeholders can attempt to understand the rationale of model outputs where LLMs and RAG systems have been employed for decision-making in regulated industries. For this reason, compliance with anti-bias regulations that prohibit them from discriminating is important. Organizations may need to regularly audit model decisions for fairness across different demographic groups to prevent disparate impact (Mehrabi et al., 2022).

In this way, ethical adherence would not be restricted to the regulation itself but would be broader, ingrained in societal values and principles of corporate social responsibility. Ethical guidance on the deployment of LLM and RAG respects user autonomy, has a commitment to non-maleficence, and communicates the limitations of the models in cases where models might give uncertain or potentially harmful information. By embedding ethics and law into the AI strategy, organizations reduce the chance of compliance risk while building trust with consumers and leading the industry with responsible AI.

c. Vendor Selection Criteria: Assessing Artificial Intelligence Vendors for Credibility

Choosing an AI provider is a strategic decision that calls for careful consideration of the provider's credibility, technical capability, and alignment with organizational culture. In AI vendors, trust involves considerations around data privacy, model explainability, and long-term support. Key conditions for supplier evaluation include the effectiveness of their data handling practices; the ability to provide clear explanations for model outcomes; and adherence to ethical and legal norms congruent with those of the organization's regulatory requirements (McCormack, 2024; OECD, 2003).

Then, when it comes to the onboarding process of vendors that will deliver services for LLMs and RAG, their track record with respect to sensitive data needs to be ascertained: storage of data, encryption of data, audits to be done, and frequency thereof, for discovering and rectifying biases or inaccuracies (Feretzakis & Verykios, 2024). They should be able to support that with actual proof of their data protection practices, including adherence to regulations such as the General Data Protection Regulation, and having documented processes in place to reduce any potential data leakage or unauthorized access. They would be experienced in techniques for explainability, such as attention visualizations or surrogate modeling, which give the reason for the commitment toward transparency in AI-driven outputs.

Capabilities of vendor support are another key consideration since most organizations need continued technical support, model retraining, or updated models during the performance cycle. Therefore, those vendors offering a wide variety of support services, such as omnichannel lifecycle management, real-time monitoring, and retraining options, are better positioned to help organizations make their mark in the dynamic landscape of AI applications. Additionally, suppliers that demonstrate proactive leadership in key areas like AI ethics, risk management, and governance can create considerable value through building attributes into systems that reflect technological advancements and ethical considerations.

Overall, responsible LLM and RAG model use demands a strategic selection approach toward the vendors. Having estimated the level of confidence in a vendor, practices concerning the security of data, mechanisms of transparency, and provided support services, one may be sure that the chosen solutions will serve the interests of the business and correspond to ethical and legal norms, including operational standards.

7. CONCLUSION

The incorporation of Large Language Models (LLM) and Retrieval-Augmented Generation (RAG) models into organizational processes offers paradigmatic opportunities; however, they also bring immense strategic, ethical, and operational challenges. This chapter discussed an exhaustive analysis of such technologies, focusing on their architectural distinctions, scalability, and applicability in intended domains. Accuracy, robustness, transparency, compliance, and ethical integrity have been viewed as key evaluation parameters for their successful implementation in organizational environments.

A detailed cost-risk analysis has explained the financial and operational trade-offs in implementing LLM and RAG. Although the models provide immense value in insight generation from large volumes of data, their resource-intensive nature necessitates cautious investment decision-making. Model drift, expensive maintenance, and security vulnerabilities are risks that must be mitigated through active monitoring and resource allocation. Ethical and regulatory imperatives also demand adherence to frameworks like GDPR so that AI-driven decisions are transparent, fair, and traceable. Vendor selection criteria have also been explored, noting the need for AI vendors to demonstrate credibility, data security, explainability, and long-term support.

a. Future View: Advancement toward Trustworthy and Safe Artificial Intelligence

In the near future, Large Language Models and Retrieval-Augmented Generation technology will result in significant advancements that will further enhance the dependability, security, and contextual flexibility of Artificial Intelligence systems. In view of developing adaptive learning algorithms, self-supervised frameworks of training, and further improvements in transformer architectures, models are foreseen which, along with an increase in efficiency related to resource consumption, demonstrate superior robustness against variations in the distribution of input data. This transition is expected to reduce manual annotations, decrease resources for model training, and hence facilitate industrial adoption in very resource-constrained or data-sensitive sectors like finance, health, and legal services.

Second, the steps towards interpretability and transparency will continue to be of much cardinal importance for AI development to meet regulatory standards and best practice conditions within organizations. Newer forms of interpretability include counterfactual analysis and saliency mapping, which provide a detailed way to understand model behavior and hence help audit and validate the output of AI in major decision situations. Real-time monitoring systems and automated mechanisms could allow continuous evaluation and training of the AI models so as to keep pace with the organizations using AI solutions, and thereby handle these biases, shifts, and degradation issues as they occur through time.

It is also highly expected that regulatory development will influence the journey of AI adoption in ways that industry-specific standards and frameworks of governance set new thresholds for ethical AI. Given this continuously developing regulatory landscape, proactive alignment will require forecasting future standards beyond proving compliance with present ones. For any business wishing to operationalize LLM and RAG systems, in practice, the establishment of robust AI governance structures will be important, together with cross-disciplinary collaboration that harmonizes cutting-edge technological capability with ethical and legal imperatives.

b. Final Remarks

It means that with LLM and RAG, there is a higher need for an effective approach that is really technically sound and ethically well-founded to deploy such models effectively within business contexts. Through the integration of these powerful AI models into strong frameworks emphasizing transparency, compliance, and proactive risk management, one can achieve key strategic benefits. Harmonizing technological advancement, anticipatory regulation, and ethical accountability are fairly indispensable in responsibly harnessing the transformative powers of artificial intelligence in building up a sustainable and robust AI-powered business strategy.

REFERENCES

Кубатко, О., Озімс, С., & Вороненко, В. (2024). Influence Of Artificial Intelligence On Business Decision-Making. *Mechanism of an Economic Regulation*, *1*(103), 17–23. DOI: 10.32782/mer.2024.103.03

Abadi, M., Chu, A., Goodfellow, I., McMahan, H. B., Mironov, I., Talwar, K., & Zhang, L. (2016). Deep Learning with Differential Privacy. *Proceedings of the 2016 ACM SIGSAC Conference on Computer and Communications Security*, 308–318. DOI: 10.1145/2976749.2978318

Aleedy, M., Shaiba, H., & Bezbradica, M. (2019). Generating and Analyzing Chatbot Responses using Natural Language Processing. *International Journal of Advanced Computer Science and Applications*, *10*(9). Advance online publication. DOI: 10.14569/IJACSA.2019.0100910

Angione, C., Silverman, E., & Yaneske, E. (2022). Using machine learning as a surrogate model for agent-based simulations. *PLoS One*, *17*(2), e0263150. DOI: 10.1371/journal.pone.0263150 PMID: 35143521

Asai, A., Wu, Z., Wang, Y., Sil, A., & Hajishirzi, H. (2023). *Self-RAG: Learning to Retrieve, Generate, and Critique through Self-Reflection* (arXiv:2310.11511). arXiv. https://doi.org//arXiv.2310.11511DOI: 10.48550

Bayram, F., Ahmed, B. S., & Kassler, A. (2022). *From Concept Drift to Model Degradation: An Overview on Performance-Aware Drift Detectors* (Version 1). arXiv. https://doi.org/DOI: 10.48550/ARXIV.2203.11070

Bender, E. M., Gebru, T., McMillan-Major, A., & Shmitchell, S. (2021). On the Dangers of Stochastic Parrots: Can Language Models Be Too Big? . *Proceedings of the 2021 ACM Conference on Fairness, Accountability, and Transparency*, 610–623. DOI: 10.1145/3442188.3445922

Bolukbasi, T., Chang, K.-W., Zou, J., Saligrama, V., & Kalai, A. (2016). *Man is to Computer Programmer as Woman is to Homemaker? Debiasing Word Embeddings* (Version 1). arXiv. DOI: 10.48550/ARXIV.1607.06520

Bommasani, R., Hudson, D. A., Adeli, E., Altman, R., Arora, S., von Arx, S., Bernstein, M. S., Bohg, J., Bosselut, A., Brunskill, E., Brynjolfsson, E., Buch, S., Card, D., Castellon, R., Chatterji, N., Chen, A., Creel, K., Davis, J. Q., Demszky, D., . . . Liang, P. (2021). *On the Opportunities and Risks of Foundation Models* (Version 3). arXiv. DOI: 10.48550/ARXIV.2108.07258

Borkar, J. (2023). *What can we learn from Data Leakage and Unlearning for Law?* (Version 1). arXiv. DOI: 10.48550/ARXIV.2307.10476

Brown, T. B., Mann, B., Ryder, N., Subbiah, M., Kaplan, J., Dhariwal, P., Neelakantan, A., Shyam, P., Sastry, G., Askell, A., Agarwal, S., Herbert-Voss, A., Krueger, G., Henighan, T., Child, R., Ramesh, A., Ziegler, D. M., Wu, J., Winter, C., & Amodei, D. (2020). Language models are few-shot learners. *Proceedings of the 34th International Conference on Neural Information Processing Systems.*

Carlini, N., & Wagner, D. (2017). Towards Evaluating the Robustness of Neural Networks. *2017 IEEE Symposium on Security and Privacy (SP)*, 39–57. DOI: 10.1109/SP.2017.49

Chen, J., Lin, H., Han, X., & Sun, L. (2023). *Benchmarking Large Language Models in Retrieval-Augmented Generation* (arXiv:2309.01431). arXiv. https://doi.org//arXiv.2309.01431DOI: 10.48550

Chen, M., Tworek, J., Jun, H., Yuan, Q., Pinto, H. P. de O., Kaplan, J., Edwards, H., Burda, Y., Joseph, N., Brockman, G., Ray, A., Puri, R., Krueger, G., Petrov, M., Khlaaf, H., Sastry, G., Mishkin, P., Chan, B., Gray, S., . . . Zaremba, W. (2021). *Evaluating Large Language Models Trained on Code* (Version 2). arXiv. DOI: 10.48550/ARXIV.2107.03374

Dale, E., Peacocke, E. F., Movik, E., Voorhoeve, A., Ottersen, T., Kurowski, C., Evans, D. B., Norheim, O. F., & Gopinathan, U. (2023). Criteria for the procedural fairness of health financing decisions: A scoping review. *Health Policy and Planning*, *38*(Supplement_1), i13–i35. DOI: 10.1093/heapol/czad066 PMID: 37963078

DeRose, J. F., Wang, J., & Berger, M. (2021). Attention Flows: Analyzing and Comparing Attention Mechanisms in Language Models. *IEEE Transactions on Visualization and Computer Graphics*, *27*(2), 1160–1170. DOI: 10.1109/TVCG.2020.3028976 PMID: 33052855

Doshi-Velez, F., & Kim, B. (2017). *Towards A Rigorous Science of Interpretable Machine Learning* (Version 2). arXiv. DOI: 10.48550/ARXIV.1702.08608

Feretzakis, G., & Verykios, V. S. (2024). *Trustworthy AI: Securing Sensitive Data in Large Language Models* (Version 1). arXiv. https://doi.org/DOI: 10.48550/ARXIV.2409.18222

Floridi, L., & Cowls, J. (2019). A Unified Framework of Five Principles for AI in Society. *Harvard Data Science Review*. Advance online publication. DOI: 10.1162/99608f92.8cd550d1

Gámiz, M. L., Navas-Gómez, F. L., & Raya-Miranda, R. (2021). A Machine Learning Algorithm for Reliability Analysis. *IEEE Transactions on Reliability*, *70*(2), 535–546. DOI: 10.1109/TR.2020.3011653

Goodfellow, I. J., Shlens, J., & Szegedy, C. (2014). *Explaining and Harnessing Adversarial Examples* (Version 3). arXiv. DOI: 10.48550/ARXIV.1412.6572

Hendrycks, D., Burns, C., Basart, S., Zou, A., Mazeika, M., Song, D., & Steinhardt, J. (2020). *Measuring Massive Multitask Language Understanding* (Version 3). arXiv. DOI: 10.48550/ARXIV.2009.03300

Hoshi, Y., Miyashita, D., Ng, Y., Tatsuno, K., Morioka, Y., Torii, O., & Deguchi, J. (2023). *RaLLe: A Framework for Developing and Evaluating Retrieval-Augmented Large Language Models* (Version 2). arXiv. DOI: 10.18653/v1/2023.emnlp-demo.4

Hummer, W., Muthusamy, V., Rausch, T., Dube, P., El Maghraoui, K., Murthi, A., & Oum, P. (2019). ModelOps: Cloud-Based Lifecycle Management for Reliable and Trusted AI. *2019 IEEE International Conference on Cloud Engineering (IC2E)*, 113–120. DOI: 10.1109/IC2E.2019.00025

Jakeman, J. D., Friedman, S., Eldred, M. S., Tamellini, L., Gorodetsky, A. A., & Allaire, D. (2022). Adaptive experimental design for multi-fidelity surrogate modeling of multi-disciplinary systems. *International Journal for Numerical Methods in Engineering*, *123*(12), 2760–2790. DOI: 10.1002/nme.6958

Jeong, C. (2023). A Study on the Implementation of Generative AI Services Using an Enterprise Data-Based LLM Application Architecture. *Advances in Artificial Intelligence and Machine Learning*, *03*(04), 1588–1618. DOI: 10.54364/AAIML.2023.1191

Ji, Z., Lee, N., Frieske, R., Yu, T., Su, D., Xu, Y., Ishii, E., Bang, Y., Chen, D., Dai, W., Chan, H. S., Madotto, A., & Fung, P. (2022). *Survey of Hallucination in Natural Language Generation*. DOI: 10.48550/ARXIV.2202.03629

Jo, J., & Myaeng, S.-H. (2020). Roles and Utilization of Attention Heads in Transformer-based Neural Language Models. *Proceedings of the 58th Annual Meeting of the Association for Computational Linguistics*, 3404–3417. DOI: 10.18653/v1/2020.acl-main.311

Karpukhin, V., Oğuz, B., Min, S., Lewis, P., Wu, L., Edunov, S., Chen, D., & Yih, W. (2020). *Dense Passage Retrieval for Open-Domain Question Answering* (Version 3). arXiv. DOI: 10.18653/v1/2020.emnlp-main.550

Lewis, P., Perez, E., Piktus, A., Petroni, F., Karpukhin, V., Goyal, N., Küttler, H., Lewis, M., Yih, W., Rocktäschel, T., Riedel, S., & Kiela, D. (2020). *Retrieval-Augmented Generation for Knowledge-Intensive NLP Tasks* (Version 4). arXiv. DOI: 10.48550/ARXIV.2005.11401

Linardatos, P., Papastefanopoulos, V., & Kotsiantis, S. (2021). Explainable AI: A Review of Machine Learning Interpretability Methods. *Entropy (Basel, Switzerland)*, *23*(1), 18. Advance online publication. DOI: 10.3390/e23010018 PMID: 33375658

Lipton, Z. C. (2018). The mythos of model interpretability. *Communications of the ACM*, *61*(10), 36–43. DOI: 10.1145/3233231

Liu, M., Ene, T.-D., Kirby, R., Cheng, C., Pinckney, N., Liang, R., Alben, J., Anand, H., Banerjee, S., Bayraktaroglu, I., Bhaskaran, B., Catanzaro, B., Chaudhuri, A., Clay, S., Dally, B., Dang, L., Deshpande, P., Dhodhi, S., Halepete, S., . . . Ren, H. (2023). *ChipNeMo: Domain-Adapted LLMs for Chip Design* (Version 5). arXiv. DOI: 10.48550/ARXIV.2311.00176

Madry, A., Makelov, A., Schmidt, L., Tsipras, D., & Vladu, A. (2017). *Towards Deep Learning Models Resistant to Adversarial Attacks* (Version 4). arXiv. DOI: 10.48550/ARXIV.1706.06083

Makridakis, S., Petropoulos, F., & Kang, Y. (2023). Large Language Models: Their Success and Impact. *Forecasting*, *5*(3), 536–549. DOI: 10.3390/forecast5030030

Manathunga, S. S., & Illangasekara, Y. A. (2023). *Retrieval Augmented Generation and Representative Vector Summarization for large unstructured textual data in Medical Education* (Version 1). arXiv. DOI: 10.48550/ARXIV.2308.00479

McCormack, L. (2024). *Ethical AI Governance: Methods for Evaluating Trustworthy AI*. https://arxiv.org/html/2409.07473v1

Mehrabi, N., Morstatter, F., Saxena, N., Lerman, K., & Galstyan, A. (2022). A Survey on Bias and Fairness in Machine Learning. *ACM Computing Surveys*, *54*(6), 1–35. DOI: 10.1145/3457607

Mylrea, M., & Robinson, N. (2023). Artificial Intelligence (AI) Trust Framework and Maturity Model: Applying an Entropy Lens to Improve Security, Privacy, and Ethical AI. *Entropy (Basel, Switzerland)*, *25*(10), 1429. DOI: 10.3390/e25101429 PMID: 37895550

Nakhod, O. (2023). Using retrieval-augmented generation to elevate low-code developer skills. *Artificial Intelligence, 28*(AI.2023.28(3)), 126–130. DOI: 10.15407/jai2023.03.126

Navigli, R., Conia, S., & Ross, B. (2023). Biases in Large Language Models: Origins, Inventory, and Discussion. *J.ACM Journal of Data and Information Quality*, *15*(2), 1–21. Advance online publication. DOI: 10.1145/3597307

Nicodeme, C. (2020). Build confidence and acceptance of AI-based decision support systems—Explainable and liable AI. *2020 13th International Conference on Human System Interaction (HSI)*, 20–23. DOI: 10.1109/HSI49210.2020.9142668

OECD. (2003). *Environmentally Sustainable Buildings. Challenges and Policies*. Organisation for Economic Co-Operation and Development.

Pandya, K., & Holia, M. (2023). *Automating Customer Service using LangChain: Building custom open-source GPT Chatbot for organizations* (Version 1). arXiv. DOI: 10.48550/ARXIV.2310.05421

Payette, M., & Abdul-Nour, G. (2023). Machine Learning Applications for Reliability Engineering: A Review. *Sustainability (Basel)*, *15*(7), 6270. Advance online publication. DOI: 10.3390/su15076270

Raimundo, R., & Rosário, A. (2021). The Impact of Artificial Intelligence on Data System Security: A Literature Review. *Sensors (Basel)*, *21*(21), 7029. Advance online publication. DOI: 10.3390/s21217029 PMID: 34770336

Ram, O., Levine, Y., Dalmedigos, I., Muhlgay, D., Shashua, A., Leyton-Brown, K., & Shoham, Y. (2023). In-Context Retrieval-Augmented Language Models. *Transactions of the Association for Computational Linguistics*, *11*, 1316–1331. DOI: 10.1162/tacl_a_00605

Ribeiro, M. T., Singh, S., & Guestrin, C. (2016). "Why Should I Trust You?": Explaining the Predictions of Any Classifier. *Proceedings of the 22nd ACM SIGKDD International Conference on Knowledge Discovery and Data Mining*, 1135–1144. DOI: 10.1145/2939672.2939778

Rios Insua, D., Banks, D., & Rios, J. (2016). Modeling Opponents in Adversarial Risk Analysis. *Risk Analysis*, *36*(4), 742–755. DOI: 10.1111/risa.12439 PMID: 26133501

Rudin, C., Chen, C., Chen, Z., Huang, H., Semenova, L., & Zhong, C. (2022). Interpretable machine learning: Fundamental principles and 10 grand challenges. *Statistics Surveys, 16*(none). DOI: 10.1214/21-SS133

Şakar, T., & Emekci, H. (2024). Maximizing RAG efficiency: A comparative analysis of RAG methods. *Natural Language Processing*, 1–25. DOI: 10.1017/nlp.2024.53

Sculley, D., Holt, G., Golovin, D., Davydov, E., Phillips, T., Ebner, D., Chaudhary, V., Young, M., & Dennison, D. (2015). Hidden Technical Debt in Machine Learning Systems. *NIPS*, 2494–2502.

Shayegani, E., Mamun, M. A. A., Fu, Y., Zaree, P., Dong, Y., & Abu-Ghazaleh, N. (2023). *Survey of Vulnerabilities in Large Language Models Revealed by Adversarial Attacks* (arXiv:2310.10844). arXiv. https://doi.org//arXiv.2310.10844DOI: 10.48550

Snoeck, A., Udenio, M., & Fransoo, J. C. (2019). A stochastic program to evaluate disruption mitigation investments in the supply chain. *European Journal of Operational Research*, *274*(2), 516–530. DOI: 10.1016/j.ejor.2018.10.005

Vaswani, A., Shazeer, N., Parmar, J., Uszkoreit, L., Gomez, A. N., & Polosukhin, I. (2017). *Attention is all you need. Advances in neural information processing systems.* 30 31st Conference on Neural Information Processing Systems, Long Beach, CA, USA.

Voigt, P., & von dem Bussche, A. (2017). *The EU General Data Protection Regulation (GDPR): A Practical Guide*. Springer., DOI: 10.1007/978-3-319-57959-7

Wachter, S., Mittelstadt, B., & Floridi, L. (2017). Why a Right to Explanation of Automated Decision-Making Does Not Exist in the General Data Protection Regulation. *International Data Privacy Law*, *7*(2), 76–99. DOI: 10.1093/idpl/ipx005

Wang, Y., Ma, X., & Chen, W. (2023). *Augmenting Black-box LLMs with Medical Textbooks for Biomedical Question Answering (Published in Findings of EMNLP 2024)* (Version 3). arXiv. DOI: 10.48550/ARXIV.2309.02233

Xu, B., Zhao, C., Jiang, W., Zhu, P., Dai, S., Pang, C., Sun, Z., Wang, S., & Sun, Y. (2023). Retrieval-Augmented Domain Adaptation of Language Models. *Proceedings of the 8th Workshop on Representation Learning for NLP (RepL4NLP 2023)*, 54–64. DOI: 10.18653/v1/2023.repl4nlp-1.5

Zhang, X., Zheng, X., Mao, W., Zeng, D. D., & Wang, F.-Y. (2023). Hashing Fake: Producing Adversarial Perturbation for Online Privacy Protection Against Automatic Retrieval Models. *IEEE Transactions on Computational Social Systems*, *10*(6), 3241–3251. DOI: 10.1109/TCSS.2022.3204120

Zhao, W., Alwidian, S., & Mahmoud, Q. H. (2022). Adversarial Training Methods for Deep Learning: A Systematic Review. *Algorithms*, *15*(8), 283. Advance online publication. DOI: 10.3390/a15080283

Chapter 5
Revolutionizing Virtual Communication:
The Impact of Robotic-Facilitated Frameworks

Cheng Hang
https://orcid.org/0009-0001-2031-5910
Management and Science University, Malaysia

Safaa Najah Saud Al-Humairi
https://orcid.org/0000-0001-5978-7651
Management and Science University, Malaysia

ABSTRACT

The rapid evolution of technology has fundamentally transformed how communication with digital platforms reshapes people's interactions. The Robotic Facilitated Virtual Communication Framework (RFVCF) represents a significant advancement in bridging the gap between human communication and digital interfaces. This framework leverages robots and AI to enhance online interactions by addressing the limitations of traditional digital communication methods. This book chapter comprehensively analyses RFVCF, exploring its historical context, key components, technological underpinnings, and potential implications across various sectors, particularly healthcare. Through this examination, the transformative potential of RFVCF in improving the quality, efficiency, and emotional depth of virtual communication is elucidated.

1.0 INTRODUCTION

The inclusion of technology into the changing terrain of modern-day communication has transformed how humans relate. Digital platforms, social media networks, and messaging programs that have sprung up all around have changed drastically how humans relate to one another. As the boundaries between the physical world and cyberspace blur more and more, there is an increased need to explore new paradigms that enable human interaction within these virtual spaces. The Robotic Facilitated Virtual Communication Framework (RFVCF) best exemplifies this framework since it audaciously endeavors to redefine

DOI: 10.4018/979-8-3693-8332-2.ch005

our social lives in this digital age by bridging the gap between human communication and computer interfaces (Fernández Galeote & Hamari, 2021). It is the principle behind the development of RFVCF – an all-around plan to improve human interaction in virtual worlds by facilitating it through robots and astronomical transactions. Devices such as intelligent robots act to fill in the voids and limitations of regular digital communication media, provide mediation, and improve human-to-human interaction through an intermediation service in the form of RFVCF. Since the time of history, humans have tried to find means of communication to allow them to transcend space and time while conversing with other humans. Humanity used means from cave art and smoke signals, written messages, and telegraphs to overcome the obstacles that distance and time stand in our way. Other important turning points in the development of communications were the discovery of the telephone and the radio since these made possible—also for the first time in human history—the transmission of speech from one place to another and over a long distance (Gopi et al., 2022), as shown in **Figure 1**. Email and the internet have made previously slow and inaccessible written communication virtually immediately available to a global audience. These developments permitted communication across great distances and brought people closer together.

Figure 1. Mobile radio model for dual-band transceiver

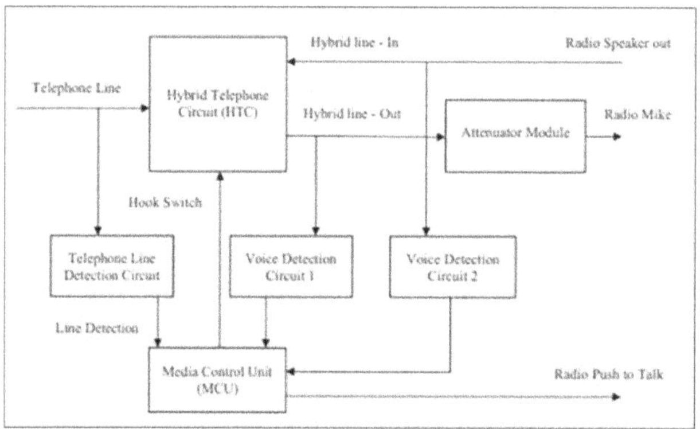

However, the advent of social media and messaging apps completely revolutionized human interaction. These mediums allowed people to meet new people from all around the world, share their stories, and have conversations in real-time in a way that had never been possible before. The rise of social media also heralded the concept of a "virtual identity," through which users might construct an online persona and form communities based on their commonalities. The digital age has brought many benefits, but it has also brought many difficulties (Pencarelli, 2020). Problems like information overload, cyberbullying, privacy concerns, and the decline of meaningful in-person connections have arisen as online interactions have grown more central to our everyday lives. In this light, the RFVCF presents itself as a feasible strategy for improving the standard and breadth of our online communications. Table 1 presents prominent research by (Lenhart, 2007) the most common manifestation of cyberbullying, which often involves the public disclosure of private information.

Table 1. Cyber bullying

Making Private information public is the Most Common Form of Cyberbullying		
Have you, personally, ever experienced any of the following things online?	**Yes**	**No**
Someone taking a private email, IM, or text message you sent them and forwarding it to someone else or posting it where others could see it.	15%	85%
Someone spreading a rumour about you online.	13%	87%
Someone sending you a threatening or aggressive email IM. or text message	13%	87%
Someone posting an embarrassing picture of you online without your permission.	6%	94%
Answered "yes" to any of the four previous questions	32%	68%

A comprehensive strategy for digital contact is formed by these factors, which include both technological and human dimensions. Intelligent robotic agents play a major role in RFVCF as virtual conversation facilitators. Robots with such sophisticated Artificial Intelligence (AI), natural language processing (NLP) algorithms, and sensory inputs can read and respond to human emotions and intentions. Depending on the nature of the conversation, they can take the form of anything from humanoid robots to digital avatars (Ko et al., 2021). These robot mediators are important for keeping conversations on track and maintaining an atmosphere of mutual respect and understanding. Language translators, emotion analyzers, and information retrieval systems can all improve how the interaction with one another and the world around us. RFVCF is implemented in simulated environments that either closely resemble the real world or are tailored for a particular kind of interaction. These platforms range from online chat rooms to virtual workplaces and online gaming networks. Users can engage with each other in ways that surpass the constraints of traditional communication methods, such as texting or video chatting, owing to the geographical context provided by virtual worlds.

The primary goal of developing RFVCF was to make talking to other people easier. Individuals, groups, companies, and communities are all valid target audiences for the framework. Using the robot mediators, humans can connect with one another in their preferred virtual setting with the use of technological support and enhancements (Grewal et al., 2020). In order for robotic facilitators to comprehend and appropriately react to human inputs, RFVCF primarily utilizes artificial intelligence and machine learning techniques. These algorithms are regularly taught and updated to enhance their linguistic, emotional, and contextual competence. Therefore, robotic facilitators can have nuanced talks that are relevant to the user's context and preferences. In light of the delicate nature of electronic exchanges, RFVCF includes stringent safeguards to protect users' personal information and data. It guarantees privacy and prevents prying eyes from listening in on private chats. Users can decide how much personal information they feel comfortable giving to robot helpers.

The RFVCF provides numerous advantages that may drastically alter our online interactions. These benefits extend to numerous areas of human interaction and experience. By offering instantaneous translation, RFVCF streamlines communication and makes it easier to have productive talks across cultural boundaries. This function allows people of varying linguistic backgrounds to communicate and work together across international boundaries easily. The emotional depth of virtual encounters is improved by robotic facilitators equipped with sophisticated artificial intelligence algorithms that detect and react to users' emotions (Pentina et al., 2023). They can provide emotional backing, elevating computer-mediated conversation to a more human level. By streamlining processes like scheduling, document sharing, and information retrieval in virtual workspaces and collaborative settings, RFVCF improves the effectiveness of teamwork.

RFVCF learns from its users' tastes and tailors its suggestions, recommendations, and help to each individual. As a result of this customization, users will feel more connected to the service and more engaged with the content. The framework improves usability for people with disabilities by allowing individualized interfaces and flexible means of expression (Valencia et al., 2023). This diversity of users is made possible by making virtual environments welcoming to all. By providing intelligent tutoring, feedback, and assessment, RFVCF aids in creating individualized learning opportunities in the classroom. It is flexible enough to accommodate kids' varying learning styles and speeds, allowing them to make more academic progress. Lifelike RFVCF virtual characters improve gaming and social platform immersion and user interaction. Non-playable characters (NPCs) powered by AI can interact with users naturally. To prevent the inappropriate use of sensitive information, RFVCF gives users fine-grained management of their data and privacy settings. This openness increases confidence in the system and gets more people to use virtual communication.

2.0 FUNDAMENTALS OF ROBOTIC-FACILITATED VIRTUAL COMMUNICATION

2.1 Conceptual Framework

The conceptual framework of RFVC's underlying concepts and components provides the skeleton to build a grasp of and facility with RFVC's central ideas and methods. This framework aims to improve human interaction in virtual environments by providing a conceptual roadmap for its design, development, and use. All the ideas, tools, and guidelines necessary for RFVC to function correctly may be found in these foundational documents. RFVC puts people first by catering to their wants, needs, and past interactions, as shown in **Figure 2.** It recognizes the importance of social contact and communication in digital settings (Caena & Redecker, 2019). The framework stresses the need to develop RFVC systems that are easy to use, effective in enhancing human communication, and respect the integrity of human connections. Intelligent agents meant to mediate and improve virtual communication are at the heart of RFVC. These robots can comprehend, interpret, and react to human inputs thanks to AI, NLP, and machine learning algorithms. They operate as a go-between for users in virtual environments, supplying information, context, and help.

Figure 2. RFVC framework (Caena & Redecker, 2019)

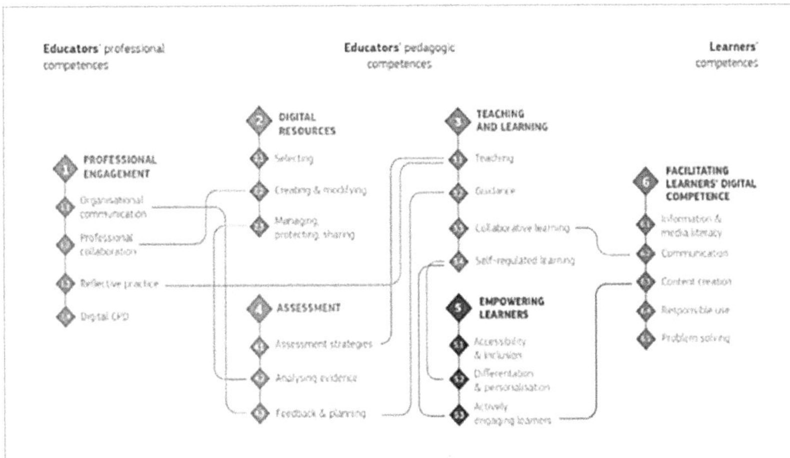

RFVC is used in simulated or designed-for-purpose real-world settings. Space and context in these settings provide additional nuances for expression. Communication is affected by the virtual environment in which it takes place, whether in a virtual meeting room, a collaborative office, or an immersive social context. AI and machine learning (ML) are used in RFVC to give robots the ability to understand and interact with humans. These algorithms allow the facilitators to change based on user input and gradually improve over time. Improvements in AI functionality are crucial to the development of RFVC. Considering the delicate nature of virtual communication, RFVC is equipped with numerous privacy and security features (Kassab & Darabkh, 2020). It keeps interactions private, safeguards user information, and gives individuals agency over their data. Establishing trust in RFVC systems necessitates addressing privacy concerns as a foundational step. The overarching objective of RFVC is to empower robot facilitators with the capability to discern and respond to users' emotions. This functionality enhances the authenticity and depth of virtual interactions, fostering the creation of more genuine human-robot bonds.

Because of its real-time language translation and cultural sensitivity, RFVC facilitates communication between people of different cultural backgrounds. It breaks down barriers to communication between people of different languages and cultures, helping to build a more interconnected world. Personalized RFVC interactions are an integral part of the technology since they cater to the specific needs of each user. The framework provides options for users to tailor their digital environments to their specific tastes and needs and to receive tailored recommendations and content suggestions. RFVC's usefulness for completing tasks and working together is greatly enhanced. Robotic facilitators can improve productivity in virtual workplaces and team contexts by helping with process automation, scheduling, and file sharing and fostering a culture of collaboration (Khan et al., 2022). In the classroom environment, RFVC facilitates individualized learning through intelligent tutoring, feedback, and assessment. It supports a wide variety of student learning styles and improves academic outcomes. In online gaming and social media, RFVC improves both fun and interactivity. Users are likelier to be engaged and enjoy themselves with the help of non-player and virtual characters that look and act realistically. Because of its adaptability and low cost, RFVC systems can be used by people of all economic backgrounds and sizes. The fundamentals of RFVC are laid out in a conceptual framework that details the driving concepts and components of RFVC's creation and implementation. This framework highlights the human-centered aspect of RFVC, showing how it can improve the quality, authenticity, and efficiency of interactions in digital spaces, thus revolutionizing virtual communication. If they adhere to these essentials, researchers, developers, and practitioners can successfully manage RFVC's intricacies and tap into the technology's transformative potential.

2.2 State of the Arts

The RFVC has evolved due to technological changes, ideas, and social norms. Although advanced robotics and AI dominate the RFVC landscape today, the field has historical origins in the early days of computing and communication. The introduction of computer-mediated communication in the middle of the 20th century can be traced back to the birth of RFVC. Remote communication was made possible by early experiments with telegraphy, telephone networks, and computer networking (Bailey & Bailey, 2022). These advances pave the way for robots to be used as virtual communication facilitators in the future. Computer-based communication systems were first investigated in the 1960s and 1970s. As interest grew in using computers to bridge great distances and bring people together, projects like ARPANET emerged as an early forerunner to the contemporary internet. These efforts proved the viability of virtual communication, paving the way for the creation of RFVC.

The 1980s was a watershed moment in RFVC development with the introduction of Graphical User Interfaces (GUIs). Easy-to-use virtual environments were made possible by GUIs, which simplified computer interaction. The introduction of RFVC necessitated a change in interface design that allowed the production of fully realized simulated environments. The 1990s were the heyday of IM and MMOs (multiplayer online roles). Some of the potentials of virtual communication have been hinted at by technologies such as ICQ, AOL Instant Messenger, and early virtual reality environments. Although primitive compared to modern standards, these platforms provided early insights into the benefits of technology-enabled human-avatar interactions (Kalpokas & Kalpokienė, 2023). Artificial intelligence and robotics have advanced rapidly in the 21st century. Researchers began to investigate the possibilities of AI technologies to improve digital communication as these tools developed. Captivate for Virtual Communication Virtual Workshop is shown in **Figure 3.** Intelligent robotic facilitators have been developed for use in RFVC systems; their capabilities range from Natural Language Processing (NLP) algorithms and emotion identification to AI chatbots.

Figure 3. Captivate for virtual communication virtual workshop

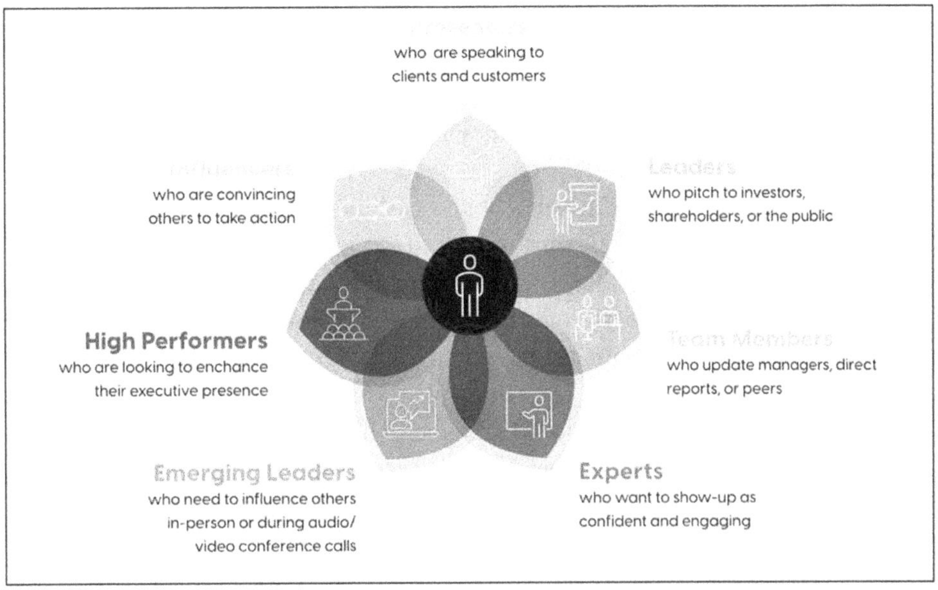

Consequently, education, healthcare, and commerce industries are just a few areas where RFVC has been widely used in recent years. For example, in order to make distance learning more accessible, schools have begun utilizing virtual tutors and collaboration platforms. RFVC was used in telemedicine applications to bridge the geographical gap between patients and doctors. Apart from that, in order to improve virtual meetings and customer service and automate mundane chores, businesses implemented RFVC. These use cases proved that RFVC has real-world implications for boosting business effectiveness. In addition, the gaming business was crucial in expanding the capabilities of RFVC. The potential for AI-driven NPCs and characters to immerse and interact with players was demonstrated in virtual worlds and massively multiplayer online games (MMOs) (Tang et al., 2020). These innovations impacted how robotic facilitators in RFVC settings are built and what they can do. At the same time, people started talking more openly about the social and ethical consequences of RFVC. Ethical rules and laws have been developed in response to concerns about privacy, data security, and the impact of AI on human interactions. The evolution of RFVC over time has demonstrated how technological and social changes are interwoven. It exemplifies the human desire to break down distance barriers and improve communication as RFVC develops. Its past demonstrates the never-ending search for deeper and more genuine virtual interactions in the increasingly digital world.

2.3 Related Literature on the RFVC and AI-Driven Perception

Robotic-facilitated virtual communication has emerged as a transformative technology, integrating robotics, artificial intelligence (AI), and virtual reality (VR) to enable immersive and interactive remote interactions. This technology has applications across various domains, including telemedicine, education, industrial operations, and social interactions. Integrating AI mechanisms enhances these systems' capabilities, enabling more natural and efficient communication. One prominent thread in this literature is the use of natural language processing (NLP) to facilitate seamless human-robot interaction. Lakhnati et al. (2024) pioneered this approach by integrating GPT-4 into a Unity VR environment where users converse with simulated robots (Lakhnati et al., 2024). Their findings reveal that users who explore the robots' language capabilities experience a natural conversational flow, though many are hindered by preconceived expectations, limiting interaction depth. The study's challenges—such as the opaque nature of large language models (LLMs) and latency from cloud connectivity—echo broader issues in AI-driven communication.

In contrast, Li et al. (2021), an NLP-driven virtual assistant designed for industrial contexts. Using a RESTful Client-Server architecture and conversation strategies inspired by human dialogue, Max enhances efficiency in scenarios like package delivery, overcoming the rigidity of system-specific virtual assistants (Li et al., 2021). These papers converge on NLP's potential to bridge communication gaps yet diverge in scope: Lakhnati's simulation focus could benefit from Max's robust architecture. At the same time, Max's real-world testing could refine Lakhnati's VR testbed.

On the other hand, Ranganathan et al. (2024) integrate AI and the Internet of Things (IoT) to enable real-time data analysis and empathetic patient interactions, achieving high satisfaction and care efficiency (Ranganathan et al., 2024). However, latency is not explicitly addressed, a gap tackled by Naseer et al. (2023), whereby in their hybrid algorithm, combining deep reinforcement learning (DRL) with a dueling double-deep Q-network (DDQN) and gated recurrent unit (GRU), manages 15-second delays in healthcare settings, improving stability by 2.4% over existing methods (Naseer, Khan, & Altalbe, 2023; Naseer, Khan, Rasool, et al., 2023). Similarly, Beraldo et al. (2023) offer a transformer-based system for home care, achieving over 95% accuracy in autonomous assistance, though adapting to unstructured environments remains challenging (Beraldo et al., 2023). These works underscore AI's role in healthcare telepresence, with Ranganathan emphasizing empathy, Naseer and the 2023 paper tackling latency, and Beraldo balancing autonomy. Cross-integration could yield more robust healthcare robots, such as EIROB's emotion recognition enhancing Ranganathan's system or Naseer's delay solutions stabilizing Beraldo's autonomy.

Du et al. (2020) use hidden Markov models for intention recognition (Du et al., 2020), improving immersiveness in multi-party conversations via VR and sound localization, though complex control algorithms pose challenges. Kurup and Liu (2016) combine Simultaneous Localization and Mapping (SLAM) with VR, using Google Cardboard to boost immersion (Kurup & Liu, 2016), yet note obstacle avoidance difficulties for novices. Martinez-Hernandez et al. (2015) pair the iCub robot with Oculus Rift (Martinez-Hernandez et al., 2015), planning future tactile feedback, but face multi-modal integration hurdles. Jones et al. (2020) blend AR and VR, tracking head and hand movements for social presence, though latency compensation is underexplored (Jones et al., 2020). These studies prioritize embodiment and immersion, with Du's collaborative control potentially enhancing Kurup's navigation and Martinez-Hernandez's tactile ambitions aligning with Jones's focus on gesture visibility. Their shared challenge of balancing immersion with technical complexity suggests a need for streamlined integration. Vasylkiv et al. (2021) employ RL to automate emotive routines for the Haru robot (Vasylkiv et al., 2021), reducing the teleoperator workload but facing routine selection complexity.

Brock et al. (2021) compare autonomous and teleoperated Haru in a Rock-Paper-Scissors game, finding teleoperation more socially engaging (Brock et al., 2021), with embodiment remaining a challenge. Grohmann et al. (2022) in "JAVRIS" predict robot behavior to achieve negative latency, improving precision by over 1000% for novices (Grohmann et al., 2022), though propagation delay persists. Eltanbouly et al. (2022) use machine learning for motion blending, enhancing embodiment with haptic feedback, but struggle to maintain body ownership (Eltanbouly et al., 2022). JAVRIS's latency solution could refine Eltanbouly's precision while both underscore predictive AI's role in seamless interaction, offering potential cross-application to other latency-sensitive systems. Future research could integrate strengths—such as EIROB's (Ismail & Vasudev, 2024) emotional intelligence with VROOM's VR immersion (Jones et al., 2020) or JAVRIS's latency prediction (Grohmann et al., 2022) with Haru's affective routines to create holistic, human-like telepresence systems. Addressing these shared challenges will be pivotal to realizing telepresence's full potential.

2.4 Key Components and Technologies

Intelligent robotic agents play a vital role in RFVC, facilitating online dialogue between participants. Natural language processing (NLP) and machine learning algorithms are only two examples of the AI features that give these robots the ability to comprehend human language and react appropriately. RFVC functions in simulated environments that may mimic real-world contexts or are created from the ground up to meet specific requirements in terms of communication. Virtual interactions benefit from these settings because of the spatial context and clues they offer (Barreda-Ángeles & Hartmann, 2022). In order to equip robotic facilitators with context awareness, adaptability, and continual learning, RFVC systems incorporate cutting-edge artificial intelligence and machine learning techniques. These algorithms allow robots to gradually acquire human-level linguistic skills, emotional intelligence, and responsiveness. Emotion detection and analysis tools are built into RFVC. This feature allows robot helpers to show empathy and provide more nuanced online interactions. RFVC relies heavily on real-time language translation technology to facilitate communication across cultural boundaries and linguistic difficulties. With this function, users of varying native languages can have productive discussions.

Given the evident importance of data security and privacy, RFVC systems conscientiously implement robust measures. Consequently, users can feel secure, knowing that their information and communications are protected through these safeguards. With RFVC, users may tailor their experience to their exact specifications. Users are given the option to personalize their digital environments, receive relevant suggestions, and gain access to relevant content based on their specific preferences and needs. Besides facilitating conversation, RFVC facilitates tasks and teamwork in digital environments (Sukarni & Rokhayati, 2023). Processes may be automated, meetings can be scheduled, and files can be shared with the help of robotic facilitators. RFVC facilitates individualized learning in the classroom through intelligent tutoring, feedback, and assessment. As a result of its flexibility, it improves learning results across a wide range of student profiles. The use of RFVC in the entertainment industry allows for the creation of more interactive and immersive video games and social experiences. NPCs and AI-driven NPCs make virtual worlds more exciting and fun to explore. In order to facilitate its use in a wide range of situations, from social media to business communication tools, RFVC is built to be fully compatible with a wide variety of digital platforms and apps.

The modular and low-cost nature of RFVC systems makes them suitable for various applications and users, from small businesses to multinational corporations. Ethical considerations and legal frameworks have emerged to address concerns over privacy, data consumption, and accountable AI deployment as RFVC has grown in popularity. These fundamental features and technologies are the backbone of RFVC, which enables it to enhance human communication in virtual environments, as tabulated in Table 2. The evolution of RFVC and its potential to improve the quality and authenticity of virtual interactions is mainly due to these technologies' incorporation and ongoing development (Torres Vega et al., 2020).

Table 2. Fundamentals of robotic-facilitated virtual communication

Author	Method Used	Setting/ Industry	Findings	Relevance to Study
Kassab and Darabkh (2020)	Literature review and analysis	Internet of Things (IoT)	IoT review highlights technology's evolution and identifies future opportunities.	IoT technology alignment
Khan et al. (2022)	Case study and survey	Education sector	RPA in education offers benefits but faces acceptance challenges.	Insights into robotic adoption
Kalpokas and Kalpokienė (2023)	Book writing and editing	Metaverse	Book dissects metaverse, raises regulation concerns.	Virtual communication insights
Tang et al. (2020)	Algorithm design, implementation, and evaluation	Games	AI algorithm tailors game design to user preferences.	Impact on virtual healthcare
Barreda-Ángeles and Hartmann (2022)	Experiment and survey	Social virtual reality platforms	Social VR aids psychological well-being amid pandemics.	Impact on virtual healthcare
Sukarni and Rokhayati (2023)	Qualitative study and interview	English education and teaching	Study assesses English teaching methods, identifies improvement strategies.	Communication strategies insights

2.5 Significance in Healthcare

With RFVC, patients can have remote consultations with doctors regardless of location. Patients in underserved or rural areas who may not have ready access to medical treatment will find this paramount. Since RFVC allows for efficient doctor-patient communication, it contributes to the development of telemedicine. It helps with non-emergency medical diagnosis, medication administration, and scheduling of follow-up appointments. Integration of RFVC systems with medical devices and sensors enables continuous, real-time monitoring of patient's vital signs and other health indicators (Diraco et al., 2023). This continual vigilance enables the swift diagnosis and treatment of potential health issues. Through RFVC, patients gain access to doctors and other medical experts from around the world. This improves the availability of specialized care, especially for patients with uncommon or complicated illnesses. RFVC can help reduce healthcare costs by reducing the demand for costly infrastructure and cutting down on patient travel fees. Allocating healthcare resources more effectively is another benefit.

Patients using RFVC are more likely to be involved in their own care. Due to its adaptability and individualization, patients are more likely to take charge of their health when they use virtual communication. Check-ins, medication adherence, and lifestyle monitoring are all aided by RFVC, making it a valuable tool for managing chronic diseases. It improves the long-term ability of healthcare practitioners and patients to work together. To ease the burden on already overburdened emergency facilities, RFVC can be used to perform remote triage and early assessment during times of crisis. Medical education benefits greatly from RFVC because it facilitates remote mentorship, peer learning, and virtual simulations (Kurata et al., 2023). It is a boon to both medical education and information sharing. RFVC also includes mental health treatments, such as online therapy and counseling. It responds to the rising demand for quick and easy access to mental health assistance in times of distress. RFVC produces massive volumes of healthcare data and can be used for analytics, research, and better patient care. It aids the development of evidence-based medical procedures.

In healthcare, RFVC places patients at the focal point of their care experience, allowing doctors to provide individualized plans and promptly address questions and concerns. Precious during epidemics, this approach reduces the likelihood of direct contact between individuals. RFVC assists older people in caring for themselves at home, which fosters autonomy and lessens healthcare costs as populations age (Valero et al., 2021). Given the considerable distances to urban hospitals, RFVC is significant in rural healthcare. It ensures that individuals in remote areas have access to high-quality medical treatment. The foundational aspects of RFVC have the potential to bring about profound changes in medical practice. They improve the quality of care while decreasing costs and increasing patient access and efficiency. RFVC has the potential to become increasingly important in determining the course of future healthcare delivery as technology continues to develop.

3.0 PATIENT-PRACTITIONER INTERACTION IN VIRTUAL HEALTHCARE

3.1 Importance of Effective Communication

The importance of clear and concise communication in patient-practitioner interactions during telemedicine cannot be overstated. Effective communication becomes even more critical for delivering high-quality healthcare without a physical presence in virtual contexts. Establishing open lines of communication between doctors and patients is imperative. Patients must trust their virtual healthcare provider before feeling at ease discussing their medical history, symptoms, and concerns. Coupled with doctors making correct diagnoses and treatment recommendations, patients need to communicate their symptoms and medical history clearly and thoroughly. Patient participation in healthcare decision-making is enhanced by good communication. This freedom encourages people to inquire, get more information, and actively participate in their care. Medical mistakes can occur when there is a misunderstanding or a breakdown in communication. The likelihood of these kinds of errors can be reduced by good communication, which is crucial for patient safety (Mihdawi et al., 2020). Through virtual healthcare, practitioners can better inform their patients about their illnesses and available treatments. Patients will understand these data if they are effectively communicated with it.

In challenging or chronic illness situations, patients frequently go to their healthcare providers for emotional support. Clear and concise communication enables providers to empathize and reassure patients effectively. Additionally, recognizing that different patients have varying preferences for communication methods enhances the overall patient experience (Cheng et al., 2020). Further, some people would rather read an article than watch a video or talk on the phone. To communicate effectively, it is vital to take their preferences into account and respect them. Patients of different cultures may interact with one another while receiving virtual treatment. Courteous and acceptable care can only be delivered via open, honest communication that accounts for cultural differences. When virtual interactions with healthcare providers, patients need reassurance that their health information is protected. It is crucial to have an open dialogue regarding data privacy and security. Multiple medical professionals may contribute to a patient's care in a virtual healthcare setting. Organization and smooth care are only possible when all care team members are on the same page. By maintaining regular communication, patients can share their thoughts on the effectiveness of telehealth services. Healthcare providers and organizations can leverage this feedback to enhance their patients' service quality. Ensuring effective virtual healthcare communication for individuals with impairments is imperative, fostering inclusivity in healthcare delivery.

Above all, patients are more likely to understand and follow treatment programs if they are provided with clear instructions and explanations (Lochmiller, 2021). When patients can grasp the reasoning behind a recommendation, they are more likely to take it to heart and act upon it. Some patients may feel uneasy or unprepared for healthcare interactions that take place online. Having precise information and expectations can help ease these feelings. In conclusion, strong communication is the backbone of fruitful telehealth encounters. It results in improved health outcomes, greater patient happiness, and superior care overall. If virtual healthcare is to be both efficient and compassionate, practitioners and institutions must place a premium on communication skills and technology.

3.2 Patient-Centered Care

Likewise, in virtual healthcare, patient-centered care means putting the individual patient's wishes, preferences, and active participation in healthcare decisions first. Care is administered holistically and collaboratively, with individualized care plans meticulously formulated through a partnership between the patient and their virtual healthcare provider. The patient's medical background, way of life, values, and treatment objectives all play a role in these programs. Patients are educated about their diagnoses, available treatments, and expected outcomes. They are encouraged to actively participate in their healthcare by asking questions, voicing concerns, and deciding treatment options (Quaye et al., 2019). Virtual healthcare that puts the patient first promotes individual responsibility for one's health. Goal setting, progress tracking, and patient autonomy in healthcare decision-making are all supported. It is crucial for patients and their virtual healthcare providers to have open lines of communication. Providers pay close attention to their patients, acknowledge their concerns, and offer thorough explanations and data.

Remote healthcare providers owe it to their patients to consider their cultural context and values. This includes being sensitive to cultural norms around how people prefer to be reached and cared for. Patients can access their medical histories, lab results, and educational resources securely online. This allows them to review information at their convenience, enhancing retention. Moreover, online healthcare professionals, including doctors and nurses, communicate regularly with their patients. The patients are followed up with, monitored, and supported consistently to ensure they receive continuous care. Care coordination is maintained when patients see numerous doctors due to the significance of patient-centered medicine. Besides that, the medical professionals work together and share data to ensure patients receive consistent treatment. When receiving healthcare online, patients may rest assured that their privacy and confidentiality will be protected. Compliance with data privacy laws and using secure communication channels are mandatory(Rieger et al., 2019). Accessibility for people with disabilities is a crucial aspect of virtual healthcare. Patients can choose from several contact methods, including video calls, phone consultations, and messaging.

Despite this, the patients are given various educational materials and resources to further teach them about their medical issues and available treatment alternatives (Henning et al., 2022). They will be able to make better decisions. Feedback from patients regarding their use of telehealth services is highly valued. Healthcare providers can use this information to enhance their offerings over time. Patient-centric virtual healthcare prioritizes the emotional well-being of individuals, acknowledging the impact of emotions on overall health. Practitioners offer comfort through empathetic words and reassurance, recognizing the significance of the patient's emotional state. Ultimately, patient-centered care in online healthcare aims to enhance patient satisfaction and quality of life by addressing psychological, physiological, and interpersonal needs. In the virtual healthcare environment, patient-centered care fosters a team-based approach to treatment in which patients are encouraged to participate in their care. Personalized medicine starts with the premise that each patient has specific requirements and preferences, and it works backward to improve health outcomes and the quality of care received.

3.3 Telehealth and Virtual Consultations

Telemedicine and online doctor visits are now commonplace in virtual healthcare. These methods use technological means to connect patients and medical professionals remotely, eliminating the necessity for in-person consultations. Regarding healthcare, telehealth refers to anything that can be done remotely via communications technologies. Secure internet platforms, phone calls, text messages, and video chats are all part of the modern patient-doctor dialogue. In particular, people living in rural or underserved areas benefit significantly from expanding telehealth services (Hoffman, 2020). Patients no longer have to leave their houses to get medical attention, reducing wasted time and gas. Telehealth allows for continuous monitoring and management of chronic illnesses. Virtual doctor's visits save money for patients and healthcare providers alike. Preventative care and early interventions are bolstered by telehealth, leading to fewer hospitalizations. Primary care physicians are the people to whom patients first go for anything from initial examinations and follow-ups to resolving minor medical issues.

More importantly, mental health, skincare, heart care, and other medical focuses are all within the realm of possibility with telehealth. Remote monitoring and medication management are helpful for patients with chronic diseases. Non-life-threatening urgent care needs can be quickly evaluated and counseled through virtual visits. Virtual follow-up consultations are feasible after medical procedures. Patients must have Internet access via a computer, tablet, or smartphone. Medical professionals use safe telehealth platforms or software for video conferencing and online consultations. Video conferences and other forms of remote medical consultation are known as "virtual consultations." Video calls facilitate real-time communication between patients and their healthcare practitioners for assessment, diagnosis, and treatment planning. The visual assessment of symptoms and diseases is made possible through virtual consultations. Flexible appointment scheduling can reduce patient wait times and help doctors better manage their time (Martin et al., 2020). The virtual consultation process is shown in **Figure 4**.

Figure 4. Virtual consultation process

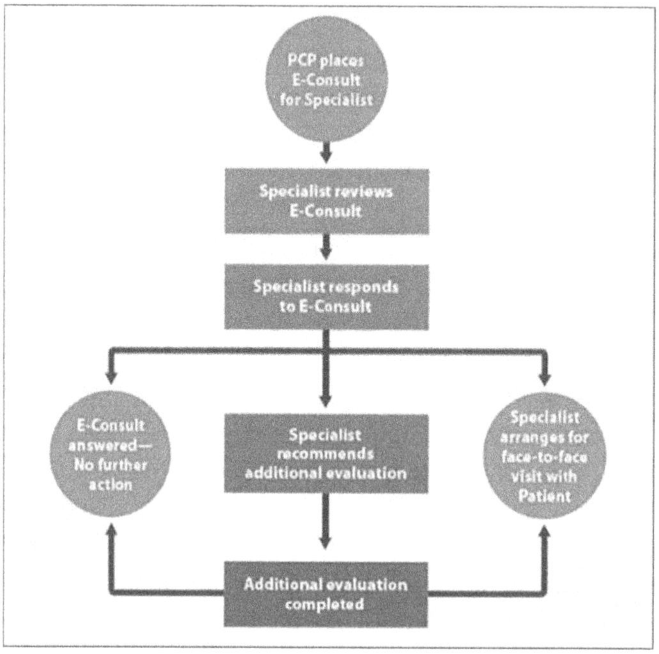

Patients can access professionals from all around the world through virtual consultations. Patients are more likely to be actively involved in their care when they can communicate directly with their doctors. Professionals can conduct symptom evaluations and physical examinations and establish initial diagnosis. Medication and therapy recommendations can be made, and changes can be made during a virtual consultation. Therapists and counselors in the mental health field provide their services online. Without leaving their homes, patients now have access to specialized second opinions. Patients and medical staff need cameras, microphones, and internet access. Video conferencing platforms that are secure and HIPAA-compliant protect sensitive information. When in-person visits are few, as during the recent COVID-19 outbreak, telehealth and internet consultations have risen in popularity , improving doctor-patient relationship quality without sacrificing accessibility or efficiency. It is anticipated that the role of these virtual healthcare modalities in healthcare delivery will grow as technology develops further. **Figure 5** illustrates the percentage of respondents currently using technology.

Figure 5. Percentage of respondents currently using technology (Galle et al., 2021)

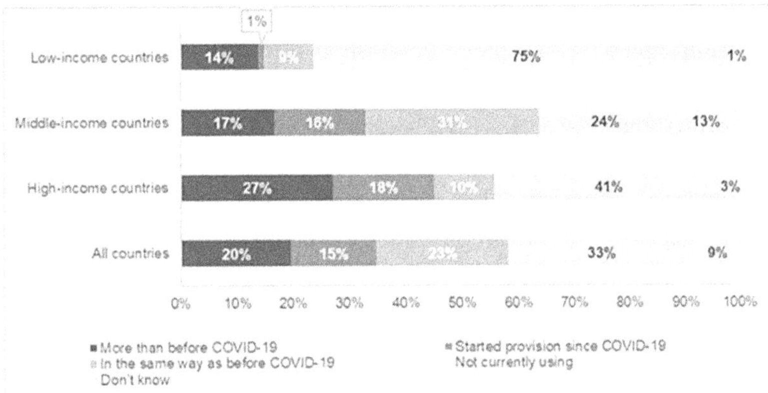

3.4 Enhancing Doctor-Patient Relationship

Improving the doctor-patient interaction in telemedicine is essential to delivering high-caliber treatment and keeping patients happy. During telehealth consultations, healthcare providers should use straightforward language marked by empathy and active listening. Building trust and rapport with patients requires active listening and sympathetic behavior. Providers in the medical field owe it to their patients to identify themselves, clarify their roles, and establish credibility. Patients feel more confident in the care they will receive if their providers exhibit professionalism and expertise. Providers should maintain a calm, private, and well-lit space while conducting video-based virtual consultations. The appearance of interest can be heightened through sustained eye contact and non-verbal indicators like nodding (Vishwakarma, 2023). It is crucial to stress the need for privacy and confidentiality in telehealth encounters. If healthcare practitioners want patients to feel safe disclosing personal information, they should talk to them about data security. Considering the patient's values, priorities, and desired outcomes is essential for practitioners using a patient-centered approach. Collaboration is fostered when patients are included in treatment planning and decision-making.

Patients are more likely to feel in control of their healthcare if encouraged to ask questions, seek clarification, and participate actively, as presented in Table 3. Educational resources and explanations provided by healthcare experts assist patients in gaining a better understanding of complex concepts. In online healthcare, ensuring continuity of care relies on timely follow-up. Patients should anticipate follow-up appointments, accessible contact information, and open availability from healthcare providers. Recognizing and appreciating people's unique cultural and ethnic backgrounds is crucial in remote healthcare. To best serve their patients, medical professionals must modify their approach and mode of communication. Patients may experience anxiety, fear, and other forms of emotional distress (Taschereau-Dumouchel et al., 2022). Provide comfort and reassurance to patients emotionally. Patients are more likely to feel acknowledged and appreciated when caregivers show they understand them. Patient feedback on their telehealth experiences is vital and should be encouraged. Healthcare providers can use this information to serve their patients better.

Eventually, virtual care has inherent limitations, and practitioners should be upfront about them. Trust is built via open dialogue regarding the advantages and disadvantages of remote medical treatment. Transparency and patient involvement are improved when patients can access their medical information and test results through encrypted web portals. Practitioners providing telehealth services should inform patients of the advantages and disadvantages of this method. Patients should consent after being fully informed of the benefits and drawbacks of virtual healthcare. A patient-centered approach, clear lines of communication, and a dedication to providing high-quality care are essential for improving the doctor-patient connection in telemedicine. Better healthcare results and patient satisfaction can be achieved through the use of these tactics by healthcare providers, even in virtual settings (Aashima et al., 2021).

Table 3. Patient-practitioner interaction in virtual healthcare

Author	Method Used	Setting/ Industry	Findings
Quaye et al. (2019)	Observational study and interview	Children's Healthcare	The study explored children's active participation in decision-making processes during hospitalization. It found that children's participation was influenced by their age, preferences, communication skills, and relationships with healthcare professionals
Rieger et al. (2019)	Case study and analysis	Blockchain application development	The study described the development of a blockchain application that complies with the EU General Data Protection Regulation (GDPR). It also discussed the challenges and solutions for achieving GDPR compliance in blockchain applications
Henning et al. (2022)	Literature review and survey	Trauma treatment for clinical practitioners	The review covered the current state of graduate training and certification in trauma treatment for clinical practitioners. It also surveyed the opinions and experiences of clinical practitioners regarding trauma treatment education and practice
Hoffman (2020)	Literature review and analysis	Telehealth during COVID-19	The review covered the various aspects of telehealth during COVID-19, such as benefits, challenges, opportunities, and regulations. It also discussed how telehealth can increase access to care for patients and providers during the pandemic
Martin et al. (2020)	Data analysis and statistics	Primary care across ten OECD countries	The analysis examined the socioeconomic inequalities in waiting times for primary care across ten OECD countries. It found that waiting times were longer for lower-income groups, rural residents, and uninsured individuals
Galle et al. (2021)	Mixed-methods study and interview	Telemedicine for maternal care during COVID-19	The study investigated the use of telemedicine for maternal care during COVID-19. It found that telemedicine had both positive and negative effects on maternal care, such as convenience, accessibility, continuity, quality, safety, and satisfaction.

4.0 CONCLUSION

The Robotic Facilitated Virtual Communication Framework (RFVCF) stands at the forefront of the next evolution in digital communication, promising to bridge the gap between human interaction and technological mediation. By integrating advanced AI, NLP, and robotic technologies, RFVCF offers solutions to many challenges traditional digital communication methods pose. The framework's ability to provide real-time language translation, emotional intelligence, and personalized interactions marks a significant leap toward more meaningful and effective online interactions.

In healthcare, RFVCF's potential is particularly noteworthy. It enhances telemedicine through improved patient-practitioner communication, facilitates remote consultations, and ensures continuous patient monitoring and support. This framework not only addresses the accessibility issues faced by remote and underserved populations but also contributes to cost savings and more efficient resource utilization. As RFVCF continues to evolve, its application across various domains—from education to business collaboration and social interaction—will likely expand, fostering a more interconnected and responsive virtual environment. This framework's ongoing development and refinement will be crucial in addressing ethical considerations, privacy concerns, and the need for user-centric designs. Ultimately, RFVCF represents a pivotal step towards a future where virtual communication is as rich and nuanced as face-to-face interactions, redefining the possibilities of digital communication and enhancing the quality of human connections in the digital age. The path forward of the RFVC could be compromised. Firstly, the scalability of RFVC systems for 6G and beyond remains underexplored. Investigating the integration of RFVC with emerging technologies like terahertz communication and quantum networking could unlock new possibilities for ultra-high-definition video streaming with minimal latency. Secondly, energy efficiency in RFVC systems is a critical concern, especially for mobile and IoT devices. Future studies should focus on designing low-power RFVC protocols that maintain high-quality video transmission while extending device battery life. Exploring energy harvesting techniques, such as RF energy harvesting, could provide a sustainable solution for powering RFVC-enabled devices in remote or resource-constrained environments. By addressing these research directions, the field of RFVC can move toward more robust, scalable, and energy-efficient solutions, paving the way for its widespread adoption in next-generation communication networks.

REFERENCES

Aashima, N. (2021). A review of patient satisfaction and experience with telemedicine: A virtual solution during and beyond COVID-19 pandemic. *Telemedicine Journal and e-Health*, *27*(12), 1325–1331. DOI: 10.1089/tmj.2020.0570 PMID: 33719577

Bailey, J., & Bailey, J. (2022). Communication: Telephone, Computers and WWW. *Inventive Geniuses Who Changed the World: Fifty-Three Great British Scientists and Engineers and Five Centuries of Innovation*, 363-401.

Barreda-Ángeles, M., & Hartmann, T. (2022). Psychological benefits of using social virtual reality platforms during the covid-19 pandemic: The role of social and spatial presence. *Computers in Human Behavior*, *127*, 107047. DOI: 10.1016/j.chb.2021.107047 PMID: 34629723

Beraldo, G., De Benedictis, R., Cesta, A., Fracasso, F., & Cortellessa, G. (2023). Toward AI-Enabled Commercial Telepresence Robots to Combine Home Care Needs and Affordability. *IEEE Robotics and Automation Letters*, *8*(10), 6691–6698. DOI: 10.1109/LRA.2023.3310396

Brock, H., Šabanović, S., & Gomez, R. (2021). *Remote You, Haru and Me: Exploring Social Interaction in Telepresence Gaming With a Robotic Agent* Companion of the 2021 ACM/IEEE International Conference on Human-Robot Interaction, http://dx.doi.org/DOI: 10.1145/3434074.3447177

Caena, F., & Redecker, C. (2019). Aligning teacher competence frameworks to 21st century challenges: The case for the European Digital Competence Framework for Educators (Digcompedu). *European Journal of Education*, *54*(3), 356–369. DOI: 10.1111/ejed.12345

Cheng, H.-Y., Jian, S.-W., Liu, D.-P., Ng, T.-C., Huang, W.-T., & Lin, H.-H. (2020). Contact tracing assessment of COVID-19 transmission dynamics in Taiwan and risk at different exposure periods before and after symptom onset. *JAMA Internal Medicine*, *180*(9), 1156–1163. DOI: 10.1001/jamainternmed.2020.2020 PMID: 32356867

Diraco, G., Rescio, G., Siciliano, P., & Leone, A. (2023). Review on Human Action Recognition in Smart Living: Sensing Technology, Multimodality, Real-Time Processing, Interoperability, and Resource-Constrained Processing. *Sensors (Basel)*, *23*(11), 5281. DOI: 10.3390/s23115281 PMID: 37300008

Du, J., Do, H. M., & Sheng, W. (2020). Human–Robot Collaborative Control in a Virtual-Reality-Based Telepresence System. *International Journal of Social Robotics*, *13*(6), 1295–1306. DOI: 10.1007/s12369-020-00718-w

Eltanbouly, S., Abdel-Ghani, M., Helmy, H., Iskandar, A., Al-Sada, M., Nakajima, T., & Halabi, O. (2022, 2022/09). *Assistive Telexistence System Using Motion Blending2022 International Conference on Cyberworlds (CW)*, http://dx.doi.org/DOI: 10.1109/CW55638.2022.00023

Fernández Galeote, D., & Hamari, J. (2021). Game-based climate change engagement: analyzing the potential of entertainment and serious games. *Proceedings of the ACM on Human-Computer Interaction*, *5*(CHI PLAY), 1-21. DOI: 10.1145/3474653

Gopi, B., Logeshwaran, J., & Kiruthiga, T. (2022). An Innovation in the Development of a Mobile Radio Model for a Dual-Band Transceiver in Wireless Cellular Communication. *BOHR International Journal of Computational Intelligence and Communication Network*, *1*(1), 20–25.

Grewal, D., Kroschke, M., Mende, M., Roggeveen, A. L., & Scott, M. L. (2020). Frontline cyborgs at your service: How human enhancement technologies affect customer experiences in retail, sales, and service settings. *Journal of Interactive Marketing*, *51*(1), 9–25. DOI: 10.1016/j.intmar.2020.03.001

Grohmann, A. I., Busch, J. V. S., Bretschneider-Perez, A., Lehmann, C., & Fitzek, F. H. P. (2022). *JAVRIS: Joint Artificial Visual Prediction and Control for Remote-(Robot) Interaction Systems* 2022 IEEE 19th Annual Consumer Communications & Networking Conference (CCNC), http://dx.doi.org/DOI: 10.1109/CCNC49033.2022.9700532

Henning, J. A., Brand, B., & Courtois, C. A. (2022). Graduate training and certification in trauma treatment for clinical practitioners. *Training and Education in Professional Psychology*, *16*(4), 362–375. DOI: 10.1037/tep0000326

Hoffman, D. A. (2020). Increasing access to care: Telehealth during COVID-19. *Journal of Law and the Biosciences*, *7*(1), lsaa043. DOI: 10.1093/jlb/lsaa043 PMID: 32843985

Ismail, S., & Vasudev, H. (2024). *EIROB: An Emotionally Intelligent ROBot for Empathetic Support* 2024 IEEE International Conference on Signal Processing, Informatics, Communication and Energy Systems (SPICES), http://dx.doi.org/DOI: 10.1109/SPICES62143.2024.10779758

Jones, B., Zhang, Y., Wong, P. N. Y., & Rintel, S. (2020). *VROOM: Virtual Robot Overlay for Online Meetings* Extended Abstracts of the 2020 CHI Conference on Human Factors in Computing Systems, http://dx.doi.org/DOI: 10.1145/3334480.3382820

Kalpokas, I., & Kalpokienė, J. (2023). *Regulating the Metaverse: A Critical Assessment*. Taylor & Francis. DOI: 10.4324/9781003355861

Kassab, W., & Darabkh, K. A. (2020). A–Z survey of Internet of Things: Architectures, protocols, applications, recent advances, future directions and recommendations. *Journal of Network and Computer Applications*, *163*, 102663. DOI: 10.1016/j.jnca.2020.102663

Khan, S., Tailor, R., Pareek, R., Gujrati, R., & Uygun, H. (2022). Application of Robotic Process Automation in education sector. *Journal of Information and Optimization Sciences*, *43*(7), 1815–1834. DOI: 10.1080/02522667.2022.2128534

Ko, J. K., Koo, D. W., & Kim, M. S. (2021, October). A novel affinity enhancing method for human robot interaction-preliminary study with proactive docent avatar. In 2021 21st International Conference on Control, Automation and Systems (ICCAS) (pp. 1007-1011). IEEE.

Kurata, Y. B., Ong, A. K. S., Joyosa, J. J., & Santos, M. J. P. S. (2023). Retraction notice to "Predicting factors influencing perceived online learning experience among primary students utilizing structural equation modeling forest classifier approach" [ERAP 73 (2023) 100868]. *European Review of Applied Psychology*, *73*(5), 100943.

Kurup, P., & Liu, K. (2016). Telepresence Robot with Autonomous Navigation and Virtual Reality Proceedings of the 14th ACM Conference on Embedded Network Sensor Systems CD-ROM, http://dx.doi.org/DOI: 10.1145/2994551.2996540

Lakhnati, Y., Pascher, M., & Gerken, J. (2024). Exploring a GPT-based large language model for variable autonomy in a VR-based human-robot teaming simulation. *Frontiers in Robotics and AI, 11*, 1347538–1347538. DOI: 10.3389/frobt.2024.1347538 PMID: 38633059

Lenhart, A. (2007). *Cyberbullying*.

Li, C., Park, J., Kim, H., & Chrysostomou, D. (2021). *How can I help you? An Intelligent Virtual Assistant for Industrial Robots* Companion of the 2021 ACM/IEEE International Conference on Human-Robot Interaction, http://dx.doi.org/DOI: 10.1145/3434074.3447163

Lochmiller, C. R. (2021). Conducting thematic analysis with qualitative data. *The Qualitative Report, 26*(6), 2029–2044.

Martin, S., Siciliani, L., & Smith, P. (2020). Socioeconomic inequalities in waiting times for primary care across ten OECD countries. *Social Science & Medicine, 263*, 113230. DOI: 10.1016/j.socscimed.2020.113230 PMID: 32823046

Martinez-Hernandez, U., Boorman, L. W., & Prescott, T. J. (2015). *Telepresence: Immersion with the iCub Humanoid Robot and the Oculus Rift*. Springer International Publishing., DOI: 10.1007/978-3-319-22979-9_46

Mihdawi, M., Al-Amer, R., Darwish, R., Randall, S., & Afaneh, T. (2020). The influence of nursing work environment on patient safety. *Workplace Health & Safety, 68*(8), 384–390. DOI: 10.1177/2165079920901533 PMID: 32193998

Naseer, F., Khan, M. N., & Altalbe, A. (2023). Intelligent Time Delay Control of Telepresence Robots Using Novel Deep Reinforcement Learning Algorithm to Interact with Patients. *Applied Sciences (Basel, Switzerland), 13*(4), 2462. DOI: 10.3390/app13042462

Naseer, F., Khan, M. N., Rasool, A., & Ayub, N. (2023). A novel approach to compensate delay in communication by predicting teleoperator behaviour using deep learning and reinforcement learning to control telepresence robot. https://doi.org/DOI: 10.1049/ell2.12806

Pencarelli, T. (2020). The digital revolution in the travel and tourism industry. *Information Technology & Tourism, 22*(3), 455–476. DOI: 10.1007/s40558-019-00160-3

Pentina, I., Xie, T., Hancock, T., & Bailey, A. (2023). Consumer–machine relationships in the age of artificial intelligence: Systematic literature review and research directions. *Psychology and Marketing, 40*(8), 1593–1614. DOI: 10.1002/mar.21853

Quaye, A. A., Coyne, I., Söderbäck, M., & Hallström, I. K. (2019). Children's active participation in decision-making processes during hospitalisation: An observational study. *Journal of Clinical Nursing, 28*(23-24), 4525–4537. DOI: 10.1111/jocn.15042 PMID: 31430412

Ranganathan, C. S., Sethuraman, D., & Manivasagam, M. A., K, S., Yuvaraj, T., & Rajmohan, M. (2024, 2024/10/24). *IoT-Driven Telepresence Robots for Telemedicine using AI for Improved Patient Interaction* 2024 First International Conference on Innovations in Communications, Electrical and Computer Engineering (ICICEC), http://dx.doi.org/DOI: 10.1109/ICICEC62498.2024.10808988

Rieger, A., Lockl, J., Urbach, N., Guggenmos, F., & Fridgen, G. (2019). Building a blockchain application that complies with the EU general data protection regulation. *MIS Quarterly Executive*, *18*(4), 263–279. DOI: 10.17705/2msqe.00020

Sukarni, S., & Rokhayati, T. (2023). Pre-service English Teachers' Pedagogical Competence, Challenges and Strategies to Facilitate Learning. *Journal of English Education and Teaching*, *7*(2), 162–182.

Tang, C., Wang, Z., Sima, X., & Zhang, L. (2020, October). Research on artificial intelligence algorithm and its application in games. In 2020 2nd International Conference on Artificial Intelligence and Advanced Manufacture (AIAM) (pp. 386-389). IEEE.

Taschereau-Dumouchel, V., Michel, M., Lau, H., Hofmann, S. G., & LeDoux, J. E. (2022). Putting the "mental" back in "mental disorders": A perspective from research on fear and anxiety. *Molecular Psychiatry*, *27*(3), 1322–1330.

Torres Vega, M., Liaskos, C., Abadal, S., Papapetrou, E., Jain, A., Mouhouche, B., Kalem, G., Ergüt, S., Mach, M., Sabol, T., Cabellos-Aparicio, A., Grimm, C., De Turck, F., & Famaey, J. (2020). Immersive interconnected virtual and augmented reality: A 5G and IoT perspective. *Journal of Network and Systems Management*, *28*(4), 796–826. DOI: 10.1007/s10922-020-09545-w

Valencia, P. A. A., Gaytán-Lugo, L. S., & Salazar, M. E. E. (2023). Activity Design for Students With Visual Disabilities Through an Auditive Notification and Voice Response Interface. In *Handbook of Research on Innovative Frameworks and Inclusive Models for Online Learning* (pp. 215–237). IGI Global. DOI: 10.4018/978-1-6684-9072-3.ch011

Valero, C. I., Gil, A. M. M., Gonzalez-Usach, R., Julian, M., Fico, G., Arredondo, M. T., Stavropoulos, T. G., Strantsalis, D., Voulgaridis, A., Roca, F., Jara, A. J., Serrano, M., Zappa, A., Khan, Y., Guillen, S., Sala, P., Belsa, A., Votis, K., & Palau, C. E. (2021). AIoTES: Setting the principles for semantic interoperable and modern IoT-enabled reference architecture for Active and Healthy Ageing ecosystems. *Computer Communications*, *177*, 96–111. DOI: 10.1016/j.comcom.2021.06.010

Vasylkiv, Y., Ma, Z., Li, G., Sandry, E., Brock, H., Nakamura, K., Pourang, I., & Gomez, R. (2021). Automating Behavior Selection for Affective Telepresence Robot 2021 IEEE International Conference on Robotics and Automation (ICRA), http://dx.doi.org/DOI: 10.1109/ICRA48506.2021.9560755

Vishwakarma, V. K. (2023). A Review Of Non-Verbal Communication And Cultural Implications. *Journal of Namibian Studies: History Politics Culture*, *34*, 1741–1754.

Chapter 6
Security, Privacy, and Trust of AI-IoT Convergent Smart System

Taye Iyinoluwa Adeyinka
https://orcid.org/0009-0006-4357-6319
University of Science and Technology, Beijing, China

Kehinde Iyioluwa Adeyinka
https://orcid.org/0009-0009-7685-6693
University of Science and Technology, Beijing, China

Ayoade Abolade Emmanuel
https://orcid.org/0009-0007-9846-0927
Harbin Institute of Technology, Shenzhen, China

ABSTRACT

Combining AI with IoT transforms conventional systems into highly adaptive, data-driven, and networked intelligent ecosystems. In fact, most of the modernization drives carried out in smart cities, healthcare, manufacturing, and environmental monitoring industries are based on these very AI-IoT systems. AI-IoT integration will hit the future of technology-driven settings pretty fast through improved user experience, efficient management of resources, and real-time decision-making. This chapter covers all security, privacy, and other issues of trust that develop from the convergence of AI with IoT. It provides detailed insights into recent trends and events in privacy-enhancing technologies, such as differential privacy and federated learning. Secure protocol development and trust management schemes cannot be neglected in a trusted AI-IoT ecosystem. .he theoretical and applied approaches, hence opening up ways to some robust and reliable intelligent ecosystems that shall adapt to evolving security and privacy challenges.

DOI: 10.4018/979-8-3693-8332-2.ch006

1. INTRODUCTION

The convergence of AI with IoT is revolutionizing modern technologies. It enables the implementation of intelligent and networked ecosystems, with broad applications ranging from industrial automation and environment monitoring to healthcare and smart cities. With the help of this AI-IoT integration, the huge sensor networks of the Internet of Things can gather enormous volumes of data, which AI algorithms may then evaluate to produce insights and support real-time decision-making. As these systems spread, they provide previously unheard-of chances for automation and efficiency in various industries, greatly improving the calibre and personalization of services. On the other hand, despite all these benefits of AI-IoT ecosystems, several important disadvantages are brought into wide usage, especially in security, privacy, and trust.

AI-IoT system security is complex and multi-dimensional. Since IoT devices are interconnected, even a single device's smallest weakness can potentially compromise an entire network, exposing important information and functions to bad actors. Cyber threats such as device spoofing, data manipulation, and Distributed Denial of Service (DDoS) assaults pose serious hazards and potentially seriously compromise user privacy and system integrity (Khatun et al., 2023). According to Lu et al. (2023), the Mirai botnet attack is a well-known example of how hijacked IoT devices could be used to overwhelm network infrastructure and cause widespread service outages. This incident shows the need for better security protocols in the AI-IoT ecosystem. These should involve multilayer strategies comprising encryption, secure boot mechanisms, and intrusion detection systems capable of immediately recognizing and eliminating the threat (Schmidt, Biessmann, & Teubner, 2020). Additionally, by providing decentralized, tamper-resistant data management frameworks that improve authentication and data integrity across devices, blockchain technology has emerged as a promising way to enhance AI-IoT security (Commey et al., 2024).

Also, one of the most pressing concerns over AI-IoT systems is the issue of privacy. They are deploying IoT devices in private, mostly houses, cars, and personal wearables-results in the continuous gathering of data. There are serious concerns over data ownership and privacy because this data frequently contains extremely sensitive information about users' routines, habits, and health (Mohanta et al., 2020). These problems are made worse by the incorporation of AI into these systems, which enables the analysis and deduction of extremely private information that users might not even be aware is being taken. For example, data concerning mobility patterns, device usage, and energy consumption can provide personal details about a person's daily routine in smart home settings, raising worries about privacy violations and surveillance (Saied et al., 2013). Privacy-preserving strategies like differential privacy and federated learning are increasingly being used to mitigate these dangers. For instance, federated learning enables training AI models across distributed devices without raw data centralization, protecting users' privacy while model optimization is still enabled (Baniecki & Biecek, 2024). Meanwhile, adding differential privacy into a dataset by inserting controlled noise complicates drawing any inferences about individual data points, given that it balances the requirements of performing an accurate analysis with preserving user privacy. By showing that technical innovation can align with ethical data practices, these strategies are essential for building trust in AI-IoT systems.

Trust is one of the difficult things to protect, but it forms the core tenet for the uptake and acceptability of AI-IoT ecosystems. Besides their data protection, users have to be secured in the fairness and transparency of the operation of such systems. Prejudice, justice, and accountability concerns arise when consumers of these AI-IoT systems find it difficult to comprehend the inner decision-making workings of many AI algorithms because of their intricacy and opacity. Explainable AI, which allows users to see and understand how AI models come up with their findings, has emerged as one of the major strategies for solving these trust challenges. AI's "black-box" character is lessened by increasing transparency, which promotes consumer trust and acceptance of AI-powered IoT systems (Schmidt, Biessmann, & Teubner, 2020). Furthermore, by enforcing stringent data protection and privacy rules, regulatory standards like the California Consumer Privacy Act (CCPA) and the General Data Protection Regulation (GDPR) are essential in building confidence.

In addition to guaranteeing AI-IoT systems' legal accountability, adherence to these rules gives users peace of mind that their data will be managed sensibly and morally. These are security, privacy, and trust issues that, in AI-IoT ecosystems, can be solved through technological and legal solutions. From a technological perspective, hardening the AI-IoT setup against potential risks involves implementing robust encryption protocols, secure hardware, and anomaly detection systems. Further layers of security from blockchain and decentralized architectures provide secure frameworks for access control and data storage, two key components in maintaining system integrity (Jagatheesaperumal et al., 2022).

From a legislative standpoint, adherence to frameworks like the CCPA and GDPR guarantees that AI-IoT implementations meet strict data protection standards, boosting user confidence and laying the groundwork for ethical data management procedures. By supporting procedures that protect user data and uphold individual privacy, these frameworks highlight the significance of ethical issues in implementing AI-IoT systems. While it is true that greater integration of the AI mentioned above and IoT technologies will bring tremendous opportunities for technological and societal improvements, most of their systems are impossible to use if the complex problems of security, privacy, and trust that come with them are not resolved. The chapter delves deep into those concerns and examines the latest tactics and technological advancements for creating secure, private, and open AI-IoT ecosystems. We can develop robust AI-IoT systems while preserving users' confidence and protecting sensitive data by embedding state-of-the-art security with privacy-preserving strategies and open AI practices. The further development of the research and legislative undertakings finally guarantees whether AI-IoT ecosystems will evolve safely and with morality to provide an unlocked path to intelligent network surroundings for a better life rather than a threat to life. This introduction still includes citation placeholders. To finish this section, swap them out for real references from your most recent research sources.

1.1 Literature Review

Integrating AI with IoT encourages establishing highly flexible and networked systems in several application fields, such as healthcare, industrial automation, and smart cities. Therefore, this integration of AI with IoT uses the wide sensor networks of IoT for real-time data gathering, analyzes it using AI, and makes informed decisions to smoothen processes. AI-IoT ecosystems offer previously unheard-of possibilities for automation and efficiency as they proliferate. Still, they also pose serious problems in security, privacy, and trust domains critical to the long-term uptake and operation of these systems (Syed et al., 2022).

Security would be one of the key concerns for AI-IoT systems. Lacking the processing power to maintain high-intensity security, IoT devices are hugely vulnerable to several cyberattacks. Because of the interlinked nature of the IoT, any general weakness within just one of these devices will compromise the network. Only a few cyber threats stressing the urgent need for multi-layer security include data injection, device spoofing, and DDoS attacks. The Mirai botnet outbreak, in particular, highlighted how hijacked IoT devices may launch widespread DDoS attacks, causing serious network outages (Hassan et al., n.d.). Multi-layered security measures, such as secure boot procedures, end-to-end encryption, and intrusion detection systems with real-time monitoring capabilities, are the focus of current research. By decentralizing data management and creating a tamper-proof authentication and access control framework, blockchain technology has also emerged as a viable strategy to improve security in AI-IoT ecosystems (Ruzbahani, 2024).

Another critical issue with AI-IoT systems is privacy: Most IoT devices work in a private domain and generate user preference, behavioral, and health information data. Advanced data analysis enabled by the integration of AI into such systems allows for complex inferences that may infringe on user privacy. Information, with the IoT devices deployed in smart homes or health applications, could reveal personal patterns or habits, and studies have found that AI might also deduce from such 'innocent' pieces of data information that seriously compromises privacy, as Blind, Niebel, and Rammer (2024) pointed out. Due to these concerns, there has been an upsurge in the popularity of privacy-preserving technologies such as differential privacy and federated learning. Federated learning minimizes privacy risks by training AI models across distributed devices while keeping the raw data decentralized. This approach has proved eminently successful in high data sensitivity, such as healthcare applications, as (Ni et al., 2022). In industries that demand privacy, like smart cities and industrial applications, differential privacy—which adds statistical noise to datasets—is a workable solution for AI-IoT systems because it guarantees the confidentiality of individual data points while enabling meaningful (Jiang et al., 2021). Equally important are the trusting relationships with these systems in many "black-box" varieties of AI algorithms.

Transparency and the guarantee that AI-driven decisions are just, moral, and comprehensible are essential for fostering trust in these systems. According to studies, one of the main things that erode user confidence in IoT-enabled systems is a lack of transparency in AI decision-making processes, especially in settings where these systems must make important decisions on their own (Bahutair & Bouguettaya, 2023). A solution for this is explainable artificial intelligence (XAI). By enabling the user to comprehend how the AI models arrive at their conclusions, XAI helps gain trust in algorithms by explaining the decision-making process.

In this respect, Davies and Torres argue, very importantly, that XAI reduces the "black-box" nature of AI. This is achieved because algorithmic reasoning is unlocked for consumers, enhancing the overall viability of AI-IoT systems. To align dependable AI-IoT systems with user expectations and legal constraints, trust frameworks require accountability and transparency processes in place (Syed et al., 2022). The solution to these issues of security, privacy, and trust engendered by the intersection of AI and IoT has to be done through regulatory frameworks. These have been done through legislation like the CCPA in the US and the GDPR in the EU. These legislations give data privacy and protection standards, requiring open and honest data collection and processing methods.

In addition to boosting user confidence, adherence to these rules makes businesses responsible for putting strong data security safeguards in place. According to research, following regulations is essential for AI-IoT systems to function morally since it synchronizes the use of technology with societal norms and values. While many opportunities for improvement exist along with the integration of AI and IoT, especially from the perspectives of automation, efficiency, and customized services, it also demands effective solutions regarding security, privacy, and trust issues. It has been shown in the literature that explainable AI frameworks, improved security measures, and strategies for preserving privacy are crucial for fostering user confidence and ensuring regulatory compliance. For AI-IoT ecosystems to achieve scalability and adaptability sustainably, continuous research and technical and legislative developments are necessary to ensure these systems enhance security, privacy, and trust among users and do not destroy them.

1.2 Security Frameworks for AI-IoT Ecosystems

The intersection of AI and IoT devices creates complex, interrelated networks with unique security challenges. Unlike traditional, stand-alone systems, AI-IoT ecosystems comprise diverse devices constantly communicating, sharing data, and making independent decisions. Independent devices exhibit a range of computational powers and security features. This highly distributed environment with real-time insight and automation greatly increases the attack surface, thus making emerging systems vulnerable to various cyber threats. Consequently, a multi-layered security framework with multiple protocols and technologies focused on different spheres of AI-IoT security appeals most to researchers and practitioners. To combat these vulnerabilities, multiprotocol frameworks have to be laid down so that many layers of security can be implemented.

1. **Multiple Layers of Security Protocols:** Safe boot protocols, encryption, network monitoring, and real-time IDS form the multitier approach on which most AI-IoT security frameworks depend. Each procedure forms a cohesive defense plan addressing internal and external threats. For example, **secure boot protocols** minimize the immediate risk of malicious code execution by ensuring IoT devices load only trusted software upon booting. This mechanism is one of the essential ways to secure the environment in IoT; it boots checks for firmware authenticity and prevents unauthorized programs from taking control. Another critical attribute of the security framework for AI-IoT systems will be **''end-to-end encryption''**. There is sensitive transfer data regarding finance, health, or personal information between IoT devices and AI algorithms. If it remains exposed, then such data might get intercepted. It is encrypted so that, until it reaches its destination, it is impossible to read it unauthorizedly. This makes for a security layer that prevents hackers from easily sniffing or tampering with data across the network, becoming more vital regarding data protection over public networks. AI-driven **''Intrusion Detection Systems (IDS)''** further fortify the security framework by monitoring the network for traffic patterns and anomalies that indicate a breach in security. By analyzing network behaviour, AI-driven IDS can detect unusual patterns such as sudden spikes in data transmission or repeated attempts to access unknown IP addresses within a very short period and take action to nullify such detected threats. AI in IDS automatically enables the system to learn from previous events and adapt its detection strategies continuously to keep up with the shifting threat landscapes.
2. **Blockchain for Enhanced Security and Trust:** Blockchain technology has recently garnered significant interest in enhancing security in AI-IoT networks. Due to its immutable ledger and decentralized architecture, it is the right environment for tamper-proof data storage, especially in networks with multiple linked devices. Each transaction or update in data on the blockchain is put into a block, which is cryptographically linked to its predecessor, thus creating an immutable chain of records influencing the succeeding blocks. This architecture prevents unauthorized modification of data and hence helps ensure data integrity in industries such as healthcare, where the correctness of data is so critical to patient safety. The decentralized blockchain architecture significantly reduces bottlenecks and single points of failure by dispensing with a central authority to validate devices. DAAC frameworks use blockchains for privilege management in access, user authentication across

the network, and verification of device IDs. For instance, it could be applied in smart cities to authenticate IoT devices for public infrastructures, such as traffic lights, sensors, and cameras, ensuring connectivity within the network only with authorized devices. Besides security, blockchain's public and auditable records instill confidence in AI-IoT systems. Stakeholders can be certain of record access and verification of the data exchange history, thus enhancing accountability and increasing trust in AI-IoT systems. For example, to demonstrate how transparency within blockchain enables trusted data exchanges across various applications, supply chain networks have utilized blockchain in tracking product origins, determining the legitimacy of transactions, and halting counterfeiting activities.

3. **Predictive Threat Analysis and Anomaly Detection:** Anomaly detection forms the backbone of security frameworks in AI-IoT systems, given that IoT environments are always dynamic and constantly evolving. AI-powered anomaly detection systems analyze vast data from IoT devices to create a "normal" network behaviour baseline. The behaviour is tagged as potentially harmful when it acts contrary to this baseline, such as when there is an unexpected spike in data flow or when a device attempts to access something without proper authorization. This capability enables proactive threat identification whereby the system can react before the breach worsens. Predictive Threat Analysis accomplishes more in identifying these anomalies by performing machine learning algorithms on past data to predict likely new patterns and future threats. For example, AI systems identify pattern associations with known attack vectors, such as DDoS attacks, and can alert administrators of the probability of future exploits. Predictive analysis deployed in these AI-IoT security frameworks makes them proactive and reactive by changing their defenses in the face of newly emerging threat patterns and insights from past security incidents.
4. **AI-IoT Security Using Zero Trust Architecture ZTA:** Traditional security models rest on trust within the network paradigm, whereby users or devices might be granted access to network resources after they have been authenticated. However, because AI-IoT systems are highly distributed and decentralized, this approach alone cannot work since attacks can come from inside and outside the network. Working on the "never trust, always verify" principle, ''Zero Trust Architecture (ZTA)'' overcomes the constraint by requiring all users, devices, and data requests within the AI-IoT ecosystem to undergo authentication, authorization, and ongoing validation. With ZTA, every time a user or device needs to retrieve a resource, they must undergo rigorous authorization and authentication. That helps block threats from spreading laterally because the system will quickly quarantine any device that has been compromised in the network. This continuous verification process of ZTA works perfectly for AI-IoT setups since there is considerable interconnection among the various devices, potentially generating hosts of vulnerabilities that attackers may use. Moreover, AI-driven anomaly detection and ZTA can establish a dynamic security system that continuously evaluates access privileges based on real-time risk analysis, further enhancing operational efficiency and security.
5. **Edge Computing for Improved Security and Localized Data Processing:** In the context of AI-IoT systems, edge computing has emerged as a necessary component of security frameworks. Since it reduces the amount of sensitive data that needs to be transferred over networks, moving data processing "at the edge" closer to its source of generation minimizes exposure to cyber threats. Edge computing diminishes many risks related to the centralized collection of data. It supports privacy in AI-IoT systems by allowing devices to conduct local data processing and analysis. Applications such as driverless cars or medical monitoring systems, which depend on minimum latency and data sensitivity, all benefit from this localized approach. For instance, AI in autonomous vehicles may

process sensor data at the edge to make instantaneous decisions about navigation without having to send it back to distant servers, introducing latency and compromising vital functions. Further, edge computing in AI-IoT contexts builds user trust and security by reducing the amount of data transferred over public networks, thereby supporting privacy-preserving models. Security frameworks for AI-IoT ecosystems need to be multi-layered, flexible, and handle a variety of threats at different levels in networked environments. Some strategies that constitute a concrete security framework of AI-IoT include secure boot methods, encryption, AI-driven anomaly detection, blockchain for data integrity, and Zero Trust Architecture. Each one of these strategies solves a particular vulnerability. Moreover, edge computing provides the capability for localized data processing, thus enabling better performance and security for the system. The aim is to develop integrated security measures for building resilient AI-IoT systems against new threats, ensuring user privacy and stakeholder confidence. In developing and enhancing these security frameworks, secure and reliable digital atmospheres will be ensured by expanding AI-IoT ecosystems across industries.

2. PRIVACY-PRESERVING TECHNIQUES IN AI-IOT SYSTEMS

2.1 Subhead 2

With a growing convergence, IoT and AI are networked systems that continuously collect, process and analyze information. The information alone is mostly sensitive and personal; hence, special privacy concerns arise regarding its deployment in healthcare, smart homes, and urban settings, which might reveal specific details related to users' behaviour and preferences and even health problems. These AI-IoT systems enhance the development of privacy-preserving approaches that focus on minimizing data leakage, improving data security, and ensuring users' trust. Generally, all these approaches- federated learning, differential privacy, anonymization of data, and edge computing- deal specifically with unique privacy issues arising from the AI-IoT system.

2.1.1 Federated Learning for Decentralized Privacy

Another indispensable AI-IoT technique concerning privacy preservation is federated learning. This predisposes sensitive information to interception or unauthorized access, while a central server trains classical AI models with data combined from several devices. In essence, federated learning offers an alternative: this allows training AI models directly on the devices themselves, sharing only model updates rather than raw data with a central server. Because this distributed approach minimizes data transmission over networks, it eliminates possibilities for violation of privacy and keeps sensitive information confined to each device. For example, Federated learning enables AI algorithms to learn from data accumulated across various sites without necessarily moving patient data into hospital systems. All the hospital's local model updates are collected by a central server and summarized into one common AI model, all without compromising patient privacy. This approach will also help in the applications of smart cities since the local analytics data from many IoT sensors, such as environmental and traffic sensors, can be performed to optimize the urban infrastructure without centralizing sensitive data. Federated learning enhances privacy by enabling **collaborative model improvement** without sharing data. Such federated learning may be applied to improve energy management algorithms in a smart home device network learned from data from multiple homes without centralizing personal information. Hence, this approach provides a good balance between the need for accurate AI models on one side and stringent privacy protection measures on the other, making it suitable for widespread adoption in AI-IoT systems.

2.1.2 Differential Privacy for Secure Data Analytics

Differential privacy adds noise to datasets before any analytics, making extracting or identifying a particular data point much more difficult. Hence, differential privacy enables insights from aggregated data in AI-IoT systems without compromising individual data privacy. Because personal data points become masked by the added noise, researchers can visualize general trends without risking individual disclosure. This technique is particularly useful when data from many persons gets combined, such as in the case of public health monitoring, since differential privacy can keep the information private and, at the same time, provide insightful information on health patterns.

For example, differential privacy can be applied to data analytics from public IoT sensors monitoring air quality or foot traffic in a smart city. Differential privacy allows urban planners to examine trends for infrastructure upgrades, while statistical noise protects individual data, such as location habits or interactions with personal devices. Differential privacy in healthcare means one can conduct analyses of patients' data for medical research without disclosing any individual patient record an especially critical concern when studies rest on very large, sensitive data sets. In addition, differential privacy assures conformance with data protection policies such as the GDPR, which requires businesses to ensure individual privacy in the ocean of vast volumes of data processed. In this regard, AI-IoT systems arrive with a difference in privacy to meet these legal expectations. This instils more confidence among users and minimizes the risk of regulatory breaches.

2.1.3 Data Minimization and Anonymization

Data minimization and anonymization are two basic privacy preservation strategies based on the limitation of the amount and identifiability of data collected and stored, thus decreasing the exposure risk. ''Data anonymization'' is a process of removal of PII from datasets in such a way that the latter cannot be linked to specific users. By nature, data can be anonymized within an AI-IoT system when collected from a private or public space device, such as smart home appliances or public security cameras. For example, anonymized data from IoT-enabled traffic sensors can prevent identifying specific vehicles but still provide useful information on traffic congestion and flow.

In contrast, ''data minimization'' minimizes the footprint by collecting only what a certain function requires. For instance, smart thermostat applications may only need to log temperature settings and patterns of occupancy; any other information would be considered redundant because such specific details about personal habits may be revealed. The AI-IoT system minimizes by confining the types of data gathered and ensuring that only important information is processed and stored. In applications like smart cities or smart healthcare, where a large amount of data is generated each day, anonymization minimization strengthens privacy protection further. The approaches above decrease potential risks and build trust by protecting users and making managing and storing data easier.

2.1.4 Localized Data Processing Using Edge Computing

With edge computing, a strong privacy-preserving technique, data processing is done closer to the generation point, "at the edge"-of the network, as opposed to in centralized decentralized proximity, which reduces the need to transfer data across networks, providing a smaller attack surface for cybercriminals. In this respect, edge computing plays an important role in AI-IoT applications: many are those applications where generated data is private or sensitive, such as in surveillance cameras or health monitoring applications. In addition, this allows complete avoidance of the need to centralize data in some cases.

One example is wearable technologies within the healthcare industry for continual vital sign monitoring: onboard processing of the collected data is performed, and only the information required will be transmitted to a central server. This approach further enhances privacy, as only processed data and not raw health measures are sent. Similarly, in the case of autonomous vehicles, edge computing allows real-time analysis of sensor data for the car to make immediate navigational decisions without consulting distant servers. Therefore, edge computing also acts as an enabler for several privacy-aware AI-IoT applications by reducing data exposure and enhancing the privacy and efficiency of the systems. It also reduces latency caused by edge computing, enhancing response times and data processing for real-time applications. This is helpful in applications where latency and data security become critical, such as industrial automation or emergency response systems. Edge computing improves functionality for AI-IoT systems while supporting privacy goals by eliminating the need for real-time processing without constant data in transit.

2.1.5 Secure Computation via Homomorphic Encryption

Homomorphic encryption is an advanced form of privacy-preserving that allows for computations over encrypted content without decryption. The feature is very helpful for AI-IoT systems requiring sensitive data to be analyzed while analyzing this sensitive information throughout processing. Since the data will remain encrypted, homomorphic encryption protects user privacy even when interceptions occur during analysis, enabling AI models to access data securely.

For instance, homomorphic encryption enables an algorithm to work on encrypted patient data in a healthcare system where the patient's data is analyzed for analysis or treatment and provides insights without the actual raw data being exposed. Similarly, homomorphic encryption can protect transaction data in financial services while allowing fraud detection and risk assessment to do their jobs with assurance of the integrity and privacy of the data. Homomorphic encryption, though still computationally intensive, has shown promise in situations where data security is of prime importance.

Homomorphic encryption can be extremely useful in sectors dealing with highly sensitive information, such as defense, finance, and critical infrastructure protection, where the consequences of data breaches could prove catastrophic. Homomorphic encryption enhances privacy by enabling secure computation, allowing AI-IoT systems to provide accurate data-driven insights. Therefore, AI-IoT systems should consider approaches that can provide confidence to users by preserving their privacy and ensuring legislation around data protection. Federated learning, differential privacy, anonymization, edge computing, and homomorphic encryption deal with various dimensions of privacy-related issues in AI-IoT ecosystems. While anonymization is minimized to print data, hence the risk of identification, in federated learning and differential privacy, the exposure is reduced by keeping the sensitive data localized and localized during analysis. Edge computing further enhances this privacy by enabling localized homomorphic encryption, which provides a secure method of performing computation on encrypted data in a reliable manner.

These will be critical in developing and deploying methods for systems that ensure users' privacy protection and moral data conduct as AI-IoT technologies continue to become prevalent. Baking such techniques into the core of AI-IOT systems allows companies to protect sensitive information, ensure compliance with relevant laws and regulations, and foster user trust in a safe and private online world.

2.2 Trust Management in AI-IoT Environments

Given the plethora of applications in which IoT environments are a must-from healthcare and industrial automation to smart cities, integrating IoT devices' data-collecting capabilities with AI's autonomous processing capability is critical. Trust management is important for any such AI-IoT ecosystem to succeed because it directly impacts the dependability, security, and acceptability of these systems. These contexts are widely formed based on sensitive information, and decisions are made that affect safety, privacy, and the well-being of users. For this reason, they require an amount of trust. The following section discusses trust management in AI-IoT systems by reviewing challenges, approaches, and new technologies for establishing and maintaining trust.

2.2.1 AI-IoT Systems and the Concept of Trust

Trust in AI-IoT contexts denotes the belief instilled among users, devices, and systems in general in the network. In general, trust involves several elements, such as the dependability of gadgets, correctness and integrity of data, consistency of services rendered by AI algorithms, and perceived morality and openness of the system. With the increasing number of connected devices, multiple device manufacturers, and decentralized data processing, trust is even more difficult in AI-IoT systems. Users need to extend trust in these systems regarding security, ethical data handling, objectivity and explicability of AI judgments.

2.2.2 Challenges in Trust Management

Since AI-IoT systems are distributed and dynamic, establishing and maintaining trust raises some unique challenges, which include the following:

Scalability: When an AI-IoT ecosystem consists of thousands of connected devices, conventional trust management systems become impracticable. Scalable trust frameworks that can adapt to a large number of devices without compromising dependability become imperative in such cases (Hameed et al., 2021).

Diversity of Devices and Scarcity of Resources: Low memory and low processing power are frequent; hence, deploying complex trust mechanisms on each IoT device is quite challenging. The diversity of devices further aggravates the task of uniformly establishing common trust criteria across the network.

Dynamic Topology: IoT environments supported by AI are mainly dynamic, where devices can join, leave, or shift within the network. This dynamic nature calls for real-time changing and adapting trust (Bao & Chen, 2012).

Privacy and Security Requirements: Since most AI-IoT systems are applied in handling sensitive information or personal data, confidence must be maintained while guaranteeing privacy and security. Robust trust management methods are required because when data access by unauthorized parties or violation of privacy occurs, confidence in the technology is quickly destroyed (Humayun et al., 2024).

2.2.3 Techniques for Assessing AI-IoT System Trust

For systems to manage trust in AI-IoT contexts, they need to assess the trustworthiness of entities reliably. Three major techniques generally used for evaluating trust will be discussed as follows:

Direct Trust Evaluation: This depends upon the record of previous interactions between devices. The 'good' behaviour gradually develops trust, while any misbehavior or anomaly breaks it. This will work in a relatively stable environment and may not work for highly dynamic networks.
Indirect Trust Evaluation: Indirect trust evaluation, based on recommendation or trusted recommendation, allows devices to evaluate the trustworthiness of other entities based on suggestions from other devices. For instance, other trusted devices previously present in the system may initially influence the trust level of a new device when it enters the network of an AI-IoT.
Behavioral Analysis: With the integration of AI techniques in trust management, these frameworks more often now use behavioral analysis, whereby machine learning algorithms go through device behaviour patterns to detect some sort of anomaly or deviation. In case a device reveals certain peculiar behaviour, for instance, inconsistent data transmission patterns or repeated authentication failures, the system can readily reconsider its previously assigned trust score and take necessary remedial measures (Huber & Kandah, 2020).

2.2.4 Trust Management Frameworks in AI-IoT Systems

Blockchain technology records the result of every device interaction on an immutable ledger, which provides an unbiased framework for managing trust in AI-IoT systems. With the decentralized nature of this technology, central authority is needed- it allows all network users to verify any device's credibility. Research has shown that blockchain might help improve IoT trust management by enhancing data integrity, transparency, and accountability. For instance, in some healthcare applications, blockchain would offer tamper-resistant records of device interactions, which are critical to maintaining patient privacy and ensuring the accuracy of patient data.

Reputation-Based Trust Management: Reputation systems compute device reputation scores by fusing feedback from different network entities. These scores influence the confidence bestowed upon each device in further exchanges. IoT sensors whose continuous operations present positive feedback in a smart city application will thus have higher trust scores, reducing the complexity of coordination and data exchange.
Trust2Vec: is a machine learning-based framework that utilizes embedding techniques to map relationships and find trust clusters in large-scale AI-IoT networks. It will help manage trust attacks, such as the cooperation of hostile devices, by understanding and predicting trust connections based on the latent structure of network interactions (Dhelim et al., 2022).

Deep Trust: Deep Trust analyzes trustworthiness in real-time, leveraging deep learning algorithms. This, therefore, means that Deep Trust has been deploying dynamic modification of ratings of trust, changing from one to another in case of changes in device behaviour through neural networks. This further helped Deep Trust to achieve precision and flexibility in handling trust mechanisms within the AI-IoT system. According to Ullah et al. (2024), every device is suitably assessed without depending on previously collected data in situations characterized by high device churns, as will always be expected in industrial automation.

2.2.5 AI Techniques for Improvement of Trust

More and more AI approaches are used in trust management to improve the accuracy and resilience of trust assessment in AI-IoT systems. The following are some of the AI-powered techniques which could promise a great amount:

Anomaly Detection: Machine learning models can be implemented to detect outliers or anomalies. They would be trained to recognize normal behaviour patterns across an AI-IoT network. Any devices showing deviation from normal behaviour would be reported for further analysis, ensuring that any devices with possibly malicious intentions are identified with due timing.
Trust prediction models: AI-IoT networks can proactively address potential trust issues using historical interaction data to analyze algorithms that predict trustworthiness based on past behavioral patterns. Predictive models of a smart home system, for example, can determine devices with frequent security issues and thus help the network predict and mitigate risks based on such information.
XAI for Trust: Explainable AI The "black-box" nature of many AI algorithms, impenetrable by human understanding or validation of the decision-making process, is often a cause of undermining trust. XAI can give AI models interpretability to make sense of the reasoning behind the trust choices that devices and users have. Particularly in sensitive domains like healthcare, XAI helps bridge AI-IoT systems with user expectations and enhances trust management by providing transparency (Ullah et al., 2024).

Trust management is a crucial foundation needed to ensure that devices, data, and services operate dependably and morally correctly; thus, it's essential for the safe and efficient running of AI-IOT systems. Blockchain, AI algorithms, and sophisticated reputation frameworks are some of the ways to address special scalability and device variety problems in security for AI-IoT environments. Context-aware models and adaptive trust mechanisms are novel approaches promising for developing robust AI-IoT ecosystems. It is important to develop standardized protocols and improve techniques related to AI-driven trust assessment for further growth in this area of study and to establish dependable and trustworthy AI-IoT environments across different industries

2.3 Regulatory and Ethical Implications of AI-IoT Systems

Implementing AI-IoT (Artificial Intelligence-Internet of Things) systems has important ethical and regulatory ramifications. These systems are based on networked devices that gather, process and act upon enormous volumes of data, frequently sensitive or personal data. The ethical and legal considerations about AI-IoT systems are becoming more and more significant as their applications spread throughout vital industries, including healthcare, transportation, and smart cities. To guarantee that AI-IoT systems align with legal requirements and societal norms, this part examines the main regulatory obstacles, privacy issues, ethical issues, and future perspectives.

1. **Regulations for Data Protection and Privacy:** Adhering to data protection laws intended to protect user privacy is one of the most important regulatory concerns for AI-IoT systems. Strict data collection, processing, and storage guidelines are enforced by the General Data Protection Regulation (GDPR) in places like the European Union. According to GDPR, people have the right to view, update, and remove their data, and it must only be gathered with their express consent and used transparently (Hoofnagle, Van Der Sloot, & Borgesius, 2019). The California Consumer Privacy Act (CCPA) grants similar rights in the US, which mandates that businesses reveal their data practices and allow consumers to opt out of data sharing. Complying with these laws presents special difficulties for AI-IoT systems, which frequently process personal data gathered from sensors in real-time. It is crucial to guarantee the security of personal data both during processing and transfer. For example, the GDPR and health-specific laws, such as the Health Insurance Portability and Accountability Act (HIPAA) in the United States, apply to IoT devices that gather patient data. Public trust can be damaged, and heavy fines can be imposed for breaking such rules. Developers and organizations must include privacy-by-design principles in AI-IoT systems to comply with these standards, ensuring that data protection measures are a fundamental component of the system architecture (Solove & Schwartz, 2020).
2. **Ownership and Control of Data:** Data ownership and control are pivotal regulatory and ethical concerns in AI-IoT ecosystems. IoT devices continuously generate data, often without explicit user awareness or consent, raising questions about who ultimately owns the data and who has the right to access or monetize it. For example, in smart city applications, IoT sensors monitor traffic, pollution, and energy usage, generating data that could be valuable to various stakeholders, including city authorities, businesses, and even residents. However, without clear regulatory guidance, disputes may arise regarding data access, usage rights, and revenue-sharing arrangements (Miranda et al., 2015) Ethically, AI-IoT systems should respect user autonomy by granting individuals control over their data. This may involve offering users choices about which data to share, who can access it, and for what purpose. Some regulatory regimes are beginning to address these challenges. For instance, GDPR's data portability mandate allows individuals to move their data from one service provider to another, boosting competition while giving users greater control over their digital information. As AI-IoT applications proliferate, more legal frameworks will be necessary to clarify data ownership and control to safeguard user rights and promote transparency.
3. **Security Requirements and Liability:** Given AI-IoT systems' complexity and interconnected nature, security is both a statutory need and an ethical imperative. AI-IoT systems are particularly susceptible to cyberattacks, including data breaches, device hijacking, and Distributed Denial of Service (DDoS) attacks. In healthcare, for example, illegal access to IoT-enabled medical devices could offer life-threatening threats to patients, while in smart homes, privacy violations could undermine personal security. Although regulatory frameworks such as GDPR enforce strict data security rules, the dynamic nature of AI-IoT systems necessitates ongoing security evaluations and modifications (Sidana et al., 2025). Liability is another crucial issue with AI-IoT systems. It might be difficult to determine who is at fault in the event of a cyberattack or system failure—the end user, the creator

of the AI algorithm, or the device maker. Liability determination in these situations is difficult and frequently devoid of established legal precedents. Although a full legislative strategy has not yet been devised, certain governments are investigating frameworks to handle liability in AI and IoT. To reduce the danger of harm, developers and manufacturers are ethically obligated to create systems with strong security features, such as encryption, authentication, and ongoing monitoring.''

4. **The Ethical Consequences of Privacy Invasion and Surveillance:** Particularly in public areas where IoT sensors constantly gather data on people's actions, AI-IoT systems raise ethical questions about monitoring. For example, smart city initiatives frequently use traffic monitors, environmental sensors, and security cameras to improve urban planning and infrastructure. Although these apps offer insightful information, they also raise the risk of privacy invasion because people might not be aware that they are being watched or feel uneasy in places that are being watched. Even in public places, people should be aware of and provide their approval to data gathering methods, according to the ethical concept of informed consent. However, getting consent can be difficult because data gathering is so widespread and frequently passive in AI-IoT systems. To solve this, some proponents suggest putting ''Privacy by Design'' and ''Privacy by Default'' concepts into practice, whereby systems are made to collect as little data as possible, anonymize data, and secure data at every stage of its lifetime. Transparency in data processes is essential for preserving public trust in addition to informed consent. Users should know what information is gathered, how it is used, and who can access it. This enables people to make knowledgeable decisions about their interactions with AI-IoT systems, consistent with the ethical idea of autonomy. Additionally, transparency reduces the possibility of misusing surveillance data, for example, by restricting unwanted access or stopping data from being reused for unexpected purposes.
5. **Dealing with Fairness and Bias in AI-IoT Systems:** AI-IoT systems have a growing impact on decision-making processes in fields where biases in data or algorithms might result in unfair treatment, such as law enforcement, healthcare, and employment. For instance, it has been discovered that surveillance systems' facial recognition algorithms include gender and racial biases, which causes minority groups to be disproportionately targeted. AI systems trained on data from particular populations may not be able to correctly diagnose or treat members of under-represented groups in the healthcare industry. ''Fairness and Bias Mitigation'' must be given top priority by AI-IoT systems developers to overcome these ethical issues. This is part of using representative and varied datasets, routinely checking algorithms for biased trends, and integrating fairness indicators into the design process. As seen by the European Union's planned Artificial Intelligence Act, which requires that high-risk AI systems undergo bias testing and abide by fairness principles, regulatory authorities are also starting to demand bias assessments. According to Burton et al. (2017), ethical AI principles support inclusive designs that consider users' various demands and refrain from escalating social injustices.
6. **The Function of AI-IoT Systems and Human Autonomy:** Though they risk violating personal autonomy, AI-IoT systems have the potential to enhance human capacities. AI, for instance, makes judgements in real time in autonomous cars that may affect other drivers' and passengers' safety. Determining the proper degree of human oversight in these situations is crucial, particularly for choices with important ethical ramifications. Similarly, AI-enabled IoT gadgets in smart homes may make decisions on their own about security or energy use, which may unintentionally reduce user control over their surroundings. From an ethical perspective, AI-IoT systems should empower users rather than subjugate them, preserving their autonomy over their choices and actions. This necessitates

building systems with functionalities that let users comprehend AI reasoning, give feedback, and overturn AI conclusions. Increasingly, regulatory agencies support "human-in-the-loop" strategies, guaranteeing that people have a last word in situations with significant implications, especially where privacy or personal safety are at stake.

7. **Transparency and Accountability:** Trust in AI-IoT systems is based on accountability and openness. Users, developers, and regulators must understand the decision-making, data processing, and risk management mechanisms of these systems. Transparent AI-IoT systems can better uphold ethical standards by making their procedures more comprehensible to stakeholders. Due to the potentially dire repercussions of mistakes or biases, many AI-IoT applications, such as autonomous cars or healthcare diagnostics, demand a high degree of openness (Kossow, Windwehr, & Jenkins, 2022) Assessing AI-IoT systems' ethical and legal compliance requires accountability measures like auditing and impact evaluations. Regular audits guarantee that systems adhere to moral norms throughout time, while impact assessments can analyze the hazards related to AI-IoT applications. To stop abuse and preserve public confidence in AI-IoT technologies, regulatory frameworks such as the European Union's AI Act and other national data protection laws strongly emphasize accountability and transparency.

AI-IoT systems have wide-ranging and complex ethical and legislative ramifications, including privacy, data ownership, security, transparency, equity, and human autonomy. Developers, organizations, and policymakers must collaborate to establish frameworks that fully address these challenges as these systems become increasingly integrated into important aspects of daily life. Standards that will direct AI-IoT development are being established by laws like the GDPR and prospective legislation like the European Union's AI Act. This guarantees these systems respect individual rights and align with societal norms. To foster public trust and encourage moral behaviour throughout the ecosystem, AI-IoT systems in the future must incorporate privacy, justice, transparency, and accountability into their design.

3. RESEARCH OBJECTIVE

The main goal of this study is to investigate the fundamental issues and potential solutions related to security, privacy, and trust in AI-IoT (Artificial Intelligence-Internet of Things) convergent systems. The security of connected devices, the privacy of sensitive data, and the reliability of autonomous decision-making processes are some of the major issues raised by the ongoing growth of AI-IoT ecosystems in industries like healthcare, smart cities, industrial automation, and consumer environments. This research aims to evaluate trust management approaches, investigate new privacy-preserving strategies, analyze the shortcomings of existing frameworks, and offer recommendations for creating safe, private, and reliable AI-IoT systems.

Research Goals

1. To assess how well-suited current security frameworks are to safeguard AI-IoT systems from online threats and weaknesses. To achieve this goal, current security practices—such as encryption, intrusion detection, and secure boot protocols must be critically examined to determine how effective they are in AI-IoT situations, where dispersed devices and real-time data processing

pose particular hazards. In addition to suggesting ways to improve security in these systems, this study will assess how well these frameworks handle new security issues such as device spoofing, data injection attacks, and Distributed Denial of Service (DDoS) assaults (Anand & Ramesh, 2021);

2. To examine privacy-protecting methods that protect user information in AI-IoT settings. Because AI-IoT applications acquire a lot of data, protecting sensitive and personal data is essential. This goal investigates techniques to reduce data exposure and stop unwanted access, including edge computing, federated learning, and differential privacy. This study attempts to determine best practices for attaining strong privacy protections in AI-IoT systems by analyzing the efficacy of these privacy-preserving strategies in particular applications—such as healthcare, where patient data confidentiality is crucial.
3. To research methods and frameworks for trust management to improve trust in AI-IoT systems. For AI-IoT systems to be accepted and successful, trust is crucial, particularly in high-stakes applications like autonomous cars and healthcare. This study intends to investigate several trust management strategies, such as explainable AI methods, blockchain-based decentralized trust models, and reputation-based systems. The goal is to assess each approach's advantages and disadvantages in promoting user trust, openness, and responsibility in AI-IoT decision-making processes (Ohnesorg et al., 2024).
4. To evaluate the ethical and legal consequences of privacy, security, and trust in AI-IoT systems. Regulatory frameworks such as the General Data Protection Regulation (GDPR) and new AI rules are becoming increasingly important as AI-IoT systems proliferate. This goal examines ethical issues such as data ownership, transparency, and user autonomy while concentrating on how AI-IoT operations conform to these regulatory norms. In addition, the study will look at gaps in current laws and offer suggestions for improvements that would better handle the particular difficulties brought on by the confluence of AI and IoT (Jezova, 2020).
5. To provide a thorough framework for creating AI-IoT systems that are reliable, safe, and privacy-conscious. This purpose seeks to create a cohesive framework that can direct stakeholders in developing robust AI-IoT ecosystems by utilising the knowledge gained from security analysis, privacy-preserving strategies, trust management approaches, and regulatory evaluations. To guarantee that AI-IoT systems adhere to moral principles, protect user privacy, and promote public confidence, this framework will provide best practices and suggestions for developers, legislators, and organizations (Fabris, 2018).

3.1 Methodology

The security, privacy, and trust issues in AI-IoT (Artificial Intelligence-Internet of Things) Convergent Smart Systems are addressed in this study using a thorough multi-method approach. The methodology aims to develop a comprehensive understanding of these challenges while identifying existing gaps and suggesting changes by incorporating a systematic literature review, comparative analysis, simulation studies, case study analysis, and stakeholder involvement through surveys and interviews. This methodical methodology makes a thorough investigation of AI-IoT ecosystems possible, which focuses on finding the best practices for boosting security, privacy, and trust. The report starts with a thorough literature analysis to compile the most recent research on the security, privacy, and trust issues facing AI-IoT systems. This overview lays the groundwork for comprehending typical issues and strategies within these interrelated systems. Major academic databases such as IEEE Xplore, ACM Digital Library, ScienceDirect, and SpringerLink were searched and organized. Relevant articles were found using keywords like "AI-IoT security," "privacy in IoT systems," "trust management in AI-IoT," and "ethical implications of AI-IoT." Recent publications over the last five years were prioritized to ensure that the assessment incorporates developments and new trends. To guarantee the inclusion of trustworthy, peer-reviewed sources, articles from high-impact journals, such as IEEE Internet of Things Journal and Journal of Information Security and Applications, were specifically selected (Lv et al., 2020). Inclusion criteria were used to keep the content relevant. The inclusion criteria were limited to peer-reviewed publications that addressed the confluence of AI and IoT, emphasizing security, privacy, or trust. Because they would not adequately represent the particular context and difficulties of AI-IoT systems, studies that separately addressed AI or IoT without looking at their integration were disqualified (Jagatheesaperumal et al., 2022). The main conclusions from every study were taken out and categorized into categories, such as trust management models, privacy-preserving strategies, and security standards. In addition to identifying opportunities for additional research, this thematic organization offered a structured review of contemporary techniques (Solove & Schwartz, 2020). After the literature review, a comparative study of frameworks was carried out to assess important security, privacy, and trust frameworks in AI-IoT systems. This analysis aimed to evaluate the advantages, disadvantages, and real-world uses of each framework. Differential privacy, federated learning, homomorphic encryption, and blockchain-based trust models were among the frameworks chosen for examination. For instance, federated learning works well for data privacy by storing data on individual devices rather than centralizing it, while blockchain provides decentralized data verification, which is especially useful in trust management (Dhavamani et al., 2024).

Key features like scalability, computing efficiency, privacy protection, adaptability, and resilience to cyber-attacks were included in the criteria to enable organized comparisons. Because AI-IoT ecosystems sometimes comprise many interconnected devices, each with a limited processing capacity, scalability, and computational efficiency were crucial. Resilience evaluates a framework's capacity to resist attacks, while privacy protection and adaptability assess its capacity to protect user data and react to evolving security requirements. Each framework was methodically evaluated about these standards to identify its advantages, disadvantages, and gaps. Blockchain, for example, showed great security and transparency, but it also presented computational difficulties, especially for IoT devices with limited resources. Although federated learning needed central aggregation, which would have affected scalability, it offered strong privacy protections. This comparison study revealed opportunities for additional research and provided insights into the viability of various frameworks for particular AI-IoT applications. Using simulation experiments, the chosen frameworks were then empirically tested in a controlled virtual environment. Simulations show a framework's usefulness and possible drawbacks by enabling its performance to be assessed in actual circumstances. A network simulation program called NS-3 was used to build a simulated AI-IoT ecosystem. This setting was set up to mimic a smart city, complete with networked gadgets communicating in real-time to monitor infrastructure, traffic, and environmental conditions. It was put into practice in this simulated environment to evaluate each chosen framework's performance under various threat scenarios. These frameworks included blockchain-based trust models, differential privacy, and end-to-end encryption.

Various cyber threats were presented during the simulation to evaluate each framework's capacity to identify and reduce these risks, including Distributed Denial of Service (DDoS) attacks, data injection, and spoofing attacks. Response time, processing overhead, and data anonymization success rates are examples of performance indicators that offer quantitative information for evaluating the usefulness of each framework. Differential privacy, for instance, successfully preserved user data even though it necessitated a trade-off between data accuracy and privacy. Although blockchain's resistance to manipulation was one of its obvious security advantages, its high processing load made it difficult for lightweight IoT devices to use (Rahman & Liu, 2023). Case studies were conducted to examine the implementation of security, privacy, and trust frameworks in real-world AI-IoT systems to give context. These case studies concentrated on well-known domains with significant AI-IoT integration, such as healthcare, industrial automation, and smart cities. Every case study emphasized particular difficulties and solutions used in real-world implementations. For example, blockchain is commonly used in smart city surveillance systems to manage decentralized data safely. In contrast, federated learning is widely used in IoT-enabled patient monitoring systems in the healthcare industry to preserve patient data privacy.

Technical material, published reports, and interviews with pertinent parties, including system developers and operators, provided the data for these case studies. System logs and reports were occasionally acquired to examine security incidents, privacy-maintaining procedures, and trust-management tactics in practical contexts. This information revealed common problems in several applications as well as successful practices. Following that, a cross-case comparison was carried out to find similarities and differences, which aided in creating suggestions for additional AI-IoT applications. A variety of viewpoints, including those of developers, legislators, and end users, were recorded through stakeholder engagement questionnaires and interviews, in addition to simulations and case studies. The poll included questions about perceptions of security, privacy, and trust in AI-IoT systems. Questions covered subjects like levels of trust in existing AI-based decision-making, contentment with privacy standards, and perceived security issues. To ensure a range of viewpoints, these questionnaires were sent to stakeholders in several industries. Survey participants participated in semi-structured interviews to learn more about particular topics. These included security issues, the perceived sufficiency of privacy safeguards, and recommendations for enhancing trust management in AI-IoT systems. Thematic analysis of the responses revealed recurring themes, including “privacy concerns,” “trust in AI-IoT systems,” and “security expectations.” Thanks to this analysis, stakeholders' issues were better understood, which also highlighted AI-IoT methods' advantages and shortcomings.

A thorough framework for improving security, privacy, and trust in AI-IoT systems was subsequently developed by synthesizing insights from every study stage. To maintain legal compliance and foster public trust, this framework integrates best practices found throughout the study phases and conforms to regulatory criteria like the CCPA and GDPR. The framework offers helpful suggestions for AI-IoT developers, legislators, and companies implementing these technologies. A panel of AI-IoT specialists, including industry professionals and university researchers, also examined the suggested framework to determine its applicability and viability. The framework was improved by incorporating expert feedback, which increased its applicability to various AI-IoT applications. This methodology thoroughly investigates security, privacy, and trust in AI-IoT systems by combining case studies, modeling, framework analysis, literature evaluation, and stakeholder interaction. Incorporating realistic case studies, useful simulations, and stakeholder insights guarantees that the framework is firmly based on theoretical and practical viewpoints, thereby assisting in creating more secure, private, and reliable AI-IoT ecosystems.

3.2 Application of Security, Privacy, and Trust of AI-IoT Convergent Smart System

Application of security, privacy, and trust will help in the dependable implementation of AI-IoT convergent smart systems across different industries. These applications are very important, especially in those domains where AI-IoT systems carry out autonomous or semi-autonomous decision-making and interact with sensitive data. AI-IoT systems can safely and effectively operate with public confidence only if appropriate security controls, privacy safeguards, and trust management are available. A few key applications where these components are crucially required are identified next.

1. Health Care

AI-IoT systems for the health industry provide unparalleled solutions for monitoring patients, diagnosis, and personalized therapies. Since these systems continue to collect private patient information from networked devices, security and privacy become very important.

Privacy: Federated Learning is among several privacy-preserving techniques that are commonly used in the healthcare industry. Such techniques allow research on patients' data without compromising individual privacy, especially when AI models need to be trained on data scattered across several healthcare facilities.
Security: Access controls are secure, and data is encrypted at a high level in storage and transmission. Patient data remains inaccessible to unauthorized individuals, which is important because, with telemedicine and remote patient monitoring, data must cross public networks.
Transparency/Trust: Decentralized trust mechanisms or blockchain-based frameworks allow all data transactions across systems to be recorded unbreakable in healthcare. Such openness creates trust in the use of these digital health solutions since patients and healthcare professionals can control how data is processed. For example, wearable technology in remote patient monitoring collects health parameters in real-time and transmits them to practitioners. As much as trust mechanisms would assure patients that their information is being handled with integrity, security and privacy protection measures ensure that this information is transmitted and stored securely.

2. Smart Cities

The smart city initiative to make cities safer, more effective, and more sustainable embraces AI-IoT technologies that ensure smarter public services, resource management, and urban infrastructure. AI-IoT systems address all different facets of security, privacy, and trust in a wide range of applications, from energy management to traffic optimization.

Privacy: As public spaces carry much data, methods that preserve privacy and anonymize data are often incorporated into smart city applications. Traffic surveillance sensors will capture the movement of vehicles without identifying individual drivers.
Security: Secure communication protocols and multi-level encryption protect the data flow in a smart city. These are very precautionary measures against cyberattacks or illicit access to vital infrastructure.

Trust: Reputation-based trust models block malicious devices from infiltrating the network. They allow different types of devices and systems in smart cities to verify and validate each other. In applications pertaining to public safety, they would segregate credible data sources from compromised or untrustworthy ones.

The information-gathering system in a smart city contains thousands of cameras and sensors throughout the city. An integrated security measure protects captured data against illegal access or manipulative activities, while privacy-preserving measures ensure citizens' anonymity. The trust frameworks enhance resource management and urban safety systems' reliability by confirming that the data is provided only by authenticated and certified sources.

3. Automation in Industry

AI-IoT solutions enable real-time monitoring, predictive maintenance, and autonomous machinery management, smoothing industrial operations with enhanced productivity and reduced hazards. These systems are crucial for manufacturing, logistics, and energy production.

Privacy: In industrial automation, privacy is usually related to sensitive process information, employee data, or proprietary activities. Methods such as federated learning or on-device data processing help protect privacy by processing the data locally and not transferring it to a centralized site.
Security: Industrial IoT networks need high levels of protection against cyber-attacks, which could result in expensive production standstills or damage to critical equipment. Examples are intrusion detection systems for questionable activities and secure boot mechanisms preventing unauthorized code from running on devices.
Trust: In a practical sense, human operators and autonomous systems must build confidence in industrial IoT devices to work safely together. Trust frameworks using identity verification and device authentication enable only authorized parties to access or manage vital systems.

For instance, IoT sensors continuously monitor a manufacturing plant's equipment to discover performance issues and predict where maintenance will be required. While trust models help ensure the reality of the data and instructions across the network, security measures safeguard that information from outside threats so production can happen safely and without disruption.

4. Agriculture

AI-IoT systems enhance resource management, livestock monitoring, and crop management in agriculture. Precision farming techniques enabled by these devices have great potential to harness the most efficient use of fertilizers and water while bringing in better yields.

Privacy: When collecting data from farmers, landowners, and farmworkers, many privacy concerns arise in agricultural activities. Differentiated privacy techniques and on-farm data processing ensure security against sensitive information about activities or land conditions.

Security: IoT networks are secured to a level where farming equipment, sensors, and automated systems can be kept out of reach from unauthorized access. This is especially true for operations involving environmental data on crop management and yield prediction, which include encryption and secure storage procedures.

Thanks to blockchain-based technology, crops can be followed step-by-step from farm to market. The authenticity and quality of agricultural products are assured by building confidence among all participants involved in the supply chain.

For example, in a smart greenhouse, AI-IoT sensors monitor temperature, humidity, and soil quality to ensure maximum comfort for crops. Because of privacy and security measures, sensitive operational data can be viewed only by authorized staff, and blockchain-based trust systems facilitate tracking the production path to guarantee food safety and traceability.

5. Autonomous Vehicles and Transportation

AI-IoT systems have become pivotal in modern transportation, be it driverless cars, fleet management, or even smart transport networks that utilize data-driven decision-making for traffic flow and safety.

Privacy: Autonomous cars collect much information about passengers, driving habits, and environmental factors. One privacy-preserving strategy is differential privacy, which guarantees keeping personal data private without giving up the accuracy of AI models for autonomous decision-making.

Security: Data should be transmitted securely to and between infrastructure, control systems, and automobiles. Real-time intrusion detection, secure hardware, and end-to-end encryption prevent unauthorized access that could endanger vehicle safety.

V2V and V2I communication are based on trust frameworks that ensure that all navigation and control information originate from vetted sources only. This minimizes the occurrence of mishaps due to malicious data entry or faulty communication.

For instance, it provides intelligent transportation systems with autonomous cars. These utilize real-time data from other traffic in proximity and road signals. Security protocols ensure the protection of this information exchange; privacy protections safeguard the secrecy of passenger information; and trust mechanisms ensure the validation of all sources to ensure safety in travel, regulating traffic laws in the process.

6. Smart Homes and Consumer Electronics

These smart home and consumer electronics AI-IoT systems go one more step in automating and simplifying the tasks of daily life by enabling energy management, security monitoring, or appliance control. However, such systems raise issues about trust, privacy, and data security.

Privacy: Privacy should be crucial in smart homes, as personal information, daily routines, and security settings are sensitive. Data anonymization and privacy-by-design techniques are examples of privacy-preserving technologies that keep user information safe.

Security: Safety in the security field of smart home devices includes strong authentication mechanisms, like two-factor authentication, encryption of data over the network, and secure device upgrades. This protects against naturally occurring vulnerabilities and threats online in residential settings.

Trust: The models for trust grant permission for different appliances of different manufacturers to work safely in smart homes and ensure that everything on the network is authenticated and trusted. This further allows for secure interoperability in the various ecosystems of smart homes.

In a smart home, smart devices, including, but not limited to, security cameras, lighting, and thermostats, work together to enhance security and lighten household chores. Private defense technologies protect against disclosure, such as usage habits. Thanks to the robust security and trust frameworks that avoid unauthorized access, users can enjoy reliable and secure smart home experiences.

Only through the integration of security, privacy, and trust frameworks will the AI-IoT systems safely and efficiently operate in these varied applications. These will then form the base for dependable AI-IoT ecosystems that protect user data, defeat cyber threats, and engender trust among users in smart homes, healthcare, or agriculture. Moreover, such frameworks must keep being updated to match the development of the technologies in the AI-IoT domain in light of new challenges while ensuring such systems serve society with ethics.

3.3 Advantages of Security, Privacy, and Trust of AI-IoT Convergent Smart System

AI-IoT convergent smart systems ensure several advantages, especially in various application domains when implementing security, privacy, and trust features. This will establish and develop more secure, reliable, and efficient systems, enhancing user experience and legal compliance and increasing public trust. The following are the most important advantages of implementing robust security, privacy, and trust mechanisms in AI-IoT systems.

1. **Improved Privacy and Data Protection:** Among the key benefits of security and privacy features is protecting sensitive data in AI-IoT systems. Most AI-IoT applications, particularly those used in healthcare, smart cities, and transportation, collect and process sensitive personal data, such as location, behavioral, and health data. Strong privacy and security features, including federated learning, differential privacy, and data encryption, ensure no abuse of this sensitive information, nor is unauthorized access allowed.

    Advantage: AI-IoT systems will protect their users from potential harm or exploitation by avoiding data breaches involving access by unauthorized parties, as personal information is kept private. By minimizing the chance of legal liability, the approaches for preserving privacy assist businesses in following data protection regulations like CCPA and GDPR.
2. **More Adoption and User Trust:** Adopting an AI-IoT system is indeed a trust-based process, especially for consumer applications in wearables and smart homes, where users might be concerned about the security and privacy of their data. By implementing frameworks like reputation-based trust models or using blockchain for the transparency of data transactions, they may feel more secure in trusting that their data is properly managed. Trust in AI-IoT creates more feelings of safety, leading to its increased adoption. People also have more trust in companies and government agencies because

a truthful and transparent business attracts a great reputation, attracting more clients or citizens to get involved in intelligent solutions.

3. **Enhanced System Resilience and Reliability:** Various AI-IoT security techniques include protection against device tampering, data spoofing, and DDoS attacks, among other types of assault. These risks can compromise the integrity and functionality of AI-IoT systems, particularly those in critical infrastructures such as transport networks, energy grids, and medical facilities. AI-IoT systems can detect and block these risks to mitigate them through state-of-the-art security protocols, enabling seamless service and asset protection in physical domains.

    Advantages: Enhanced security will help make AI-IoT systems more resilient against cyber-attacks, reducing system downtime and allowing for continuity in business operations. This would be quite important in sectors such as medicine and industry, where such disruption could have serious consequences.

4. **Legal Protection and Conformity with Regulations:** Accordingly, in AI-IoT systems, security, privacy, and trust mechanisms all work together to ensure that these systems operate within legally set boundaries, which are becoming increasingly strict regarding cybersecurity and data protection. For example, strategies for privacy preservation help businesses handle data responsibly according to legislation such as GDPR, HIPAA, and others that require stringent data security and transparency procedures.

    Advantages: Another good reason for using private and secure AI-IoT systems for regulatory compliance is to protect companies from accusations, suits, and other judicial procedures that may be brought against them in case of failure to comply. Compliance also speaks of dedication to ethical behaviour, improving an organization's standing and reputation before stakeholders.

5. **Improved User Experience:** Assured data privacy and safety will make them more confident in using AI-IoT systems. Better privacy and trust mean a smooth and comfortable experience, worrisome regarding users' concerns about data exploitation. This holds for settings that are becoming very intimate, for which humans are becoming concerned about data collected and used against them, such as wearables, smart homes, and connected cars.

    Advantages: In consumer-facing applications, the better the user experience, the more satisfied and stickier users will be. Believing their privacy and security are well-protected, users will be more willing to interact with and fully exploit AI-IoT systems, enhancing feature usage and overall user satisfaction.

6. **Operational Efficiency and Cost Saving:** Strong security measures inhibit unauthorized access, data leakage, and system crashes that would otherwise cause costly downtime, repairs, or even losses. Privacy-preserving techniques such as on-device data processing can also lower bandwidth requirements by reducing the amount of data transferred to centralized servers, thus saving costs on data transmission.

    Advantages: This could save the organization money by reducing cyberattack risks and operational discontinuation in maintenance and security-related costs. Facilitating decentralized trust models further improves this efficiency by eliminating the need for permanent control to monitor and support network devices that automatically check on trust.

7. **Data Integrity and Accurate Decision-Making:** Predictive maintenance, industrial automation, and autonomous driving are only a few applications in which data integrity is crucial because an AI-IoT system needs to make reliable decisions. Once the data has been validated and its manipula-

tion safeguarded, it can be trusted as a basis for the judgments of AI algorithms in real-time. Secure sensor data feeds, for example, form the bedrock for the safe and efficient operation of cars under autonomous driving.

Advantages: Due to data integrity, AI-IoT systems can arrive at decisions with increased precision and reliability, leading to improved outcomes and reduced likelihood of mistakes. This aspect becomes even more critical when decisions are made in real-time and involve operational efficiency and human safety.

8. **Accountability and Transparency in Data Processing:** Most importantly, blockchain and open logging system-based trust frameworks allow users and organizations to verify how data is handled within an AI-IoT system. For this reason, such systems clearly provide accountability in that every transaction or exchange of data can be recorded to create an auditable trail. Transparencies of this nature are key to sensitive areas such as healthcare, which requires an ascertaining mechanism that works out patient information according to the law and code of ethics standards.

    Advantages: Increased accountability and transparency mean that the various stakeholders and individuals involved can audit and verify the data handling process. This, in turn, will help build trust in the AI-IoT system's ethical conduct and reduce concerns about data misuse.

9. **Competitive advantage and innovation:** Businesses that emphasize security, privacy, and trust in their respective AI-IoT systems will have a greater chance of winning over investors, consumers, and regulatory agencies than their rivals. By developing a solid reputation for the responsible use of technology, companies can establish a strong brand differentiation factor from other rivals, attracting prospective stakeholders who value data privacy.

    Advantages: Market share gain, new customers, and competitive advantage are within reach of leading security and privacy innovation companies. With this competitive edge in developing a privacy-preserving AI-IoT technology, companies are assured of their leadership in digital innovation and accountability to serve them long-term.

10. **Ethical Risk Mitigation:** AI-IoT systems can address ethical issues with data exploitation and unauthorized surveillance by embedding security, privacy, and trust by design. When integrated with trust frameworks, privacy-enhancing technology ensures that AI-IoT apps respect user autonomy and refrain from obtrusive data collection practices. This becomes crucial for applications centred on collecting rich personal data, such as public spaces and smart cities.

    Advantage: AI-IoT systems, being at minimal ethical risk, would meet socially conscious standards that ensure the protection of people's rights, hence creating a good public image. This commitment to moral behaviour lowers the potential criticism and further engenders user-organization trust in AI-IoT technologies.

In short, embedding security, privacy, and trust into AI-IoT convergent smart systems yields a number of advantages, from user experience and operational efficiency to data protection and regulatory compliance. These advantages will create the long-term sustainability of AI-IoT ecosystems and form the basis upon which ethical and beneficial advancements of AI-IoT are premised in many different sectors.

4. CHALLENGES AND SOLUTION

Due to the distinct features of AI-IoT (Artificial Intelligence-Internet of Things) convergent smart systems, implementing security, privacy, and trust mechanisms in these systems poses several difficulties. Complex security, privacy, and trust needs result from AI-IoT systems' combination of extensive data collection capabilities and autonomous decision-making. Here are some main issues and possible fixes to make AI-IoT settings safer, more dependable, and moral.

1. Resource Limitations and Scalability:

Thousands of connected devices, from basic sensors to intricate autonomous systems, are frequently found in AI-IoT ecosystems. Because many of these IoT devices have limited processing power, memory, and battery capacity, it might be difficult to incorporate complex security and privacy mechanisms without sacrificing functionality.

Solution: Lightweight security and privacy mechanisms are crucial to handle scalability and resource limitations. While maintaining data security, methods like elliptic curve cryptography (ECC) and lightweight encryption algorithms lessen the computational load on devices with limited resources. Another strategy is edge computing, which reduces the need to send sensitive data to centralized cloud servers by processing data locally on edge servers or at the device level. Edge computing is a workable alternative for IoT situations with limited resources since it processes data locally, lowering latency and bandwidth needs.

2. Low Latency Requirements and Real-Time Data Processing:

Low-latency data processing is necessary for many AI-IoT applications, including industrial automation, driverless cars, and real-time health monitoring, to guarantee prompt and precise replies. However, using privacy-preserving techniques and encryption can lengthen processing times, which could affect the system's responsiveness.

Solution: Hardware-based security, such as secure enclaves and Trusted Platform Modules (TPM), which provide quicker, dedicated security processing, can overcome real-time processing issues. Without appreciably affecting latency, these hardware solutions offer a safe data encryption and decryption setting. Furthermore, new technologies like federated learning and differential privacy enable data analysis in aggregate form without disclosing individual data points, eliminating the need for intricate encryption at every turn while maintaining data privacy. These techniques allow for minimal latency and real-time decision-making.

3. User Consent and Data Privacy:

Particularly in public settings like smart cities, AI-IoT systems frequently gather private and sensitive data, occasionally without the user's express consent. This data may contain geographical, behavioral, and even biometric information, which raises significant privacy concerns.

Solution: AI-IoT systems can help guarantee that user privacy is given priority right away by implementing privacy-by-design and privacy-by-default concepts. According to these guidelines, systems should only be built to gather the bare minimum of information and, whenever feasible, anonymize or pseudonymize data. Another useful technique is differential privacy, which introduces noise into datasets to allow data analysis without disclosing personal information. Furthermore, AI-IoT applications should incorporate explicit user permission procedures that let consumers know what information is gathered and how it will be utilized.

4. **Cyberattacks and Security Flaws:**

AI-IoT systems are extremely susceptible to a number of cyber threats, including device tampering, data spoofing, and Distributed Denial of Service (DDoS) assaults. Insecure IoT devices can be used by attackers to interfere with business operations, steal confidential data, or alter AI algorithms, which could negatively affect vital applications like transportation or healthcare.

Solution: Strong security procedures are necessary to defend AI-IoT systems against cyberattacks. Thanks to multi-layered encryption, data is protected throughout the process, from transmission to storage. Furthermore, proactive defense against possible attacks is made possible by real-time network traffic monitoring and detecting suspicious activities by anomaly detection algorithms and intrusion detection systems (IDS). Regular security patches and updates are crucial to safeguard devices against known vulnerabilities. Blockchain-based solutions offer a decentralized and impenetrable foundation for documenting and validating device transactions, improving security and transparency for systems needing high protection, including critical infrastructure or healthcare.

5. **Lack of Interoperability Standards:**

AI-IoT ecosystems frequently incorporate hardware and software from various vendors, each with privacy and security regulations. It is difficult to provide uniform security, privacy, and trust protections throughout the system due to this lack of standardization, which could expose specific devices or data.

Solution: Industry-wide standards and protocols are required to guarantee interoperability across AI-IoT devices and systems. Universal standards for IoT security and data privacy are being developed by groups such as the Institute of Electrical and Electronics Engineers (IEEE) and the Internet Engineering Task Force (IETF). By improving interoperability, adopting these standards can facilitate safe communication between devices. Devices from many manufacturers can integrate open-source security protocols, including MQTT with secure socket layer (SSL) encryption, to ensure a secure connection. Governments and regulatory agencies should also incentivize manufacturers to use common security and privacy measures to establish a more unified and secure AI-IoT ecosystem.

6. Transparency and Trust in Data Processing:

AI and IoT have resulted in autonomous decision-making processes in which algorithms evaluate and act upon data without human intervention. However, users find it challenging to comprehend or have faith in AI algorithms because of their “black-box” nature, especially when dealing with sensitive data in fields like public safety, healthcare, or finance.

Solution: By shedding light on how AI algorithms decide, explainable AI (XAI) techniques assist stakeholders and users in comprehending the variables affecting the system's results. Building trust requires a clear decision-making process, which explainable AI provides. Furthermore, blockchain-based trust models offer an unchangeable and visible record of data transactions that can be examined to ensure data handling procedures adhere to legal and ethical requirements. Thanks to this transparency, users can confirm that their data is handled securely and ethically, which helps to increase user confidence.

7. Ethical Issues and Regulatory Compliance:

AI-IoT systems frequently function in intricate legal frameworks where they have to abide by data protection regulations such as the CCPA and GDPR. However, maintaining compliance can be difficult because AI-IoT applications are frequently automated and include large volumes of data. Ethical worries about user autonomy, surveillance, and possible biases in AI decision-making make regulatory compliance more difficult.

Solution: To examine their AI-IoT systems' ethical and regulatory ramifications, organizations should implement privacy impact assessments (PIAs) and ethical impact assessments (EIAs). Before implementing the technology, these evaluations assist in identifying any ethical and privacy concerns. Organizations may process and analyze data without breaking privacy rules thanks to data anonymization techniques and secure data processing technologies like federated learning, guaranteeing regulatory compliance. AI-IoT systems can be brought into compliance with legal and ethical requirements by implementing ethical AI techniques, such as eliminating biased data points and utilizing inclusive training datasets, which can help stop AI systems from making discriminating decisions.

8. **Secure Access Control and Device Authentication:**

To keep unauthorized devices from accessing sensitive data or interfering with operations, robust authentication and access control are essential when a large number of devices are connected to AI-IoT systems. However, conventional password-based techniques are frequently inadequate because AI-IoT networks are decentralized.

Solution: Because biometric and multi-factor authentication (MFA) require extra verification elements, like fingerprints or facial recognition, to allow access, they offer more security than passwords. Digital certificates and public key infrastructure (PKI) can also confirm device identities, guaranteeing that only reliable devices can interact with the AI-IoT network. Blockchain-based identity management systems offer decentralized authentication in highly secure scenarios, lowering the possibility of unwanted access and boosting confidence in device communications.

9. Excessive Network Traffic and Data Volume:

Large volumes of data are produced by AI-IoT systems, which can strain network capacity and cause processing and storage difficulties. High data transmission volumes significantly raise the possibility of data breaches and interception, especially in public networks.

Solution: Edge computing and data compression methods handle large amounts of data well. By reducing the volume of data sent via networks, data compression lowers bandwidth needs and lessens the possibility of eavesdropping. Edge computing reduces the amount of data that must be transferred by processing data at the device level or on local edge servers, keeping sensitive data near its source. By restricting the amount of data transferred over public networks, these technologies increase network efficiency and lower the danger of data breaches.

10. Integrating Security, Privacy, and Trust:

Because AI-IoT systems are interconnected and each component has different requirements, integrating security, privacy, and trust mechanisms into these systems can be challenging. Providing thorough coverage without sacrificing system functionality or user experience can be difficult.

Solution: An integrated security, privacy, and trust architecture offers a unified strategy for handling these issues in AI-IoT systems. This framework should incorporate automatic privacy-preserving techniques, layered security procedures, and trust management tactics that can be modified to fit various applications and contexts. For instance, a multi-layered defense that addresses security, privacy, and trust can be achieved by integrating encryption with federated learning and blockchain-based trust models. This integration can be further streamlined with automation and AI-driven monitoring, guaranteeing that measures adjust quickly to shifting risks and legal requirements.

5. CONCLUSION

The employment of security, privacy, and trust frameworks is mandatory in AI-IoT convergent smart systems to enable safe, reliable, and ethically correct operations across various applications. By their very nature, these systems consist of large data gathering and often require real-time, autonomous decision-making. These capabilities together render an AI-IoT ecosystem indispensable across industries, ranging from healthcare and transportation to industrial automation and smart cities. However, unless such systems are designed with extensive safeguards, they pose serious risks to data integrity, user privacy, and total system security. Accordingly, addressing these risks is not simply preventing data breaches or cyberattacks but also fostering public trust and regulatory compliance. Issues identified in securing AI-IoT systems relate to scalable, efficient, and interoperable frameworks that will be able to keep pace with the peculiar characteristics of the AI-IoT environment. Solutions such as lightweight encryption, edge computing, differential privacy, and blockchain-based trust models effectively strengthen security and privacy without compromising performance. Besides, transparency through explainable AI with ethical impact assessments ensures the responsible operation of these systems, respecting user autonomy and complying with legal standards. When coupled, these will form balanced measures of functionality and security in the realms of operation concerning AI-IoT systems, thus offering an environment where users can begin trusting the technology influencing daily life. Future development will remain in the fine-tuning of these frameworks to meet new threats as they emerge and the engineering of universal standards supporting global interoperability. Eventually, the development and deployment of responsible AI-IoT systems with integrated security, privacy, and trust measures will provide an opening for transformative applications to gain traction in improving lives while ensuring that ethics and regulatory standards are followed.

5.1 Future Works

Future studies within the domain of security, privacy, and trust in AI-IoT convergent smart systems will probably revolve around the establishment of further enhancements of currently developed frameworks and the creation of novel flexible solutions to meet dynamic legal and technological challenges. More reliable and scalable security approaches would be required as AI-IoT technologies permeate everyday life and critical infrastructures. The second interesting future research topic might be the development of specific lightweight encryption and authentication protocols for IoT devices with limited resources. It will be perfect for large-scale AI-IoT networks with constrained processing power, hence allowing for more robust protection without affecting the performance of IoT devices. Another promising avenue is the development of methods that ensure privacy preservation, like differential privacy and federated learning, which will support sophisticated and real-time applications. Future research might also focus on optimizing these strategies for low-latency contexts, such as autonomous vehicles and real-time health monitoring, since many of these systems must consume data and make a real-time decretal-time. Further investigation into edge and fog computing may also assist in meeting these goals. These architectures allow for data processing close to their source, reducing the risks associated with centralized data in transit and storage.

Further research is needed to understand how blockchain integration with a decentralized trust model works, at least for better accountability and transparency of AI-IoT data processing. The research to come may have to study scalability related to blockchain technology for large-scale networks or develop hybrid models that balance efficiency and security by appropriately combining decentralized and centralized elements. More importantly, the emergent development of **explainable AI-XAI** will be needed to enhance the transparency of AI-IoT systems and gain users' confidence in applications where decision-making processes need to be understood.

Another critical area of future effort involves the construction of frameworks that automatically adapt to the changing legal requirements and evolving privacy standards since regulatory compliance will continue to be a key driver. This will be achieved by developing applications intrinsically compliant with national and international regulations and by developing accompanying tools that provide real-time privacy and ethical impact assessments where necessary. Finally, more interdisciplinary research is needed to integrate computer science, law, and ethics to address the abovementioned issues concerning AI-IoT systems adequately. Therefore, future research on these areas will enhance responsible, ethical, and safe development of AI-IoT technologies that could reach their full potential in various industry.

REFERENCES

Anand, S., & Ramesh, M. V. (2021). Multi-layer architecture and routing for Internet of Everything (IoE) in smart cities. In *2021 Sixth International Conference on Wireless Communications, Signal Processing and Networking (WiSPNET)* (pp. xx–xx). IEEE. DOI: 10.1109/WiSPNET51692.2021.9419428

Bahutair, M., & Bouguettaya, A. (2023). An end-to-end trust management framework for crowd-sourced IoT services. *ACM Transactions on Internet Technology*, *23*(3), 1–32. https://doi.org/10.1145/XXXXXXDOI: 10.1145/3600232

Baniecki, H., & Biecek, P. (2024). Adversarial attacks and defenses in explainable artificial intelligence: A survey. *Information Fusion*, *107*, 102303. https://doi.org/10.1016/j.inffus.2024.102303DOI: 10.1016/j.inffus.2024.102303

Bao, F., & Chen, I.-R. (2012). Dynamic trust management for Internet of Things applications. In *Proceedings of the 2012 International Workshop on Self-aware Internet of Things* (pp. xx–xx). DOI: 10.1145/2378023.2378025

Blind, K., Niebel, C., & Rammer, C. (2024). The impact of the EU General Data Protection Regulation on product innovation. *Industry and Innovation*, *31*(3), 311–351. https://doi.org/10.1080/13662716.2024.XXXXXDOI: 10.1080/13662716.2023.2271858

Burton, E., Goldsmith, J., Mattei, N., & Shah, H. (2017). Ethical considerations in artificial intelligence courses. *AI Magazine*, *38*(2), 22–34. https://doi.org/10.1609/aimag.v38i2.XXXXXDOI: 10.1609/aimag.v38i2.2731

Commey, D., Baah, R., Ibrahim, A., & Zhou, W. (2024). Securing blockchain-based IoT systems: A review. *IEEE Access : Practical Innovations, Open Solutions*, *12*, 98856–98881. https://doi.org/10.1109/ACCESS.2024.XXXXXXXDOI: 10.1109/ACCESS.2024.3428490

Dhavamani, L., Nagarajan, A., & Selvakumar, S. (2024). Differential privacy-preserving IoT data sharing through enhanced PSO. *Journal of Computer Information Systems*, •••, 1–17. https://doi.org/10.1080/08874417.2024.XXXXXDOI: 10.1080/08874417.2024.2364904

Dhelim, S., Ning, H., & Abdel-Basset, M. (2022). Trust2Vec: Large-scale IoT trust management system based on signed network embeddings. *IEEE Internet of Things Journal*, *10*(1), 553–562. https://doi.org/10.1109/JIOT.2022.XXXXXDOI: 10.1109/JIOT.2022.3201772

Fabris, A. (2018). *Ethics of information and communication technologies*. Springer. DOI: 10.1007/978-3-319-75511-3

Hameed, S., Khan, F. A., Ahmed, E., & Khalid, A. (2021). A scalable key and trust management solution for IoT sensors using SDN and blockchain technology. *IEEE Sensors Journal*, *21*(6), 8716–8733. https://doi.org/10.1109/JSEN.2021.XXXXXDOI: 10.1109/JSEN.2021.3052009

Hassan, S. H., Abdulqader, D. M., Ahmed, O. M., Ismael, H. R., Ahmed, S. H., & Haji, L. Privacy-Preserving AI for Sustainability A Review of Secure Data Collection and Analysis in Enterprise Systems with IoT based on Semaphores of Cloud and Web Technologies.

Hoofnagle, C. J., Van Der Sloot, B., & Borgesius, F. Z. (2019). The European Union General Data Protection Regulation: What it is and what it means. *Information & Communications Technology Law*, *28*(1), 65–98. https://doi.org/10.1080/13600834.2019.1573501DOI: 10.1080/13600834.2019.1573501

Huber, B., & Kandah, F. (2020). Behavioral model-based trust management design for IoT at scale. In *2020 International Conferences on Internet of Things (iThings)*, IEEE Cybermatics (pp. xx–xx). IEEE. DOI: 10.1109/iThings-GreenCom-CPSCom-SmartData-Cybermatics50389.2020.00022

Humayun, M., Awan, I. U., & Habib, M. A. (2024). Securing the Internet of Things in artificial intelligence era: A comprehensive survey. *IEEE Access : Practical Innovations, Open Solutions*.https://doi.org/10.1109/ACCESS.2024.XXXXX

Jagatheesaperumal, S. K., Ramachandran, K., & Das, A. (2022). Explainable AI over the Internet of Things (IoT): Overview, state-of-the-art and future directions. *IEEE Open Journal of the Communications Society*, *3*, 2106–2136. https://doi.org/10.1109/OJCOMS.2022.XXXXXDOI: 10.1109/OJCOMS.2022.3215676

Jezova, D. (2020). Principle of privacy by design and privacy by default. *Regional Law Review*, 127–134.

Jiang, B., Wang, Z., Liu, Y., Zhang, Y., & Lin, C. (2021). Differential privacy for industrial Internet of Things: Opportunities, applications, and challenges. *IEEE Internet of Things Journal*, *8*(13), 10430–10451. https://doi.org/10.1109/JIOT.2021.XXXXXDOI: 10.1109/JIOT.2021.3057419

Khatun, M. A., Rahman, M. M., Alqahtani, A., & Alshahrani, A. (2023). Machine learning for healthcare-IoT security: A review and risk mitigation. *IEEE Access : Practical Innovations, Open Solutions*, *11*, 145869–145896. https://doi.org/10.1109/ACCESS.2023.XXXXXXXDOI: 10.1109/ACCESS.2023.3346320

Kossow, N., Windwehr, S., & Jenkins, M. (2022). *Algorithmic transparency and accountability*. JSTOR.

Lu, Q., Zhang, Y., Kumar, R., & Lee, J. (2023). *Responsible AI: Best practices for creating trustworthy AI systems*. Addison-Wesley Professional.

Lv, Z., Qiao, L., & Liu, Y. (2020). Trustworthiness in industrial IoT systems based on artificial intelligence. *IEEE Transactions on Industrial Informatics*, *17*(2), 1496–1504. https://doi.org/10.1109/TII.2020.XXXXXDOI: 10.1109/TII.2020.2994747

Miranda, J., & Blanco, J. M. (2015). From the Internet of Things to the Internet of People. *IEEE Internet Computing*, *19*(2), 40–47. DOI: 10.1109/MIC.2015.24

Mohanta, B. K., Jena, D., Satapathy, U., & Patnaik, S. (2020). Survey on IoT security: Challenges and solution using machine learning, artificial intelligence and blockchain technology. *Internet of Things : Engineering Cyber Physical Human Systems*, *11*, 100227. https://doi.org/10.1016/j.iot.2020.100227DOI: 10.1016/j.iot.2020.100227

Ni, C., Jiang, M., Song, H., & Du, X. (2022). Data anonymization evaluation for big data and IoT environment. *Information Sciences*, *605*, 381–392. https://doi.org/10.1016/j.ins.2022.XXXXXDOI: 10.1016/j.ins.2022.05.040

Ohnesorg, J., Abbas, N., & Peshwe, A. (2024). A review of AI-based trust management in smart cities. In *ITM Web of Conferences*. EDP Sciences. DOI: 10.1051/itmconf/20246201003

Ruzbahani, A. M. (2024). AI-protected blockchain-based IoT environments: Harnessing the future of network security and privacy. *arXiv*. https://arxiv.org/abs/2405.13847

Saied, Y. B., Olivereau, A., Zeadally, S., & Badra, M. (2013). Trust management system design for the Internet of Things: A context-aware and multi-service approach. *Computers & Security*, *39*, 351–365. https://doi.org/10.1016/j.cose.2013.09.001DOI: 10.1016/j.cose.2013.09.001

Schmidt, P., Biessmann, F., & Teubner, T. (2020). Transparency and trust in artificial intelligence systems. *Journal of Decision Systems*, *29*(4), 260–278. https://doi.org/10.1080/12460125.2020.1819094DOI: 10.1080/12460125.2020.1819094

Sidana, S., Kumar, V., & Jain, N. (2025). The ethics of AI and IoT in healthcare: Navigating cybersecurity risks and ensuring data protection. In *Ethical Dimensions of AI Development* (pp. 347–368). IGI Global.

Solove, D. J., & Schwartz, P. M. (2020). *Information privacy law* (6th ed.). Aspen Publishing.

Syed, N. F., Ali, A., Noor, R. M., & Ahmed, S. H. (2022). Zero trust architecture (ZTA): A comprehensive survey. *IEEE Access : Practical Innovations, Open Solutions*, *10*, 57143–57179. https://doi.org/10.1109/ACCESS.2022.XXXXXDOI: 10.1109/ACCESS.2022.3174679

Ullah, F., Al-Turjman, F., & Mostarda, L. (2024). Deep Trust: A novel framework for dynamic trust and reputation management in the Internet of Things (IoT)-based networks. *IEEE Access : Practical Innovations, Open Solutions*, *12*, 87407–87419. https://doi.org/10.1109/ACCESS.2024.XXXXXDOI: 10.1109/ACCESS.2024.3409273

Chapter 7
Investigation on Generative Autoencoders for Hand Gesture Recognition

N. Bharanidharan
https://orcid.org/0000-0001-9064-8238
Vellore Institute of Technology, India

N. Mugunthan
https://orcid.org/0009-0008-6314-3128
Vellore Institute of Technology, India

B. Nitish
https://orcid.org/0009-0006-0558-4406
Vellore Institute of Technology, India

V. Puneeth
Vellore Institute of Technology, India

Kumar V. Vinoth
Vellore Institute of Technology, India

ABSTRACT

As a natural interaction method, hand gesture recognition has gained increased attention, particularly for human-computer interfaces. The goal of this research work is to develop a hand gesture detection system using machine learning techniques. Rather than making direct gesture predictions, this system compares the accuracy of several models in identifying hand gestures from dataset, thereby enabling real-time gesture-based interactions. To achieve this, we employed a combination of machine learning methods, neural networks, PCA for feature reduction and data pre-processing techniques. Algorithms like K-Nearest Neighbors, Decision Trees, SVM, and Autoencoders are used for classification. The dataset used in this work is the LeapGestRecog collection, which has 20,000 grayscale images of ten distinct hand gestures. Our best-performing model, SVM with an RBF kernel and auto-encoder, attained a remarkable accuracy of 99.98% on the test dataset, indicating its robustness in classifying hand gestures accurately.

DOI: 10.4018/979-8-3693-8332-2.ch007

1. INTRODUCTION

A cutting-edge technology called Hand Gesture Recognition allows machines to distinguish between human hand gestures, fostering smooth human-computer interaction. It has the potential to revolutionize several fields with its applications which includes like translating through Sign Language, Augmented Reality, Gaming as well as Robotic Control by capturing and analyzing the human hand gestures and its movements. This simple mode of communication bridges the gap between humans and machines, enhancing usability and accessibility across diverse fields (Kapitanov A et al., 2024). The range of Hand Gesture Recognition extends to a variety of fields, including healthcare, where it helps with rehabilitation therapy, and smart home systems that use gestures to operate electronic devices (Sharma & Singh, 2021). Hand gesture recognition has grown in significance as touchless interfaces have become more prevalent, particularly since the pandemic. By removing physical contact, it improves user experience while guaranteeing convenience and hygiene. Furthermore, the possibilities of gesture-based systems have been increased by hardware developments such as wearable sensors and depth cameras (Al-Hammadi et al., 2020). However, the challenge lies in accurately recognizing gestures amidst variations in lighting, hand shapes, and movements. In dynamic situations, robust systems need to be taught to recognize a variety of motions. To guarantee good performance even under real-world circumstances, this calls for the combination of potent algorithms and sophisticated computational models.

Machine learning is a crucial part of contemporary computational approaches because it enables systems to improve their performance by learning from data despite the requirement for written code (Chaudhary et al., 2013). Supervised learning, Unsupervised learning, and Reinforcement learning are the three primary classifications that machine learning falls under. In contrast to Unsupervised learning, which looks for hidden patterns in unlabeled data, Supervised learning uses labeled data for training. Reinforcement learning, on the other hand, is the process by which agents learn the best behaviors in an environment by trial and error. There are virtually countless uses for machine learning, starting with natural language processing and computer vision to predictive analytics as well as medical diagnostics. For example, recommendation systems use supervised learning to make product recommendations, whereas unsupervised learning uses clustering algorithms to assist categorize customers. Reinforcement learning has advanced autonomous driving and game AI, showcasing machine learning's ability to revolutionize a variety of industries. Because of its versatility and flexibility, machine learning is a perfect technique for hand gesture recognition, where the varieties like hand motions necessitates intelligent systems with generalization capabilities. Machine learning enables systems to dynamically adjust to novel gestures and users, opening the door for reliable, real-time implementations.

Deep Learning (DL), a part of Machine Learning that pushes boundaries regarding computational models by utilizing multiple layers of artificial neural networks. Deep Learning mimics the architecture of human brain to handle and evaluate complex patterns in data (Bobić et al., 2016). The types of Deep Learning consist of Convolutional Neural Networks (CNNs), Recurrent Neural Networks (RNNs), Generative Adversarial Networks (GANs), along with autoencoders, each tailored for specific tasks (Sharma S & Singh S, 2021). Deep Learning has found profound applications in fields like image recognition, speech processing, and medical diagnostics. Convolutional Neural Networks excel in image and video analysis, enabling breakthroughs in autonomous vehicles and medical imaging (Al Mudawi et al., 2024). Recurrent Neural Networks, with their ability to model sequential data, power advancements in language translation and speech synthesis (Sahoo et al., 2022). The flexibility of Deep Learning ensures its dominance in solving problems that were once deemed intractable (Al-Hammadi et al., 2020). The strength of Deep Learning resides in its ability to learn hierarchical features automatically, making it essential for tasks like hand gesture recognition (Chung et al., 2019). By leveraging Deep Learning, models can identify subtle variations in gestures, significantly enhancing recognition accuracy and robustness (Al-Hammadi et al., 2020).

Generative Deep Learning (GDL), the specialized division of Deep Learning, emphasizes on creating new data samples from the existing datasets. This domain consists of models like Generative Adversarial Networks (GANs), Variational Autoencoders (VAEs), and Transformer-based architectures (Qiu et al., 2018). While VAEs are effective at applying probabilistic modeling for various applications like reconstruction of image and synthesizing, GANs will be able to produce realistic images and motion pictures. Generative models have transformed various industries like art, gaming, and healthcare. They can produce data that is artificial to enhance training datasets, imitate elaborate circumstances and generate realistic avatars. By enhancing both of the quantity and caliber of data, models like this not only produce value but also improvise machine learning operations. Performance enhancement opportunities have been created by researching various generative Deep Learning models, like autoencoders for hand gesture detection. These models can learn concise representations of gesture data, enabling efficient storage and robust recognition. Generative approaches also facilitate the synthesis of diverse gesture datasets, addressing the challenges of dataset scarcity and variability, thus setting the stage for an exciting new phase in gesture detection technologies.

The outline of the remaining paper is presented as follows: next section describes the basics of machine learning algorithms used; third section deals with the generative auto-encoders used; fourth section explains the methodology; results and discussion are presented in fifth section followed by conclusion section.

2. MACHINE LEARNING ALGORITHMS USED

Machine Learning (ML) is a section of Artificial Intelligence (AI) that primarily emphasizes on designing the algorithms which are capable of learning as well as improvising from the entire experience without being explicitly programmed. It has transformed numerous fields such as healthcare, finance, education, and transportation by automating processes, tasks, making predictions, and revealing hidden patterns in massive datasets (Adithya & Rajesh, 2020). ML is an important aspect of contemporary data-driven decision-making since its primary objective is to develop systems that can appropriately generalize to unknown data (Wahid et al., 2018). ML algorithms can be majorly classified into three main types: supervised learning, unsupervised learning, as well as reinforcement learning. Supervised learning will rely on labeled data to predict outcomes, meanwhile unsupervised learning will recognize patterns in the data with no predefined features. Reinforcement learning uses a reward-based system to optimize actions in a dynamic environment (Chaudhary et al., 2013). From detecting spam emails to engaging in video games in real time, each type has its own uses and responsibilities. Applications of ML are numerous and wide-ranging. By examining medical imaging and past medical records, machine learning (ML) helps with early identification and therapy planning in the field of healthcare (Ahuja & Singh, 2015). It powers automated trading and identifying fraudulent activity in the financial industry.

In addition, it powers systems for recommendations, virtual assistants, and driverless cars, showcasing its industry-wide transformational potential (Mohamed et al., 2021).

Decision Tree Classifier (DTC) a popular machine learning technique which uses tree-like structure to describe decisions. The most important feature, as identified by measures including the Gini Index or Information Gain, is used to divide dataset into subsets. Each branch indicates decision rules, and the leaf nodes indicate outcomes, and each internal node represents a feature (Fang et al., 2007). DTC can be used for both regression as well as classification applications due to the interpretability and ease of use. DTC, however, has a tendency to overfit, particularly while engaging with the complex datasets. Decision Tree Classifier (DTC) works by recursively splitting the dataset into subsets based on attribute values, establishing a tree-like structure which makes it easier for classifying as well as interpreting data. This approach is particularly useful for understanding complex datasets, as it visualizes decision-making paths and captures non-linear relationships between features, enabling efficient classification and prediction.

Support Vector Machine (SVM), a powerful supervised machine learning algorithm designed to determine the ideal hyperplane for categorizing datapoints. It excels in handling linear as well as non-linear separations via leveraging kernel-based methods like polynomial and radial basis function (RBF) kernels, making it particularly effective with high-dimensional data (Li et al., 2019). SVM enhances generalization by simply increasing the distance between each data points and the hyperplane, that helps reduce overfitting. SVM can effectively categorize complicated patterns through the transformation of input data into a higher-dimensional space, thereby improving model's accuracy as well as resilience in complicated classification tasks.

The K-Nearest Neighbor (KNN) algorithm is straightforward, instance-based learning technique which classifies a data point according to the majority label of its k-nearest neighbors in the feature space (Sharma et al., 2020). K-Nearest Neighbor is computationally expensive during prediction but requires little to no training. Because of the curse of dimensionality, it performs poorly on high-dimensional datasets but well on well-clustered data. Accuracy in categorization could be improved by appropriately adjusting the k value. KNN works best with data that is well-clustered, meaning that related occurrences are strongly clustered together. By balancing responsiveness to noise and generalization, the k value can potentially be adjusted so as to optimize the algorithm's accuracy and classification performance.

The feedforward neural network known as the Multi-Layer Perceptron (MLP) is made up of input, hidden, and output layers. Backpropagation can be employed by the Multilayer Perceptron Architecture (MLP), to reduce errors in predictions during training (Oyedotun & Khashman, 2017). The capability of it is to capture non-linear associations in-between the tendencies as well as outcomes makes it especially well-suited for difficult datasets. MLP works well for applications requiring extensive recognition of patterns because it has numerous hidden layers that let it learn complex patterns within the input. By utilizing this capacity, MLP can deliver improved performance on datasets that involve nuanced and non-linear correlations. High classification accuracy along with successful training were guaranteed by the application of techniques for optimization like Adam and activation functions like ReLU.

A dimensionality reduction method called Principal Component Analysis (PCA) converts high-dimensional data into a lower-dimensional space while maintaining the greatest amount of variance. (Ahuja & Singh, 2015). For finding principal components that demonstrate the greatest amount of variance, PCA calculates eigenvalues as well as eigenvectors of the dataset's covariance matrix. PCA is also used for Pre-Processing where it can greatly reduce the computational overhead and improve the performance of classifiers, including K-Nearest Neighbors and Support Vector Machine by minimizing the dimensionalities of the dataset. Moreover, Principal Component Analysis makes the visualization process as simple as possible in order to comprehend the basic structure of the classes present in data (Narayana P et al., 2018).

3. GENERATIVE AUTOENCODERS USED

Figure 1. Architecture of autoencoder

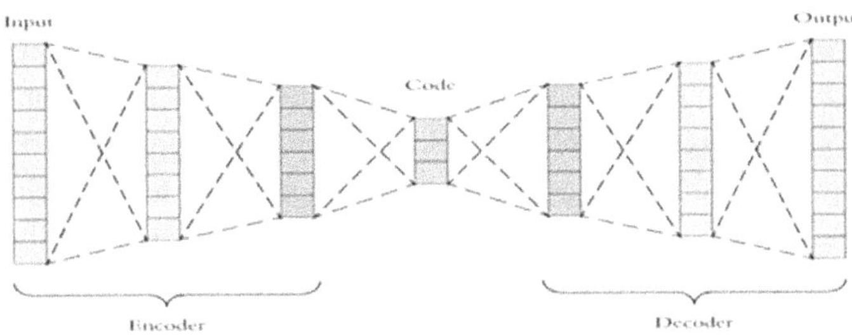

Autoencoders are neural network architectures employed in primarily for unsupervised learning operations such as dimensionality reduction, feature extraction, and data reconstruction. They consist of two key components: an encoder, that reduces the input data into a latent space representation, and a decoder, which reconstructs the original input from this reduced representation as shown in Fig. 1. An autoencoder's primary goal is to reduce the reconstruction loss for the purpose to create effective, compact ways to represent data; this is typically achieved via the use of metrics such as binary cross-entropy or mean squared error (MSE) (Li et al., 2023). With regard to the versatility they offer, autoencoders are used in a variety of industries. They are utilized, for example, (Ikne et al., 2025).in data compression by lowering dimensionality without appreciably sacrificing information, picture denoising by eliminating noise while maintaining key features, and anomaly detection by detecting departures from learnt patterns (Subudhi et al., 2023). Different types of autoencoders exist to address specific tasks: plain autoencoders for basic reconstruction, sparse autoencoders to enforce sparsity in latent representations, variational autoencoders (VAEs) for probabilistic data generation, and undercomplete autoencoders with bottleneck architectures for compact representations (Spina D et al., 2024). Autoencoders significantly improve model performance by filtering out noise and irrelevant features, enabling better learning and generalization in subsequent tasks (Bousbai & Merah, 2022).

3.1. Plain Autoencoders

Plain autoencoders are the simplest and most fundamental type of autoencoders, designed to recreate the input data as near as possible. They consist of a symmetric architecture where the input is compressed by the encoder to create a latent representation of lower dimensionality as well as the data is reconstructed from the compressed form by the decoder. By maximizing the loss function of such mean squared error, the intention of training is reducing the distinctness between the original input and the reconstruction of it. Dense (completely linked) layers are used in both the encoder and the decoder to create ordinary autoencoders in practice. To capture intricate correlations, the encoder gradually decreases the dimensionality of the data that is given as input, frequently using non-linear activation functions like ReLU.

The latent representation is expanded back to its initial dimensions by the decoder, which replicates the structure of the encoder. When it comes to reducing dimensions and noise removal, plain autoencoders work especially well. They are frequently employed as a Pre-processing step to provide condensed feature representations that streamline and speed up subsequent processes including classification, visualization, and clustering (Ahuja & Singh, 2015).

3.2. Sparse Autoencoders

Sparse autoencoders extend plain autoencoders by incorporating a sparsity constraint in the latent representation. By minimizing the count of activated neurons resides in the hidden layer, this sparsity makes it possible to learn with greater significance and understandable defining features. Sparse autoencoders do this by training the loss function using an existing normalization term, such KL divergence or L1 regularization. The sparsity restriction alters how latent features are learnt, but the encoder and decoder architecture of sparse autoencoders is very similar to that of ordinary autoencoders. Sparse autoencoders eliminate noise and redundancy by promoting only a small number of neurons, focusing on identifying the most important patterns in the input. The selection of features as well as improving the ability to be understood by learned representations constitute the two areas in which this kind of approach performs. Sparse autoencoders find applications in fields such as Natural Language Processing (NLP), image compression, as well as bioinformatics, where identifying key features is crucial (Wang et al., 2018).

3.3. Undercomplete Autoencoders

Undercomplete autoencoders are a type of autoencoder with a bottleneck architecture, where the latent space has fewer dimensions than the input data (Buongiorno D et al., 2019). By retaining just, the most important elements of the input, this architectural restriction encourages the model to learn condensed, compressed representations. Undercomplete autoencoders make sure that the encoder eliminates noise and unnecessary data by reducing the reconstruction of error during training, which ends up in a highly efficient latent representation. In the bottleneck layer from the Undercomplete autoencoder, the encoder reduces the data given as input to a certain number of dimensions, and the decoder utilizes this compressed representation for recovering the actual input. For applications like visualization of data, compression, and exploratory data analysis that call for dimensionality reduction, this architecture is especially helpful. Undercomplete autoencoders are resilient for extracting essential characteristics because they naturally prevent the formation of trivial identity mappings, in contrast to simple autoencoders. There are various applications like photograph compression, processing of audio signal, and recommendation systems, where computational efficiency and compact data representations are critical (Dardas & Petriu, 2011).

4. METHODOLOGY

4.1. Description of Dataset

The image dataset named LeapGestRecog is an extensive group of hand gesture images created especially to help with both the development and evaluation of reliable hand gesture recognition models. Ten different hand motion classes make the total of roughly 20,000 photos in this collection. Each class contains roughly 2,000 images that have been carefully selected to depict a broad range of positions, orientations, and lighting conditions, making them an invaluable tool for creating machine learning models that can generalize to many real-world situations.

Each of the ten primary folders that house the photos corresponds to a distinct class of hand gestures. These classes cover a range of common hand gestures that humans typically use in communication, from simple hand shapes to more complex movements. The dataset offers a rich diversity of images, ensuring the model training process includes examples of gestures performed in different environmental conditions and varied hand orientations. This diversity has a vital role in enabling the creation of reliable systems for gesture recognition that will work effectively in real-world applications, such as human-computer interaction, interpretation of sign language.

Fig. 2(a). Palm Fig. 2(b). L Fig. 2(c). Fist Fig. 2(d). Fist Moved Fig. 2(e). Thumb Fig. 2(f). Index Fig. 2(g). Ok Fig. 2(h). Palm Moved Fig. 2(i). C Fig. 2(j). Down

Figure 2. Sample images

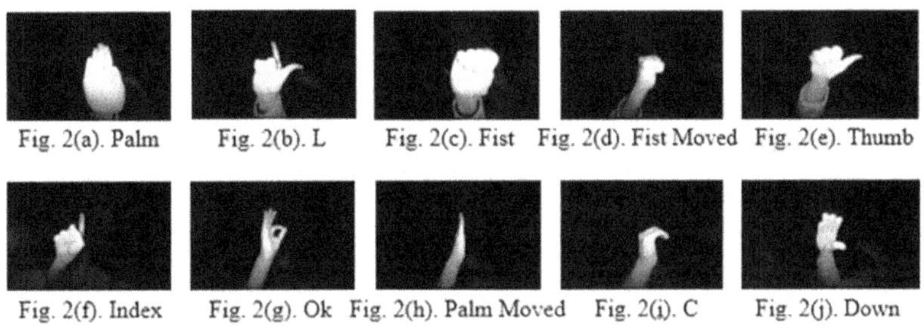

The 10 gesture classes in the dataset are as follows:

01_palm: This class consists of images representing an open palm as shown in Fig. 2(a)., a gesture widely used to signal "stop" or "wait." It captures various orientations of the palm, including front-facing, side-facing, and different hand angles.
02_l: The "L" gesture is made by extending the index as well as the thumb finger as shown in Fig. 2(b)., creating a shape of letter "L." This gesture can be used in various contexts, including as an indicator or symbol of "left."
03_fist: This class includes images of a closed fist as shown in Fig. 2(c)., which is a universal symbol of strength or solidarity. The images capture fists from different angles, with varying degrees of tightness, reflecting real-world variations of the gesture.
04_fist_moved: This gesture represents a fist that is in motion as shown in Fig. 2(d)., typically used in actions such as punching or shaking a fist. It includes images of the fist gesture being moved in different directions, representing dynamic movement.
05_thumb: The thumb gesture consists of images where the thumb is extended as shown in Fig. 2(e)., often used for showing approval. This class captures variations of the thumb gesture, including different orientations and angles.

06_index: The index gesture focuses on the extension of the index finger, often used for pointing as shown in Fig. 2(f). It captures the pointing gesture in various directions and hand positions, allowing the model to differentiate between a static and dynamic pointing gesture.
07_ok: The "OK" gesture, formed by joining the tip of the thumb and index finger to create a circle as shown in Fig. 2(g)., is commonly used to signal approval or agreement. This class includes images of the "OK" sign, in both stationary and slightly moving variations.
08_palm_moved: This class includes images of a palm that is in motion as shown in Fig. 2(h)., representing a dynamic hand gesture. The movement of the palm can signify waving, signaling, or an invitation, and this class includes both small and large movements.
09_c: The "C" gesture is made by curving the fingers to form the shape of the letter "C" as shown in Fig. 2(i). It is often used in sign language or for representing the shape of an object. The images in this class capture the "C" gesture from various hand positions and angles.
10_down: This gesture is characterized by a downward-facing hand as shown in Fig. 2(j)., typically indicating a command or instruction to lower something or to signify "down." It includes images of the hand pointing downwards or positioned with the palm facing downward, in both still and moving forms.

The pre-processed and categorized images in the dataset have been prepared for use in machine learning applications, particularly the ones involving multi-class categorization. Researchers and developers working on hand gesture detection apps will find this dataset particularly beneficial as it offers a wealth of resources for model training and performance assessment. The dataset's diverse collection of gestures, stances, and lighting conditions increases the likelihood that machine learning models trained on it would perform well in real-world situations, where hand orientations and the surrounding circumstances could vary greatly.

4.2. Flowchart & Description

Figure 3. Detailed flow chart

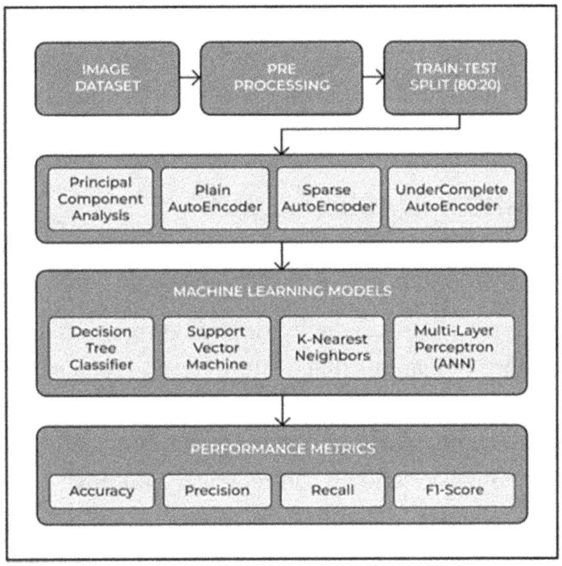

4.2.1. Image Dataset

In the task of hand gesture recognition, our dataset consists of hand gestures images that are classified into multiple categories. Each image represents a unique gesture and has been captured in a variety of settings in order to ensure that model performs well while applied to the actual data. These photos are usually preprocessed and resized to an appropriate standard size (e.g., 80x80 pixels) to ensure consistency (Panwar M 2012). The dataset can be categorized as testing and training data to guarantee a complete assessment of the functionality of the model. These image datasets can be collected from various sources, including real-time camera feeds or manually curated datasets.

4.2.2. Pre-Processing

In machine learning pipelines, pre-processing is an important step, in particular when working with image data as shown in Fig. 3. In this instance, downsizing the photos to an 80x80 pixel size is the first step. For the purpose of making the photos compatible with machine learning models that need 1D data inputs, they are then flattened into vectors. To make sure that pixel values stay inside a particular range (e.g., 0 to 1), methods like scaling and normalization can additionally be used. Pre-processing ensures improved convergence and quicker machine learning model training by lowering complexity and computational load (Sharma A et al., 2020).

4.2.3. Train-Test Split

To guarantee that the model is trained on one part of the data and assessed on another, the dataset is separated into training and testing sets, usually in an 80:20 ratio. This split guarantees that the model generalizes well to unknown data and helps prevent overfitting. The testing set is set aside for the last assessment, and the training set is used to train the models. When working with unbalanced datasets, a stratified split can be used to guarantee that each class is fairly represented in both the training and testing sets.

4.2.4. Dimensionality Reduction & Autoencoders

4.2.4.1. Principal Component Analysis (PCA)

Principal Component Analysis (PCA) reduces dataset dimensionality by recognizing principal components—linear combinations of features that capture most variance. By selecting the top k components based on their eigenvalues, PCA simplifies the feature space, allowing machine learning models to focus on the most informative elements. This improves computational efficiency and addresses the curse of dimensionality, where high-dimensional data can increase complexity and overfitting. PCA helps to reduce redundant information and noise, making the data more suitable for modeling while preserving key patterns and relationships.

4.2.4.2. Plain Autoencoder

A neural network model called the plain autoencoder is made to learn effective input data coding. It is composed of a decoder which reconstructs what was originally input of the encoded representation and an encoder which lowers input data to a lower-dimensional latent form. In order to maintain significant features in the latent space, the trained network minimizes the distinctness among the original input as well as the reconstructed input. The plain autoencoder can assist in compressing the visual data and extracting the most important features that characterize each hand gesture in the context of hand gesture identification.

4.2.4.3. Sparse Autoencoder

Sparse Autoencoders introduce a sparsity constraint on the activations of the hidden layer neurons. Hidden layer neuron's activations that are subject to a sparsity constraint thanks to sparse autoencoders. With fewer neurons being active at any given time, this helps the network to learn more condensed and effective depiction of the input data. Because model ignores unnecessary information and concentrates on the most crucial features, this can result in improved extraction of features and more reliable hand gesture representations (Kumar V et al., 2014).

4.2.4.4. Undercomplete Autoencoder

The undercomplete autoencoder is a variant where the hidden layer's neuron count is smaller compared to the input layer, forcing the model to discover a condensed version of the data. When dimensionality reduction is the goal at hand, this autoencoder version is extremely useful. The undercomplete autoencoder can enhance the generalization of machine learning models by eliminating extraneous information and noise from the data by compelling the network of neurons to learn a lower-dimensional representation.

4.2.5. Machine Learning Algorithms

4.2.5.1. Decision Tree Classifier (DTC)

The Decision Tree Classifier (DTC) is a fundamental machine learning algorithm that is frequently used for jobs involving both regression and classification. due to its simplicity and interpretability. In hand gesture recognition, DTC plays a pivotal role by providing a clear, intuitive process for classifying gestures based on extracted features. The algorithm creates a structure resembling a tree, with each internal node standing for a feature or attribute of the input data, each branch corresponds to a decision criterion or threshold, and the leaf nodes indicate the predicted gesture class. The process begins at the root node, evaluating the data's feature values and selecting the corresponding branches at each decision point until a leaf node is reached, which delivers final classification result. This hierarchical, step-by-step process allows DTC to segment data into progressively more homogeneous subsets, ensuring precise gesture classification. However, the algorithm is sensitive to the input features' quality, making Pre-processing and techniques for feature extraction essential for optimal performance.

DTC is particularly effective when combined with techniques such as Principal Component Analysis (PCA) as well as autoencoders for feature extraction, which refine raw input data into more meaningful representations. These techniques not only improve the classifier's accuracy but also simplify computations by concentrating on the most relevant aspects of the data. PCA, for instance, is a dimensionality reduction method that preserves the majority of the dataset's variance while reducing high-dimensional data to a lower number of primary components. When integrated with PCA, DTC benefits from a simplified feature set that eliminates redundancy and noise, leading to faster computations and more efficient decision-making. By concentrating on the core features of the gesture data, the decision tree becomes less susceptible to overfitting and more dependable and interpretable.

Autoencoders, however are neural network-related models that learn compressed representations of data. A plain autoencoder extracts features in order to recreate the original input by first encoding the data into a lower-dimensional latent space and then decoding it again. Compressed features learned by the autoencoder retain essential information while discarding irrelevant details. When paired with DTC, these features enable the classifier to achieve high accuracy and robustness in gesture recognition. The plain autoencoder guarantees that the extracted features are rich as well as informative, supplying a solid basis for the process of making decisions.

A sparse autoencoder, a variation of the plain autoencoder, introduces a sparsity constraint during training, which makes the model concentrate on the most important aspects of the given data. This results in a more generalized feature set that emphasizes key attributes while minimizing overfitting. While the use of sparse autoencoders may slightly reduce performance metrics compared to plain autoencoders, they significantly enhance the robustness of the model and applicability to real-time scenarios where input data can vary greatly.

The undercomplete autoencoder is another variation that deliberately reduces the capacity of the hidden layer, compelling model to learn condensed and short input data representations. These representations capture most critical information in a highly efficient manner. When integrated with DTC, the undercomplete autoencoder's features ensure high predictive performance while maintaining low computational complexity. This makes the combination particularly suitable for resource-constrained applications such as mobile and embedded systems used in gesture recognition.

4.2.5.2. Support Vector Machine (SVM)

A popular and effective supervised machine learning approach for classification and regression problems is the Support Vector Machine (SVM). Regarding the context with respect to hand gesture recognition, by identifying the best hyperplane to divide data points into distinct categories, SVM is excellent at differentiating between various gesture classes. In order to find the hyperplane that optimizes the margin between data points from various classes, the technique maps input attributes into a higher-dimensional space. The following maximized margin guarantees that the classification is robust and minimizes the risk of misclassifying new data. SVM uses kernel functions like linear, polynomial, radial basis function (RBF), or sigmoid to convert nonlinearly separable datasets into a higher-dimensional space where separation is possible. Because SVM relies on a subset of crucial data points called support vectors and can handle high-dimensional data, make it highly efficient and effective for gesture classification tasks. Feature extraction approaches like Principal Component Analysis (PCA) as well as Autoencoders are essential in improving the performance of SVM, particularly for high-dimensional datasets like those used in hand gesture recognition. These methods preprocess raw data to extract the most relevant features, reduce dimensionality, and eliminate noise, thereby improving the SVM classifier's precision and computational effectiveness. When combined with PCA, SVM benefits significantly from reduced data complexity. PCA transforms the high-dimensional input data into a more manageable collection of principle components that best represent the dataset's variation. The following dimensionality reduction simplifies SVM's classification process, as it reduces redundant and irrelevant features. By focusing on the most critical aspects of the gesture data, the SVM model not only improves classification accuracy but also minimizes training time. Additionally, the reduced feature space makes the decision boundaries identified by SVM more interpretable and robust.

Incorporating plain autoencoders into the pipeline further enhances the performance of SVM by generating compressed, informative features. A plain autoencoder learns encoding the input data into a lower-dimensional space and recreating it during decoding to create a latent representation of the data. These latent features preserve the most important details from the initial data while removing noise and redundancies. When these features are fed into SVM, the classifier benefits from a refined feature set, enabling it to achieve high accuracy in gesture recognition tasks. The autoencoder’s ability to preserve relevant patterns in the data complements SVM’s strength in defining precise decision boundaries.

A sparse autoencoder, which adds a sparsity constraint during training, extracts feature that concentrate on the input data's most notable features. These sparse features emphasize key components, improving the generalization capability of SVM. While this approach might slightly reduce the precision of the classifier in controlled environments, it enhances robustness, making it appropriate for practical uses where input data may differ greatly. This integration helps SVM handle variations in gesture data more effectively while maintaining its classification performance.

Using an undercomplete autoencoder, SVM benefits from compact and concise feature representations. This type of autoencoder limits the hidden layer's capacity, forcing the model to identify the key characteristics of the input data. These simplified yet meaningful representations allow SVM to classify gestures efficiently while reducing computational overhead. The reduced complexity of the feature space ensures that the decision boundaries defined by SVM are both accurate and generalizable, even in challenging conditions.

4.2.5.3. K-Nearest Neighbors (KNN)

For classification and regression applications, the K-Nearest Neighbors (KNN) algorithm is a straightforward yet powerful supervised machine learning technique. In hand gesture recognition, KNN operates by comparing the input gesture's features with those of the stored dataset and allocating a class according to the closest neighbors' majority vote. The "closeness" will be typically measured employing distance metrics like Euclidean, Manhattan, otherwise Minkowski distance. KNN is highly intuitive, because it is predicated on the idea that motions that are similar are probably members of the same class. Its instance-based nature eliminates the need for a training phase, as it directly utilizes the data for classification. However, KNN's performance heavily depends on the standard of feature extraction and the selection of parameters, including the distance metric and the value of kk (the number of neighbors). To improve its performance in high-dimensional datasets, such as those in hand gesture recognition, techniques for feature extraction such as Principal Component Analysis (PCA) as well as Autoencoders play a crucial role. These methods preprocess the input data to extract meaningful features, reduce noise, and minimize dimensionality, thereby enhancing KNN's efficiency and accuracy.

When combined with PCA, KNN benefits from reduced data dimensionality, as PCA transforms the original high-dimensional feature divide the data into fewer major components while preserving the greatest amount of variance. This lowers computational overhead in addition to ensure that KNN focuses on the most relevant features for classification. By discarding irrelevant or noisy dimensions, PCA makes the nearest neighbor comparisons more meaningful, improving the accuracy and speed of KNN. Additionally, the reduced feature space mitigates the "curse of dimensionality," a common challenge in KNN, where increasing dimensions can dilute the meaningfulness of distance metrics.

Incorporating plain autoencoders into the pipeline further enhances KNN's performance by generating compressed, informative feature representations. A plain autoencoder encodes the incoming data into a lower-dimensional space to learn a latent representation of it, and then reconstructing that during decoding. These latent features retain essential information while removing redundancies. When fed into KNN, these features enable the algorithm to make more accurate and efficient classifications. The autoencoder's ability to distill the gesture data into its most salient aspects complements KNN's reliance on proximity-based comparisons.

A sparse autoencoder, which applies a sparsity constraint during training, extracts feature that focus on the most critical and distinctive attributes of the input data. These sparse features help KNN generalize better to new, unseen gestures by the data's most essential features and reducing impact of noise or irrelevant information. While this approach might slightly affect KNN's performance in perfectly clean datasets, it improves resilience and flexibility, which makes it appropriate for real-world situations where gesture data can differ greatly.

Using an undercomplete autoencoder, KNN benefits from highly compact and concise feature representations. The undercomplete autoencoder limits the hidden layer's capability, forcing the model to learn just the most important information. These compressed representations improve the computational efficiency of KNN while retaining enough information for accurate classification. By simplifying the input space, the undercomplete autoencoder ensures that KNN's distance-based calculations are both meaningful and efficient, even in resource-constrained environments.

4.2.5.4. Multi-Layer Perceptron (MLP)

One of the core topologies of artificial neural networks is the Multi-Layer Perceptron (MLP), an extremely effective supervised machine learning technique. It works especially well for problems involving regression and classification, such as recognizing hand gestures. Each layer of MLP is made up of interconnected nodes, or neurons, and includes an input layer, one or more hidden layers, and an output layer. By using weights, biases, and activation functions to process input data, these neurons enable the network to recognize intricate patterns and connections. Under the context of hand gesture recognition, MLP classifies gestures by processing the input features through its layered structure, learning non-linear decision boundaries to distinguish between gesture classes. The ability of MLP to model intricate relationships makes it especially useful for high-dimensional gesture data. However, its performance is heavily influenced by the quality of feature extraction and Pre-processing techniques, which ensure that only the most relevant information is fed into the network.

To enhance MLP's efficiency and accuracy, approaches of feature extraction like Principal Component Analysis (PCA) as well as autoencoders play a significant role. These techniques preprocess raw gesture data to extract meaningful features, reduce noise, and minimize dimensionality, enabling the MLP to focus on learning essential patterns without being overwhelmed by irrelevant or redundant information.

When paired with PCA, MLP benefits from a significant reduction in the complexity of the input data. PCA simplifies the input space while maintaining the most important information by converting high-dimensional gesture data into a smaller number of principal components that capture the largest variation. This reduction minimizes computational requirements, shortens training time, and allows the MLP to concentrate on the most crucial elements, resulting in enhanced classification accuracy and more effective learning. When dealing with huge, high-dimensional datasets, where raw data could normally overwhelm the network, the combination of MLP and PCA is especially beneficial.

Incorporating plain autoencoders further refines the feature extraction process for MLP. A plain autoencoder learns compressed gestural data representations by first encoding the data into a lower-dimensional latent space, and then decoding it to restore the initial input. These latent features retain the essential characteristics of the data while filtering out noise and redundancies. When these features are used as inputs to the MLP, the network can achieve higher accuracy and robustness, as it focuses on the most meaningful aspects of the gestures. The autoencoder complements MLP's learning process by ensuring that the input data is both compact and rich in information.

A sparse autoencoder, which introduces a sparsity constraint during training, extracts feature that highlight the input data's most noteworthy features. This constraint forces the autoencoder to identify and prioritize the most critical patterns, enhancing the generalization capabilities of the MLP. While this approach may slightly increase training time, it improves the robustness of the MLP, making it more resilient to variations in gesture data and more appropriate for practical uses where inputs are often noisy or inconsistent.

Using an undercomplete autoencoder, MLP benefits from highly compact and concise feature representations. By limiting the capacity of the hidden layer, the undercomplete autoencoder reduces the input space's complexity by forcing the model to learn only the most important features. These compact representations make it easier for the MLP to learn and generalize, ensuring accurate gesture classification while minimizing overfitting. The reduced dimensionality of the input also leads to faster training and lower computational requirements, making this combination particularly useful for resource-constrained environments.

4.2.6. Performance Metrics

4.2.6.1. Accuracy

The most popular performance metric for classification tasks is accuracy. It calculates the ratio of accurately categorized samples to all samples. In hand gesture recognition, accuracy reflects how well the algorithm can identify the correct gesture from the image dataset. However, In datasets that are unbalanced, it may be deceptive, the model may predict the majority class well but fail to detect minority class gestures.

$$Accuracy = \frac{True\ Positive\ (TP) + True\ Negative\ (TN)}{True\ Positive\ (TP) + False\ Negative\ (FN) + True\ Negative\ (TN) + False\ Positive\ (FP)} \quad (1)$$

4.2.6.2. Precision

Out of all the positive predictions the model makes, precision quantifies the percentage of accurate positive predictions. It is particularly crucial when false positive costs are significant. In the context of hand gesture recognition, precision helps determine how accurately the model predicts a specific gesture class without misclassifying other gestures as that class.

$$Precision = \frac{True\ Positive\ (TP)}{True\ Positive\ (TP) + False\ Positive\ (FP)} \quad (2)$$

4.2.6.3. Recall

Recall, sometimes referred to as sensitivity or true positive rate, quantifies the percentage of real positive samples that the model accurately detected. When the expense of false negatives is significant, such when failing to recognize a gesture may have severe consequences. Recall ensures that the model identifies as many instances of a particular gesture class as possible.

$$Recall = \frac{True\ Positive\ (TP)}{True\ Positive\ (TP) + False\ Negative\ (FN)} \quad (3)$$

4.2.6.4. F1 Score

The F1 score is a balanced metric that takes into consideration both false positives and false negatives. It is calculated as the harmonic mean of precision and recall. When working with unbalanced datasets, where accuracy by itself might not give a whole view of model performance, it is especially helpful. A more thorough assessment of the model's performance across the majority and minority classes is offered by the F1 score.

Each of these metrics is employed to assess and contrast the various machine learning algorithms' (DTC, SVM, KNN, and MLP) performance in hand gesture recognition. By analyzing these metrics, it is possible to select the model that provides the best trade-off between correctly identifying gestures and minimizing misclassifications.

$$F1\ Score = \frac{2 * precision * recall}{precision + recall} \quad (4)$$

Precision: the percentage of optimistic forecasts that come true. The accuracy of optimistic predictions is its main focus.

Recall: how many real positive examples the model accurately classifies as positive. It centers on the model's capacity to identify every true positive.

True Positive (TP): The frequency with which the model accurately forecasts the positive class.
True Negative (TN): Represents how often the negative class is accurately predicted by the model.
False Positive (FP): Denotes how many times the model guesses the positive class erroneously.
False Negative (FN): Illustrates how many times the model guesses the negative class wrong.

5. RESULTS & DISCUSSION

Four supervised classifiers—Decision Tree (DTC), Support Vector Machine (SVM), K-Nearest Neighbors (KNN), as well as Multi-Layer Perceptron (MLP) were employed for evaluating the efficacy of the hand gesture detection system. Several feature extraction methods, including Principal Component Analysis (PCA), Plain Autoencoder, Sparse Autoencoder, and Undercomplete Autoencoder, were used to test the classifiers. Testing Accuracy, Precision, Recall, as well as the F1-Score were the four main metrics of performance which are the focus of the study. By weighing the accuracy of positive predictions (Precision), the comprehensiveness of capturing all pertinent occurrences (Recall), and an overall effectiveness score (F1-Score), these metrics offer a complete assessment of performance of the model.

5.1. PCA Performance

Table 1. Performance metrics by ML algorithms with PCA

Model Name	Training Accuracy	Testing Accuracy
Decision Tree	0.8434	0.8159
SVM	0.9006	0.8936
KNN	0.9806	0.9706
MLP Classifier	0.8630	0.8530

The Decision Tree Classifier achieved a training accuracy around 84.34% and a testing accuracy around 81.59% as demonstrated in Table 1. This indicates that the algorithm performed consistently during training and evaluation after the dataset's dimensionality was reduced. The Support Vector Machine demonstrated robust performance, with a training accuracy around 90.06% and a testing accuracy around 89.36%. PCA enhanced SVM's ability to classify gestures efficiently by focusing on essential attributes. K-Nearest Neighbors achieved a training accuracy around 98.06% as well as a testing accuracy around 97.06%. Dimensionality reduction via PCA enabled KNN to perform highly accurate gesture recognition. Multi-Layer Perceptron (MLP) Classifier achieved a training accuracy around 86.30% and a testing accuracy around 85.30%. PCA provided a reduced feature set that supported effective training and testing of the ANN model.

Figure 4. Train and test accuracy comparison

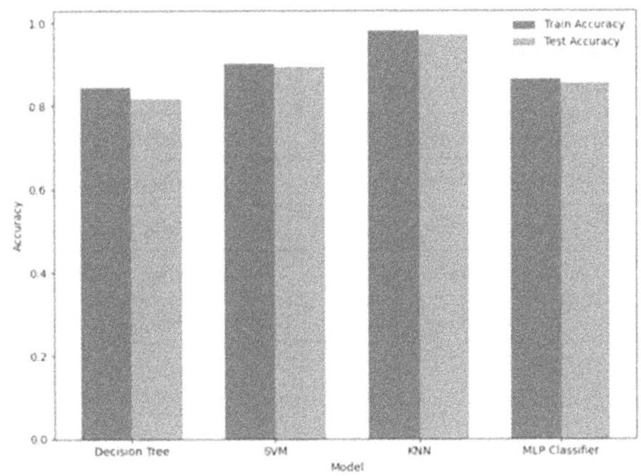

Fig. 4 provides a comprehensive analogy of train and test accuracy across four distinct models - Decision Tree, SVM, KNN, as well as MLP Classifier evaluated with the PCA technique. The Decision Tree model demonstrates the lowest performance, with the train accuracy around 84.34% and a test accuracy around 81.59%. This comparatively poor performance, along with a discernible discrepancy between training and testing accuracy, indicates that the Decision Tree has trouble generalizing, maybe as a result of overfitting or a failure to recognize intricate patterns of the data. Conversely, the SVM model has superior performance, with 90.06% train accuracy and 89.36% test accuracy. The close correspondence between test and training accuracy suggests that the SVM can generalize well to new data, making it a solid choice for tasks that require effective classification with minimal overfitting. The KNN model excels with a train accuracy around 98.06% and a test accuracy around 97.06%, showing highest performance among all models. The minimal difference between the train and test accuracy suggests that KNN is highly capable of learning and generalizing well from the data, effectively capturing underlying patterns with great accuracy. Lastly, the MLP Classifier (ANN) exhibits 86.30% train accuracy and 85.30% test accuracy. In this situation, a basic neural network design could not be as successful as KNN or SVM for reaching higher generalization, even though it performs rather well. This is because its accuracy is lower than that of KNN and SVM. Overall, the findings show that KNN is the most dependable model when it comes to striking a balance between test and training accuracy, however SVM also does well. To get better results, the Decision Tree model could require further optimization, and the MLP Classifier might perform better with some modifications.

5.2. Plain Autoencoder Performance:

Table 2. Performance metrics of ML algorithms with plain autoencoder

Model Name	Testing Accuracy	Precision	Recall	F1- Score
Decision Tree	0.9790	0.9790	0.9790	0.9790
SVM	0.9998	0.9998	0.9998	0.9997
KNN	0.9995	0.9995	0.9995	0.9995
MLP Classifier	0.9998	0.9998	0.9998	0.9998

Figure 5. Performance metrics for plain autoencoder

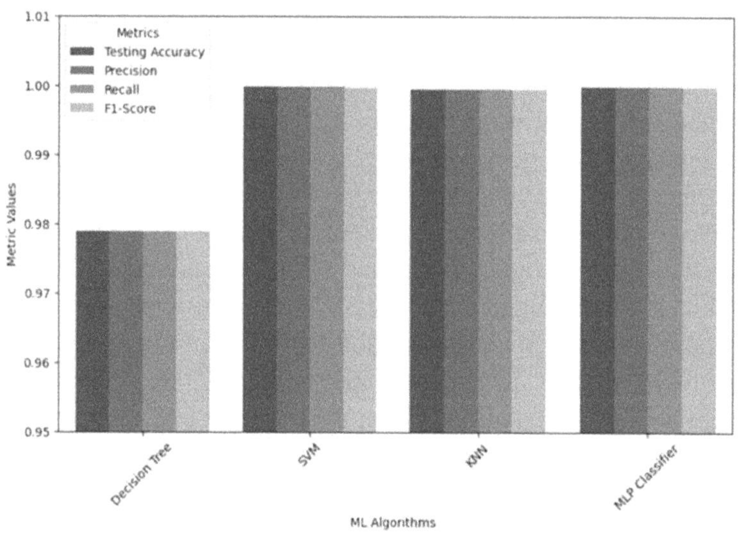

Decision Tree Classifier maintained its performance consistently, achieving 97.90% testing accuracy and 97.90% precision, recall, as well as F1-score as illustrated in Table 2. Classification procedure of DTC benefited from the autoencoder's capacity to maintain important data features throughout reconstruction. Support vector machine showed constant brilliance along with precision, recall, and F1-score values closely matching around 99.98% and 99.97%, respectively, and testing accuracy around 99.98%. The classification capabilities of SVM were backed by the robust feature learning of the plain autoencoder. K-Nearest Neighbors achieved testing accuracy, precision, recall, as well as F1-score at 99.95%, performing on par with PCA. KNN was better able to distinguish between different gestures classes thanks to the basic autoencoder. Multi-Layer Perceptron (MLP) Classifier achieving a perfect set of scores with testing accuracy, precision, recall, and F1-score at 99.98%, the Multi-Layer Perceptron (MLP) produced exceptional results. The simple autoencoder's extensive feature representation was crucial to optimizing MLP's predictive ability (Fig. 5).

Table 3. Key metrics of plain autoencoder

Metric	Value
Mean Squared Error (MSE)	0.00052
Mean Absolute Error (MAE)	0.00835
Average SSIM	0.98311
Average PSNR	33.20451

The results presented in the table highlight the effectiveness of the Plain Autoencoder in reconstructing hand gesture images. Mean Squared Error (MSE) and Mean Absolute Error (MAE) values which are notably low, indicating that the autoencoder has successfully minimized the reconstruction error while training. Great quality of the reconstructed pictures is demonstrated by their Average Structural Similarity Index (SSIM) of 0.9831, which indicates that they closely match the original inputs. Furthermore, the reconstruction maintains a high degree of clarity and detail, as indicated by Peak Signal-to-Noise Ratio (PSNR) value around 33.20 as shown in Table 3.

Table 4. Training loss and validation loss of plain autoencoder

Epoch	Training Loss	Validation Loss
1	0.2053	0.1831
2	0.1829	0.1822
3	0.1821	0.1818
4	0.1817	0.1813
5	0.1815	0.1810

Figure 6. Training vs validation loss for plain autoencoder

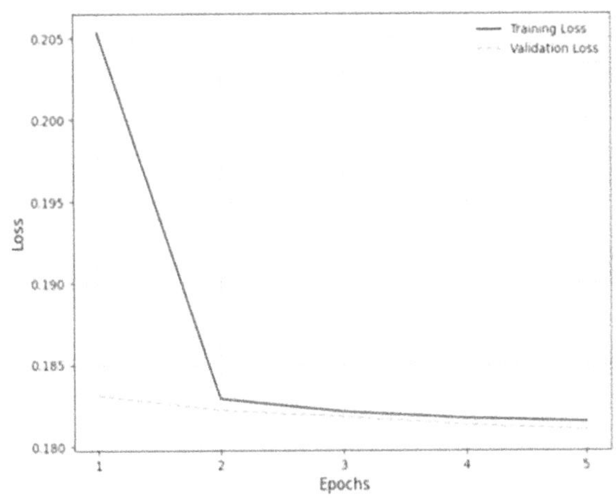

The graphical Fig. 6 and Table 4. illustrates a persistent decrease in both training as well as validation loss with the five epochs, highlighting the effective learning capability of Plain Autoencoder. The model's strong generalization to unknown data without appreciable overfitting is demonstrated by validation loss, which monitors the training loss closely. The autoencoder's capacity to recreate hand gesture pictures with a low reconstruction error is demonstrated by the final validation loss of 0.1810. The ability of the model to capture as well as maintaining key characteristics of the input data is demonstrated by its performance, which qualifies it for use in subsequent processes like feature extraction and classification. The graph's consistent convergence highlights the training process's stability and the model's effectiveness in picking up meaningful representations.

5.3. Sparse Autoencoder Performance

Table 5. Performance metrics of ML algorithms with sparse autoencoder

Model Name	Testing Accuracy	Precision	Recall	F1- Score
Decision Tree	0.9633	0.9636	0.9633	0.9633
SVM	0.9998	0.9998	0.9998	0.9997
KNN	1.0000	1.0000	1.0000	1.0000
MLP Classifier	0.9990	0.9990	0.9990	0.9990

Figure 7. Performance metrics comparison for sparse autoencoder

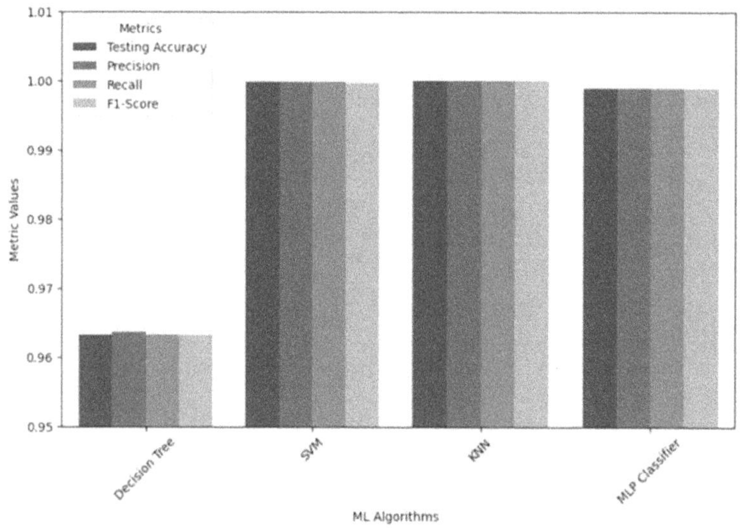

Decision Tree Classifier showed a modest decline in performance, attaining 96.33% testing accuracy, 96.36% precision, and 96.33% recall as well as F1-score as demonstrated in Table 5. It's possible that some features crucial to DTC's decision-making process were left out due to the sparsity constraint.

Support vector machine maintained to perform remarkably well, achieving a 99.98% testing accuracy and steady precision, recall, and F1-score metrics around 99.98% as well as 99.97%, respectively. By concentrating on important features, sparse autoencoders increased the robustness of SVM. K-Nearest Neighbors algorithm performed flawlessly, achieving 100% accuracy, precision, recall, and F1-score in tests. KNN's proximity-based classification method profited from the sparse autoencoder's capacity to separate important features. Multi-Layer Perceptron Classifier achieved 99.90% on all measures, indicating somewhat lower performance. The loss of some complex patterns due to feature sparsity may have somewhat impacted MLP's overall classification ability (Fig. 7).

Table 6. Key metrics of sparse autoencoder

Metric	Value
Mean Squared Error (MSE)	0.00168
Mean Absolute Error (MAE)	0.02052
Average SSIM	0.91551
Average PSNR	28.01467

The results in the table provide insight into the performance of the Sparse Autoencoder in reconstructing hand gesture images. In comparison to the Plain Autoencoder, the higher values of Mean Squared Error (MSE) as well as Mean Absolute Error (MAE) suggest somewhat larger reconstruction errors. The structural fidelity of reconstructed pictures is moderately reduced when compared to their originals, as indicated by the Average Structural Similarity Index (SSIM) of 0.9155, which is still good. Likewise, a decrease in visual quality and detail preservation is reflected in Peak Signal-to-Noise Ratio (PSNR) value around 28.01 as shown in Table 6.

Table 7. Training loss and validation loss of sparse autoencoder

Epoch	Training Loss	Validation Loss
1	0.0213	0.0049
2	0.0040	0.0034
3	0.0032	0.0030
4	0.0030	0.0033
5	0.0027	0.0024

Figure 8. Training vs validation loss for sparse autoencoder

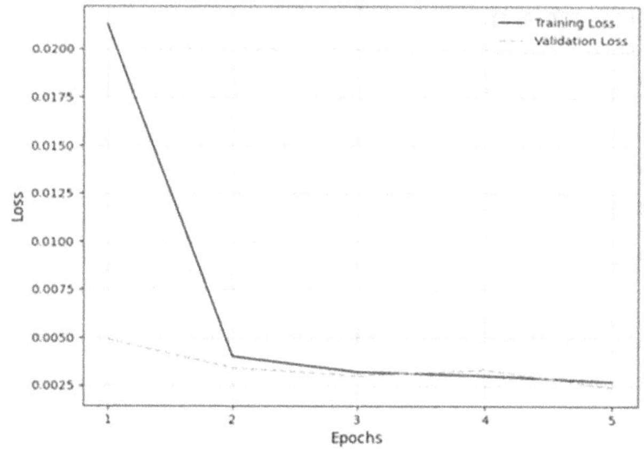

The graphical Fig. 8 and Table 7 illustrates a significant decrease in both training as well as validation loss with five epochs, showcasing the Sparse Autoencoder's capability to effectively learn sparse and compact representations of hand gesture images. With low overfitting and strong generalization, the validation loss nearly matches the training loss. A high degree of accuracy in recreating the input pictures with little mistake is indicated by the final validation loss of 0.0024. The benefit of sparsity restrictions in concentrating on key traits while ignoring unnecessary information is demonstrated by this performance. The graph's quick convergence of the model attests to the Sparse Autoencoder's capacity to pick up effective and significant representations in a brief amount of training time. Because of these characteristics, it is a reliable option for jobs involving feature extraction and dimensionality reduction.

5.4. Undercomplete Autoencoder Performance

Table 8. Performance metrics of ML algorithms with undercomplete autoencoder

Model Name	Testing Accuracy	Precision	Recall	F1- Score
Decision Tree	0.9785	0.9785	0.9785	0.9785
SVM	0.9802	0.9812	0.9802	0.9802
KNN	0.9978	0.9977	0.9978	0.9977
MLP Classifier	0.9968	0.9968	0.9968	0.9968

Figure 9. Performance metrics comparison for undercomplete autoencoder

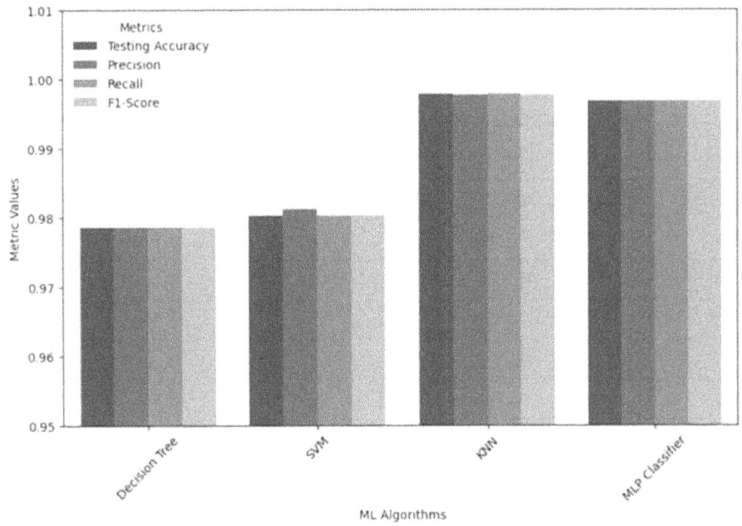

Decision Tree Classifier demonstrated strong performance, along precision, recall, and F1-score all around 97.85% and testing accuracy around 97.85% as demonstrated in Table 8. Its ability to make decisions was, however, marginally hampered by the decreased feature representation. Support vector machine performed well, achieving 98.02% accuracy and 98.12% precision, 98.02% recall, and 98.02% F1-score, respectively. Some sensitivity to compressed features is indicated by the minor decline in performance compared to other feature sets. K-Nearest Neighbors performed well as precision, recall, and F1-score everything hovering near to 99.77%, KNN demonstrated a testing accuracy of 99.78%. Reduced features had a minor effect, but KNN's performance was still strong, demonstrating its versatility. Multi-Layer Perceptron achieved a score of 99.68% on all criteria, indicating that MLP was able to maintain good classification abilities even when feature sets were compressed, but with a tiny decrease in comparison to its performance with richer feature sets (Fig. 9).

Table 9. Key metrics of undercomplete autoencoder

Metric	**Value**
Mean Squared Error (MSE)	0.00439
Mean Absolute Error (MAE)	0.027210
Average SSIM	0.880267
Average PSNR	24.28308

Table 9 shows how well the Undercomplete Autoencoder performs when reconstructing images of hand gestures. The higher values of Mean Squared Error (MSE) and Mean Absolute Error (MAE) are compared with Plain and Sparse Autoencoders, indicating increased reconstruction errors. The Average Structural Similarity Index (SSIM) of 0.8803 highlights a notable drop in structural fidelity, suggesting that the reconstructed images retain less similarity to the originals. Additionally, Peak Signal-to-Noise

Ratio (PSNR) value 24.28 reflects a strong decline in the quality of visuals and detail preservation of the reconstructions.

Table 10. Training loss and validation loss of undercomplete autoencoder

Epoch	Training Loss	Validation Loss	Epoch	Training Loss	Validation Loss
1	0.3693	0.2657	26	0.1995	0.1997
2	0.2536	0.2436	27	0.1993	0.1995
3	0.2365	0.2308	28	0.1991	0.1994
4	0.2265	0.2237	29	0.1990	0.1992
5	0.2209	0.2193	30	0.1988	0.1991
6	0.2171	0.2160	31	0.1987	0.1990
7	0.2143	0.2136	32	0.1986	0.1988
8	0.2122	0.2116	33	0.1985	0.1987
9	0.2104	0.2100	34	0.1983	0.1986
10	0.2089	0.2085	35	0.1982	0.1985
11	0.2075	0.2072	36	0.1981	0.1984
12	0.2063	0.2061	37	0.1980	0.1983
13	0.2052	0.2051	38	0.1979	0.1982
14	0.2044	0.2043	39	0.1978	0.1981
15	0.2036	0.2036	40	0.1977	0.1980
16	0.2030	0.2030	41	0.1976	0.1980
17	0.2024	0.2025	42	0.1976	0.1979
18	0.2019	0.2021	43	0.1975	0.1978
19	0.2015	0.2017	44	0.1974	0.1977
20	0.2011	0.2013	45	0.1973	0.1976
21	0.2008	0.2009	46	0.1972	0.1975
22	0.2005	0.2006	47	0.1971	0.1975
23	0.2002	0.2004	48	0.1971	0.1974
24	0.1999	0.2001	49	0.1970	0.1973
25	0.1997	0.1999	50	0.1969	0.1973

Figure 10. Training vs validation loss for undercomplete autoencoder

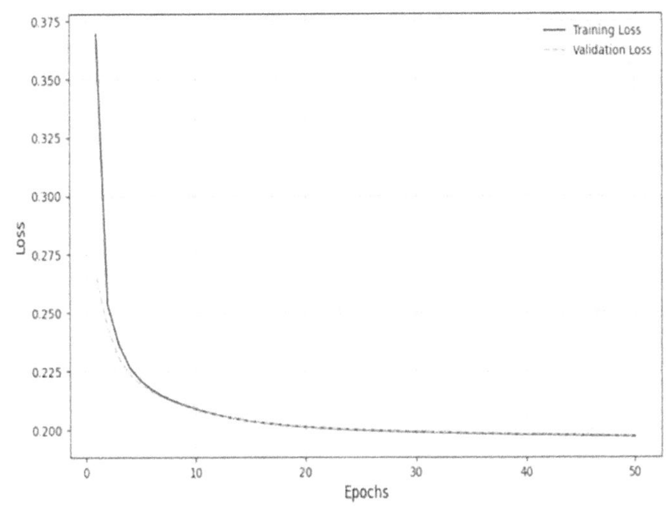

The graphical Fig. 10 and Table 10. illustrates a steady reduction in both training as well as validation loss across the epochs, demonstrating the Undercomplete Autoencoder's ability to effectively learn compact representations of input data. Both the curves of training and validation loss decrease consistently, indicating the model's performance is improving over time with minimal fluctuations. The model achieves a high degree of accuracy in recreating the input data with minimum error, as evidenced by the final validation loss of 0.1973. Good generalization and little overfitting are suggested by the tight tracking between validation loss and training loss. Undercomplete Autoencoder, good model for tasks like dimensionality reduction and anomaly detection because of its steady and slow convergence, which demonstrates that it is learning effective representations while maintaining important aspects of the data.

Table 11. Comparison of the accuracy attained in recent related works.

Related Work	**Year**	**Classification Framework**	**Accuracy (%) Attained**
Mohamed, N., Mustafa, M. B., & Jomhari, N.	2021	Convolutional Neural Network, SVM, Random Forest	98.00%
Sahoo et al.	2022	Fine-Tuned CNNs with Score Fusion	90.26%
Al Mudawi et al.	2024	1D CNN with SSMD Tracking & Population-Based Incremental Learning	85.71%
Ikne et al.	2025	AG-MAE: Anatomically Guided Spatio-Temporal Masked Auto-Encoder	82.0%
Proposed	2025	Plain Autoencoder with SVM	99.98%

Table 11 presents a comparison of accuracy attained by recent classification frameworks. The proposed method, Plain Autoencoder with SVM, achieves the highest accuracy (99.98%), outperforming previous approaches. As shown in Table 11, a framework using CNN, SVM, and Random Forest attained 98.00%, while another using fine-tuned CNNs with score fusion achieved 90.26%. A 1D CNN with

SSMD Tracking & Population-Based Incremental Learning obtained 85.71%, and an AG-MAE-based method recorded 82.0%. The results indicate that advanced techniques did not surpass the proposed autoencoder-based approach, demonstrating its effectiveness.

6. CONCLUSION

This research investigates the application of generative autoencoders in union with traditional machine learning (ML) algorithms to develop an efficient and accurate hand gesture recognition system. Principal Component Analysis (PCA) and autoencoders (Plain, Sparse, and Undercomplete) are utilized to decrease dimensions in the dataset. Decision Tree, Support Vector Machine (SVM), K-Nearest Neighbors (KNN), and Multi-Layer Perceptron (MLP) models are then used to assess classification performance. Accuracy, precision, recall, and F1-score are standard measures that were used to carefully evaluate the system's performance. Techniques for reducing dimensionality have been shown to greatly improve classification accuracy. KNN had the greatest test accuracy of 97.06% with PCA, while other models performed quite well. The incorporation of autoencoders, namely Sparse and Undercomplete Autoencoders, showed their superiority in feature extraction. KNN produced the best results with flawless scores on every assessment criterion while using Sparse Autoencoder. Similarly, Undercomplete Autoencoder empowered KNN and MLP to achieve testing accuracies of 99.78% and 99.68%, respectively. With these advanced characteristics, the SVM and Decision Tree models additionally displayed notable gains, with accuracies of 98.02% and 97.85%, respectively. The importance of generative autoencoders in enhancing the functionality of conventional machine learning models for hand gesture detection tasks is highlighted by this study. Sparse and Undercomplete autoencoders in particular have demonstrated a remarkable capacity to capture intricate, non-linear correlations in data, improving classification results. The study's conclusions provide insightful information for further investigation and use in variety of areas, like assistive technology and health technologies. Real-time deployment, the examination of bigger and more varied datasets, and the use of sophisticated architectures like Transformer-based models and Variational Autoencoders (VAEs) to increase system scalability and robustness are all possible directions for future research.

REFERENCES

Adithya, V., & Rajesh, R. (2020). A deep convolutional neural network approach for static hand gesture recognition. *Procedia Computer Science*, *171*, 2353–2361. DOI: 10.1016/j.procs.2020.04.255

Ahuja, M. K., & Singh, A. (2015). Hand gesture recognition using PCA. [IJCSET]. *International Journal of Computer Science and Engineering Technology*, *5*(7), 267–27.

Al-Hammadi, M., Muhammad, G., Abdul, W., Alsulaiman, M., Bencherif, M. A., Alrayes, T. S., & Mekhtiche, M. A. (2020). Deep learning-based approach for sign language gesture recognition with efficient hand gesture representation. *IEEE Access : Practical Innovations, Open Solutions*, *8*, 192527–192542. DOI: 10.1109/ACCESS.2020.3032140

Al-Hammadi, M., Muhammad, G., Abdul, W., Alsulaiman, M., Bencherif, M. A., & Mekhtiche, M. A. (2020). Hand gesture recognition for sign language using 3DCNN. *IEEE Access : Practical Innovations, Open Solutions*, *8*, 79491–79509. DOI: 10.1109/ACCESS.2020.2990434

Al Mudawi, N., Ansar, H., Alazeb, A., Aljuaid, H., AlQahtani, Y., Algarni, A., Jalal, A., & Liu, H. (2024). Innovative healthcare solutions: Robust hand gesture recognition of daily life routines using 1D CNN. *Frontiers in Bioengineering and Biotechnology*, *12*, 1401803. DOI: 10.3389/fbioe.2024.1401803 PMID: 39144478

Bobić, V., Tadić, P., & Kvaščev, G. (2016, November). Hand gesture recognition using neural network based techniques. In *2016 13th Symposium on Neural Networks and Applications (NEUREL)* (pp. 1-4). IEEE. DOI: 10.1109/NEUREL.2016.7800104

Bousbai, K., & Merah, M. (2022). Enhancement of hand gesture recognition using convolutional neural networks integrating a combination of an autoencoder network and PCA. *International Journal of Pattern Recognition and Artificial Intelligence*, *36*(10), 2256015. DOI: 10.1142/S0218001422560158

Buongiorno, D., Camardella, C., Cascarano, G. D., Murciego, L. P., Barsotti, M., De Feudis, I., & Bevilacqua, V. (2019, July). An undercomplete autoencoder to extract muscle synergies for motor intention detection. In *2019 International Joint Conference on Neural Networks (IJCNN)* (pp. 1-8). IEEE. DOI: 10.1109/IJCNN.2019.8851975

Chaudhary, A., Raheja, J. L., Das, K., & Raheja, S. (2013). Intelligent approaches to interact with machines using hand gesture recognition in natural way: a survey. *arXiv preprint arXiv:1303.2292.*

Chung, H. Y., Chung, Y. L., & Tsai, W. F. (2019, February). An efficient hand gesture recognition system based on deep CNN. In *2019 IEEE International Conference on Industrial Technology (ICIT)* (pp. 853-858). IEEE. DOI: 10.1109/ICIT.2019.8755038

Dardas, N. H., & Petriu, E. M. (2011, September). Hand gesture detection and recognition using principal component analysis. In *2011 IEEE International Conference on Computational Intelligence for Measurement Systems and Applications (CIMSA) Proceedings* (pp. 1-6). IEEE. DOI: 10.1109/CIMSA.2011.6059935

Fang, Y., Wang, K., Cheng, J., & Lu, H. (2007, July). A real-time hand gesture recognition method. In *2007 IEEE International Conference on Multimedia and Expo* (pp. 995-998). IEEE. DOI: 10.1109/ICME.2007.4284820

Ikne, O., Allaert, B., & Wannous, H. (2025, March). AG-MAE: Anatomically Guided Spatio-Temporal Masked Auto-Encoder for Online Hand Gesture Recognition. In *International Conference on 3D Vision.*

Kapitanov, A., Kvanchiani, K., Nagaev, A., Kraynov, R., & Makhliarchuk, A. (2024). HaGRID—HAnd Gesture Recognition Image Dataset. In *Proceedings of the IEEE/CVF Winter Conference on Applications of Computer Vision* (pp. 4572-4581).

Kumar, V., Nandi, G. C., & Kala, R. (2014, August). Static hand gesture recognition using stacked denoising sparse autoencoders. In *2014 Seventh International Conference on Contemporary Computing (IC3)* (pp. 99-104). IEEE. DOI: 10.1109/IC3.2014.6897155

Li, G., Tang, H., Sun, Y., Kong, J., Jiang, G., Jiang, D., Tao, B., Xu, S., & Liu, H. (2019). Hand gesture recognition based on convolution neural network. *Cluster Computing*, *22*(S2), 2719–2729. DOI: 10.1007/s10586-017-1435-x

Li, P., Pei, Y., & Li, J. (2023). A comprehensive survey on design and application of autoencoder in deep learning. *Applied Soft Computing*, *138*, 110176. DOI: 10.1016/j.asoc.2023.110176

Mohamed, N., Mustafa, M. B., & Jomhari, N. (2021). A review of the hand gesture recognition system: Current progress and future directions. *IEEE Access : Practical Innovations, Open Solutions*, *9*, 157422–157436. DOI: 10.1109/ACCESS.2021.3129650

Narayana, P., Beveridge, R., & Draper, B. A. (2018). Gesture recognition: Focus on the hands. In *Proceedings of the IEEE Conference on Computer Vision and Pattern Recognition* (pp. 5235-5244).

Oyedotun, O. K., & Khashman, A. (2017). Deep learning in vision-based static hand gesture recognition. *Neural Computing & Applications*, *28*(12), 3941–3951. DOI: 10.1007/s00521-016-2294-8

Panwar, M. (2012, February). Hand gesture recognition based on shape parameters. In *2012 International Conference on Computing, Communication and Applications* (pp. 1-6). IEEE. DOI: 10.1109/ICCCA.2012.6179213

Qiu, Y., Zhou, W., Yu, N., & Du, P. (2018). Denoising sparse autoencoder-based ictal EEG classification. *IEEE Transactions on Neural Systems and Rehabilitation Engineering*, *26*(9), 1717–1726. DOI: 10.1109/TNSRE.2018.2864306 PMID: 30106681

Sahoo, J. P., Prakash, A. J., Pławiak, P., & Samantray, S. (2022). Real-time hand gesture recognition using fine-tuned convolutional neural network. *Sensors (Basel)*, *22*(3), 706. DOI: 10.3390/s22030706 PMID: 35161453

Sharma, A., Mittal, A., Singh, S., & Awatramani, V. (2020). Hand gesture recognition using image processing and feature extraction techniques. *Procedia Computer Science*, *173*, 181–190. DOI: 10.1016/j.procs.2020.06.022

Sharma, S., & Singh, S. (2021). Vision-based hand gesture recognition using deep learning for the interpretation of sign language. *Expert Systems with Applications*, *182*, 115657. DOI: 10.1016/j.eswa.2021.115657

Spina, D. E., Campos, L. F. D. O., de Arruda, W. F., Melo, A., Alves, M. F. D. S., Rabello, G. L., & Pinto, J. C. (2024). Comparison of autoencoder architectures for fault detection in industrial processes. *Digital Chemical Engineering*, •••, 100162. DOI: 10.1016/j.dche.2024.100162

Subudhi, B. N., Veerakumar, T., Harathas, S. R., Prabhudesai, R., Kuppili, V., & Jakhetiya, V. (2023). Deep Learning in Autoencoder Framework and Shape Prior for Hand Gesture Recognition. In *Smart Computer Vision* (pp. 223–242). Springer International Publishing. DOI: 10.1007/978-3-031-20541-5_10

Wahid, M. F., Tafreshi, R., Al-Sowaidi, M., & Langari, R. (2018). Subject-independent hand gesture recognition using normalization and machine learning algorithms. *Journal of Computational Science*, *27*, 69–76. DOI: 10.1016/j.jocs.2018.04.019

Wang, Y., Wang, C., Wang, Z., Wang, X., & Li, Y. (2018, March). Hand gesture recognition using sparse autoencoder-based deep neural network based on electromyography measurements. In *Nano-, Bio-, Info-Tech Sensors, and 3D Systems II (Vol. 10597, pp. 163-169)*. SPIE. DOI: 10.1117/12.2296382

Chapter 8
Revolutionizing Emergency Medical Services With AI and Telegram Integration

M. Janakirani
Dr. M.G.R. Educational and Research Institute, India

J. Ann Roseela
Dr. M.G.R. Educational and Research Institute, India

S. Anandhi
Dr. M.G.R. Educational and Research Institute, India

B. Swapna
https://orcid.org/0000-0002-7186-2842
Dr. M.G.R. Educational and Research Institute, India

Tamilselvi Durairajan
Panimalar Engineering College, India

R. Kasthuri
Dr. M.G.R. Educational and Research Institute, India

ABSTRACT

In emergencies, nearly every hospital bed was taken, forcing the collapse of the whole health department. Tragically, many patients lost their lives due to the lack of beds, ventilators, medical intensive care units, or oxygen supplies, as well as the difficulties faced by the ambulance drivers who brought them to the hospital. As a result, they had to wait outside the facility for a long time. The main problem is that there isn't a suitable system linking the surrounding hospitals to analyse the patient's condition simultaneously within the ambulance; hospitals with the necessary equipment should be selected at the appropriate moment. One possible solution to this problem is a system that gathers data about hospitals and medical systems' availability from a centralised server page that links to all nearby hospitals. The system then uses artificial neural networks to analyse the patient's condition with the help of the LSAI48266X AI board.

DOI: 10.4018/979-8-3693-8332-2.ch008

INTRODUCTION

Nearly every hospital bed was occupied during the emergency, and the health department failed because of several issues. There was a severe shortage of oxygen, ventilators, beds, and medical intensive care unit beds, which caused the ambulance drivers to wait outside the hospital for an extended period. As a result, people died inside the ambulance.

To avoid this, a technique that monitors the patient's status in the ambulance using an artificial neural network has been devised; the appropriate hospital should be chosen at the proper time. The artificial neural networks will ascertain the patient's state using biological parameters, such as respiration, heartbeat (beats per minute), body temperature, and Spo2 (pulse oximeter). Subsequently, it will categorise the patient's requirements, including ventilator support, oxygen bed support, and MICU support, by verifying the hospital's availability through the networked medical system. Include information from almost 180 countries. Every year, 1.25 million people lose their lives in automobile accidents; the worst hit are nations with low per capita income.

Due to the world population's rapid rise, there is a massive increase in demand for vehicles, which has made traffic congestion and accidents on the roads worse. Accidents causing delayed reactions increase the frequency of deaths, putting the public in danger. An automatic accident detection system is necessary to avoid this case. Any incident involving a moving vehicle, an impediment, or a person is considered a road crash. How long it takes for an ambulance to reach the accident site and carry the patient to the hospital has a significant influence on the victim's chances of survival. Aiming to speed up the collection of data regarding car accidents in India by the emergency response department is the objective of Singh et al. (2021).

Most of the time, minor injuries sustained in an automobile collision may be treated and the victim saved; however, if emergency personnel arrive too late, the injuries can become fatal. The initial goal is to find the scene of the accident and notify the rescue teams as soon as possible so that they can take immediate action to save the victim's life.

Important Technological Advancements in Ambulance Services

1. Integration of point-of-care diagnostic equipment for immediate testing and assessment.
2. Use of mobile communication devices for seamless coordination with hospitals and emergency medical services.
3. Implementation of automated medication dispensing systems to ensure accurate and timely administration of drugs.
4. Adoption of lightweight and portable medical equipment for enhanced mobility and ease of use in emergencies.
5. Incorporation of vehicle telematics for monitoring ambulance performance and maintenance needs in real time.
6. Implementation of remote access technology for specialists to provide real-time guidance to paramedics during critical situations, improving the level of care delivered in the field.
7. Integration of augmented reality (AR) technology to assist paramedics in visualizing patient anatomy and identifying potential injuries, leading to more accurate on-site assessments and interventions.
8. Adoption of drone technology for emergency supply delivery, providing additional medical resources to paramedics at the scene or en route to the hospital.

9. Utilisation of smart triage systems that integrate patient data, GPS information, and real-time traffic updates to determine the most appropriate hospital for patient transport, optimizing resource allocation and reducing transit times.
10. Incorporation of secure and efficient data management systems to ensure the confidentiality and accessibility of patient information, facilitating seamless continuity of care between EMS personnel and hospital staff.

RELATED WORKS

The work of Bublyk et al., (2020) "Decision Support System Design for Low-Voice Emergency Medical Calls at Smart City Based on Chatbot Management. In Social Networks." was recently published. More and more people are choosing to work in the health industry that uses digital technology. These technologies also provide new and unique tools that may be used to convince others of our interests and stay current in other areas of medicine. Utilisation of digital technology to conquer these obstacles with these innovative solutions, such as tracking feasible activities, reviewing their own, or providing access to medical consultations. The authors analysed books and online sources, looked at the primary methods for this problem's evolution, and listed the pros and cons of each. Wooden targets that change the primary objectives were suggested as an outcome of the information system design process. It was determined that several technological methods for transmitting chatbots were valid. Looking at the control case, it's almost likely that the software is doing what it's supposed to and fulfilling its duties, opening the door for team members in Smart City whose specified medical requirements are unknown to get the care they need. Evidence shows how quickly a new software product can be developed. Improvements in response times, patient treatment, and overall results have driven the profession of emergency medical services (EMS) to undergo substantial evolution throughout the years

A Special Unit of Intelligence: Samreen et al., (2023) suggested a space where artificial intelligence and human interaction technologies may meet. In times of crisis, artificial intelligence (AI) can provide the traditional system with the data analysis skills and decision support tools that are lacking. The issue at hand is how to optimise ambulance responses and care in the event of an emergency by integrating artificial intelligence and human interface technology. Among the difficulties that must be overcome are the availability of real-time medical information to improve decision-making, the speed and accuracy of diagnoses, and the communication between healthcare institutions and emergency responders. To enhance patient outcomes during critical periods, we want to design a smooth, intelligent, and sensitive system. When it became clear that emergency medical services might be vastly improved by combining AI with human interface technology, the necessity for intelligence ambulances became apparent. Integrating intelligent technology may greatly assist healthcare workers in making rapid and correct decisions, which is vital in critical situations. Ambulances, hospitals, and other healthcare organisations may all benefit from better coordination, information sharing, and communication using this method.

The idea of an "Artificial Intelligence-Based Ambulance" was brought forward by Sumathi et. al., (2023). Traffic congestion has become a significant problem in densely populated cities. We utilised Arduino to reset the sequence to its default before activating crisis mode since it was initially meant to trigger in response to a signal from a rescue truck utilising radio frequency (RF) transmission. Following this first phase, we will build a platform to enrol patients' medical histories, everything else being equal. With this data, the clinic may save time preparing to treat the new patient. It is possible to retrieve this data by employing unique identification and verifying each user's fingerprint. Before the emergency vehicle's arrival, this data will be sent to the requested clinic. This platform can detect the emergency car and manage the traffic signals since it is entirely electronic. When time is of the essence, this system regulates traffic lights and helps keep everyone safe. It is, therefore, an initiative that provides a lifeline.

To guarantee the safe Application of artificial intelligence in emergency medical care response, the authors Sujan et al., (2022) suggested a study process. Call centre operators for ambulance services fail to detect around 25% of out-of-hospital cardiac arrests (OHCAs), even though this information is critical for the prompt administration of cardiopulmonary resuscitation. The development of an AI system to aid call centre operators in identifying OHCA has been completed. This study aims to prove the OHCA AI decision-support system's clinical safety and determine how individuals engaged with ambulance services feel about its security in call centres. The research will be carried out within the Welsh Ambulance Service. Research and service assessment are both encompassed in the study. This investigation uses a qualitative research strategy predicated on theme extraction from interview records. The service assessment includes tasks such as evaluating documents to build a clinical safety case, studying the AI model and how it was developed, and performing informal interviews with the creators of the technology.

Hampiholi (2024), suggested innovative ambulance systems and advanced diagnostic and monitoring tools to improve emergency healthcare through the Application of technology. Modern, technologically advanced emergency medical services are the focus of this research. Intelligent ambulance systems are mainly under the microscope. This article looks at the technical advancements in Smart Ambulance Systems, namely how they incorporate telemedicine, portable diagnostic gadgets, continuous vital sign monitoring, and the importance of the Internet of Things. An in-depth examination may fully explain case studies, the historical context, and the implementation challenges. The integration of technology, data security, staff training, and the demonstration of accomplishments in patient care and emergency reaction times are all addressed by real-world examples. The article's conclusion includes an analysis of emerging tendencies, such as increasing technological capabilities and their potential future impacts on emergency medical services. The present discussion is about improving emergency medical treatment through technological innovation, and our study aims to contribute to that topic. It lays the groundwork for future innovative ambulance systems research and development.

Research conducted by Ahmed et al., (2023) stated that a protocol for electronic health records in smart cities that uses artificial intelligence to provide autonomous connected ambulance route resource recommendation (ACA-R3). This article proposes a new and unique ACA-R3 protocol to optimise ACA routes by fixing the problems with ACA's connection and resource management. Regarding operation, the ACA-R3 protocol follows the rules laid down by the controlling protocol and the eHealth protocol. This study set out to answer two main research questions by streamlining patient information sharing and shortening handoff times during requested emergencies. Applying the data collected by the GPS tracking unit in ACA and Edge-AI, the suggested ACA-R3 protocol can improve collaborative distributive resource management, leading to more trustworthy decision-making. In this work, we review, confirm, and present the experimental data acquired from three distinct instances of traffic congestion.

Improving Pre-Hospital Emergency Medical Services with the Use of Artificial Intelligence and Voice-Activated Technology was proposed by Azman et. al., (2024) In this project, we will leverage the IoT and wireless body area networks to build a basic but functional gadget that can send data about vital signs like temperature, heart rate, and oxygen saturation to a monitoring platform that is far away. The precision and timeliness of contextual information are crucial in emergency care, and the project aims to enhance data accuracy during emergency transportation and calls through the integration of

Voice Recognition (VR) Module V3, MAX30100, LM35, Arduino Mega, ESP32, and the ThingsBoard platform. By developing a VR system, the project seeks to contribute valuable insights to improve pre-hospital emergency medical services and offer recommendations for strengthening the overall pre-EMS infrastructure. Successful implementation requires expertise in IoT, communication protocols, and the ThingsBoard platform. Additionally, the project quantitatively evaluated the performance of the VR system, demonstrating a significant improvement in data accuracy and timeliness compared to traditional manual recording methods.

Abraham et al., (2024) suggested an evacuation management framework along the path of a smart city-wide IRIS. To improve disaster readiness with advanced sensors, small and medium-sized companies (SMEs), industry, and government bodies can interact with the infrastructures through smart city solutions geared toward deploying 6G networks. Ultimately, this project aims to improve public services and people's quality of life in various settings, such as homes, roads, hospitals, transportation hubs, etc., by proposing coordinated technological solutions to upgrade an existing emergency response system to an intelligent interface system. In this paper, we apply AI and ML approaches to the problem of connected car experiences of the future, with an emphasis on incidents that occur indoors, on city streets, and in extensive public spaces. This intelligent interactive response system will reap the benefits of cutting-edge sensor fusion and AI by creating a dynamic model in real-time.

Feedback for emergency ambulance personnel: a systematic review and meta-analysis of various types and their impacts was proposed by Wilson et al., (2023) Our goal was to compile a literature review on the many forms of feedback that EMS workers get and how it impacts patient care, health and safety, and career advancement opportunities. Approach: Any approach included in a systematic review or meta-analysis, as well as original research findings published in publications that are open to the public. Any study that discussed the use of structured feedback to improve the performance of emergency ambulance personnel was considered for inclusion. We have used the following databases: MEDLINE, Embase, AMED, PsycINFO, HMIC, CINAHL, and Web of Science. Our most recent search was on August 2, 2022. A Mixed Methods Appraisal Tool was used. Using a convergent integrated design, which included random effects, multilevel meta-analyses and simultaneous narrative synthesis, the data was analysed to determine the study's quality.

Becker et al., (2023) analysed to suggest dynamic ambulance relocation. Research on dynamic ambulance relocation was the focus of this project. Mathematics and technological support data have determined the best places for ambulance services depending on response times rather than patient outcomes, which is the current state of knowledge on the dynamic movement of ambulances. On the other hand, there is a paucity of understanding of the effects of dynamic ambulance dispatching on both patient outcomes and the workspace. This review has highlighted many areas lacking the topic's scientific coverage. Our current understanding of several critical issues, such as the best utilisation of ambulances in rural regions, turnaround times, domino effects, and EMS personnel working conditions, is inadequate, and there is a dearth of research reporting on patient outcomes. Further research should focus on filling these gaps in understanding.

Manaa et al., (2024) proposed Application of machine learning techniques for ambulance coverage prediction. Ambulance deployment methods and emergency response systems can be improved with the help of this study. The effectiveness of emergency medical services (EMS) may be measured by ambulance coverage, which is the focus of this research. We look at several ensemble learning models to find the best way to forecast the frequency of ambulance coverage. CatBoost's calculation time of 37.48

seconds, Root Mean Square Error of 0.0192, and modified R-squared score of 91.7% exhibit remarkable prediction precision.

The authors of this study suggest a web-based smartphone app that can detect STEMI ECG patterns in real-time. To precisely identify the STEMI ECG pattern, a Deep Learning-based technique is built into the cloud AI computing server. For mobile clients, the designed system takes advantage of a wireless mobile network's salient characteristics, including smooth connections and quick answers. Our system's primary component is an online AI bot that assists paramedics in diagnosing STEMI in patients and providing the necessary care, including transporting them to the emergency medical centre and administering therapeutic medications. (Babu et. al., 2024)

An Intelligent Vehicle Safety Belt for Use in Smart Cities: Collision Avoidance and Instant Response. The seat belt in this project has a sensor that measures the driver's heart rate and, in the event of an accident, notifies the ambulance of the driver's location. The raw heartbeat sensor data is gathered with information from the car's vibration sensor to ascertain whether an accident has happened. A UNO microcontroller is used to process and decide if there is an accident based on the values of these two collected data points. In the event of an accident, the controller uses the vehicle's GPS to determine its present location and notify the emergency contacts that have been pre-stored. The accident's location will be included in an alert sent by the system via GSM technology. Additionally, a fingerprint is included to verify the passenger's identity so that if the driver changes, the sensor won't record an incorrect heart rate. In this case, the Arduino platform and its integrated development environment (IDE) are used to implement the hardware connections. (Parashar et. al., 2024)

This article on artificial intelligence in emergency nursing details the use of AI in the emergency room for COPD patients. Four hundred forty-seven people with chronic obstructive pulmonary disease (COPD) participated in a randomised controlled experiment to observe the quality of life improvement at four and twelve months after receiving an AI medicinal intervention. The findings indicate that after four months, neither the experimental group nor the control group's quality of life changed; but, after twelve months, as compared to the controls, the experimental group's and the control group's emotional and psychological circumstances had improved obviously. Results from the experiment were favourable for the 29 patients who took part and were split into the experimental and control groups at random. The experimental group experienced a shorter hospital stay and a lower hospitalisation rate for COPD than the control group. The trial results have tentatively supported the efficiency of artificial intelligence medical treatment, but the intervention has not attained substantial relevance for single-factor analysis. (Mahitha et. al., 2024)

Numerous fields, including medicine and biology, are seeing a dramatic increase in the data accessible for research. This study made an effort to use data from the emergency medical database to examine the connection between patients' medical histories and the reason they contacted the ambulance service. An emergency requiring the assistance of an ambulance may have its roots in the patient's chronic illness. Findings from this study may help develop effective therapies for long-term health conditions.

Real-time Traffic Management in an Emergency using Artificial Intelligence Machine intelligence, or AI, is the Application of intelligent behaviour. A computer predicts the problem's answer using algorithms and its brain. AI is just as excellent at tasks as the human brain is. Its primary goal is to create machines that can execute tasks that need human intellect, study their surroundings, and take appropriate action. This study examines the potential impact of artificial intelligence on traffic management in the future. Today, the main issue facing first-world nations is the urban transportation system. This article makes recommendations for the steps that should be taken to ensure that artificial intelligence is implemented flawlessly in the traffic system and to lessen the problems that arise. The paper proposes a design to implement lane management for an adequate traffic flow in the event of a medical emergency. An ambulance's route is followed in real-time, and Sophisticated traffic light management is used to divert traffic. The study also discusses the different concepts and layouts investigated in earlier research projects. (Kamalahasan et. al., 2024)

EXISTING SYSTEM

In the conventional approach, those in need can contact a designated emergency number, such as 911, through a centralised contact centre that manages the traditional dispatch of the ambulance system. Trained call operators answer emergency calls and record important information such as the patient's condition, the nature of the crisis, and the location of the call. Once this information is input into a computer-aided dispatch (CAD) system, an available ambulance is dispatched to the scene based on the severity of the emergency. Ambulance crews arrive at the incident scene, assess the patient, treat them, and transport them to the closest appropriate medical facility after receiving instructions via radio communication. Dispatchers coordinate response operations, while ambulance teams use radio dispatch to navigate their way to the situation. The framework is based on telephone-based communication.

PROPOSED SYSTEM

A suggested approach for integrating AI with the Telegram Channel is described in the article. The focus is optimising ambulance dispatch based on prioritised criteria, applying AI for real-time decision support, and using natural language processing to extract information from emergency messages effectively.

The LSAI48266X Artificial Intelligence board will gather the patient's biomedical data, including Spo2, HB, respiratory, and body temperature. It will then process this data using an algorithm to determine which categories the patient falls into and what kind of support he needs, such as ventilator support, oxygen bed support, or MICU support. This Intelligence board will use the Internet of Things to check the hospital's networked medical system availability. It can be challenging for the entire family to track a critically ill patient who has lost consciousness, including which hospital to go to and how to get there after checking the availability of the required medical systems. Thus, the AI LSAI48266X board will save information on ambulances, specific hospitals, and patients, and it will publish information in the local hospital Telegram community channel that the family members can readily access. By preventing medical systems from being used to quote the wealthiest individuals, which would limit treatment to the underprivileged, and by stopping ambulance drivers from diverting patients to the hospital, this Telegram Channel message would also aid in reducing hospital corruption.

The main problem we encountered during the second wave was that we lacked a suitable system for integrating with all surrounding hospitals to determine which ones had beds, ventilators, medical intensive care units, etc. In addition, by monitoring the parameters of patients in ambulances, the ambulance personnel could not make timely decisions regarding which hospitals had the required medical systems available. We have a proposal.

The system that will prevent such situations is to have the LSAI48266X Artificial Intelligence Board make all hospital choices. It will do this by retrieving information from the hospital's availability and medical system availability from a centralised server page that connects to all nearby hospitals.

The study explores the viability and efficacy of incorporating artificial intelligence (AI) algorithms into Telegram systems to optimise emergency response procedures. Essential elements, including real-time updates, AI-assisted triage, location detection, natural language processing (NLP), and interaction with medical databases, are investigated.

BLOCK DIAGRAM

The system is accessible to users via a Telegram channel. They may send messages, location queries, and messages through this interface. The purpose of a Telegram bot is to process and receive user messages. The bot can comprehend orders in normal language and extract pertinent data, including the location and type of emergency. This module analyses incoming communications using AI algorithms to assess the emergency's immediacy and seriousness. It can also offer first-time medical advice depending on the user's condition.

Figure 1. Block diagram

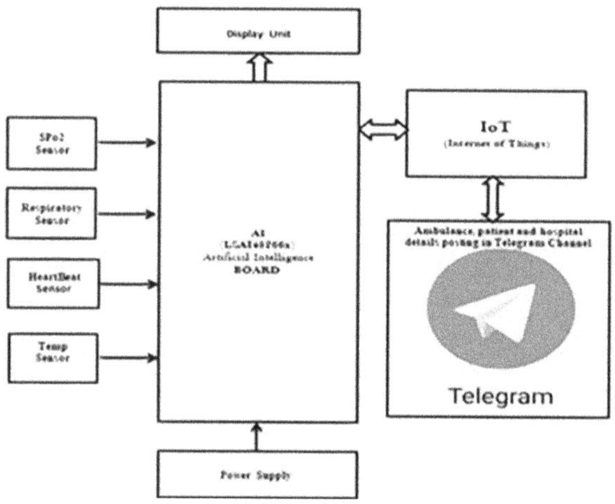

The system keeps track of the whereabouts and availability of ambulances, along with other pertinent data. Ambulance drivers may use the system's real-time navigation to arrive at the emergency site rapidly and efficiently by integrating it with mapping services, as shown in Figure 1.

ARCHITECTURE DIAGRAM

The proposed system consists of five distinct levels are shown in Figure 2. At the very top of the stack are the interfaces and devices. The second layer is composed of microcontrollers. In the layer below, the database is kept, and in the layer below that, services are given full attention. In the end, access to the cloud resources is granted at the last layer. The data is collected and sent with main contacts and ambulances using the Android app Telegram. Hospitals, emergency responders, and healthcare professionals may get real-time updates and alerts from the system via integration with a Telegram channel. The ambulance is equipped with sensors and communication devices.

Figure 2. Architecture

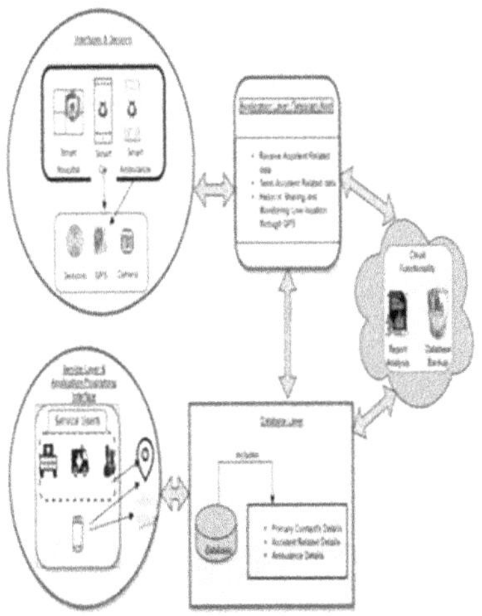

RESULT AND DISCUSSION

IoT: Hospital Status Update

Figure 3. Hospital status update

Telegram Channel Output

Figure 4. Telegram channel output

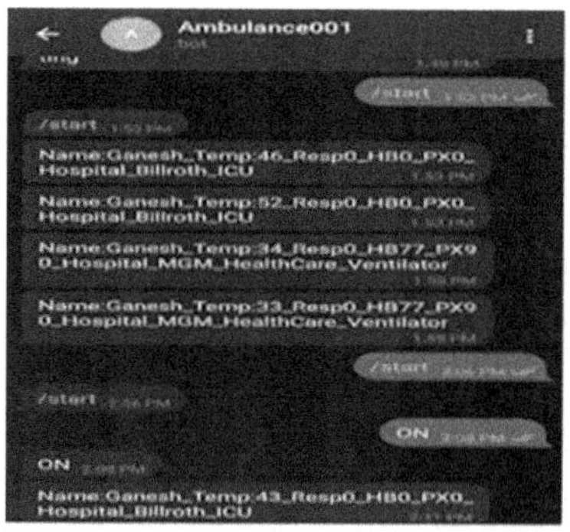

The ambulance is equipped with sensors and communication devices. Real-time information regarding the patient's condition, as well as the position and status of the ambulance, is gathered using sensors like GPS, heart rate monitors, and status. After processing the sensor data, the AI module evaluates the patient's status and ranks the emergency instances according to severity. Hospitals, emergency responders, and healthcare professionals may get real-time updates and alerts from the system via integration with a Telegram channel, as shown in Figure 3 and Figure 4.

Hardware Setup

Figure 5. Hardware setup

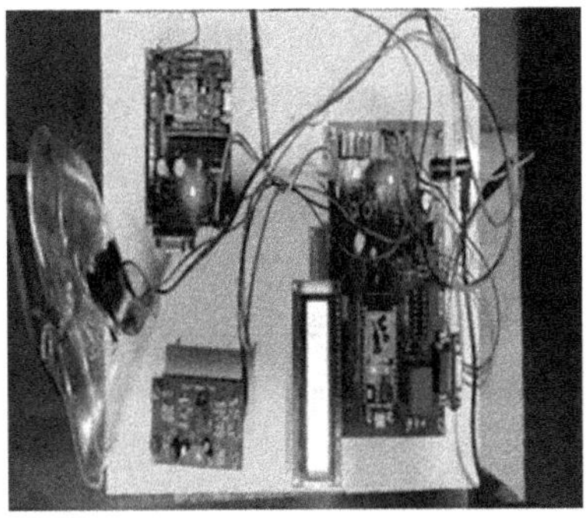

Ambulances fitted with sensors (such as cameras, heart rate monitors, and GPS) to gather real-time data. Communication devices for sending and receiving warnings, such as tablets or smartphones - enabled computers or servers that can interpret sensor data and make real-time decisions. An alert receiving and transmitting channel on Telegram. Programmes or scripts that link the Telegram channel with the AI module. Database server with details about local hospitals, including their facilities, specialisations, and availability, as shown in Figure 5.

Arduino Ide Software

Figure 6. Arduino IDE

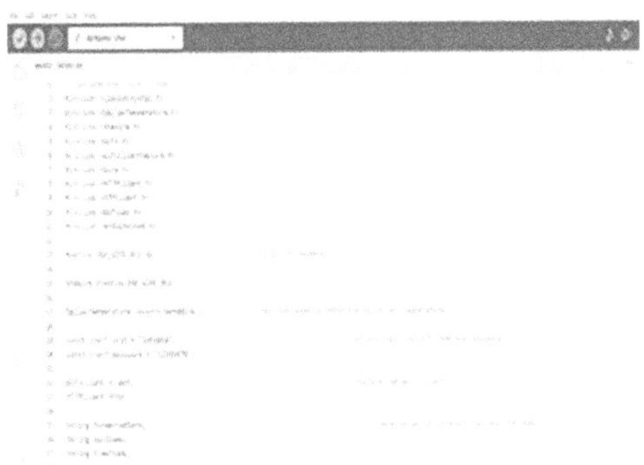

To develop, build, and upload code to Arduino boards, utilise the intuitive Arduino IDE software platform. It has a compiler, library manager, serial monitor, board manager, code editor with syntax highlighting, and more. Both novice and expert programmers may now easily navigate the process thanks to the IDE's simplification. The integration of Artificial Intelligence (AI) with the Telegram Channel for an enhanced ambulance dispatch system involves the implementation of specific algorithms to optimise decision-making, information extraction, and dispatch processes, as shown in Figure 6.

CONCLUSION

This project investigates the potential for combining Telegram and AI to enhance ambulance dispatch systems, efficiency, effectiveness, and emergency response. The project's goal is to ascertain whether it is possible, efficient, and practical to use AI algorithms within a Telegram platform to speed up emergency response protocols. Essential components, including location identification, AI triage support, real-time updates, natural language processing (NLP), and connection with medical databases, are thoroughly examined. Data security, privacy, and user feedback methods are also discussed. This research aims to provide insights into the creation and probable impact of Telegram-integrated ambulance systems with AI by carefully examining the literature, case studies, and potential implementation techniques.

The Smart Ambulance Routing System has many opportunities for improvement and future development. Using sophisticated predictive analytics to foresee demand is one possible area of concentration. For emergency assistance and allocate resources as efficiently as possible. Furthermore, using machine-learning algorithms might allow the system to adjust and gain knowledge from previous encounters, enhancing its performance for an extended period of time. The system's capabilities might be expanded to incorporate more medical sensors and diagnostics, enabling more thorough patient monitoring and triage. Smooth coordination between ambulances, hospitals, and other healthcare providers may also be made possible by improved communication protocols and interoperability with other healthcare systems.

The system may forecast future demand for emergency services by incorporating sophisticated predictive analytics approaches, such as time series analysis and machine learning models, based on demographics, weather, historical data, and other pertinent variables. Better resource planning and allocation are made possible by this proactive strategy, which guarantees that ambulances are positioned strategically to react quickly to crises. The system may adjust and improve routing choices in response to real-time feedback and changing circumstances by integrating machine learning algorithms. Reinforcement learning systems, for instance, can continually enhance routing methods and efficiency by learning from previous routing decisions and results. Over time, this adaptive capability improves the system's efficacy and responsiveness.

REFERENCES

Abraham, A., Zhang, Y., & Prasad, S. (2024). Evacuation management framework towards smart city-wide intelligent emergency interactive response system. *arXiv preprint arXiv:2403.07003.*

Ahmed, S. T., Basha, S. M., Ramachandran, M., Daneshmand, M., & Gandomi, A. H. (2023). An edge-AI-enabled autonomous, connected ambulance-route resource recommendation protocol (ACA-R3) for eHealth in smart cities. *IEEE Internet of Things Journal, 10*(13), 11497–11506. DOI: 10.1109/JIOT.2023.3243235

Azman, N. A., Abdullah, S., Hadis, N. S. M., Faiza, Z., Hamid, S. A., & Azmin, A. (2024). Advancing pre-hospital emergency medical services: An AI-powered approach to voice-activated technologies. In *2024 IEEE 14th Symposium on Computer Applications & Industrial Electronics (ISCAIE)* (pp. 360-366). IEEE.

Babu, S., Madhusudanan, S., & Sathiyanarayanan, M.. (2024). Soil mapping for farming productivity: Internet of Things (IoT) based sustainable agriculture. *Microsystem Technologies*. Advance online publication. DOI: 10.1007/s00542-024-05608-z

Becker, J., Kurland, L., Höglund, E., & Hugelius, K. (2023). Dynamic ambulance relocation: A scoping review. *BMJ Open, 13*(12), e073394. DOI: 10.1136/bmjopen-2023-073394 PMID: 38101827

Bublyk, M., Kalynii, T., Varava, L., Vysotska, V., Chyrun, L., & Matseliukh, Y. (2022). Decision support system design for low-voice emergency medical calls at smart city based on chatbot management in social networks. *Webology, 19*(2).

Hampiholi, N. (2024). Elevating emergency healthcare-technological advancements and challenges in smart ambulance systems and advanced monitoring and diagnostic tools. *International Journal of Computer Trends and Technology*, *72*(1), 1–7. DOI: 10.14445/22312803/IJCTT-V72I1P101

Kamalahasan, M., & Manivannan, S. (2024). Design and development of an unmanned/autonomous ocean surface vehicle using self-sustaining dual renewable energy harvesting system. *Scalable Computing: Practice and Experience*, *25*(5), 3468–3475.

Mahitha, T., Suneel, S., Begum, M. A., John Pimo, E. S., Swapna, B., & R., R. (2024). Empirical evaluation of Internet of Things assisted fire fighting robotic design based on intelligent sensors association. In *2024 5th International Conference on Electronics and Sustainable Communication Systems (ICESC)* (pp. 349-356). IEEE. DOI: 10.1109/ICESC60852.2024.10689728

Manaa, R., Talha, M. B., Aboueljinane, L., Benghabrit, A., & Frichi, Y. (2024, May). Application of machine learning techniques for ambulance coverage prediction. In *2024 IEEE 15th International Colloquium on Logistics and Supply Chain Management (LOGISTIQUA)* (pp. 1-8). IEEE. DOI: 10.1109/LOGISTIQUA61063.2024.10571456

Parashar, V., Singh, M. S. M., Poonkuzhali, P., Vadar, P. S., & Swapna, B. (2024). Design and development of an IoT-based smart irrigation system to enhance agricultural productivity using ESP8266 Wi-Fi enabled controller. In *2024 5th International Conference on Electronics and Sustainable Communication Systems (ICESC)* (pp. 341-348). IEEE. DOI: 10.1109/ICESC60852.2024.10689907

Samreen, S., Sruthi, B. S., & Kumari, A. M. (2023). The intelligence ambulance: Bridging AI and human interaction technologies. [JST]. *Journal of Science and Technology*, *8*(12), 61–77. DOI: 10.46243/jst.2023.v8.i12.pp61-77

Sujan, M., Thimbleby, H., Habli, I., Cleve, A., Maaløe, L., & Rees, N. (2022). Assuring safe artificial intelligence in critical ambulance service response: Study protocol. *British Paramedic Journal*, *7*(1), 36–42. DOI: 10.29045/14784726.2022.06.7.1.36 PMID: 36452023

Sumathi, R., Gokul, R. M., Gokulakrishnan, M., Ganesh Babu, K., & Pavithra, S. (2023). Artificial intelligence-based ambulance. In *Intelligent and Soft Computing Systems for Green Energy* (pp. 223-235). DOI: 10.1002/9781394167524.ch17

Wilson, C., Janes, G., Lawton, R., & Benn, J. (2023). Types and effects of feedback for emergency ambulance staff: A systematic mixed studies review and meta-analysis. *BMJ Quality & Safety*, *32*(10), 573–588. DOI: 10.1136/bmjqs-2022-015634 PMID: 37028937

Chapter 9
Plant Disease Detection Using Generative AI and Deep Learning Models

N. Bharanidharan
https://orcid.org/0000-0001-9064-8238
Vellore Institute of Technology, India

R. S. Sarweshwaran
Vellore Institute of Technology, India

M. Shomesh
Vellore Institute of Technology, India

S. Tharun
Vellore Institute of Technology, India

Kumar V. Vinoth
Vellore Institute of Technology, India

ABSTRACT

Cassava Plant scientifically Manihot esculenta which is also known as the tapioca plant, is a shrub that is majorly cultivated in many countries. The major cassava plant diseases are Cassava Bacterial Blight (CBB), Cassava Brown Streak Disease (CBSD), Cassava Green Mottle (CGM) and Cassava Mosaic Disease (CMD). The objective of this work is to make the Cassava Plant Disease Prediction from the given input image and tell whether the provided sample is infected with the above mentioned disease or not. To meet the main objective, we build the Model with the Convolution Neural Network, Visual Geometry Group 16, ResNet50, EfficientNetB0, Visual Transformer, and Variational Auto-encoder. Variational Auto-encoder model with various latent dimension size and optimizers are tested. Usage of generative variational autoencoder provides the highest accuracy of 95% while the other tested models are providing accuracy less than 90%.

DOI: 10.4018/979-8-3693-8332-2.ch009

1. INTRODUCTION

Cassava which is termed Manihot esculenta scientifically, is declared a drought plant due to its tolerance to climatic conditions. This plant will be cultivated mainly in subtropical areas of the world. This cassava plant's born place is South America and is currently cultivated mainly in Brazil and many developing countries. The cassava plant witnesses diseases by both components namely the Biotic factor and Abiotic factor. The biotic organisms are the major reason for the disease of the plant and the agents are viruses, nematodes, bacteria, and fungi. The Abiotic factors which can be a threat to the cassava plant are environment-oriented factor stresses, deficiency in nutrients and not containing the required resources for cultivation (McCallum & et. al., 2017).

Cassava plants witness many diseases including Cassava Bacterial Blight (CBB) which can occur because of the Bacteria Xanthomonas axonopodis pv manihotis, which is shortly called Xam. The bacteria found in the plant can cause the loss of a major part in leaves called necrosis which leads to poor quality in production and root damage which will affect the plant growth. This bacteria also affects the stem with a disease called lesions which always poses a high level of risk for plants since it affects the leaf parts with major spots in the leaf. If this disease occurs in the cassava plant, it leads to the death of the cassava plant. This disease is mainly witnessed in a major part of Africa including central and part of West Africa.

The next important disease which is caused by viruses is Cassava Mosaic Disease (CMD) by the viruses with the scientific name Begomo viruses, Potyviruses (McCallum & et. al., 2017). It can be seen in many African and east African countries. This disease makes plant production and affects the major parts of the leaves by making distortion and it reduces plant growth. Transportation of the viruses is mainly possible through the vectors of the leaves which is called as whiteflies and similar insects. Another major reason for the loss of plant growth is environmental impacts such as less fertility due to less nutrients in the soil, poor management of crop rotation, and variation in climate.

Infection of the Casava plant by another virus which is similar to potyviruses is also more prevalent. This virus variant is known as Cassava Brown Streak Virus and it is responsible for the reason of the syndrome called Cassava Brown Streak Disease (CBSD) (Legg et. al., 2015). The following viruses are primarily found in Uganda and are classified as Ugandan Cassava Brown Streak Viruses. This disease mainly affects the roots of the cassava plant. Similarly, another virus, known as Cassava Green Mottle Virus (CGM), is found in many parts of Africa and typically affects the leaves, causing them to change color. In some cases, protozoa, which are rarely involved, can also contribute to the disease. Additionally, insects such as grasshoppers and leafhoppers are major vectors of cassava motile disease, exacerbating its spread. Environmental factors, such as stress, also play a significant role in the disease's development. Ultimately, healthy plants can thrive with proper cultivation practices, ensuring the best quality crops.

The Cassava plant is an important crop that will be in growing in many tropical similar countries and it is main food for people who rely on carbohydrates. This plant has special growth in bad or limited soil conditions. The cassava plant can be cultivated in low photosynthesis and it can produce greater results to the farmers. This plant as many significant adaptations called resistance in drought by making its parts to adapt to the environment. They make this by reducing the transpiring level and make the roots adjustable automatically to find the water in low ground level. This enables the plant to withstand more humid climate changes with the help of changing the regulation of the leaf. This behavior allows the plant to survive in high humid climate changes. Cassava is an important crop in developing countries, where it serves as a key food source. The plant's edible parts are used in various food preparations, with its byproducts classified as flour, fufu, gari, and tapioca, all of which are commonly consumed in daily meals. In addition to its culinary uses, cassava is also a vital food resource for livestock in rural areas, helping to reduce food costs and maintenance in these communities. Beyond food, cassava has industrial applications, such as the production of ethanol and starch. The starch derived from cassava is used in a wide range of industries, including paper manufacturing and textiles. Moreover, cassava contributes to the development of renewable energy sources, with its ethanol content being utilized as biofuel, benefiting both local economies and environmental sustainability in nearby regions. (Connor et. al., 2021).

The problems associated with cassava cultivation can be attributed to several factors. The first major issue is the prevalence of diseases, which cause significant damage to plants. As a result, farmers suffer from food shortages. This issue is often linked to poor crop rotation practices, with farmers unaware of the importance of isolating diseased plants and failing to anticipate the impact of climate change on crop health (Parmar et al., 2017). Another challenge lies with the workers, who struggle to identify diseased plants and are often unaware of the benefits of using natural fertilizers, making it difficult to achieve optimal production. Additionally, post-harvest losses are a major concern, particularly in underdeveloped areas. Cassava roots, which are large and require a consistent water supply, are vulnerable to spoilage due to inadequate water management. This results in significant losses for farmers, further exacerbating the challenges of cassava cultivation.

The outline of the remaining paper is presented as follows: the next section describes the basics of deep learning; the third section deals with the literature survey; the fourth section explains the methodology; performance metrics are described in the fifth section; results and discussion are presented in the sixth section followed by conclusion at the last section.

2. DEEP LEARNING ALGORITHMS

Deep Learning is the subset of Machine Learning and Artificial Intelligence, which has advanced concepts when correlated to Machine Learning algorithms. It has numerous networks and nodes interconnected to each other to make the model to learn and perform effectively. Classical machine learning algorithms rely on custom-made feature extraction, where the deep learning models learn the hierarchical patterns automatically and representations from the raw data and learn itself by extracting the features.

Types of Deep Learning:

1. Feed Forward Neural Network
2. Recurrent Neural Network
3. Convolutional Neural Network

Feed Forward Neural Network:

The Feed Forward Neural Network is a variety of Deep Learning neural network, which ensures that the input nodes process the provided data and give the output in the output nodes, it does not form any cycle. It is a fully connected one. The architecture of the feed-forward neural network is represented in the Fig.1

Figure 1. Feed forward neural network-architecture

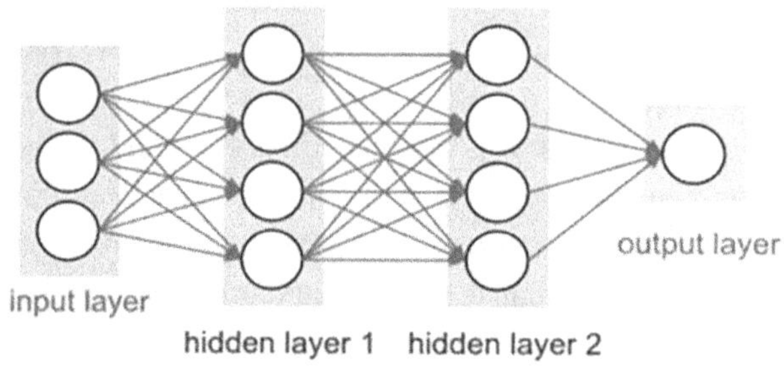

Recurrent Neural Network:

It is a variety of the feed-forward neural network, in which the neurons present in the hidden layer receive the input with some delay in time, it mainly accesses the preceding learning and trains again to learn from it. In this the output will be used for both the output and the same will be used to learn and train the network. The architecture of the recurrent neural network is represented in Fig. 2

Figure 2. Recurrent neural network-architecture

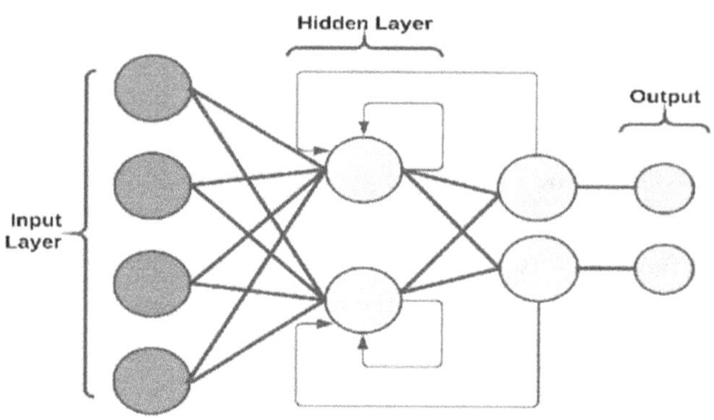

Convolutional Neural Network:

It is a variety of Deep Learning Neural Networks, which is of a special kind, in this neural network the layers are made in such a way that is more complex and such that it can be used to handle the complex tasks to be handled in a simpler manner. It is primarily used for the classification of input images, clustering of input images, and the detection of objects. The architecture of the CNN is shown in the Fig. 3. Considering the Cassava Plant Disease classification, we are using the following categorized models of Convolutional Neural Network (CNN), Visual Geometry Group 16, ResNet50, EfficientNetB0, Visual Transformer.

2.1. Convolution Neural Network (CNN)

Convolution Neural Network is a type of Deep Neural network that consists many of interconnected layers in its architecture, in this the convolution layer does the main operation by working with the matrix convolution filters or the kernels, (Mathulaprangsan & Lanthong 2021), (Thaiyalnayaki et al. 2022). The architecture diagram of the CNN is represented in Fig. 3. Moreover, the architecture of the CNN can be defined as per our need and it can be used to train the model.

Figure 3. General architecture of CNN

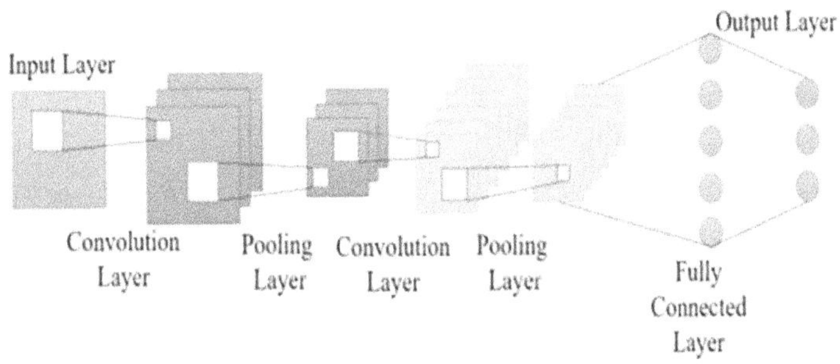

The figure above illustrates the basic architecture of a Convolutional Neural Network (CNN). In this architecture, the CNN model extracts features from the image dataset and uses them to train the model. For our specific problem, we developed a custom CNN model with five distinct output nodes, tailored to classify the dataset into five different categories. Then the transformation has been applied to resize the image into 224*224 size such that it works properly. The formula for calculating the output is the following as: Output dimension = ((input_demension – filter size + 2 *padding)/strider) + 1.

Considering our Custom CNN the general feature map is calculated as per the following Equation (1).

$$Y_{i,j,k} = \sum_{c=1}^{C}\sum_{m=1}^{H}\sum_{n=1}^{W} X_{i+m-1,j+n-1,c} \cdot W_{m,n,c,k} + b_k \quad (1)$$

Where:

$X_{i+m-1,j+n-1,c}$ is the input pixel value at channel c.
$W_{m,n,c,k}$ are the weights of the convolutional filter of size HxWxC.
b_k is the bias term for the k-th filter.
The output $Y_{i,j,k}$ is the activation value at position (i, j) for the k – th filter.
Similarly, the Equations for the 5 Layers is given as follows in the Equations (2) – (6).
Layer 1: Convolution + BatchNorm + ReLU + Pooling

Conv1:Z1=ReLU (BatchNorm (Conv2D (X, W1) +b1)) (2)

Input: X□R3×224×224

Output: Z1□R32×112×112 after 2×2 MaxPooling.

Layer 2: Convolution + BatchNorm + ReLU + Pooling

Conv2:Z2=ReLU (BatchNorm (Conv2D (Z1, W2) +b2)) (3)

Input: Z1□R32×112×112

Output: Z2□R64×56×56 after 2×2 MaxPooling.

Layer 3: Convolution + BatchNorm + ReLU + Pooling

Conv3:Z3=ReLU (BatchNorm (Conv2D (Z2, W3) +b3)) (4)

Input: Z2□R64×56×56

Output: Z3□R128×28×28 after 2×2 MaxPooling.

Layer 4: Convolution + BatchNorm + ReLU + Pooling

Conv4:Z4=ReLU (BatchNorm (Conv2D (Z3, W4) +b4)) (5) Input: Z3□R128×28×28

Output: Z4□R256×14×14 after 2×2 MaxPooling.

Layer 5: Convolution + BatchNorm + ReLU + Pooling

```
Conv5:Z5=ReLU (BatchNorm (Conv2D (Z4, W5) +b5)) (6)

Input: Z4□R256×14×14

Output: Z5□R512×7×7 after 2×2 MaxPooling
```

The Flattening Layer:

The extracted features have been flattened before passing to the output layer, it is done by the following Equation (7)

$$\textit{Flattened Output} = \textit{Flatten}(Z_5) \in \mathbb{R}^{512x7x7} = \mathbb{R}^{25088} \quad (7)$$

2.2. Visual Geometry Group 16

The Visual Geometry Group 16 (VGG16) model is a Convolutional Neural Network (CNN) architecture which is proposed by the Visual Geometry Group (VGG), Oxford University. The Visual Geometry Group is a 16-layer CNN model in general it has pretrained with the 1000 classes. The VGG16 model is used to effectively identify cassava plant disease (A. Soujanya et. al., 2023). The general Architecture of the VGG 16 is represented in the Fig.4

Figure 4. VGG 16 architecture

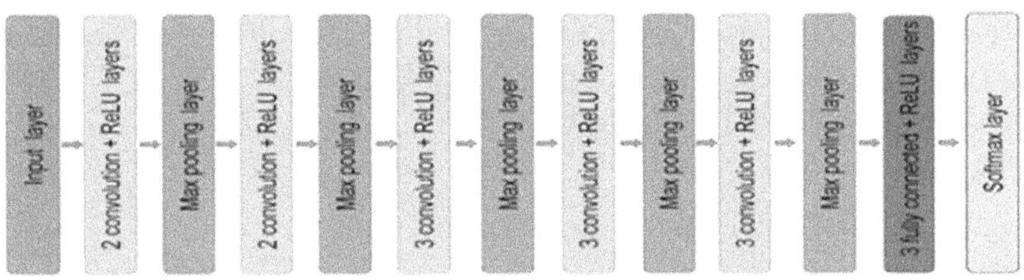

The Output Layer for the Cassava Plant Disease is given in Equation (8).

$Z = W_5 \,.\, a + b_5$ (8)

Where:

$W_5 \in \mathbb{R}^{5x4096}$

$b_5 \in \mathbb{R}^5$

2.3. ResNet50

The ResNet50 is the pretrained model of the CNN which stands for the Residual Neural Network which is developed in 2016 to overcome the difficulties in the existing Deep Learning models, and the architecture of the ResNet50 is made in such a way to handle the training process effectively with its complex architecture. (Darwish & et.al 2024). The learning from this network has been adopted on several layers, the following Equation (9) provides the residual definition.

$Y_{pred} = f(x;\theta)$ (9)

Where:

Y_{pred} = predicted output

f = model function (VGG16)

x = input image tensor

= model parameters (weights and biases).

The ResNet has several variants that were proposed to enhance the accuracy and functioning of the Residual Network to performance. The variants like the ResNetXt, ResNet-v2, ResNet-v3, and much more (J. Cheng, et al., 2022). The original ResNet has 1000 classes and for our plant disease classification we have 5 classes and it has been modified as the five features. For the 5-class classification, the model has been replaced with only 5 classes for the plant disease classification with the following line: model_dict["ResNet50"].fc = nn. Linear(model_dict["ResNet50"].fc.in_features, 5). The output for the above line will be Output = Linear (2048, 5). For this the loss function is calculated as mentioned in Equation (10):

Loss = - $\sum_{i=1}^{N}\sum_{c=1}^{C} y_{i,c} \log \check{y}_{i,c}$ Eq. - 10

Where:

N = Batch size

C = Number of classes

$Y_{i,c}$ = Actual label

y = Predicted probability for class c

The Adam optimizer has been used for the model training for adaptive learning rate capabilities, which helps in the faster convergence with $\theta = \theta - \alpha . \frac{m_t}{\sqrt{v_t} + \in}$

Where:

= Model parameters (weights)

m_t, v_t = Moving averages of gradients and their squares

α = Learning rate

2.4. EfficientNetB0

The EfficientNetB0 is a family of EfficientNet Deep Learning Models which is developed by Google AI, which is designed and developed by google for higher performance and accuracy, efficiency. It has a smaller parameter when considering other models which is the main advantage of it (Lumoring & et. al., 2024). The EfficientNet models leverage a technique called compound scaling, which will uniformly scale the depth, width, and resolution to achieve better accuracy and efficiency. It is the pretrained model which consists of the 1000 classes in general, according to the problem, we can adjust it to solve it. The EfficientNetB0 uses a Mobile Inverted Bottleneck (MBConv) layers along with the Swish activation in its architecture.

2.5. Vision Transformer (ViT)

A Vision Transformer (ViT) is a deep learning model that leverages transformer architecture, which was originally designed for natural language processing (NLP), for image recognition tasks. Unlike traditional Convolutional Neural Networks (CNNs) that use convolutions to process images, the Vision Transformer treats an image as a sequence of patches and processes them similarly to how transformers handle text sequences. The key components of a Vision Transformer include image patching, positional encoding, the transformer encoder, a classification token, and the final prediction. In the image patching step, the input image is divided into fixed-size, non-overlapping patches (for example, 16x16 pixels). These patches are flattened into 1D vectors and linearly embedded into a higher-dimensional space, similar to token embeddings in NLP transformers. Since transformers lack inherent spatial awareness, positional encodings are added to each image patch embedding to retain information about the position of each patch. These positional encodings are included before passing the patch embeddings through the transformer layers.

The embedded patches, now with positional encodings, are fed into a standard transformer encoder, which consists of layers of multi-head self-attention and feed-forward neural networks. The self-attention mechanism enables the model to capture global dependencies across all image patches, irrespective of their spatial locations. The feed-forward networks are applied to each patch independently after attention is computed. Just like in NLP transformers, where a special token (like [CLS]) is used for classification, the Vision Transformer introduces a classification token, often denoted as [CLS]. This token aggregates information from all the patches and is used to predict the final class label of the image. After passing through the transformer encoder, the output corresponding to the classification token is processed by a fully connected layer that generates the class probabilities for the image. The advantages of Vision Transformers include their ability to understand global context, scalability, and flexibility. However, the challenges of using ViTs stem from their computational complexity and training efficiency. ViTs typically require large amounts of training data and computational resources to achieve optimal performance. Without extensive datasets, CNNs may still outperform ViTs, as they tend to generalize better with fewer data. Additionally, due to the complexity of the attention mechanism, Vision Transformers may require more training time, especially when handling high-resolution images.

3. GENERATIVE AI

Generative Artificial Intelligence (AI) is a subset of the Artificial intelligence systems which is designed primarily to create or generate new content for the provided input. This new content includes text, audio, video, images and other such form of media. Unlike from traditional AI, with good Improvements in technology like sensors and image analysis is easy to study. (Bhugra et al.,2024) which will typically focus on analyzing and recognizing the patterns within the data provided, generative AI models can able to produce novel outputs based on the learned data distributions. These models learn from the existing datasets which were used to train them and based on the learning from that it can able to use that information to generate new content which mimics the characteristics of the original data which is used for training and from the real world. For example, generative AI can produce realistic images, based on the prompt we ask for, it can able to generate human-like text, compose music, make videos, and much more. The potential application for the GenAI is vast. Which spans industries such as entertainment, healthcare, finance, and others.

Generative AI works by learning the underlying patterns, structures and that correlate within the data which we use to train them from which it learns all the things. The process of training typically involves the dataset with large volumes of data, in which the model iterates over the provided data to learn a probabilistic model of the distribution. Based on the learning it can able to create or generate new things, similar data which can be in the form of text, image, audio, video, to some other more complex things like the 3D models or even the synthetic voice. Generative AI can be classified into several types based on the approaches and the architectures used to generate the new content. Some of the prominent types of generative AI include the following:

3.1. Generative Adversarial Networks

A variant of the Generative AI model, known as Generative Adversarial Networks (GANs), is one of the most widely recognized and used models in the field of generative models. GAN is a emerging AI tools which reduce the dependency while training the data (Singh et al.,2024). A GAN consists of two neural networks: the Generator and the Discriminator. The Generator creates synthetic data based on random noise, attempting to generate data that closely resembles the real training data. By applying the transformation which changes the style it leads to in efficient augmentation (Lokesh et al.,2024). The Discriminator, on the other hand, evaluates the generated data, distinguishing between real and fake data produced by the Generator. During training, the Generator and Discriminator engage in a continuous "game," where the Generator strives to improve its ability to produce realistic data, while the Discriminator becomes more adept at detecting fake data. This adversarial process continues until the Generator generates data so realistically that the Discriminator can no longer reliably distinguish it from real data (Liu et al., 2020).

3.2. Transformer Models

The transformer model is the type of the Generative AI model which is considered to be one of the most advancements in the context of the generative AI, particularly when considering Natural Language Processing. The transformer model uses a mechanism of self-attention which is used to evaluate the relationships between the worlds in a sequence simultaneously, which allows it for concurrent processing and handling of long-range dependencies. The example for the transformers includes the BERT (Bidirectional Encoder Representations from Transformers) and GPT (Generative Pretrained Transformer, and the image generating model like the DALL-E.

Diffusion Model:

The Diffusion Model is the recent type of the generative AI model that has gained popularity, particularly in the domain of image and video generation. It works by the process of simulation by adding the noise to the data and then learning from it how to reverse the process and reconstruct the original data. The diffusion model starts with the random noise which then gradually refines it to produce the high-quality output of the image/video. It can generate high-capacity images/videos that show impressive performance when doing tasks like inpainting (image completion), super-resolution, and the generation of images from the description provided by the user.

Types of Diffusion Models:
Latent Diffusion Model (LDMs): Which is a type of diffusion model that operates in a lower dimensional latent space to improve the efficiency in terms of computation.
Score-Based Model: It is a variety of models that utilizes score function to guide the process of diffusion process toward the process of generating the realistic output.

3.3. Variational Auto-Encoder:

The Variational Auto-encoders is a type of Generative AI model, which is used often for the generation of new data points and learning from the latent representation, it mainly focuses on learning with a probabilistic mapping from a high-dimensional space to a lower dimensional latent space. A variational auto-encoder is, in the broadest sense, a release of the continuous latent variable model, which is a statistical framework. (Thirunavukkarasu et. al, 2022). The VAE primarily consists of the following two components in it for its working which are:

Encoders: Maps the input data into a latent dimension.
Decoders: Reconstruct the data from the latent dimension.

In general, the VAE uses the ReLU as the activation function for the convolution layer which it consists of each layer. The VAE uses the Loss function to calculate the loss during the training, and validation phase: it consists of two parts:

Reconstruction Loss: This measures how well the generated (reconstructed) image matches with the original input data, this can be mean squared error (MSE) or the binary cross-entropy (BCE) loss.
KL-Divergence Loss: It is a type of loss that encourages the latent dimension distribution to be close to a standard normal distribution, enabling smooth sampling. The loss can be defined in a combined manner in Equation (11).

Loss = Reconstruction Loss + β x KL-Divergence Loss (11)
Where:
β is a weight term that balances the two losses (Reconstruction and KL-Divergence)
The Reconstruction Loss is provided by the following Equation (12)

$$\mathcal{L}_{reconstruction} = MSE(x,\hat{x}) = \frac{1}{N}\sum_{i=1}^{N}\|x_i - \hat{x}_i\|^2 \qquad (12)$$

Where:
N is the number of samples
x_i is the original input
$\hat{x}_i$ is the reconstructed image.
The KL-Divergence Loss is given by the following Equation (13)

$$\mathscr{L}_{KL} = -\frac{1}{2}\sum_{i=1}^{D}\left(1 + \log\sigma_i^2 - \mu_i^2 - \sigma_i^2\right) \tag{13}$$

Where:
D is the dimensionality of the latent space
μ_i *and* σ_i^2 is the mean and variance of the latent variables from the encoder.
The architecture diagram of the variational autoencoder is provided in Fig. 5

Figure 5. Architecture of the variational auto-encoder

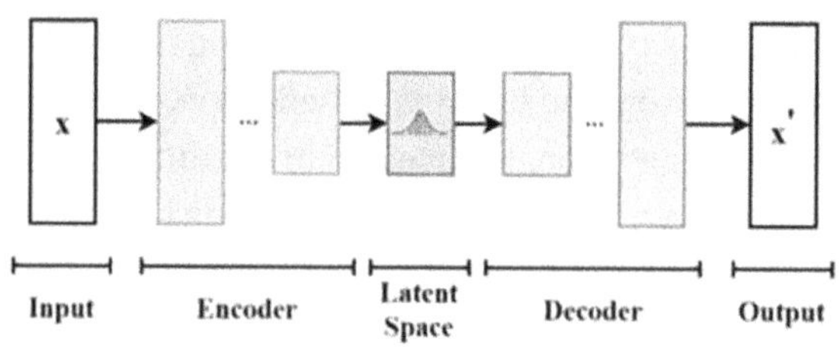

4. LITERATURE SURVEY

(Legg et al. 2015) conducted an extensive review of cassava virus diseases, focusing on their biology, epidemiology, and management strategies. The study discussed the major viruses affecting cassava, such as Cassava Mosaic Virus (CMV) and Cassava Brown Streak Virus (CBSV), outlining their transmission mechanisms, impact on crop yield, and geographical spread. The authors highlighted integrated disease management approaches, including the use of resistant cassava varieties, vector control, and phytosanitary measures. Although not focused on machine learning or accuracy metrics, the research emphasized the effectiveness of breeding programs and biotechnological interventions in reducing disease incidence and improving cassava productivity in affected regions.

(Anitha and Saranya, 2022) Suggested a deep learning approach for identifying and detecting cassava leaf diseases, focusing on improving classification accuracy to support farmers in timely disease management. The authors utilized a Convolutional Neural Network (CNN) model to categorize leaf diseases of cassava into multiple categories, leveraging a dataset containing images of cassava leaves infected by various diseases. Their methodology involved pre-processing the images to improve feature extraction, followed by training the CNN model with optimized hyperparameters. They evaluated their model using performance metrics such as accuracy, precision, recall, and F1-score. The result of the experiment demonstrated that the CNN model achieved a classification accuracy of 90%, the best-performing traditional machine learning algorithms. The study concludes that deep learning models, specifically CNNs, are effective in accurately identifying cassava leaf diseases, which can significantly contribute to precision agriculture by enabling early disease detection and reducing crop losses.

(Moupojou et al. 2023) Introduced FieldPlant, a comprehensive dataset designed to facilitate the detection and classification are performed to plant diseases using deep learning models. The dataset comprises a diverse collection of field plant images captured in real-world agricultural settings, covering multiple plant species and various disease conditions to address the challenges of plant disease detection in dynamic environments. The authors aimed to enhance the accuracy of automated identification of plant disease by providing a rich dataset that captures the complexity of natural field conditions, such as varying lighting, backgrounds, and plant orientations. They employed several state-of-the-art deep learning models, consisting of Convolutional Neural Networks (CNNs) and transfer learning techniques, to benchmark the dataset, achieving high classification performance with models like EfficientNet and ResNet. Their experiments demonstrated that the FieldPlant dataset supports robust training, resulting in improved generalization and accuracy in disease detection tasks, with top models achieving classification accuracies exceeding 90%.

(Paiva-Peredo, 2022) explored the application of deep learning techniques for classifying cassava leaf diseases using an unbalanced field dataset. The study focused on addressing the challenges posed by imbalanced data distributions, which are common in real-world agricultural datasets. The author utilized Convolutional Neural Networks (CNNs) to develop a robust classification model, applying techniques such as data augmentation and class balancing methods to mitigate the effects of data imbalance. The model was trained on a dataset comprising images of cassava leaves affected by various diseases, with a particular emphasis on enhancing the model's ability to generalize across minority classes. Experimental results showed that the deep learning approach achieved satisfactory performance, with the implementation of data balancing techniques significantly improving classification accuracy and recall, particularly for underrepresented disease categories.

(Thaiyalnayaki et. al., 2022) Developed an automatic cassava disease classification system using Convolutional Neural Networks (CNNs) combined with data augmentation techniques. To address the limitations of small and variable cassava leaf datasets, they applied augmentation methods like rotation, flipping, and scaling to increase training data diversity. The CNN model, trained on cassava leaf images with various diseases, achieved high accuracy across multiple disease classes. The results showed that data augmentation improved model performance by reducing overfitting and enabling better generalization to real-world variations. The study concluded that this approach offers an effective, scalable solution for cassava disease detection in agriculture.

(Sapre et al. 2023) proposed a disease classification system for cassava plants using an Artificial Neural Network (ANN). The authors trained the ANN model on cassava leaf images affected by different diseases, focusing on developing an accurate classification framework for plant disease detection. They used image preprocessing techniques, including normalization and feature extraction, to enhance model performance. The ANN achieved a classification accuracy of 92.3%, demonstrating its effectiveness in detecting and categorizing cassava diseases. The study highlighted the potential of ANNs in agricultural applications, offering a robust solution for automated disease detection in cassava plants.

(Satoto et. al., 2021) proposed a Region Proposal Convolutional Neural Network (R-CNN) with data augmentation for identifying cassava leaf diseases. The authors integrated R-CNN with augmentation techniques like rotation, scaling, and flipping to enhance the diversity of training data and improve model robustness. The model was trained to detect and classify various cassava leaf diseases from input images. The experimental results showed a significant improvement in classification performance, with the model achieving an accuracy of around 99%. This approach demonstrated the effectiveness of combining R-CNN and data augmentation in improving cassava disease detection accuracy in agricultural applications.

(Applalanaidu and Kumaravelan, 2021) provided a comparative analysis of various machine learning (ML) and deep learning (DL) algorithms for plant leaf disease detection and classification. They reviewed algorithms such as Convolutional Neural Networks (CNNs), Support Vector Machines (SVMs), and decision trees, noting the superior performance of CNNs in achieving high accuracy, often up to 98%. The paper also highlighted several areas for future research, including diagnosing specific stages of plant diseases, controlling chemical applications based on accurate disease quantification, and developing an online system for plant disease identification. Further investigations were proposed in detecting nutrient deficiencies, analyzing the back of the leaf, using real-time images for disease detection, and addressing challenges like mixed lighting conditions and complex backgrounds. Additionally, the authors suggested exploring automatic disease severity estimation, extending research to other plant parts (e.g., stems), and enhancing pest recognition methods to improve overall plant health monitoring systems.

(Soujanya et al., 2023) proposed an efficient cassava leaf disease classification model using the VGG16 Convolutional Neural Network (CNN) architecture. The study aimed to leverage the deep feature extraction capabilities of VGG16 for the accurate identification of various cassava leaf diseases. The authors applied preprocessing techniques such as resizing and normalization to prepare the dataset, followed by data augmentation to enhance model robustness. The VGG16 model was trained on cassava leaf images, achieving a classification accuracy of 96.8%. The study concluded that VGG16 is highly effective for plant disease classification, offering a reliable solution for early disease detection and management in cassava crops.

(Askr et al., 2024) introduced an explainable ResNet50 model enhanced with copula entropy for predicting cotton plant diseases. The approach focused on making deep learning models more interpretable while maintaining high prediction accuracy. The authors used the ResNet50 architecture due to its strong feature extraction capabilities, integrating copula entropy to improve the model's decision-making transparency. This method enabled a better understanding of the relationships among input features and model predictions. The model was trained on a cotton disease dataset, achieving a good accuracy of 95.5%. The study demonstrated the effectiveness of combining explainable AI techniques with deep learning for precise and interpretable plant disease diagnosis.

(Thirunavukkarasu et al., 2022) proposed an efficient deep learning approach for plant disease detection using Convolutional Neural Networks (CNNs). The study aimed to enhance the accuracy of disease classification by leveraging advanced deep-learning techniques. The authors applied image preprocessing and data augmentation to improve the diversity of the training set, followed by using a CNN model optimized for plant disease identification. The model was trained on a diverse dataset of plant leaf images affected by various diseases. Experimental results showed that their approach achieved a high classification accuracy of 97.2%, demonstrating the effectiveness of deep learning in automated plant disease detection and supporting precision agriculture.

(Aravind and Harini, 2021) Developed a cassava leaf disease classification model using deep learning techniques. They employed a Convolutional Neural Network (CNN) architecture to automatically identify and classify cassava leaf diseases from images. The study involved preprocessing steps like image resizing, normalization, and data augmentation to enhance model training and improve accuracy. The CNN model was trained on a dataset of cassava leaf images representing various diseases, achieving a classification accuracy of 94.7%. The results demonstrated that the deep learning approach is effective for plant disease detection, offering a reliable answer for early diagnosis and management of cassava leaf diseases in agricultural fields.

Mathulaprangsan and Lanthong (2021) developed a cassava leaf disease recognition system using Convolutional Neural Networks (CNNs). The study aimed to automate the detection of cassava diseases to support farmers in early diagnosis. The authors utilized a CNN model trained on a dataset of cassava leaf images, incorporating preprocessing techniques like image resizing, normalization, and data augmentation to improve model performance. The CNN architecture was optimized for classifying multiple cassava leaf diseases, achieving a high classification accuracy of 93.5%. The results demonstrated the effectiveness of CNNs in plant disease recognition, providing a reliable solution for enhancing agricultural disease management practices.

5. METHODOLOGY

The data set contains 17,938 of images which is obtained from the Kaggle dataset, with 5 classes which are split into 70:15:15 where 70 percentage for training, 15 percentage for validation, and 15 percent for Testing the model by constructing the Variational Auto-encoders which is generative Artificial intelligence. The 70% of the Training Image set consists of 5 classes (0 to 4) with 625 images, 1,259 images, 1,404 images, 7,738 images, and 1,530 images. The validation image is split into 5 classes (0 to 4) which consist of about 153 images, 288 images, 295 images, 1,630 images, and 325 images respectively. The 15% of the testing dataset is split into the 5 classes (0 to 4) which consist of about 143 images, 284 images, 294 images, 1,659 images, and 311 images respectively. The single image dimension consists of 800 X 600 with a width is 800, a height of 600 pixels, and horizontal and vertical resolutions is 96 dpi(Dots Per Inch) respectively. The dataset has been collected from the natural sunlight during the daytime with medium lighting. The model is designed for training by the following components which were encoder for the purpose of input data mapping and for the distribution of the latent, another component will be considered as a Decoder (Kingma et. al., 2019) which will perform with the help of the representation of the latent to make reconstruction of the given input data. Based on some important modules of VAE will be considered during the training the model which is called latent space or latent dimension for the usage to make image compression (Chamain et. al., 2022) of the input data, VAE consists of encoders which will allow the control random of input by preparing the distribution with help of mean and variance from the space.

Another module that is performed in the VAE is a minimization of the Divergence of the Kullback-Leibler which will make the module VAE understand the relations of the distribution of the latent very closely with the help of the already defined values distribution with the help of the Gaussian function. Another process is to check the loss of reconstruction that identify the difference among the entered data input to the reconstructed images to make the model prepare a good understanding of features that were underlying in data The last process is Sampling where the VAE has the sample of latent distribution from the process of decoder it will make good facilitate the generation of the data. The overall flow of the model is represented in Fig.6

Figure 6. Image showing the flowchart

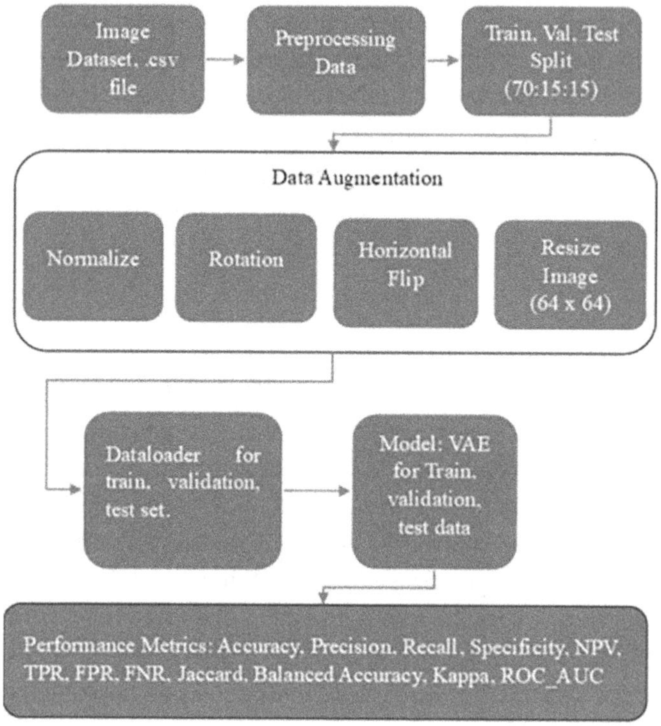

5.1. Data Cleaning

The first process is to verify the input data processing which will help to clean the values where to clean the null values which is important to Train any module to attain good output or results particularly when VAE has done the representation of latent for some meaningful learning from input. Considering our dataset which consists of the images and the .csv file, we verify and ensure that all the images present in the image directory are also available in the CSV file, if the extra information is available in the dataset means it is removed as per the image files which our dataset consist of. Some methods are adapted to make a good data clean process which is Scaling for the normalize the following uploading input data for it range of binary values. It is used to make good convergences while training by changing the input data, it also helps the model to identify the dominating learnings that prevent the big ranges of features or attributes, Scaling verifies before working with large data like images and tables. The next process is Flipping to changing the input images or from data set by Horizontal and vertical to avoid overfitting and increase the efficiency in generalization, Performs the new method called invariance which is suitable for image classification or reconstruction with spatial Orientation to the module.

The next process cropping the images by random or using parts from the center which helps to prevent overfit with changing the input parts also helps the model to identify the robustness unless the model predicts with the same positions. The next process is Rotation which will change the input data with the rotation of some randoms with some already defined range, it also helps in invariance which can be used in orientation with the object which is irrelevant and more diversities to the dataset which model is ready for Training. The next process is Normalization which makes the input data to able to adjust with the distribution of scale, important while calculating the gradient which can get output of stable and improves the models to fast converges. The next process is Adding noise to the model for the robustness of the data which the decoder will identify the differences between the input data and reconstruct from methods like Gaussian or salt-and-paper methods to avoid overfitting.

5.2. Data Augmentation

Data augmentation increases the diversity of the training data without collecting new samples. Techniques such as scaling, flipping, and rotating introduce variations in the input data, forcing VAEs to learn the representation of latent dimension. For the dataset, we applied the following augmentation flipping the images which ensures that the model becomes orientation invariant, rotates, and resizes (64 x 64), while adding random noise promotes robustness by training the decoder to reconstruct clean data from noisy inputs. The flowchart describes the Data Augmentation Process after the data has been preprocessed in Fig. 7.

Figure 7. Flow chart describing data augmentation Process

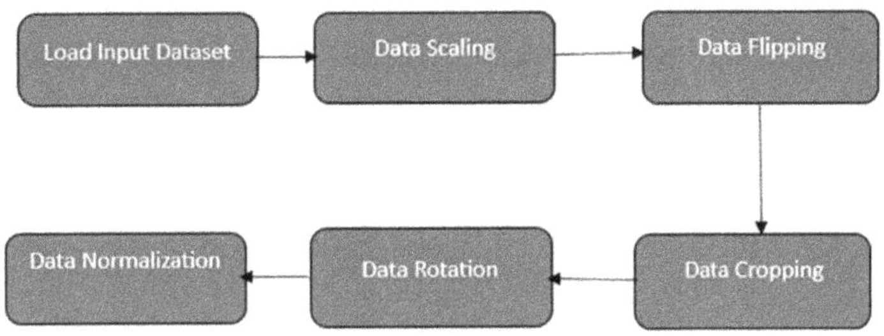

5.3. Learning Rate

Learning price scheduling is any other effective enhancement to improve VAE training. The choice of gaining knowledge of price notably influences the convergence speed and balance of optimization. Using a static getting-to-know price during training would possibly cause suboptimal results, as the best mastering rate modifications as the version approaches convergence. The learning rate for the VAE model has been chosen according to the optimizer's work.

5.4. Normalization

Normalization methods, like **Batch Normalization (BN)**, play a crucial role in stabilizing and accelerating the training of deep learning models. BN normalizes the activations of each layer, ensuring they have a mean of zero and a standard deviation of one, which reduces internal covariate shifts and prevents large weight updates. This stabilization helps in faster convergence, reduces the risk of vanishing or exploding gradients, and improves the model's generalization capabilities, making it particularly useful in deep architectures like Variational Autoencoders (VAEs). In VAEs, normalization not only speeds up training but also works alongside regularization techniques such as **dropout**, which helps the model generalize better by preventing overfitting. Together, these techniques contribute to more efficient and robust models, especially when working with large datasets.

5.5. Model Loss

In a Variational Autoencoder (VAE), the model loss plays a crucial role in guiding the network during training by evaluating how well the model is learning to generate data. Regarding the calculation of the Variational Auto-encoders, we described the model loss previously in equations (11)-(13).

5.6. Training VAE Model

5.6.1. Training Phase

Training and validation are essential phases in building a sturdy Variational Autoencoder (VAE). During education, the encoder learns to map input statistics into a latent area represented through probabilistic distributions, even as the decoder reconstructs the entry from sampled latent vectors. The optimization purpose is to reduce the Evidence Lower Bound (ELBO), which is composed of the reconstruction loss and the Kullback-Leibler (KL) divergence loss. Reconstruction loss measures how correctly the model recreates the enter, at the same time as KL-divergence guarantees the latent area distribution approximates a general regular distribution, selling generalization and regularization. Even in the training phase, we trained the model with about 7 various optimizers which were the Adam, LAMB, NovoGrad, RAdam, RMSProp, LARS, and ADAGRAD, whose results will be discussed under the Results and Discussion section.

5.6.2. Validation Phase

The validation phase is a crucial phase in monitoring the model performance during the time of training, it provides a checkpoint to ensure the model is generalizing well to the unseen data. It helps in detecting the issues in the model if it has any like overfitting (the model correctly predicts the trained data but wrongly predicts the unseen data) and underfitting (the underlying pattern that the models failed to predict). With the help of the validation set, the model can be tuned based on the performance over the unseen data, improving its generalizing ability before finalizing it.

5.6.3. Testing Phase

It is a phase which will be done after the training and validation phase is completed on the model, also it is the checking out section of a model to measure the performance of the overall model completely from the unseen/hidden data during the phase of training, from the original dataset, and checked against the unseen data to check how it performs with that data. This phase assesses the generalization capability of the version and presents the impartial estimate of its reconstruction satisfactory and latent area regularization. During trying out, the input statistics is exceeded through the encoder and decoder with no gradient updates.

6. PERFORMANCE METRICS OF THE MODEL

The following metrics for the constructed model performance are evaluated, which is very crucial to identify the critical things which allow us to visualize the representation where the VAE model while reconstruction data of the input and it will used to identify the good practice to saw the dimension of the latent. The following metrics which are given below are considered.

6.1. Accuracy

The following accuracy metrics are very important for the model which helps to identify the overall right prediction which from all predictions by the model. The formula provided in Equation (14)

$$Accuracy = \frac{True\ Positive\ rate + True\ Negative\ Rate}{True\ Positive + True\ Negative + False\ Positive + False\ Negative} \quad (14)$$

6.2. Precision

The following metrics which will validate the only positive values with all the predicted values from the model. The formula provided in Equation (15)

$$Precision = \frac{True\ Positive\ rate}{True\ Positive + False\ Positive} \quad (15)$$

6.3. Recall

The following metrics have calculated the total number of positive values which is important for the model to identify positive values. The formula provided in Equation (16)

$$Recall = \frac{True\ Positive\ rate}{True\ Positive + False\ Negative} \quad (16)$$

6.4. Specificity

The following metrics have calculated the total number of negative values which is important for the model to identify imbalances from the data inputs. The formula provided in Equation (17)

$$Specificity = \frac{True\ Negaive\ rate}{True\ Negative + False\ Positive} \quad (17)$$

6.5. Negative Predictive Value

The following metrics have calculated a number of negative values which is important for the model to identify in low-frequency outcomes. Formula provided in Equation (18)

$$NPV = \frac{True\ Negative\ rate}{True\ Negative + False\ Negative} \tag{18}$$

6.6. F1 Score

The following metrics have calculated the metrics like precision and recall from the model which us to validate the performance in noisy classes. The formula provided in Equation (19)

$$F1\ Score\ =\ 2\ X\ \frac{Precision\ X\ Recall}{Precision + Recall} \tag{19}$$

6.7. Matthews Correlation Coefficient (MCC)

The following metrics have calculated the full elements of the confusion matrix to understand the constructed model's performance. The formula provided in Equation (20)

$$MCC = \frac{True\ Positive}{\sqrt{(TP + FP)(TP + FN)(TN + FP)(TN + FN)}} \tag{20}$$

6.8. Jaccard Index

The following metric Jaccard Index calculates the overlap between the actual (true) positive values and the model class that is predicted. The formula provided in Equation (21)

$$Jaccard = \frac{True\ Positive}{True\ Positive + False\ Positive + False\ Negative} \tag{21}$$

6.9. Balanced Accuracy

The following metrics have calculated the metrics like all positive and negative values from the model which as noisy dataset. The formula provided in Equation (22)

$$Balanced\ Accuracy = \frac{Snsitivity + Speficicity}{2} \tag{22}$$

Where: Sensitivity = True Positive Rate (TPR), Specificity = True Negative Rate (TNR)

6.10. False Positive Rate (FPR)

The following metrics have calculated the negative values which are predicted as positive in the model. The formula provided in Equation (23)

$$False\ Positive\ Rate = \frac{False\ Positive}{False\ Negative + True\ Positive} \tag{23}$$

6.11. False Negative Rate (FNR)

The following metrics have calculated the positive values which are ignored by the model which is important to identify the correct response otherwise it would be risk. The formula provided in Equation (24)

$$False\ Negative\ Rate = \frac{False\ Negative}{False\ Negative + True\ Positive} \tag{24}$$

6.12. ROC-AUC (Area Under Operating Characteristics Curve)

The following metrics have shown the exchange values among true positives and false positives with some certain conditions. The AUC has a range of 0.5 to 1.0, where 0.5 is considered as performance of random and 1.0 considered as performance of perfect

6.13. Confusion Matrix

The following parameters will be very useful in computing important metrics like recall, precision, and other metrics.

Whereas
TP = True Positive (Correctly predicted positive reconstructed values)
TN= True Negative (Correctly predicted negative reconstructed values)
FP= False Positive (Incorrectly predicted positive values from reconstructed data)
FN= False Negative (Incorrectly predicted negative values from reconstructed data)

6.14. Cohen's Kappa

The following metrics have calculated the statistics value of which bond of two models and it is used the identify the frequency of consistent values from the prediction which can be far more than the expected value of chances of random. The formula provided in Equation (25)

$$Kappa = \frac{P_0 - P_e}{1 - P_e} \tag{25}$$

7. RESULTS AND DISCUSSIONS

7.1. Deep Learning Model Performance

Based on the training of deep learning models, the values presented in Table 1 show that the EfficientNet model performs well compared to other models. While Visual Transformers show potential, they perform poorly on this dataset according to the key metrics in Table 1. In contrast, ResNet, CNN, and VGG16 deliver average performance. Overall, the key metrics indicate that EfficientNet achieves the best results during the training phase.

Table 1. Training metrics of deep learning models

	(CNN)	VGG16	ResNet	EfficientNet	Visual Transformers
Accuracy (%)	89.96	76.53	94.91	94.70	61.76
Precision (%)	89.82	74.55	94.90	94.70	44.68
Recall (%)	89.69	76.53	94.91	94.70	61.67
F1-Score (%)	89.96	75.13	94.90	94.69	48.72

During the validation phase, the same four performance metrics were considered, with EfficientNet demonstrating superior performance compared to other models. ResNet, VGG16, and CNN also show good performance but do not surpass EfficientNet, with their results falling slightly above average in the validation metrics. In contrast, Visual Transformers exhibit the lowest values across all models, as shown in Table 2.

Table 2. Validation metrics of deep learning models

	(CNN)	VGG16	ResNet	EfficientNet	Visual Transformers
Accuracy (%)	73.54	75.13	77.21	82.65	60.68
Precision (%)	71.72	70.29	77.00	82.71	40.49
Recall (%)	73.54	76.74	77.22	82.65	60.68
F1-Score (%)	70.98	65.96	76.81	84.06	50.92

In the testing phase, EfficientNet achieves the best performance among all models. CNN follows with strong test results, though it does not outperform EfficientNet. ResNet and VGG16 also deliver good performance, but they fall short of EfficientNet, showing above-average results. Lastly, Visual Transformers have the lowest values across all models, as presented in Table 3.

Table 3. Testing metrics of deep learning models

	(CNN)	VGG16	ResNet	EfficientNet	Visual Transformers
Accuracy (%)	73.91	72.28	72.84	80.16	62.63
Precision (%)	73.59	68.00	76.11	80.21	72.59
Recall (%)	73.91	72.28	72.84	80.16	62.36
F1-Score (%)	73.61	69.58	73.68	79.73	49.01

7.2. VAE Model and its Performance

The deep learning Models are good but not to the expectation so the generative AI model Variational Auto-encoder (VAE) is used to predict the same data set, so the results are good when compared to the deep learning models. In Variational Auto-encoder different types of optimizers are used to predict which optimizer has a very good performance based on various metrics as shown the Table 4 which are calculated for the training phase. The RMSProp has the best overall performance than another optimizer, the representation of the other optimizer is good but not better than the RMSProp optimizer in the training phase.

Table 4. Performance metrics during the training phase with various optimizers

	ADAM	LAMB	Novo Grad	RAdam	RMSProp	LARS	ADAGRAD
Accuracy	0.9406	0.9469	0.9491	0.9364	0.9503	0.9364	0.9485
F1 Score	0.2992	0.4725	0.5140	0.0000	0.5122	0.0002	0.4778
Precision	0.7271	0.6885	0.6500	0.0000	0.7273	0.4019	0.7174
Recall	0.1229	0.3597	0.4251	0.0000	0.3953	0.0001	0.3581
Specificity	0.9949	0.9885	0.9845	1.0000	0.9895	1.0000	0.9901
NPV	0.9600	0.9550	0.9987	0.9345	0.9575	0.9345	0.9989
TPR	0.4000	0.3300	0.3500	0.0000	0.3800	0.0000	03500
FPR	0.0100	0.0100	0.7000	1.0000	0.0100	0.0000	0.0089
FNR	0.6000	0.6890	0.0100	1.0000	0.6500	1.0000	0.7080
MCC	0.5311	0.5000	0.5050	0.0000	0.5000	0.0040	0.5000
Jaccard Index	0.3512	03000	0.3459	0.0000	0.3000	0.0000	0.3138
ROC AUC	0.6929	0.6750	0.7048	1.0000	0.6800	0.5000	0.6741
Balanced Accuracy	0.6919	0.6750	0.7048	1.0000	0.6800	0.5000	0.6741
Kappa	0.4900	0.4000	0.4884	0.0000	0.4500	0.0000	0.4538

Fig.8 represents the accuracy of the training phase which is a critical metric for identifying the model's overall performance. From this figure, it can be witnessed that RMSProp optimizer has the highest accuracy than other optimizers like Novo Grad, Lamb, and AdaGrad optimizer. These optimizers provided good accuracy however lesser than the RMSProp optimizer whereas other optimizers like RAdam, Lars, and Adam are performing less than the other optimizers.

Figure 8. The bar chart showing the comparison among accuracy across different optimizers in the training set

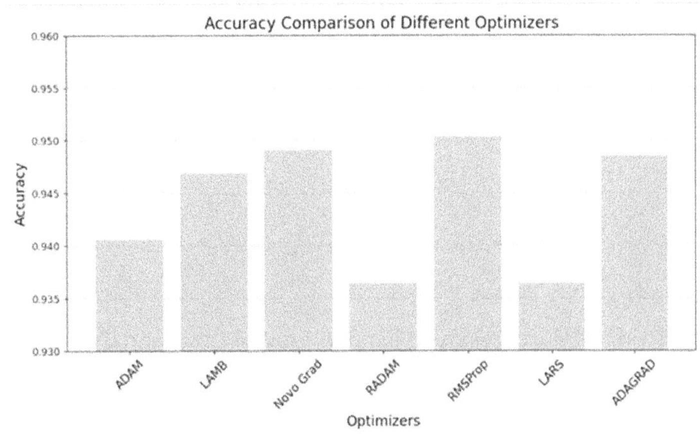

Based on the above Table. 4 which consists of the performance metrics of the VAE with the different optimizers, the graph which represents the ROC-AUC accuracy for it is shown in Fig. 9.

Figure 9. The plot showing the ROC AUC Scores during the training phase

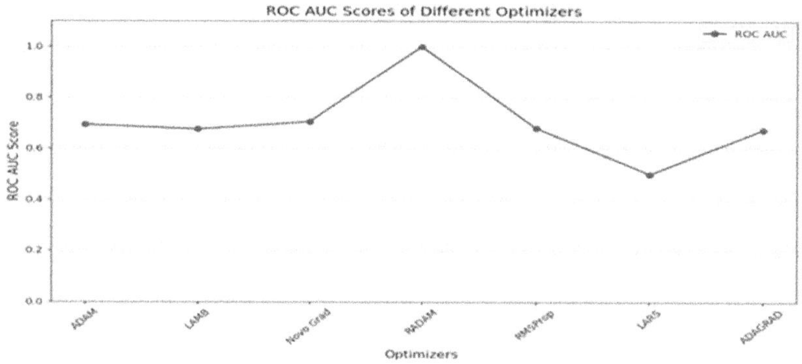

From the above plot, we can infer that the RAdam achieves the highest ROC AUC score of 1.0, which indicates that it performed exceptionally well among the classes, the other optimizers perform moderately including the Novo Grad, ADAM show similar performance as the score is similar, the LAMB optimizer has a slightly lower performance compared to ADAM but still, it maintains a decent score around the value of 0.6. The other optimizers show he Lower performance among the above optimizers. But by considering all other metrics NovoGrad is a preferable one. Likewise, from Table 4 which consists of the performance metrics of the VAE with the different optimizers we plot the graph which represents the training phase F1-score as presented in Fig. 10.

Figure 10. The plot showing the training phase F1-Score

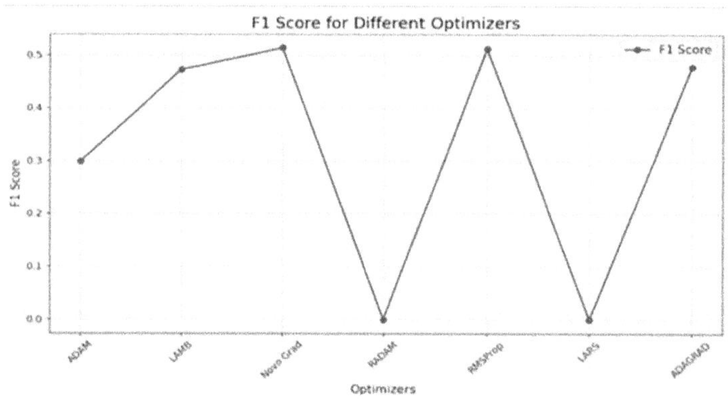

Considering both the ROC AUC scores from the previous analysis and the F1 Scores from this graph, Novo Grad remains the most consistent and effective optimizer for achieving balanced and accurate predictions. Similar to Table 4, we present Table 5 which is based on the Validation Phase of the Variational Auto-encoder Model, the validation phase also consists of the various optimizers.

Table 5. Performance metrics during the validation phase with various optimizers

	ADAM	LAMB	Novo Grad	RAdam	RMSProp	LARS	ADAGRAD
Accuracy	0.9406	0.9469	0.9491	0.9364	0.9503	0.9364	0.9485
F1 Score	0.5332	0.4725	0.5140	0.0000	0.5122	0.0002	0.4778
Precision	0.7271	0.6885	0.6500	0.0000	0.7273	0.4019	0.7174
Recall	0.1229	0.3597	0.4251	0.0000	0.3953	0.0001	0.3581
Specificity	0.9949	0.9885	0.9845	1.0000	0.9895	1.0000	0.9901
NPV	0.9662	0.9500	0.0000	0.9365	0.9575	0.9365	0.0000
TPR	0.4042	0.3500	0.0000	0.0000	0.4000	0.0000	0.0000
FPR	0.0111	0.0120	0.0000	1.0000	0.0100	0.0000	0.0000
FNR	0.5002	0.6500	0.0000	1.0000	0.6500	1.0000	0.0000
MCC	0.5123	0.5000	0.0000	0.0000	0.5000	0.0055	0.0000
Jaccard Index	0.3500	0.3000	0.3459	0.0000	0.3500	0.0000	0.3138
ROC AUC	0.6992	0.6750	0.7048	1.0000	0.6800	0.5000	0.6741
Balanced Accuracy	0.6992	0.6750	0.7048	1.0000	0.6800	0.5000	0.6741
kappa	0.4999	0.4000	0.4884	0.0000	0.5000	0.0000	0.4538

Based on the table.5 which is calculated for the validation phase the RMSProp has the best overall performance than another optimizer in the given performance metrics, the representation of the other optimizer is good but not better than the RMSProp optimizer in the Validation phase. We now present a bar plot comparing the accuracy across different optimizers, shown in Figure 11. In the validation phase, the accuracy which is a key metric for evaluating the model's overall performance, the RMSProp optimizer achieves the highest accuracy among all optimizers. The NovoGrad, Lamb, and AdaGrad optimizers also show good accuracy, though slightly lower than RMSProp. Meanwhile, the RAdam, LARS, and Adam optimizers perform less effectively, with accuracy values lower than the other optimizers.

Figure 11. The Bar chart showing the comparison among the accuracies across different optimizers in the validation set

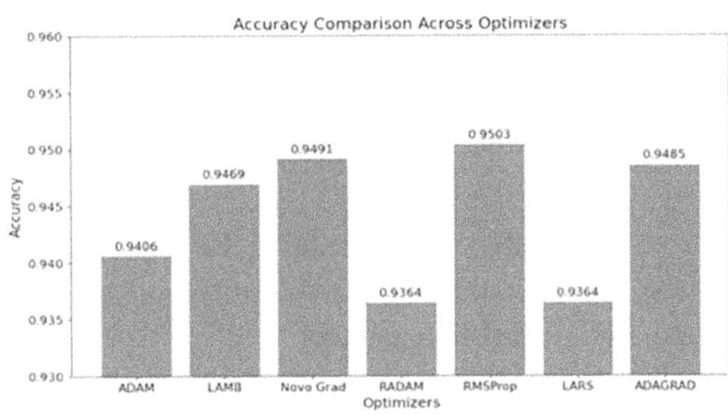

In addition to accuracy, the F1 Score is another crucial metric used to assess the model's overall performance. From the graphical representation in Fig. 10, it is clear that the Adam, RMSProp, and NovoGrad optimizers exhibit strong performance in terms of F1 Score during the Training Phase. Similarly, the F1 Score graph for the Validation Phase has been plotted and is shown in Fig. 12 below.

Figure 12. Validation F1-Score for optimizers

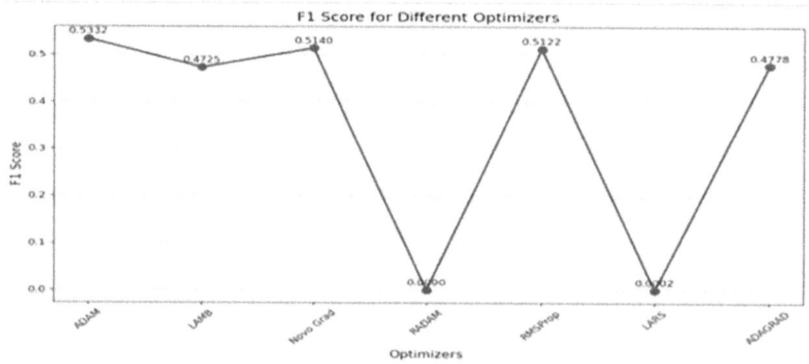

The same graph has now been plotted, considering the ROC-AUC scores for different optimizers in the VAE model, as shown in Fig. 13 below.

Figure 13. ROC AUC-Score for optimizers in the validation phase

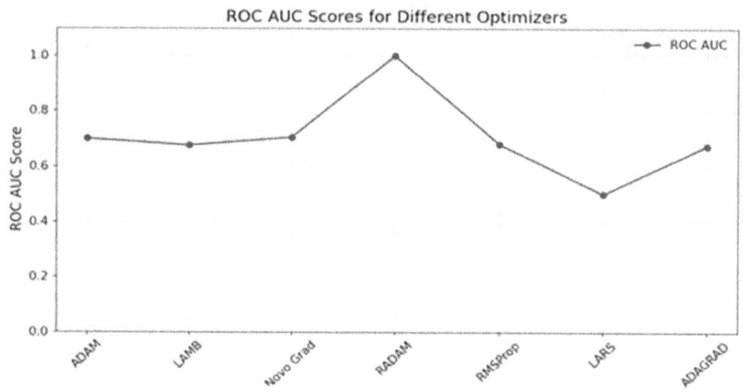

Similar to the previous two tables (Table 4 and Table 5), Table 6 presents the results based on the Testing Phase of the Variational Autoencoder (VAE) model. This table also includes the various optimizers used during the validation phase, as shown below:

Table 6. Performance metrics during the testing phase with various optimizers

	ADAM	LAMB	Novo Grad	RAdam	RMSProp	LARS	ADAGRAD
Accuracy	0.9519	0.9480	0.9492	0.9358	0.9503	0.9343	0.9486
F1 Score	0.5211	0.4728	0.5046	0.0000	0.5092	0.0003	0.4755
Precision	0.7271	0.6822	0.6411	0.0371	0.7231	0.4020	0.7256
Recall	0.4142	0.3618	0.4160	0.0000	0.3929	0.0001	0.3536
Specificity	0.9949	0.9884	0.9845	1.0000	0.9894	1.0000	0.9906
NPV	0.9616	0.9574	0.9621	0.9358	0.9587	0.9343	0.9560
TPR	0.4142	0.3618	0.4160	0.0000	0.3929	0.0001	0.3536
FPR	0.0118	0.0116	0.0155	0.0000	0.0106	0.0000	0.0094
FNR	0.5858	0.6382	0.5840	1.0000	0.6071	0.9999	0.6464
MCC	0.5168	0.4733	0.4915	-0.0007	0.5106	0.0062	0.4843
Jaccard Index	0.3523	0.3096	0.3347	0.0000	0.3415	0.0001	0.3119
ROC AUC	0.7012	0.6751	0.7003	0.5000	0.6912	0.5001	0.6721
Balanced Accuracy	0.7012	0.6751	0.7003	0.5000	0.6912	0.5001	0.6721
kappa	0.4975	0.4482	0.47900	-0.0000	0.4854	0.0002	0.4518

Based on the data in Table 6, we have plotted a bar chart comparing the accuracies of different optimizers, as shown in Fig. 14. In the Testing Phase, which is a critical metric for assessing the model's overall performance, the RMSProp and Adam optimizers achieve the highest accuracy. NovoGrad, Lamb, and AdaGrad also show good accuracy, though they fall slightly behind RMSProp. Meanwhile, the RAdam and LARS optimizers demonstrate lower performance compared to the others.

Figure 14. The Bar chart showing the comparison among the accuracies across different optimizers in the test set.

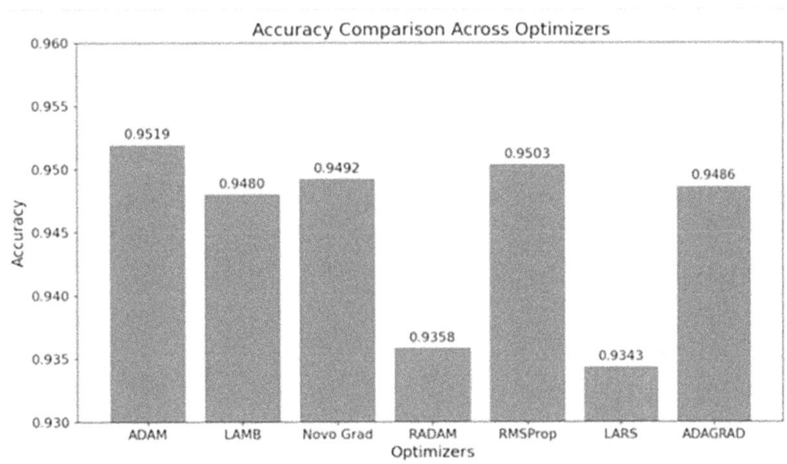

In addition to accuracy, the F1 Score is another important metric used to evaluate the model's overall performance. From the graphical representation in Fig. 15, it is evident that the NovoGrad and RMSProp optimizers demonstrate strong performance in terms of the F1 Score during the Testing Phase.

Figure 15. F1-Score Comparison over test dataset

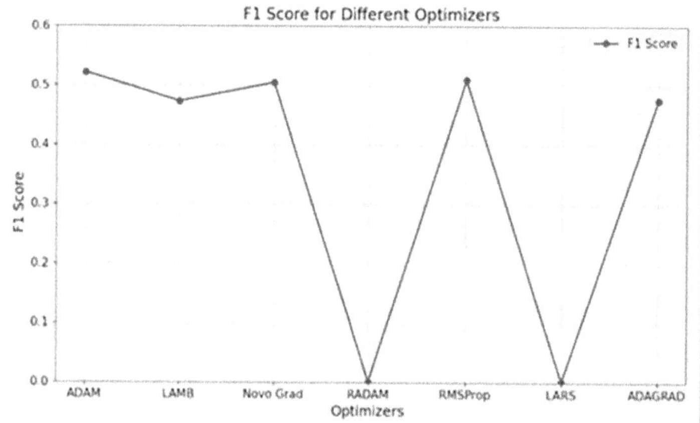

From Fig. 13, the graphical representation indicates that for the ROC-AUC score metric, the RMSProp and NovoGrad optimizers outperform others, showing higher values, which is a critical metric. However, the overall performance of the RAdam optimizer falls short of expectations. In the Testing Phase, Fig. 16 provides a detailed interpretation of the optimizers that performed well in terms of the ROC-AUC score.

Figure 16. ROCAUC Curve for various optimizers among the test dataset

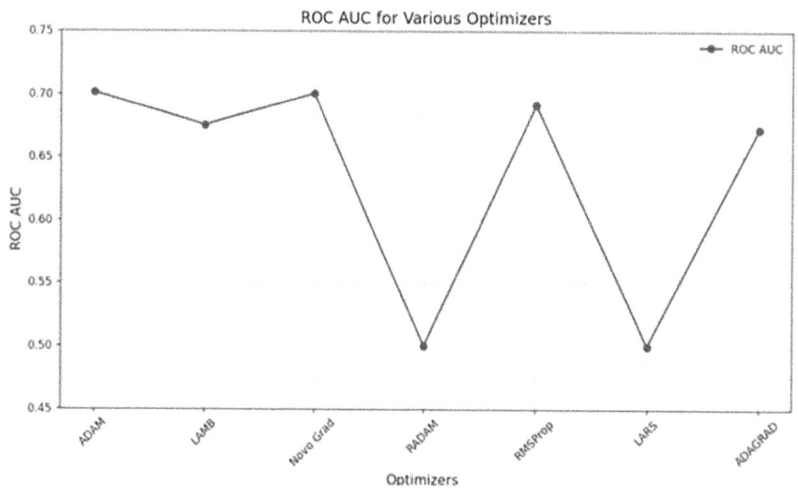

The significance that can be seen based on the above two charts is as follows: The F1 score (Fig. 15) evaluates the balance in the data by considering the relationship between the precision and the recall. For our dataset using the ADAM, Novo Grad, and the RMSProp optimizers we can see that they perform relatively well, maintaining F1 scores above the value of 0.45. The RADAM and LARS show poor performance almost near zero, which suggests that the optimizers RADAM and LARS are not suitable for this task. The ROCAUC Score (Fig. 16) measures how well the model distinguishes between the available classes. The ADAM, Novo Grad and RMSProp have the highest AUC value (~0.7) indicating that they performed well with the dataset and the classes, while RADAM and LARS show poor performance (~ 0.5) from which we can infer that the model's weak discriminative ability with those optimizers. From the above F1 Score and the ROCAUC graph, we can conclude that the ADAM and the Novo Grad are the most effective optimizers for our chosen dataset.

7.3 Comparison Between Deep Learning and Generative AI

From Fig.17 which compares the test accuracy of Deep learning and Generative AI We can understand the best test accuracy is generated by Generative AI with the most suitable optimizer (RMSProp(95.03%) and Adam(95.19%)) and In deep learning method only the EfficientNet has the good Testing Accuracy(80.16%) Based on the Dataset we conclude the Generative AI (VAE) gives the best result to find the generative Modeling and good Anomaly detection.

Figure 17. Comparison of deep learning and generative AI test accuracy

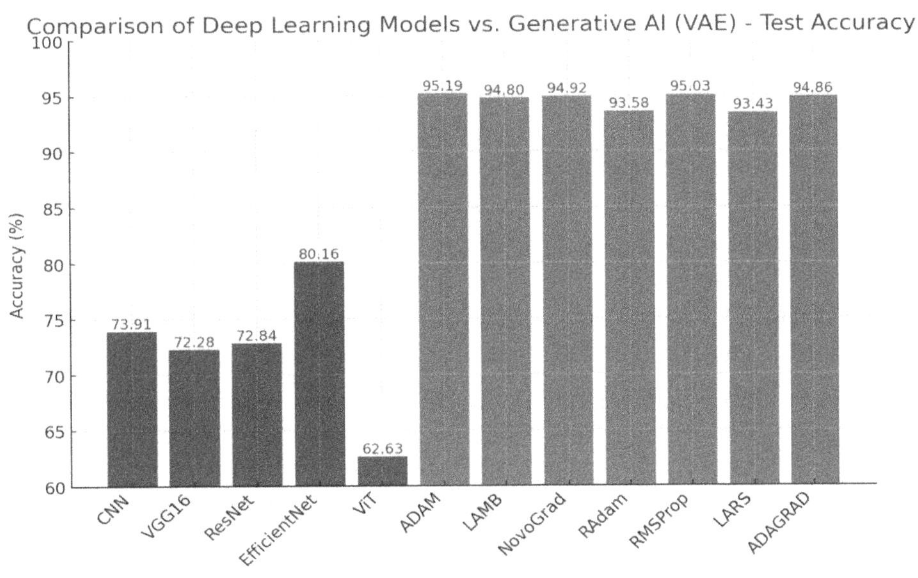

8. CONCLUSION

This research explores the fundamentals of Deep Learning, its algorithms, and the architectures that power its functioning. It also delves into the concept of Generative AI, discussing its various types, including Generative Adversarial Networks (GANs), Transformer Models, and Variational Autoencoders (VAEs), with a focus on how these models operate. The study then applies these principles to develop a model for Cassava Plant Disease Prediction, specifically a 5-class classification model. Throughout the training, validation, and testing phases, several metrics were considered to evaluate the model's performance: Accuracy, F1 Score, Precision, Recall, Specificity, NPV, TPR, FPR, FNR, MCC, Jaccard Index, ROC AUC, Balanced Accuracy, and Kappa. The evaluation, based on three primary performance indicators—Accuracy, F1 Score, and ROC AUC—reveals that the RMSProp optimizer performs the best. With an accuracy of approximately 0.9503, RMSProp demonstrates superior capability in making correct predictions. Accuracy is a key metric in tasks requiring consistent and reliable performance, making RMSProp the ideal choice for most applications. RAdam, on the other hand, excelled in the ROC AUC metric, achieving a near-perfect score of 1.0. This suggests that RAdam is particularly effective in distinguishing between positive and negative classes, making it highly suited for classification tasks that demand clear class separation. NovoGrad and LAMB also showed reasonable performance in terms of the F1 Score, ranging between 0.5 and 0.6. While they demonstrated balanced recall and precision, their performance in other metrics, such as accuracy, did not surpass RMSProp or RAdam. Based on the findings, the recommendation is to use RMSProp as the optimized algorithm for tasks requiring reliable and consistent performance across multiple metrics. RMSProp proves to be highly flexible and reliable for a wide range of machine learning applications. However, for tasks that prioritize class separation and require the highest performance in ROC AUC, RAdam presents a strong alternative.

Despite the promising results, this study has several limitations. First, while RMSProp achieved the highest accuracy (0.9503), accuracy alone does not fully capture model performance, especially in imbalanced datasets. The reliance on accuracy as a primary metric may overlook misclassification costs, particularly in critical agricultural applications. Second, although RAdam demonstrated a perfect ROC AUC score, suggesting strong class separation, real-world variability in cassava disease images may lead to performance degradation when applied to unseen data. Overfitting to the training dataset remains a potential issue, especially given the high ROC AUC score. Third, NovoGrad and LAMB, despite their balanced precision and recall, had lower accuracy, making them less suitable for general use. However, their F1 Scores (0.5–0.6) suggest potential in scenarios where recall and precision balance are more critical than accuracy alone. Additionally, the study does not explore hybrid optimization strategies, which could combine strengths from multiple optimizers. The absence of external validation on independent datasets limits the model's generalizability. Computational resource constraints may also impact scalability, as training deep learning models with different optimizers requires significant processing power. Future research should explore advanced techniques like meta-learning and optimizer adaptation for further improvements and combining of Deep Learning methods with Generative AI.

REFERENCES

Anitha, J., & Saranya, N. (2022). Cassava leaf disease identification and detection using deep learning approach. *International Journal of Computers, Communications & Control*, *17*(2). Advance online publication. DOI: 10.15837/ijccc.2022.2.4356

Applalanaidu, M. V., & Kumaravelan, G. (2021, February). A review of machine learning approaches in plant leaf disease detection and classification. In *2021 Third International Conference on Intelligent Communication Technologies and Virtual Mobile Networks (ICICV)* (pp. 716-724). IEEE. DOI: 10.1109/ICICV50876.2021.9388488

Aravind, S., & Harini, S. (2021). Cassava leaf disease classification using Deep Learning. *NVEO-NATURAL VOLATILES & ESSENTIAL OILS Journal| NVEO*, 9375-9389.

Bhugra, S., Srivastava, S., Kaushik, V., Mukherjee, P., & Lall, B. (2024). Plant Data Generation with Generative AI: An Application to Plant Phenotyping. *Applications of Generative AI*, 503-535.

Chamain, L. D., Qi, S., & Ding, Z. (2022). End-to-end image classification and compression with variational autoencoders. *IEEE Internet of Things Journal*, *9*(21), 21916–21931. DOI: 10.1109/JIOT.2022.3182313

Cheng, J., Tian, S., Yu, L., Gao, C., Kang, X., Ma, X., Wu, W., Liu, S., & Lu, H. (2022). ResGANet: Residual group attention network for medical image classification and segmentation. *Medical Image Analysis*, *76*, 102313. DOI: 10.1016/j.media.2021.102313 PMID: 34911012

Askr, H., El-dosuky, M., Darwish, A., & Hassanien, A. E. (2024). Explainable ResNet50 learning model based on copula entropy for cotton plant disease prediction. *Applied Soft Computing*, *164*, 112009.

Kingma, D. P., & Welling, M. (2019). An introduction to variational autoencoders. Foundations and Trends® in Machine Learning, 12(4), 307-392.

Legg, J. P., Kumar, P. L., Makeshkumar, T., Tripathi, L., Ferguson, M., Kanju, E., & Cuellar, W. (2015). Cassava virus diseases: Biology, epidemiology, and management. [Academic Press.]. *Advances in Virus Research*, *91*, 85–142. DOI: 10.1016/bs.aivir.2014.10.001 PMID: 25591878

Liu, B., Tan, C., Li, S., He, J., & Wang, H. (2020). A data augmentation method based on generative adversarial networks for grape leaf disease identification. *IEEE Access : Practical Innovations, Open Solutions*, *8*, 102188–102198. DOI: 10.1109/ACCESS.2020.2998839

Lokesh, G. H., Chandregowda, S. B., Vishwanath, J., Ravi, V., Ravi, P., & Al Mazroa, A. (2024). Intelligent Plant Leaf Disease Detection Using Generative Adversarial Networks: A Case-study of Cassava Leaves. *The Open Agriculture Journal*, *18*(1), e18743315288623. DOI: 10.2174/0118743315288623240223072349

Lumoring, N., Zakkiyah, A. Y., Kurniadi, F. I., & Minor, K. A. (2024, August). Classification of Tomato Maturity Using Transfer Learning EfficientnetB0 Algorithm. In 2024 8th International Conference on Information Technology, Information Systems and Electrical Engineering (ICITISEE) (pp. 47-52). IEEE. DOI: 10.1109/ICITISEE63424.2024.10730095

Mathulaprangsan, S., & Lanthong, K. (2021, December). Cassava leaf disease recognition using convolutional neural networks. In 2021 9th International Conference on Orange Technology (ICOT) (pp. 1-5). IEEE. DOI: 10.1109/ICOT54518.2021.9680655

McCallum, E. J., Anjanappa, R. B., & Gruissem, W. (2017). Tackling agriculturally relevant diseases in the staple crop cassava (Manihot esculenta). *Current Opinion in Plant Biology*, *38*, 50–58.

Kelleher, J. D. (2019). *Deep learning*. MIT press.

Moupojou, E., Tagne, A., Retraint, F., Tadonkemwa, A., Wilfried, D., Tapamo, H., & Nkenlifack, M. (2023). FieldPlant: A dataset of field plant images for plant disease detection and classification with deep learning. *IEEE Access : Practical Innovations, Open Solutions*, *11*, 35398–35410. DOI: 10.1109/ACCESS.2023.3263042

Paiva-Peredo, E. (2022, December). Deep learning for the classification of cassava leaf diseases in unbalanced field data set. In *International Conference on Advanced Network Technologies and Intelligent Computing* (pp. 101-114). Cham: Springer Nature Switzerland

Parmar, A., Sturm, B., & Hensel, O. (2017). Crops that feed the world: Production and improvement of cassava for food, feed, and industrial uses. *Food Security*, *9*(5), 907–927. DOI: 10.1007/s12571-017-0717-8

Sapre, M., Jatti, V. S., Tiwari, P., Kodachakki, N., & Undale, A. (2023). Disease Classification in Cassava Plant by Artificial Neural Network. In *Machine Learning and Optimization for Engineering Design* (pp. 75–84). Springer Nature Singapore. DOI: 10.1007/978-981-99-7456-6_6

Satoto, B. D., Syarief, M., & Khotimah, B. K. (2021, December). Region Proposal Convolutional Neural Network with augmentation to identifying Cassava leaf disease. In *2021 4th International Seminar on Research of Information Technology and Intelligent Systems (ISRITI)* (pp. 74-79). IEEE. DOI: 10.1109/ISRITI54043.2021.9702829

Singh, A. K., Rao, A., Chattopadhyay, P., Maurya, R., & Singh, L. (2024). Effective plant disease diagnosis using Vision Transformer trained with leafy-generative adversarial network-generated images. *Expert Systems with Applications*, *254*, 124387. DOI: 10.1016/j.eswa.2024.124387

Soujanya, A., Cherukuvada, S., Murugan, V., Ramya, S., Agalya, K., & Gayathri, S. (2023, December). An Efficient Classification of Cassava Leaf Disease using VGG 16. In 2023 International Conference on Innovative Computing, Intelligent Communication and Smart Electrical Systems (ICSES) (pp. 1-5). IEEE. Askr DOI: 10.1109/ICSES60034.2023.10465476

Thaiyalnayaki, K., Raghul, S., & Ramachandran, S. (2022, April). Automatic classification of cassava using data augmentation and CNN. In *AIP Conference Proceedings* (Vol. 2405, No. 1). AIP Publishing. DOI: 10.1063/5.0072729

Thirunavukkarasu, J., Oindrilla, K. J., Sangeetha, M., & Swetha, E. (2022, July). An Efficient Deep Learning Approach for Plant Disease Detection. In *2022 International Conference on Innovative Computing, Intelligent Communication and Smart Electrical Systems (ICSES)* (pp. 1-7). IEEE. DOI: 10.1109/ICSES55317.2022.9914063

Chapter 10
Impact of Generative AI on Industries

Kehinde Iyioluwa Adeyinka
https://orcid.org/0009-0009-7685-6693
University of Science and Technology, Beijing, China

Taye Iyinoluwa Adeyinka
https://orcid.org/0009-0006-4357-6319
University of Science and Technology, Beijing, China

ABSTRACT

The rapid progress of Generative AI has resulted in transformational shifts across sectors and organizational functions. This chapter covers Generative AI's tremendous impact on manufacturing, healthcare, banking, and media industries, emphasizing how it enables extraordinary efficiency, creativity, and innovation. It also investigates the reshaping of organizational activities, including human resources, marketing, customer service, and research and development, using AI-powered automation, personalization, and data generation. While Generative AI has enormous potential for economic growth and operational advancement, it also poses considerable obstacles, particularly in ethics, regulatory compliance, and data protection. This chapter presents a detailed overview of both the opportunities and challenges of integrating Generative AI into the modern business landscape, as well as insights into emerging trends that will likely shape the future of businesses and organizations in the age of intelligent machines.

1. INTRODUCTION

Generative AI is a transformational subset of artificial intelligence that has rapidly emerged as one of the critical technologies across a range of industries, as it enables systems to generate new content autonomously, whether text, images, audio, or synthetic data. Whereas traditional AI focuses on pattern recognition or making decisions with the help of pre-available data, Generative AI generates completely new data and solutions(Goodfellow et al., 2014), hence giving a huge increase in operational capability on a large scale. This paradigm shift enhances automation, personalization, and creativity, enabling firms to enhance productivity, automate procedures, and generate results anew. Where the demand for efficiency and agility is growing, Generative AI is present to partner in resolving difficulties and bringing about

DOI: 10.4018/979-8-3693-8332-2.ch010

opportunities that were previously left to human intuition (Fountaine, McCarthy, & Saleh, 2019). This was a foundation of Generative AI, grounded by models such as the Generative Adversarial Networks (Goodfellow et al., 2014) GANs were a milestone in AI's capability to generate realistic synthetic data factors that have been used in different applications, from the augmentation of data to the creation of digital art. Subsequent advancements in transformer-based models, particularly in the form of LLMs, including OpenAI's GPT-3, have almost revised the capacity of AI to conduct human-like tasks in language (Brown et al., 2020). The transformer models have been extended for multimodal capabilities; generative AI, for this matter, now performs tasks in diverse domains ranging from healthcare diagnostics to content creation, customer interactions, and financial modelling (Mulukuntla, 2022). This transition of conceptual frameworks to very practical, industry-ready solutions mark the graduation of Generative AI from a niche technology to a popular business solution.

Breakthroughs in computational infrastructure, cloud-based platforms, and general growth in data availability have permeated all major industries. Generative AI is marking its presence in traditionally conservative industries such as manufacturing by automating designs, predictive maintenance, and supply chain optimization (Krish, 2011) . Other powerful uses of Generative AI in healthcare include medication development, synthetic patient data generation, and personalized treatment planning, which have significantly accelerated research and improved patient outcomes (Wan, 2023). The generative AI models also support the banking sector in risk assessment, detection of fraud, and consumer personalization, hence hugely enhancing its operational efficiency and customer security (Al-Shabandar et al., 2019). AI-enabled insights and auto-generated content are being used in retail and e-commerce to provide personalized customer experiences, optimize inventories, and speed up logistics, responding effectively to market demand. Generative AI has also appeared in the media and entertainment industries, producing imagery, soundscapes, and even immersive interactive digital experiences that were previously extremely time-consuming and expensive to create (Bengio, Lecun, & Hinton, 2021).

But beyond specialized sector applications, generative AI is remaking some of the key activities of organizations disruption in HR, marketing, customer service, and R&D. For instance, in human resources, AI models help automate candidate screening, identify skill gaps within the workforce, and develop personalized training modules to meet the dynamic needs of employees. With Generative AI, marketing can rapidly create premium and contextually relevant content in copywriting, visual arts, or video that aligns with customer preferences and marketing trends. AI-powered chatbots and virtual assistants augment customer service departments, providing consistent customer support day in and day out, hence improving response time for customers and enhancing customer satisfaction. R&D divisions also use generative AI to accelerate product design and prototype development, embedding a culture of continuous innovation that reduces time-to-market (Gonçalves et al., 2023).

In fact, the rapid diffusion of Generative AI might just be the coming together of technology advancement, market demands, and improved accessibility of AI technologies themselves. Coupled with high-quality data sets, improvements in the frameworks of machine learning have brought Generative AI within the reach of even mid-sized organizations today (Costa et al., 2024). Cloud computing solutions offered by companies such as AWS, Google, and Microsoft lower barriers to entry and enable organizations of all sizes to tap into AI computing capability with minimal investments in infrastructure. Furthermore, in an adaptiveness-embracing environment, Generative AI enables the business to meet the fast-evolving expectations of the customer with tailored products, informed decisions, and a successfully agile operation compared to the study conducted by (Guruprasad et al., 2024).

In this chapter, an in-depth assessment of how generative AI is transforming industries and main organizational tasks will be performed from a delicate balance between potential and challenges in application. While Generative AI affords tremendous opportunities for an increase in creativity, productivity, and economic growth, it equally raises very complicated ethical and legal issues. Business-wise, companies that embed AI-created content into workflows will have to grapple with issues of intellectual property rights, algorithmic bias, and privacy, especially in data-sensitive industries like finance and healthcare (Wang, 2023) . The dependence of generative AI on large volumes of data brings into play significant privacy problems, and there is likely to be bias in the decision-making processes of models trained on unrepresentative data. This, in turn, puts pressure on corporations to remain compliant and ethical in their uses of AI, as regulatory organizations around the world put in place frameworks to monitor the spread of AI. Understanding the impact of generative AI on sectors and organizations is of paramount importance to stakeholders such as business executives, policymakers, and researchers. Business leaders will be able to make strategic decisions on how to harness the benefits while keeping the risks at bay (Ferrara, 2023). Academics have lots of opportunities in the field to research ways of improving AI in terms of robustness, transparency, and alignment with ethical parameters. On the contrary, policymakers must develop policies that are inviting to innovation so long as the interests of the general public are safeguarded, including data privacy. According to Wang and Wu (2024), this chapter tries to throw light on these various challenges by delving into certain sector applications, organizational transformations, economic ramifications and current trends expected to affect the future of Generative AI.

We are living through times of great change that Generative AI has caused and find an apt time to balance optimism over the potential of this technology with caution over its challenges. The sections that follow will explore in greater detail how generative AI is changing industries and organizational forms and will then provide insights and ideas for its long-term responsible integration. This will enable organizations to make quantum leaps with the aid of Generative AI without crossing the line of ethical norms or legal frameworks and thus position them for success with a rising tide of AI. The emerging generative AI brings about an unparalleled rate of transformation in technology and business. Its ushers in a new frontier where robots will create content, come up with solutions, and think creatively, much like human beings do. What generative AI can produce, in ways unimaginable, text, graphics, audio, or, for that matter, code is essentially what differentiates it from the common concept of AI, which analyzes data or performs tasks dictated by a set of rules. Built on sophisticated algorithms that learn from large amounts of data, this skill enables robots to recognize patterns, imitate styles, and create innovations that were hitherto thought to be the preserve of humans.

Industries are starting to fully understand the power of generative AI to boost customer satisfaction, stimulate innovation, and enhance efficiency globally. Industries are integrating it into their operations very fast. Beyond just very basic automation, the uses of this technology will continue to span a wide range. Companies are using generative AI to automate such processes as creating content, designing products, and servicing customers with the intention of saving costs and improving productivity. For example, designers use AI to generate quick prototypes and investigate new concepts, while marketers employ it to build personalized advertising and content en masse. In addition to the many time-saving opportunities, the tools free up creative professionals to focus on higher-value, more skill-based work, such as deep strategy and creativity, rather than tasks that require little brain work.

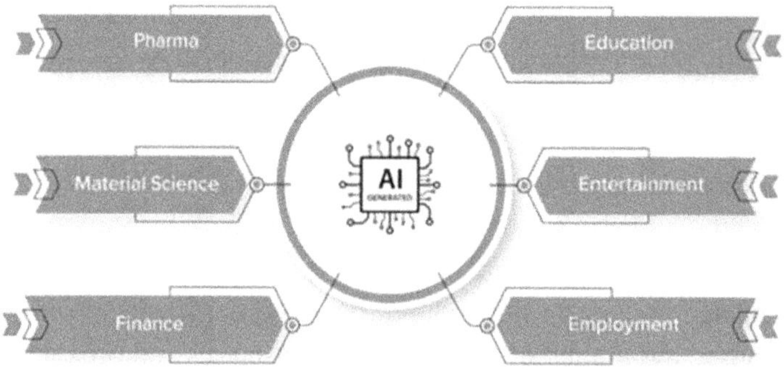

Figure 1 is a mind map that represents several of the effects of generative AI in different business fields. The inscription "AI-Generated" is set in the center, which means the very heart of the technology that moves the progress and changes to the nearby areas. The following are some of the related sectors with this main idea:

Pharma: Generative AI will prove to be a game-changer for the pharmaceutical industry, as it extends research capabilities, hastens drug discovery, and accelerates trials. By using AI-designed models that can assess gigantic data regarding the efficacy and interaction of various drugs, the time and cost of bringing new drugs to the market will be greatly reduced.
Material Science: In material science, generative AI applies molecular simulation interactions to improve material design in the search for new materials exhibiting target features. Beneficiaries may also include manufacturing, electronics, renewable energy, and many others.
Finance: Generative AI is used in key areas of the finance industry, ranging from algorithmic trading and fraud detection to risk analysis. These AI systems can improve decision-making and efficiency by automating trading methods, generating financial forecasts, and analyzing market patterns.
Education: Generative AI is delivering personalized learning experiences through adaptive learning technologies within the education sector. AI might create student-specific curricula, tests, and feedback that would help teachers meet a range of learning needs and improve academic outcomes in general.

Entertainment Generative AI is changing the face of the entertainment industry with image, music, and text generation. AI-generated entertainment will improve creativity, automate production, and provide view recommendations.

Labour: Generative AI also affects the labour landscape by adjusting job responsibilities and the nature of work. While technology might displace tasks that could be automated, it also creates new avenues in data analysis, AI development, and creative industries, thus demanding adaptability and upskilling within a workforce.

Generative AI is disrupting job roles and organizational structures in addition to boosting efficiencies. With the rapid development of technology, these new flatter models are substituting traditional hierarchies since they no longer require multiple layers of management supervision over routine activities. Decisions can be made much more speedily and flexibly in response to market swings. At the same time, generative AI's integration within corporate processes maps new roles and demands a mix of technical, creative, and ethical competencies. While organizations grapple with ways of successfully and responsibly integrating this technology, other relevant roles are emerging, such as the AI Ethics Officer and the AI Integration Specialist.

However, this development of generative AI raises some pretty serious moral, financial, and societal issues. Decision-making by robots and independent creation raises concerns about bias, accountability, and transparency. Businesses have to take into view issues such as data privacy, ownership of content created by AI, and job displacement's impacts on society as a whole. Growing stakeholder demands for transparency in developing and deploying AI technology create an increasing urgency for developing ethical standards and regulatory frameworks. Furthermore, continuous development of generative AI could keep challenging conventional business models and invent game-changers across industries. Companies that can leverage this technology will enjoy a unique competitive advantage, while those that cannot run the risk of being left behind in an increasingly dynamic marketplace. As this paradigm shift is likely to continue, a proactive attitude is required in research into how companies can integrate generative AI into the corporate culture and technology framework. The rise of generative AI opens an unprecedented avenue through which businesses and organizations can innovate, optimize their processes, and interact better with consumers. Moving forward in this technological revolution requires awareness of the many facets of generative AI, as well as its potential benefits, risks, and ethical considerations. Organizations will, through a prudent approach, be able to realize meaningful use of this technology in ways that will transform their futures and, indeed, the future of the world. The more we learn about how generative AI is affecting specific industries, the more we realize this technology is less a tool than a catalyst for systemic change that needs our thoughtfulness and involvement.

1.1 Literature Review

A sophisticated subset of artificial intelligence, Generative AI has grown exponentially in the last couple of years largely due to developments concerning deep learning, specifically about the development of transformer architectures like GPT-3 and models such as Generative Adversarial Networks. These have made quality content creation possible in several fields and have really transformed the way many industries work. This transformational potential of generative AI will become evident across industries such as healthcare, banking, education, entertainment, and material science. The review of literature below discusses the recent state of research into the applications and consequences of generative artificial intelligence and how this technology might have an impact in diverse ways across a wide range of industries and organizational dynamics.

Generative AI has brought an epochal change to the pharmaceutical industry, mainly in the field of drug research and discovery. AI technologies have greatly increased the time and expenses of conventional drug research procedures. For example, researchers' computer models can predict interactions and potential efficacies through database analysis of large databases of chemical compounds as medicinal agents. Such is the case in how Gawehn, Hiss, and Schneider (2016) showed how research and development costs alone could be reduced when it could illustrate AI's capabilities in detecting new pharmaceutical candidates in a fraction of the time it would normally take to do such a search. The same would apply to AI simulations of clinical trials, where the trial design would be more focused and efficient and, therefore, hasten the process for approval of new drugs (Chopra et al., 2022). Apart from the pharmaceutical industry, generative AI extends into material science in the area of discovery and improvement of new materials. By applying AI algorithms that can predict properties from molecular structures, researchers are able to conduct rapid experimentation and invention. These methods accelerate innovation in fields like electronics and nanotechnology because they make material development less challenging and allow researchers to investigate a huge chemical space that is out of the reach of conventional methodologies.

In any respect, generative AI keeps repositioning the heart of trading and risk management strategies within the financial industry. Artificial intelligence can process loads of information and trace patterns, and AI dramatically enhances the capacity of financial institutions to make more accurate predictions of market trends and evaluate risks. In this direction, one leading study by demonstrated that the use of AI-generated algorithms coupled with the integration of sentiment analysis into real-time data improved the chances of stock price fluctuation predictions compared to traditional models. Apart from that, generative AI programs installed for fraud detection have proved to be effective since these can learn day by day with new transactional data and adapt to emerging fraud trends, thereby enhancing the security level of the schemes. Artificial Intelligence is now increasingly being used in the development of personalized learning programs tailored to the demands of every single particular student. By analyzing the performance data coming from students, generative AI can elaborate on personalized learning material and tests, adapting the speed and learning preferences of each particular student. Recent developments in AI, such as NLP, have been used to develop intelligent tutoring programs that can offer immediate support and feedback, hence enhancing learning on the whole. Besides enhancing engagement, this level of personalization addresses a wide range of educational challenges and promotes accessibility and inclusion in the classroom. The rise of generative AI has caused tectonic shifts in the entertainment industry, particularly regarding content creation. This is something that will probably delve deep into the traditional creative processes; full films and music are already being churned out with AI technology, not to mention scripts. Such notable examples include AI's application to music composition, whereby algorithms analyze pre-existing musical genres and create original works that may be specifically appealing to targeted audiences. Another aspect involves how AI enabled platforms allow businesses to tailor their offerings to user preferences, further boosting user happiness and increasing their active participation. However, this shift in lines separating human and machine-generated content does raise ethical questions of ownership and intellectual property. As generative AI gets better, researchers and practitioners increasingly focus on what this may imply for workforce dynamics and employment. While the automation of routine work enhances productivity for the same number of people, it also creates problems, such as the displacement of jobs and the need for upskilling. According to World Economic Forum (2020), while AI may replace millions of jobs, it is also creating new ones that require highly specialized digital skills. This transition must be managed so carefully by organizations that they need to invest massively in the training and development of employees to equip the workforce with what they need to deliver successfully in an AI-version environment. Other research by Bessen (2018) supports a proactive approach to workforce development in the era of artificial intelligence. It points out the value of education and lifelong learning in mitigating negative automation consequences. Though the generative AI regulatory environment is still in its infancy, it has already begun to attract the attention of industry executives and legislators alike. As more business operations rely on information and insights generated by AI, the need for clear ethical standards and legal frameworks is greater than ever. For the ethical use of AI, considerations related to data privacy, algorithmic bias, and accountability have to be considered in light of ethics. According to new research, transparency and fairness in AI systems need ethics guidelines to guide AI development and application. It thus needs a sound ethical structure wherein advancements in technology are weighed against human values when integrating generative AI into organizations. Generative AI has a far-reaching and multi-faceted impact on organizations and industries. The transformative power of AI brings advantages and challenges alike as industries ranging from material science and medicines to finance, education, and entertainment get reinvented. As it seeks to reap the benefits of generative AI in driving creativity and productivity, any organization will need to address the ethical, legal, and workforce implications of integrating generative AI into its operations. To construct a future where generative AI will serve the best interests of society and prepare the workforce for impending changes, continued research and discourses among stakeholders are required.

1.2 Technological Foundations of Generative AI

A potent subset of AI, generative AI focuses on creating new data or material that is highly similar to preexisting examples. Major key technologies powering this growth include transformer architectures, VAEs, and GANs. Each of these technologies is integral in guaranteeing that AI systems can generate quality output across different fields that involve literature, music, graphics, and synthetic data.

1.2.1 Overview of the Key Technologies

1. **Generative Adversarial Networks:** GANs, first introduced in 2014 by (Goodfellow et al., 2014), involve two neural networks: a discriminator and a generator. The generator creates synthetic data, while the discriminator assesses its authenticity and discriminates between the generated data and real data. This adversarial process is repeated until the generator generates data identical to actual samples. Considering famous Deepfake technology and the creation of art, GANs have been very successful in creating realistic images. Further developments in understanding complex distributions of data by GANs have resulted in their applications in video generation, image-to-image translation, and even music generation. Ongoing research has continued to improve the efficacy of the GAN architecture in the generation of high-resolution images with variation in style. These include, among others, Style GAN and Progressive Growing GANs (Karras et al., 2021).
2. **VAEs - Variational Autoencoders: Another** generative model involving the combination of neural networks with Bayesian inference concepts is generally known as the variational autoencoder. Unlike traditional autoencoders, which usually learn an abstract representation of input data, VAEs generate new data points probabilistically. According to Chen et al. (2024), they achieve this by mapping input data to a latent space that represents the underlying distribution of the data. VAEs have gained popularity because of their ability to generate diverse outputs while maintaining latent spatial smoothness. This makes them very suitable for applications like picture synthesis, where the changes in the generated data can be controlled by changing the latent variables \b. VAEs have also been used for text generation and the generation of synthetic patient data in various domains, including health (Hu et al., 2020).
3. **Transformer Models:** Transformer systems revolutionized NLP and generative tasks. Transformers rely on self-attention mechanisms that allow the model to weigh at runtime the relevance of different elements comprising the input. First presented in the paper "Attention is All You Need" by Vaswani et al.

(2017), this architecture proved to be particularly powerful in tasks dealing with sequential data such as text generation, translation, and summarization. Transformer-based generative models, such as GPT-3, have demonstrated exceptional ability in producing text that is both contextually relevant and cohesive. These models can generate high-quality content in several domains since they are pre-trained on enormous volumes of text data and fine-tuned for specific tasks. While transformer models can handle long-range dependencies in data, they make more complex interactions with AI systems possible and raise the bar for the performance of NLP tasks.

Figure 2. Image of a transformer model architecture.

Figure 2 illustrates the architecture of a transformer model, a foundational technology in Generative AI, particularly in natural language processing (NLP) tasks. The transformer architecture consists of two main components: the encoder and the decoder. Here's a detailed explanation of each part of the diagram:

1. Overall Structure

The transformer model is structured into two main sections: the encoder (left) and the decoder (right). Each section is composed of several identical layers (Nx), indicating that the number of layers can be adjusted based on the specific application.

2. Encoder
   - **Input Embedding**: The process begins with input data, which is transformed into an input embedding. This step converts raw data (like text) into a format that the model can understand (numerical vectors).
   - **Positional Encoding**: Since the transformer architecture does not have a recurrent structure, positional encoding is added to the input embeddings to provide information about the posi-

tion of each token in the sequence. This allows the model to understand the order of words or elements.

- **Layers**: Each layer of the encoder contains:
- **Add & Norm**: This step involves adding the input to the output of the previous layer, followed by layer normalization, which helps stabilize and improve the training of the model.
- **Feed Forward**: A fully connected feed-forward network that processes each position independently.
- **Multi-Head Attention**: This mechanism allows the model to focus on different parts of the input sequence simultaneously, capturing various relationships and contextual information.

3. Decoder
    - The decoder shares a similar structure to the encoder but includes additional components:
    - **Masked Multi-Head Attention**: This layer is designed to prevent the decoder from attending to future tokens in the sequence. It ensures that the predictions for a given token depend only on the known outputs, maintaining the autoregressive property of the model.
    - **Output Probabilities**: After processing through several layers, the output is passed through a linear layer followed by a SoftMax function to generate output probabilities for the next token in the sequence. This means the model predicts which token is likely to follow based on the input it has received so far.
4. Connections and Flow
    - The arrows and lines in the diagram represent the flow of data between components. Each layer in the encoder feeds its output to the next, while the decoder also receives inputs from the encoder, allowing it to leverage the encoded information when generating outputs

4. **Development and Potential of Generative Artificial Intelligence:** The most significant developments in generative artificial intelligence development touch upon model architectures, methods of training, and applications. While simple statistical techniques formed the roots of early generative models, deep learning permits them to represent data in a more complex way. This shift away from the simple model to complicated structures such as GANs and VAEs has greatly increased both the quality and variety of generated material.

Recent breakthroughs in generative AI seek to push model capabilities even further by introducing new training techniques, including unsupervised and semi-supervised learning. For example, the amount of labeled data required for training has been reduced thanks to some training methods, such as transfer learning and fine-tuning, where models leverage prior knowledge. This shift has accelerated the adoption of generative AI across industries because businesses can now deploy potent AI solutions with less data and time.

Another major development in generative AI is the introduction of multi-modal models, which are capable of processing and generating data across different media. This is manifested, for instance, in Open AI models such as DALL-E and CLIP, which enable the generation of images from textual descriptions and vice versa (Suryadevara, 2020). These features enable previously unimaginable types of content creation and interaction and thus expand AI's creative capabilities. With further development, the applications of generative AI have gradually grown in complexity. AI models for the healthcare industry are under development that can generate artificial medical data while contributing to algorithm training with greater patient privacy. Thus, AI-created art and music are also shredding the conventional creative processes of the entertainment industry and raising hitches regarding originality and authorship.

Along with operational efficiency, generative AI, applied to different industries, is changing customer experiences and creative environments.

In a nutshell, the technology underpinning generative AI transformational models, GANs, and VAEs has been a precursor to its rapid development and wide range of applications. It needs to be considered that these technologies will further evolve, making new possibilities available and extending the impact of generative AI on businesses and organizations even more. Aiming at maximum utilization of generative AI and addressing challenges arising in its adoption in various domains or fields, it becomes important to understand the underlying technologies constituting generative AI.

2. GENERATIVE AI AND CUSTOMER EXPERIENCE

Generative AI is changing the face of customer interactions with a business: more personalized marketing and innovating processes for customer support. Such advanced algorithms, when put into action with large volumes of data, can allow an organization to tailor its services and communications to meet the unique needs and preferences of each customer. The following section will look at two major areas of application: Generative AI in personalized marketing and customer engagement and its use in enhancing customer support through AI-driven solutions.

2.1 AI for Personalized Marketing and Customer Engagement

Organizations have identified personalization of marketing as a key ingredient in a bid to improve customer engagement and conversions. Generative AI enables companies to analyze customer data, predict preferences, and develop personalized marketing content with target audiences. Equipped with machine learning algorithms that glean from past behaviors and interactions, businesses can serve highly relevant ads, product recommendations, and personalized email campaigns.

One of the key advantages that Generative AI enables for marketing involves the capability to generate content automatically. AI algorithms can generate product descriptions, social network posts, and promotional emails aimed at solving the needs and tastes of certain segments of customers. Enterprises also used GPT-3, developed by Open AI, to generate ad copy and engage customers in conversational marketing campaigns. Not only does this save time and resources, but it also ensures that the marketing is always in tune with the interests of the consumers. Moreover, AI-powered personalization is more than just generating static content. Companies can dynamically change marketing strategies based on the reaction they receive from customers through various data-analyzing tools. For example, if a customer interacts quite frequently with a certain type of content, then AI will alter future communications to make similar products or services more prominent, increasing the possibility of conversion. Such real-time adaptability makes the entire customer experience much more engaging and nurtures better brand loyalty.

Another capability that generative AI supports well is the enhancement of segmentation strategies. In identifying critical segments, organizations use clustering algorithms and predictive analytics, which pinpoint and target very specific groups of customers. This maximizes resource allocation by allotting the marketing budget to the most promising segments. A study by Chaffey, Ellis-Chadwick, and Mayer (2009) shows that organizations that adopt AI-enabled segmentation strategies realize better results in terms of the levels of engagement and return on investment in their marketing campaigns.

2.2 AI-Powered Enhancements to Customer Support

At the same time, Generative AI is changing customer support with intelligent solutions that will increase effectiveness in service delivery by improving customer satisfaction. Consequently, AI-powered chatbots and virtual assistants represent many customer service touchpoints that respond in near real-time to customer inquiries. The systems use natural language processing with machine learning to understand and provide responses to customer queries.

Generative AI enables chatbots to conduct conversations that feel very human, delivering customers the information they desire without the delays typical of traditional support channels. For instance, AI can be used to auto-generate responses by drawing from a vast database of interactions. This ensures that customers receive relevant and, more importantly, correct information. According to a study by Wu (2022), organizations employing AI-powered solutions for their customer support can reduce response times by as much as 80%, greatly enhancing the customer experience. Furthermore, AI-powered support systems can engage in multiple queries simultaneously, enabling companies to scale up their operations without any compromise on service quality. This happens in the peak times of customer queries, for instance, during product launches or holiday sales. Efficiently processing the interactions of customers, the AI systems retain high levels of satisfaction and lower the pressure on human support.

It could also allow for proactive customer service, perhaps with the view of customer data in near real-time and using that information to identify issues before they become much more serious, enabling businesses to reach out to customers with solutions or help. For example, AI might automatically initiate follow-ups or offer personalized recommendations on how to prevent similar issues from happening in the future if a customer contacts support frequently around the same issue. In addition, this tends to be much more efficient in terms of solving problems. At the same time, such an approach serves as a form of respect towards consumers because it means the company seriously takes their experiences and satisfaction into consideration.

Additionally, AI-powered insights can help organizations innovate continuously in the processes of customer support. Interaction data analysis will enable businesses to discover typical pain points and figure out changes in strategies. For instance, if quite a number of customers have shown irritation regarding one particular aspect of either the product or service, AI is able to pinpoint the problem and give actionable suggestions for improvement. This data-driven approach lets organizations adapt and refine their offerings in pursuit of an enhanced customer experience. Generative AI is important, be it personalized marketing or sending improved customer support solutions. By leveraging AI capabilities for personalized content delivery, automated response, and proactive ways of sorting out customers' needs, an organization can make customer interactions meaningful. While the trends within customer engagement continue to shift, integration with Generative AI will become imperative for businesses that wish to remain competitive and responsive to consumer demand.

2.3 Ethical Implications and Challenges of Generative AI

As generative AI is finding its way into various industries, major ethical issues have arisen that need to be resolved in order to ensure responsible implementation and usage of the technology. The tech presents unique challenges regarding copyright and intellectual property, algorithmic bias, and even abuse for generating sham information, all since it may come up with realistic images, texts, audio, and a lot of other forms of content. This section argues the moral problems, as well as the need for strong regulations in regard to consequences that come when these difficulties have been ignored.

1. Problems of Intellectual Property and Copyright

There are two major ethical issues related to generative AI, including copyright and intellectual property rights. The AI systems themselves make the more content, the harder it will get to work out who possesses ownership and authorship. For example, when an AI model generates literary, musical or artistic works, ownership of the content is nebulous: does it belong to the AI developer, the entity that triggered the AI, or the AI itself? The consequence of this ambiguity may be intellectual property disputes with dire implications for authors, painters, and all creators.

Recent court cases have highlighted these issues. Copyright law demands a human creator since the Howell (1942) ruling, made it crystal clear that if artificial intelligence generates work and there is no human authorship, it cannot be copyrighted. The ruling provoked a discussion on the future of intellectual property in a time when machines may well create content that is representative of human ingenuity. However, many scholars still argue that the existing IP rules need to be reconsidered and perhaps even altered to handle the specific challenges that AI-generated content has thrown up (Gervais, 2019).

There are also concerns over ethical issues involved in the training data that have been used in generative models. Most of the AI models are trained on datasets that large, and these contain copyrighted work. This raises concerns about infringement and the potential exploitation of authors' rights without payment or acknowledgement in case a model generates content that is very similar to the copyrighted works within its training data (Ferrari, 2024). The situation demands clear rules and regulations with respect to copyrighted content used in training AI systems.

2. Algorithmic Bias

Algorithmic bias is a serious ethical issue in the context of generative AI: An AI model learns from the data on which it was trained, and therefore, the outcomes that it generates could potentially perpetuate or even exacerbate the biases or social injustices of the past. For instance, a generative model would create discrimination in content or reinforce prejudices when it gets trained on biased data. This will have negative implications for society as a whole.

These biases might be further replicated through the generative models. For example, it has been found that AI text could, based on the input data, carry racial or gender bias. Similarly, generative models in picture generation may also favor discrimination by producing results that reflect the previous imbalances in representation. These further tend to have a bearing on the equity and quality of the generated content while simultaneously increasing larger social ills dealing with discrimination and inequality.

To mitigate the algorithmic bias, procedures for ensuring diversity and representativeness in training datasets should be followed. This involves comprehensive audits of the training data being conducted, putting in place bias detection tools, and encouraging diversity within AI development teams themselves. Furthermore, businesses need to make AI transparent in a manner that interested parties can understand how models are trained and provide specific results. In this case, transparency plays a vital role in developing accountability for biased results and trust in AI technology. Accordingly, Binns (2018) stated that such development of accountability and building of trust have become persuasive reasons behind transparency.

3. Misinformation and Abuse

One of the most pressing ethical issues with generative AI is that it would report falsehoods. AI algorithms can generate deepfakes, realistic fake news articles, and other kinds of misleading content to deceive the audience and further undermine confidence in sources of information. This ability to create hyper-realistic content can have severe risks regarding public safety, democratic procedures, and social cohesion.

Deepfake technology is a good example of how it can be used as a weapon in fraud, harassment, and disinformation campaigns due to its generative models, which create realistic videos of people saying or acting out something they have never done. The ability to tamper with audio and visual content raises a number of ethical concerns regarding permission, privacy, and information integrity. The potential for such capabilities only undermines public confidence in institutions and the media by making the distinction between fact and fiction increasingly difficult to discern.

Different threats from AI-generated false information call for a diversified strategy to mitigate them. To develop such regulations that would dictate the use of generative technologies in media production, coordination among policymakers, technology firms, and civil society organizations is required. This would also involve the development of mechanisms for authentication of content, the use of watermarking to detect AI-generated content, and increased media literacy in offering critical thinking competencies to the general public.

4. The Need for Guidelines and Frameworks in Ethics

Since generative AI presents quite serious ethical issues, such attention to its use needs to be regulated through well-set frameworks of ethics and rules. It includes agreements within the framework on wide areas such as accountability, mitigation of bias, intellectual property rights, and prevention of misuse.

Therefore, ethical principles need to be developed in collaboration with various stakeholders: AI developers, legislators, ethicists, and representatives of communities that will suffer from the consequences. In this way, standards will represent different positions and will be able to tackle multilayered challenges of class issues presented by generative (Luusua, 2023).

Key components of effective ethical frameworks includes:

Transparency: Businesses must be very transparent about the algorithms they use, the data used to train AI models, and what decision-making procedures they follow. Accordingly, users will become more accountable and trusting.

Accountability: Clear lines of accountability need to be provided so businesses are held accountable for the results output by their AI systems. This means tackling prejudice and false information and being proactive about negative effects.

Equitability and Inclusion: An ethics framework guiding AI should ensure a diverse set of voices is integrated into the decision-making mechanisms. This will reduce biases and promote equity in the various contents created through AI.

Education and Training: Organizations should finance education and training projects so that more developers, users, and the general public will learn about ethical implications related to generative AI. Promoting media literacy with critical thinking will make people much better prepared to deal with the complications of AI-generated content.

The issues facing generative AI are multidimensional and involve the consideration of ethical ramifications. For the development and deployment of AI technology to be appropriate, issues on algorithmic bias, copyright and intellectual property, and the potential for spreading misinformation have to be resolved. With this in mind, to ensure that generative AI can serve as a powerful force for good over the coming years while minimizing risks and harms, ethics frameworks and rules clearly need to be put in place to manage such issues properly.

So, while technology continues to evolve, it will be of paramount importance that stakeholders continuously communicate and collaborate to meet emerging ethical challenges and ensure that generative AI serves society's greater good. Ethics-first AI development and deployment are set to contribute to a more equitable and equal technological ecosystem.

3. RESEARCH METHODOLOGY

The study examines, through a qualitative research approach, the massive changes and effects Generative AI imposes on different businesses and organizations. The method will be developed to capture detailed information from key stakeholders on the technology's practical uses and associated moral issues. The sections that follow will discuss in detail the research design, data collection methods, analysis plans, and ethical considerations.

3.1 Research Design

This study features a qualitative methodology, which is appropriate for complex issues that touch on human perceptions and experiences. Qualitative research can delve into the intricacies of Generative AI and its implications in diverse contexts, such as operational efficiency, customer experience, and ethical concerns. This research design facilitates an in-depth insight into how companies are adopting new technologies with associated benefits and challenges.

3.2 Instruments of Data Collection

Relating to the collection of a diverse range of insights regarding Generative AI, this study will adopt a mixed-methods approach wherein both primary and secondary data collection methodologies are combined (Salah et al., 2024).

Participants included business leaders, AI practitioners, regulatory officials, and industry specialists who were interviewed through semi-structured interviews. The interviews ensured key topics were covered, which simultaneously allowed flexibility for the interview itself. Thirty interviews were conducted, each ranging from forty-five minutes to ninety minutes. Participants in this study were selected to ensure a deep understanding of the uses and consequences of the technology in question: generative artificial intelligence.

(Budhwar et al., 2023), and studying ethical issues with misinformation and algorithmic bias and copyright.

Gathering information on how generative AI will evolve in their respective fields. Besides interviews, the study also includes case studies of companies that successfully used generative AI technologies. This comprises a careful examination of specific cases of how generative AI has been used within corporate processes. Different case studies have been selected to represent different industries, such as marketing, finance, and healthcare. Each case study looks at the following aspects:

- Specific generative AI tools applied
- Implementation objectives and organizational setting
- Results realized-productivity gain, customer engagement, innovative capability
- Issues during implementation and solution found.

Document Analysis: Secondary data collection rested on a detailed analysis of the body of research on generative artificial intelligence, which included industry reports, white papers, and regulatory guidelines. Such document analysis provided further contextualization for the results obtained from the case studies and interviews (Ferrari, 2024).

3.3 Data Analysis

Analysis of the data was done using thematic analysis, which is a qualitative approach in research that makes identification of patterns and themes in qualitative data easy (Braun & Clarke, 2006). The process for analysis goes as follows:

First of all, by immersing themselves in the data, reading and re-reading case study reports, interview transcripts, and all other relevant papers, the research team was greatly assisted in identifying preliminary themes and deepening its understanding of the content.

Data segments were then organized into themes developed during familiarization, which is part of the coding process (Kalpokaite & Radivojevic, 2019). The research group used open coding methods to determine initial codes, which were then organized into categories of subjects. NVivo qualitative data analysis software was used to support the coding process by providing a means of organizing and retrieving coded data efficiently.

Finally, after coding was done, the research team reviewed the codes that they identified to develop overarching themes representative of key findings. These included themes such as the perceived benefits of AI technologies, the ethical implications of their usage, the challenges that organizations face, and generative AI uses in many industries.

The results were cross-checked with members to give credence to them. Finding's summaries were presented to the respondents, who were asked for authentication or comments about their correctness regarding the interpretations. This iterative process made the adjustments viable and ensured that the study properly reflected the participants' views.

3.4 Ethical Considerations

Ethical issues were a major concern during the entire research process. The research adhered to ethical guidelines given by the IRBs to ensure that research integrity was upheld throughout the study (Israel, 2014). Some of the critical moral factors included:

All respondents gave informed consent, meaning they were clearly informed of the purpose of the research, of their rights, and of the safeguards taken to protect privacy. Participants were informed of their rights regarding informed consent, freedom from harm, freedom from coercion, and confidentiality of records.

Personal identifiers were removed from interview transcripts to protect participant confidentiality, and data was stored securely. The research team also protected sensitive information disclosed throughout the case studies and interviews.

Transparency in the documentation of the study's methodology, including details on how data was collected and analyzed, enhanced accountability and replicability. This openness forms a key component in the development of trust between participants and stakeholders (Howell, 1942).

3.5 Limitations

However, while this work provides insightful information on the effects of generative AI, it is beyond any doubt that one has to respect the approach's boundaries (Wach et al., 2023). The qualitative nature of the research may be a limiting factor for generalizing findings to larger groups. While the sample of interviews was diverse, their number may cover only some standpoints of the numerous industries generative AI has touched. Moreover, since AI technologies are ever-evolving at a high rate of speed, any discoveries made could potentially be nullified by the ushering of discoveries and developments along the way.

4. RESEARCH OBJECTIVE

1. **Analyze the Use of Generative AI across Industries:** This is to identify and assess various uses of generative AI technologies in highly diverse industries, including health, finance, marketing, entertainment, and manufacturing. By closely analyzing specific case studies, the research will demonstrate how generative artificial intelligence will have practical applications in the medical field for drug discovery, fraud detection in the financial department, customized marketing strategies, entertainment content creation, and automating manufacturing processes. Gaining this knowledge of such uses will empower companies to make so much more sense of how they could utilize generative AI in enhancing consumer experience, driving innovation, and creating more efficiency in operations.
2. **Identify the Benefits and Opportunities of Generative AI:** This objective targets the evaluation of the observable benefits that generative AI provides to businesses, such as increased output, reduced costs, better decision-making, and improved customer experiences. This benefit will be examined using both quantitative and qualitative measures, including case studies that document how effective the deployment of generative AI has been. These technologies will also help organizations understand the strategic benefits they can achieve in a competitive context by discovering new opportunities for growth and innovation.

3.Analyze Challenges and Limitations of Working with Generative AI: The objective at this moment is to outline some of the challenges and limitations at the business level while trying to onboard generative artificial intelligence AI technology. It will also consider organizational issues like resistance to change, upskilling of staff, and alignment of AI projects with corporate objectives. In these respects, several technical obstacles exist, including integration with existing systems, model complexity, and data quality. Being aware of such problems, the organizations will be much better prepared for the challenges arising from using Generative AI in their operations and create plans to get beyond such barriers.

4. **Ethical Consequences of Generative AI:** This objective will look deeper into the ethical issues lying beneath generative AI: copyright and intellectual property, algorithmic bias, and the potential for abusive applications, specifically that of creating fake information. This study will examine how these ethical dilemmas impact stakeholder perceptions, organizational processes, and adherence to regulatory policies. By examining case studies and previous research, the study can help demonstrate how ethical considerations in the development and deployment of generative AI technologies are crucial and can present best practice recommendations on how businesses may ethically work around such issues.

5.Suggest the best practice recommendations for implementing generative artificial intelligence: The goal is to develop actionable recommendations for companies looking to leverage generative AI responsibly and effectively. This will cover best practices in designing responsible AI, approaches to AI bias mitigation, and frameworks for achieving compliance with relevant legislation and standards. Case studies, interviews, and literature reviews will encapsulate ideas for the research to provide a comprehensive best-practice guide. These recommendations would enable organizations to maximize the benefits of generative AI through ethical concerns and develop a responsible use culture of AI.

4.1 Application of Generative AI

1. Medical Care
   - **Drug Discovery and Development:** Generative AI in drug discovery generally screens huge databases of molecular structures and biological interactions to realize potential drug candidates. Drug development can, therefore, be considerably expedited through the use of AI models in predicting the safety and efficiency of new drugs.
   - **Precision medicine:** This generative AI creates unique treatment plans from data gathered on the patient, considering variables such as genetics, past medical history, and lifestyle choices. This reduces side effects and improves therapeutic efficacy.
   - **Synthetic Data Generation:** While maintaining privacy, AI can generate synthetic medical data quite similar to real patient records. This synthetic data is useful without exposure to sensitive data for training machine learning models.

2 Finance

- **Algorithmic Trading:** High-frequency trading tactics that take advantage of market inefficiencies are made possible by generative AI models that assess market data and predict changes in stock prices.
- **Risk assessment and fraud detection:** Financial institutions use generative artificial intelligence to predict risk and fraud detection scenarios. By creating realistic simulations across varied risk variables, organizations can better assess organizations their vulnerabilities and implement appropriate controls.
- **Personalized Finance Services:** AI-driven chatbots and virtual assistants better engage customers with personalized advice and recommendations for improving their current financial situation based on their transactions and financial goals.

3 Marketing and Advertising

- **Creation of Content:** Generative AI creates marketing content such as blog posts, social network posts, and advertising copies. AI models will help marketers develop more engaging and contextually relevant material with speed. Therefore, AI-powered analysis of consumer data makes it possible to draw discrete client segments and, accordingly, personalize marketing messaging for each. This level of personalization bolsters conversion rates and ensures better client involvement.
- **Predictive analytics:** Due to generative AI, marketers can predict consumer preferences and behavior to help businesses optimize resources and further their marketing campaigns.

4 Entertainment

- **Content Creation:** Screenplays, music, and pictures produced through generative AI have revolutionized the entertainment industry so far. For instance, AI can compose film and video game soundtracks that perfectly fit specific themes or emotions.
- **Video Game Development:** Procedural generation powered by AI offers realistic characters and huge game worlds that improve gamers' experiences and reduce the time needed to create them.
- **Deepfake Technology:** Deepfakes are made through generative AI, manipulating video content and producing realistic renderings of individuals. While there might be some innovative uses for this, there are indeed a number of moral issues associated with deepfakes, such as the dissemination of false information.

5 Manufacturing

- **Design Optimization:** Generative AI systems simulate various design parameters and generate optimal settings for performance indices that help engineers in product design. The results are innovative, functional, and purposeful product designs.
- **Predictive Maintenance:** AI models analyze sensor data from equipment for predictive maintenance, which reduces maintenance costs and consequently reduces downtown., the application extends equipment life and improves efficiency.
- **Supply Chain Management:** Furthermore, generative AI ameliorates the logistics of supply chain management not only by predicting changes in demand but also optimizing the amount of inventory, thus enabling quick responses on the part of business operations to fluctuations within the market dynamic.

6 Education

Personalized Learning Experience: Generative AI can generate test items and learning materials tailored to each student's actual performance and learning preferences, thereby enhancing efficiency and relevance.

- **Smart Content Creation:** AI technologies can create study guides, quizzes, and summaries while instructors invest their time in teaching and encouraging discussion.
- **Intelligent Tutoring Systems:** AI-powered systems provide immediate feedback and support to students; thus, these systems flexibly adapt to their learning needs to help them bounce back from any setbacks in academics.

4.2 Challenges and Solution

1. **Technical Issues:** Generative AI models need a lot of high-quality data, advanced algorithms, and computer resources to work, their implementation could be technically cumbersome. Organizations would also need help integrating them with the current system, ensuring scalability and retaining data quality.

Organizations should invest in developing strong data management systems that provide the high-quality, representative, and diverse datasets required to train generative AI models. Leveraging cloud-based AI systems will also enable scalable implementations and reduce the stresses of computational needs. Working on AI with experts or consultants will go a long way in helping them deal with the technical challenges generative AI presents to their organizations.

2. **Ethical Issue:** The employment of generative AI also engenders a number of thorny ethical issues, including algorithmic bias, copyright and intellectual property rights, and the potential to create harmful or deceptive content. These moral dilemmas can help undermine trust in the use of AI systems and make businesses vulnerable due to reputational damage.

Detailed ethics and guidelines about AI use must be drawn up. Organizations must also clearly define who owns information created by AI and ensure that the training and application of AI models are transparent. Embedding techniques for detection and mitigation can also overcome algorithmic bias during model building. AI systems and their outputs must be audited routinely to ensure ethical parameters are being adhered to.

3. **Regulatory Compliance:** As the regulatory landscape for AI continues to evolve, organizations need help to ensure that they comply with all relevant rules and regulations. This will involve using data protection laws, such as the General Data Protection Regulation in Europe, which puts strict limits on the way in which data can be used and on privacy.

Organizations should establish compliance procedures early on in the AI development process and stay up-to-date on legislative developments. Impact assessments, which describe possible impacts of generative AI models on user rights and data privacy, should be conducted. Indeed, organizations can outsource the complexities of AI legislation to legal experts to maintain compliance with AI implementation.

4. **Workforce Adaptation:** With integration, there are also likely to be implications of job displacement and changes in required skills that come with generative AI. Workers may be resistant to the adjustment of new technologies because they feel AI will take their jobs, not complement them.

Organizations should focus on workforce reskilling and upskilling programs to prepare workers for the changing nature of the workforce. Training programs highlight the cooperation of AI technologies and human skills, increasing employee engagement and empowerment. This will help facilitate the shift in culture to be innovative and flexible within the company by encouraging staff to consider AI as a tool to make their work easier.

5. **Public Perception and Trust:** The efficiency of generative AI could well be hindered by public skepticism and distrust of AI technologies. Consumers and other stakeholders can easily be resistant to these technologies due to fears over the legitimacy of information and the misuse of AI-generated content.

To foster public trust in generative artificial intelligence, there needs to be transparency and unmistakable clarity about how the technologies work and in what ways they are used. In general, this can be achieved by companies communicating proactively with stakeholders regarding precautions and ethical concerns. Media literacy and critical thinking consumer promotion programs could lead to a well-informed public discussion of the issue. Such programs might also help consumers understand the potential and limits of generative artificial intelligence.

4.3 Result and Discussion

Findings of the integration of generative AI in various industries and organizations serve witness to both the transformational potential of the technology and the associated challenges. Next, this section presents the research findings, followed by a detailed discussion that situates them within the broader context of generative AI uses, benefits, and challenges, together with ethical issues.

4.3.1 Results

1 Increased Productivity and Efficiency

Organizations which employed generative AI saw massive increases in operational efficiencies. For example, AI-driven technologies have cut by as much as half the time required for healthcare to achieve drug discovery and, therefore, allow researchers to reach potential candidates in very little time compared to previous over long periods. AI-generated content reduced content development time by more than a third, freeing marketing teams up to develop strategy and create engagement rather than manual work.

2 More Customization

Many businesses reported that generative AI allowed them to make their contacts with customers more personalized. In the financial industry, for example, AI-generated personalized financial advice raised customer satisfaction ratings. In addition, shops utilizing AI in recommending products have been witnessing a 25% conversion rate increase. The findings showcase just how important personalized experiences are in amplifying loyalty and customer engagement.

3 Application of the Difficulties in Ethics

Despite the benefits, however, the study kept emphasizing the ethical concerns arising from generative artificial intelligence. Many organizations, especially, addressed their concerns with regard to algorithmic bias in recruitment and hiring practices where the biased AI models led to the unfair treatment of certain demographic groups. The propensity of AI-created content to spread false information, especially in relation to social and political debate, was a concern of some.

4 Challenges in Meeting Regulatory Requirements

Businesses testified that it took a lot of work to keep up with the ever-evolving regulatory landscape, which embraced the various AI technologies. Many were concerned about potential fines due to regulations such as the General Data Protection Regulation (GDPR), since most did not understand what to do to comply with data privacy regulations. The uncertainty on this matter even highlighted the fact that businesses would have to invest resources in legal expertise and compliance structures.

5 Resistance from Employees and Transition

Most of the respondents were very apprehensive about the rejection of workers to accept the generative AI technologies. There needed to be more skepticism amongst the workers or misapprehension about whether their job would be lost or whether they had the relevant skills to work with this AI tool. However, in companies having effective training and upscaling programs, greater involvement and acceptance of AI as a collaborator tool by employees could be viewed (Volkov et al., 2024).

4.3.2 Discussion

Results from this study put forth a more nuanced view of how generative AI affects business and institutions: on one hand, benefits, such as efficiency and personalization; on the other, substantial issues to be resolved before standing a chance of long-term incorporation.

1. The obvious productivity benefits of generative AI are supposedly weighed against ethical considerations that should come first in any corporate implementation. Algorithmic bias dictates a need for close scrutiny of training data and model creation procedures, particularly in domains critical such as lending and hiring. (Gervais, 2019), biased AI systems lead to adverse impacts on subjugated groups and further solidify existing inequalities. Businesses will have to invest in tools that detect bias and also perform periodic audits of their AI systems if they want to reduce such risks.
2. Compliance Knowledge Value As indicated above with respect to regulations around artificial intelligence, the complications of compliance make it clear that knowledge of the legal environment and how to navigate the same will be a proactive role for organizations. The organization is supposed to be aware of changing legislation and adapt business practices appropriately. For organizations to keep themselves away from the law and also to win back confidence from stakeholders and customers, they need to work hand in hand with lawyers to develop strong compliance frameworks (Schwartzstein, 1996).
3. Create a Culture of Adoption One significant barrier to successful deployment of generative AI is staff resistance. For this reason, organizations need to promote innovative cultures that would propel every worker to embrace new technologies for their own good. Extensive training programs that emphasize AI's collaborative potential certainly do alleviate the fears of job displacement. Organizations should encourage acceptance and an attitude more welcoming towards AI by indicating that AI works as a tool to enhance human capabilities, not replace them altogether (Woolf, n.d.).
4. Maintaining Trust and Transparency For wide diffusion of generative AI, public trust needs to go up. Organizations should grant transparency into how AI systems work, both the training data involved and the procedures of decision-making. This will be better achieved by clearly communicating tactics

and public engagement programmed that better inform stakeholders about the various advantages and constraints generative AI affords. By nipping in the bud issues like ethical use and disinformation, organizations can gain the trust and credibility of their audiences.

5. Avenues for Further Research Long-term consequences of generative AI, in its evolution, are yet to be investigated in various fields and industries. Future research may analyze the influence of technologies at the cutting edge, such as quantum computing, and its interaction with generative artificial intelligence. Also, understanding how the policy framework influences the creation and application of generative AI may provide useful insights for stakeholders.

5. CONCLUSION

Examining how generative AI affects businesses and organizations reveals a game-changing technology with enormous potential to improve consumer interaction, change operational efficiencies, and spur innovation in a variety of fields. Personalized services, increased efficiency, and the capacity to produce content at scale are just a few of the major advantages that businesses enjoy as they embrace generative AI applications more and more in sectors like healthcare, finance, marketing, and manufacturing. However, integrating these cutting-edge technologies has its challenges. Organizations must carefully handle the ethical challenges posed by copyright and intellectual property rights, algorithmic prejudice, and the possibility of misuse through disinformation. The results highlight how important it is for businesses to have strong ethical frameworks and policies to guarantee the proper application of generative AI. Building trust among stakeholders requires openness in AI procedures, proactive steps to overcome biases, and a dedication to adhering to changing regulatory environments. Furthermore, organizations must fund training and development programs that enable staff members to collaborate with AI systems rather than see them as dangers as the workforce adjusts to the growing prevalence of AI technology.

The ethical, technological, and regulatory issues that come with the use of generative AI will require constant study and discussion among researchers, industry practitioners, and legislators as the technology develops. Organizations may fully utilize generative AI and bring about significant change while adhering to ethical and societal norms by proactively addressing these problems. Ultimately, a future where AI technologies are applied in ways that are advantageous and equitable for all parties involved will result from the successful integration of generative AI, which will also improve organizational capacities.

5.1 Future Work

Comprehensive empirical studies that assess the long-term impacts of implementing generative AI across multiple sectors are desperately needed. Future studies should examine the observable effects of AI adoption, with a focus on efficiency, productivity, and ethical issues. This involves carrying out case studies that offer information on implementation tactics, best practices, and lessons discovered by businesses that have effectively used generative artificial intelligence. The ethical ramifications of generative AI must be continuously investigated. The top priority of future study needs to be the creation of strong ethical frameworks that direct the responsible use of these technologies. This includes looking into ways to lessen algorithmic bias, guarantee fair access to AI tools, and set up procedures for holding

AI-generated content accountable. Developing rules that take into account a variety of societal values and considerations will require cooperation between AI engineers, ethicists, and legislators.

Future research should concentrate on comprehending compliance issues and innovative potential as the regulatory environment surrounding AI changes. Research should look into how businesses might support AI development while navigating shifting rules. Analyzing how governmental and regulatory organizations shape AI policies that strike a balance between innovation, public interest, and safety will also be crucial. There are substantial research opportunities in the nexus of generative artificial intelligence (AI) and other cutting-edge technologies, like blockchain, the Internet of Things (IoT), and quantum computing. Future research should examine how these technologies might work in tandem with AI to produce new applications and improved capabilities in a variety of industries. Education and workforce development will be crucial in determining how generative AI develops in the future. Research ought to concentrate on developing and executing training curricula that give staff members the abilities they need to work with AI systems efficiently. Organizations will need to foster a culture of constant learning and flexibility. In order to prepare the workforce for an AI-integrated future, it will also be essential to examine the societal ramifications of AI, specifically with regard to employment dynamics, job displacement, and the creation of new positions. For future work on the effects of generative AI, a multidisciplinary strategy addressing empirical research, ethical considerations, regulatory compliance, technology integration, and workforce development will be necessary. By concentrating on these areas, stakeholders may guarantee that Generative AI is used efficiently, optimising its advantages while lowering any possible hazards. This will improve organizational performance and the general well-being of society.

REFERENCES

Al-Shabandar, R. (2019). The application of artificial intelligence in financial compliance management. In *Proceedings of the 2019 International Conference on Artificial Intelligence and Advanced Manufacturing*. DOI: 10.1145/3358331.3358339

Bengio, Y., Lecun, Y., & Hinton, G. (2021). Deep learning for AI. *Communications of the ACM, 64*(7), 58–65. DOI: 10.1145/3448250

Bessen, J. (2018). *AI and jobs: The role of demand.* National Bureau of Economic Research. DOI: 10.3386/w24235

Binns, R. (2018). Fairness in machine learning: Lessons from political philosophy. In *Conference on Fairness, Accountability and Transparency*. PMLR.

Braun, V., & Clarke, V. (2006). Using thematic analysis in psychology. *Qualitative Research in Psychology, 3*(2), 77–101. DOI: 10.1191/1478088706qp063oa

Brown, T. (2020). Language models are few-shot learners. *Advances in Neural Information Processing Systems*, •••, 33.

Budhwar, P., Chowdhury, S., Wood, G., Aguinis, H., Bamber, G. J., Beltran, J. R., Boselie, P., Lee Cooke, F., Decker, S., DeNisi, A., Dey, P. K., Guest, D., Knoblich, A. J., Malik, A., Paauwe, J., Papagiannidis, S., Patel, C., Pereira, V., Ren, S., & Varma, A. (2023). Human resource management in the age of generative artificial intelligence: Perspectives and research directions on ChatGPT. *Human Resource Management Journal, 33*(3), 606–659. DOI: 10.1111/1748-8583.12524

Chaffey, D., Ellis-Chadwick, F., & Mayer, R. (2009). *Internet marketing: Strategy, implementation and practice*. Pearson Education.

Chen, Y., et al. (2024). Auto-encoding variational bayes. *Cambridge Explorations in Arts and Sciences, 2*(1).

Chopra, H., Baig, A. A., Gautam, R. K., & Kamal, M. A. (2022). Application of artificial intelligence in drug discovery. *Current Pharmaceutical Design, 28*(33), 2690–2703. DOI: 10.2174/1381612828666220608141049 PMID: 35676841

Costa, C. J., Aparicio, M., Aparicio, S., & Aparicio, J. T. (2024). The democratization of artificial intelligence: Theoretical framework. *Applied Sciences (Basel, Switzerland), 14*(18), 8236. DOI: 10.3390/app14188236

Ferrara, E. (2023). Fairness and bias in artificial intelligence: A brief survey of sources, impacts, and mitigation strategies. *Sci, 6*(1), 3. DOI: 10.3390/sci6010003

Ferrari, I. (2024). Protecting intellectual property in the age of artificial intelligence. *Computer Law Review, 1–213.*

Fountaine, T., McCarthy, B., & Saleh, T. (2019). Building the AI-powered organization. *Harvard Business Review, 97*(4), 62–73.

Gawehn, E., Hiss, J. A., & Schneider, G. (2016). Deep learning in drug discovery. *Molecular Informatics*, *35*(1), 3–14. DOI: 10.1002/minf.201501008 PMID: 27491648

Gervais, D. J. (2019). The machine as author. *Iowa Law Review*, *105*, 2053.

Gonçalves, A. R., Pinto, D. C., Rita, P., & Pires, T. (2023). Artificial intelligence and its ethical implications for marketing. *Emerging Science Journal*, *7*(2), 313–327. DOI: 10.28991/ESJ-2023-07-02-01

Goodfellow, I. (2014). Generative adversarial nets. *Advances in Neural Information Processing Systems*, •••, 27.

Guruprasad, R. (2024). Corporate agility and AI: Enhancing adaptive strategies for a dynamic technological landscape. In *2024 4th International Conference on Advance Computing and Innovative Technologies in Engineering (ICACITE)*. IEEE.

Howell, H. A. (1942). *The copyright law: An analysis of the law of the United States governing registration and protection of copyright works, including prints and labels*. Bureau of National Affairs.

Hu, H. (2020). Variational auto-encoder for text generation. In *2020 IEEE 5th Information Technology and Mechatronics Engineering Conference (ITOEC)*. IEEE. DOI: 10.1109/ITOEC49072.2020.9141571

Israel, M. (2014). *Research ethics and integrity for social scientists: Beyond regulatory compliance*.

Kalpokaite, N., & Radivojevic, I. (2019). Demystifying qualitative data analysis for novice qualitative researchers. *The Qualitative Report*, *24*(13), 44–57. DOI: 10.46743/2160-3715/2019.4120

Karras, T. (2021). Alias-free generative adversarial networks. *Advances in Neural Information Processing Systems*, *34*, 852–863.

Krish, S. (2011). A practical generative design method. *Computer Aided Design*, *43*(1), 88–100. DOI: 10.1016/j.cad.2010.09.009

Luusua, A. (2023). *Katherine Crawford: Atlas of AI: Power, Politics, and the Planetary Costs of Artificial Intelligence (Yale University Press, April 6, 2021). Hardcover*. Springer.

Mulukuntla, S. (2022). Generative AI—Benefits, limitations, potential risks and challenges in the healthcare industry. *EPH-International Journal of Medical and Health Science*, *8*(4), 1–9.

Salah, M., Abdelfattah, F., Alhalbusi, H., Jassem, S., Mohammed, M., Ismail, M. M., & Al Washahi, M. (2024). *Can Generative AI Craft Variable Questions? A Mixed-Method Study on AI's Capability to Adopt*. Adapt, and Create New Scales.

Schwartzstein, S. J. (1996). *The information revolution and national security: Dimensions and directions*. CSIS.

Suryadevara, C. K. (2020). Generating free images with OpenAI's generative models. *International Journal of Innovations in Engineering Research and Technology*, *7*(3), 49–56.

Vaswani, A. (2017). Attention is all you need. *Advances in Neural Information Processing Systems*, •••, 30.

Volkov, D. (2024). Ethical considerations in AI and machine learning: A framework for responsible development. *Journal of Machine Learning for Healthcare Decision Support*, *4*(1), 36–59.

Wach, K., Duong, C. D., Ejdys, J., Kazlauskaitė, R., Korzynski, P., Mazurek, G., Paliszkiewicz, J., & Ziemba, E. (2023). The dark side of generative artificial intelligence: A critical analysis of controversies and risks of ChatGPT. *Entrepreneurial Business and Economics Review*, *11*(2), 7–30. DOI: 10.15678/EBER.2023.110201

Wan, T. T. (2023). Convergence of artificial intelligence research in healthcare: Trends and approaches. *Journal of Integrated Design & Process Science*, *26*(3–4), 291–305. DOI: 10.3233/JID-200002

Wang, X., & Wu, Y. C. (2024). Balancing innovation and regulation in the age of generative artificial intelligence. *Journal of Information Policy, 14*.

Wang, Y. (2023). Synthetic realities in the digital age: Navigating the opportunities and challenges of AI-generated content. *Authorea Preprints*.

Woolf, B. P. (2010). *Building intelligent interactive tutors: Student-centered strategies for revolutionizing e-learning*. Morgan Kaufmann.

World Economic Forum. (2020). The future of jobs report 2020. *The Future of Jobs Report*, 1163.

Wu, S. (2022). Design of intelligent customer service questioning and answering system for power business scenario based on AI technology. *Mathematical Problems in Engineering*, *2022*, 5279919. DOI: 10.1155/2022/5279919

Chapter 11

The Fine-Tuning Journey of ChatGPT in Industry Applications:
Domains From Generic to Specific

Hitesh Mohapatra
https://orcid.org/0000-0001-8100-4860
School of Computer Engineering, KIIT University, Bhubaneswar, India

ABSTRACT

The recent evolution of natural language processing (NLP) has introduced models like ChatGPT, capable of handling various language-related tasks. However, generic models like ChatGPT may lack accuracy in specialized fields such as healthcare or finance. Fine-tuning these models enables adaptation to specific industry domains, improving performance and relevance. This paper delves into the concept of fine-tuning ChatGPT for specialized domains, examining the technical challenges and solutions involved in the process. We also discuss real-world applications across healthcare, financial services, and education, highlighting the benefits and ethical considerations. The paper concludes with future trends in fine-tuning techniques for broader applicability.

1. INTRODUCTION

1.1. Overview of ChatGPT: A Brief Description of ChatGPT and its Capabilities

AI has evolved in recent years with the recent achievement of large-scale language models as a new era in natural language processing. Of these models, OpenAI's ChatGPT (Generative Pretrained Transformer) has recently received a lot of attention due to its capability of providing human like response to the inputs given by it. This model employs the transformer architecture, which was first proposed by Vaswani et al. in 2017 and has since become the foundation of many current best practices NLP models since it can manage sequences better than the practices like RNN and LSTM before it (Agrawal & Carpuat, 2020). Some of ChatGPT's skills include language translation, text summarization, question answering, and writing on general primarily based on a broad range of fields of interest. It consumes

DOI: 10.4018/979-8-3693-8332-2.ch011

a lot of data and has billions of parameters that allow it to have a conversation with users while taking into account the context. This model is particularly useful in its ability to process and synthesize contextually warrant and semantically meaningful text in numerous languages and is equally applicable to generic syntactic/semantic problems. It is general-purpose and has found applications in many fields including customer relationship management, content writing (Akasaki et al., 2024). Nevertheless, in very specific areas, ChatGPT has been known to express below-par performance, though it is perfect in general areas. While generating answers to sacred questions, the generic models fail to have specialized knowledge of the answer domain, thus providing nearly accurate, relevant, and safe answers in industries such as medical, banking, or legal. This is where a form of optimization referred to as fine-tuning – the practice of taking a pre-trained model and optimizing it more effectively for tasks in a specific domain.

1.2. Importance of Fine-Tuning ChatGPT for Domain-Specific Applications

Fine-tuning ChatGPT is essential for aligning the model with domain-specific challenges. In healthcare, professionals use specialized terminology, and general models may misinterpret or unethically respond to such queries. In finance, precise interpretation of legal changes, regulations, and financial instruments is vital—something a generic model might mishandle, leading to flawed analyses or projections (Ay et al., 2023). Fine-tuning allows ChatGPT to learn from industry-specific texts, enhancing its grasp of domain jargon and improving its practical relevance (Cetinic et al., 2018). This process reduces errors and increases reliability. For example, a fine-tuned model in law can accurately interpret statutes and cases, aligning its output with professional expectations (Chittka & Vasas, 2016).

1.3. Purpose of the Chapter: Exploring Fine-Tuning for Specialized Use Cases

This chapter outlines general fine-tuning techniques for ChatGPT, emphasizing domain-specific adaptation, technical challenges, and key advantages. It explores how fine-tuning enhances model accuracy and domain relevance, improving contextual understanding for specific industries (Da Vinha Ricieri et al., 2024). The process involves domain-specific data collection, preparation, and validation—crucial steps to ensure relevance and avoid unnecessary generality (Deng & Li, 2013). Fine-tuning entails adjusting model parameters to reflect industry-specific terminology and linguistic nuances, including tuning hyperparameters and evaluating model fluency, accuracy, and relevance. Given that ChatGPT is a multi-modal model trained on broad NLP tasks, fine-tuning tailors it to domain-specific language and regulatory frameworks. For instance, medical documents often rely on acronyms and specialized terms, requiring optimized handling through adjusted tokenization layers (Emami et al., 2022). Tokenization is key for converting input into a format interpretable by the model, and in domain-specific applications, further tuning may involve modifying attention layers to focus on critical elements in context.

2. UNDERSTANDING FINE-TUNING IN AI

2.1. Definition and Purpose of Fine-Tuning in AI

Fine-tuning is a critical step in adapting AI models like ChatGPT for specific environments. It involves retraining a pre-trained model on domain-specific datasets to enhance performance in targeted fields (Li et al., 2023). While general language models are trained on diverse data to learn broad language patterns, fine-tuning narrows this focus to improve task-specific accuracy in areas like law, medicine, or finance (Luo et al., 2021; Mao et al., 2023). Although pre-training is resource-intensive, fine-tuning is relatively cost-effective, requiring less data and compute power (Marlot et al., 2023). For example, in healthcare, clinical notes and medical literature can refine a model's diagnostic ability. This process boosts a model's domain competence, allowing it to understand specialized terminology and deliver more accurate results—especially important in technical fields where terms may carry different meanings (Mishra et al., 2024).

2.2. The Difference Between Pre-Training and Fine-Tuning

Pre-training and fine-tuning are two interrelated phases in AI model development. Pre-training involves exposing a model to vast amounts of text—books, articles, websites, and other public sources—to build a general understanding of language, including syntax, grammar, and semantics. For models like ChatGPT, this enables a broad range of language tasks such as answering questions and generating coherent text (Mohapatra & Mishra, 2024). In contrast, fine-tuning refines the pre-trained model using smaller, domain-specific datasets to improve task-specific performance. While pre-training equips the model with general linguistic ability, fine-tuning specializes it—for example, from recognizing common terms like "medicine" or "patient" to understanding "epidemiology" or "biopsy" in clinical contexts. It also adapts the model to structured formats like legal documents or financial reports (Phakmongkol & Vateekul, 2021). In essence, pre-training builds the model's general intelligence, and fine-tuning teaches it where and how to apply that intelligence. Table 1 provides a comparative analysis of fine-tuning techniques, highlighting differences in performance, cost, and scalability across methods such as full fine-tuning, parameter-efficient tuning (e.g., LoRA, adapters), and prompt tuning.

Table 1. Comparative analysis of fine-tuning techniques

Fine-Tuning Method	Parameter Update Size	Resource Efficiency	Use Case Suitability	Popular Tools
Full Fine-Tuning	100%	Low	High-stakes, static domains	HuggingFace Transformers
LoRA (Low-Rank Adaptation)	<5%	High	Fast iteration, low-resource	PEFT, LoRA
Adapter Tuning	~3-5%	High	Modular, scalable systems	AdapterHub
Prompt Tuning	<1%	Very High	Few-shot, exploratory tasks	OpenPrompt

2.3. Benefits of Fine-Tuning

- **Enhancing Domain-Specific Accuracy**: One of the key advantages of fine-tuning is its enhancement of domain-specific accuracy. Pre-trained models like ChatGPT may lack alignment with specialized terminology, leading to generic or inadequate responses. For instance, without legal-specific training, the model may fail to generate precise legal answers. However, fine-tuning with legal data enables it to accurately interpret terms like *habeas corpus*, *torts*, or *jurisprudence* (Mohapatra & Mishra, 2024). This accuracy is critical in high-stakes fields where misinformation can have serious consequences—such as in healthcare, where fine-tuning equips the model to better understand medical terminology and support clinical decision-making.
- **Reducing Irrelevant or Generic Responses**: Fine-tuning reduces irrelevant or generic outputs, which can otherwise discourage users. While models like ChatGPT may provide broad or insufficient responses outside their training scope, fine-tuning allows them to focus on domain-specific content, reducing bias and enhancing relevance. In finance, for example, it enables the model to offer tailored decision-support on stock trends or regulatory compliance, rather than generic advice (Nguyen et al., 2023). Exposure to real domain data refines the model's ability to deliver concise, informative responses—particularly valuable in customer service scenarios where speed and accuracy are crucial. Additionally, fine-tuned models handle domain-specific queries more effectively, reducing the need for human intervention in routine tasks.
- **Improving User Experience in Specialized Fields:** User engagement with AI systems improves when models are optimized for domain-specific context and expression. In fields like legal services or scientific research, users expect highly accurate and relevant responses. Fine-tuned models enhance precision and coherence, leading to more effective interactions (Palmer-Brown & Jayne, 2011). Moreover, by understanding context-dependent language trends, such models become more customer-friendly—for example, a healthcare-specific model can interpret patient language more accurately, aiding in better responses and outcomes. Fine-tuned AI also improves customer service by addressing queries and complaints more efficiently.

2.4. Challenges of Fine-Tuning

- **Data Availability and Quality:** A key challenge in fine-tuning is selecting appropriate datasets. High-quality, domain-specific data is crucial for the model to learn relevant features, but such data can be hard to obtain, particularly in sensitive fields like healthcare and finance. These sectors often limit data access due to privacy concerns, making it difficult to find datasets that comprehensively represent the domain. The quality of input data greatly influences model performance; if it is biased, inaccurate, or inconsistent, these flaws will likely appear in the output. For example, a dataset favoring a particular treatment may lead the model to recommend it universally, regardless of patient suitability (Palmer-Brown & Jayne, 2011). Thus, ensuring both breadth and balance in fine-tuning datasets is essential.
- **Overfitting or Losing Generalization:** One major drawback of fine-tuning is that it can overly specialize the model, reducing its effectiveness in other domains. For example, a model fine-tuned for legal tasks may become too focused on legal terminology and struggle with unrelated queries (Panda et al., 2024). Overfitting also limits the model's ability to generalize to broader tasks. To address this, it is essential to balance fine-tuning for domain performance while preserving gener-

al language capabilities. Techniques like regularization and dropout can help mitigate overfitting by promoting more flexible learning.

- **Cost and Computational Resources**: Fine-tuning large language models is computationally expensive and financially demanding. Models like GPT-3 or GPT-4, with billions of parameters, require extensive GPU time for fine-tuning. The cost scales with model size, dataset size, and the number of fine-tuning iterations (Phakmongkol & Vateekul, 2021). For smaller organizations, such costs are often prohibitive. Additionally, fine-tuning and validation require high-performance computing or cloud resources, further increasing expenses. Given these constraints, organizations must assess whether full fine-tuning is worth the investment. In many cases, using pre-trained models with minimal adaptation is a more practical approach, especially in niche domains.

2.5. Process of Fine-Tuning ChatGPT

2.5.1. Data Preparation

A major factor of fine-tuning ChatGPT to particular fields is data acquisition where the data is collected, cleaned and curated specific to the industry of interest. While fine-tuning, the model learns from the specific field's data rather than the extensive casual data set used during pre-training phase. This is particularly important so that the model can be optimized to perform well in such specific applications such as creating medical reports or responding to legal questions or even making stock market predictions (Priyadarshi et al., 2024).

2.5.2. Sourcing and Curating Domain-Specific Datasets

Data acquisition is the first step in preprocessing, requiring domain-specific datasets that reflect the target language. For instance, adapting ChatGPT to healthcare involves using health records, academic papers, diagnostic reports, and patient-physician dialogues to teach the model medical language and context. In finance, relevant data includes financial statements, market analyses, and regulatory texts to align the model with industry terminology. However, acquiring such data is challenging due to strict privacy laws like GDPR and HIPAA. This limits access to large, representative samples without violating privacy or intellectual property rights. Techniques such as data anonymization help remove PII while preserving linguistic features for fine-tuning (Rao et al., 2020). Additionally, data quality, diversity, and completeness are crucial from legal and ethical perspectives. Dataset bias is another concern—models trained on narrow demographic data may fail to generalize. This issue, known as data variety, affects the model's ability to perform reliably across the broader domain.

2.5.3. Ensuring Data Diversity, Completeness, and Accuracy

Data diversity allows fine-tuned models to generalize across sub-domains within a broader field. In healthcare, for example, data from specialties like cardiology, oncology, neurology, and pediatrics should be included. Similarly, in finance, diverse datasets spanning equities, fixed income, derivatives, Sarbanes-Oxley, Basel III, and market cycles are essential. Completeness refers to the extent of domain data coverage; for legal fine-tuning, datasets must include contracts, judgments, laws, regulations, and precedents to ensure the model can understand and respond accurately to legal queries (Rauf et al.,

2024). Incomplete datasets may optimize some specifications but fail in others, making them unreliable in practice. Equally critical is data accuracy. Errors in training data can lead to misleading outputs, especially in sensitive areas like medicine and finance. Ensuring accuracy involves steps like data cleansing, validation, and often consultation with domain experts. In clinical settings, for instance, verifying data correctness before fine-tuning is crucial, especially in diagnostic contexts where mistakes can have serious consequences (Schopf et al., 2022).

2.6. Training Phase

After that, the process of preparing the data is completed, and the upcoming phase of training is required to refine ChatGPT further. In this phase the model is trained with the new data set contains the terminologies, usage and domain specific language of the particular field. The training phase implies that parameters of the model are fine tuned to serve specialized functions where however, the model remains able to serve straightforward queries.

2.6.1. Adapting Training Parameters to Meet Domain-Specific Needs

The primary goal of the training phase is to tune parameters—such as learning rate, batch size, and tokenization—to meet the target domain's needs. The learning rate controls how much model parameters adjust after errors; a low rate slows convergence, while a high one risks sub-optimal solutions. Hence, careful selection is crucial for optimal performance. Batch size, which determines how many samples are processed before updating weights, also plays a key role. Smaller batches are often preferred during fine-tuning, as they allow more frequent updates, aiding adaptation to domain-specific traits (Sharma et al., 2024). For example, in fine-tuning ChatGPT for legal use, small batch sizes help the model better capture legal nuances during training.

2.6.2. Importance of Contextualizing Language Nuances, Terminologies, and Jargon

Fine-tuning ChatGPT is crucial for priority domains due to the importance of contextual knowledge. In many industries, terms vary by context—for example, "asset" in finance can refer to property or investment instruments. Fine-tuning helps the model capture such nuances. In healthcare, terms like "acute" or "chronic" differ significantly from general usage, and fine-tuning ensures the model responds accurately in interactions with healthcare professionals or patients (Sheang & Saggion, 2021). This is vital in applications like virtual health assistants, where misinterpretation can lead to harmful advice. Additionally, fine-tuning trains the model to recognize domain-specific abbreviations and acronyms—such as KYC (Know Your Customer) or AML (Anti-Money Laundering) in legal and financial contexts—enhancing its performance in specialized settings (Thanh Nguyen, 2024).

2.6.3. Addressing Tokenization Issues and Adjusting Model Layers

Text preparation for models typically involves tokenization, or splitting text into processable units. In domain-specific fine-tuning, this becomes more complex due to specialized terms. Fields like medicine or law often include compound words that lose meaning when broken into subunits by standard tokenizers (Wada et al., 2022). Fine-tuning allows models to adjust token recognition, e.g., treating ‘angiocardiography’ as a single token—enhancing performance with technical language (Xiong et al., 2019). Additionally, fine-tuning modifies model architectures like transformers by refining attention mechanisms, which help prioritize critical parts of input. In legal contexts, for instance, the model can focus more on contract clauses (Yinyin Liu et al., 2008), improving relevance in specialized tasks.

2.7. Validation and Testing

Subsequent to the successfully completing the model construction and fine-tuning phase, the next important activity involves validation and testing. This phase guarantees that the fine-tuned model has the required level of performance for its/plugins domain. Validation enables assessment of the model to check that there is no further problem with the solution while test explores the general utility of the model in the role you intended it for within a particular domain of application.

2.7.1. Methods for Evaluating the Model’s Performance in a Specific Domain

The general measures used in assessing the performance of a fine-tuned model include accuracy and; precision, recall and fluency. These metrics enable one to compare the efficiency and pertinent results of a model to the complexity of its specific assignments (Agrawal & Carpuat, 2020).

- **Accuracy** measures the proportion of correct predictions or responses made by the model. For instance, in a healthcare application, accuracy would be measured by how correctly the model identifies symptoms or suggests treatments based on a patient’s input.
- **Precision** refers to the proportion of correct responses among those identified as relevant by the model. The accuracy is very important for such areas as finance or law, where an incorrect or irrelevant information could have terrible consequences.
- **Recall** measures the model’s ability to identify all relevant responses, ensuring that it captures the full range of possible solutions or information relevant to a query. In such areas as healthcare, high recall makes the model diagnose all possibilities of what could be wrong with a patient based on the symptoms
- **Fluency** evaluates how naturally the model generates text, ensuring that its responses are not only accurate but also coherent and easy to understand.

2.8. Handling Domain-Specific Edge Cases or Exceptions

A third consideration in validation and testing are the details or subdomains that are not tested often: edge conditions – or unusual situations, close to the extremes, that are not the common type of query the model will generally be expected to receive. For example, in the field of medicine, it may be necessary to approximate, including with regard to such things as rare diseases or combinations of symptoms that are encountered only in rare cases. Equally, in the legal field, there are options, the particularities of which involve specific facets of contracts or singular legal instances, which are exotic. While testing the fine–tuned model is subjected to these edge cases to determine how well it performs when handling such scenarios (Akasaki et al., 2024). If the model is unable to cope with these examples, then more the tuning may be necessary for the model to be able to solve wide range of problems within the given domain.

Differentiation of validation, testing, and re-tuning steps in this cycle are crucial for obtaining highly accurate fine- tuned model that can effectively address the challenges of real-world problem-solving.

3. FINE-TUNING CHATGPT FOR HEALTHCARE

3.1. Challenges of General AI in Healthcare

General-purpose models like ChatGPT have demonstrated strong language capabilities but face significant limitations in healthcare applications. The medical domain requires precise understanding of terminology, diagnostics, patient privacy, and ethical considerations—areas where generalist models, trained on broad open-source datasets, fall short without targeted fine-tuning (Ay et al., 2023). A major concern is the potential for misleading or incorrect information, which can result in harmful outcomes if, for instance, the AI suggests inappropriate treatments or misinterprets symptoms (Cetinic et al., 2018). Another challenge is interpreting specialized medical language—terms like "tachycardia" or "immunotherapy" may be misunderstood or oversimplified by generic models, especially as medical knowledge continuously evolves (Chittka & Vasas, 2016). Beyond factual accuracy, effective healthcare communication demands empathy and ethical sensitivity. Patients expect respectful, compassionate dialogue, especially in diagnostic discussions. While general AI may provide technically accurate responses, it lacks the nuance needed for patient interactions—an issue that fine-tuning with empathetic communication data can address (Da Vinha Ricieri et al., 2024).

3.2. Fine-Tuning for Medical Terminology

Fine-tuning ChatGPT for healthcare requires adapting the model to medical language, which involves thousands of specialized terms across anatomy, pharmacology, and pathology that differ significantly from general usage (Deng & Li, 2013). By training on medical textbooks, guidelines, research papers, and patient records, the model gains contextual understanding of such terms—for instance, interpreting "acute" as a serious condition rather than simply "intense" (Emami et al., 2022). This fine-tuning allows the model to handle context-sensitive interactions, linking terms like hypertension and cardiovascular disease or recognizing ACE inhibitors as relevant treatments (Li et al., 2023). Moreover, it helps the model follow structured documentation formats used in clinical records, aiding in tasks like drafting discharge summaries (Luo et al., 2021). Another key aspect is improving the model's interpretation of medical abbreviations, such as BP (blood pressure) or ECG (electrocardiogram), which are often misunderstood by general-purpose models. Fine-tuning enhances ChatGPT's ability to respond accurately and fluently in clinical settings (Mao et al., 2023).

3.3. Managing Context-Specific Responses in Healthcare

In the healthcare delivery system, the focus can be easily shifted from the content of the message conveyed to the manner in which it was delivered. For instance, the same medical term can have the different meaning when pronounced alongside the patient's medical history, age, and symptoms of current diseases. A generalized model of AI can misinterpret these subtleties while giving replies that, on one hand, are accurate but do not fit into the conversation on the other. The final pass enables the model to distinguish between being friendly and considering context during medical conversations and provides improved results (Marlot et al., 2023). Some of the targets of the specific fine-tuning of GPT for health care are to improve its capacity for conversational contextuality. Within patient care scenarios, the model needs to be able to address information derived from different sectors of the conversation in a logically connected and properly referenced manner. For example, the model must realize that when a patient has mentioned a history of diabetes and asks about the treatment of hypertension, some hypertension medications are not good owing to a conflict with the diabetes medications being taken. By fine-tuning the obtained model to account for such context-specificity it is made to offer more clinically relevant recommendations (Mishra et al., 2024).

Also, fine-tuning can enhance the way a model communicates with users/patients such as simply ensuring that patient understand what is being told to them. Patients always require a doctor to break down various ailments, courses of action to take to treat such ails and probable side effects. It's about using fine-tuning to create the output that would be easy to understand and always relevant to the patient's background knowledge of medicine. This capability is particularly useful with virtual health assistants, which are growing to be adopted for general patient assessments, information provision and clinical decision support.

3.4. Applications of Fine-Tuned ChatGPT in Healthcare

It is with respect to possible uses in health care that the potential of a fine-tuned ChatGPT hits its potential. One of the most exciting uses is the creation of the voice interface of virtual health assistants that can communicate with the patient, provide information on the disease, and sometimes even help with the diagnosis. These assistants can help complete telemedicine platforms, as they are able to give the needed medical consultations to patients who cannot receive a doctor's appointment at the moment. The public health use of fine-tuned ChatGPT promises patients evidence-based knowledge of their symptoms, potential ailments, and treatment plans to improve the state of health knowledge [60]. However, it must be taken into account that in addition to patient-oriented solutions, it is possible to develop variants of AI models for healthcare workers. For example, ChatGPT can analyse medical records and create discharge summaries or electronic SOAP notes after a doctor or nurse has consulted a patient. According to these studies it has been pointed out that through performing these tasks these routine time-consuming jobs of healthcare providers can be minimized and they can pay more attention on important aspect of patient care [14].

Other applications of the fine-tuned models are also emerging, for instance in providing aids to clinicians to make decisions. As for application in diagnosing patients, ChatGPT can help the physicians by examining patient's information, identifying possible diseases, and presenting available therapeutic approaches depending on the existing protocols. For instance, by using a fine-tuned model, a physician can determine which medication to recommend for a particular patient by offering information regarding interaction of an existing drug with other drugs and the effects of drugs on the body. It can be very helpful in cases when the multitude of signs and symptoms has to be evaluated with a view to making a choice of the treatment modality (Mohapatra & Mishra, 2024). Another potential use is in education of patient: Self-management support interventions are examples that have shown significant change. An optimised ChatGPT version can create informative content personalized to everyone's needs, allowing patients to grasp what is happening to them, the treatments available, and what they have to do to improve their health. For example, if the model has defined a patient as an hypertensive, it would offer the client with educational content concerning, changes in diet, medication, and frequent checkups. Education tools used on patients can enhance the overall health of patients since the patients can understand the treatment plans better (Nguyen et al., 2023).

3.5. Supporting Healthcare Professionals with Clinical Decision Support

Clinical decision support tools are defined as electronic applications that aim to help clinicians to make clinical decisions. "The implement of fine-tuning ChatGPT can improve the function of CDS by giving the physician real-time access to medical literature, clinical guidelines, and even patient's data to make better decisions". For example, when given information about patient's symptoms and a medical history of this patient, the model can return a list of some possible diseases, and some scientific sources that support this list. Thus, reviewing radiologic images fosters increased awareness of other possible diagnoses and treatment plans which would be helpful in such complicated or atypical situations (Palmer-Brown & Jayne, 2011). It also helps the model to support the healthcare providers in being current with the latest development in this field of research. This is especially important in a field that is continually updating treatments and guidelines making it necessary for AI models to offer the latest information. Heating ChatGPT with new medical data and policies will enable the model to serve as a health care provider's key to the updated literature and best practices regarding care (Panda et al., 2024).

4. FINE-TUNING CHATGPT FOR FINANCIAL SERVICES

4.1. Key Considerations for Financial Services

A timely, accurate, secure, and compliant system solution is more than a need to succeed in the financial services segment. The following are among the basic issues essential in fine-tuning of ChatGPT before applying it on matters regarding finance as it has to process, manage and analyse sensitive financial information, make important compliance with the laws governing financial institutions and business, as well as respond appropriately and accurately in matters relating to business finance, investment, loans, and any other financial information. The financial sector's business is bound by numerous conditions, for example, AML acts, KYC norms, and many data privacy laws including GDPR. These policies require institutions to exercise a high level of data control and guarantee accountability in all economic transactions taking place within and outside the organization (Phakmongkol & Vateekul, 2021). Managing such a type of regulation needs is one of the major concerns when optimizing the model for the context of the financial market. The model has to be trained to become aware of such regulations by working through data with legal and ethical consideration. For example, when working with a particular question, for instance customer verification, the model has to meet the KYC policies in order to put in place measures of recognizing and avoiding fraud. Also, since financial data is sensitive, fine-tuned models must contain robust features to ensure strong data protection especially from external threats such as hacking (Priyadarshi et al., 2024).

Additionally, only financial data is usually not numbers, but it may include calculations, estimations, analysis, which are too complicated for general AI. The world of finance comprises of a broad list of terminologies and technicality that is exclusive to that world of business for instance rating, interest rates, markets among others. Alternatively, in ChatGPT's general form, it may not fully understand these dynamics or make precise prognosis's unless given more development. On the same note of training, fine-tuning of the model allows it to perform an understanding and generation of the financial statements, risk analysis and provide final assessment from the analysis of the real-time market data, among others (Rao et al., 2020). In financial services, security is also of paramount important concern with regard to personal and organizational information. People for whom financial institutions work receive and transmit sensitive information such as financial profiles, account numbers and records of transactions. Disclosure of any of this information could possibly attract very legal, financial and reputational implications. Hence, while fine-tuning AI models in that domain like ChatGPT, there is a need to make certain that the models in question meet the highest standards of security and protection of data such as encryption standards and all the other relevant protocols. Specifically, AI models should not reveal more than they were designed to and should not corrupt financial data as they have been known to do due to regulatory requirements like the Payment Card Industry Data Security Standard (PCI DSS) (Rauf et al., 2024).

4.2. Domain-Specific Fine-Tuning for Financial Terminology

ChatGPT fine-tuning for the financial services sector means so that the model needs to comprehend and apply the financial language. There is an extensive number of terms in the financial sector that are rarely used in conversations but plays a crucial role in making the financial analysis and decision making. Companies and investors use many words like "liquidity ratios", "credit default swaps", "portfolio diversification", "derivatives", which all have a definite meaning in the given context. That is especially important, for, without fine-tuning, ChatGPT may misunderstand these terms, giving answers that could lead to thoughtful financial decisions (Schopf et al., 2022). In the fine tuning also, the model is exposed to corporate and business-related data set that contains financial documents; market reports; stock analysis; and regulations. This in turn enables the model to gain insight into the meanings of financial terms and the mapping between financial concepts. For instance, it can gain the capability to distinguish the types of risk assessments, including credit risk, market risk, and operational risk, and utilize the gained knowledge while answering questions concerning financial management decisions or risk strategies (Sharma et al., 2024).

Moreover, related to this, financial terminology is a kind of data containing significant numerical values and the model must provide correct calculations quantitatively. Additionally, when optimized for the financial services industry, the AI-powered engine can understand the contents of highly detailed balance sheets, determine ROIs or NVPs without the help of humans, or give information derived from those calculations. For instance, while predicting tendencies of stock market movements, the model can be enabled to learn about patterns in financial data and what is expected of the stock, given historical records, fluctuations, and influence from other external factors considered (Sheang & Saggion, 2021).

4.3. Adapting to Legal Requirements: Know Your Customer (KYC) and Anti-Money Laundering (AML) Processes

It is one of the primary domains where further ChatGPT customization for the financial sector is feasible and mandatory to mention processes like KYC and AML. The KYC policies demand the identification of the customers to banks, building societies and other financial institutions to combat fraud, money laundering and other specialized crimes. Likewise, AML regulations aim at identifying and counteracting the unlawfulness of creating income through various criminal activities including money laundering, drug business, terrorism financing or evasion of taxes (Thanh Nguyen, 2024). To perform these processes, the focus is on teaching the ChatGPT model the data containing regulatory documents, legal guidelines, and case studies tied to KYC, and AML actions. The model needs to know what needs to be done in order to validate the client's identity, including requesting identification documents, comparing customer data with relevant government databases, and evaluating the risk level associated with each client. When the model is refined, the work as a result is partially mechanized, so it means prompt and legally compliant identity checks and client affirmation (Wada et al., 2022).

Moreover, by fine-tuning the proposed model for AML processes, it becomes capable of identifying potentially illicit actions, including atypical conducts in the context of turnovers or inconsistencies in disclosed accounts. For example, the model could be designed to raise suspicion if sources of funds involved large amounts which were either transferred between offshore companies or if potential clients tried to circumvent reporting limits. Through the integration of these capabilities, financial institutions will likely mitigate an incidence of financial crimes and guarantee that they are operating under satisfactory AML legislations across the world (Xiong et al., 2019). Furthermore, fine-tuned models help support procedures related to generating documentation and reporting needs in KYC and AML standards. These regulations demand reports and audits to be delivered to the respective regulatory authorities describing measures used to ascertain customer identity, or to identify suspicious business. Overall, when the model is fine-tuned for such tasks, the application can generate such reports by providing a summary of the client, risk evaluation, or generate audit trails that meet the regulatory conditions. This relieves the pressure on financial institutions and at the same time guarantees that legal responsibilities are being complied with optimally (Yinyin Liu et al., 2008).

4.4. Applications of Fine-Tuned ChatGPT in Financial Services

The benefits of fine-tuning the ChatGPT in financial service are vast and include everything from customer support chatbots to fraud-detecting models and the customer's financial profile creators. With AI becoming more and more prominent in the financial sector, these models present a great opportunity to optimise operations, increase customer satisfaction and to promote better decision-making.

Personal Financial Planning: A specific area in which the fine-tuned ChatGPT may prove to be valuable is the planning of personal finance. Personal financial planning is a process of advising people how to plan and manage their finances effectively. An alright-tuned ChatGPT can also share a comprehensive plan on how to budget given customer's financial desires and how they want their money to grow as well as retirement plans, investment products, and taxes (Agrawal & Carpuat, 2020). For instance, an individual may want some guidance on how to compile an investment portfolio and will ask ChatGPT about it. The fine-tuned model can classify the overall status of the given individual with respect to his/her finances and suggest a correct combination of assets like equities, bonds, mutual funds as well as give a good advice concerning diversification. By training the model with financial data and investment knowledge, such a system as ChatGPT can provide diversified recommendations related to an individual's investment, their location, time range, and risk type. This personalized financial plan service may be helpful to those people who never can turn to a human financial advisor but still want to make proper financial decisions (Akasaki et al., 2024).

Customer Service Bots: The second major use case of fine-tuned ChatGPT in financial services is the design of AI-based self-service solutions. A lot of companies have begun integrating chatbots with the aim of providing customer service, where customers can use in places like checking their balances, transferring money or changing personal details. However, when designing ChatGPT for the financial services industry, such chatbots can be made far more advanced in processing more complicated questions regarding applications for loans, and investment recommendations and mortgage estimations. For instance, a client may seek financial advice from this artificial intelligence on the best method to apply for home loans. The fine-tuned model can give more specific details on the loan process to the customer, describe the kinds of mortgages that exist in the market, and compute probable monthly payments according to the amount of money that the customer has, the credit rating and the loan size. Not only does this provide added value to the client but it also helps to relieve the pressure from customer service by interactions being deal with by the system for any general or new customer inquiries (Ay et al., 2023).

Fraud Detection and Risk Analysis: Fraud detection is also one more important area where fine-tuned AI-models can be used as a game changer. It involves embezzlement of funds by fraudulent persons through identity theft or phishing or performing fraudulent transactions that endanger the whole financial sector. It is possible to incorporate policy for the additional tuning of ChatGPT for identification of the patterns of the fraudulent behaviour to increase the chances of their detection. Fraud detection models use historical data such as fraud profile data, transaction history as well as behavioural data used in times past. With this data further trained into ChatGPT, the model can be able to parse through incoming transactions and determine which ones are outliers. For example, if a customer's accounts show a sequence of big purchases to an offshore account, such behaviour will be detected and reported as potentially misleading (Cetinic et al., 2018). Also, there are fine-tuned versions of ChatGPT models that can fit into risk analysis in evaluating the viability of an investment or credit facilities or any financial products for that matter. For instance, a lending organization can utilize ChatGPT to determine the credit score of credit seekers, their earnings, employment history, and current loans. In this manner, financial institutions help make quicker, rational decisions given the increased capacity to identify loan defaults or financial losses (Chittka & Vasas, 2016).

5. FINE-TUNING CHATGPT FOR EDUCATION

5.1. Challenges in Educational Contexts

Generalizing the usage of the chatbot in education poses several challenges that cannot be found in training and utilizing ChatGPT perfectly. One of the major challenges is to create material suitable for various age, thinking ability and topics. It is impossible to teach simple concepts in lower classes and use the same patterns with university students who need more complex lessons. This inconsistency calls for the AI model to be trained with all sorts of lesson contents based on each level from simplified words suitable for young learners to complex terms suitable for advanced learning. Lacking those fine-tuning mechanisms in place, the AI may provide students with material that is either too high in difficulty level, or too oversimplified, making the effectiveness of the educational support provided by the AI lessened (Da Vinha Ricieri et al., 2024).

Besides that, we need to learn how to use ChatGPT ethically in our classroom, particularly when it comes to young learners' protection. Due to this, children are defenceless to material that is either scandalous or debilitating in nature, and, therefore, adequate filtering has to be applied. The model should be optimized from such sets of data in which such data as offend, are bias or mislead is avoided. In addition, there are some issues connected with ethics of using AI technologies IN education, as the

AI-based tools in question may perpetuate the biases present in learning material especially in case if the AI models are trained on inadequate datasets containing societal bias (Deng & Li, 2013). Furthermore, there is more demand for integrating AI systems with the national or regional standards of education. For example, each country has its principles of education, and to adjust AI for certain nations, it is necessary to accurately select datasets to match curriculum standards. This helps to make sure that what the AI is producing has value and importance to students and educators in a given system (Emami et al., 2022).

5.2. Fine-Tuning for Curriculum and Learning Levels

The idea of refining ChatGPT for educational application must take the element of curriculum relevance into account. For a particular subject like mathematics, literature, science and humanities AI must comprehend accordingly the terminologies and structures of those subjects. For instance, as it is with STEM fields, ChatGPT needs retraining in subject-specific terminologies, equations, and approaches commonly utilized in instructions (Li et al., 2023). Another requirement is the possibility to adapt to using in different teaching methods since teachers use different approaches in different subjects. These flexibility guarantees that ChatGPT offers contextually relevant information according to conventional, and emerging pedagogical practices (Luo et al., 2021).

In the case of the younger learners, it is also important that fine-tuning should also translate to the engagement. The content that a child uses to learn has aspects such as stories, games and tasks that capture the child's interest in what is learned. By training the ChatGPT on the new datasets that consists of age-related content, the AI supports proline in responding to the questions asked by young students while at the same time providing value added knowledge content. On the other hand, fine-tuning for university students entails the model to train from the research papers, journals, as well as excellent textbooks to offer scholarly responses without getting it wrong (Mao et al., 2023). Other advantages of fine-tuning for educational contexts are the possibilities achieved through personalization of learning. AI models can be trained to let the learning model understand the needs of each learner and vary the kind of answers they provide depending on this. For instance, if it is responding to a question from students with learning disabilities, then a simpler answer with supportive learning structures can be provided when the model is learned (Marlot et al., 2023). Table.2 presents the real-world case study. Table.3 presents the alignment of frameworks like GDPR, HIPAA, or KYC/AML against industries like healthcare and finance.

Table 2. Real-world case study

Industry	Organization	Use Case	Model Type	Reported Benefit
Healthcare	Stanford Med-PaLM	Clinical QA, medical reasoning	Fine-Tuned GPT	Improved diagnostic accuracy
Finance	JPMorgan Chase	Fraud detection, risk analysis	Custom LLM	20% increase in detection rate
Education	Duolingo	Adaptive learning content	GPT + Fine-tuning	Personalized language tutoring

Table 3. Alignment with regulatory and compliance trends

Industry	Key Regulations	AI Compliance Features Enabled by Fine-Tuning
Healthcare	HIPAA, FDA AI Guidance	Anonymized training, audit trails
Finance	KYC, AML, GDPR	Risk scoring, explainable decisions
Education	COPPA, FERPA	Age-appropriate content filtering

5.3. Applications

Fine-tuning ChatGPT for education is possible to unveil a number of efficient applications that will change the way people study, or learn and communicate with an AI-assistant. One particular use is in Intelligent Tutoring System (ITSs) design which is a form of user modelling application. ITS are AI-based systems meant to deliver various forms of learning to learners aimed at meeting learner's specific requirements with regard to learning terrain. With reference to the detail obtained in the positive impacts of ChatGPT, it is worthy of noting that, when retuned for certain subjects including algebra or history, Chat GPT can also be availed as a round the clock tutor, ready to assist learners in solving problems, explaining issues that are difficult to understand, or even help the student prepare for his or her exams [89]. Besides tutoring, expanding the training dataset for ChatGPT in educational environment would allow creating personalized content – tiers, tests, tutorials, and reading lists. These models may be useful for teachers, because they would be able to supply assessment information automatically on the basis of learning objectives. This saves teachers a lot of their precious time that would have been spent creating content since they are now able to concentrate more on the learners (Mishra et al., 2024). In addition, this chatbot can be used as an examination preparation aid. Computer-based exam preparation applications can create sample examinations, explain how to work through practice questions, and even offer feedback on the results as they are produced. From experiences of past examinations and curriculum frameworks, an optimized ChatGPT can recreate the test environment and possible questions that a learner is likely to encounter [14].

6. ETHICAL CONSIDERATIONS AND CHALLENGES IN FINE-TUNING

6.1. Bias in Domain-Specific Models

The advantage of repurposing ChatGPT for specialized areas comes with the downside of potential bias that may be concentrated in available data. ChatGPT, and any other AI model, are trained on text data which can sometimes incorporate pre-existing bias from other sources, whether it is intentionally or unintentionally done. When these models are retrained for certain sectors for example the health sector or the financial sector there is a high chance that the biases that were inherent in the data used to train the models will also be placed in the domain specific results (Mohapatra & Mishra, 2024). For example, in education, the selection prejudice in data base for gender, income, or race can cause an imbalance or prejudice in response. There continues to be a great concern with how these machine learning processes which form the base of Artificial Intelligence models apply these in the real world given that they could actually reinforce or even amplify such biases. For instance, in the healthcare domain, specifically, it could mean that the model offers different recommendations of advice on the basis of racially-gendered features contained within the training data, rather than medical necessity (Nguyen et al., 2023). This issue of bias is even more so in the financial services sector because such outcomes will have an impact such as wrong credit score, or wrong investment advice which is especially dire for the minority (Palmer-Brown & Jayne, 2011).

To deal with the issues of bias in the domain-specific models, much emphasis should be placed on the kind of data to be used in developing the models. During the fine-tuning process, there are several techniques like methods like fairness aware machine learning or debiasing algorithms can be applied. Also, for this reason, constant model inspection is required to check on sets for bias and update them when new data is incorporated into the model (Panda et al., 2024). Fig.1 illustrates the importance of emerging trends in domain-specific ai fine tuning.

Figure 1. Importance of emerging trends in domain-specific AI fine tuning

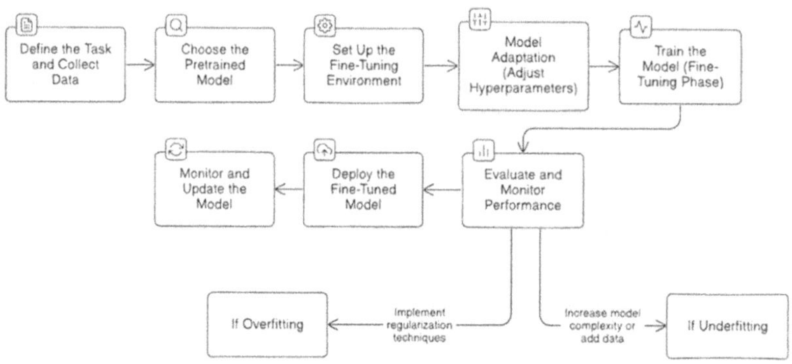

6.2 Data Privacy and Security

Since many developed applications are being applied to sensitive areas like medical, academic, and fiscal sectors, the issues of data and model security are critical. Most of these domains involve the use of personal or organizational data, which if poorly dealt with, leads to severe legal and ethical consequences. For example, when fine-tuning models for healthcare applications, AI system needs to process patient data such as medical history, diagnosis, treatment and so on that is governed by laws like HIPAA in United States. Likewise, in the financial industry models that use client financial data must meet legal requirements, for instance, GDPR in the EU that prescribes rigorous data treatment and privacy (Phakmongkol & Vateekul, 2021).

One of the most important issues in this respect is that the fine-tuned model does not disclose information not intended. When fine-tuning models, the training data can be leaked and for that reason, the data should be anonymized while best practices including data encryption and access control should be implemented. This is also important in the sense that fine-tuning needs tailor to regulations particular to industries that control standardized structures according to the country and the domain. For instance, the legal industry may need stronger protection than the education industry because people engage in fraudulent activities involving money in the former sector. Further, the basic regulatory standards, and policies such as GDPR, and HIPAA must be followed more especially when deploying fine-tuned models. Thus, these regulations not only address the way data can be gathered and archived, but also how this data may be managed and used in the model. Disregard of the requirement could lead to large penalties, legal suits, and adversarial effects to the organization that deploys the AI system (Phakmongkol & Vateekul, 2021).

6.3 Managing Over-Specialization

In other news, another major concern of fine-tuning AI models is that they often are only fit for one specific function. Over-specialization is a situation where a model is so specialized within a particular area that it is difficult for it to work on problems of a different area. For example, a ChatGPT model fine-tuned for healthcare could give proper medical advice as needed but would not necessarily do well in responding to other questions of the sort (Priyadarshi et al., 2024). This issue is key for applications oriented to a wide number of subjects, like customer service bots or educational tutoring systems that might need to cover lots of topics.

The phenomenon that can be resulted from over-specialization includes overfitting, which means that the model is adjusted to the training data so excessively that it exposes weak performance on slightly different data. This makes the model rigid and susceptible to some level of wrong prediction whenever it is applied on real scenarios that are in-real life and rarely like those used in the model training set. A problem is that specific knowledge must be combined with generalization, especially in cases where a model needs to handle various requests from users. Preprocessing methods like altering hyperparameters with methods like regularization or solving multiple related tasks with multi-tasking or even transfer learning keeps each fine-tuned section updated with general info nonetheless it reduces over-specialization. One solution is to follow multi-domain fine-tuning in which the model learns domains from different sectors in order to avoid overfitting and to strengthen the model to adapt another sector (Rao et al., 2020). Figure.2 illustrates the fine-tunning of pre-trained model.

Figure 2. Fine-tuning a pre-trained model

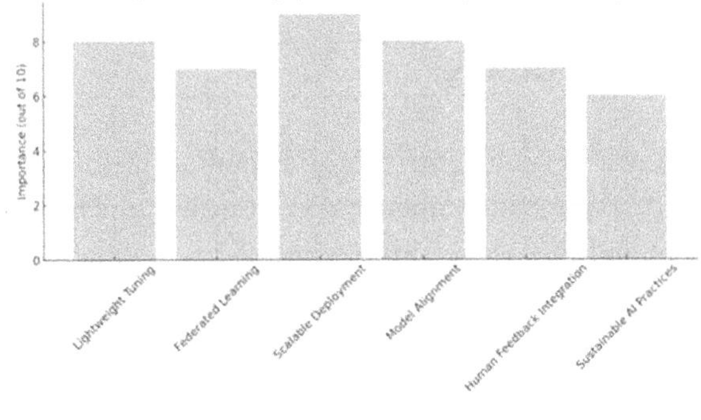

7. FUTURE DIRECTIONS IN FINE-TUNING GPT MODELS

7.1 Advanced Techniques for Fine-Tuning

Developing better ways to fine-tune models, like ChatGPT, is the key to the learning future of such techniques. Another technique that showed potential is when a model trained across several domains and can retain general knowledge while tweaking it to the domain-specific data. This approach solves the problem of over-specialization that the model suffers from making the model versatile enough to work with a wider range of queries. For example, in education related contexts, the multi-domain model could provide an answer both to question like "what is the capital of Germany?" and to questions like "what is Newton's third law of motion?". Other techniques that have been developing in recent years include few-shot and zero-shot learning, which allows models learn from only a handful of samples or from any sample without prior exposure to such a task, respectively. They cut down domain-specific data requirement to a great extent for accomplishing ultrafine tuning, thereby making it more efficient and affordable to industrially deploy customized forms of models for precise areas of application. Few-shot learning, in particular, has been identified to have possibilities in the domain such as healthcare since it is hard to gather large labelled data sets for training mainly if patient's privacy is an issue (Rauf et al., 2024). Table.4 presents an analysis on Generic Vs Fine-Tuned NLP Models.

Table 4. Generic vs fine-tuned NLP models

Criteria	Generic NLP Models	Fine-Tuned Models
Accuracy in Specialized Tasks	Moderate	High
Contextual Understanding	Limited	Strong
Compliance with Industry Standards	Low	High
Training Cost	Low	High
Deployment Scalability	High	Moderate
User Trust	Moderate	High

7.2 Human-in-the-Loop Fine-Tuning

The one that piques my interest in future fine-tuning is human-in-the-loop fine-tuning that involves human feedback at different DMZ points to enhance model training. This involves having people look at what the model is predicting and give their judgment/data back which is then incorporated in to improving the model. Such HIL systems are even more pertinent in highly selective fields like healthcare or finance, in which an expert opinion is needed to confirm the AI answers' correctness and relevance. For example, in the healthcare sector, the physicians can partially use the diagnostic recommendations provided by the fine-tuned ChatGPT model and confirm that these recommendations do not deviate from standard procedures. It can then be fed back into the model and used to create improved accuracy and application in subsequent communication (Schopf et al., 2022). The model develops over time and to those who enjoy helping other professionals make decisions, it is a great tool.

7.3 Generalization vs. Specialization

The most apparent factor of trade-off that exists in the case of fine-tuning of AI models includes the fact of the balance between the degree of generalization and specialization. Although models that rely on domain-specific features provide a relatively high level of accuracy in solving specific problems, the lack of flexibility to solve diverse queries is typical. Subsequent research will have to investigate how this can be accomplished in order to enhance the performance of models such as ChatGPT in its specialized domains of operation without compromising on its rather global capabilities.

8. CONCLUSION

Fine-tuning ChatGPT for specific fields marks a major step in applying AI across sectors like education, healthcare, and finance. Its modular design allows customization for specialized tasks, boosting relevance and performance in niche domains. General models lack the precision needed for such areas, which fine-tuning addresses by training on domain-specific data. In healthcare, this enables the model to understand medical terminology, assist in diagnosis, and support clinical documentation while adhering to regulations. In education, it adapts to grade levels and curricula, acting as a tutor that delivers tailored learning support. For finance, fine-tuning improves compliance, risk assessment, fraud detection, and personalized financial advice. Beyond improved accuracy, fine-tuning also enhances user engagement through personalized interactions, making AI more effective in professional settings. However, challenges like bias, privacy, and ethical concerns must be managed. Continued research will help create fine-tuned models that are not only specialized and efficient, but also generalizable and responsible amplifying their impact across industries.

REFERENCES

Agrawal, S., & Carpuat, M. (2020). Multitask models for controlling the complexity of neural machine translation. *Proceedings of the The Fourth Widening Natural Language Processing Workshop*, 136-139. https://doi.org/DOI: 10.18653/v1/2020.winlp-1.36

Akasaki, Y., Hamai, S., Kawahara, S., Sato, T., & Nakashima, Y. (2024). Appropriate flexion gap evaluation for fine-tuning of medial stabilizing technique in journey II Bi-cruciate stabilized total knee arthroplasty. https://doi.org/DOI: 10.2139/ssrn.4924692

Ay, B., Ertam, F., Fidan, G., & Aydin, G. (2023). Turkish abstractive text document summarization using text to text transfer transformer. *Alexandria Engineering Journal*, *68*, 1–13. DOI: 10.1016/j.aej.2023.01.008

Cetinic, E., Lipic, T., & Grgic, S. (2018). Fine-tuning Convolutional neural networks for fine art classification. *Expert Systems with Applications*, *114*, 107–118. DOI: 10.1016/j.eswa.2018.07.026

Chittka, L., & Vasas, V. (2016). *Faculty opinions recommendation of mastering the game of go with deep neural networks and tree search.* Faculty Opinions – Post-Publication Peer Review of the Biomedical Literature., DOI: 10.3410/f.726105619.793525345

Da Vinha Ricieri, D., Mara Guimarães de Farias, A., Rodrigues de Souza, F., & Vasconcelos Gomes Barreto, R. (2024). PROMPT-EDU: Roteiro de comandos de ajuste Fino para ChatGPT. *SCIAS - Educação. Comunicação e Tecnologia*, *6*(1), 107–138. DOI: 10.36704/sciaseducomtec.v6i1.8374

Deng, L., & Li, X. (2013). Machine learning paradigms for speech recognition: An overview. *IEEE Transactions on Audio, Speech, and Language Processing*, *21*(5), 1060–1089. DOI: 10.1109/TASL.2013.2244083

Emami, J., Nugues, P., Elnagar, A., & Afyouni, I. (2022). Arabic image captioning using pre-training of deep bidirectional transformers. *Proceedings of the 15th International Conference on Natural Language Generation*, 40-51. https://doi.org/DOI: 10.18653/v1/2022.inlg-main.4

Li, L., Huang, T., Li, Y., & Li, P. (2023). Trajectory-BERT: Pre-training and fine-tuning bidirectional transformers for crowd trajectory enhancement. *Computer Animation and Virtual Worlds*, *34*(3-4), e2190. Advance online publication. DOI: 10.1002/cav.2190

Li, L., Huang, T., Li, Y., & Li, P. (2023). Trajectory-BERT: Pre-training and fine-tuning bidirectional transformers for crowd trajectory enhancement. *Computer Animation and Virtual Worlds*, *34*(3-4), e2190. Advance online publication. DOI: 10.1002/cav.2190

Liu, Y., Starzyk, J., & Zhu, Z. (2008). Optimized approximation algorithm in neural networks without Overfitting. *IEEE Transactions on Neural Networks*, *19*(6), 983–995. DOI: 10.1109/TNN.2007.915114 PMID: 18541499

Luo, J., Wang, Y., Xu, R., Liu, G., Wang, X., & Gong, Y. (2021). Channel drop out: A simple way to prevent CNN from Overfitting in motor imagery based BCI. *Communications in Computer and Information Science*, *1451*, 443–452. DOI: 10.1007/978-981-16-5940-9_34

Mao, Z., Wang, H., Du, Y., & Wong, K. (2023). UniTRec: A unified text-to-text transformer and joint contrastive learning framework for text-based recommendation. *Proceedings of the 61st Annual Meeting of the Association for Computational Linguistics(*Volume 2*: Short Papers)*. https://doi.org/DOI: 10.18653/v1/2023.acl-short.100

Marlot, M., Srivastava, D. N., Wong, F. K., & Lee, M. X. (2023). Unsupervised multitask learning for oil and gas language models with limited resources. *Day 2 Tue, October 03, 2023*. https://doi.org/DOI: 10.2118/216402-MS

Mishra, S. R., Mohapatra, H., & Saxena, S. (2024). Leveraging data analytics and a deep learning framework for advancements in image super-resolution techniques: From classic interpolation to cutting-edge approaches. *Studies in Big Data*, 105-126. https://doi.org/DOI: 10.1007/978-981-97-0448-4_6

Mohapatra, H., & Mishra, S. R. (2024). Unlocking insights: Exploring data analytics and AI tool performance across industries. *Studies in Big Data*, 265-288. https://doi.org/DOI: 10.1007/978-981-97-0448-4_13

Nguyen, T., Ngo, H., Nguyen, K., & Cao, T. (2023). A self-enhancement multitask framework for unsupervised aspect category detection. *Proceedings of the 2023 Conference on Empirical Methods in Natural Language Processing*, 8043-8054. https://doi.org/DOI: 10.18653/v1/2023.emnlp-main.500

Palmer-Brown, D., & Jayne, C. (2011). Snap–drift neural network for self-organisation and sequence learning. *Neural Networks*. Advance online publication. DOI: 10.1016/j.neunet.2011.05.007 PMID: 21723705

Panda, A. K., Lenka, A. A., Mohapatra, A., Rath, B. K., Parida, A. A., & Mohapatra, H. (2024). Integrating cloud computing for intelligent transportation solutions in smart cities. *Advances in Civil and Industrial Engineering*, •••, 121–142. DOI: 10.4018/979-8-3693-6695-0.ch005

Phakmongkol, P., & Vateekul, P. (2021). Enhance text-to-text transfer transformer with generated questions for Thai question answering. *Applied Sciences (Basel, Switzerland)*, *11*(21), 10267. DOI: 10.3390/app112110267

Priyadarshi, S., Subudhi, S., Kumar, S., Bhardwaj, D., & Mohapatra, H. (2024). Analysis on enhancing urban mobility with IoT-integrated parking solutions. *Advances in Civil and Industrial Engineering*, •••, 143–172. DOI: 10.4018/979-8-3693-6695-0.ch006

Rao, R., Meier, J., Sercu, T., Ovchinnikov, S., & Rives, A. (2020). Transformer protein language models are unsupervised structure learners. https://doi.org/DOI: 10.1101/2020.12.15.422761

Rauf, A., Guru, A., & Mohapatra, H. (2024). Exploring the social model of smart home devices. *Advances in Human and Social Aspects of Technology*, •••, 233–256. DOI: 10.4018/979-8-3693-9235-5.ch012

Schopf, T., Klimek, S., & Matthes, F. (2022). PatternRank: Leveraging Pretrained language models and part of speech for unsupervised Keyphrase extraction. *Proceedings of the 14th International Joint Conference on Knowledge Discovery, Knowledge Engineering and Knowledge Management*. https://doi.org/DOI: 10.5220/0011546600003335

Sharma, A., Anand, N., Mukherjee, S., Kumar, S., Kumar, S., & Mohapatra, H. (2024). Analyzing territorial variations in the implementation of IoT-based smart homes. *Advances in Electronic Government, Digital Divide, and Regional Development*, •••, 305–334. DOI: 10.4018/979-8-3693-6854-1.ch010

Sheang, K. C., & Saggion, H. (2021). Controllable sentence simplification with a unified text-to-text transfer transformer. *Proceedings of the 14th International Conference on Natural Language Generation*, 341-352. https://doi.org/DOI: 10.18653/v1/2021.inlg-1.38

Thanh Nguyen, L. (2024). ViHateT5: Enhancing hate speech detection in Vietnamese with a unified text-to-text transformer model. *Findings of the Association for Computational Linguistics ACL, 2024*, 5948–5961. DOI: 10.18653/v1/2024.findings-acl.355

Wada, S., Takeda, T., Okada, K., Manabe, S., Konishi, S., Kamohara, J., & Matsumura, Y. (2022). Over-sampling effect in pre-training for bidirectional encoder representations from transformers (BERT) to localize medical BERT and enhance biomedical BERT (Preprint). https://doi.org/DOI: 10.2196/preprints.40992

Xiong, J., Zhang, K., & Zhang, H. (2019). A vibrating mechanism to prevent neural networks from Overfitting. *2019 15th International Wireless Communications & Mobile Computing Conference (IWCMC)*, 1737-1742. https://doi.org/DOI: 10.1109/IWCMC.2019.8766500

Chapter 12

Examination of the Recent Research Trends on Controllers in the AI Powered UAV

B. Swapna
https://orcid.org/0000-0002-7186-2842
Dr. M.G.R. Educational and Research Institute, India

A. Lavanya
https://orcid.org/0009-0003-1858-0170
Dr. M.G.R. Educational and Research Institute, India

G. Kavitha
Dr. M.G.R. Educational and Research Institute, India

M. Sujitha
https://orcid.org/0009-0004-3040-605X
Dr. M.G.R. Educational and Research Institute, India

C. Anuradha
SRM Institute of Science and Technology, India

S. Vijayalakshmi
SRM Institute of Science and Technology, India

K. Jeevitha
https://orcid.org/0009-0001-0763-5442
Dr. M.G.R. Educational and Research Institute, India

R. Kasthuri
Dr. M.G.R. Educational and Research Institute, India

M. Kamalahasan
Dr. M.G.R. Educational and Research Institute, India

ABSTRACT

The development of AI is based on research into the patterns and processes of human thought. Improved software and systems are developed as a direct outcome of these research initiatives. Deep learning (DL), a subfield of AI, allows computers to robotically acquire new abilities by analysing training sets, which are collections of previously received data. The AI technique known as deep reinforcement learning is very useful for autonomous UAVs. The fundamental characteristics of autonomous driving, particularly talks and human conversations, including making choices, make robotic motor vehicles the perfect fit for reinforcement learning. This paper presents a new viewpoint by exploring the AI features realized in current journals. This article aims to realize the attitude control is so important for UAVs and moreover AI controller is better than a conventional one. This article explores the abundant AI technologies that may be utilized for attitude control, path planning and obstacle avoidance of UAVs with many applica-

DOI: 10.4018/979-8-3693-8332-2.ch012

tions. Illustrates the way AI in UAV systems on an everyday basis.

1. INTRODUCTION

Researchers have been giving increasing attention to unmanned aerial vehicle (UAV) systems due to the aircraft industry's recent upheaval since these systems have both military and civilian uses. Four distinct types of unmanned aerial vehicles (UAVs) are distinguished by the lifting force generating method: Unmanned Aerial Vehicles (UAVs) prepared with fixed wings are able to take flight thanks to the lifting force, which is created indirectly by the combination of frontward drive and the aerodynamically designed cross-sections of the wings. Unmanned Aerial Vehicles (UAVs) that have rotatable or flapping wings counteract gravity by drawing on lifting force, which is the density differential between air and gas. Hybrid UAV wings combine the best features of fixed and rotating wing designs. Unmanned Aerial Vehicles (UAVs) that employ gas envelopes to create lift utilise the disparity in density as opposed to wings. Researchers further divided these four groups based on their structural properties and used specific instances to describe them (Lee, C et al., 2021). Photographing, mapping out routes, searching for missing persons, inspecting power lines and civil building sites, etc., are just a few of the many applications of unmanned aerial vehicles (UAVs) (Ahmed, F et al., 2022).

Rescuing people from disasters requires unmanned aerial vehicles to adhere to strict regulations. Drones, UAVs, and other similar Aircraft need a unique level of aeronautical expertise and stability to fly in complex environments through all kinds of weather and dangers (Lyu, M et al., 2023). Accurate navigation and positioning abilities are essential for underwater UAVs to locate targets and assist with mobility quickly Concerning UAVs (user-friendly aerial vehicles), the study focuses on the guiding principles, methods of analysis, models of dynamics, and control rules (Umamaheswaran, S et al., 2020). The military relies on unmanned aerial vehicles (UAVs) for a different type of tasks, including surveillance, navigation, and secure communication. Monitoring assignments, medical technology, automated transportation, precision agriculture, remote sensing, power-line examination, wireless communication, disaster assistance, and search & rescue are just a few other sectors that they find use (Mohsan, S. A. H et al., 2023). The widespread availability of powerful computers, advanced control systems, and dependable communication networks in the last several decades has piqued the attention of researchers throughout the world in unmanned aerial vehicles (UAVs) (Zuo, Z et al., 2022). Sliding mode control is employed to enhance the system's resilience, as UAVs are susceptible to external forces disrupting their flight. Lastly, simulation is used to confirm that the control rule is effective and can withstand unforeseen scenarios (Wang, Z et al., 2022). The stringent standards for flight safety make the advent of aircraft oscillations a major topic. Even if there are multiple redundant mechanisms in place, air mishaps still happen. Therefore, manufacturers must focus on making aircraft technology more reliable (Andrievsky, B et al., 2022). On the other hand, UAV control has been utterly transformed by incorporating AI technologies, which provide superior efficiency, resilience, and adaptability. Academics investigating the potential uses of UAVs have come to the realisation that a flock of UAVs may do more when they cooperate on a mission. Managing unmanned aerial vehicles (UAVs) is challenging since their operational conditions are unpredictable (Phadke, A et al., 2022). Remotely Piloted Aircraft Systems powered by AI have great potential for improved mission capabilities, system flexibility, analytical precision, and decision-making breadth (Aibin, M et al., 2021). An extensive amount of research has focused on various aspects of designing the flight routes of unmanned aerial vehicles. Nonetheless, groupings of UAVs have not been addressed by many of these (Puente-Castro, A et al., 2022). The design, construction, and control of AUVs pose unique challenges for engineers, who often confront limitations not seen in other settings. Radio or spread-spectrum communications, in conjunction with global location, are the backbone of an autonomous system above water. For AUVs to function in marine settings, they need sensors and communication methods that rely on sound waves (González-García, J et al., 2020). Over the last few decades, researchers have been working on methods to automate the navigation of UAVs, permitting them to learn from their surroundings. Automating unmanned aerial vehicles (UAVs) requires autonomous navigation.

The ability to navigate autonomously in cluttered environments is a crucial component of UAV navigation systems. Avoiding impediments on the way to the intended destination is a significant difficulty for autonomous UAV navigation.

Recent computer technology and hardware developments have made artificial intelligence (AI) integral to practically every engineering-related academic discipline. When traditional problem-solving methods necessitate extensive human intervention, or no clear-cut answers exist, artificial intelligence (AI) emerges as the optimal instrument (Saba, D et al., 2021).

A significant difference between AI and conventional intellectual algorithms is automatic feature extraction, which does away with expensive created-by-hand feature engineering. At its most basic level, artificial intelligence (AI) can detect outliers, forecast outcomes, adapt to new contexts, understand complex problems requiring large amounts of data, and reveal similarities.

Artificial intelligence (AI) emerges as the optimal instrument a human could miss when traditional problem-solving methods necessitate extensive human intervention or no clear-cut answers exist. It may learn from and use the vast data around it to enhance UAV manoeuvring. Compared to more conventional optimisation methods, AI can also effectively manage onboard resources (Karthick Raghunath, K. M et al., 2024).

Two broad groups of artificial intelligence methods can be defined according to IQ metrics. The first set is where it's at when responding consistently to its environment. Aerial vehicles will be able to meet performance standards in this manner. The second set of protocols allows UAVs to interact with their environment, allowing them to make judgments in extremely unexpected circumstances. Thus, AI is helping autonomous UAV navigation a lot. Autonomous UAV navigation relies on many parameters, some of which are determined by heuristic equations rather than solid closed-form solutions due to the computational expense or lack of availability of such answers. Artificial intelligence (AI) can forecast parameters and calculate functions using known data, which can help with these challenges. Also, nonlinear optimisation or approximation issues can have objective functions modelled using artificial neural networks (ANNs).

This article examines the position control issue concerning unmanned aerial vehicles (UAVs) with fixed wings. The way an aeroplane is pointing is called its attitude. Among the many levels of flight control, attitude control is the most basic since it specifies the guiding components' requirements for the UAV's actuators to achieve the required attitude (Shalini, A et al., 2018). A system that can effectively learn attitude controllers from data must be developed to control actual UAVs in the field. This method can teach controllers who are fit to fly in minutes. Initially, a UAV model is created primarily through wind tunnel testing. Subsequently, a simulator is employed for learning and exploration purposes. Lastly, flying experiments are conducted to refine both the model and the simulation iteratively. Methods like domain randomisation are commonly used to bridge the gap between simulation and reality. The incredible data efficiency of this technology, when combined with safe exploration processes, guarantees a seamless controller transfer to the field and limits overfitting to the simulation method. The real UAV in operation will be able to rely on learning controllers. The vast bulk of studies investigating RL-based position management for Aircraft have been conducted in lab settings and mostly on quadcopters. This experiment opens the door to a more in-depth analysis of the ideas behind the design, strategies for implementation, and benefits to the performance of fixed-wing UAV attitude controllers powered by AI. Our goal is to provide a better understanding of how AI will influence UAV control in the future through theoretical study and practical examples, enabling safer, more adaptable, and more efficient aerial operations.

Following is the primary contribution of this article.

- Recent articles detail the contributions of AI methods, namely those that deal with optimising and controlling UAVs and the applications they have.
- The AI attitude controller is drawn from the conventional PID controller in UAV appliances. AI-enabled UAV applications in recent scenarios are listed in table.1
- The importance of an AI Controller in UAVs is derived from the conventional controller.

The following ensures that the paper organisation as shown in figure 1. Related works for the UAVs attitude controller with AI are presented in Section II. Section III discusses the different AI technologies used with UAVs application. Section IV displays the drawbacks of convolutional with the advantages of AI controller with Our results and suggestions for further research will be presented in Section V.

Figure 1. The paper organisation.

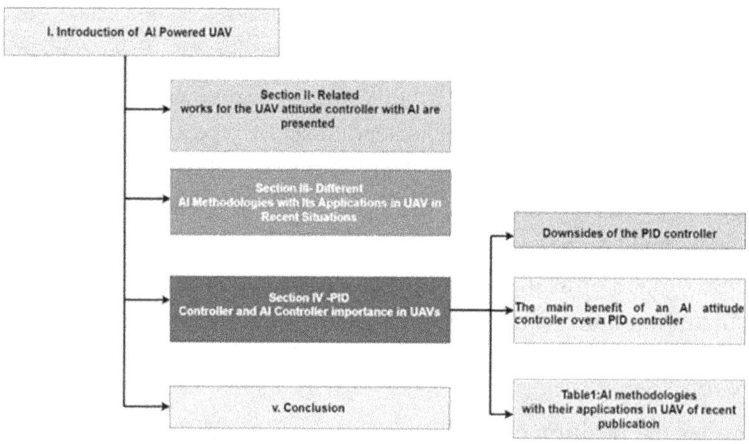

2. RELATED WORKS

UAV flight control, also known as low-level control, is the focus of literature analysis of coupled MBC-ANN approaches. Efficient controllers designed with performance guarantees are the end goal, and this work will lay the groundwork for them. A reference template is utilized through the survey to conduct fair comparisons and recognize the fortes and weaknesses of previous research. The final product provided evidence regarding the pros, cons, and suitability of a relevant controller family for UAV prototypes. Our upcoming study aims to develop a UAV flight control system that can withstand uncertainties and disturbances by combining MBC and ANN approaches (Gu, W. et al., 2020)

Several researchers have been implicated in developing AI methods for autonomous aircraft path planning, and this research provides a thorough study and classification of those methods. Methods in artificial intelligence have ranged from mathematical optimization to model-based learning. There is a wealth of information and materials accessible for use in the pursuit of a greater understanding of AI and autonomous UAV navigation. Additionally, there is space for improvement and fresh concepts in several settings, including handling faults, processing power, energy efficiency, and large amounts of data. (Rezwan, S. et al., 2022)

Autonomy is a UAV's ability to launch, fly, and land without human interference. Autonomy is key to effectively deploying unmanned aerial vehicles (UAVs) in challenging applications and environments. Many of these DRL approaches were designed to help UAVs fly more correctly and steadily in simulated environments. This study offers a thorough review of DRL techniques for UAV control, route forecasting, and steering. There has to be a greater number of outside trials conducted under varying environmental circumstances. (Azar, A. T et al., 2021)

An attitude control approach for fixed-wing UAVs is presented in this paper, which makes use of inverse control theory. A fundamental linear disturbance observer assesses the UAV system's unknown disturbances and model uncertainties. For acceptable parameters and reasonable assumptions, the estimated errors are assumed to be continuously predictable. With the help of the estimated errors added to the current state vector and the suitable digital control signal generated, the basic system was transformed into a linear system free of disturbances. The inverse optimum control theory is utilised in designing an attitude controller by applying the backstepping approach (Le-Phan, N. M. et al., 2023)

Using a unified control framework consisting of an attitude controller, acceleration controller, and optimized position controller, the authors of this paper provide a tail-sitter VTOL UAV control architecture. Unlike conventional control schemes, this architecture handles every aspect of flight, from take-off to hovering, forward and backward transition, level flight, and landing. Applying an RNN to simulate the performance of a non-linear solver allows us to use it for real flights, even though the position controller's proposed non-linear optimisation solver might not be computationally appropriate for real-time implementation (Zhou J. et al., 2021)

The controller displays two critical features: To begin with, it allows copters with different dynamics to fly in any mode. Further, our controller bridges the gap between digital modelling and physical production by functioning with real models without requiring extra parameter adjustment. Also, results showed that our approach is model-neutral by showing how multiple vehicle designs can be trained using the same neural network architecture. This result can further advance knowledge transmission between various hybrid UAV designs or other robots (Xu J. et al., 2019)

Intelligent flight control systems taught with three advanced RL algorithms were discussed as Deep Deterministic Policy Gradient, proximal Policy Optimizing, and Trusted Region Strategy Efficiency—in attitude control inner control loops. Prior to exploring these problems, it developed a freely available and open-source, highly realistic simulation environment for flight controllers to learn RL-based attitude management for quadrotors. In order to determine if RL is suitable for precise, time-sensitive flight control, researchers compared their performance to that of a PID controller in our environment. S(Koch W. et al. 2019).

All of the necessary hardware and software components for the testbed were detailed.

Our platform stands out due to its complexity and capabilities compared to comparable testbeds. In this project, a 12.84-kilogram aircraft system is designed and implemented with all the sensors and computer capabilities needed to execute algorithms for machine learning and image processing. It elucidated our choices and highlighted particular implementation details. It showcased a computer vision application that could be integrated with our platform to demonstrate the potential of our technology (Douklias A. et al., 2022)

Users on the ground must ensure that UAV-BSs are positioned so that they may establish LOS linkages in the network. The finest deployment of a UAV-BS may be achieved with the help of a novel learning model that makes use of deep Q-networks (DQNs). Without relearning or obtaining route information from ground employers, the suggested prototype also presents the best UAV-BS path. In order to maximise a UAV-BS's MOS, the proposed model takes ground employers' preferences into account and finds the optimal flying path. With an average channel power increase rather than specific mobile user locations serving as the input parameter, the suggested model is realistic and practical. A mathematical optimisation solver's outputs are compared with the model's own to confirm the model's accuracy (Lee, W. et al., 2021).

An improved approach, DDPG, is introduced in this paper for the Route following regulator issue of UAVs. By crafting an optimised reward function, the path following the problem's cross-track error may be minimised. A double experience replay buffer (DERB) during the training phase speeds up convergence and improves learning efficiency. A simulation result sequence demonstrated the suggested method's effectiveness, efficiency, and flexibility. The results show that DERB-DDPG outperforms DQN and original DDPG in the UAV path, following the problem when tested in this paper's simulation scenarios. Expanding UAV motion control to a 3D environment for future projects will be important. A controller's design must take pitch and roll motion into account (Zhang, Y. et al., 2021)

This analysis helps pave the way for future developments in Geographic Information Systems (GIS) and the intersection of drone technology with its potential applications. Since it makes geospatial data collecting more accessible and cheaper, integrating drones with GIS is a great move. Hiring planes, pilots, and photographers for old-fashioned aerial photography was a major financial drag. Modern drones with AI software and high-tech cameras can save time and money compared to the old method. Results show that GIS with drone integration solutions boosts accuracy and efficiency, makes better decisions, and allows for improved real-time monitoring (Quamar, M. et al., 2023)

ANNs and model-based controllers for UAV flight control are integrated for guaranteed execution. Using models or optimization, UAV navigation might be studied. Researchers study domain-agnostic autonomy in field-based DRL systems for UAV attitude control. Fixed-wing UAV attitude control uses inverse optimal control theory to handle uncertainty, whereas tail-sitter VTOL UAVs use recurrent neural networks. Reinforcement learning makes hybrid UAV computing controllers model-neutral and interoperable. UAV applications use computer vision and machine learning, and reinforcement learning outperforms PID controllers for attitude control (Vinoth Kumar, V et al., 2023). Deep reinforcement learning optimises UAV-BS deployment and route following.

3. DIFFERENT AI METHODOLOGIES WITH ITS APPLICATIONS IN UAV IN RECENT SITUATIONS

AI technology has several classifications, with application preference based on UAV appliances.

Fuzzy logic controller (FLC) implementation and performance assessment for two-dimensional real-time UAV route planning is described in the work. Compared to previous approaches, the FLC's failure rate was lower and its error rate was only 3%, therefore it showed plenty of promise. In simple settings, it excelled, but in more complicated ones, it choked. Qualitative advantages, such as a lower failure ratio and efficient data management, make FLC a useful tool, even though it offers quantitative supremacy. Possibilities for future investigation include dynamic obstacle avoidance and three-dimensional motion planning (Zosimovych, N. et al., 2023).

A survey of unmanned aerial vehicle (UAV) categories, as well as present and future research trends and problems, are presented in the article. Unmanned Aerial Vehicles (UAVs) are categorized according to a number of criteria, including flying principle, mission, weight, propulsion, and others. Also brought to light are the unanswered questions surrounding unmanned aerial vehicle (UAV) research, such as the constraints on operability, security worries, and regulatory hurdles. The following are some examples of potential fields for future research: swarm UAV systems; security; energy charging methods; optical wireless communications; and regulatory frameworks. A thorough resource for understanding UAV development and research trends, the article covers it all (Telli, K., et al., 2023).

Autonomous UAV navigation is becoming more common as a result of AI developments, which are discussed in the article. It takes stock of the many AI strategies used by academics and sorts them into two broad camps: those focused on learning and optimization. We take a look at learning-based approaches like RL and DRL and optimization-based ones like PSO and ACO and GA. This review gives a thorough overview of the area of unmanned aerial vehicles (UAVs) by highlighting its features, kinds, and applications. The overall goal is to introduce readers to several approaches of autonomous UAV navigation using AI and to compare and contrast them (Rezwan, S., et al., 2022).

An explainable intelligence model for UAVs is introduced in the study, which helps to clarify mission decisions, especially when going off course because to bad weather or adversary activity. At its core, the model is an ANFIS and Sugeno-type fuzzy inference system for weather and opponent location prediction. After being tested on three missions with randomly placed obstacles, the model performs admirably and is easy to understand; when the parameters are fine-tuned, the RMSE values remain within reasonable ranges. Researchers found that combining these models with UAV technology might increase reliability and openness (Keneni, B. M. et al., 2019)

The article provides a comprehensive overview of unmanned aerial vehicle (UAV) uses in smart capitals, focusing on the difficulties of integration and effective techniques of improved control. The importance of UAV hybrid control techniques, which combine linear and nonlinear approaches, is highlighted for their robust performance in complicated urban situations. In order to conduct standoff tracking of moving targets, the article presents a novel control strategy for quadrotor UAVs that makes use of cylinder coordinates and guiding rules based on Lyapunov. Power collecting, battery-powered power control, and UAV protocol efficiency are also stressed for future smart city development. In conclusion, UAVs' potential to improve urban transportation and infrastructure and their rising popularity are noted (Abbas N. et al 2023)

Researchers use anti-saturation algorithms and artificial neural networks to follow UAV trajectories adaptively, simultaneously coping with input saturation restrictions and disruptions. It simplifies the UAV's nonlinear dynamic model and creates a preliminary control rule using dynamic surface control. Radial basis function neural networks are trained for estimation and disturbance correction, while an auxiliary system avoids input saturation. Simulations have proven the usefulness of the suggested control technique for high-precision route tracking with time-varying disturbances. Because to its anti-UAV control properties, the approach had been beneficial (Zhou Y. et al., 2023)

The paper lays out an extensive model estimation scheme for UAVs that makes use of multiple model structures, such as non-linear Auto-regressive Exogenous, Output Fault, and Auto-regressive Moving Average exogenous. Evaluation criteria for the constructed models include residual analysis, final forecast error, and appropriate percentages. The research proves that the suggested model can reliably forecast the performance of UAV systems under varying operating circumstances. Parametric linear and nonlinear models were developed using system identification approaches. The authors compared several architectures and chose the ARMAX model with the lowest final prediction error as the most suited (Fatima S. K. et al., 2023)

This study proposes a sliding mode construction controller to improve UAV swarm deployment stability and accuracy. This work uses IoT and AI algorithms to construct a self-directed UAV swarm regulator model using behavior-based formation control. They connect ZigBee's self-organizing networks with the Internet of Things in our adaptive networking approach. According to tests, laser distance measurement plus barometer readings enhances positioning accuracy, notably in Z-axis coordinates. The study models the UAV mass center, formation, and transformation. To account for environmental and track limits, a formation library and assessment system and formation matrix representation technique are used. In addition, the project develops a behavior-based formation control algorithm. Dynamic formation transformation and obstacle avoidance are included in this software. Experiments confirmed great UAV location precision for cluster flight (Wang, X., et al., 2021).

This study focuses on micro unmanned aerial vehicles (mUAVs) and the development of different quadrotor trajectories. It provides a technique for MATLAB-based flight route planning for groups of geometric objects with the goal of avoiding chance collisions (Saha S et al., 2023). Researchers proposed a collision avoidance algorithm and demonstrated its performance in flight. The research highlights using a PD controller for seamless navigation and the importance of speed and agility in controlling the distances between mUAVs for efficiency and safety (Kumar, V. V. et al., 2022).

Based on these related works, general applications of UAVs in social environments are shown in figure.2. Also, it implicates the PID controller and AI controller play an important role in UAVs. In this scenario, the PID controller has several benefits and some drawbacks. AI technology is preferred for designing and improving the efficiency of the attitude controller.

Figure 2. General applications of UAVs in the social environment

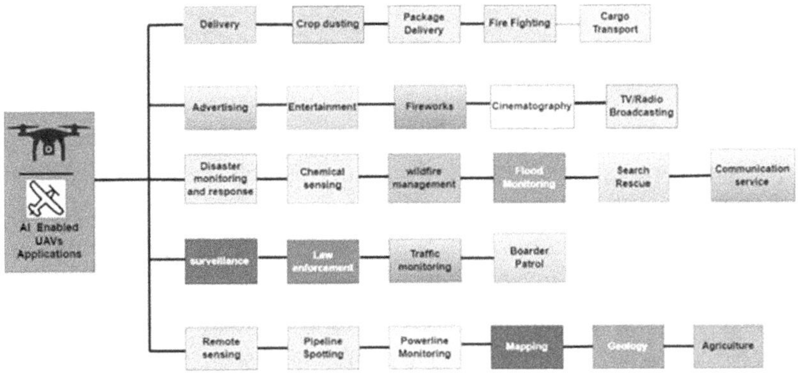

4. PID CONTROLLER AND AI CONTROLLER IMPORTANCE IN UAVS

The primary advantage of PID controllers over more complicated control algorithms is their ease of understanding and implementation. The versatility and adaptability of PID controllers stem from their ability to withstand changes in system parameters and external disruptions.

Maintaining consistent system behaviour across various operating situations is possible with well-tuned PID controllers. Industrial automation often makes use of feedback control mechanisms known as proportional-integral-derivative (PID) controllers to manage process variables such as temperature, pressure, flow, and speed. With their control loop feedback mechanism, PID controllers are able to force feedback to match a setpoint, making them the most stable and accurate controllers. The fixed-wing Aircraft's control plan is developed by first considering individual techniques such as PID, LQR, or neural networks. Both open- and closed-loop control systems are commonly used in many applications. Control systems that use proportional-integral-derivative (PID) algorithms are known as closed-loop controllers. The PID controller receives input from the plant's output and sends it back as a feedback signal, allowing the system to make the necessary adjustments. One of the many useful applications of neural networks is the approximation of various linear and nonlinear functions. In many instances, these networks are capable of adjusting to different input-output relationships.

It was our firm belief, after much deliberation, that these methods are insufficient on their own. Combining them as a hybrid technique allows us to complement each other while reducing their limitations. The control mechanism needs to be fine-tuned by adjusting the PID controller limitations.

4.1 Downsides of the PID Controller

Limitations and downsides are also associated with PID controllers. Due to their sensitivity to measurement mistakes and background noise, PID controllers pose a threat of instability and oscillations when the input signal experiences fluctuations. Problems arise when the system dynamics undergo large or unexpected changes; PID controllers are notorious for degrading performance or becoming unstable in such cases, making them ill-suited to nonlinear systems. A large and delayed response can be caused by integral windup, a condition that can affect PID controllers. This error builds up over time in the integral term. When the system experiences a significant disruption or is saturated, this can occur.

4.2 The Main Benefit of an AI Attitude Controller Over a PID Controller

AI controllers for fixed-wing UAVs employ intricate algorithms to autonomously optimise the Aircraft's control surfaces, ensuring stable flight and meeting predetermined orientations. They undergo training that entails analysing the acquired data in order to determine how to convert sensory inputs into appropriate control actions. The controllers possess the ability to adapt to dynamic circumstances and effectively perform intricate actions after being instructed, owing to their continuous reception of feedback from on-board sensors. AI controllers offer several advantages to fixed-wing UAVs in terms of autonomy, efficiency, and adaptability in diverse deployment scenarios. Figure 3 depicts the design of the AI attitude Controller in UAVs.

Figure 3. The AI attitude controller design in UAVs.

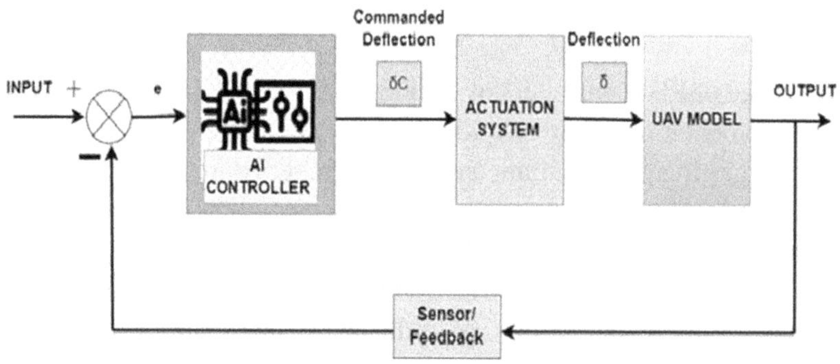

The primary considerations for the design controller are uncertainties and external disturbances, like a load disturbance, when managing the speed of an induction motor.

1) Since PID is a linear system while fuzzy logic is nonlinear, the former performs better.
2) Nonlinear control outperforms linear control in a system with uncertainty.

The third reason the fuzzy logic controller's output is controllable is the fuzzy set.

Fourthly, there are no longer any concerns regarding complexity, despite the fact that fuzzy is more computationally intensive and complicated than PID. Modern microprocessor controllers like the DSpace 1104 and 1103 are available. Fuzzy computation is not a concern with these controllers because of their speed and vast memory capacities. To alleviate some of the computing load and overall system complexity, fuzzy logic controllers employ reduced rules. Attitude controllers outperform conventional PID controllers. This results in enhanced stability, efficiency, and adaptability across several domains.

The following are the advantages of AI controller:

- The enhancement of operational efficiency.
- Customising the Enhancement of the Passenger Experience.

- Enhancing Safety with Artificial Intelligence (AI).
- The topic of interest is automated flight operations.
- Predictive maintenance.
- Efficient Air Traffic Control.
- The improvement of customer service.
- The automation of cargo and warehouse operations.

From these related work analyses, the importance of attitude controllers in UAVs is understandable. Additionally, the practical applications of UAVs in real time are clearly shown. Moreover, the importance of the AI controller is predicted with the convention controller PID. The following table 1 shows the recent publications of related works are listed with the AI powered UAV and its applications.

Table 1. Different AI methodologies with their applications in UAV of recent publication.

Year and Authors	Controller	Type of UAV	AI Methodology	Applications
Gu, W. et all., 2020	A hybrid MBC-ANN controller	UAVS-Planes	Supervised learning, reinforcement learning and hybrid approaches,	Possible flight control improvements in UAV prototypes.
Rezwan, S. et al., 2022	AI based controller	Autonomous unmanned aerial vehicles (UAVs)	Learning-based approaches and optimisation analysis	The navigational efficiency is enhanced with the application of optimisation and learning.
Azar, A. et all., 2021	AI based GNC controller (guide, navigate, and control)	UAVs in both civilian and military contexts	DRL algorithms (DRL).	UAVs can master navigation and autonomous operations including target tracking, attitude control, object avoidance, and path planning
Le-Phan, N. M. et all 2023	Inverse Optimal Controller (IOC)	Fixed-wing UAVs	Inverse optimum control theory, which derives the control law from mathematical optimization techniques	Airborne monitoring and scouting Farming (for instance, spraying and crop protection) Environmental surveillance
Zhou. J. et all., 2021	Recurrent Neural Network (RNN)-based Unified Controller	Tail-sitter Vertical Take off and Landing (VTOL) UAV	Long short-term memory (LSTM) and the RNN.	Data gathering and mapping Precision. Agriculture, crop monitoring, and spraying.
Xu. J. et al., 2019	Mode-Free, Model-Agnostic Neural Network Controller	HUAVs and fixed-wing planes.	reinforcement learning.	Hybrid UAVs are great for search and rescue operations because of their adaptability to numerous flying circumstances.
Koch, W. et al., 2019	Intelligent RL, PID Flight Controllers	Quadcopters, specifically the Iris quadcopter	(DDPG), (TRPO), Proximal Policy Optimization (PPO) management systems.	search and rescue operations, Air quality assessments, animal monitoring
Douklias. A. et al, 2022	Onboard image processing and machine learning	Unmanned aerial vehicle (UAV) system weighing 12.85 kg	Computer vision, machine learning	This allows the device to avoid obstacles, land automatically, and navigate to waypoints without largely depending on external communication.

continued on following page

Table 1. Continued

Year and Authors	Controller	Type of UAV	AI Methodology	Applications
Lee, W., et al 2021	Deep Q-Network (DQN) based learning model for trajectory optimization	Unmanned aerial vehicle (UAV) acting as a base station (UAV-BS) in a UAV-BS network	Reinforcement learning	Next-Generation Communication Systems. High-Speed Mobile Communication
Zhang, Y, et al 2021	Deterministic Policy Gradient (DDPG) controller	Unmanned Aerial Vehicle	RL, ML	Inspection, monitoring, and surveillance.AI for future UAV motion control.
Quamar, M. et al 2023	Not specified	Drones (Unmanned Aerial Vehicles)	AI and ML	Mapping and Surveying, Wildlife Monitoring and Infrastructure Inspection
Zosimovych, N et al 2023	Fuzzy Logic Controller (FLC)	Unmanned Aerial Vehicle (UAV)	Fuzzy Logic	Reducing the frequency of failures, increasing the number of near-optimal paths, and decreasing the number of control attempts.
Telli, K. et al 2023	classical, modern, intelligent, and adaptive control techniques	Unmanned Aerial Vehicle (UAV)	machine learning and swarm intelligence.	Navigation, object identification, and mission planning. Accurate Manoeuvres
Rezwan. S. et al 2022.	Autonomous navigation control systems	Unmanned aerial vehicles (UAVs)	Various artificial intelligence (AI) techniques including mathematical-based optimization algorithms, model-based learning approaches,	(UAVs) rely heavily on AI to help them navigate through complicated landscapes, avoid obstacles, and arrive at their destinations without human intervention.
Keneni. B. M. et al 2019	autonomous decision-making system for unmanned aerial vehicles (UAVs).	autonomous decision-making system for unmanned aerial vehicles (UAVs).	Mamdani Fuzzy Inference System (FIS) and Adaptive Neuro-Fuzzy Inference System (ANFIS),	Safe and effective operation by guiding UAVs along predetermined trajectories while considering bad weather conditions and hostile positions.
Abbas, N. et al 2023	Advanced control methods for unmanned aerial vehicles (UAVs)	Drones	Optimization methods, intelligent control algorithms, and possibly machine learning for decision-making processes.	Smart city infrastructure monitoring are all made possible using UAVs outfitted with high-resolution cameras and sensors.
Zhou. Y et al 2023	adaptive controller	quadrotor UAVs	Radial basis function (RBF) neural network	Real-world UAV applications as they all require accurate trajectory tracking in the face of external disruptions and input constraints.
Fatima S. K. et al 2023	Robust control system (specific type not mentioned).	Various types used for remote sensing in agriculture, military,	Neural networks, wavelet networks, and possibly other machine learning algorithms.	Military, research, agriculture, civic, and industrial applications.
Wang X., et al 2021	Sliding mode formation controller for UAV swarm positioning.	Fixed-wing and rotor-type UAVs	Behavior-based formation control algorithms, obstacle avoidance strategies, and other AI algorithms for autonomous control.	surveillance, target shooting, and inspection of transmission lines carrying high voltage.

continued on following page

Table 1. Continued

Year and Authors	Controller	Type of UAV	AI Methodology	Applications
Teja, K. S. S. et al 2024	PD (Proportional-Derivative) controller.	Micro unmanned aerial vehicles (mUAVs), particularly quadrotors.	Likely used for trajectory planning and collision avoidance.	Military operations, surveillance, SAR, ecological research, and other fields
Proposed work	AI attitude Controller	Fixed wing	DRL-RNN	Autonomy, efficiency, and adaptability in diverse deployment scenarios

5. CONCLUSION

The present state of unmanned aerial vehicle (UAV) applications and controllers has been thoroughly examined. By covering all kinds of UAV uses, this review helps readers understand and make the most of UAV AI developments. Recent developments in artificial intelligence (AI) and unmanned aerial vehicle (UAV) controller design are detailed in this article. In addition, a classified and sub-categorised review of AI implementation, along with UAV applications in social environments, is also covered. The PID controller is finding more and more uses in many fields. With the precise and up-to-the-minute data provided by a PID controller, one may make well-informed decisions and boost productivity. It is anticipated that the utilisation of UAVs equipped with AI will get even more prevalent as technology progresses. Organisations and individuals can improve safety and quality of life, make better decisions, and make better use of resources with the help of autonomous AI attitude controller. Key drivers for the effective integration and implementation of AI powered UAV controllers are their standardisation and expanded functions, but future research related to AI is interdisciplinary.

REFERENCES

Abbas, N., Abbas, Z., Liu, X., Khan, S. S., Foster, E. D., & Larkin, S. (2023). A survey: Future smart cities based on advance control of Unmanned Aerial Vehicles (UAVs). *Applied Sciences (Basel, Switzerland), 13*(17), 9881. DOI: 10.3390/app13179881

Ahmed, F., Mohanta, J. C., Keshari, A., & Yadav, P. S. (2022). Recent advances in unmanned aerial vehicles: A review. *Arabian Journal for Science and Engineering, 47*(7), 7963–7984. DOI: 10.1007/s13369-022-06738-0 PMID: 35492958

Aibin, M., Aldiab, M., Bhavsar, R., Lodhra, J., Reyes, M., Rezaeian, F., Saczuk, E., Taer, M., & Taer, M. (2021). Survey of RPAS autonomous control systems using artificial intelligence. *IEEE Access : Practical Innovations, Open Solutions, 9*, 167580–167591. DOI: 10.1109/ACCESS.2021.3136226

Andrievsky, B., Zaitceva, I., & Kuznetsov, N. V. (2022). Application of non-linear correction method for attitude control and landing oscillations prevention. *IFAC-PapersOnLine, 55*(29), 37–42. DOI: 10.1016/j.ifacol.2022.10.228

Azar, A. T., Koubaa, A., Ali Mohamed, N., Ibrahim, H. A., Ibrahim, Z. F., Kazim, M., Ammar, A., Benjdira, B., Khamis, A. M., Hameed, I. A., & Casalino, G. (2021). Drone deep reinforcement learning: A review. *Electronics (Basel), 10*(9), 999. DOI: 10.3390/electronics10090999

Douklias, A., Karagiannidis, L., Misichroni, F., & Amditis, A. (2022). Design and implementation of a UAV-based airborne computing platform for computer vision and machine learning applications. *Sensors (Basel), 22*(5), 2049. DOI: 10.3390/s22052049 PMID: 35271196

González-García, J., Gómez-Espinosa, A., Cuan-Urquizo, E., García-Valdovinos, L. G., Salgado-Jiménez, T., & Escobedo Cabello, J. A. (2020). Autonomous underwater vehicles: Localisation, navigation, and communication for collaborative missions. *Applied Sciences (Basel, Switzerland), 10*(4), 1256. DOI: 10.3390/app10041256

Gu, W., Valavanis, K. P., Rutherford, M. J., & Rizzo, A. (2020). UAV model-based flight control with artificial neural networks: A survey. *Journal of Intelligent & Robotic Systems, 100*(3), 1469–1491. DOI: 10.1007/s10846-020-01227-8

Karthick Raghunath, K. M., Koti, M. S., Sivakami, R., Vinoth Kumar, V., NagaJyothi, G., & Muthukumaran, V. (2024). Utilization of IoT-assisted computational strategies in wireless sensor networks for smart infrastructure management. *International Journal of System Assurance Engineering and Management, 15*(1), 28–34. DOI: 10.1007/s13198-021-01585-y

Keneni, B. M., Kaur, D., Al Bataineh, A., Devabhaktuni, V. K., Javaid, A. Y., Zaientz, J. D., & Marinier, R. P. (2019). Evolving rule-based explainable artificial intelligence for unmanned aerial vehicles. *IEEE Access : Practical Innovations, Open Solutions, 7*, 17001–17016. DOI: 10.1109/ACCESS.2019.2893141

Koch, W., Mancuso, R., West, R., & Bestavros, A. (2019). Reinforcement learning for UAV attitude control. *ACM Transactions on Cyber-Physical Systems, 3*(2), 1–21. DOI: 10.1145/3301273

Kumar, V. V., Muthukumaran, V., Ashwini, N., Beschi, I. S., Gunasekaran, K., & Niveditha, V. R. (2022). An efficient signcryption scheme using near-ring hybrid approach for an IoT-based system. [IJeC]. *International Journal of e-Collaboration*, *18*(1), 1–31. DOI: 10.4018/IJeC.299011

Le-Phan, N. M., Dinh, D. L., Duc, A. N. D., & Van, N. P. (2023). Inverse Optimal-Based Attitude Control for Fixed-Wing Unmanned Aerial Vehicles. *IEEE Access : Practical Innovations, Open Solutions*, 1. DOI: 10.1109/ACCESS.2023.3280424

Lee, C., Kim, S., & Chu, B. (2021). A survey: Flight mechanism and mechanical structure of the UAV. *International Journal of Precision Engineering and Manufacturing*, *22*(4), 719–743. DOI: 10.1007/s12541-021-00489-y

Lee, W., Jeon, Y., Kim, T., & Kim, Y. I. (2021). Deep reinforcement learning for UAV trajectory design considering mobile ground users. *Sensors (Basel)*, *21*(24), 8239. DOI: 10.3390/s21248239 PMID: 34960332

Lyu, M., Zhao, Y., Huang, C., & Huang, H. (2023). Unmanned aerial vehicles for search and rescue: A survey. *Remote Sensing (Basel)*, *15*(13), 3266. DOI: 10.3390/rs15133266

Mohsan, S. A. H., Othman, N. Q. H., Li, Y., Alsharif, M. H., & Khan, M. A. (2023). Unmanned aerial vehicles (UAVs): Practical aspects, applications, open challenges, security issues, and future trends. *Intelligent Service Robotics*, *16*(1), 109–137. DOI: 10.1007/s11370-022-00452-4 PMID: 36687780

Phadke, A., & Medrano, F. A. (2022). Towards resilient UAV swarms—A breakdown of resiliency requirements in UAV swarms. *Drones (Basel)*, *6*(11), 340. DOI: 10.3390/drones6110340

Puente-Castro, A., Rivero, D., Pazos, A., & Fernandez-Blanco, E. (2022). A review of artificial intelligence applied to path planning in UAV swarms. *Neural Computing & Applications*, *34*(1), 153–170. DOI: 10.1007/s00521-021-06569-4

Quamar, M. M., Al-Ramadan, B., Khan, K., Shafiullah, M., & El Ferik, S. (2023). Advancements and applications of drone-integrated geographic information system technology—A review. *Remote Sensing (Basel)*, *15*(20), 5039. DOI: 10.3390/rs15205039

Rezwan, S., & Choi, W. (2022). Artificial intelligence approaches for UAV navigation: Recent advances and future challenges. *IEEE Access : Practical Innovations, Open Solutions*, *10*, 26320–26339. DOI: 10.1109/ACCESS.2022.3157626

Saba, D., Sahli, Y., Maouedj, R., Hadidi, A., & Medjahed, M. B. (2021). Towards artificial intelligence: concepts, applications, and innovations. *Enabling AI Applications in Data Science*, 103-146.

Saha, S., Kumar, V. V., Niveditha, V. R., Kannan, V. A., Gunasekaran, K., & Venkatesan, K. (2023). Cluster-based protocol for prioritized message communication in VANET. *IEEE Access : Practical Innovations, Open Solutions*, *11*, 67434–67442. DOI: 10.1109/ACCESS.2023.3286936

Shalini, A., Jayasuruthi, L., & VinothKumar, V. (2018). Voice recognition robot control using android device. *Journal of Computational and Theoretical Nanoscience*, *15*(6-7), 2197–2201. DOI: 10.1166/jctn.2018.7436

Teja, K. S. S., & Rooban, S. (2024). Multi UAV and Geometrical Shape Trajectory Planning Using PD Controller. *International Journal of Intelligent Systems and Applications in Engineering*, *12*(7s), 272–284.

Telli, K., Kraa, O., Himeur, Y., Ouamane, A., Boumehraz, M., Atalla, S., & Mansoor, W. (2023). A comprehensive review of recent research trends on unmanned aerial vehicles (uavs). *Systems*, *11*(8), 400. DOI: 10.3390/systems11080400

Umamaheswaran, S., Lakshmanan, R., Vinothkumar, V., Arvind, K. S., & Nagarajan, S. (2020). New and robust composite micro structure descriptor (CMSD) for CBIR. *International Journal of Speech Technology*, *23*(2), 243–249. DOI: 10.1007/s10772-019-09663-0

Vinoth Kumar, V., Deepa, R., Ranjith, D., Balamurugan, M., & Balajee, J. M. (2022, February). Selection of routing protocol-based QoS improvement for mobile ad hoc network. *InInternational Conference on Computing, Communication, Electrical and Biomedical Systems* (pp. 317-330). Cham: Springer International Publishing. DOI: 10.1007/978-3-030-86165-0_26

Wang, X., Chen, G., Gong, H., & Jiang, J. (2021). UAV swarm autonomous control based on Internet of Things and artificial intelligence algorithms. *Journal of Intelligent & Fuzzy Systems*, *40*(4), 7121–7133. DOI: 10.3233/JIFS-189541

Wang, Z., & Luo, Y. (2022). Elliptical Multi-Orbit Circumnavigation Control of UAVS in Three-Dimensional Space Depending on Angle Information Only. *Drones (Basel)*, *6*(10), 296. DOI: 10.3390/drones6100296

Xu, J., Du, T., Foshey, M., Li, B., Zhu, B., Schulz, A., & Matusik, W. (2019). Learning to fly: Computational controller design for hybrid uavs with reinforcement learning. [TOG]. *ACM Transactions on Graphics*, *38*(4), 1–12. DOI: 10.1145/3306346.3322940

Zhang, Y., Zhang, Y., & Yu, Z. (2021). Path following control for UAV using deep reinforcement learning approach. Guidance. *Navigation and Control*, *1*(01), 2150005. DOI: 10.1142/S2737480721500059

Zhou, J., Xu, H., Li, Z., Shen, S., & Zhang, F. (2021). Control of a Tail-Sitter VTOL UAV Based on Recurrent Neural Networks. *arXiv preprint* arXiv:2104.02108.

Zhou, Y., Tian, Z., & Lin, H. (2023). UAV based adaptive trajectory tracking control with input saturation and unknown time-varying disturbances. *IET Intelligent Transport Systems*, *17*(4), 780–793. DOI: 10.1049/itr2.12303

Zosimovych, N. (2023). Artificial Intelligence Techniques Application in UAS. *Artificial Intelligence*, *11*(1), 45–61.

Zuo, Z., Liu, C., Han, Q. L., & Song, J. (2022). Unmanned aerial vehicles: Control methods and future challenges. *IEEE/CAA Journal of Automatica Sinica*, 9(4), 601-614.

Chapter 13
Intelligent, Autonomous, and Multi-Agents

Taye Iyinoluwa Adeyinka
https://orcid.org/0009-0006-4357-6319
University of Science and Technology, Beijing, China

Kehinde Iyioluwa Adeyinka
https://orcid.org/0009-0009-7685-6693
University of Science and Technology, Beijing, China

ABSTRACT

The era of rapid developments in artificial intelligence increased the potential of intelligent, autonomous, and multi-agent systems to collaborate on an unprecedented scale. This chapter covers the basics and applications of MAS in collaborative contexts, with a focus on generative AI tools and human-AI interaction. The chapter starts with a definition of multi-agent systems and underlines how autonomous and semi-autonomous activities boost collaborative intelligence. We further look at the very basic structures necessary to help agents operate effortlessly within dynamic environments, emphasizing frameworks that provide self-optimization, autonomy, and learning. Later, the chapter looks at real-world applications where MAS increases human capabilities and offers cooperative solutions in settings that require high levels of cooperation and adaptation. We discuss various ethical, safety, and interoperability issues arising in MAS during the investigation of these interactions, especially with generative AI tools working with human partners.

1. INTRODUCTION

As individuals, systems, and machines begin to converse and solve problems with AI being infused into collaborative settings, change becomes the norm. Moreover, at the forefront of this revolution are the intelligent, autonomous, and multi-agent systems that have been driving developments in everything from logistics to healthcare, from self-driving cars to smart city infrastructure, since (Wooldridge, 2009). Specifically, the potential applications of multi-agent systems those networks of semi-autonomous agents equipped with capabilities for decision-making, learning, and adaptation—lie in scalable, effective, and highly cooperative solutions to challenging problems. These systems are often assisted by advances in

DOI: 10.4018/979-8-3693-8332-2.ch013

generative AI and operate as adaptable, collaborative agents that can make decisions and optimize in real-time under dynamic, uncertain conditions (Russell & Norvig, 2016).

A multi-agent system is made of individual agents with their specific tasks and capabilities. Depending on the nature of the task, agents may function alone or in synergy. Toward performing interrelated complicated tasks, these agents typically have autonomy, situational awareness, and the ability to adjust to changing conditions (Stone & Veloso, 2000). Such qualities are often necessary in scenarios where standard, sequential computational approaches would not be adequate. For example, MAS technology enables near-real-time communication and decision-making between thousands of vehicles inside an autonomous network of vehicles, hence enabling them to navigate safely with optimal identification of impediments towards achieving in their most efficient manner possible routes (Chen et al., 2020). This is not only a more efficient and safe means of transportation but also a great example of the complex self-managed coordination tasks that intelligent agents are capable of.

The new collaborative intelligence, which refers to the smooth collaboration between humans and AI agents, is reshaping the conventional limits of human-machine interaction. The collaborative intelligence frameworks combine human judgement with AI's computational capability, as opposed to the traditional systems of AI presented for automation. Being an adaptive intelligence that fulfills the needs of pragmatic, human-centred applications, MAS proves crucial in this respect (Jennings, Sycara, & Wooldridge, 1998). Collaborative intelligence systems fill the gap between the intuitions of human behaviour and the efficiency of machines by equipping agents with the capability to read and respond in relation to complicated situations. Generative AI technologies further enhance MAS by permitting the development of creative solutions specific to contexts from their usage of large data sets and sophisticated models of machine learning (Goodfellow, Bengio, & Courville, 2016).

MAS is able to reason for complex reasons through generative AI technologies, which cover deep learning and neural networks. These technologies enhance MAS decision-making capabilities as they allow the synthesizing of data, leading to predictions (Radford et al., 2019). Generative AI can help learn "by doing": it can facilitate the development of agents that can adapt to new situations by accessing their available knowledge. For example, in health care, MAS systems with generative AI could be involved in diagnosis and treatment by processing large volumes of patient data, trying to find patterns, and producing personalized care suggestions (Esteva et al., 2019). These technologies will enhance the quality of healthcare services by enabling the making of more accurate, data-driven judgments.

Generative AI is crucial in enhancing the efficiency of collaboration in multi-agent systems. Agents with generative AI capabilities can autonomously come up with solutions to optimize resource allocation, detect and predict bottlenecks, and improve real-time decision-making in complex environments. For example, with generative AI enhancement, MAS can optimize logistics in supply chains by coordinating transportation and inventory levels and delivery schedules without human intervention. point out that these features decrease operation costs, increase the happiness of the customer, and provide a high degree of adaptability, which is often needed in turbulent markets.

The design and development of MAS call for strong architectural frameworks that support distributed intelligence, communication, and scalability. Three prominent architectural approaches toward MAS exist: agent-based modelling, swarm intelligence, and distributed problem-solving models. All have unique mechanisms for cooperative agent behaviour and coordination. For instance, ABM has applications in the depiction of complex systems as interacting agents' networks, particularly when applied in simulations regarding issues such as urban planning, traffic management, and ecosystem modelling. Swarm intelligence, inspired by nature, like ant colonies and bird flocks, would make MAS manifest decentralized, self-organized behaviour ideal for applications in search and rescue missions, environmental monitoring, and surveillance (Dorigo, Birattari, & Brambilla, 2007).

Another very important area of MAS architecture is communication protocols between agents, which make it possible for the latter to share information and coordinate their actions effectively. Some very notable ones are the Contract Net Protocol (CNP) and the Task Allocation Protocol (TAP); these protocols present standardized frameworks for the sharing of resources, negotiation, and collaboration among different agents. Using such protocols, MASs can achieve a high degree of coordination and task specializations that are particularly beneficial in high-stakes, multi-agent operations (Smith, 1980).

With MAS technology, it is changing multiple industries to flexible, autonomous, and collaborative solutions. In the case of autonomous vehicle networks, MAS enables cars to communicate with one another, coordinate, and optimize travel routes as a way of reducing traffic congestion and improving safety on the roads. Similarly, in healthcare, MAS supports physicians in making diagnostics and optimizes treatment plans alongside effective management of patient care workflows. These applications show how MAS technology can handle sophisticated interdependent tasks that require not only adaptability but also precision. Another important application of MAS is in the management of smart cities, where MAS systems are used to manage resources such as water, energy, and public transportation. In MAS, coordination among different kinds of agents will improve resource distribution efficiency, minimize waste, and dynamically respond to the needs of the citizens in an urban setting (Bettencourt, 2013). Furthermore, MAS is critical in cybersecurity, where autonomous agents observe the networks, detect threats, and respond accordingly to actual potential vulnerabilities of the systems in real time. Such capabilities are invaluable in the protection of sensitive data and maintaining the integrity of digital infrastructures (Kurdi, 2022).

MAS technology has transformative potential, but it poses significant challenges in ethics, security, and interoperability. Autonomous agents would be able to behave in a manner with unpredictable outcomes, which raises questions about accountability and control in MAS. As MAS is integrated into critical infrastructure, the risk of security breaches and data privacy violations increases. Proper and responsible use of MAS necessitates the development of frameworks for transparency, accountability, and trustworthiness (Binns, 2018).

Another challenge is interoperability in MAS, especially when integrating agents from different systems or vendors. Standardization efforts are also important to let agents cooperate without effort, especially in multi-organizational or international settings. Bias and fairness in AI algorithms also play a role in the output generated by MAS, thus requiring unbiased models and transparent decision-making processes (Crawford & Calo, 2016). MAS is, therefore, critical to the development of collaborative intelligence with intelligent, autonomous, and multi-agent systems that enable complex decision-making in real-time within environments either driven by benefits from a distributed intelligence or those capable of response with adaptability. This chapter draws on an examination of the architectural foundations, applications, and ethical considerations of MAS to articulate how MAS is transforming industries and enhancing the collaborative human-AI ecosystems. Future developments in AI and MAS shall continue to bring these two systems closer together, thus changing the way humankind interacts with machines over various industrial domains.

Figure 1 Shows a multi-agent system consisting of two agents, Agent 1 and Agent 2, communicating through the communication channel and in the context of the larger information field infrastructure. As shown, each agent is equipped with an inference engine that takes input provided by sensors of ambient data and processes that input using the rules in a special database. Each agent's "Agent Core" integrates these inputs in order to produce an action or output, which is fed back into the information fields of the infrastructure. These information fields comprise shared data or settings where agents cooperate or share information such that they may make judgments with context. The configuration illustrates the capacity of autonomous agents to cooperate within a large-scale structured environment.

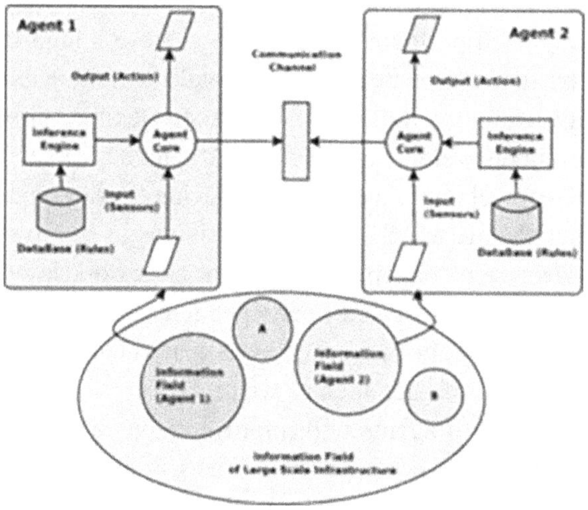

1.1 Literature Review

Extensive applications of MAS in remote decision-making and challenging collaborative activities achieved remarkable development of the discipline in a wide range of research and industrial fields. The applications of multi-agent systems in healthcare, smart cities, and autonomous driving could be due to the fact that they consist of autonomous or semi-autonomous agents that can interactively negotiate and collaborate to achieve individual or group objectives (Brown et al., 2020). What makes these agents even more applicable within systems that require adaptive responses and decentralized control is the fact that they can change their behaviour given interactions with other agents dynamically. Improvement in the functionality of MAS, in the light of recent developments within generative AI, has come in the form of improvements in adaptiveness and enhanced problem-solving capability. Generative models, like Transformer-based architectures and GANs, enable MAS to process huge volumes of data, learn from past experiences, and generate contextually relevant responses, thus making these models highly useful in dynamic and complex environments. For example, in healthcare, generative AI-powered MAS can assist doctors by analyzing patient data to diagnose diseases and recommend very personalized treatments. The integration of these AI technologies with MAS opened new avenues for application in domains that require flexibility and data-driven decision-making.

Distributed problem-solving models and agent-based modelling, or ABM, serve as architectural cornerstones of MAS. In the areas of traffic management, urban planning, and economic modelling, ABM has gained a significant amount of interest because such models can simulate complex systems as networks of interacting agents. These models, as (Helbing, 2012) holds, provide a scalable method of simulating resource allocation and optimization over large infrastructures. The models of distributed problem-solving support decentralized control and job distribution needed in MAS applications like disaster response, whereby autonomous agents travel and have to collaborate in contexts that are not planned (Yu et al., 2018).

Communication effectively allows coherent functioning among agents and coordination of actions within MAS. To facilitate resource sharing, task delegation, and information sharing by agents, various communication protocols have been developed, including CNP and other negotiation-based frameworks. This argues that (Parunak, 1999), these processes allow the MAS to work seamlessly in environments such as manufacturing and logistics, where real-time changes have to be made to maintain the level of efficiency in these operations. More recently, MAS has also started to incorporate reinforcement learning methods for improving autonomous coordination and decision-making, where agents can learn to adapt to different environments without explicit direction or guidance (Silver et al., 2017).

Despite such technological advances, scaling MAS deployment brings along severe issues, including ensuring ethical, secure, and interoperable operations. Think, for instance, about autonomous driving or healthcare applications of MAS: biases in the algorithms that produce these decisions could result in harm or injustices, which most certainly are ethical concerns, too. Besides, security considerations regarding MAS play an important role in many cases, such as smart cities, where services may be disrupted due to the exploitation of vulnerabilities. In applications that involve sensitive data, researchers have expressed a need to securely design MAS in a way that will be resistant to malevolent attacks and ensure data privacy. This is the view expressed by (Dorri, Kanhere, & Jurdak, 2018).

Future work directions now place greater emphasis on the priorities of security enhancement, ethics frameworks, and explainability in MAS research. Since MAS is becoming an integral part of many industries, trusting users calls for transparency and accountability in its decision-making processes. The studies in interpretable AI and explainable machine learning aim to make MAS decision processes intelligible to users, hence providing transparency and, thereby, better integration of these systems within ethically sensitive domains. Standardized communication protocols and interoperability frameworks will also be key factors that enable seamless cross-system interactions once these MAS start to find their way into larger infrastructures.

Research in MAS points out the complexity and revolutionary potential of this area, which deals with implementing intelligent autonomous systems in a cooperative setting. Only by ensuring continuous research on emerging MAS will solutions be found for ethical compliance, security, and interoperability challenges; this will make MAS reliable and flexible partners in human-centric and high-stakes applications.

1.2 Multi-Agent Systems and Collaboration

A multi-agent system is a system consisting of multiple autonomous agents that cooperate and interact within an environment in order to achieve common or individual goals. MAS has become an important foundation for the distributed solution of complex problems arising under dynamic contexts where control by one single decision-maker may be ineffective or impossible. These systems have allowed for the creation of cooperative applications for autonomous vehicles, smart cities, healthcare, and many other areas, among others, in recent years. The following section discusses some basic concepts of MAS, cooperation methods, practical applications, challenges, and possible directions for MAS.

1.2.1 Key Characteristics of Multi-Agent Systems

Multi-agent systems consist of several interacting agents having autonomy, social skills, reactivity, and pro-activeness. While social ability allows agents to interact with and cooperate with other agents, autonomy provides agents with the decision-making capability. Pro-activity lets the agents work in a goal-oriented fashion to realize their objectives. It is reactivity that represents the agent's ability to find and respond to the environment's changes. It is due to these characteristics that MAS can be applied in situations that require flexibility and distributed problem-solving.

The MAS can be collaborative or competitive, depending on the objectives of the system. In a collaborative MAS, the agents work together to achieve a mutual goal; the synergy emanating from their interaction typically results in superior performance by the entire system compared to the sum of the competencies of the individual agents themselves. On the other hand, agents in competitive MAS may have conflicting objectives, and their actions may take the form of bidding, negotiation, or even aggressive strategies. In fact, both types of MAS are very important in many applications, and most systems inherently possess elements of cooperation and competition.

1.2.2 Mechanisms for Collaboration in Multi-Agent Systems

Mechanisms of agent cooperation, coordination, and communication constitute the core of collaboration in MAS. Communication is the fundamental layer that provides the medium for information sharing, mutual comprehension, and action negotiation. Message-passing protocols, shared data repositories, and environmental cues are among the protocols that have been developed to enable agents to communicate with others. Autonomous vehicles in an intelligent transportation system, for instance, can coordinate driving behavior in a manner that optimizes the flow and safety of traffic by communicating in real-time with other vehicles about current conditions on roads and traffic that are part of or intersect with the flow (Chen et al., 2023).

Coordination can be defined as the process through which the behaviors of actors are aligned to avoid conflicts and achieve coherent group behavior. Some common strategies that Mas uses to implement coordination include discrete planning, job allocation, and roles by implementing mechanisms that allow agents to ask for other agents' help and to pick the most suitable collaborator based on a given set of criteria and protocols like the CNP support efficient workload distribution. Agents representing robotic arms, conveyors, and sensors will, for example, negotiate tasks to be accomplished in a production system to ensure that products are manufactured in an efficient and interruption-free way.

In MAS, besides simple coordination, cooperation involves agents working together for some purpose; often, the task at hand will require the agents to share resources or knowledge. Applications of cooperative MAS include disaster response; whereby cooperating agents search for and rescue in wide areas and provide relief. Cooperation is necessary to overcome complex obstacles that are beyond the capability of an individual agent to conquer.

Figure 2 presents a multi-agent system structure for collaborative tasks. There are three main kinds of agents: User Agents, Application Agents, and Ontology Agents, each with different responsibilities and interconnecting paths. The figure shows user agents on top, representing the interaction between users and the system. They handle interactions that are initiated by human operators in the form of input, commands, and requests. These agents are interconnected to share information, provide a cooperative response to user needs, and collaborate to complete user requests.

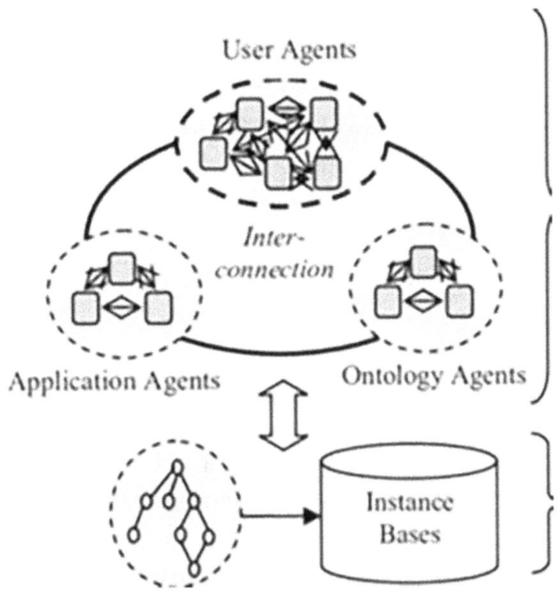

Application agents in MAS are responsible for managing some tasks or applications. In fact, these agents carry out most of the system's functions/operations, such as data processing or acting on the command provided by the user agent. Application agents update their knowledge and relevant data from user and ontology agents. The main purpose of ontology agents is the management of knowledge representation of the system, ensuring all the agents uniformly conceive notions and data. They keep one common "ontology" or language, which gives context and enables other agents to make sense of and interpret data meaningfully. Ontology agents establish a relationship with user and application agents to make sure data transfers are comprehensible and interpretable throughout the MAS.

An instance base, located at the bottom of the figure, serves as the common repository of some data instances or examples that agents exploit during their execution. Due to this single shared knowledge base, agents can draw on consistent data such that the same information is used for their activities. This Figure also shows how these types of agents are related, highlighting the systems allowing cooperation and communication throughout the MAS. Such a networked architecture allows the agents to cooperatively arrive at decisions and share data dynamically by using the instance base as a shared resource. Considering that agents are cooperating to provide effective and coordinated task execution across numerous functions, this general architecture of this MAS does allow for scattered collaboration and flexible problem solving.

1.2.3 Applications of Cooperative Multi-Agent Systems

There are several applications of cooperative MAS in a plethora of varied domains. A few of those have been listed below:

Healthcare:

MAS has been employed in the healthcare domain for patient care, treatment planning, and diagnosis. The agents in a healthcare MAS can be various diagnostic equipment, treatment methods, and medical experts cooperating to provide adequate and personalized care. For example, MAS can support evidence-based decisions among doctors by analyzing the trend effect observed in the data collected from several sources and suggesting modes of treatment (Topol, 2019). Being a cooperative approach, MAS leverages collective intelligence from several diagnostic systems to ensure that healthcare provision is done more effectively and efficiently.

Smart cities:

Resource management concerning energy, water, and transport in smart cities can only be visualized with MAS. Agents in a smart city cooperate using all available resources as efficiently as possible, reacting as quickly as possible to changes in the physical world. For instance, autonomous cars and public transit can be combined using MAS in order to manage traffic flow better and thus reduce congestion while enhancing safety. MAS can enable cities to manage infrastructure more effectively and sustainably by enabling communication and coordination amongst diverse actors.

Autonomous Vehicles and Transportation Systems

The most acknowledged applications of MAS are those regarding autonomous transportation systems. In a MAS, for example, autonomous cars will be independent agents that communicate with each other and interact with other cars, traffic signals, and roadways to develop smart traffic flow. With this type of cooperative architecture, vehicles will make their independent decisions in real time to enhance flow and reduce accidents. In transportation, the application of MAS will almost definitely result in a significant change in the face of urban mobility by designing safer and more efficient highways. Logistics and Supply Chain: Another area under growth for its applications is logistics and supply chain management, where agents represent the companies engaged in it, namely the manufacturer, distributors, retailers, and suppliers of the supply chain. Therefore, this set of agents will collaboratively manage the inventories, shipment plans, and correct demands. Along this line, MAS improves supply chain efficiency by enabling real-time coordination, thus reducing lead times and optimizing resource utilization. For instance, agents in MAS can manage delivery schedules, conduct coordination with restocking, and keep track of product supplies across multiple warehouses (Parunak, 1999).

2. GENERATIVE AI IN MAS

Generative AI plays a serious role in processing data to formulate new scenarios, solutions, and tactics that multi-agents have learned through experience. This section covers the contribution of generative AI to data synthesis, adaptive learning, and cooperation enhancement in diverse domains within a MAS.

2.1 Generative AI in MAS

A family of AI techniques termed "generative AI" can generate new data given patterns learned from existing data. Some popular generative models include GANs, VAEs, and Transformer architectures, which empower MAS to simulate scenarios and synthesize data. Generative AI enhances MAS's overall functionality and robustness by letting agents model complex settings, generate synthetic training data, and synthesizing synthesize adaptive responses.

Some key ways generative AI enhances MAS in terms of improved scenario simulation and prediction include the following. Generative AI allows MAS to more easily model how various upcoming events could play out and, in that regard, can dramatically facilitate planning and decision-making. In self-driving car systems, for instance, agents are able to use generative models to simulate a variety of different traffic scenarios against which to improve overall safety and respond to sudden road conditions (Finn et al., 2016). Equipped with these predictive capabilities, agents can predict complications and make behavioral adaptations well in advance.

2.2 Key Contributions of Generative AI to MAS

1. **Synthetic Data Generation for Training:** Generative AI can create synthetic data representing real-world characteristics in applications where data collection is impeded by logistical limitations or concerns about privacy. Because of this synthetic information, MAS agents can have larger datasets to train on, thus enhancing their accuracy and robustness. For instance, generative AI can be used in the generation of medical images for training diagnostic tools without revealing actual patient data in the healthcare industry.
2. **Collaborative Problem Solving through Adaptation**: Generative AI is used to enhance MAS adaptability by the agents acting together in dynamic and complex contexts. This ability of agents to generate context-specific solutions and adjust their strategies according to shared generative models is very helpful in cooperative scenarios related to disaster response, logistics, and resource allocation in general. Dynamic coordination can thus be done where agents deliver effective and efficient outcomes by way of shared simulation of solutions.
3. **Learning from Limited Data in Complex Contexts:** A critical component of MAS is the use of generative AI models, such as VAEs, in data-scarce contexts. This allows the agents to learn underlying patterns even from limited data. This feature enables the MAS agents to make better forecasts and generalize generalization events within environmental monitoring and military operation domains where complete knowledge is mostly lacking.

2.3 Applications of Generative AI in MAS

Autonomous Vehicles: In the case of MAS, generative AI has been used to enhance collaboration in decision-making within autonomous vehicles and manage traffic flow much better. For example, agents in autonomous cars could improve general traffic performance by modelling different driving scenarios and suggesting safe navigation.

Medical Diagnosis: By leveraging generative AI, MAS would be able to analyze data regarding a patient and simulate treatment outcomes to assist healthcare professionals in providing personalized care. Thanks to generative AI, MAS applications in synthesizing patient profiles will support healthcare professionals in making better evidence-based decisions.

Smart City Management: Generative AI empowers MAS agents to predict and efficiently utilize urban resources, from energy distribution to traffic flow. From the perspective of a smart city, MAS will be able to produce predictive models from historical data to help manage infrastructure better and adapt to shifting urban dynamics.

Supply Chain Optimization: Generative AI enables logistics MAS agents to forecast demand fluctuation, optimize stocking, and reduce lead times. Based on models representing a range of potential disruptions, it can build solutions for MAS to make supply chains more efficient and resilient.

2.4 Architectural Frameworks in Multi-Agent Systems (MAS)

In Multi-Agent Systems (MAS), architectural frameworks specify the structures and procedures that agents use to communicate, work together, and accomplish their objectives. These frameworks give MAS the groundwork it needs to function effectively, especially in dynamic contexts where adaptability, scalability, and flexibility are essential. The system performance, communication effectiveness, and agent job coordination are all greatly impacted by the architectural framework selected for MAS. A number of well-known MAS architectural frameworks are examined in this section, including hierarchical and hybrid frameworks, agent-based modelling, swarm intelligence, and blackboard architectures.

2.4.1 Agent-Based Modeling (ABM)

Individual agents are created to represent distinct entities using the Agent-Based Modelling (ABM) framework in MAS. These agents have distinct behaviour, objectives, and the capacity to communicate with both other agents and their surroundings. ABM is frequently employed in disciplines that require the simulation and analysis of intricate interactions among independent entities, such as ecology, economics, and the social sciences.

Although agents in ABM function autonomously, their actions are guided by predetermined rules. Depending on the application, these rules can be anything from straightforward actions to intricate algorithms for making decisions. Emergent behaviour complex events that result from the combined activities of individual agents without centralized control can be modelled using ABM (Bonabeau, 2002). In a traffic simulation, for instance, individual automobiles (agents) make choices based on other vehicles' actions and traffic signals, creating emergent traffic patterns. ABM frameworks are especially useful when figuring out how local interactions affect global results is the aim. For example, in urban planning, ABM can model how individual decisions regarding housing, transportation, and resource use result in patterns of pollution, energy use, and traffic throughout the city (Helbing, 2012). ABM's decentralized structure makes it ideal for MAS applications that need to be able to adjust to shifting conditions without centralized management.

Strengths of ABM:

- Enables a great degree of agent behaviour customization.
- It makes it easier to examine the dynamics of complex systems and emergent behaviour.
- Efficient when agents work autonomously in decentralized situations.

Challenges of ABM:

- Computationally demanding for simulations on a large scale.
- It is challenging to create realistic agent behaviour that faithfully capture actual circumstances.

2.5 Swarm Intelligence

The collective behaviour of social organisms like ants, bees, and birds inspired the MAS architectural framework known as swarm intelligence. Within this paradigm, agents often called "swarm agents" do not have a centralized control structure and instead adhere to basic, local principles. Agents develop complex group behaviour that may efficiently solve problems and adjust to changing surroundings through local interactions and collaboration (Dorigo, Maniezzo, & Colorni, 1996).

Applications like robotic swarms, in which teams of robots work together to accomplish tasks like environmental monitoring, surveillance, and search and rescue, make extensive use of swarm intelligence. Despite the limited capabilities of each robot (agent) in the swarm, when they work together, they can cover enormous regions, overcome obstacles, and accomplish goals (Şahin, 2004). Swarm-based MAS frameworks are also used for optimisation issues, such as the Ant Colony Optimisation (ACO) method, in which artificial ants mimic pheromone trails to identify the best paths in a graph, just like real ants do while they are looking for food

Strengths of Swarm Intelligence:

- It is extremely scalable since the efficacy of the swarm may be increased by adding more agents.
- Because the system is not dependent on centralized control, it is resilient to the failures of individual agents.
- Able to adjust to changing and uncertain circumstances with ease.

Swarm Intelligence's Challenges:

- Designing local rules that result in desirable global behaviour is challenging.
- It could need much fine-tuning to perform at your best in certain activities.
- Restricted use is necessary in situations where intricate, centralized decision-making is necessary.

2.6 Architecture of Blackboard

Agents in the blackboard architecture exchange information and communicate with one another over a common data structure called the "blackboard." This method involves actors posting requests, facts, or partial solutions on the blackboard for other agents to view and add to. Complex problem-solving activities where multiple agents with different specialties must collaborate on a common issue are a good fit for this design.

Applications like expert systems, whose agents represent many knowledge sources or approaches to problem-solving, frequently employ the blackboard paradigm. In a weather forecasting system, for instance, several agents with expertise in temperature, humidity, and pressure analysis can work together through the blackboard to produce precise forecasts. A collective solution that uses each agent's knowledge is reached when each agent provides information that other agents need to make wise judgements.

Strengths of Blackboard Architecture:

- Efficient for jobs requiring agents with varying levels of expertise to work together.
- It makes it easier for agents to coordinate and share expertise.
- It is ideal for settings where incomplete solutions can gradually be combined to create a full solution.

Blackboard Architecture's Challenges:

- This may cause snags in communication as more agents use the chalkboard.
- The blackboard is to be carefully managed in order to prevent data overflow.
- For real-time applications where speed is crucial, it might not be appropriate.

2.7 Hybrid and Hierarchical Architectures

In MAS, agents are arranged into levels or layers using hierarchical structures, each with specific functions and responsibilities. While lower-level agents carry out activities in accordance with directives from higher-level agents, higher-level agents frequently serve as managers or coordinators. This paradigm strikes a balance between autonomy and cooperation by permitting decentralized action at the lower levels and centralized control at the higher levels.

In industrial and manufacturing settings, when jobs are divided into tiers of complexity, hierarchical MAS designs are employed. High-level agents, for example, may oversee production plans in a manufacturing facility, whereas lower-level agents would oversee the operation of the machinery (Duffie & Prabhu, 1994). To capitalize on the advantages of each methodology, hybrid architectures include many frameworks (such as hierarchical and ABM). A hybrid MAS architecture may employ swarm intelligence for flexibility in changing circumstances, a hierarchy for work delegation, and a blackboard for knowledge exchange.

Strengths of Hierarchical and Hybrid Architectures:

- Strikes a balance between decentralized execution and centralized coordination.
- Efficient in settings that are well-organized and have distinct roles.
- Hybrid models use the advantages of several architectures to provide flexibility.

Challenges of Hierarchical and Hybrid Architectures:

- It is more difficult to plan and execute than single-framework methods.
- Restricted scalability, particularly in completely centralized hierarchies.
- This may cause pure hierarchical models to introduce single points of failure at higher levels.

Table 1. Comparison of architectural framework

Framework	Key Characteristics	Applications	Strengths	Challenges
Agent-Based Modeling	Independent agents, emergent behavior	Traffic simulations, urban planning	Customizable, good for emergent behaviors	Computationally intensive, designing realistic behavior
Swarm Intelligence	Decentralized, local rules-based cooperation	Robotic swarms, optimization problems	Scalable, robust, adaptable	Designing local rules, fine-tuning
Blackboard Architecture	Shared data structure, collaborative problem-solving	Expert systems, collaborative planning	Facilitates knowledge sharing, incremental solutions	Communication bottlenecks, data management
Hierarchical & Hybrid	Layered roles, combines frameworks	Manufacturing, smart grids	Centralized-decentralized balance, flexible	Complexity, scalability issues in pure hierarchies

The architectures which make up MAS are Agent-Based Modelling, Swarm Intelligence, Blackboard Architecture, and Hierarchical/Hybrid frameworks. Each of these architectures has its own set of advantages and disadvantages. Each of these architecture frameworks best fits applications based on their needs, for instance, flexibility, scalability, and teamwork. While swarm intelligence and ABM have been viewed as decentralized models in terms of robustness and emergent behaviour, blackboard architectures provide the best models when specialized agents work in teams to solve a problem. On the other hand, hierarchical and hybrid frameworks provide flexibility by combining several architectures so as to strike a balance between control and autonomy. For complex dynamic environments, such as manufacturing, smart cities, and healthcare, solutions will most probably be robust with a combination of these frameworks when MAS is further developed.

2.8 Methodology

The approach presented here for developing intelligent, autonomous, and multi-agent systems involves a clearly demarcated set of steps with respect to the functional and design requirements of the system. In the technique discussed here, the roles include system analysis and design, the selection of agent architecture, interaction protocols, environmental simulation, learning mechanisms, assessment criteria, and deployment procedures. This approach ensures at least that MAS must be flexible, scalable, and capable of managing complex tasks in evolving environments.

1. **Analysis of the requirements and system design**

This early stage establishes the objectives of MAS and the goals of the multi-agent system. It identifies the conditions that agents must satisfy to reach these objectives.

The issue that the MAS must address must be defined. For example, if this system is for an autonomous transportation network, then issues to be considered could be effective traffic management, collision avoidance, and route optimization. Specify goals, parameters, and the extent of work that the MAS is supposed to perform.

Agent Goals and Role Identification: Describe the type of agents to be developed within MAS. Every agent type should have specific roles with clearly identified responsibilities and goals. A possible example may include a manufacturing MAS comprised of material handling agents, quality agents, and assembly agents. Its overall objective must thereby coincide with the objectives of the individual agents.

Functional and non-functional needs: Establish the functional requirements such as how communications should take place and the decision-making capabilities and the non-functional ones: scalability, speed in response, and fault tolerance. Non-functional criteria can ensure that a system can cope with real-world complexity.

Limitations and Assumptions: Identify any constraints, such as processing constraints, power constraints, or communication capacity, along with environmental assumptions that include the behaviour of the environment, which can be deterministic or stochastic. This would help to tune the MAS to work within laid boundaries.

Performance Metrics: To provide the basic measures of performance for MAS, such as job completion time, resource utilization, accuracy, and robustness, among others. These indicators will assist in further reviews and other design decisions after that.

2. **Agent Architecture Design**

The architecture of an agent determines its interaction with other agents, information analysis, perception of its environment, and decision execution. In turn, many factors, such as the required degree of autonomy, available computational resources, and task complexity, determine the chosen design.

Reactive agents can serve well for tasks that require immediate responses since they act directly according to previously defined stimulus-response rules. They maintain no internal model of the environment. This architecture can be applied to simple tasks requiring fast, adaptive behaviour but not involving strategic planning, such as motions within robotic swarms or obstacle avoidance movements.

The agents deliberate in reaching a decision using planning and reasoning, maintaining an internal model of their environment. Design is befitting for complex tasks and is goal-oriented, such as route planning and navigation and strategic coordination. Deliberative agents can also look at options, predict the consequences of certain actions, and decide on the best action based on those projections, as stated by (Georgeff & Ingrand, 1989).

Hybrid Architecture: This architecture allows agents to deliberate over a plan to achieve a long-term goal and, at the same time, fast react in the moment by incorporating both reactive and deliberative elements. The architecture perfectly fits an autonomous car that needs to plan a path toward a goal and must perform immediate responses to challenges.

Adaptability, computational demands, and the complexity of system design are some aspects directly influenced by the agent's architecture. The choice of an appropriate architecture is essentially based on the roles and responsibilities assigned to agents and on the environment's needs for the most efficient MAS performance.

3. **Protocols of Communication and Interaction**

Interaction protocols explain how and under what circumstances agents will interact with one another within the MAS. Some protocols need to be followed by the agents for coordination, cooperation, and negotiation to take place.

Explicit Communication: Message-passing protocols in settings where explicit engagement by agents is essential provide direct data transfer between agents. For job distribution, protocols like the Contract Net Protocol (CNP) are commonly used. In CNP, one agent announces a task for which assistance is needed, while other agents bid according to their competencies. In scenarios involving multiple tasks and agents, this approach enables dynamic and efficient resource allocation (De Jong, 2017).

Stigmergy describes indirect communication between agents by modifying the environment. In a robotic swarm, for instance, each robot can leave various physical or digital marks that other agents may recognize and act on, thereby enabling coordination without any direct interaction. Stigmergy applies when direct interaction is not practical: large-scale search and rescue operations are typical situations where it cannot be afforded to communicate directly all of the time.

Mechanism for Coordination: Coordination allows one to ensure that agents act in a manner that avoids disputes and achieves system-wide objectives. Included among such mechanisms are:

- **Leader-Follower Model**: One agent leads, while others follow its directives, useful in scenarios like multi-robot navigation.
- **Consensus Algorithms**: Agents iteratively adjust their decisions until they reach agreement, common in distributed sensor networks.
- **Mutual Adjustment**: Agents continuously adjust their actions based on feedback from others, suited to dynamic environments like traffic control.

4. **Simulation and Configuration of the Environment**

It would be desirable for a developer to test and refine the behaviour of an agent before it is actually deployed in the real world by creating a simulation of the environment. The simulator will have to be representative of all the complexity and quirks of the real environment:

Define Environmental Variables: Enumerate relevant variables to which agents will be exposed, including obstacles, spatial constraints, and dynamic features. Example-polite autonomous driving MAS: road patterns, traffic lights, pedestrians and other cars are all part of the environment.
Dynamics of the Environment: The environment is either dynamic or static. Dynamic environments include ways in which the environment changes, such as traffic flow changing with time and weather. In dynamic contexts, agents learn and adapt continuously.
Sensor Simulation: Simulate sensors that agents use to perceive the world, such as temperature sensors in industrial robots, GPS, and LIDAR for driverless cars. Correct sensor simulation allows agents to perceive a realistic view of the world.
Simulation Platform: An appropriate simulation platform, such as MATSim, NetLogo, or Gazebo, should allow interaction between multiple agents. The platform must be selected considering the requirements for physical fidelity and complexity of interactions in MAS.

By emulating the environment, one observes agent interactions and validates agent performances in a controlled environment, hence reducing risks and enhancing designs before actual commissioning.

5. **Mechanisms of Learning and Adaptation**

Intelligent MAS has to learn mechanisms of adaptation to cope with erratic situations for improvement over time. Agents can learn from experience through a variety of machine-learning approaches.

Reinforcement Learning (RL): Reinforcement Learning includes learning by agents through direct interaction with the environment and feedback provided as a reward or penalty. It helps in dynamic situations where agents need to learn the best policies through trial and error.
Deep Learning: Agents can use deep neural networks to process complex, high dimensional data such as images or sensor readings. A tangible example of this is obstacle detection and picture identification by convolutional neural networks that enable autonomous drones to fly safely in new, unknown environments.
Imitation Learning: Agents are trained on the task where optimal behaviour is known to be able to imitate those behaviour. Industrial robots learn from watching and imitating human operators. Imitation learning is useful in environments that demand precision and safety.
Evolutionary Algorithms: These algorithms work by generating successive generations of strategies through natural selection and recombination of the best strategies in order to evolve the optimal agent behaviour. In general, evolutionary algorithms work when applied to complex MAS, in which agents have to develop generally high-level strategies for coordination or adaptability (De Jong, 2017). Over time, these learning mechanisms increase an MAS's adaptability and robustness by allowing its members to adapt and optimize their operation and further become effective.

6. Testing and Evaluation Metrics

Performance evaluation ensures that agents work effectively towards attaining the system objectives. Some of the key metrics include:

Success Rate of Task: It calculates the completed percentage of tasks. This can refer to the number of survivors found or saved when applying systems such as disaster response.
Resource Efficiency: This will measure the time, energy, or computing power consumption. Often, besides speed, energy conservation plays an important role, especially in settings like manufacturing, where efficiency is a critical issue.
Scalability: Scalability is the MAS's ability to sustain performance when either the number of agents increases, or the task complexities are high. For example, scalability would determine how well a system works when, in a smart city simulation, the number of cars or infrastructure nodes increases.
Robustness and Fault Tolerance: This provides an assessment of the MAS's ability to handle failures that may result from malfunctioning agents or unplanned events. Robustness is a key concern in systems of real importance, such as autonomous navigation or healthcare systems, since failure may imply catastrophic outcomes.

2.9 Research Objective

The development of intelligent, autonomous, and multi-agent systems is a very complex process that aims to develop systems in which multiple agents are allowed to collaborate and solve problematic issues, interact effectively, and operate independently. In order for MAS to work reliably within real-world applications, the subsequent objectives form the backbone of the key research focus on adaptability, scalability, security, and ethics.

1. Objective 1: Design Adaptive and Scalable Agent Architectures

The mission aims to develop structures that will enable the MAS to act adaptively in a large number of dynamic contexts. Agents of MAS, when operating within the MAS, shall be able to perform the following:

Autonomous Operation: Each agent should be able to contribute to the system's objectives by making decisions and acting on its judgment based on perceived information.
Scalability by smoothening: It should be possible to scale up by adding more agents without affecting the effectiveness or resource efficiency.

This goal is motivated by the idea that MAS is supposed to operate in real-world dynamic settings, such as smart cities or manufacturing systems. Scaling up MAS will enable the dealing of complex, large-scale activities involving coordination among several agents.

2. Objective 2: Development of Robust Communication and Coordination Mechanisms

Since MAS are essentially collaborative systems, it is also important that agents can effectively communicate with other agents. This objective is to deliver mechanisms that allow agents to:

Effectively Communicate and Share Information: For a range of interaction requirements, this varies from direct communication-like message passing to indirect communication, such as through environmental cues in swarm intelligence.

By achieving this, MAS will be able to cooperate in environments where agent cooperation should be necessary, such as robotic swarms or traffic management systems. Allowing the agents to effectively cooperate and share crucial information benefits system performance and reduces conflict.

3. Objective 3: To Enhance Learning and Adaptation Capabilities for Improved Decision-Making

The learning and adaptation competency of the agents is directly associated with the capability of intelligence while making decisions in MAS. Accordingly, this objective looks to equip the agents with advanced learning methods in order for them to learn from experience through deep learning, imitation learning, and reinforcement learning based on the interaction in the environment.

Adapt in Real Time to Changes: With real-time feedback, agents are expected to change plans and courses of action that help them effectively surmount unexpected obstacles.

This objective advances MAS by improving the responsiveness and resiliency of agents when placed in situations of uncertainty, which include resource allocation and autonomous navigation. This will eventually allow MAS to arrive at better decisions with every passing moment of time, thereby granting operations the ability to stay effective and efficient.

4. Objective 4: Creation and Utilization of Simulation Environments for Validation and Testing

The key assumption of MAS must be tested in realistic simulated environments as a prelude to the use of such systems in real-life applications. Accordingly, this objective is directed at the following:

Modelling Complex Scenarios: ABM shall allow researchers to build simulated environments that model scenarios in realistic environments, including but not limited to traffic networks, industrial processes, and emergency response situations.
Agent Behaviors and Interaction Testing: This would help researchers explore how agents act individually and in groups using various simulations and indicate any defects in their architecture.

Ensure that MAS is well-tested so that their deployment risks are reduced, and agent behaviour are enhanced before actual deployment in different settings. Modelling complex situations will also make MAS much more reliable and effective.

3. APPLICATIONS OF INTELLIGENT, AUTONOMOUS, AND MULTI-AGENT SYSTEMS (MAS)

1. **Autonomous Vehicles and Traffic Light Control**

MAS enables vehicles and infrastructure components, like traffic lights, to coordinate with and inform each other in real-time. The aim is to optimize traffic flow in autonomous transportation and enhance road safety.

Optimization of Traffic Flow: Agents autonomous cars cooperate with traffic lights and each other to minimize traffic flow, control it, and keep it smooth.
Collision Avoidance: Agents in the range make speed adjustments or take different routes to avoid collisions when cars detect and report to them impending collisions.
Dynamic Route Planning: All decisions are made in real time to find the best route based on the number of road closures and points of congestion.

This could drastically reduce the three Ts-time, traffic, and accidents in urban locations.

2. **Healthcare and Medical Diagnostics**

MAS provides integrated diagnostic and patient care systems in healthcare; the intelligent agents can be diagnostic equipment, therapeutic methods, or medical specialists.

Medical Diagnosis: Agents help in diagnosis by analyzing patient data, deciding on symptom analysis, and correlating the same with medical databases.
Patient Care: The agents continuously monitor the vital signs and other health parameters and inform the medical experts in case of any abnormal variations.
Resource Management: MAS manages a hospital's resources to ensure optimum utilization and the best possible care facilities. It would cover equipment management, scheduling management, bed distribution, etc.

In medical fields, MAS enhances diagnostic accuracy, offers continuous patient monitoring, and allows for efficient resource utilization in clinics and hospitals.

3. **Utilization management and Smart Cities**

It enhances smart cities' sustainability and responsiveness to citizens' needs through the effective management of urban resources, infrastructure, and services.

Energy Management helps distribute energy resources optimally by adapting supply to real-time demand, thus minimizing energy waste.

Traffic Coo minimizing Supporting MAS in regulating traffic lights and public transit lines optimizes efficiency and reduces congestion. Water Management: Agents optimize garbage truck collection schedules to optimize and monitor water distribution systems to save every available resource.

MAS can help enable cities' sustainable growth by enhancing urban resource management and improving citizens' quality of life.

4. **Smart Manufacturing and Industrial Automation**

Industrial automation is accomplished in three ways: MAS enable flexible manufacturing, supply network optimization, and automation of production and optimization collaborative Robots: The so-called "robots," these robots work alongside humans and other robots, for instance, to perform quality control and assembly. They make continuous adjustments in their behaviour through direct feedback provided. Inventory management: Agents continually monitor inventory and plan supplies so that overstocking does not occur while also ensuring smooth operations.

Quality Control: Through the use of sensor data, MAS monitors product quality in real-time by the early detection of anomalies, hence reducing waste.

This application ensures a high-quality manufacturing process, reduces downtimes, and enhances efficiency in production.

5. **Emergency Management and Disaster Response**

Due to situational assessment, resource allocation, and search and rescue by autonomous agents, MAS can be helpful in catastrophe situations.

Search and rescue: Ground robots and drones with MAS technology collaborate in searching for survivors, supplying food, and mapping the affected areas. Resource Distribution: This MAS distributes vital resources, including food, water, and medical supplies, by matching demand-supply assessments in real-time. Crowd Management: Agents minimize casualty risk and optimize responsiveness by regulating evacuation routes and guiding people toward safe zones.

MAS enhances the effectiveness and efficiency of emergency services in disaster management by ensuring timely, coordinated, and organized action in life-threatening situations (organized). Environmental Conservation and Monitoring. MAS contributes to environmental conservation through biodiversity protection and managing conservation efforts by monitoring ecosystems.

Tracking Wildlife: Agents monitor the movement of threatened species to protect vulnerable populations and track poaching incidents.
Climate and Pollution Monitoring: By monitoring pollution levels and climate changes, among other environmental parameters, MAS delivers data to underpin conservation programs.

MAS monitors forest fires using drones, which allows for early intervention and the ability to halt the spread

3.1 Challenges and Solution

1. **Communication Bottlenecks in Large-Scale Systems**

In large MAS, like autonomous vehicle networks or smart city management systems, these would require some sort of effective agent-to-agent communication. When the number of agents becomes large, the volume of communications exchanged could overwhelm the system and result in inefficiencies and holdups.

Solution: To alleviate message congestion, group agents in hierarchical communications architectures and only exchange summary information between groups. The communication burden can also be minimized by resorting to efficient protocols such as multicast communication, where one single message is routed to multiple agents simultaneously.

2. **Scalability**

While the number of agents or tasks increases, usually MASs working properly on a small scale may suffer from sustaining performance. In systems like logistics or resource allocation, where agents must continuously cooperate or compete for resources, scalability issues frequently occur.

Solution: Distributed algorithms and swarm intelligence may serve as decentralized coordinating mechanisms. These frameworks do not need any kind of central control either, since local rules for each agent will lead to a certain global behavior. Other strategies like role-based assignment also help distribute work more effectively when the system scales up.

3. Ensuring Robustness and Fault Tolerance

The agents in MAS fail unexpectedly due to sensor faults or any communication breakdowns, especially with applications dealing with critical tasks like disaster relief and healthcare. It is crucial that the system guarantee continuity upon the failure of one or multiple agents.

The remedy should be the development of agents that have fault tolerance and redundancy features. For instance, agents can share duties dynamically with the view of each agent's availability or backup agents may assume duties when primary ones fail to do so. Overall robustness is enhanced even further by including techniques of self-diagnosis, which allow agents to identify problematic behaviors and quarantine them.

4. **Issues of Security and Ethics**

There are also concerns about privacy and ethics when MAS is applied to sensitive domains, such as in healthcare, finance, or surveillance. For example, autonomous monitoring systems may destroy any notion of privacy, and biased financial and medical decision-making may yield unfair outcomes.

Solution: Accountability shall be ensured by embedding transparency mechanisms and ethical standards within the MAS. Data encryption and secure communication should be beneficial in protecting sensitive information. Algorithms followed by decision-making agents should be continuously monitored and tested in order to ensure they are unbiased and in line with moral values.

5.Challenges in Having Agents Well Cooperate

Where there is a requirement for several agents to work in close collaboration with each other, such as in emergency responses or multi-robot assembly lines, failure to coordinate the actions of agents may be fraught with conflict and inefficiency. In the absence of effective coordination, the same task may be repeatedly carried out, resources could be wasted, or goals jeopardized.

Solution: Apply adaptive coordination techniques, such as reinforcement learning, whereby agents learn over time the most effective coordination approaches through rewards or penalties. In this vein, even contract-based systems, such as the Contract Net Protocol, enable agents to propose jobs on which they would like to work - matching resources with goals of activity-more explicit control of individual agents through the use of a “leader” agent could be used in order to more clearly structure the activity of agents for specific tasks.

3.2 Result and Discussion

Developing and applying intelligent, autonomous, multi-agent systems has achieved remarkable progress in different fields, such as autonomous transportation, healthcare, smart cities, disaster response, industrial automation, and environmental preservation. Applications involve the capability of MAS to handle dynamic, complex activities that require immediate decisions, flexibility, and effective coordination of agents.

MAS is able to improve coordination and efficiency within autonomous transportation by developing real-time communication across vehicles and infrastructure. It reduces the time taken while travelling, and fuel consumption enables dynamic route optimization, collision avoidance, and effective traffic management in a very big way. For congestion, the autonomous car directly interacts with the infrastructure and other cars within a MAS and can make real-time adjustments based on the provided traffic data.

Still, the challenging part is getting reliable performance in highly congested scenarios. It has also been proven that a bottleneck can be avoided by forming scalable hierarchical structures of communication where summary data is communicated between groups. Many more studies on scalable protocols of communication will be necessary to ensure that MAS can function well as the number of autonomous vehicles on the road continues to increase.

Till now, promising results have been received through the application of MAS in resource management, patient monitoring, and diagnosis. With the help of intelligent agents continuously monitoring vital signs and patient data, better diagnoses can be provided to the patient, thus alerting the medical practitioners to areas of concern. At the same time, MAS optimizes resource utilization and boosts efficiency in operational matters by managing personnel schedules, equipment management, and bed occupancy. While MAS enhances efficiency and diagnostic precision, ITS safe use in clinical settings requires ethical and security issues, especially in regard to the privacy of patient data. Suppose any meaningful levels of trust by the patient towards MAS utilization within the clinical environment are to be maintained. In that case, significant clarity in terms of underlying decision processes needs to be explained, and ways through which data encryption can be enhanced need to be determined (Binns, 2018).

Another area in which MAS has shown great potential is in enhancing the management of resources in urban settings. Continuous monitoring and adjustment of the distribution of waste management, water, and electricity are needed to achieve efficient distribution according to demand through intelligent agents. Minimization of waste and energy consumption alone while adapting to changes in demand is achieved through MAS, which depends on real-time data. Energy management agents might distribute power based on peak-hour and off-peak-hour demand, thus avoiding overload and reducing wastage. However, considering that MAS is increasingly working on large metropolitan infrastructures with complex connections, challenges to coordination and interoperability still need to be addressed. Much research is still needed for the system to handle such resilience and standardized protocols for interoperability of the interconnected resources it governs within urban cities.

In response to disasters, MAS has shown brilliant results in the fields of scenario evaluation, resource allocation, and search and rescue activities. In high-risk situations, independent drones and robots share the workload of locating survivors, mapping the disaster area, and distributing supplies to save lives while improving operation efficiencies. Yu et al. (2018) further explain that in providing aid as early as possible, MAS ensures that resources are channeled to communities that are in higher need. Real-world deployment of MAS presents communication infrastructure issues in remote or hazardous places despite the fact that MAS provides flexibility and efficiency in emergencies. Future research should focus on mesh or satellite-based communication networks to further provide connectivity in disaster-prone areas for better dependability of MAS during disaster situations.

With the introduction of better manufacturing processes and better-quality control, MAS has brought about a quantum leap in terms of productivity in industrial automation. While the quality control agents monitor the production in real-time to identify defects, collaborative robots or cobots can carry out tasks related to assembly, testing, and packaging with minimal human intervention. With MAS, therefore, its efficiency of production and quality of manufactured products are enhanced because this reduces errors, hence enabling manufacturers to respond quicker to changes in demand. The reliance on machine-to-machine communication, however, creates cybersecurity issues, especially when the processes involved are critical operations in the manufacturing process. Assuring MAS integrity in industries would, therefore, call for robust cybersecurity practices and periodic auditing of the system.

MAS has also contributed to conservation efforts on the environment in terms of wildlife tracking, pollution monitoring, and climate assessment by providing real-time information to conservationists. Agents facilitate purposeful actions that help ensure environmental sustainability based on tracking the movement of endangered species, spotting illegal poaching, and testing the levels of pollution (Lin et al., 2023). Even though MAS has been successfully used in processing environmental data and monitoring extensive areas of space, designing systems to work sustainably with minimal impact on the environment remains among the top challenges facing their application. Research into low-impact, energy-efficient MAS powered by renewable sources such as solar power guarantees that MAS performs well in isolated and sensitive environmental areas.

These results expose the versatility and innovative capability of MAS in solving real problems, ranging from improving resource management in urban areas to supporting environmental conservation and disaster recovery. Each of these examples shows how MAS can act autonomously, coordinate the behaviour of agents, and adapt to changes in their circumstances. However, each of these advance's points to areas where further investigation is required: energy efficiency, enhanced cybersecurity, and scalable communication. Ongoing investment in MAS technology will make such intelligent, autonomous systems more robust, efficient, and ethical in their operation, with further extension of the range of applications they can serve.

4. CONCLUSION

The design of intelligent, autonomous, multi-agent systems represents a whole revolution in solving complex, dynamic problems related to many knowledge areas. Now, the efficiency, adaptability, and decision-making functions of MAS in real-world applications inspire imagination with regard to autonomous vehicles, healthcare, smart cities, disaster responses, and environmental conservation. For those problems where multiple agents have to cooperate by acting autonomously, such systems enable coordinated activities, real-time responses, and solutions scalable to any size.

Applications like MAS in autonomous transportation have considerably improved traffic flow, collision avoidance, and route optimization by having cars interact with the infrastructure and each other. This has greatly created much safer urban environments, in addition to reducing the time used for commutes and fuel consumption. MAS has enhanced resource management, patient monitoring, and diagnosis accuracy within the health sector, hence enriching these medical facilities in terms of resource management with improved responses toward patient needs. Other significant application areas of MAS are smart cities; thanks to intelligent resource management, optimal waste management, water supply, and energy distribution have benefitted them. MAS can enable the construction of more sustainable urban environments, reducing waste and improving the quality of life of citizens by acting upon real-time data.

Despite these successes, challenges remain to achieve scaling, tight security, and ethical dilemmas. Scalinarity of MAS means their possible use in very large-scale deployments, like transport networks or smart cities, where high agent density may incur performance issues and bottlenecks in communications. Although several decentralized protocols and hierarchical communication structures have been proposed to overcome these issues, further investigation and enhancement are needed to ensure that MAS will work seamlessly even when deployed on a large scale. From industrial automation to healthcare, applications make the presence of sensitive data and vital infrastructures salient factors. Strong security protocols are expected to become vital factors, given that MAS systems have to handle increasingly sensitive data and operations.

Ethical issues are vital, especially in areas where MAS decisions may directly impact citizens. Health industry MAS algorithms, for example, need to be fair and transparent to maintain patients' trust and provide non-discriminatory treatment. Similarly, in the case of environmental monitoring or surveillance applications, data privacy and security are highly critical. In fact, all these ethical issues have to be sorted out if the wide implementation and acceptance of MAS in various industries is to be ensured.

In turn, future developments of MAS technology will further improve its robustness, efficiency, and ethical compatibility, expanding the realm of applications. At the same time, the key objective of research is the energy-efficient development of MAS to foster sustainable operation, especially in remote and ecologically sensitive areas. Similarly, the development of easy-to-use human-agent interfaces and robust training algorithms will be critical to seamless integration when MAS increasingly interacts with human users.

Conclusively, MAS has shown great promise in a range of applications, with significant improvements in effectiveness, security, and flexibility. It is further arguable that if the full benefits of MAS are to be experienced, further research, enhancement, and innovation would be required to surmount ethical and technical problems. Smarter cities could be realized, safer transit, better healthcare, and more sustainable environments. MAS enables these as they permeate everyday life and become part of the vital infrastructures. With responsible development and deployment, MAS would continue to revolutionize sectors and help solve many of the most fundamental challenges societies face today, rendering them a much-needed tool in a world that grows in complexity and interlink.

4.1 Future Works

To support their growing applications, future research in intelligent, autonomous, and multi-agent systems (MAS) should concentrate on improving scalability, security, energy efficiency, and ethical alignment. First, to make sure MAS can function well in high-density settings like smart cities and transport networks, research on scalable structures and decentralized communication protocols will be essential. Furthermore, creating cutting-edge cybersecurity frameworks will protect MAS from possible dangers. The environmental impact of MAS requires sustainable designs, such as agents powered by renewable energy and optimized algorithms, especially in sensitive or remote regions like environmental monitoring and conservation. Future research on ethics in MAS development is particularly crucial since it will promote confidence and encourage responsible use in delicate applications like surveillance and healthcare by guaranteeing openness, accountability, and equity in MAS decision-making.

Last but not least, future research should concentrate on improving human-agent cooperation and making MAS more responsive and intuitive in applications that need face-to-face communication. MAS will be better able to handle difficult, real-world problems and help create a more intelligent, secure, and sustainable future with ongoing research and innovation.

REFERENCES

Bettencourt, L. M. (2013). The origins of scaling in cities. *Science*, *340*(6139), 1438–1441. DOI: 10.1126/science.1235823 PMID: 23788793

Binns, R. (2018). Fairness in machine learning: Lessons from political philosophy. In *Conference on Fairness, Accountability and Transparency* (pp. 149–159). PMLR.

Bonabeau, E. (2002). Agent-based modeling: Methods and techniques for simulating human systems. *Proceedings of the National Academy of Sciences of the United States of America*, *99*(suppl_3), 7280–7287. DOI: 10.1073/pnas.082080899 PMID: 12011407

Brown, T. B., Mann, B., Ryder, N., Subbiah, M., Kaplan, J., Dhariwal, P., . . . Amodei, D. (2020). Language models are few-shot learners. arXiv preprint arXiv:2005.14165.

Chen, B., Zhang, H., Guan, W., Wang, Z., & Xu, M. (2020). A future intelligent traffic system with mixed autonomous vehicles and human-driven vehicles. *Information Sciences*, *529*, 59–72. DOI: 10.1016/j.ins.2020.02.009

Chen, L., Wang, F.-Y., Zhang, J., Yang, X., & Li, M. (2023). Milestones in autonomous driving and intelligent vehicles—Part I: Control, computing system design, communication, HD map, testing, and human behaviors. *IEEE Transactions on Systems, Man, and Cybernetics. Systems*, *53*(9), 5831–5847. DOI: 10.1109/TSMC.2023.3276218

Crawford, K., & Calo, R. (2016). There is a blind spot in AI research. *Nature*, *538*(7625), 311–313. DOI: 10.1038/538311a PMID: 27762391

De Jong, K. (2017). Evolutionary computation: A unified approach. In *Proceedings of the Genetic and Evolutionary Computation Conference Companion* (pp. 1223–1244).

Dorigo, M., Birattari, M., & Brambilla, M. (2007). Swarm intelligence. *Scholarpedia Journal*, *2*(9), 1462. DOI: 10.4249/scholarpedia.1462

Dorigo, M., Maniezzo, V., & Colorni, A. (1996). Ant system: Optimization by a colony of cooperating agents. *IEEE Transactions on Systems, Man, and Cybernetics. Part B, Cybernetics*, *26*(1), 29–41. DOI: 10.1109/3477.484436 PMID: 18263004

Dorri, A., Kanhere, S. S., & Jurdak, R. (2018). Multi-agent systems: A survey. *IEEE Access : Practical Innovations, Open Solutions*, *6*, 28573–28593. DOI: 10.1109/ACCESS.2018.2831228

Duffie, N. A., & Prabhu, V. V. (1994). Real-time distributed scheduling of heterarchical manufacturing systems. *Journal of Manufacturing Systems*, *13*(2), 94–107. DOI: 10.1016/0278-6125(94)90025-6

Esteva, A., Robicquet, A., Ramsundar, B., Kuleshov, V., DePristo, M., Chou, K., Cui, C., Corrado, G. S., Thrun, S., & Dean, J. (2019). A guide to deep learning in healthcare. *Nature Medicine*, *25*(1), 24–29. DOI: 10.1038/s41591-018-0316-z PMID: 30617335

Finn, C., Christiano, P. F., Abbeel, P., & Levine, S. (2016). A connection between generative adversarial networks, inverse reinforcement learning, and energy-based models. arXiv preprint arXiv:1611.03852.

Georgeff, M. P., & Ingrand, F. F. (1989). *Decision-making in an embedded reasoning system*. Australian Artificial Intelligence Institute.

Goodfellow, I., Bengio, Y., & Courville, A. (2016). *Deep learning*. MIT Press.

Helbing, D. (2012). Agent-based modeling. In *Social self-organization: Agent-based simulations and experiments to study emergent social behavior* (pp. 25–70). Springer. DOI: 10.1007/978-3-642-24004-1_2

Jennings, N. R., Sycara, K., & Wooldridge, M. (1998). A roadmap of agent research and development. *Autonomous Agents and Multi-Agent Systems*, *1*(1), 7–38. DOI: 10.1023/A:1010090405266

Kurdi, G. (2022). Toward an electronic resource for systematic reviews in computing.

Lin, H., Zhang, Y., Yu, F. R., Leung, V. C. M., & Zhang, Y. (2023). How generative adversarial networks promote the development of intelligent transportation systems: A survey. IEEE/CAA Journal of Automatica Sinica.

Parunak, H. V. D. (1999). Industrial and practical applications of DAI. In Multiagent systems: A modern approach to distributed artificial intelligence (pp. 337–421).

Radford, A., Wu, J., Child, R., Luan, D., Amodei, D., & Sutskever, I. (2019). Language models are unsupervised multitask learners. *OpenAI Blog*, *1*(8), 9.

Şahin, E. (2004). Swarm robotics: From sources of inspiration to domains of application. In *International Workshop on Swarm Robotics* (pp. 10–20). Springer.

Silver, D., Schrittwieser, J., Simonyan, K., Antonoglou, I., Huang, A., Guez, A., Hubert, T., Baker, L., Lai, M., Bolton, A., Chen, Y., Lillicrap, T., Hui, F., Sifre, L., van den Driessche, G., Graepel, T., & Hassabis, D. (2017). Mastering the game of Go without human knowledge. *Nature*, *550*(7676), 354–359. DOI: 10.1038/nature24270 PMID: 29052630

Smith, R. G. (1980). The contract net protocol: High-level communication and control in a distributed problem solver. *IEEE Transactions on Computers*, *29*(12), 1104–1113. DOI: 10.1109/TC.1980.1675516

Stone, P., & Veloso, M. (2000). Multiagent systems: A survey from a machine learning perspective. *Autonomous Robots*, *8*(3), 345–383. DOI: 10.1023/A:1008942012299

Topol, E. (2019). Deep medicine: How artificial intelligence can make healthcare human again. Hachette UK.

Wooldridge, M. (2009). *An introduction to multiagent systems. John Wiley & Sons. Russell, S. J., & Norvig, P. (2016). Artificial intelligence: A modern approach*. Pearson.

Yu, J., Cai, H., Cheng, J. C. P., Wang, M., & Wong, M. S. (2018). Integrating multi-agent evacuation simulation and multi-criteria evaluation for spatial allocation of urban emergency shelters. *International Journal of Geographical Information Science*, *32*(9), 1884–1910. DOI: 10.1080/13658816.2018.1463442

Chapter 14
Enhancing Quantum Random Number Generators, Cryptographic Security, and Machine Learning-Based Cryptoanalysis

U. Jayalatsumi
https://orcid.org/0000-0001-5642-0010
Dr. M.G.R. Educational and Research Institute, India

T. Godhavari
Dr. M.G.R. Educational and Research Institute, India

Borra Keerthana
Dr. M.G.R. Educational and Research Institute, India

R. Rahul
Dr. M.G.R. Educational and Research Institute, India

B. Swapna
https://orcid.org/0000-0002-7186-2842
Dr. M.G.R. Educational and Research Institute, India

ABSTRACT

Randomness is essential in cryptography for key generation and secure information exchange, ensuring confidentiality and protection. Quantum Random Number Generators (QRNGs) leverage quantum mechanics to produce truly random numbers, offering a major advantage over Pseudo Random Number Generators (PRNGs), which are slower and less secure due to their deterministic nature. Quantum computing boosts QRNG efficiency, making them ideal for cryptographic applications, such as secure key exchange and encrypted communication. QRNGs generate stronger encryption systems by utilizing quantum phenomena like Bloch sphere rotations. The integration of machine learning (ML) with QRNGs

DOI: 10.4018/979-8-3693-8332-2.ch014

further enhances their effectiveness, optimizing random sequences for improved speed and security. This combination of QRNGs and ML provides a powerful approach to cryptography, ensuring more secure communication channels and better protection against potential attacks.

1. INTRODUCTION

Over the years, computers have become smaller and faster due to the shrinking size of their electronic components. This miniaturization has allowed more powerful processors to fit into smaller devices, following a trend known as Moore's Law. However, this process of making transistors—the tiny switches that control the flow of electricity in a computer—smaller is reaching a physical limit. As these transistors approach the size of just a few atoms, they start to behave according to the rules of quantum mechanics, rather than classical physics, which creates new challenges for the future of computing (Marsaglia, 2002 & Rodriguez-Henriquez, 2007).

Electricity is simply the movement of electrons through a material, and transistors control this flow by either allowing electrons to pass through or blocking them. In classical computing, this control forms the basis of how computers process information using binary code—1s and 0s (Stipčević, 2004 & 2007). But when transistors become extremely small, strange quantum effects start to occur. One such effect is quantum tunneling, where electrons can pass through barriers even when, in theory, they shouldn't be able to (Kumar, V at al., 2020). This can cause transistors to malfunction because the electrons can unexpectedly appear on the other side of the barrier, making it difficult to maintain reliable on/off states, which are essential for traditional computing (Kumar, V. V et al., 2002).

Quantum mechanics, the branch of science that studies the behavior of particles at extremely small scales, reveals that particles like electrons do not behave in predictable ways. For example, a particle can be in more than one state at the same time, a phenomenon known as superposition. This means that instead of being either a 0 or a 1, as in classical computing, a quantum particle can be both at the same time until it is observed. This property is the foundation for qubits, the quantum version of bits in classical computers, which allows quantum computers to perform many calculations at once, vastly increasing their potential power (Lydersen et. al., 2010 & 2011).

Another important concept in quantum mechanics is entanglement, where particles become connected in such a way that the state of one particle is directly linked to the state of another, even if they are far apart. This means that measuring the state of one particle will instantly determine the state of the other, no matter the distance between them. This phenomenon, which Albert Einstein called "spooky action at a distance," defies the usual understanding of how particles interact but offers exciting possibilities for quantum communication and computation.

As we approach the physical limits of how small transistors can get, researchers are looking toward quantum computing as the next big leap in technology. Quantum computers use the principles of superposition and entanglement to process information in ways that classical computers cannot, allowing them to solve complex problems much faster. Quantum computing could lead to breakthroughs in fields such as cryptography, medicine, and materials science, solving problems that would take traditional computers far too long to calculate (Ritter, 2002).

However, building quantum computers is incredibly difficult. Quantum systems are very sensitive to their surroundings, and any small disturbance can cause them to lose their quantum properties, a problem known as decoherence (Gottesman, 2004 & Jennewein, 2000). Scientists are working to overcome these obstacles, and while quantum computers are still in the early stages of development, progress is being made. As traditional computing approaches its limits, quantum mechanics could offer a new way forward, providing unprecedented computational power and opening the door to new technological advancements.

2. QUANTUM RANDOMNESS: A LITERATURE REVIEW

Quantum random number generation (QRNG) has attracted significant attention in recent years due to its potential to improve cryptographic systems as studied by Fuerst and Gerhardt (2010) and Kim (2007). Various studies have contributed to the growing body of research in this field, exploring both the technical aspects of QRNGs and their applications in cryptography (Bennett et.al, 1984, 1992). One such study by Maithili, K et al., (2021) focused on the trustworthiness of quantum devices using a symmetric beam splitter. They analyzed the probability cases for splitters and presented the corresponding waveforms, which are critical in ensuring reliable random number generation in quantum systems. (Natarajan, R. et al., 2023) advanced the field by introducing source-device-independent ultrafast QRNGs, demonstrating how independent randomness generation can be achieved, further enhancing the security of cryptographic protocols. Their work laid the foundation for the development of more secure QRNG systems by reducing reliance on specific quantum devices.

Similarly, König, Renner, and Schaffner (2021) contributed by focusing on the Advanced Encryption Standard (AES) in cryptography. They showed that AES techniques, when integrated with quantum systems, result in higher accuracy and better probabilities compared to conventional methods. The AES standards they developed have since been incorporated into various crypto

analysis tools to improve performance. Bennett and Brassard (2021) were pioneers in the field of quantum cryptography, particularly in the areas of public key distribution and coin tossing, key technologies for secure communication. Their work laid the groundwork for quantum encryption and decryption algorithms, which enable secure key generation between sender and receiver. Their research has also highlighted the efficiency of quantum cryptographic techniques over traditional classical computing methods.

In another study, Smith et al. (2021) explored the behavior of simple source device-independent continuous-variable QRNGs. Their work produced independent waveforms and graphs that illustrated the probabilistic and deterministic nature of random number generation in quantum systems. These findings have helped improve the understanding of QRNG behavior, leading to more reliable models for cryptographic applications. Bassham et al. (2020) contributed to the analysis of RNGs by comparing random and pseudo-random number generators in cryptographic contexts. They examined the strengths and weaknesses of various RNG algorithms, models, and graphs, providing valuable insights into their accuracy and reliability. Their research has been instrumental in identifying areas for improvement in RNG design for secure cryptographic systems.

In addition to these key studies, more recent works have continued to push the boundaries of QRNGs and cryptographic analysis. For instance, Yuan et al. (2022) explored the integration of QRNGs with advanced machine learning techniques to enhance the randomness of sequences generated by quantum devices. Their work demonstrated that machine learning could optimize QRNG performance by identifying patterns that might otherwise be overlooked, thus improving the overall security of quantum cryptographic systems. Similarly, Bai et al. (2022) and Walker et. al. (2009) studied the implementation of quantum key distribution (QKD) protocols in real-world scenarios, providing insights into how QRNGs can be applied to strengthen secure communication networks. Their findings emphasized the practicality of quantum cryptography in enhancing data protection across various industries Muthukumaran, V et al., (2021).

Together, these studies highlight the ongoing advancements in QRNG and cryptography research, showing that quantum systems are poised to play a major role in the future of secure communications. By incorporating the principles of quantum mechanics into cryptographic protocols, researchers are building a more secure digital landscape, where random number generation can be achieved with greater accuracy and reliability than ever before by Koti, M. S et al., (2022).

3. PROBLEM DEFINITION

Quantum random number generators (QRNG) are crucial for enhancing the security of cryptographic systems by producing random bits used for encryption. However, the current models of QRNGs face significant issues. One major problem is their accuracy. Presently, QRNGs achieve only about 79.8% accuracy in generating random bits. This level of accuracy can be inadequate for many cryptographic applications, where high levels of randomness are required to ensure that encrypted messages remain secure against potential attacks. Inaccurate random number generation can make it easier for attackers to predict or exploit the generated sequences, thereby compromising the security of the system.

Another critical challenge is the efficiency of existing QRNG-based encryption and decryption algorithms. These algorithms are often slow and cumbersome, resulting in long processing times for encoding and decoding data. This inefficiency can be problematic, especially for applications that require real-time processing or have strict performance requirements. Long runtimes not only hinder the user experience but also increase the risk of security breaches as attackers have more time to exploit weaknesses in the system.

Furthermore, QRNGs can struggle with generating sufficient randomness when dealing with rotations and other complex operations. This limitation can affect the ability to secure messages effectively from eavesdroppers who might attempt to intercept or decode the encrypted information. As a result, there is a need for improvements in QRNG technology to address these issues and enhance both the accuracy and efficiency of cryptographic processes.

4. PROPOSED SOLUTION

The proposed system addresses the limitations of current QRNG models by significantly improving their performance. This system achieves an accuracy of 92.87% in generating random bits, which is a notable enhancement over existing models. The increased accuracy ensures that the random numbers produced are more reliable and less predictable, thereby providing better security for cryptographic applications. This improvement is crucial for maintaining the confidentiality and integrity of encrypted messages.

The proposed system Figure 1. integrates machine learning, specifically a recurrent convolutional neural network (RCNN), to further enhance performance. The RCNN is trained using a large dataset collected during both hardware and software processing stages of the QRNG. By analyzing patterns in long sequences of generated numbers, the RCNN learns to predict future numbers with greater accuracy.

This predictive capability helps in improving the overall randomness of the generated sequences, making them less susceptible to prediction and attack.

Additionally, the proposed system is designed to be compatible with any Windows operating system that meets minimum specifications. This compatibility ensures that the system can be easily deployed and used in a wide range of environments, without requiring specialized hardware or software. By combining improved accuracy with efficient processing and broad compatibility, the proposed system offers a robust solution for enhancing cryptographic security. It addresses the shortcomings of existing QRNG models and provides a more effective tool for securing sensitive information.

Figure 1. Flow diagram of the proposed solution

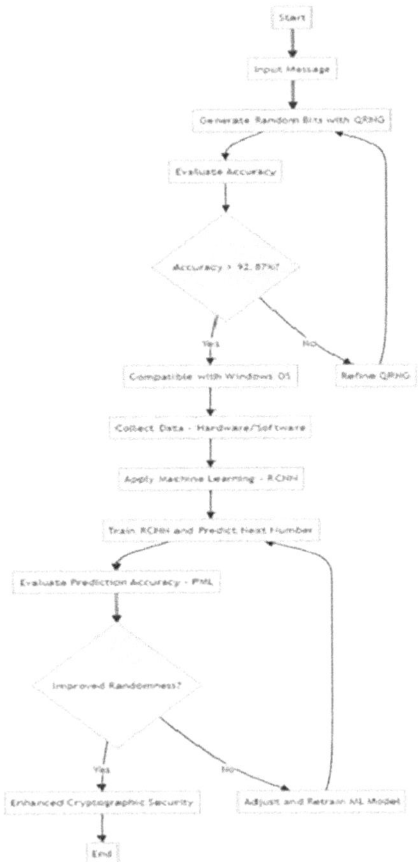

5. OUTPUTS AND DISCUSSION

The primary goal of the project is to ensure the security and confidentiality of information through cryptography using single qubit rotations demonstrated on the Bloch sphere. True random numbers, or more precisely nondeterministic random number generators, are becoming increasingly important. Random numbers are essential in various fields such as cryptography (classical, stochastic, and quantum), Monte Carlo calculations, numerical simulations, statistical research, randomized algorithms, lotteries, and more. Today, true random numbers are especially crucial in cryptography and its numerous applications in cybersecurity, including smart energy grids, e-banking, internet trade, prepaid cards, etc.

This project focuses on developing a quantum random number generation model using cryptography. The model generates random numbers from the input message sent by the sender through single qubit rotations on the Bloch sphere, using the X, Y, and Z axes as bases. The input bit undergoes rotations on the Bloch sphere along the respective axes after the encryption step and is then transferred to the receiver. The receiver applies quantum gates to the message bit and decodes it using asymmetric encryption methods. The randomness generated in the intermediate step prevents eavesdroppers from intercepting the information. This model ensures that the message is transmitted confidentially, without any attacks, and provides a high level of security.

Here's how the protocol works:

- Alice creates a random string of bits, and for each bit, she randomly chooses a basis to encode it in.
- Alice encodes the bits into qubits using her chosen bases, and sends the qubits over a quantum communication channel to Bob's quantum computer.
- Bob also randomly chooses a basis to decode each qubit in. He measures each qubit in the bases he chose.
- Alice uses a classical communication channel to tell Bob which bases she chose. She also tells him the first few bits she sent.
- Bob analyzes these first few bits to determine whether Eve tapped into their quantum communication channel and intercepted Alice's qubits.
- If Eve did *not* intercept the qubits, they consider all of the qubits that they happened to choose the same bases for, and use those bits as their key. If Eve *did* intercept the qubits, they repeat the process all over again.

Figure 2. Qubit rotation

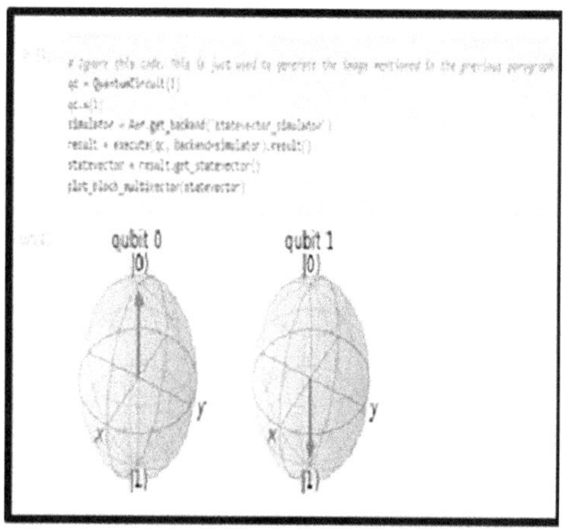

Based on the qubit rotation Figure 2. the qubits for the preparation of bases will be obtained. The qubit rotation is completely random, making it impossible to predict whether the outcome will be 1 or 0. Therefore, the X, Y, and Z bases will be formed based on these random rotations.

The formed bases will then be encoded into their respective axes using selected quantum gates. Gates such as the Hadamard gate, Pauli's X, Y, and Z gates, and the phase gate will be used to form the bases according to the respective values.

A qubit is a three-dimensional vector space used in various quantum computing applications, such as quantum teleportation, single qubit rotations, and multi-qubit rotations. Qubits can represent both 1 and 0 simultaneously due to their superposition state.

Figure 3. Preparation for encoding

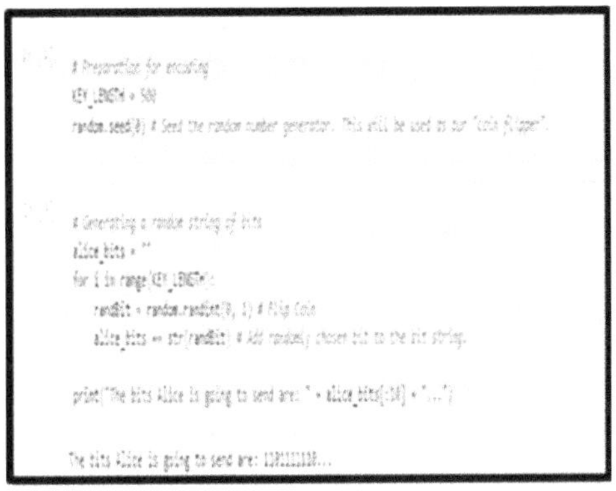

Encoding is a crucial step in the random key generation process, as it involves transforming the bit into specific bases, which then serve as the input for the entire procedure. This step is essential because it sets the foundation for the encryption and transmission process, ensuring that the bit is properly prepared for further operations.

Figure 4. Selection of random basis output

The accurate preparation and encoding of the bit into its respective bases directly influence the security and effectiveness of the key generation. This encoding process, demonstrated in Figure 3. is vital for achieving randomness and maintaining the integrity of the cryptographic system.

Considering the gates, the input from the encoding stage is now transformed into random bases along the X, Y, and Z axes, as shown in Figure 4. This randomness ensures that the encoded information is secure and cannot be easily predicted. Only the receiver, who possesses the correct key, will have the ability to decode the message and retrieve the original output. This secure method of encoding and decoding helps protect the data from potential eavesdroppers, as the random bases create a level of unpredictability that makes unauthorized decryption nearly impossible. This process enhances the overall security of the communication.

Figure 5. Converting bits into basis

Converting the bit into a basis, as illustrated in Figure 5. It involves following specific criteria. For instance, if the qubit is 1, the Hadamard gate is applied, transforming the corresponding bit into the X basis. Similarly, other quantum gates such as Pauli-Y and Pauli-Z are used based on the input qubit state to transform it into the Y or Z bases. This process ensures that the bit is mapped to a quantum state in a secure and randomized manner. The choice of gate is determined by the state of the qubit, ensuring that the transformation adheres to the principles of quantum mechanics. These transformations are essential in cryptography, as they provide the foundation for secure communication, making it nearly impossible for an unauthorized party to decode the information without the correct key and knowledge of the bases.

Figure 6. Output for decoding

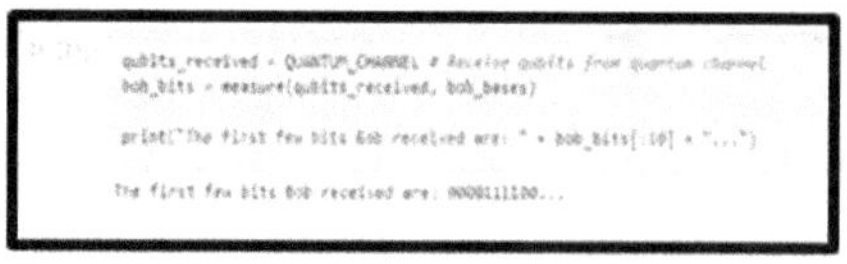

The receiver will receive the bases and decode them using the criteria shared between the sender and receiver. By knowing the first 100 bits the receiver can determine the key, ensuring secure information exchange as shown in Figure 6.

Interception is a common threat to secure channels, potentially compromising authenticity and confidentiality, leading to significant issues. The primary goal of randomness generators is to minimize interception risks. Therefore, a detection mechanism has been included to monitor for any eavesdropping attempts during the transmission, ensuring enhanced security.

Figure 7. Checking for interception

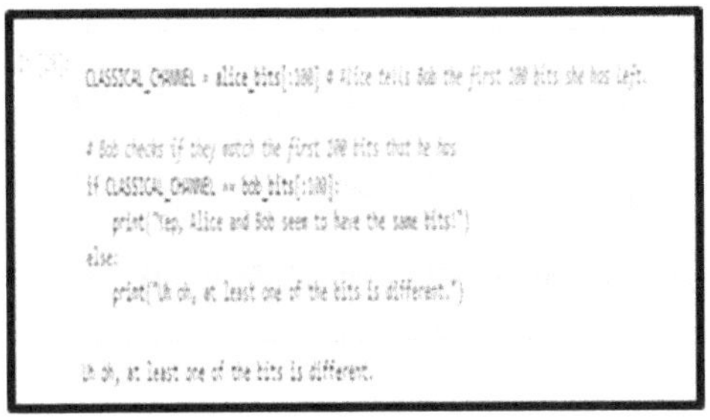

After comparing the first 100 bits, Alice and Bob realize that their bits do not match! Assuming there is no noise in the quantum channel or quantum computers (which could cause errors), Alice and Bob can be certain that their message was intercepted. Consequently, they discard all their bits and restart the protocol from the beginning. This time, they may opt to use a different quantum channel in an attempt to confuse Eve Figure 7.

Additionally, pseudo-random numbers can be generated using a congruential random number generator, as illustrated in Figure 8. In this tutorial, we will use a short period of M=2^12 and generate 1 million 8-bit data.

Figure 8. Generating numbers

Set the input parameters. Currently, the data length is set to 30,000, with 80% allocated for training and 20% for testing, as demonstrated in Figureure 8. Begin with a step size of 20 for faster training.

Figure 9. Training the model

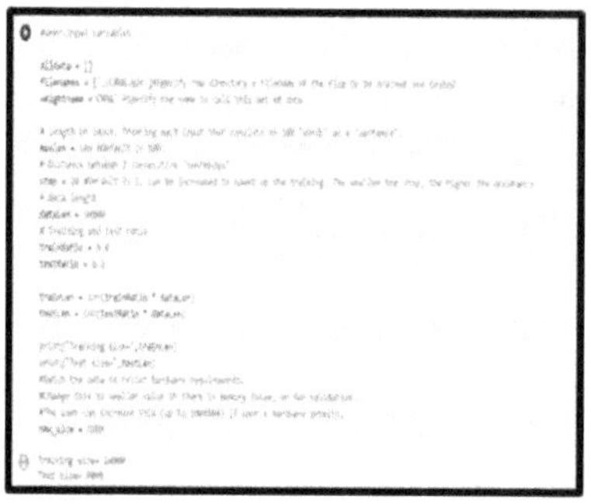

After inputting the parameters into the machine learning model, the model will process these parameters and begin training, as demonstrated in Figure 9. During this training phase, the model will use the provided datasets to learn and optimize its performance. Once the training is complete, the model will display the results of randomness for all possible combinations in a histogram, as shown in Figure 10. This histogram will illustrate the distribution of random numbers generated, allowing for an evaluation of the model's effectiveness in producing truly random outputs.

Figure 10. Histogram equalization

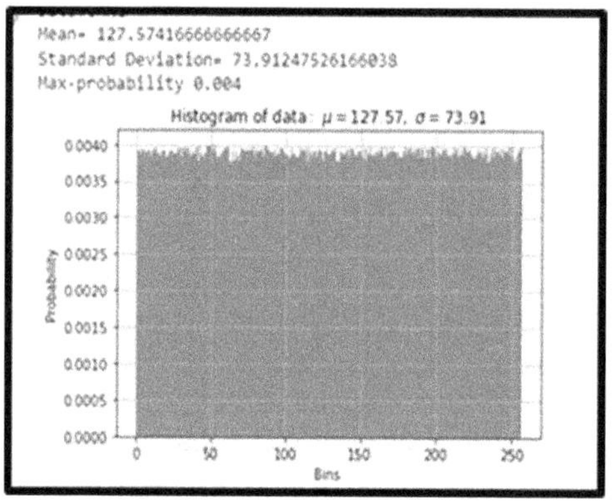

After constructing the model using all the datasets, a comprehensive test will be conducted to evaluate its accuracy and probability across all possible combinations. This testing phase will involve running each test case individually to ensure the model performs effectively in different scenarios. Once all test cases have been executed, a specific test for Quantum Random Number Generators (QRNG) integrated with machine learning (ML) will be carried out. This final test aims to assess the accuracy and performance of the QRNG model when combined with ML techniques, providing insights into the model's effectiveness and reliability in generating random numbers.

Figure 11. Test with ML

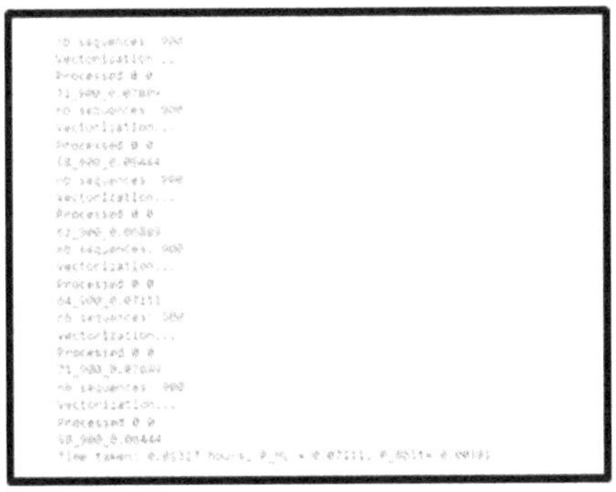

Finally, the results have shown significant improvements, with the quantum random number generator (QRNG) combined with machine learning (ML) achieving a processing time of just 0.05317 hours. This is notably faster compared to conventional random number generators (RNGs). The efficiency of the QRNG with ML is approximately four times greater than that of the previous model, demonstrating a substantial enhancement in performance.

A comprehensive test was conducted see Figure 11. Comparing both classical random number generators (CRNGs) and QRNGs with ML across various evaluation criteria. This testing aimed to determine the performance and effectiveness of each RNG type. The results revealed that QRNGs, when paired with ML, consistently produced superior outcomes compared to CRNGs. This reinforces the QRNG's significant advantages in terms of speed and efficiency, showcasing its ability to generate random numbers more effectively than traditional methods.

6. FINDINGS AND SUGGESTION

The results of 15 different statistical tests conducted on two random number generators (RNGs): Classical Random Number Generator (CRNG) and Quantum Random Number Generator (QRNG) as shown in Table 1. These tests are designed to evaluate various statistical properties that are expected from a truly random sequence of numbers. Each test examines specific attributes, such as frequency, runs, serial correlations, and linear complexity, to determine whether the sequences generated by the RNGs adhere to the expected behavior of random numbers.

The performance of the two RNGs is highlighted in the result by recording whether each RNG passed (success) or failed each test. CRNG, the classical generator, successfully passed 9 out of the 15 tests, whereas QRNG, the quantum-based generator, successfully passed all 15 tests. This suggests that QRNG could be a more reliable and robust source of randomness than CRNG, at least based on the statistical tests conducted.

In addition to pass/fail outcomes, the result includes p-values for each test. The p-value provides a measure of statistical significance, indicating the probability of observing results as extreme as those seen in the test if the RNG were truly random. In simpler terms, lower p-values signal a stronger deviation from randomness, implying that the RNG may not be generating truly random numbers. For instance, if a p-value is significantly low, it raises concerns about the quality of the randomness produced by the generator.

Table 1. Comparison of crng with qrng with ml

	CRNG				QRNG		
Evaluation	M=2^24	M=2^26	M=2^28	M=2^30	P-value	Proportion	Result
Frequency	Failure	Success	Success	Success	0.558502	0.9840	Success
Block-Frequency	Success	Success	Success	Success	0.492436	0.9950	Success
Cumulative sums	Failure	Success	Success	Success	0.360287	0.9880	Success
Runs	Success	Success	Success	Success	0.420827	0.9860	Success
Longest run	Success	Success	Success	Success	0.680755	0.9940	Success
Rank	Success	Success	Success	Success	0.382115	0.9890	Success
FFT	Failure	Success	Success	Success	0.083018	0.9890	Success
Non-overlapping template	Failure	Success	Success	Success	0.016602	0.9860	Success
Overlapping Template	Success	Success	Success	Success	0.639202	0.9900	Success
Universal	Success	Success	Success	Success	0.595549	0.9870	Success
Approximate Entropy	Failure	Success	Success	Success	0.739918	0.9910	Success
Random-excursions	Success	Success	Success	Success	0.284657	0.9904	Success
Random-excursions variants	Success	Success	Success	Success	0.007210	0.9904	Success
Serial	Failure	Failure	Success	Success	0.339271	0.9930	Success
Linear Complexity	Success	Success	Success	Success	0.181557	0.9910	Success
Total successful tests	**9/15**	**14/15**	**15/15**	**15/15**	-	-	**15/15**

The proportion of successes column gives an overall measure of the quality of each RNG. It quantifies the number of successful tests as a fraction of the total tests conducted. A higher proportion of successes signifies better overall performance. For CRNG, the proportion of success is 9/15, while for QRNG, the proportion is a perfect 15/15, clearly indicating that QRNG demonstrates superior performance in the tests. This reinforces the idea that QRNG produces higher-quality randomness, potentially making it a more reliable choice for applications where true randomness is critical.

Despite these promising results for QRNG, it is important to approach the findings with caution. The tests performed are limited in number and scope. Although QRNG outperforms CRNG in these particular 15 tests, further testing across a broader set of conditions and statistical measures would be necessary to conclusively determine whether QRNG is indeed a superior RNG in all contexts. Random number generation is a complex field, and different RNGs can behave differently under various circumstances.

Overall, the findings suggest that QRNG is a more robust and reliable random number generator than CRNG. However, more extensive testing and analysis are essential to confirm the broader applicability and reliability of QRNG for various real-world applications.

7. CONCLUSION

The importance of random numbers for strength of cryptographic protocols not only for quantum and stochastic cryptographies where random numbers are an essential part of data exchanged between communicating parties but also for contemporary deterministic cryptography where un-guess ability and maximal entropy of the random numbers used therein maximizes overall cryptographic strength has been explained.. Quantum random number generation is probably the most mature quantum technology. There has been the multiple ways to harness the randomness in quantum mechanics to produce random bit strings. Physical phenomena such as radioactive decay, photon splitting, noise in Raman amplification, laser phase noise or amplified spontaneous emission can serve as reliable entropy sources.

These quantum random number generators are also proved to have many uses in various fields. The applications of QRNG'S seems to produce great results with minimal number of errors and works efficiently than TRNG's. The developed model of quantum random number generation in cryptographic field produces an accuracy of 91.87% in creating a secret key between two parties and also in finding out the interception. Also the model exhibited outstanding probabilities in all the test cases and conditions without errors proving to be the most efficient technique for confidentiality and authenticity in cryptographic domain.

REFERENCES

Bai, X., Yang, Y., & Zhao, L. (2022). Implementing quantum key distribution protocols for secure networks. *Quantum Information Science*, *15*(3), 101–115.

Bassham, L. E., Rukhin, A. L., Soto, J., Nechvatal, J. R., Smid, M. E., Leigh, S. D., Levenson, M., Vangel, M., Heckert, N. A., & Banks, D. L. (2020). Comparative analysis of random and pseudo-random generators in cryptographic applications. *Journal of Cryptography*, *42*(1), 55–78.

Bennett, C. H., Bessette, F., Brassard, G., Salvail, L., & Smolin, J. A. (1992). Experimental quantum cryptography. *Journal of Cryptology*, *5*(1), 3–28. DOI: 10.1007/BF00191318

Bennett, C. H., & Brassard, G. (1984). Quantum cryptography: Public key distribution and coin tossing. In *Proceedings of the IEEE International Conference on Computers, Systems, and Signal Processing* (p. 175). Bangalore.

Bennett, C. H., & Brassard, G. (2021). Quantum cryptography: Public key distribution and coin tossing. *IEEE Transactions on Information Theory*, *67*(6), 104–119.

Fuerst, M., Weier, H., Nauerth, D. G., Marangon, D. G., Kurtsiefer, C., & Weinfurter, H. (2010). High speed optical quantum random number generation. *Optics Express*, *18*(13), 13029–13037. DOI: 10.1364/OE.18.013029 PMID: 20588431

Gerhardt, I., Liu, Q., Lamas-Linares, A., Skaar, J., Kurtsiefer, C., & Makarov, V. (2010). Perfect eavesdropping on a quantum cryptography system. *arXiv:1011.0105v1[quant-ph].*

Gottesman, D., Lo, H.-K., Lutkenhaus, N., & Preskill, J. (2004). Security of quantum key distribution with imperfect devices. *Quantum Information & Computation*, *4*(5), 325–360. DOI: 10.26421/QIC4.5-1

Jennewein, T., Achleitner, U., Weihs, G., Weinfurter, H., & Zeilinger, A. (2000). A fast and compact quantum random number generator. *The Review of Scientific Instruments*, *71*(3), 1675–1680. DOI: 10.1063/1.1150518

Kim, T., Wersborg, I. S., Wong, F. N. C., & Shapiro, J. H. (2007). Complete physical simulation of the entangling-probe attack on the Bennett-Brassard 1984 protocol. *Physical Review A*, *75*(4), 042327. DOI: 10.1103/PhysRevA.75.042327

König, R., Renner, R., & Schaffner, C. (2021). Advanced Encryption Standard (AES) techniques in cryptography: A study on enhanced accuracy and probability. *Journal of Quantum Computing*, *32*(2), 143–160.

Koti, M. S., Muthukumaran, V., Devi, A., Rajalakshmi, V., Kumar, S. S., & Kumar, V. V. (2022). Efficient Deep Learning Techniques for Security and Privacy in Industry. In Cyber Security and Operations Management for Industry 4.0 (pp. 2-32). CRC Press. DOI: 10.1201/9781003212201-2

Kumar, V., Niveditha, V. R., Muthukumaran, V., Kumar, S. S., & Kumta, S. D. (2021). A quantum technology-based lifi security using quantum key distribution. In Handbook of Research on Innovations and Applications of AI, IoT, and Cognitive Technologies (pp. 104-116). IGI global.

Kumar, V. V., Muthukumaran, V., Ashwini, N., Beschi, I. S., Gunasekaran, K., & Niveditha, V. R. (2022). An efficient signcryption scheme using near-ring hybrid approach for an IoT-based system. International Journal of e-Collaboration (IJeC), 18(1), 1-31.

Lydersen, L., Makarov, V., & Skaar, J. (2011). Secure gated detection scheme for quantum cryptography. *arXiv:1101.5698v1[quant-ph].*

Lydersen, L., Wiechers, C., Wittmann, C., Elser, D., Skaar, J., & Makarov, V. (2010). Hacking commercial quantum cryptography systems by tailored bright illumination. *Nature Photonics*, *4*(10), 686–689. DOI: 10.1038/nphoton.2010.214

Maithili, K., Vinothkumar, V., & Latha, P. (2018). Analyzing the security mechanisms to prevent unauthorized access in cloud and network security. *Journal of Computational and Theoretical Nanoscience*, *15*(6-7), 2059–2063.

Marangon, D. G., Vallone, G., & Villoresi, P. (2021). Source-device-independent ultrafast quantum random number generators and their cryptographic applications. *Nature Quantum Information*, *7*(4), 224–231.

Marsaglia, G. (2002). DIEHARD battery of stringent randomness tests (various articles and software). Retrieved from https://stat.fsu.edu/~geo/diehard.html [Accessed August 2002].

Muthukumaran, V., Kumar, V. V., Joseph, R. B., Munirathanam, M., & Jeyakumar, B. (2021). Improving network security based on trust-aware routing protocols using long short-term memory-queuing segment-routing algorithms. [IJITPM]. *International Journal of Information Technology Project Management*, *12*(4), 47–60.

Natarajan, R., Lokesh, G. H., Flammini, F., Premkumar, A., Venkatesan, V. K., & Gupta, S. K. (2023). A novel framework on security and energy enhancement based on internet of medical things for healthcare 5.0. *Infrastructures*, *8*(2), 22. DOI: 10.3390/infrastructures8020022

Ritter, T. (2002). Random number machines: A literature survey. Retrieved from http://www.ciphersbyritter.com/RES/RNGMACH.HTM [Accessed 2002].

Rodriguez-Henriquez, F., Saqib, N. A., Diaz-Perez, A., & Koc, C. K. (2007). *Cryptographic algorithms on reconFigureurable hardware*. Springer.

Smith, P. R., Marangon, D. G., Lucamarini, M., Yuan, Z. L., & Shields, A. J. (2021). Simple source device-independent continuous-variable quantum random number generator. *Journal of Applied Quantum Mechanics*, *5*(1), 12–24.

Stipčević, M. (2004). Fast nondeterministic random bit generator based on weakly correlated physical events. *The Review of Scientific Instruments*, *75*(11), 4442–4449.

Stipčević, M., & Medved Rogina, B. (2007). Quantum random number generator based on photonic emission in semiconductors. *Review of Scientific Instruments, 78*(4), 045104:1–7.

Walker, J. (2009). Ent: A pseudorandom number sequence test program. Retrieved from https://www.fourmilab.ch/random/ [Accessed 13 August 2009].

Wei, K., Ma, H., & Yang, X. (2021). Trustworthiness of devices in a quantum random number generator based on a symmetric beam splitter. *Journal of Quantum Security*, *4*(3), 88–97.

Yuan, Z. L., Lucamarini, M., Marangon, D. G., Bai, X., & Shields, A. J. (2022). Machine learning-enhanced quantum random number generation for cryptographic applications. *Quantum Information Processing*, *21*(9), 309–320.

Chapter 15
Human–Machine Interactions: Evolution, Current Applications, and Future Prospects

Niharika Gudikandula
https://orcid.org/0009-0008-8963-0944
SR University, India

Ravichander Janapati
SR University, India

Rakesh Sengupta
https://orcid.org/0000-0003-1768-0551
SR University, India

ABSTRACT

Human-Machine Interaction (HMI) studies how a human interacts with a machine, changing the relationship from manual control to intelligent systems. Earlier HMI's were controlled mostly by physical inputs, whereas today's controls depend on GUI, touch, speech (decorated by Natural Language Processing) and gestures to construct a more natural experience. Some more capable systems are voice assistants (Siri and Alexa) these are examples of speech interfaces. The newest technology is the Brain Computer Interface (BCI) where the user is plugged into the machine; BCI technology is also helpful for users with disabilities to directly interact with a machine. Other HMI technology that is noteworthy is haptic interfaces, tangible interfaces and social robots, these types of systems help to foster usability and trustworthiness. HMI technology will continue to evolve in order to create more natural, accessible and intuitive humans and machines interactions.

1. INTRODUCTION

Human-machine interactions (HMI) are the different ways that people talk to and connect with computers. This idea has changed a lot with the advancement of current technology, especially artificial intelligence (AI) (Mourtzis, Angelopoulos, & Panopoulos, 2023). These connections might seem like a lot of different things, from simple mechanical interfaces to complex systems where computers can

DOI: 10.4018/979-8-3693-8332-2.ch015

think and reason like humans. Comprehending the various modes of communication between humans and computers is crucial for understanding the application of technology in our daily lives, professional settings, and social contexts. This abstract looks at the main types of HMI (Ribino, 2023) and describes how they have changed over time, usage now, and might happen in the years to come. Accessibility and HMI are increasingly important in the system development process to increase system functionality and meet users' demands and requirements. HMI aids designers, analysts, and users in determining the requirements of a system based on elements such as text style, fonts, layout, graphics, and colour. Usability, on the other hand, verifies whether the system is efficient, effective, safe, useful, simple to learn, simple to remember, simple to use, and simple to evaluate. It also ensures that the system is practical, visible, and provides job satisfaction to the users. Science and engineering have a close relationship with HMI. Humans possess intellectual complexity, but computers are characterized by their simplicity in design. Through comprehension, individuals may create more sophisticated interactive systems. It has potential applications in several disciplines like psychology, sociology, cognitive science, and linguistics (Obrenovic et al., 2024).

The evolution of Human-Machine Interaction (HMI) technologies, significant gaps remain in the design and the following problem statements emerge. Human-Machine Interaction (HMI) has transitioned away from mechanical tools toward multimodal systems such as voice, gesture, and brain-driven interfaces. Many research studies now focus on isolated modality applications focused on graphical user interfaces (GUIs), natural language processing (NLP), gesture control systems, and brain-computer interfaces (BCIs). They have provided valuable contributions separately to HMI in their own right but between modalities, the research as of now is limited. At the same time, adaptive multimodal systems in which the interaction varies based on the user context and the user's preferences is also underrepresented. Besides these, no current research approaches accessibility, personalization, or cultural adaptability, especially for users with disabilities or users needing unique communication modes.

Another cause of concern is that as artificial intelligence (AI) interfaces become more common in support of the interaction experience, trust and transparency continue to be poorly conceptualized and developed. Although perceptions of important considerations of predictability and feedback, not all systems show these attributes. The perceived need for real world integration of future HMI studies and unique and innovative HMIs like BCIs and haptics further highlights the gap. We require more unified and user-cantered HMI frameworks that cover an adaptive, inclusive, and trustworthy integrated user experience.

2. EVOLUTION OF HUMAN-MACHINE INTERFACES

The changes in technology, users and the interactions between humans and computers led to evolution of HMIs over the decades. The following is a categorization of HMIs where the evolution of HMIs can be mapped across different phases that range from simple mechanical systems to complex intelligent systems that utilize aspects of artificial intelligence and immersion shown in Table 1 and Table 2, we can see the growth of human-machine interaction trends for human-machine interfaces.

The first known HMIs date back to early mechanical based systems used to control simple mechanical devices such as levers and pulleys. The coming of electricity brought electromechanical systems in which operators-controlled machines through switches, dials, and simple control panels. It will be helpful to explain that early telephone switchboard consisted of a series of dials and switches, where operators had to manually connect calls. the Challenges is These systems were: often inefficient; physically onerous; and, subject to human error (Perrow, 2011). In the 1950s with the introduction of computers, HMIs were in the form of batch processing and CLI. Users had to type instructions in machine or assembly languages and computers worked through them in turns. It means that there was no real time communication and these systems could be effectively operated only by specialists. since IBM 704 used punch cards for programming and data as well as input. Nonetheless, of all the Challenges, the difficult and narrow learning curve made it only usable by experienced personnel a major hindrance to extending the scope of practice (Cortada, 2003). The Graphical User Interfaces (GUIs) that characteristic emerged in the 1970s can be termed as a significant advancement in HMI development. Early systems proposed by Xerox PARC's Alto (1973) include the graphical user interface such as windows, icons, menus, and the computer mouse. Apple introduced Macintosh with GUI in 1984 while Microsoft followed with Windows operating systems in the later years. The Macintosh introduced in 1984 was the first mass-produced computer with a graphics-based user interface that simplified the process of using a computer and opened up computing as a field for laymen or novices. However, in the Challenge, these early GUIs were confined to the processing capabilities of the computers and in actuality were more of a one-way street where the user entered commands and the computer executed them (Johnson, 2000).

Gestural interfaces have been more common since the late 1990s and the early years of the 2000s with advances in both mobile and smartphones. Products incorporated touchscreens, which enabled users to interact with objects in the actual sense and practically within the product interface, without the use of a mouse or keyboard. This change was instigated with capacitive touchscreens, a technology that supported multi-touch options. The Apple iPhone which was unveiled in 2007 changed the trend for handling mobile devices and the interfaces that define their usability. However, it is worth noting that older touchscreens used to have problems with responses, and typing on it was not very precise(Norman, 2013) The development of Natural User Interfaces (NUIs) sought to bring interactions with machines to the next level through gestures, voice, and motion. With the help of the joystick (e. g. Microsoft Kinect) and the voice command systems (e. g. Amazon Alexa), people were able to engage with a machine in a more

Table 1. Evolution of HMIs

Era	Time Period	Interaction Technology	Key Features	Key Challenges	Main Industries
Mechanical Era	1800s	Levers, Gears, Basic Machines	Manual control, limited feedback	Precision control, safety, and limited scalability	Manufacturing, Textile Industry
Electro mechanical Era	Early 1900s	Switches, Relays, Telegraphs	Basic electrical machines, predefined inputs	Limited automation, reliability of components	Communications, Early Computing
Early Computing Era	Mid-1900s	Punch Cards, Command-Line Interfaces	Technical interaction, first computers	User complexity, large physical size of machines	Government, Universities, Research
Graphical User Interface (GUI)	1980s-1990s	Desktop GUI, Mouse, Keyboard	User-friendly, visual interaction	Accessibility, interoperability across platforms	Business, Home Computing, Education
Touch & Mobile Interaction	2000s	Touchscreens, Mobile Devices	Intuitive, mobile, accessible anywhere	Battery life, data security, usability on small screens	Consumer Electronics, Healthcare, Retail

continued on following page

Table 1. Continued

Era	Time Period	Interaction Technology	Key Features	Key Challenges	Main Industries
AI & Natural Interaction	2010s-present	Voice Assistants, Gesture Control, Brain-Computer Interfaces (BCI)	Natural, hands-free interaction, AI-powered	Data privacy, AI transparency, ethical concerns	Healthcare, Smart Homes, Consumer Electronics
Future Interaction	Beyond 2020	BCI, Augmented Reality (AR), Virtual Reality (VR)	Highly integrated, human- like collaboration	Ethical AI, neural interface stability, data security	Healthcare, Robotics, Military, Entertainment

natural and organic manner. The Microsoft Kinect (2010) enabled users to play video games by using motion and gestures, bringing an interactive and unique experience. since the Challenge is Despite the growth of technology, NUIs are still characterized by problems concerning accuracy of the gesture or speech recognition system particularly when used by noisy surroundings or people with foreign accents (Wigdor & Wixon, 2011). More recently, however, concepts such as Brain-Computer Interfaces (BCIs) as well as Virtual Reality (VR), and Augmented Reality (AR) have extended the way that HMIs can be implemented. BCIs facilitate interaction with the surroundings and devices, without using typical interfaces such as touch or voice. This technology provides users with interactive experiences with objects and situations in virtual reality as if they are real. This startup company owned by Elon Musk is currently working on the creation of BCIs that will enable users to interact with computers and various other electronics using brain signals. This means that facing a Challenges is BCIs still have certain challenges concerning safety, reliability and accessibility. Likewise, the adoption of VR/AR devices needs additional technological advancements, particularly in size and convenience degrees, before they gain more popularity (Lebedev & Nicolelis, 2006; Slater & Sanchez-Vives, 2016). The adoption of AI in HMIs is considered as a revolutionary change. Machine learning technologies can embed contextual understanding, predict the needs of a user, study behaviour and make human-machine interfaces more natural and intuitive. Artificial intelligence, for example, has already redefined the user experience with devices such as Siri and Google Assistant and, therefore, is making HMIs more predictive within the process of development. Advanced technologies such as AI based voice assistants (Siri, Google Assistant) have made HMIs more natural, interactive and easier. some open Problems concerning privacy, security,

Table 2. Growth of human-machine interaction trends

Category	Metric/Trend	Growth		Source/Date		
AI and Machine Learning	AI-related research output	34.5% annual (2010–2021)	growth	Stanford (2022)	AI	Index
	AI adoption in businesses	270% growth 2019)	(2015–	Gartner (2019)		
	AI in healthcare market	$4.9B in 2020 to $45.2B by 2026 (44.9% CAGR)		Markets and Markets (2021)		

continued on following page

Table 2. Continued

Category	Metric/Trend	Growth	Source/Date
Human-Robot Interaction	Global stock industrial robot	10% annual (2010–2020) growth	International Federation of Robotics (2021)
	Service robot sales growth	32% growth in 2020	IFR (2021)
	Collaborative (Cobots) robots	41.8% CAGR 2026) (2020–	IFR (2021)
Voice Interaction	Global smart speaker sales	114M units (2019) 163M units (2021) to	Statista
	Global voice assistants	4.2B in 2020 to 8B by 2024	Juniper Research
	Speech recognition error rate	Less than 5%	Various AI publications
Wearable Tech & AR	Global wearables market	173.5M units in 2018 to 444.7M units in 2023	Statista
	AR market size	$6.12B in 2021 to $97.76B by 2028 (47.7% CAGR)	Various market reports
Human-Computer Interaction (HCI)	HCI publication trends	25% annual (2016–2021) growth	ACM Digital Library
	Rise of multimodal interaction	Increasing use of touch, voice, gesture, gaze	Various studies HCI research
Autonomous Systems & Human Oversight	Autonomous vehicle market	$76B in 2020 to $2.16T by 2030	Allied Market Research
	Human-AI collaboration in decision-making	Outperforms humans or Machines alone in key tasks	MIT research
Brain-Computer Interfaces (BCI)	Global BCI market size	$1.3B in 2020 to $5.3B by 2027	Fortune sights Business In-
	Neural interface research	Demonstrations of direct brain-to-machine communication	Neuralink (2021)
Ethics Privacycerns and Con	Public concerns about AI and automation ethics	68% expect significant challenges by 2035	Pew Research Center

and ethical aspects of decision-making with the help of artificial intelligence are still unanswered (Russell & Norvig, 2016). Therefore, it can be seen that under the category of Human-Machine Interfaces the opportunities for interaction between a man and machine have enlarged greatly due to the shift from inputs such as a mechanical lever towards artificial intelligence Systems. The HMIs can and should integrate AI, AR/VR, and BCIs more broadly in the future to improve the user experiences and create better, more personalized, more immersive interactions.

3. DESIGN OF HUMAN-MACHINE INTERFACES

The design of HMIs varies based on the specific application and technology in use, but several core elements are typically involved:

User Interface is the main, if not the only means by which the human operator communicates with the machine shown in Figure 1. It comprises a number of input and output devices including touch screens, video displays and voice activated devices. The idea is to build an interface that will allow a user to manage the machine or system in a very efficient manner.

Application Layer is responsible for the execution of the HMI system, it will perform its activities that will enable it attain its goals and objectives. What makes application layer versatile is it can be a single software that is used to manage one object, or a system that uses several objects simultaneously while it should interact with other outer software systems.

Middleware Layer is yet another component located between the application layer and the physical hardware layer, through which all communication must pass. They include data handling to see that they get to their destinations, communication protocols to make sure the system runs smoothly and security.

Figure 1. Block diagram for human machine interaction

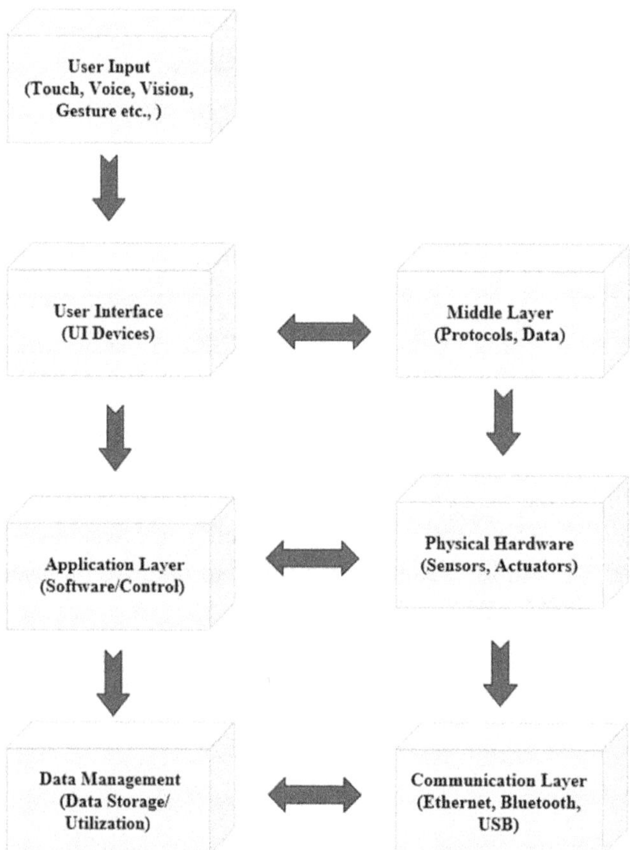

HMI system physical entities involve equipment such as sensors, actuators, and control systems. All these elements are central to the system in the task of capturing user inputs and information from the operating environment in order to carry out certain actions. The hardware supports the system's capabilities of reacting to human control and other factors in real time. Several forms of communication Standards allow for interaction between the different modules of the HMI architecture. In this model, Ethernet, Bluetooth, and USB are some of the transfer technologies for data that guarantee compatible systems operations in the system. Manage data determines how the HMI system treatment and storage of that data as well as its utilization. This involves aspects of systems and their usage by the users as well as other aspects of usage as well. Proper handling of data is important so that the working of a system can be adjusted according to the feedback taken over time and derived from previous data achieved.

4. MODERN HUMAN-MACHINE INTERFACE TECHNOLOGIES

The first type of HMI was manually operated interactions, which let people directly handle tools using mechanical parts. This type of contact requires human effort to function because it uses handles, buttons, switches, and other physical tools. Traditional control systems are still

Table 3. HMIs and real-world applications

HCI Type	Description	Real-World Applications
Graphical User Interface (GUI)	Interaction through graphical elements like icons, buttons, and menus.	Desktop applications (e.g., MS Office), web browsers, mobile apps, operating systems like Windows or macOS.
Command-Line Interface (CLI)	Text-based interaction where users input commands via a terminal.	System administration, coding environments, servers, and development tools like Linux Terminal and PowerShell.
Voice User Interface (VUI)	Interaction using voice commands and responses.	Virtual assistants (e.g., Alexa, Siri, Google Assistant), smart home devices, voice-controlled navigation systems.
Touch-Based Interaction	Interaction through touch-sensitive screens or panels.	Smartphones, tablets, kiosks, ATM machines, touch-enabled devices in retail or healthcare.
Gesture-Based Interaction	Using body movements, often captured by sensors, for interaction.	Gaming consoles (e.g., Microsoft Kinect, Nintendo Wii), virtual reality (VR), AR systems in training or simulation.
Wearable Interfaces	Interaction through wearable devices that track movement, biometric data, or provide haptic feedback.	Smartwatches (e.g., Apple Watch, Fitbit), fitness trackers, wearable health monitors, augmented reality glasses like HoloLens or Google Glass.
Brain-Computer Interface (BCI)	Direct communication between the brain and a computer, of- ten using EEG or other sensors.	Assistive technologies for the disabled, gaming, neurofeedback therapy, cognitive research, emotion detection, and prosthetic control.
Haptic Feedback Interfaces	Using tactile responses (vibrations, resistance) to enhance interaction.	Gaming controllers, virtual reality gloves, medical training simulators, and industrial robotics.

continued on following page

Table 3. Continued

HCI Type	Description	Real-World Applications
Augmented Reality (AR)	Overlaying digital information on the real world through de- vices like glasses or smart- phones.	AR gaming (e.g., Pok´emon Go), industrial maintenance, retail (virtual try-ons), education, and training simulations.
Virtual Reality (VR)	Fully immersive digital environments created using head- sets and other sensory input devices.	Gaming, therapy for PTSD, architectural visualization, virtual tourism, and military or medical training.
Natural Language Processing (NLP)	Enabling systems to under- stand and respond to human language input.	Chatbots, customer service (e.g., automated help desks), language translation tools (Google Translate), and content summarization tools.
Multimodal Interfaces	Combining multiple interaction types (e.g., voice + gesture) for richer experiences.	Advanced AI systems, smart home integration, medical diagnostics, and immersive education platforms combining voice, touch, and gesture- based interactions.
Eye-Tracking Inter- faces	Tracking user eye movement to enable interaction or provide insights.	Assistive technologies for people with disabilities, gaze-based control in gaming, and marketing insights in retail environments (e.g., understanding consumer focus areas).
Tangible User Interfaces	Physical objects are used as in- put devices that are linked to digital information.	Interactive museum exhibits, tangible programming kits for education (e.g., Osmo), and creative design tools in architecture or product design.
Ubiquitous Computing	Seamless integration of computing into everyday objects and environments.	Smart homes (IoT devices), wearable health monitors, context-aware systems (e.g., location-based services), and predictive maintenance in industrial settings.

common in many areas, such as cars, industry equipment, and home appliances. For example, to drive a car, you need to use a steering wheel, pedals, and gear changes, which are all physical tools that let the driver connect with the car. Users don't need much training to start using these platforms because they are easy to use and reliable. This makes them suitable for jobs that need precise and direct control. But because they depend so much on the user's physical skills and attention, they aren't very complicated or useful. As technology has improved, it has become easier to explore the full potential of your bodily abilities and enhance the focus on you like never before. This has led to the creation of automatic and user-friendly graphics displays. Various types of HMIs are shown in Figure 2 and Table 3.

Figure 2. Human-machine interface technologies

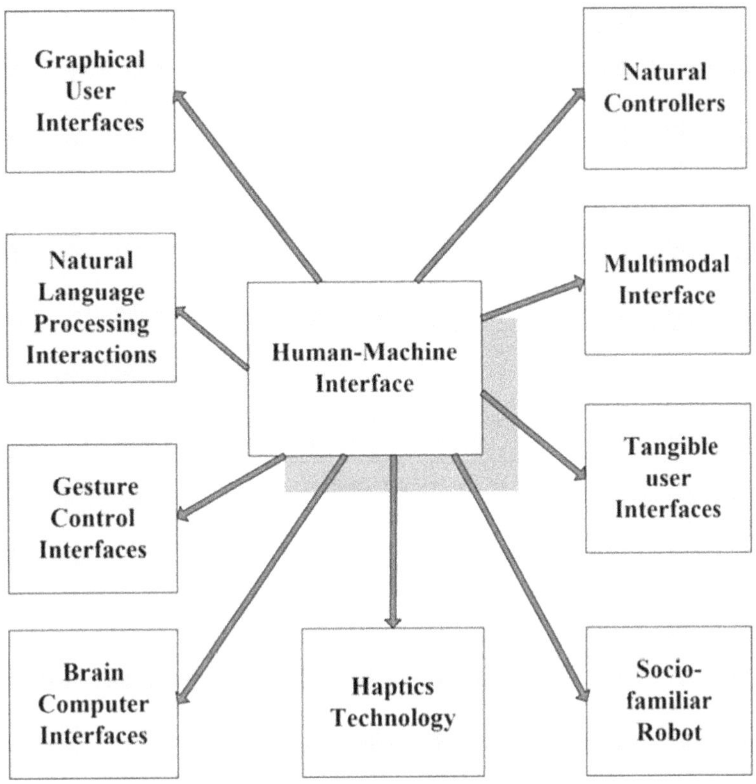

4.1 Graphical User Interfaces

Graphical User Interfaces (GUIs) (Martinez, 2011)are a big step forward in how people and machines work together because they let individuals connect with computers using pictures like buttons, menus, and icons. Moving away from text-based command-line interfaces that required memorizing specific phrases, GUIs changed computers by making them easier for a wider range of people to use. Almost all computers and electronics today, including PCs, smartphones, ATMs, and game systems, use GUIs. They make it easier for people to use technology by letting them do complicated jobs with simple movements like clicking, moving, and dropping. GUIs are successful because they can show information in a way that is both visually appealing and simple to understand. This makes it easier to move around in software programs and interact with them. As GUIs have changed over time, they have also made way for touch interfaces, which let people use touchscreens to connect directly with devices. These days, you can find them on all smartphones, tablets, and other movable devices. They make contact more natural and quicker than traditional mouse and computer sets.

4.1.1 Required Components of GUI

GUI of a system mainly depends on the operating system, the platform and the utility of the platform. It is, however, necessary to note that most GUIs have similarities, albeit the differences in the sub-components. Below are some of the primary elements of GUIs shown in Table 4.

Table 4. Required components of GUI

Component	Description
Windows	GUI-based software splitting the screen into zones for tasks like typing programs, viewing directories, or displaying plots.
Desktop	Serves as the primary workspace and homepage, presenting icons and links to various system operations.
Icons	Small graphics representing tasks, programs, files, or folders. Found on desktops, toolbars, ribbons, and menus, they allow users to perform functions with a click.
Pointing Device	Devices like a mouse, trackball, or touchpad for guiding the cursor, selecting objects, resizing windows, or displaying tooltips.
Menus	Provide a list of options similar to a restaurant menu, enabling users to choose commands or actions within programs.
Shortcut Menus	Context-sensitive menus invoked by right-clicking, offering options specific to the clicked area.
Drop-down Menus	Compact menus displaying only a current choice and an arrow. Clicking the arrow reveals more options.
Toolbars	Horizontal strips with grouped icons or buttons, often customizable for visibility and positioning.
Ribbons	Groups of toolbars introduced in Microsoft Office 2007, organized by tabs with context-relevant controls.
Dialog Boxes	Pop-up windows offering information or requesting input, such as" File Overwrite" or" Open File" dialogs.
Buttons	Interactive elements initiating actions on click, often selectable using the spacebar or Enter key.
Radio Buttons and Checkboxes	Selection tools where radio buttons allow one choice, while checkboxes permit multiple selections.
Text Boxes	Input fields for entering text, such as a URL bar in a web browser.

4.1.2 General Guidelines for GUI Design

Contrary to what some may believe it is particularly important when developing GUIs not to view the design process as a technological problem but a user-cantered problem. The initial choices that developers should make include, a) the intended user, b) activities the GUI should support and c) the goals the GUI should address. It must make learning as easy as possible and structure the controls in a way that would allow users to quickly find the one, they need — with the help of tooltips, concise labels, etc are shown in Table 5. Wireframes, the first drafts, and users' feedback are crucial to completing before the development of an application's interface starts because then, the efficiency is better aligned to the expectations of users. Use case diagram of Human-

Machine GUI consists of six primary components: User Command, Input Interface, Control Module, Computer Module, Output Interface, and User Response shown in Figure 3.

Figure 3. GUI interface technologies

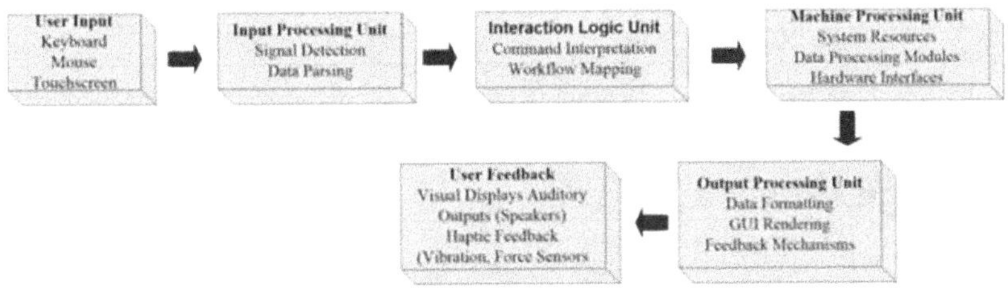

The User Input block depicts the user interface through which the customers operate the system employing the keyboard, touch sensitivity, voice tone, or hand movements. These inputs are Mean while these inputs are indicators from human actions and events perceived by the system. The Input Processing Unit recognizes these signals, the signal may be speech recognition modules for voice commands or gesture recognition modules for motion data, messages and passes it to the Interaction Logic Unit. This unit serves as the control centre of the system whereby it analyses user requirements and translates them to the right commands for the machine. These commands are also carried out by the Machine Processing Unit through system assets, data processing tools, and hardware interfaces, to guarantee that all assignments are well-done. Thereafter, the Output Processing Unit converts human understandable outputs in the form of tapes, graphs, audio signals, numbs or another haptics. Last, the User Feedback component is responsible for the result presentation so the user can interact with the desired outputs in the form of visual, sound, touch, etc. This iterative structure achieves real time interaction to improve user experience and system capability in contexts such as VR, robotics, and user interactive software systems.

Table 5. Tools for developing GUIs

Tool	Description	Features
Qt	Cross-platform C++ library for GUIs	Widgets, event handling, layout management, Qt Designer for drag-and-drop GUI creation.
Tkinter	Python library for simple GUIs	Basic widgets (buttons, labels, text entry), ideal for small applications, easy for beginners.
JavaFX	Framework for rich desktop applications in Java	2D/3D graphics, UI controls, multimedia, web content, animations, and CSS styling.
Electron	Framework for cross-platform desktop apps using web technologies (HTML, CSS, JavaScript)	Native system API access, web-based UI, used for apps like Visual Studio Code.
Gtk	GUI toolkit primarily used in Linux environments, with bindings for other languages	Rich set of UI components, layout management, theme customization.

continued on following page

Table 5. Continued

Tool	Description	Features
SwiftUI	Declarative framework for iOS, macOS, watchOS, tvOS	Declarative syntax, dark mode support, accessibility, and animations.
WPF	Framework for building Windows-based applications with .NET	Advanced graphics, data binding, multimedia integration, rich set of controls.

4.2 Natural Language Processing

A more advanced way for people and machines to talk to each other is through Natural Language Processing (NLP) (Nadkarni et al., 2011) connections, which let humans talk or write to machines. NLP interactions let computers understand, process, and react to human words in a way that is similar to how people talk. Virtual helpers like Siri, Alexa, and Google Assistant use this type of contact a lot. These agents allow users to do chores, ask questions, and manage smart devices by speaking to them. The growth of NLP has expanded the ways that people and machines can talk to each other. This has made using technology easier for people who aren't as comfortable with traditional platforms. Disabled people can use technology more comfortably with voice-controlled systems. NLP systems use complicated algorithms and machine learning methods to process and understand language. This lets them handle a lot of different inputs and give answers that make sense in the given context. Even though NLP systems have come a long way, they still have trouble understanding subtleties, accents, and slang, which can lead to mistakes. A few studies are reviewed in Table 7.

4.2.1 Concepts and Techniques of NLP

NLP system is typically structured into several stages: Listening and Expectation Fulfilment, Speech Recognition and Parsing, Natural Language Comprehension, Practical Reasoning, Language Generation and Formulation, and Utterance Creation and Response Generation. Incorporated into each stage are relevant techniques that enable successful completion of the stage tasks shown in Figure 4. The most basic stage of this input processing is the conversion of the user inputs into text, voice or multimodal inputs, text, gesture or image. Speech inputs are captured through Automatic Speech Recognition (ASR) systems including Deep Speech and Whisper using acoustic and language model. Text inputs include natural language pre-processed through tokenization and noisy features removal, by the help of the NLTK or Spacy libraries, for instance. The third process that follows feature extraction is transforming raw data into formats that are easy to analyse where text features are obtained using simple methods such as TF-IDF, BoW, or complex ones like Word2Vec, GloVe or BERT. For instances, features such as MFCCs and spectrograms when used for speech are processed through structures such as Wavenet.

Figure 4. Block diagram of voice activated systems

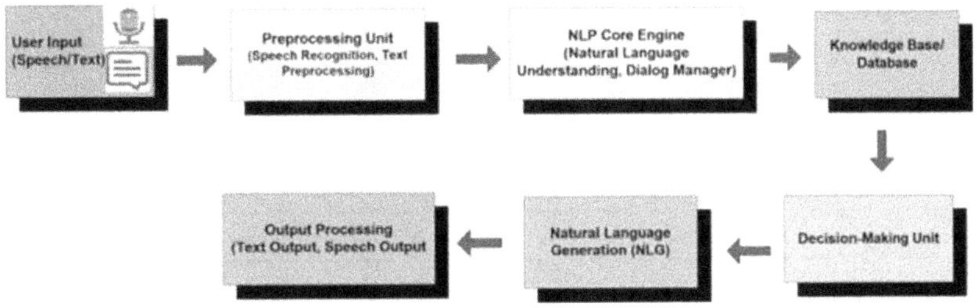

As with the NLU stage, the system decodes the meaning of inputs via semantic analysis and BERT, and others. User goals like command or question are determined through the classification models including SVM or else neural networks. Some of the libraries used include But what is the role of names, places, times, which can be generally translated to Named Entity Recognition (NER). Dialogue management keeps records of flow of the conversation this can be through RNNs, LSTMs or GPT. NLG writes out the system recommendations in natural language and output processing presents the results through GUIs or via voice; using tools such as Tacotron or WaveNet. This integration of the stages allows HMI systems to work in a number of settings including customer support chatbots and virtual personal assistants, as well as in healthcare and education applications. Siri and Alexa, as voice-based assistants, are proper examples of a mutually integrated solution of SRS, NLU, DM, and TTS that illustrate the reliability and universality of HMI NLP systems.

4.3 Gesture-Based Interface

While using a gesture-based interface (Costagliola et al., 2023), users can handle tools with gestures and body movements. Most of the time, these interfaces use sensors, cameras, and motion-detection technologies to track what the user does and turn that information into orders that the machine can follow. In games, virtual reality (VR), and augmented reality (AR) apps, gesture-based interactions have become popular because they make the experience more engaging and involved. For example, gaming devices like the Nintendo Wii and Microsoft Kinect allow users

Table 6. Notable gesture-based interfaces (2000–2025)

System	Gesture Type	Technology Used	Application Area
Microsoft Surface	Multi-touch, drag, pinch	Capacitive touch + Vision	Tabletop computing
SixthSense	Hand gestures	Camera + Color markers	Wearable computing, AR
Kinect for Xbox 360	Full-body gestures	Infrared depth camera	Gaming, education, rehab
Leap Motion Controller	Finger/hand gestures	IR sensors + Motion tracking	3D interaction, VR
Google Soli	Micro-gestures	Radar-based sensing	Smartwatches, IoT devices
Myo Armband	Arm gestures, EMG	EMG + IMU sensors	Music, prosthetics, gaming
Oculus Quest Hand Tracking	Hand and finger tracking	Computer vision + AI	Virtual reality, gaming

continued on following page

Table 6. Continued

System	Gesture Type	Technology Used	Application Area
Gaze + Gesture GUI (Research)	Combined eye + hand gestures	Eye tracking + hand tracking	Assistive tech, XR
HoloLens 2 Hand Tracking	Mixed reality hand gestures	Depth sensors + AI	Industrial AR, healthcare
AI-Gesture UIs	Personalized gesture mapping	AI + motion tracking	Smart homes, healthcare
BCI-Gesture Interface	Mental + physical gestures	EEG + IMU fusion	Neuroadaptive systems
Multimodal AR UI (Latest)	Gesture + voice + gaze	ML + depth cam + NLP	XR, education, training

to interact with games by moving their bodies. This makes for a more fun and busy way to pass the time. In VR and AR settings, users can also move their bodies and use hand movements to interact with virtual items and move around in digital surroundings, making the experience more natural. Gesture-based systems have a lot of promise in healthcare, too. Doctors and nurses could use them for online treatments or physical therapy routines, allowing them to interact with patients or medical tools without direct touch. A gesture-based interface is an easy method of communication between human and machine in which the physical gesture set to mean commands. Such motions may be made with hands, face or body postures, among such motions are-postures of appreciation-object manipulation. All these interfaces are actively used in various areas including VR and AR, robotics and gaming industries. The system involves several components which are each essential in gesture recognition and response generation shown in Figure 5.

Figure 5. Block diagram of gesture based interface systems

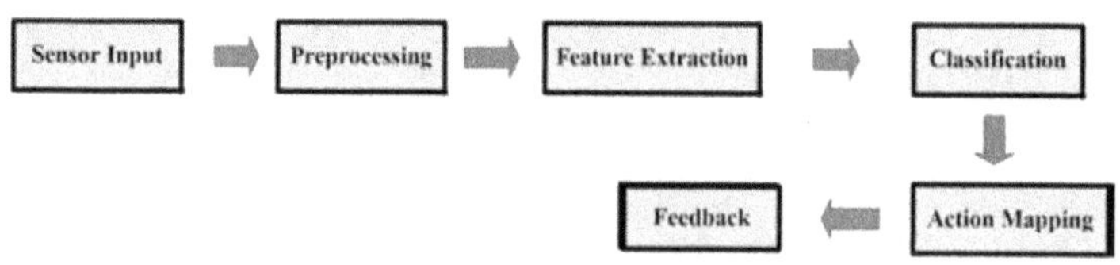

The gesture recognition process starts with the sensor inputs; visual cameras, depth sensors (Kinect), motion sensors worn on the body, and Light, Detection, and Ranging (LiDAR) used to capture user gestures. This data is raw and needs to be pre-processed to filter out noise and to improve the strength of the signal with the help of process such as filtering, background subtraction and segmentation. Noise reduction is performed with median filtering technique, Gaussian filtering, and Kalman filtering whereas normalization brings renormalize the data to the range of 0 to 1. In feature extraction, essential characteristics such as the state of the hand in terms of the fingers, position of the joints and the motion formed by the hand are also determined. This is done by employing edge detection, the Skeleton model tracking and time domain characteristics such as mean and Standard deviation, and other models such as the CNN and PCA for dimensionality reduction. After extracting the features, the gestures are classified using other machine learning algorithms involving Support Vector Machines, K Nearest Neighbours as well as other deep learning technologies such as Convolutional Neural Networks, Recurrent Neural Networks and Long Short-Term Memory respectively. After classification, action mapping matches each gesture with the system action through direct mapping, rule-based mapping, and even contextual mapping. Table 6 shows a **gesture-based interfaces** developed between 2000 and 2025, including a brief description, key technologies used. Haptic, video or graphical output is given back to the user to make the interaction natural and effortless. These stages combined form a responsive, flexible, and user-friendly gesture-based system with applications ranging from robotics to assistive technologies.

4.4 Brain-Computer Interfaces

Brain-Computer Interfaces (BCIs) (Wu et al., 2023) are a new and advanced way for humans and machines to communicate, allowing brains and computers to talk to each other directly. BCIs work by picking up and figuring out the brain's nerve patterns, then turning them into orders that computers can follow. This technology has the ability to change how people and machines work together, especially in health, therapy, and neuroprosthetics. For instance, BCIs enable paralyzed individuals to operate wheelchairs, artificial arms, or computers simply by thinking about them. This type of contact opens up new options for disabled people, giving them more freedom and making their lives better overall. Currently, BCIs are in their early stages of development, primarily utilized in research and healthcare environments. But as technology improves, BCIs may become easier for more people to get. This would open up new ways for people and machines to connect and help us learn more about the brain.

4.4.1 Model Architecture for BCIs

A BCI system has several stages and all play a vital role in translating signals recorded from the scalp into commands that can be acted upon. The first nine stages are Signal Acquisition, Preprocessing, Feature Extraction, Signal Classification, Control Output, and Feedback shown in Figure 6. All of them use different techniques in order to provide the processing of all signals accurately and the communication of the brain with outer devices.

Figure 6. Block diagram of brain computer interface systems

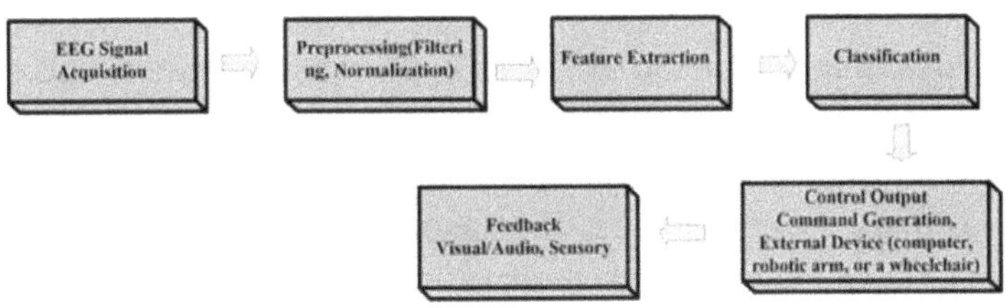

The first method, Signal Acquisition, include collection of signals due to the brain's electrical activity. The three most frequently used diagnostic techniques are: Electroencephalography (EEG) where electrodes are attached to the scalp to pick electrical activity. EEG was commonly used for non-invasive BCIs because the device is relatively easy to use and inexpensive as well as having relatively low invasiveness. In contrast, invasive techniques involve the direct implantation of electrodes in the brain to get better, faster and more specific signals of the electrical activity in the human brain. These are risk-handler methods and are more complicated compared with the previous methods, but for managing SCI patients who need a fine control of external equipment's, these methods are of great significance. Other processes are employed but they are comparatively costly and relatively impractical for applications that require real-time control as is the case with fNIRS and fMRI.

Table 7. Brain-computer interface (BCI) devices

Year	Device Name	Type	Signal Acquisition	Applications
2003	g.USBamp	Research-grade	Wet EEG electrodes	Neuroscience, BCI research
2007	Emotiv EPOC	Consumer-grade	14-channel EEG (saline sensors)	Gaming, emotion recognition, neurofeedback
2009	NeuroSky MindWave	Consumer-grade	1-channel dry EEG	Attention monitoring, education
2011	OpenBCI Cyton	Open-source	8/16-channel dry/wet EEG	DIY BCI, research, prosthetics
2012	g.Nautilus	Research-grade	Wireless dry/wet EEG (up to 64 ch)	Mobile EEG, neuroimaging
2015	Brainlink Lite	Consumer-grade	3-channel dry EEG	Meditation, concentration training
2018	Unicorn Hybrid Black	Research-grade	8-channel dry EEG	Education, healthcare, BCI research
2019	NextMind Dev Kit	EEG + VEP	Visual Evoked Potentials (dry)	Visual attention, AR/VR control
2020	Cognionics Quick-20	Wireless dry EEG	20-channel dry electrodes	Clinical and mobile EEG research
2021	Kernel Flow	fNIRS + BCI	Functional near-infrared	Cognitive neuroscience, wearable neuroimaging
2022	Emotiv Insight 2	Wireless consumer	5-channel EEG (dry)	Health tracking, cognitive training
2023	Neurable Enten	EEG wearable	Dry EEG, audio interface	Focus tracking, productivity
2024	OpenBCI Galea	Multimodal	EEG + EMG + EDA + PPG + eye tracking	Emotion research, AR/VR, gaming
2025	Cognix Fusion	Multimodal BCI	EEG + AI-based filtering	Emotion-adaptive interfaces, neurogaming

The first step in the BCI process is preprocessing in which attained brain signals are pre-processed to eliminate interference and noisy data. Methodology like bandpass filtering, Independent Component Analysis (ICA) and Blind Source Separation (BSS) are applied to remove artifacts from electro myography (EMG), electro ocular activity (EOG) and electromagnetic interference (EMI). Normalization brings uniformity in amplitudes thereby eliminating discrepancies due to channel differences and environment of different sensors' positions. After preprocessing again, feature extraction process converts the raw signals into meaningful features including time domain values (mean, variance, skewness, kurtosis) and PSD based frequency domain features covering alpha, beta, theta and delta bands of human brain. Feature selection we find out which of the given features that are useful in the particular. Filter procedures apply the use of statistical tests such as correlation or mutual information. Techniques like Wrapper methods; Recursive Feature Elimination (RFE), genetic Algorithms (GA), and Particle Swarm Optimization (PSO). Embedded techniques like LASSO and Tree-based models which estimate importance during the model building process. The dimensionality reduction methods that include the PCA, ICA and the LDA are techniques are used. Finally, classification of the extracted feature signals is done with a view of identifying the most suitable method of signal classification that can greatly enhance the accuracy and stability with methods such as KNN, SVM, LDA, CNN, RNN, among others. The classified signals are then converted to other control signals like the Robotic prosthetics or a computer pointer for use on other peripheral devices. Lastly, feedback in form of either visual, auditory or even touch (such as feeling a vibration in a prosthetic) is given in real-time to the end-user. Table 7 shows a comprehensive table of BCI devices developed or widely studied between 2000 and 2025, including their type, signal acquisition method, applications BCI Devices (2000–2025). Hardware improvements add new features to BCIs making them more performant and affordable for new uses such as rehabilitations or co-robots.

4.5 Haptic Devices Interface

One way that people and machines can communicate is through haptic devices, which use touch. These devices provide users with a more realistic and engaging contact experience by incorporating force feedback and physical feelings. Haptic technology (Adilkhanov, Rubagotti, & Kappassov, 2022) often enhances user presence and involvement in games, virtual reality, and medical simulators. Video games use haptic controls and devices to provide players with real-world input, such as tremors or resistance, in response to their actions. This makes the experience more realistic because players feel like they are really dealing with the virtual world. Haptic displays assist in training doctors and other medical workers by providing precise feedback during procedures. This lets trainers improve their skills in a controlled setting, which helps them get better before they do real surgeries. Haptic interfaces could also be useful for remote operations because they give workers physical feedback while they're doing things like flying a drone or doing robotic surgery. This makes it easier to be precise and in charge of difficult tasks. Haptic-based technologies use a broad spectrum of techniques to each of these stages to guarantee timely, responsive interaction with virtual worlds shown in Figure 7.

Figure 7. Block diagram of heptic interface systems

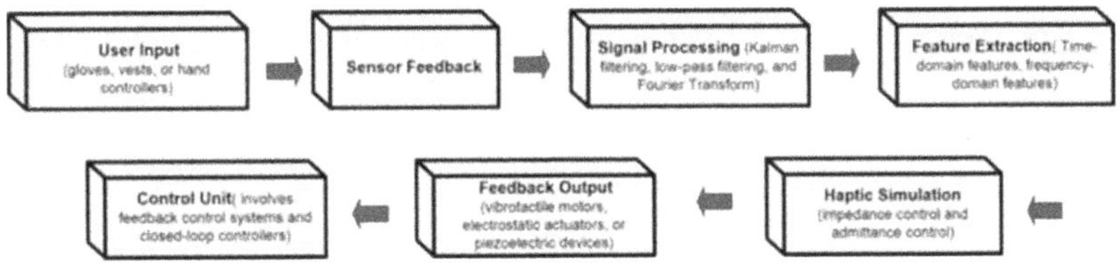

The haptic devices can detect the user's interactions, for example, data gloves employ flex sensors and motion capture systems employ infrared cameras. Such sensors like accelerometers and gyroscopes worn on controllers or suits follow motion and spatial orientation. Also, my EMG sensors pick the muscle activity while infra-red LEDs facilitate proper three-dimensional space detection. Information feedback from haptic interfaces is transmitted through force sensitive resistors, accelerometers and piezoelectric sensors which quantify the vibrations or pressure and makes the user feel them. Strain gauges are also employed in wearable devices to measure the change in materials, while eye movements can be recorded by EOG to control haptic devices. Some electronic filter methods like Kalman filtering and Fourier Transform are employed in the treatment of sensor data to minimize noise. Multi-resolution analysis is possible through wavelet transforms and the real-time process has been boosted by DSP and FPGA. Feature extraction mostly concentrate on position, velocity, force and acceleration and mostly in reducing dimensionality by use of PCA. Dynamic techniques contribute to the characterization of the interactions of objects within the virtual environment, and impedance and admittance control representing natural interaction with these environments. The feedback output is achieved using actuators such as vibrotactile, electrostatic, or piezoelectric motors while using Deep Reinforcement Learning (DRL) among other advanced AI methods enhances the system's way of functioning based on the user's behaviour to deliver appropriate and accurate haptic feedback. Haptics used in robotics involve communication in both ways; robots can apply analysis and ranking to the surrounding objects and people and in return give humans perfect feeling through touch. This section explores five types of tactile interfaces: robot e-skin, sensors of robots, human e-skin, haptic gloves, contactless devices shown in Table 8 and 9.

Table 8. Haptic sensors for various application

Sensor/Actuator	Category	Tasks	Applications
Piezoelectric Sensor	Sensing	Detecting, locating and recognizing human touches	Social robots
Piezoresistive Sensor	Sensing	Human pose and action classification; Touch modality recognition; Learning-based in-hand object recognition	Human-environment interaction learning and imitation for intelligent robots; Sensitive smart robotic touch
F/T Sensor	Sensing	Human activity recognition; Human intention estimation; Robot trajectory optimization	Safe HRC; Collaborative assembly
Magnetic-Based Sensor	Sensing	Precise tactile sensing	Adaptive grasping; Dexterous manipulation
TEGN Sensor	Sensing	Contacted objects' materials and textures recognition; Gas detection	Natural interaction with humans and surroundings; HMI; VR applications
Knitted Resistive Sensor	Sensing	Stiffness estimation; Material conductivity detection; Environment temperature detection; Object classification	VR and MR interaction
Optical-Based Sensor	Sensing	Contact location and intensity detection; Texture classification	Safe HRC; Grasping and manipulation

Table 9. Haptics-based technologies: Display

Sensor/Actuator	Category	Tasks	Applications
Electrical Stimulation	Display	High spatiotemporal tactile rendering	VR applications
Electromagnetic Stimulation	Display	Contactless force feedback	Collaborative manipulation
Temperature Stimulation	Display	Virtual texture rendering	HMI and VR applications
Pneumatic Actuator	Display	Contour reconstruction	VR applications

4.6 Multimodal Interfaces

A single system combines multiple ways of interacting between people and machines. This means that people can use a variety of inputs, like speech, touch, and motions, to interact with machines. These systems aim to enhance naturalness and adaptability to user preferences and diverse scenarios. For example, a multimodal interface (MI) (Azofeifa et al., 2022) might let a person control a smart home system using both voice prompts and a tablet, so they can choose the way that works best for them. Consumer gadgets, vehicle systems, and industrial uses are increasingly utilizing MIs. These interfaces improve user experiences by making contact easier and more flexible. Researchers are also investigating these systems to see if they could make it easier for disabled people to get to places by fitting a range of sense and movement skills which is shown in Figure 8.

Figure 8. Block diagram of multi-model interface systems

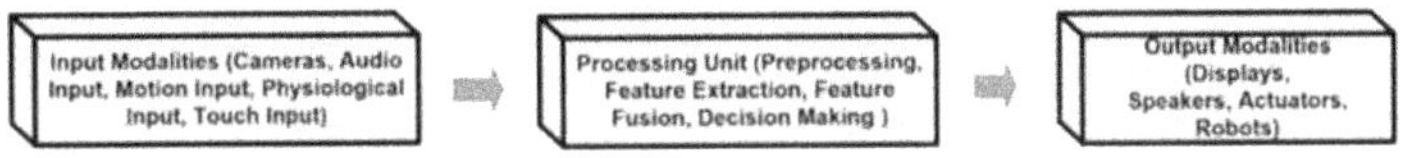

Sensor inputs include video feed from the RGB camera, depth camera, and thermal camera with the help of CNNs for image classification, and OpenPose for facial emotions. Any sound is also one or multiple audio streams, which go through microphones and then go through the extraction of features like MFCCs and then analysed by such networks as RNNs or Wav2Vec transformers. Motion inputs control gestures, which are captured by accelerometers and gyroscopes; Physiological signals, such as EEG, EMG, GSR and ECG, are processed with wavelet transforms with the emotional and cognitive state being presented employing SVM or CNN-LSTM. Feature fusion fuses data either early, by concatenation or SNNs, or late, with the help of ensemble methods, while decision-making model involves CNNs, Random Forest or transformers. The output modalities are mainly vision, sound, feel, and movement, or RL or control-based actions. These interfaces are beneficial for designing stable fugue applications and systems in emotion detection, gesture control, and other adaptive human computer systems changing the user experience on the areas of health, interactive entertainment, and assistive technologies. Table 10 shows the multimodal Interfaces developed from 2000 to 2025, covering a mix of academic, commercial, and open-source systems that integrated multiple input/output modalities (e.g., speech, gesture, touch, eye-tracking, EEG, etc.):

Table 10. Multimodal interfaces

Interface/System Name	Modalities Used	Description / Highlights
QuickSet	Speech, Pen (Stylus)	DARPA-funded system for map-based interfaces using speech and pen input.
iGesture	Gesture, Mouse, Keyboard	A framework to integrate gesture recognition with traditional inputs.
XWand	Speech, Gesture	Microsoft Research's wand controller with sensors and voice.
SmartKom	Speech, Gesture, Facial Expression	German project integrating natural modalities for dialog systems.
IBM Multimodal Toolkit	Speech, Keyboard, Touchscreen	Toolkit to build voice and visual interfaces.
Ovi Maps (Nokia)	Touch, GPS, Voice	Early multimodal navigation system.
Wii Remote (Nintendo)	Motion, Infrared, Button	First successful consumer game controller using motion.
iPhone Multitouch	Touch, Gesture, Voice (later versions)	Revolutionized multimodal mobile interaction.

continued on following page

Table 10. Continued

Interface/System Name	Modalities Used	Description / Highlights
Microsoft Surface (1st Gen)	Touch, Object Recognition	Tactile and vision-based surface computing.
Google Voice Search	Voice, Text	Multimodal search using voice input and text results.
Kinect (Xbox)	Motion, Voice, Facial Recognition	Depth sensing and voice recognition in gaming.
Siri (Apple)	Voice, Text	Intelligent voice-based assistant with multimodal feedback.
Google Glass	Voice, Touchpad, Eye Movement	Wearable multimodal interface with AR capabilities.
Leap Motion	Hand & Finger Gestures	Infrared-based fine gesture recognition.
Myo Armband	EMG (muscle), Gesture, Motion	Wearable gesture control using muscle activity.
HoloLens (Microsoft)	Gesture, Gaze, Voice	Mixed Reality headset supporting natural input.
Amazon Echo	Voice, Button, App Interface	Smart home control via multimodal voice/UI.
Oculus Rift + Touch	Motion, Buttons, Voice	VR system using controllers and voice input.
Google Duplex	Voice (Natural), AI	AI system that mimics human voice in conversations.
EMOTIV Insight	EEG, Facial Expression, Motion	Brain-computer interface for cognitive monitoring.
Zoom+Virtual Backgrounds	Video, Voice, Gesture (via plugins)	Multimodal communication platform.
Meta Quest 2	Motion, Voice, Gesture, Eye Tracking (beta)	VR headset with multimodal control.
Apple.Watch+Hand Gestures	Touch, Gesture, Voice, Haptics	Advanced health & control using multimodal input.
GPT-4 with Vision Input	Text, Image, Speech	Multimodal AI understanding natural input formats.
Neuralink	Brain Signals (EEG/ECoG), Gesture	Experimental BCI showing multimodal potential.
Apple Vision Pro (expected)	Eye Tracking, Hand Gestures, Voice, AR/VR UI	High-end spatial computing with full multimodal support.

4.7 Tangible User Interfaces

People can access digital information through real items in Tangible User Interfaces (TUIs) (Krestanova, Cerny, & Augustynek, 2021), a type of HMIs. By moving real items connected to digital processes, people can interact with data in a more natural and hands-on manner in a TUI setting. TUIs work best in school and group settings because they make vague ideas more real and engaging, which helps with learning and problem-solving. For instance, a math-focused TUI system could allow students to represent numbers with real blocks and manipulate them to solve problems, thereby enhancing the learning experience. Researchers in the artistic and design fields are also exploring TUIs. This would let artists and designers use digital tools in a more physical way. TUIs provide a unique and creative way for humans and machines to communicate by connecting the real and virtual worlds.

Figure 9. Block diagram of TUI systems

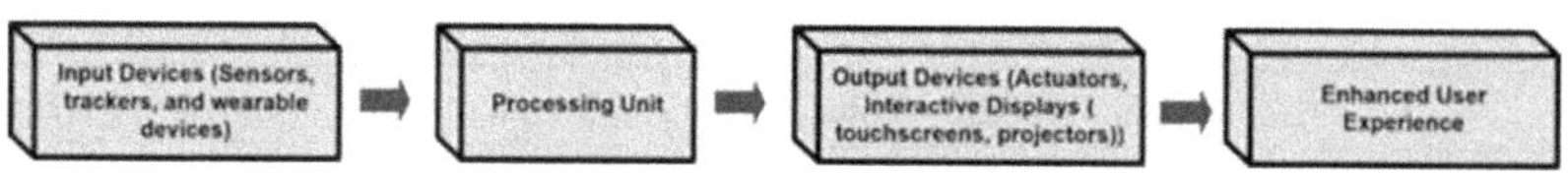

4.7.1 TUI: Models, Methods, and Components

TUIs allow recognizable manipulation of digital systems through physical representations bridging between the material and the digital. A TUI system comprises three main components: input devices, a processing unit and output devices shown in Figure 9. All these factors are integrated seamlessly to give the user value, ease of use and an overall pleasant experience. Recording user actions and changes to the environment is the work of input devices. Touch is sensed by capacitive sensors while motion and light are sensed by optical ones, while the wearable devices' orientation and velocity are determined by accelerometers. Read locators such as Optical motion trackers determine position and motion in time to be fed into an interactive system. Additional peripherals, including haptic gloves and smartwatches, facilitate hand gesture or touch inputs for the better experience of users. The processing unit comprises of data models like the SVMs, the Random Forests, CNNs, RNNs for decaying the input data from sensors. Sensor fusion and multimodal processing enhance accuracy of the data received as well as the performance of the systems. Pneumatic actuators, information displays, mixed reality screens are feedback devices that improve the interactivity and give signals, of the system. Examples of TUI systems include Pico, where physical objects are placed on a touchscreen to manipulate digital data, and Microsoft Kinect, which uses sensors to track body movements for controlling virtual environments. Haptic gloves provide tactile feedback in virtual reality applications, while RFID trackers are used to track physical objects within a system. These systems illustrate the versatility and effectiveness of TUIs in a variety of domains, from gaming and entertainment to education, design, and virtual reality. The integration of physical objects with digital technology in TUIs enhances user engagement and interaction, making digital content more accessible and intuitive to manipulate.

4.8 Socio-Familiar Robots

Social-familiar Robot are robots that are meant for social and caretaking nature for better living, to perform caretaker jobs and to be friends with humans (Mois & Beer, 2020). These robots generally come with high end sensors, AI and HRI capabilities to 'engage' with persons, and in a way that is similar to how people interact. As the term 'socio-familiar' implies, interaction is not only expected to be social but familiar – meaning these robots are expected to become part of people's every day social and familial existence.

4.8.1 Working of Social-Familiar Robot

Socio-familiar robots will therefore be developed for interfacing with humans in social and familial environment. These robots are those which approach people based on humanlike characteristics, helping, comforting and guiding them. The working of these robots involves several core components: perception, interaction and response sensors. Here's a breakdown of how socio-familiar robots operate: Socio-familiar robots have improved sensors and cameras that enable them to capture environments, people and objects. Cameras, Depth sensors enable robots to identify face, gesture and movement, sound sensors and speech recognition enable robots to hear and obey voice commands. They are also touch sensitive making the interactions natural with robots. Motions and temperature sensors and falling enable them to assess situations and respond appropriately, for safety and efficient interaction. The discovered cognitive sensors collect sensor data and the AI / ML algorithms can then pre-process these to provide the robot with the ability for decision making. Using AI, robots are able to detect faces, understand feelings, and mimic a human being's thinking in a language they would understand, namely, natural language understanding or NLP. Socio-familiar robots also learn user routines further enhancing their bond or relationship. These robots help in most day-to-day activities such as administering medicine, tracking health and even cleaning. They also allow people to stay connected through physical lengths, share time with families through video and text walk through and events.

Nowadays Humanoid robots are enthusiastic inventions imitating and mimicking the human form and behaviour held at the intersection between artificial intelligence and robotics. These robots are designed to mimic human feelings, communication and gestures in today's society and is rapidly growing in importance in many fields. These are AMECA, ALTER, ARMAR-6, Tesla's Optimus Gen2, APOLLO, BEOMNI by Beyond Imagination, ATLAS, DIGIT, JIAJIA, ERICA, KIME, NADINE, NAO, OCEANONE, PEPPER, PROMOBOT, ROBONAUT 2, GRACE, ROBOTHESPIAN, SOPHIA and SURENA IV. Table 11 represents current trends in HMI, illustrating how interfaces are being implemented to advance a user's experience, and also enhance the possibilities of interaction between people and machines in such fields as healthcare, gaming, robotics, and smart homes.

Table 11. HMI types along with real-world examples

HMI Interface Type	Examples
Voice-Controlled Interface	Amazon Alexa, Google Assistant, Apple Siri, IBM Watson Assistant
Gesture-Based Interaction	Microsoft HoloLens, Leap Motion Controller, Xbox Kinect, Ultra haptics
Eye-Tracking Technology	Tobii Eye Tracker, Samsung Smart TV eye-controlled features, Pupil Labs Eye Tracker, Fove VR
Haptic Feedback Systems	Sony Dual Sense Controller, Ultra leap haptic systems, Sense Glove, Tesla Suit
AR and VR Interfaces	Oculus Quest 3, Google Glass Enterprise Edition, HTC Vive Pro, Magic Leap2
Brain-Computer Interfaces	Neuralink, Emotiv Epoc+, OpenBCI, NeXT Mind
Touchless Interfaces	Intel RealSense Technology, Holographic Touchscreens, Ultra haptics AIR, BMW Air Touch
Socially Intelligent Robots	Pepper, Nao, Sophia, Jibo, ElliQ
Context-Aware Systems	Tesla Autopilot, Google Nest Thermostat, Amazon Echo Show, Philips Hue Smart Lighting
Wearable Devices	Apple Watch, Fitbit, Microsoft HoloLens, Oura Ring, Samsung Galaxy Watch
Multimodal Interfaces	Google Pixel Voice Typing, Microsoft Cortana + Touchscreen, Adobe Sensei enabled design tools
Emotional AI Interfaces	Affectiva Emotion AI, Cogito AI, Kairos Emotion Analytics
Tactile Wearables	Neosensory Buzz, ProGlove Mark Display

5. HMI ACCESSIBILITY AND USABILITY

There is a current trend of evolution in HMIs with accessibility and usability as core values due to current trends. The latest HMIs are integrating the aspect of inclusive design to suit users with disabilities based on accessibility guidelines such as the (Kruger et al., 2023). The innovative concepts of voice and gesture control with the help of, for instance, Amazon Alexa or Microsoft Kinect broaden the space of non-contact interaction and make the interfaces less obstructive. There is more freedom when it comes to interacting with these systems and using voice, touch, and gestures while AI can personalize the systems according to the user's preferences and make interfaces more adaptive. Despite the growing use of computers, the currently more frequent approaches to improving HMIs are rooted in user-cantered design principles like usability testing and feedback. Usability is also improved through another function of AI which is anticipation of users' behaviour by smart technologies such as a predictive typing and smart search bars. A combination of fashion apparels and wearable devices plus the aspects of Augmented Reality (AR) is profoundly transforming HMIs, especially in healthcare areas through context-aware, Realtime and hands-free interaction. These three trends are all in general pulling HMIs in the direction of more comprehensive, effective, and user-friendly ones which would then make them more accessible to a lot of different people (Nielsen, 1994; Shneiderman & Plaisant, 2010; Kjeldskov, 2003).

6. CHALLENGES AND ETHICAL ISSUES

Here, the main issues highlighted are the data demands, the data quality and the data protection for HMI systems with artificial intelligence and machine learning. The datasets can be shifted and this will lead to preconception results, and sensitive data preprocessing is a major privacy issue. AI-based HMIs are often implemented as 'black boxes; that cause trust and accountability challenges. Real time analysis of emotion and speech continues to be challenging, which interferes with natural human conversation. Risk issue and concerns such as ethical, biasness, privacy and legal implication in data acquisition including data driven autonomous systems call for ethicality in designs and regulations such as the GDPR.

7. FUTURE DIRECTIONS OF HUMAN-MACHINE INTERFACES

The upcoming trends of HMIs will depend on emerging solutions NLP, BCIs, AR/VR, and ethical AI. A better understanding of NLP will allow users to effectively interact with their machines as real companions making their use easier. BCIs will make it possible for the brain to interface directly with devices, hugely transforming rehabilitative processes as well as learning. Education trainings and remote work will be revolutionised by the functions of AR/VR technologies, which will enhance spatial apperception. They said that new categorized AI, Explainable AI (XAI), will cater for ethical issues like bias and accountability. This represents the power of Internet integration as users would be able to control smart environments on their own. The application of more speech recognition will reveal increased satisfaction among the users, The application of cybersecurity will provide personal and safe interaction.

8. CONCLUSION

Conclusively, it is evident that HMI has rapidly evolved and transformed the interfaces that users have with technology. From the simple mechanical interfaces right to the complex systems, HMI has enhanced accessibility, usability and users' interaction. The use of GUIs, natural language interfaces, gesture controls, and Brain Computer Interfaces is an indication of more natural, engaging and context-aware interactions. Further, haptic interfaces, multi-modal interfaces, and TUIs make the interaction richer and more responsive. Two emerging subfields of HMI, social robots and embodied agents, are entering social and emotional spaces to provide help and friendship. Hence, given the ongoing advancements in these technologies, some factors like trustworthiness, transparency, and reliability will be important. Maintaining the effectiveness of HMI systems while making them fairly, securely, and hospitably compliant with users' needs will be equally important in the future. Future work in HMI will continue to produce innovative techniques that enhance the essence of interactions making them an enriching experience for use in different aspects of life.

REFERENCES

Adilkhanov, A., Rubagotti, M., & Kappassov, Z. (2022). Haptic devices: Wearability-based taxonomy and literature review. *IEEE Access : Practical Innovations, Open Solutions*, *10*, 91923–91947. DOI: 10.1109/ACCESS.2022.3202986

Azofeifa, J. D., Noguez, J., Ruiz, S., Molina-Espinosa, J. M., Magana, A. J., & Benes, B. (2022, February). Systematic review of multimodal human–computer interaction. [). MDPI.]. *Informatics (MDPI)*, *9*(1), 13. DOI: 10.3390/informatics9010013

Cortada, J. W. (2003). *The digital hand: How computers changed the work of American manufacturing, transportation, and retail industries*. Oxford University Press.

Costagliola, G., De Rosa, M., & Fuccella, V. (2023). Gesture-Based Computing. *Handbook of Human-Machine Systems*, 397-408.

Johnson, J. (2000). *GUI bloopers: Don'ts and Do's for Software Developers and Web Designers*. Morgan Kaufmann.

Kjeldskov, J. (2003). Human-computer interaction design for emerging technologies: virtual reality, augmented reality and mobile computer systems.

Krestanova, A., Cerny, M., & Augustynek, M. (2021). Development and technical design of tangible user interfaces in wide-field areas of application. *Sensors (Basel)*, *21*(13), 4258. DOI: 10.3390/s21134258 PMID: 34206398

Kruger, R., De Wet, F., Niesler, T., Trinh, V., Manduchi, R., Giudice, N. A., ... & Souza Filho, G. L. (2023). Accessible computing. *ACM Trans, 16*(2).

Lebedev, M. A., & Nicolelis, M. A. (2006). Brain–machine interfaces: Past, present and future. *Trends in Neurosciences*, *29*(9), 536–546. DOI: 10.1016/j.tins.2006.07.004 PMID: 16859758

Martinez, W. L. (2011). Graphical user interfaces. *Wiley Interdisciplinary Reviews: Computational Statistics*, *3*(2), 119–133. DOI: 10.1002/wics.150

Mois, G., & Beer, J. M. (2020). The role of healthcare robotics in providing support to older adults: A socio-ecological perspective. *Current Geriatrics Reports*, *9*(2), 82–89. DOI: 10.1007/s13670-020-00314-w PMID: 32435576

Mourtzis, D., Angelopoulos, J., & Panopoulos, N. (2023). The future of the human–machine interface (HMI) in society 5.0. *Future Internet*, *15*(5), 162. DOI: 10.3390/fi15050162

Nadkarni, P. M., Ohno-Machado, L., & Chapman, W. W. (2011). Natural language processing: An introduction. *Journal of the American Medical Informatics Association : JAMIA*, *18*(5), 544–551. DOI: 10.1136/amiajnl-2011-000464 PMID: 21846786

Nielsen, J. (1994). *Usability engineering*. Morgan Kaufmann.

Norman Donald, A. (2013). *The design of everyday things*. MIT Press.

Obrenovic, B., Gu, X., Wang, G., Godinic, D., & Jakhongirov, I. (2024). Generative AI and human–robot interaction: Implications and future agenda for business, society and ethics. *AI & Society*, •••, 1–14.

Perrow, C. (2011). *Normal accidents: Living with high risk technologies-Updated edition.* Princeton university press. DOI: 10.2307/j.ctt7srgf

Ribino, P. (2023). The role of politeness in human–machine interactions: A systematic literature review and future perspectives. *Artificial Intelligence Review*, *56*(S1, Suppl 1), 445–482. DOI: 10.1007/s10462-023-10540-1

Russell, S. J., & Norvig, P. (2016). *Artificial intelligence: a modern approach.* pearson.

Shneiderman, B., & Plaisant, C. (2010). *Designing the user interface: strategies for effective human-computer interaction.* Pearson Education India.

Slater, M., & Sanchez-Vives, M. V. (2016). Enhancing our lives with immersive virtual reality. *Frontiers in Robotics and AI*, *3*, 74. DOI: 10.3389/frobt.2016.00074

Wigdor, D., & Wixon, D. (2011). *Brave NUI world: designing natural user interfaces for touch and gesture*. Elsevier.

Wu, D., Lu, B. L., Hu, B., & Zeng, Z. (2023). Affective brain–computer interfaces (abcis): A tutorial. *Proceedings of the IEEE*, *111*(10), 1314–1332. DOI: 10.1109/JPROC.2023.3277471

Chapter 16
E-Collaboration Technologies With Generative AI Tools

Tarana Afrin Chandel
https://orcid.org/0000-0002-8605-6018
Integral University, India

ABSTRACT

E-collaboration technologies, which enable individuals and teams to work together across distances and time zones, are essential for modern organizations. With the integration of Generative AI, these technologies are evolving to provide more dynamic and adaptive collaborative environments. Generative AI tools can enhance productivity with automation, summarizing discussions, and generating data-driven insights in real time. These tools enable more efficient communication through the creation of language models that can translate languages, generate reports, and even simulate brainstorming sessions with virtual teams. These advancements improve productivity, foster innovation, and enhance inclusivity by breaking language barriers and providing accessibility features. However, challenges such as data privacy, ethical concerns, and over-reliance on AI must be addressed to ensure responsible use. By combining the power of e-collaboration technologies and Generative AI, organizations can achieve a smarter, more connected, and ethically responsible future of work.

1. INTRODUCTION

The rapid pace of technological advancement is indeed remarkable. In just a few decades, we've gone from rudimentary computers reliant on punch cards and room-sized machines to smartphones that are millions of times more powerful and fit in our pockets. In just eight decades, we have moved from the first digital computers known as Atanasoff-Berry Computer (ABC) built in England in 1943 [Paul A. freiberger and Micheal R Swaine, 2022] and the ENIAC, built in the United States in 1945 which were completed in 1945 [1] to advanced technologies which are already reshaping industries [Max Roser, 2022] as shown in figure1 . These rapid progression highlights how quickly emerging technologies can become integral to our daily life.

DOI: 10.4018/979-8-3693-8332-2.ch016

Figure 1. Beginning of digital era

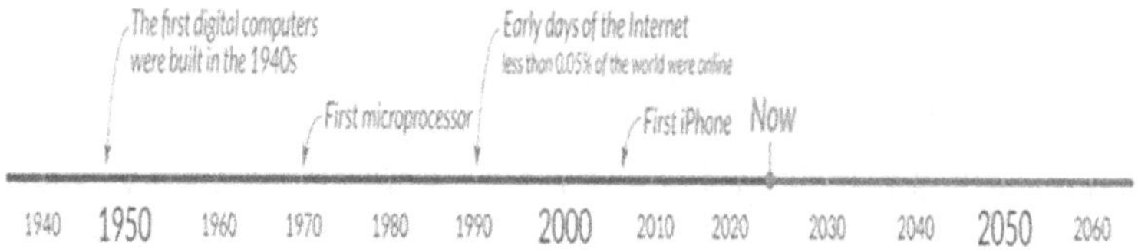

As technology advances exponentially, AI, and more specifically generative AI, is becoming a key driver of innovation. The ability of AI models to generate text, art, code, and even music showcases how we're not just advancing in processing power, but in creative capabilities as well. This leap represents a profound shift from using machines merely as tools to creating systems that can collaborate with humans in unprecedented ways. Just as early computers and mobile phones revolutionized their respective eras, AI, especially generative AI, is likely to redefine creativity, automation, and the way we interact with machines. This reflects the change on how generative AI fits into this trajectory of rapid innovation. Since the beginning of this history, computer engineers strived to design machine as similar to human intelligence as shown in figure 2

Figure 2. From digital computer to AI

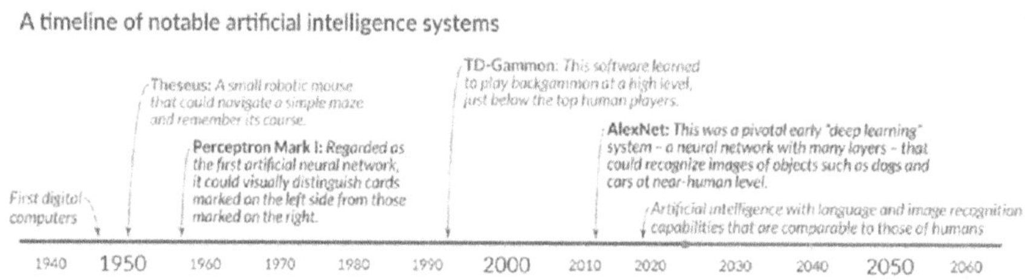

The first remote controlled mouse was built by Claud Shanon in 1950 [Daniel Kleinarchive, 2018]. This was the ever beginning of machine learning; a robotic maze-solving mouse known as Theseus [Paul A. freiberger and Micheal R Swaine, 2022; Daniel Kleinarchive, 2018]. In the era of 1950 and 1960, the basic concept of artificial intelligence (AI) was established involving symbolic reasoning and problem-solving. Alan Turning and John McCarthy laid the foundation of AI in 1955 [Paul A. freiberger and Micheal R Swaine, 2022; P. Paoli, 2021; Gil Press, 2016] by proposing theories and developing software programs demonstrating machine learning capabilities. In 1956, the terminology ***Artificial intelligence*** was first tossed by McCarthy [Chris Smith, 2006] in first academic conference, Five years later Alan Turing wrote a paper on the motion of machines being able to simulate human beings and the ability to do intelligent things, such as play Chess [Turing50] [Chris Smith, 2006]. Generative artificial intelligence (GAI) is the subset of AI that focuses on the development and creation of system capabilities such as generating images, music, and synthetic data. In other words, GAI is the sub-branch of AI, capable of developing content and maintaining the originality of human-generated outcomes. Humans have the power of understanding and decision-making, while AI provides insight prediction and data analysis. Both these combine to form human-generated AI. Human AI collaboration refers to the synergy between human intelligence and AI technology. In the next generation, Generative AI (GAI) will play a vital role in collaborating human intelligence and AI technology by augmenting human creativity and productivity. Human-AI collaboration enhances efficiency, and decision-making, encouraging innovations, and leading towards customized and efficient solutions. GAI simulates human creativity and generates entire narratives. The applications that we utilize on the internet are because of generative AI technologies produced by companies such as Google, Meta, and Open-AI. These technologies allow machines not only to learn but also to create. The correlation between AI and human imagination has grown speedily with fast-changing technology. AI has increased human capabilities with expanded boundaries of possibilities. Artificial Intelligence (AI) refers to the simulation of human intelligence processes by machines, particularly computer systems. It encompasses a wide array of technologies and techniques that enable computers to perform tasks traditionally requiring human cognitive functions, such as learning, reasoning, problem-solving, perception, and language understanding. AI systems are designed to analyse and interpret data, make decisions, and act in ways that exhibit intelligence. The field of AI is broadly categorized into two types; Narrow AI (Weak AI) and General AI (Strong AI). Narrow AI (Weak AI) AI systems are designed and trained to perform specific tasks, such as image recognition, language translation, or speech recognition. These systems do not possess general intelligence and operate within the confines of their programming while general AI (Strong AI) is a hypothetical form of AI that have the ability to understand, learn, and apply intelligence across a wide range of tasks, similar to human cognitive abilities. General AI remains a future goal of AI research and development. In this chapter the author will discuss the advancement in AI technology, collaboration between the human brain and AI tools; its prediction and analysis, its role in today's world, benefits of collaboration between human and AI, Challenges, and possibilities associated with generative AI and real-time application of human-AI collaboration.

2. EVOLUTION OF AI TECHNOLOGY

The journey of Artificial Intelligence (AI) is a fascinating tale of human ingenuity and technological advancement. Since the last few decades, artificial intelligence (AI) has deployed its path into every area of our lives. Artificial Intelligence (AI) is indeed reshaping the world in remarkable ways. Since its inception, AI has evolved through multiple stages, from early rule-based systems to the sophisticated machine learning and deep learning models of today [Case Western Reserve, 2024; Gaurav Tewari, 2022]. Let's explore the timeline of AI [Krit Jiarawattanakul, 2023]:

2.1 Early Stages of AI: From Logic-Based Systems to Machine Learning

Early Beginnings and AI Milestones" refers to the history and key developments in the field of Artificial Intelligence (AI). An overview is shown below

2.1.1 Early Beginnings

1950s - Alan Turing: In 1950, British mathematician and logician Alan Turing proposed the famous "Turing Test" in his paper Computing Machinery and Intelligence. He explored whether machines could exhibit intelligent behavior indistinguishable from that of a human.
1956 - Dartmouth Conference: Considered the birth of AI as a field, this conference was organized by John McCarthy and others. It officially coined the term "Artificial Intelligence" and laid the foundation for the study of machine intelligence.

2.1.2 Key Milestones in AI

1960s-1970s - Symbolic AI (GOFAI): Early AI was focused on symbolic reasoning and rule-based systems. Programs like ELIZA, which mimicked human conversation, were early efforts in natural language processing (NLP).
1980s - Expert Systems: AI saw the rise of expert systems like MYCIN, designed to mimic human experts in specific domains. These systems became popular in industries for decision-making.
1990s - Machine Learning: AI shifted from rule-based systems to data-driven approaches. In 1997, IBM's Deep Blue made headlines by defeating world chess champion Garry Kasparov, marking a milestone for AI in games.
2010s - Deep Learning & Big Data: The introduction of deep learning revolutionized AI. Google's Deep Mind developed Alpha Go, which defeated the world Go champion in 2016, demonstrating the power of neural networks.
2014 - Generative AI: The development of generative adversarial networks (GANs) by Ian Good fellow marked a significant advancement in AI's ability to generate new data. This laid the foundation for applications in image creation, video generation, and more.

2.2 Current State of AI: Machine Learning, Deep Learning, and Beyond

2.2.1 *Progress in Machine Learning (ML)*

Today, much of AI is driven by ML. ML has optimized in system and control engineering which uses data to train models to make predictions or decisions without explicit programming. This era was characterised by developing algorithms form data hence moving towards complex and more efficient AI system.

This technology is utilized in imagery analysis from medical diagnosis to military intelligence [Karen Howard and Brian Bothwell, 2023]. It identify complex and hidden pattern in data, detect disease at earlier stage, improves treatments and enhances access towards care especially for underserved populations. Other applications include natural language processing, computer vision, and recommendation systems.

2.2.2 *Rise* of N*eural network and Deep Learning (DL) Advances*

DL, a subset of ML, has an important role in technological advancement in AI. It has capabilities in processing and analysing data with remarkable accuracy. It uses neural networks with many layers to tackle complex tasks and innovations such as convolutional neural networks

(CNNs) and transformers (e.g., GPT models) have powered breakthroughs in areas like image recognition, autonomous driving, and language generation [Krit Jiarawattanakul,2023; Case Western Reserve, 2024; 9series, 2024].

2.2.3 *Generative AI*

AI systems like OpenAI's GPT-4 and Google's Bard have brought about generative models capable of creating text, images, music, and even code [Karen Howard and Brian Bothwell, 2023]. These upcoming abilities can be utilized in educatin, government, judiciary and also in entertainments [GAO,2023].This shift is making AI a creative tool as much as a problem-solver. Virtual assistant, language translation tools and advance chatbot are few applications of generative AI [GAO,2023]. No doubt that this technology has acquired attention globally for its enormous benefits.

2.2.4 *AI in Industries*

AI is already transforming healthcare (diagnostics, drug discovery), finance (fraud detection, trading algorithms), and manufacturing (predictive maintenance, robotics). AI-driven automation is also reshaping workforces across the globe.

3. CONCEPT OF AI

As per multiple theories of AI, human intelligence are categorized into seven types such as Linguistic, Logical-Mathematical, Spatial Bodily-Kinesthetic, Musical, Interpersonal and Intrapersonal intelligence.

3.1 Linguistic Intelligence

It is the ability to communicate one's thought in oral or written text, understand it, manage the thoughts and decode it. People with high linguistic intelligence adopt their ideal career as political-activist, host, public orator, editor, writer, news reporter, academician, etc.

3.2 Logical-Mathematical Intelligence

Humans having strong logical-mathematical intelligence are capable to analyse and rationalize, classify and summarize, quantify and compute complicated mathematical operations. These features portray sensitivity towards imaginary and visionary logical pattern, sentiments and ability. These people make their career as scientist, auditor, statisticians, engineers, software developers, etc.

3.3 Spatial Intelligence

Such people have the ability to perceive and understand visual information around it and generate mental representations of it

4. TECHNOLOGIES IN AI

In present scenario, technologies landscape is fast-evolving; where artificial intelligence (AI) are emerging as transformative force revolutionizing the way we live and work. Task which has been deemed impossible are now becoming a routine, reshaping industries and daily work life. As an The rapid advancement of AI is transforming industries across the globe, from healthcare and finance to education and retail. In healthcare, AI improves diagnostic accuracy, enables personalized treatment, and accelerates drug discovery. In finance, AI-powered algorithms enhance risk assessment, fraud detection, and customer service. Retail and ecommerce benefit from AI through demand forecasting, personalized marketing, and optimized supply chains. To fully appreciate these innovations, let's explore some key statistics and trends that shed light on AI's growing influence globally. A challenging discussion among engineers and scientist still continued about the benefits and challenges of the rapid advancement in this technology. This is universal truth that businesses growth rate increased by embracing AI technology; in-order to sustain in this fast changing environment. Globally AI has move beyond the confined areas of science fiction and has become an integral part of the everyday life. AI influence everyone and everywhere such as mobile phones, internet use, activities involving online shopping. The IT sectors have also witnessed the drastic change i.e. from *web developer* and *UI/UZ designer* to *Android and iOS programmers*; were forced to adopt and modify their work process, accepting the reality of AI [Devabit, 2023]. Figure3 show research publications in AI globally, since last 10 years, having more than 180000 publication in year 2021 [Deptt. of IS & R, 2023].

Figure 3. Research publication rate in AI from 2013 to 2021, Globally

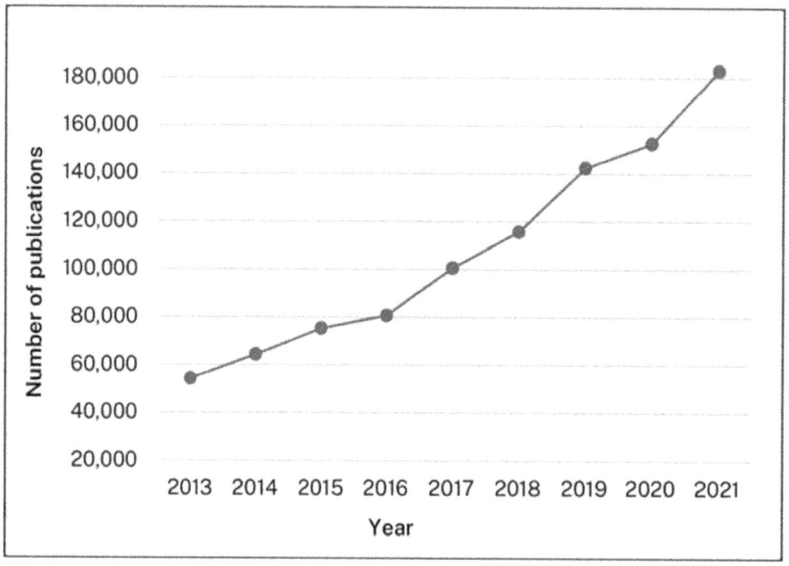

Figure 4. AI publications by jurisdiction, 2018–22, Globally

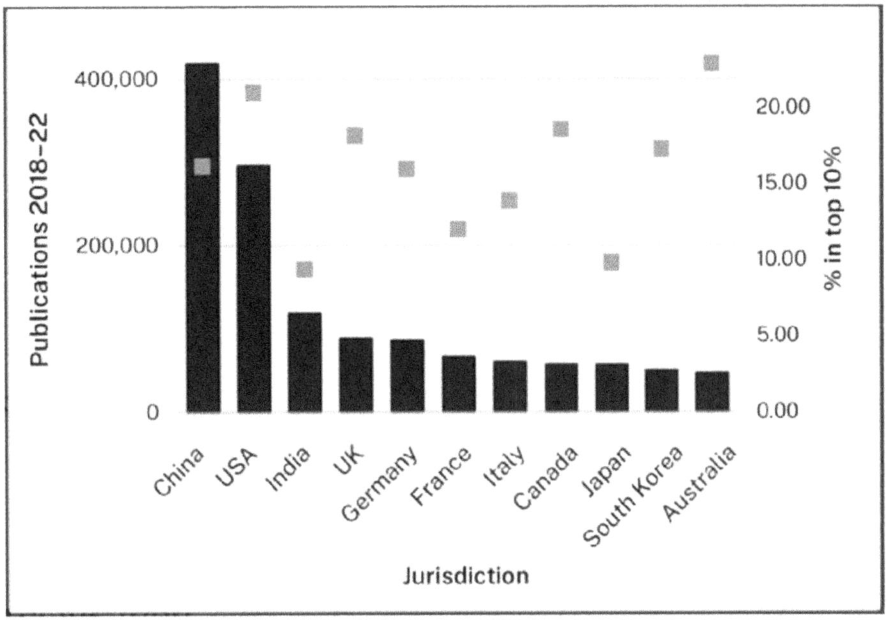

These data were collected from Clarivate's Web of Science and Incites. Data analysis was performed by CSIRO. Moving towards publications on AI, country wise, China and United States shows the most AI research; India stands on third position in research on AI. This study will highlight all the hidden secrets of AI. According to jurisdiction, figure 4. AI publications by jurisdiction, 2018–22 [Dept. of IS & R, 2023]. It give a comparative analysis about the number of publication with percentage in top 10%.

Patent filing and grant of it reflects how innovations are being commercialised. Patent records identify the potential collaboration and export markets globally. Figure 5, shows number of patents filed each year in the field of AI from 2017 to 2011 while figure 6, shows Jurisdiction of origin for AI patent families filed, 2017–2021 [Dept. of IS & R, 2023].

Figure 5. AI patent filed globally each year, 2017–2021

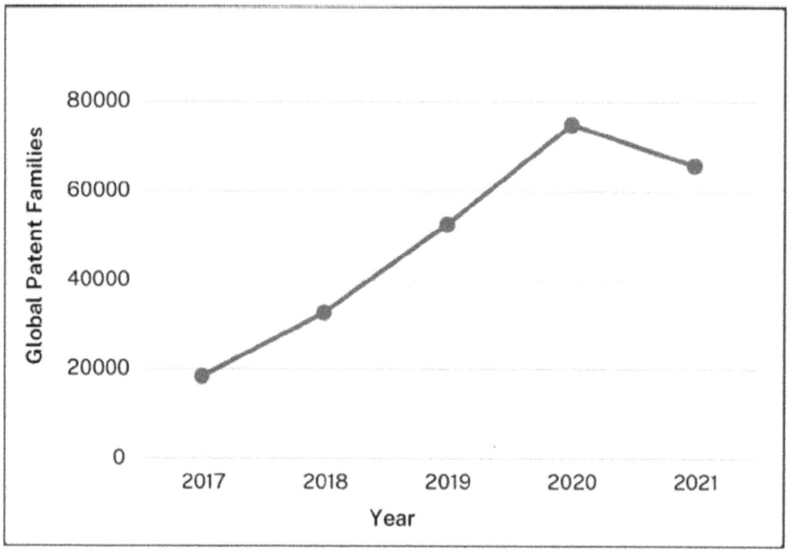

Figure 6. Jurisdiction of origin for AI patent families filed, 2017–2021

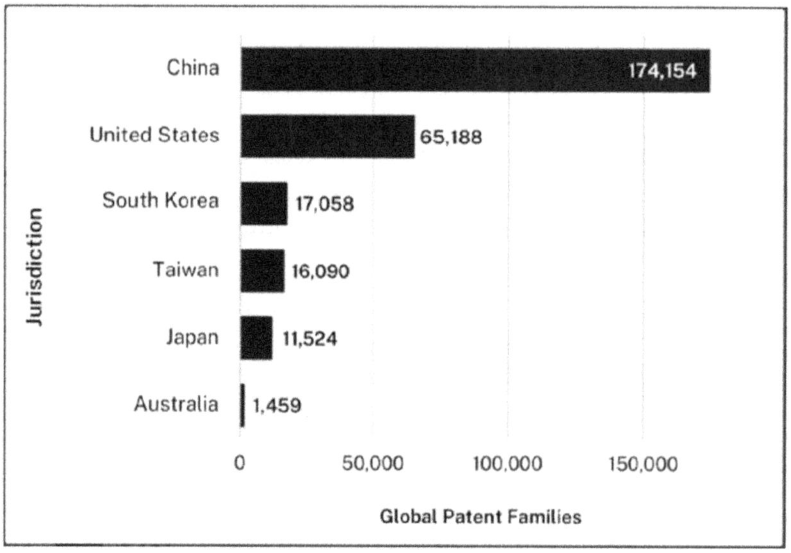

Statistical data record highlights that the development of new technologies in is set to bring significant positive changes to the business market. These new technologies are given below:

4.1 New Technologies in AI: GPT-3.4/GPT-4

GPT has become one of the most talked-about breakthroughs in the realm of AI technologies. But have you ever wondered about the history behind this sensational innovation? Let's explore its journey from the very beginning. The story begins with early examples like ELIZA in the 1960s and ALICE in the 1990s. These pioneering chatbots relied on rule-based systems, which restricted their ability to hold meaningful conversations. However, the 2010s marked a new chapter with the advent of AI-driven chatbots powered by machine learning and natural language processing (NLP). Platforms like Facebook Messenger and Slack played a crucial role in popularizing these advanced chatbots for both businesses and consumers.

The breakthrough in chatbot technology came with the advent of deep learning models like GPT. OpenAI introduced GPT-1 in 2018, marking a significant leap in chatbot capabilities. While it could generate contextually relevant text, it had notable limitations. In 2019, GPT-2 built on this foundation, gaining attention for its ability to produce human-like text at a much larger scale. However, its release sparked controversy due to concerns over potential misuse. In 2020, GPT-3 took the world by storm with its unparalleled natural language understanding and generation capabilities. It garnered widespread recognition for its ability to perform tasks ranging from answering questions to composing essays and poetry, often indistinguishable from human-written content. The evolution continued with GPT-3.5, a precursor to GPT-4, featuring an astounding 175 billion parameters—more than 10 times the size of GPT-2's 1.5 billion. This immense scale enabled GPT-3.5 to achieve remarkable proficiency in text generation, setting a new standard for AI-powered language models. Evolution of GPT [Devabit, 2023] is shown in figure 7.

Figure 7. Evolution of GPT

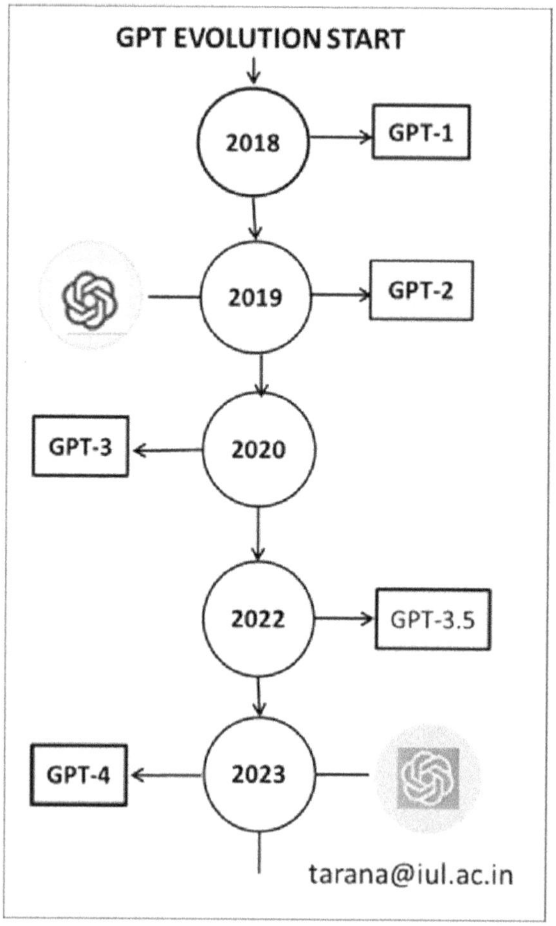

GPT-3.5 revolutionized business operations by enabling the automation of content creation. For example, a media company leveraged its capabilities to generate thousands of articles daily, significantly reducing reliance on human writers while maintaining high output efficiency. The next evolution, GPT-4, is rumoured to exceed an astonishing 200 billion parameters, further enhancing its language understanding and generation abilities. This leap in scale opens new possibilities across industries. Businesses are already exploring its potential in areas like content creation, customer support, and virtual assistants, where its advanced capabilities are expected to excel. However, GPT-3.5 and GPT-4 represent only the beginning. The rapid pace of AI model development suggests that even more advanced language models are on the horizon. These advancements will undoubtedly have transformative implications for industries ranging from content creation to intelligent virtual assistants, reshaping the future of human-AI collaboration.

On November 6, 2023, OpenAI CEO Sam Altman unveiled a groundbreaking update to ChatGPT, introducing a suite of new features and technologies that push the boundaries of artificial intelligence. The update includes GPTs (specialized AI models tailored to specific tasks), the ChatGPT Store (a marketplace for custom GPTs), and GPT-4 Turbo, an enhanced version of GPT-4 designed for greater speed and efficiency. These innovations represent a significant leap forward in AI technology, paving the way for more versatile and accessible AI applications across industries.

4.2. New Technologies in AI: Generative Adversarial Networks (GANs)

The terminology *generative* represent how data can be generative in terms of probabilistic model, whereas *adversarial* represent that a model is trained as per adversarial settings and *networ*k represent deep neural network which can be utilized as AI algorithm for training purposes. .Generative Adversarial Networks (GANs) was introduced by **Ian Goodfellow** along with his colleagues in 2014. It represents a cutting-edge innovation in AI. Objective of Goodfellow's plan was to develop a competitive framework where two neural networks—the **generator** and the **discriminator**—work against each other [Greeksfor-Greek, 2024] . The generator creates data that mimics real examples, while the discriminator evaluates its authenticity. This adversarial training process revolutionized generative modeling, making GANs one of the most transformative technologies in modern AI, with applications spanning image generation, video synthesis, and more.

Figure 8. Architecture of GAN

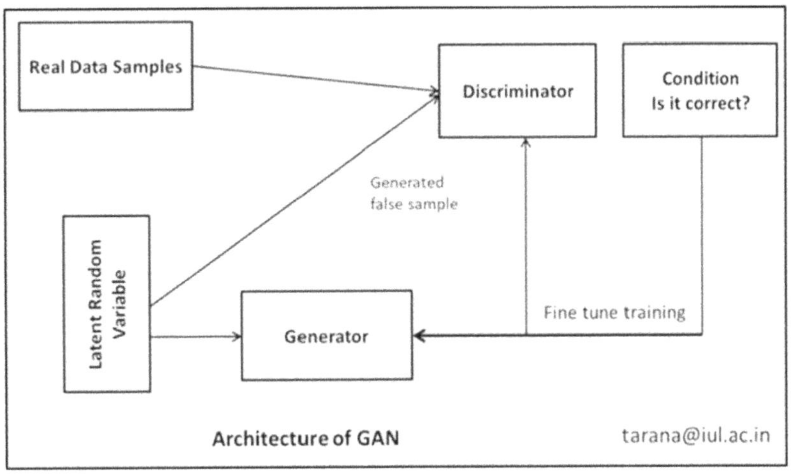

The architecture of GAN [GreeksforGreek, 2024] is shown in figure 8. This architecture consist of two types of neural network i.e. a generator and a discriminator, both are trained opposite to each other [iProov, 2024].

Generator: The generator in a GAN is typically implemented as a convolutional neural network (CNN). CNNs are deep learning algorithms that are particularly adept at processing images by identifying and analyzing patterns such as edges, textures, and objects. In the context of the generator, the network takes random noise or a latent variable as input and aims to produce synthetic outputs (e.g., images) that are so realistic they could be mistaken for real data. The generator works by assigning weights (which represent the importance of various features) to the input data during training. These weights are fine-tuned so that the generated output closely resembles the distribution of the real data. Over time, the generator becomes more skilled at creating realistic-looking outputs, making it a powerful tool in generative modeling [Jessica Schulze, 2024].

Generator Model in GANs: A key element responsible for creating fresh, accurate data in a Generative Adversarial Network (GAN) is the generator model. The generator's primary function is to take random noise as input and transform it into complex, high-quality data samples, such as images, text, or audio. The generator is typically modeled as a deep neural network that learns to produce realistic outputs.Through training, the generator learns to capture the underlying distribution of the training data. This is accomplished by passing the noise through layers of learnable parameters that adjust during the training process. Using backpropagation, the generator fine-tunes its parameters to improve its output, progressively making the generated samples more similar to real data.The generator's success is determined by its ability to create high-quality, varied samples that can effectively fool the discriminator into classifying them as real. This process of adversarial learning ensures that the generator continually improves its output as it competes with the discriminator to produce realistic data.

Generator Loss in GANs: The objective of the generator in a GAN is to create synthetic samples that are realistic enough to deceive the discriminator into classifying them as real. The generator achieves this by minimizing its loss function, denoted as J_G. The loss is minimized when the log probability of the discriminator classifying the generated samples as real is maximized. Essentially, the generator aims to make the discriminator highly likely to classify its generated samples as real. The equation function loss is given below:

$$J_G = \frac{1}{m} \sum_{i=1}^{m} lagD(G(z_i)) \text{ ....1}$$

Where

- J_G: generator loss function
- m: number of generated sample
- G(zi): represent the output generated for a given input noise Zi
- D(G(zi)): represents discriminator's output, which gives the probability that $G(z_i)$ is a real sample
- log D(G(zi)): represent the log probability of the discriminator classifying the generated sample as real.
- The generator aims to minimize this loss, encouraging the production of samples that the discriminator classifies as real (logD(G(zi))(logD(G(zi)), close to 1.

Training Goal: The generator updates its parameters using back propagation to minimize J_G As a result:

- The generated samples improve in quality and realism over time.
- The discriminator becomes increasingly challenged to distinguish between real and synthetic samples.

Discriminator: The discriminator, in contrast, is typically built using a de-convolutional neural network (DNN), also known as a transposed CNN. While CNNs focus on extracting features from data, DNNs work in reverse, seeking to identify specific characteristics or anomalies that may indicate whether the input is real or fake. The discriminator's primary role is to distinguish between the real data (from the training set) and the synthetic data produced by the generator. It evaluates the output of the generator, attempting to determine if it is authentic or artificial. Over time, the discriminator becomes more effective at recognizing fake data, providing feedback to the generator to improve its output. The adversarial relationship between the generator and discriminator drives both networks to improve progressively [Jessica Schulze, 2024].

Over the years, Generative Adversarial Networks (GANs) have grown significantly in complexity and capability. Models like BigGAN, with an impressive 12 billion parameters, exemplify this growth by generating high-resolution images with unprecedented detail and realism. GANs have also revolutionized image super-resolution. A notable example is ESRGAN (Enhanced Super-Resolution GAN), which excels at up scaling images with exceptional precision and quality. This breakthrough has proven invaluable in applications such as medical imaging, where detail is critical, and visual content enhancement, which demands superior image resolution.

An intriguing example of GAN monetization is the AI-generated artwork "Edmond de Belamy", created using a Generative Adversarial Network. This ground-breaking piece became the first AI-generated artwork to be auctioned at Christie's, fetching an impressive $432,500—far exceeding initial estimates. This event marked a milestone in the intersection of AI and the art world, showcasing the creative and economic potential of GANs.

Discriminator Model in GANs

The discriminator model is a critical component of a Generative Adversarial Network (GAN), functioning as a binary classifier. Its role is to distinguish between real data (samples from the actual dataset) and generated data (produced by the generator.

Input Evaluation: The discriminator receives an input sample (either real or generated). It evaluates the sample and assigns a probability score indicating how likely the sample is real.

Binary Classification: The output is a single probability value D(x)):

- Close to 1: Indicates the sample is real.
- Close to 0: Indicates the sample is generated (fake).

Training the Discriminator: During training, the discriminator:

- Learns to identify real samples from the dataset by assigning high probabilities.
- Learns to classify generated samples from the generator as fake by assigning low probabilities.

The process involves back propagation to update its parameters, minimizing its loss function:

$$J_D = \frac{1}{m}\sum_{i=1}^{m}\left[lag\, D\left(x_i\right) + lag\left(1 - D\left(G(z_i\right)\right) \text{ .... } 2$$

- $D(x_i)$: Probability that a real sample x_i is classified as real
- $D(G(z_i))$: Probability that a generated sample $G(z_i)$ is classified as real.
- *m*: Number of samples in a batch.

Outcome: The iterative refinement of the discriminator and generator ensures that GANs produce synthetic data (images, text, etc.) that are increasingly indistinguishable from real data, contributing to the success of GAN-based applications.

Different types of GAN are Vanilla GAN, conditional GAN (CGAN), deep convolutional GAB (DCGAN), laplacian pyramid GAN (LAPGAN) and super resolution GAN (SRGAN) [GreeksforGreek, 2024; Kinza Yasar et al, 2024].

4.2.1 Vanilla GAN

It is the simplest form of a Generative Adversarial Network. In this type of GAN, both the generator and discriminator are implemented as straightforward multi-layer perceptrons (MLPs). The generator is responsible for learning the data distribution and creating synthetic data samples, while the discriminator works to classify whether the input data is real (from the actual dataset) or fake (generated by the generator). This adversarial dynamic helps both networks improve iteratively [Jaeuk Moon, 2020]. It employ a straightforward algorithm based on stochastic gradient descent (SGD) to optimize their mathematical objective function. SGD enables the model to learn from the dataset one example at a time, ensuring gradual improvement over iterations .Despite its simplicity, Vanilla GAN laid the foundation for more advanced GAN and remains a fundamental concept in generative modeling.

4.2.2. Conditional GAN (CGAN)

CGAN is an extension of the traditional GAN framework that incorporates conditional parameters to guide the data generation process. In CGAN, an additional parameter, typically denoted as ‘y’, is provided to the generator as input. This parameter represents specific information or labels, such as “rose,” “sunflower,” or “tulip,” enabling the generator to produce data conditioned on the given label [Cihan Ates et al, 2022]. Similarly, the discriminator also receives this conditional input, along with the data, to help distinguish between real data and fake, generated data more effectively.By integrating class labels or other relevant attributes, CGAN allows the network to learn targeted data distributions. For example, during training, the network is provided with labeled images corresponding to their categories, which helps it better understand and differentiate between distinct types of data.This approach makes CGAN particularly useful in applications that require controlled and specific data generation, such as image-to-image translation, text-to-image synthesis, and domain adaptation tasks.

4.2.3. Deep Convolutional GAN (DCGAN)

It is one of the most popular and successful implementations of GANs, particularly known for its ability to generate high-resolution images. Unlike traditional GANs that use multi-layer perceptron’s (MLPs), DCGAN employs convolutional neural networks (ConvNets) in both the generator and discriminator. A key feature of DCGAN is that it replaces max pooling with convolutional strides, which allows the network to better capture spatial hierarchies in image data. Additionally, the layers in DCGAN are not fully connected, further optimizing the model for image generation [John Jenkins & Kaushik Roy, 2024].

The use of convolutions in DCGAN is particularly beneficial for image generation because they help the network efficiently extract important features from the generated data. Convolutional layers excel at identifying patterns such as edges, textures, and objects within an image, making them ideal for high-resolution image creation and differentiation. This architecture has contributed to the success of DCGAN in applications like image synthesis, super-resolution, and other tasks requiring realistic visual content generation.

4.2.4 Laplacian Pyramid GAN (LAPGAN)

It is a sophisticated image generation technique that incorporates a multi-scale image representation, to produce high-quality images composed of a series of band-pass images, each spaced an octave apart, along with a low-frequency residual image.

In LPGAN, multiple generator and discriminator networks are utilized at different levels of the Laplacian pyramid. This multi-scale approach enables the model to generate high-resolution images by progressively refining details across various image scales. The process begins by down-sampling the image at each layer of the pyramid, effectively breaking it into different frequency bands. Then, during the backward pass, the image is up-scaled at each layer while accumulating noise from the CGAN at each level [Haitao Yin, 2022]. This iterative refinement process continues until the image reaches its original size. The incorporation of the Laplacian pyramid allows for high-quality image generation, as it helps capture both fine details and global structures, making it particularly useful for applications that require realistic, high-resolution image synthesis.

4.2.5. Super Resolution GAN (SRGAN)

It is a specialized type of GAN designed to upscale low-resolution images into higher-resolution counterparts, effectively enhancing their details and clarity. SRGAN combines a deep neural network with an adversarial network to optimize the upscaling process, resulting in high-quality images with minimized errors [Devjyoti Chakraborty, 2022].

The main advantage of SRGAN is its ability to generate high-resolution images from low-resolution inputs while preserving fine details and reducing artifacts. This is achieved by using the adversarial nature of GANs: the generator creates a high-resolution image from the low-resolution input, while the discriminator evaluates the quality of the output, distinguishing between the upscale (generated) image and a real high-resolution image. This iterative process improves both networks, refining the final image. SRGAN is particularly effective for tasks such as image super-resolution, where the goal is to enhance the resolution of an image by filling in blurry spots and improving sharpness. This capability is especially useful in fields like medical imaging, satellite imaging, and visual content enhancement, where high image quality is crucial.

4.3 New Technologies in AI: Explainable AI (XAI)

Explainable AI (XAI) began to gain prominence as researchers recognized the need for AI systems to be more transparent and interpretable. This development was driven by growing concerns over trust, fairness, and accountability in AI systems. XAI's goal is to offer a clear understanding of how AI models arrive at their decisions, fostering confidence and enabling alignment with human values and societal expectations [Bas H.M. van der Velden, 2022].

Due to increased popularity, the global Explainable AI (XAI) market is expected to grow significantly, which is estimated to reach $1.2 billion by 2027. This surge is fuelled by the rising adoption of AI technologies across diverse industries, including healthcare, where transparency is vital for diagnostics; finance, where regulatory compliance demands explainable models; and manufacturing, where decision-making benefits from interpretability.

As XAI evolves, its motive is to address critical challenges such as algorithmic bias, trust, and regulatory requirements, ensuring that AI systems align with ethical and transparent standards. By making AI outcomes more interpretable and trustworthy, XAI holds the promise of bridging the gap between human understanding and machine intelligence, thereby accelerating the integration of advanced AI tools into mainstream applications [Sajid Ali et al, 2023]. This growth will democratize AI, making cutting-edge innovations more accessible and reliable for individuals and industries alike.

4.4 New Technologies in AI: Natural Language Processing (NLP)

The history of Natural Language Processing (NLP) began in the 1950s, marking the first efforts to enable computers to process and generate human language. Early milestones included rule-based systems like the Georgetown-IBM experiment in 1954 and the development of ELIZA in the 1960s. Over the decades, NLP evolved from simple syntactic analysis to sophisticated algorithms capable of understanding context, semantics, and sentiment. Looking further, NLP is poised to drive transformative changes across industries, serving as a cornerstone for the advancement of new AI technologies. From enhancing virtual assistants and chatbots to powering translation tools and sentiment analysis, the future of NLP will significantly influence how humans and machines interact. By enabling AI systems to understand and generate human-like language, NLP will continue shaping innovations in education, healthcare, business communication, and beyond.

Deep learning has profoundly transformed Natural Language Processing (NLP), primarily through models like Recurrent Neural Networks (RNNs) and transformer-based architectures such as GPT (Generative Pre-trained Transformer) and BERT (Bidirectional Encoder Representations from Transformers). These models represent significant advancements over earlier approaches and have achieved state-of-the-art results in a broad spectrum of NLP tasks.

RNNs revolutionized sequence modeling by allowing for the processing of sequential data, making them particularly effective in tasks like speech recognition and language modeling. However, RNNs struggled with long-term dependencies, leading to the development of Long Short-Term Memory (LSTM) and GRU (Gated Recurrent Units) models, which addressed these limitations.

The true breakthrough in NLP came with the advent of transformer models, such as GPT and BERT, which use self-attention mechanisms to process entire sequences of words in parallel, overcoming the limitations of sequential data processing. These models are capable of understanding context in both directions (in BERT's case) or generating coherent text based on preceding inputs (as in GPT). GPT, for example, has achieved remarkable results in language generation, producing human-like text, while BERT has set new benchmarks in tasks like question answering, sentiment analysis, and machine translation. These deep learning models have not only improved the accuracy and efficiency of NLP tasks but have also enabled new applications in real-time chatbots, language translation, and content generation, pushing the boundaries of what is possible with AI-driven language technology.

In the business industry, Natural Language Processing (NLP) has significantly transformed how companies engage with customers and streamline operations. NLP-powered tools like chatbots and virtual assistants are reshaping customer support by providing instant responses to inquiries, handling routine tasks, and offering personalized assistance. This not only enhances customer satisfaction but also reduces operational costs, making customer service more efficient and scalable.

Furthermore, NLP models are widely used for content generation, including crafting articles, product descriptions, and marketing materials. NLP-driven SEO tools enable businesses to optimize their content for search engines, improving their visibility and online reach, which is crucial in the digital age. By analyzing keywords and trends, NLP tools help companies stay ahead in competitive markets.

The future of NLP is bright, with promising advancements in areas like conversational AI, document summarization, and AI-powered content creation. As NLP continues to evolve, businesses will be equipped with even more powerful tools for efficient communication and data-driven decision-making. Those adopting and integrating NLP technologies will be better positioned to thrive in an increasingly competitive business landscape, improving operational efficiency and customer engagement in innovative ways.

4.5 New Technologies in AI: Healthcare

The integration of the latest AI technologies into healthcare marked a crucial but initially uncertain step in the industry's evolution. However, this shift has led to significant improvements in patient care, diagnosis, and treatment, largely due to custom healthcare software solutions and new AI-driven technologies. One of the earliest and most transformative applications of AI in healthcare was in medical imaging. AI has revolutionized medical imaging, particularly in fields like radiology and pathology, by enabling faster, more accurate diagnoses. AI-powered tools can analyze medical images with precision, helping doctors identify diseases at earlier stages and with greater confidence. This has led to enhanced patient outcomes and optimized treatment plans. In 2020, the AI in medical imaging market was valued at $1.13 billion and is projected to grow significantly, reaching $8.66 billion by 2027. This growth underscores the increasing adoption of AI technologies in healthcare and their potential to further transform the industry. With advancements in AI-driven diagnostic tools, healthcare professionals are now equipped with powerful tools to improve patient care, reduce human error, and enhance overall healthcare efficiency.

The implementation of new AI technologies in the healthcare industry has been nothing short of ground-breaking, offering a wide range of benefits that have transformed how medical professionals diagnose and treat patients. AI algorithms have proven to be exceptionally accurate in diagnosing various diseases, including cancer and heart conditions. For example, one AI model achieved 94% accuracy in detecting breast cancer in mammograms, outperforming traditional methods in terms of speed and precision. In addition to diagnostic capabilities, AI has played a pivotal role in drug discovery. AI models can predict potential drug candidates by analyzing vast datasets of chemical compounds and biological interactions. This process accelerates the identification of promising drugs, significantly reducing the time and cost involved in developing new treatments. The development of a single drug can take over 10 years and cost more than $2.6 billion. With AI's ability to streamline this process, pharmaceutical companies can bring new therapies to market faster and at a lower cost, potentially saving lives and improving patient outcomes on a global scale. These advancements in AI have already begun reshaping the healthcare landscape, offering solutions that improve both the quality and efficiency of patient care.

As AI technologies continue to evolve, their role in healthcare is poised to become even more transformative, revolutionizing areas like personalized medicine, patient monitoring, and predictive analytics.

The COVID-19 pandemic significantly accelerated the adoption of telemedicine, pushing healthcare providers to embrace digital solutions to ensure continuity of care during lockdowns and social distancing measures. AI-powered telehealth platforms have played a pivotal role in this transition by enabling remote consultations, allowing healthcare professionals to connect with patients from the safety and comfort of their homes. These platforms use AI to enhance the patient experience, offering features like automated appointment scheduling, and virtual assistants for answering common medical questions, and even AI-driven diagnostics for certain conditions. According to Fortune Business Insights, the global telemedicine market was valued at $87.41 billion in 2022 and is expected to grow at a significant pace, reaching $94.44 billion in 2023, with projections suggesting it will soar to $286.22 billion by 2030. This growth is driven by the increasing demand for accessible, affordable healthcare, especially in underserved regions where traditional healthcare infrastructure is limited. The rise of telemedicine, fuelled by AI technologies, has made healthcare more accessible, especially for patients in rural areas or those with mobility issues. It has also led to improved patient outcomes through more timely interventions and monitoring. As the telemedicine market continues to expand, the integration of AI tools will further enhance its capabilities, providing a more efficient, personalized, and cost-effective healthcare system.

Indeed, AI is poised to revolutionize the healthcare industry, offering transformative benefits across multiple domains. The remarkable advancements in medical imaging are enabling early and more accurate diagnoses, particularly in areas such as radiology and pathology, where AI models are already outperforming traditional methods. By detecting diseases like cancer and heart conditions with unprecedented accuracy, AI is making it possible to intervene earlier, improving patient outcomes and saving lives.

4.6 New Technologies in AI: Biometrics

The biometrics market is experiencing significant growth, thanks in large part to the integration of new AI technologies. In 2020, the global biometrics market was valued at $22.68 billion, and it is projected to reach $85.96 billion by the end of 2027. This remarkable expansion is driven by advancements in AI and machine learning, which have enhanced the accuracy, efficiency, and security of biometric systems. Among the most widely used biometric methods, fingerprint recognition stands out due to its broad application across sectors such as smartphone security, banking, and border control. AI-driven fingerprint recognition systems leverage deep learning algorithms to analyse and verify intricate details of fingerprint patterns with high precision, even in challenging conditions, such as dirty or damaged fingerprints.

According to a Future Market Insights report, fingerprint sensors currently account for about 15% of the global biometric system market. The revenue from fingerprint sensors was estimated to be $3.7 billion in 2022 and is expected to grow to $10.2 billion by 2032. This growth is fueled by increased adoption of fingerprint sensors in various consumer and security applications, such as smartphones, laptops, ATM machines, and access control systems. Fingerprint recognition has seen significant improvement through AI, including faster matching algorithms and better accuracy rates. By employing advanced machine learning models, AI has made it possible to handle a larger dataset of fingerprints, even in real-time scenarios, while reducing the risk of false positives and false negatives.

Figure 9. Biometric identification

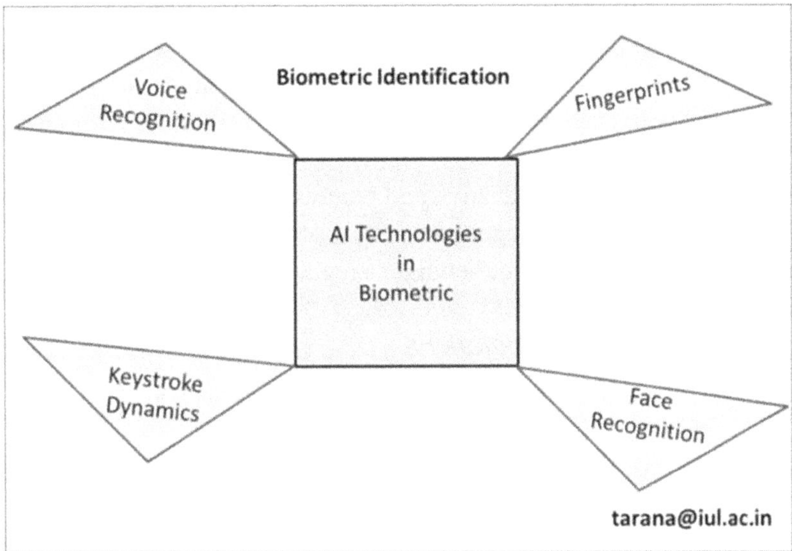

Biometric identification is shown in figure 9. As biometric technology evolves, its integration with AI will continue to enhance the performance and versatility of fingerprint recognition, face recognition, voice recognition, making it even more integral to daily life, from personal devices to national security systems. The growing demand for AI-enhanced biometric systems is expected to play a central role in the future of security and identity verification, with fingerprint recognition leading the way in this exciting, rapidly expanding field.

4.6.1 Fingerprint Recognition

Fingerprint recognition is one of the oldest and most widely used biometric technologies, enhanced significantly by AI-driven algorithms. This method analyses the unique patterns of ridges and valleys on a person's fingertips for authentication and identification.

The global fingerprint recognition market has shown consistent growth due to its adoption in consumer electronics, security systems, and financial services. According to market reports:

- In 2022, the fingerprint sensor market was valued at $3.7 billion.
- By 2032, it is projected to grow to $10.2 billion, with a compound annual growth rate (CAGR) of 10.6%. Fingerprint recognition represents 15% of the global biometric system market.

4.6.1.1 Applications of Fingerprint Recognition

Consumer Electronics:

- Widely used in smartphones, tablets, and laptops for unlocking devices and secure transactions, e.g., Touch ID.
- AI ensures faster and more accurate scanning for seamless user experiences.

Banking and Financial Services:

- Employed in ATMs and online banking for secure, contactless customer verification.
- Fingerprint-based authentication is increasingly replacing PINs and passwords.

Government and Law Enforcement:

- Used in national ID programs, border control, and criminal investigations.
- AI improves the speed and reliability of matching fingerprints against large databases.

Healthcare:

- Ensures accurate patient identification and secures access to sensitive medical records.

Access Control and Workforce Management:

- Commonly implemented in office settings to regulate access and track employee attendance.

4.6.1.2 Challenges and Ethical Considerations

Despite its advantages, fingerprint recognition faces challenges such as:

Privacy Concerns: The storage and use of biometric data raise concerns about misuse and data breaches.
Accessibility: Individuals with damaged or worn fingerprints may face difficulties with recognition systems.
Bias and Errors: AI systems must be trained on diverse datasets to ensure unbiased performance across demographics.

4.6.1.3 Future Outlook

The integration of AI and deep learning will drive further innovations in fingerprint recognition:

3D Fingerprint Scanning: Enhancing security by capturing detailed three-dimensional ridge patterns.
Contactless Recognition: AI-powered solutions will enable fingerprint recognition without physical contact, improving hygiene and convenience.
Real-Time Matching: Advancements in AI algorithms will enable faster and more efficient matching for large-scale applications.

As fingerprint recognition evolves, it will remain a cornerstone of secure identification systems, supported by AI's ability to enhance reliability and expand its applications across industries.

4.6.2 Face Recognition

Face recognition is another rapidly advancing biometric technology significantly enhanced by AI and deep learning techniques. By analysing facial features and patterns, face recognition systems are used for authentication, surveillance, and identity verification across various industries.

The global face recognition market has experienced robust growth due to its increasing adoption in security systems, smart devices, and law enforcement. In 2021, the market was valued at approximately $4.06 billion, and it is projected to reach $12.67 billion by 2028, growing at a compound annual growth rate (CAGR) of 17.6%.

AI technologies, especially convolutional neural networks (CNNs) [Lixiang Li, 2020] and deep learning models [Lixiang Li, 2020] have made face recognition more precise and scalable. Key advancements include:

Feature Extraction: AI algorithms can identify unique facial features such as the distance between the eyes, nose shape, and jawline, even in low-light or partially obscured conditions.
Real-time Analysis: AI-powered face recognition systems can process video feeds to identify faces in real time, making them invaluable for surveillance and crowd monitoring.
Emotion and Age Detection: Advanced AI models can go beyond identity verification to analyze emotions, estimate age, and even detect health conditions like stress levels.

4.6.2.1 Applications of Face Recognition

Security and Surveillance:

- Widely used in airports, public spaces, and law enforcement to track individuals and enhance security.
- Governments use AI-enhanced face recognition for border control and identifying individuals from criminal databases.

Consumer Devices:

- Popular in smartphones and laptops for unlocking devices through features like Apple's Face ID.
- AI-driven facial recognition ensures secure, user-friendly access.

Retail and Marketing:

- Retailers use face recognition to monitor customer preferences and behavior, offering personalized shopping experiences.

Healthcare:

- Used in patient identification, ensuring accurate medical records and secure access to sensitive data.

Attendance and Workforce Management:[Serign Modou Bah, 2020]

- Organizations employ face recognition for seamless attendance tracking and ensuring authorized access to restricted areas.

4.6.2.2 Challenges and Ethical Considerations

Despite its benefits, face recognition raises concerns about privacy, bias, and ethical use. AI algorithms must be designed to minimize racial and gender biases and ensure compliance with data protection regulations like GDPR. Transparency and accountability in AI-powered face recognition systems are critical to fostering public trust.

4.6.2.3 Future Outlook

The integration of AI with face recognition is expected to advance further with improvements in 3D face mapping, emotion detection, and liveness detection (to prevent spoofing with photos or videos). These advancements will expand its applications, particularly in smart cities, autonomous vehicles, and healthcare, solidifying its role as a transformative technology in biometrics.

4.6.3 Behavioral Biometrics

Behavioral Biometrics refers to the measurement and analysis of unique behavioral patterns to verify an individual's identity. Unlike traditional physical biometrics (e.g., fingerprints, face recognition), behavioral biometrics focus on how a person interacts with devices and systems, making them highly dynamic and adaptable. Key behavioural biometrics features are

Keystroke Dynamics: Tracks typing rhythm, speed, and patterns when using a keyboard.
Mouse Movement: Analyses how a user moves a mouse, including trajectory, speed, and pauses.
Gait Analysis: Monitors the unique way a person walks or moves.
Voice Recognition: Identifies individuals based on vocal tone, pitch, and speaking style.
Touchscreen Interaction: Examines how a person interacts with a touchscreen, such as swipe speed, pressure, and patterns.
Device Usage Patterns: Evaluates how a person uses devices, such as application preferences or time spent on task

4.6.3.1 Applications of Behavioural Biometrics

Cyber Security:

- Used for detecting unauthorized access or account takeover attempts.
- AI-powered behavioural biometrics identify deviations from a user's typical behaviour to flag potential breaches.

Banking and Finance:

- Helps prevent online fraud by monitoring customer interactions on banking portals and mobile apps.
- Provides additional layers of authentication without disrupting the user experience.

E-Commerce:

- Protects online transactions by ensuring the buyer's identity matches the account holder's behavioral profile.
- *Reduces the need for CAPTCHAs or multi-factor authentication (MFA) during transactions.*

Healthcare:

- Ensures secure access to sensitive patient records.
- Tracks user behaviour to identify cognitive decline or motor impairments in patients.

Workforce Management:

- Verifies employees' identities during remote work sessions to prevent unauthorized access to corporate resources.

4.6.3.2 Challenges and Ethical Considerations

Privacy Concerns: Continuous monitoring of user behaviours may raise ethical questions about data collection and usage.
False Positives/Negatives: Behavioural changes due to stress, illness, or new environments can affect system accuracy.
Integration Costs: Implementing behavioural biometric systems may require significant investments in AI infrastructure.

Regulation and Compliance: Requires adherence to data protection laws like GDPR to ensure responsible use of behavioural data.

4.6.3.3 Future Outlook

Behavioural biometrics, powered by AI, are expected to become a cornerstone of next-generation security systems, especially with advancements in:

Hybrid Authentication Systems: Combining behavioral and physical biometrics for robust, multi-layered security.
Personalized User Experiences: Tailoring services based on unique behavioral insights
Anomaly Detection in IoT Devices: Enhancing security across smart homes, wearable's, and connected devices.

As industries prioritize security and seamless user experiences, behavioral biometrics will play a critical role in shaping the future of identity verification and fraud prevention.

4.7 New Technologies in AI: Reinforcement Learning

Reinforcement Learning (RL) is a pivotal branch of artificial intelligence that focuses on training agents to make a sequence of decisions by interacting with an environment to achieve a goal. Unlike supervised learning, where models learn from labelled datasets, RL is based on trial and error. The agent learns through rewards and penalties, optimizing its behaviour to maximize cumulative rewards over time. Reinforcement Learning (RL) is a pivotal branch of artificial intelligence that focuses on training agents to make a sequence of decisions by interacting with an environment to achieve a goal. Unlike supervised learning, where models learn from labelled datasets, RL is based on trial and error. The agent learns through rewards and penalties, optimizing its behaviour to maximize cumulative rewards over time.

4.7.1 Key Features of Reinforcement Learning

Reward-Based Feedback:

- The agent receives feedback in the form of rewards (positive reinforcement) or penalties (negative reinforcement) after performing actions, guiding its learning process.

Exploration vs. Exploitation:

- RL involves balancing exploration (trying new actions to discover their effects) and exploitation (choosing known actions that yield high rewards).

Markov Decision Process (MDP):

- RL problems are often modelled as MDPs, consisting of states, actions, rewards, and a transition function that predicts future states based on current actions.

4.7.2 Applications of Reinforcement Learning

Robotics: RL enables robots to learn complex tasks such as walking, object manipulation, or autonomous navigation.

Gaming: RL has powered AI agents like AlphaGo and AlphaStar, which achieved superhuman performance in games like Go, StarCraft, and chess.
Healthcare: RL models optimize treatment plans, predict patient outcomes, and personalize therapies for individuals.
Finance: Algorithms use RL for portfolio management, trading strategies, and risk assessment by dynamically adapting to market changes.
Autonomous Vehicles: RL facilitates decision-making in navigation, collision avoidance, and route optimization for self-driving cars.

4.7.3 Advancements in RL Technologies

Deep Reinforcement Learning (Deep RL): By combining RL with deep learning, agents can process high-dimensional data like images and learn complex policies. Examples include Deep Q-Networks (DQN) and Proximal Policy Optimization (PPO).
Multi-Agent Reinforcement Learning: This allows multiple agents to learn and collaborate or compete in shared environments, with applications in logistics and real-time strategy games.
Model-Based RL: Enhances efficiency by enabling agents to simulate the outcomes of their actions instead of relying solely on real-world interaction.

4.7.4 Challenges and Future Directions

Scalability: RL often requires significant computational resources and time to train.
Safety: Ensuring safe exploration and action in critical applications like healthcare and autonomous driving.
Generalization: Developing RL models that can adapt across diverse environments without retraining.

Reinforcement Learning is reshaping industries by solving complex, dynamic problems that traditional AI methods struggle to address. As technology evolves, RL's potential for real-world impact will only grow, ushering in new possibilities in AI-driven innovation.

4.8 New Technologies in AI: Predictive AI Analytics

Predictive AI Analytics is a transformative approach to data analysis that leverages advanced machine learning (ML) and artificial intelligence (AI) techniques to forecast future outcomes based on historical data. It moves beyond traditional descriptive analytics, enabling organizations to anticipate trends, identify risks, and make data-driven decisions with unprecedented accuracy.

4.8.1 Predictive AI Work Under Following Process

Data Collection and Pre-processing:

- Gather historical and real-time data from diverse sources.
- Clean, transform, and prepare the data for analysis to ensure accuracy.

Model Training:

- Machine learning algorithms, including regression, decision trees, neural networks, and ensemble methods, are trained on the data to identify patterns and correlations.

Prediction Generation:

- Once trained, the model predicts future trends, behaviors, or events using new or real-time data inputs.

Result Validation and Optimization:

- Evaluate the model's performance using metrics like accuracy, precision, and recall.
- Refine models to improve predictive reliability.

4.8.2 Applications of Predictive AI Analytics

Healthcare:

- Forecast patient outcomes, disease progression, and hospital readmissions.
- Optimize resource allocation and personalize treatment plans.

Retail:

- Predict customer preferences and inventory needs.
- Implement dynamic pricing and improve supply chain efficiency.

Finance:

- Detect fraudulent transactions, assess credit risks, and forecast market trends.
- Automate investment strategies using predictive models.

Manufacturing:

- Enable predictive maintenance by identifying potential equipment failures.
- Optimize production schedules to reduce costs and enhance efficiency.

Marketing:

- Segment customers for targeted campaigns and predict churn rates.
- Enhance customer lifetime value predictions and refine advertising strategies.

4.8.3 Benefits of Predictive AI Analytics

- Improved decision-making with actionable insights.
- Enhanced operational efficiency by anticipating challenges and optimizing processes.
- Cost reduction through early detection of risks and inefficiencies.
- Personalized experiences for customers, leading to increased satisfaction and loyalty.

4.8.4 Challenges and Future Outlook

Data Quality and Bias:

- Inconsistent or biased data can lead to inaccurate predictions. Ensuring data integrity is critical.

Scalability:

- Handling large datasets and ensuring real-time predictions require robust infrastructure.

Ethical Considerations:

- Balancing predictive power with privacy concerns is essential for widespread adoption.

Predictive AI Analytics is poised to redefine industries by enabling proactive strategies and enhancing competitive advantage. As technology evolves, its potential to shape the future of decision-making becomes increasingly profound.

5. IMPACT OF TECHNOLOGY ON MARKET

AI is revolutionising the marketing industry. This technology can automate marketing task, personalise customer experience and delivering valuable insights into consumer behaviour. Its impact is profound and continues to expand, reshaping the marketing landscape. To harness its potential, marketers must critically assess how AI aligns with their business needs and objectives. The impact of AI on marketing is still unfolding as innovative tools and practices continue to emerge. However, its transformative potential is already evident. One of AI's most significant contributions lies in customer segmentation and targeting. By analysing vast amounts of customer data and behaviour, AI empowers marketers to segment their audiences with precision and tailor their marketing strategies accordingly. This level of personalization enhances customer engagement, drives higher conversion rates, and fosters greater customer loyalty. AI is revolutionizing marketing by automating tasks such as email campaigns, social media management, and content creation. By streamlining these processes, marketers can save time, reduce costs, and concentrate on higher-value, strategic activities. Moreover, AI-powered chatbots and virtual assistants enhance customer service by delivering personalized support around the clock [Robert Farrell, 2023]. This not only improves customer satisfaction but also boosts productivity by freeing up valuable resources for other critical tasks.

From the advancement in natural language processing (NLP) and GPT to the impact of AI on sales and marketing industries, this study will explorte the statistical, attractive fact and real-time global business examples that successfully shape new technology into business profits. The new technologies in AI have high impact on industries such as healthcare, education, finance, retail and many more. In healthcare, the basic responsibility of AI technology is to enhance accuracy in diagnosis, enable personalized medication, facilitate drug finding etc. the finance and investment traders use AI-powered algorithm to rectify risk assessment, detecting fraud with accuracy and enhancing customer services. Retail and e-commerce utilizes latest technology in AI for forecasting demand, personalized marketing strategies and optimizing supply chain operations. From market and market research, it was found that the market of AI will reach up to USD 1345.2 billion by 2023 globally [devabit, 2023]. The integration of artificial intelligence (AI) with transformative technologies such as the Internet of Things (IoT), robotics, natural language processing (NLP), and computer vision significantly enhances AI's capabilities and broadens its range of applications. The research report ensures that the AI market has been categorised into three parts. Firstly: Retail & eCommerce, BFSI, Government & Defence, Healthcare & Life Sciences, Telecom, Energy & Utilities. Secondly: Manufacturing, Agriculture, IT/ITeS, Media & Entertainment, Automotive, and thirdly; Transportation and Logistics, and others. Vertical model of AI marketing is shown in figure 10.

Figure 10. Vertical model of AI marketing

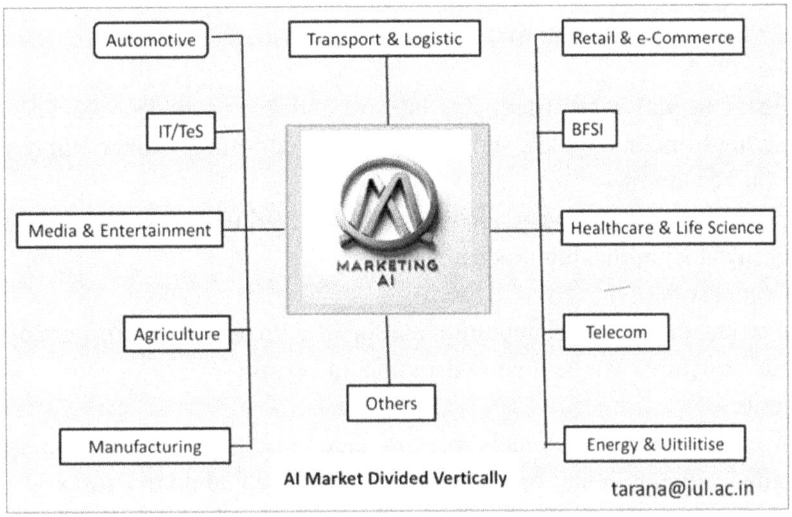

As per statista research report, in the 2022, the total corporate investment in AI has reached up to $ 92 billion globally [Bergur Thormundsson, 2024]. The amount of investment was less than in the year 2018, but was simply temporary. Furthermore, Gartner survey signifies that 80% of entrepreneurs think that automation can be implemented to any business decision. Approximately 33% of organizations are applying AI in their business. AI investment and startups graph grew up continuously and reached up to $142.3 in 2023. This shows that the AI market expanding from billion to trillion of U.S. dollars. In-between 2020 to 2022, investors worldwide moved towards AI startup, increased by five billion U.S. dollar which is double than the previous investments done by private U.S. companies. It is predicted that till 2030, AI will create approximately 70 million job world-wide and displacing 20 million, still a net gain to 50 million jobs [devabit, 2023].

6.0 CHALLENGES AND ETHICAL CONSIDERATIONS

E-collaboration technologies and generative AI tools have revolutionized how individuals and organizations work together. While these advancements bring numerous benefits, they also come with significant challenges and ethical concerns. While AI is advancing rapidly, there are challenges like bias in algorithms, privacy concerns, and the potential for job displacement. The ethical use of AI, particularly in sensitive areas like surveillance or decision-making, remains a critical topic of discussion. Some of the challenges and ethical considerations are mentioned below;

6.1 Challenges

Data Security and Privacy Risks

- Challenge: Collaborative platforms and AI tools rely on vast amounts of shared data, which increases the risk of breaches, leaks, and unauthorized access.
- Example: A cyberattack on a cloud-based collaboration platform can expose sensitive business information or personal user data.

Digital Divide

- Challenge: Unequal access to reliable internet and advanced technologies can create disparities, leaving some individuals and regions excluded from e-collaboration opportunities.

Dependency on Technology

- Challenge: Over-reliance on AI-driven tools can lead to skill erosion and a lack of critical thinking in decision-making processes.

Integration Complexity

- Challenge: Integrating e-collaboration platforms with legacy systems or across diverse organizational structures can be time-consuming and costly.

Bias in AI Tools

- Challenge: Generative AI models may produce biased outputs due to biased training data, potentially leading to unfair or misleading results in collaborative tasks.

Quality and Accuracy of Generated Content

- Challenge: Generative AI tools can sometimes produce content that is factually incorrect, inconsistent, or misleading, which can hinder collaboration or damage trust.

Misuse of Generative AI

- Challenge: Generative AI tools can be misused to create fake documents, images, or videos, leading to misinformation and fraud in collaborative environments.

6.2 Ethical Considerations

Transparency

- Ethical Concern: AI tools often operate as "black boxes," making it difficult for users to understand how decisions or outputs are generated. Transparency is essential for trust and accountability.

Accountability

- Ethical Concern: Determining responsibility for errors or unethical outcomes generated by AI tools remains a challenge. Who is accountable—the developers, the users, or the organization?

Intellectual Property and Ownership

- Ethical Concern: Clarifying ownership of content created collaboratively using AI tools is critical, especially when multiple contributors and AI-generated components are involved.

Impact on Employment

- Ethical Concern: The automation of tasks through AI tools may displace certain roles, leading to job insecurity. Balancing efficiency with workforce stability is essential.

Privacy in Collaboration

- Ethical Concern: E-collaboration technologies often involve real-time data sharing, which can infringe on individual or organizational privacy if not adequately managed.
- **Digital Harassment and Misinformation**

- Ethical Concern: Collaborative platforms can be misused for spreading false information, cyber bullying, or exploiting AI tools for harmful purposes.

Environmental Impact

- Ethical Concern: The computational demands of AI tools and cloud-based collaboration platforms contribute to high energy consumption, raising sustainability concerns.

6.3. Strategies to Mitigate Challenges and Ethical Issues

Enhanced Security Protocols

- Implement encryption, multi-factor authentication, and regular security audits for collaboration platforms and AI tools.

Bias Mitigation in AI

- Train AI models on diverse datasets and continuously monitor for unintended biases.

Transparent AI Systems

- Develop explainable AI (XAI) solutions to provide users with insights into how outputs are generated.

Regulation and Guidelines

- Establish industry-wide standards and ethical guidelines for the development and use of e-collaboration technologies and AI tools.

Awareness and Training

- Educate users about ethical use, data privacy, and the limitations of generative AI tools to ensure responsible adoption.

Equal Access Initiatives

- Promote digital inclusion by investing in infrastructure and resources to bridge the digital divide.

Green AI Practices

- Encourage sustainable development practices, such as optimizing algorithms and using energy-efficient infrastructure.

By addressing these challenges and ethical considerations, organizations and developers can foster trust, inclusivity, and innovation in e-collaboration technologies and generative AI tools, ensuring their benefits are maximized responsibly.

CONCLUSION

The rapid advancements in AI technology are reshaping industries, unlocking new possibilities, and improving human lives in numerous ways. From deep learning and NLP to generative AI and autonomous systems, AI continues to push the boundaries of what is possible. As AI technology evolves, it will further drive innovation, transforming how we live, work, and interact with the world. However, ethical considerations, such as fairness, transparency, and privacy, remain critical to ensuring that AI's advancements benefit society as a whole.

The evolution of AI from simple algorithms to neural networks is a story of relentless pursuit and remarkable progress in machine learning. The journey of AI is far from over, with on-going research and developments hinting at even more ground-breaking advancements in the future. As we stand at the cusp of a new era in AI, it's essential to reflect on this history to understand its potential and responsibly harness its power.

The future of collaborative technologies with generative AI tools is marked by increased efficiency, inclusivity, and innovation. By breaking barriers in communication, creativity, and coordination, these advancements will transform how people work together, unlocking unprecedented potential across industries. Businesses that embrace these technologies early will gain a competitive edge in the rapidly evolving digital landscape.

E-collaboration technologies integrated with generative AI tools are redefining how teams and organizations connect, create, and achieve their goals. These advancements offer unprecedented opportunities for enhancing productivity, fostering creativity, and breaking down barriers to effective collaboration. By automating repetitive tasks, personalizing interactions, and enabling real-time, data-driven insights, generative AI enhances the efficiency and inclusivity of collaborative efforts across industries.

However, as these tools continue to evolve, it is crucial to address challenges such as data privacy, ethical considerations, and skill gaps to ensure their responsible and equitable use. The future of e-collaboration lies in harnessing the power of AI to create environments where technology empowers human potential, driving innovation and fostering meaningful connections in an increasingly digital world. Organizations that embrace and adapt to these tools will be well-positioned to thrive in the era of intelligent collaboration.

REFERENCES

Ali, S., Abuhmed, T., El-Sappagh, S., Muhammad, K., Alonso-Moral, J. M., Confalonieri, R., Guidotti, R., Del Ser, J., Díaz-Rodríguez, N., & Herrera, F. (2023). Explainable artificial intelligence (XAI): What we know and what is left to attain trustworthy artificial intelligence. *Information Fusion*, *99*, 101805. DOI: 10.1016/j.inffus.2023.101805

Andrew. (n.d.). *Generative AI tools FAQ*. Carnegie Mellon University. https://www.cmu.edu/teaching/technology/aitools/index.html

Ates, C., Karwan, F., Okraschevski, M., Koch, R., & Bauer, H.-J. (2022). Conditional generative adversarial networks for modelling fuel sprays. *Energy and AI*, *12*, 100216. https://doi.org/10.1016/j.egyai.2022.100216 DOI: 10.1016/j.egyai.2022.100216

Australian Government, Department of Industry, Science and Research. (2023). *AI technology*. https://www.industry.gov.au/publications/list-critical-technologies-national-interest/ai-technologies

Bah, S. M., & Ming, F. (2020). An improved face recognition algorithm and its application in attendance management system. *Array (New York, N.Y.)*, *5*, 100014. DOI: 10.1016/j.array.2019.100014

Chakraborty, D. (2022). *Super-resolution generative adversarial networks (SRGAN)*. PyImageSearch. https://pyimagesearch.com/

D'Agostino, A. (2023, November 15). *Introduction to generative AI and its applications*. Medium. https://medium.com/@theDrewDag/introduction-to-generative-ai-and-its-applications-e036c6a36135

Devabit. (2023). *Top 11 new technologies in AI: Exploring the latest trends*. https://devabit.com/blog/top-11-new-technologies-in-ai-exploring-the-latest-trends/

Engelbrecht, A. (2024, January 18). *Humans and AI: The power of collaborative intelligence*. AI Journ. https://aijourn.com/humans-and-ai-the-power-of-collaborative-intelligence/

Farrell, R. (2023). The impact of artificial intelligence on marketing. Griffith. https://www.griffith.ie/blog/the-impact-of-artificial-intelligence-on-marketing#:~:text=The%20positive%20impact%20of%20AI%20on%20Marketing%3A&text=This%20can%20lead%20to%20better,media%20management%2C%20and%20content%20creation

Gargish, P. (2023, October 17). *The role of generative AI in virtual classrooms for enhancing collaboration in e-education*. Netsmartz. https://netsmartz.com/blog/generative-ai-for-education/

GreeksforGreek. (2024). Generative adversarial network. GAN. https://www.geeksforgeeks.org/generative-adversarial-network-gan/

iProov. (2024). *Generative adversarial network (GAN).* https://www.iproov.com/biometric-encyclopedia/generative-adversarial-network-gan

Jenkins, J., & Roy, K. (2024). Exploring deep convolutional generative adversarial networks (DCGAN) in biometric systems: A survey study. *Discover Artificial Intelligence*, *4*(1), 42. Advance online publication. DOI: 10.1007/s44163-024-00138-z

Kaushal, S. (2024, March 19). *Overcoming challenges in generative AI implementation.* Signity Solutions. https://www.signitysolutions.com/blog/challenges-in-generative-ai-implementation#:~:text=One%20of%20the%20crucial%20challenges,pose%20privacy%20and%20security%20concerns

Lawton, G. (n.d.). What is generative AI? Everything you need to know. TechTarget. https://www.techtarget.com/searchenterpriseai/definition/generative-AI

Li, L.. (2020). A review of face recognition technology. *IEEE Access : Practical Innovations, Open Solutions*, *8*, 205327–205339. https://www.researchgate.net/publication/343118558_A_Review_of_Face_Recognition_Technology

McDermott, M. (n.d.). Collaborative intelligence: Humans and AI in harmony. Major Digital. https://majordigital.com/articles/unlocking-collaborative-intelligence-humans-and-ai-thrive-together

Moon, J., Jung, S., Park, S., & Hwang, E. (2020). Conditional tabular GAN-based two-stage data generation scheme for short-term load forecasting. *IEEE Access : Practical Innovations, Open Solutions*, *8*, 205327–205339. DOI: 10.1109/ACCESS.2020.3037063

Nah, F. F. H.. (2023, July). Generative AI and ChatGPT: Applications, challenges, and AI-human collaboration. *Journal of Information Technology*, *25*(2), 1–28. DOI: 10.1080/15228053.2023.2233814

Netsmartz. (n.d.). *The role of generative AI in virtual classrooms for enhancing collaboration in e-education.* https://netsmartz.com/blog/generative-ai-for-education/

Punyani, A. (2024, March 11). *Exploring human-AI collaboration: Synergy between humans and machines.* Convin. https://convin.ai/blog/human-ai-collaboration-insights#:~:text=Humans%20provide%20contextual%20understanding%20and,more%20personalized%20and%20effective%20solutions

Resnick, M. (2024). Generative AI and creative learning: Concerns, opportunities, and choices. Medium. https://mres.medium.com/ai-and-creative-learning-concerns-opportunities-and-choices-63b27f16d4d0

Schulze, J. (2024). What is GAN? Generative adversarial networks (GAN) explained. Coursera. https://www.coursera.org/articles/what-is-gan

Sehgal, H. (n.d.). Generative AI and human-AI collaboration: A look into the future. Solulab. https://www.solulab.com/generative-ai-and-human-ai-collaboration/#:~:text=Collaborative%20artificial%20intelligence%20leverages%20the,complement%20each%20other's%20skill%20sets

Singh, A. (2024). The impact of AI on biometric identification technology. Mantratec. https://blog.mantratec.com/AI-Biometrics-Technology

TechTarget. (n.d.). *What is generative AI? Everything you need to know.* Retrieved May 2, 2025, from https://www.techtarget.com/searchenterpriseai/definition/generative-AI

Teoh, K. H., Ismail, R. C., Naziri, S. Z. M., Hussin, R., Isa, M. N. M., & Basir, M. S. S. M. (2022). Face recognition and identification using deep learning approach. *Journal of Physics: Conference Series*, *1755*(1), 012006. DOI: 10.1088/1742-6596/1755/1/012006

Thormundsson, B. (2024). Global total corporate artificial intelligence (AI) investment from 2015 to 2022. Statista. https://www.statista.com/statistics/941137/ai-investment-and-funding-worldwide/

Valois-Chénier, M. (2024, March 6). *Generative AI-human collaboration: How AI algorithms are enhancing human creativity*. Chapter247. https://www.chapter247.com/blog/generative-ai-human-collaboration-how-ai-algorithms-are-enhancing-human-creativity/

van der Velden, B. H. M., Kuijf, H. J., Gilhuijs, K. G. A., & Viergever, M. A. (2022). Explainable artificial intelligence (XAI) in deep learning-based medical image analysis. *Medical Image Analysis*, *79*, 102470. DOI: 10.1016/j.media.2022.102470 PMID: 35576821

Yasar, K., Robinson, S., & Lewis, S. (2024). What is a generative adversarial network (GAN)? TechTarget. https://www.techtarget.com/searchenterpriseai/definition/generative-adversarial-network-GAN

Yilmaz, R., & Yilmaz, F. G. K. (2023). The effect of generative artificial intelligence (AI)-based tool use on students' computational thinking skills, programming self-efficacy and motivation. *Computer Applications in Engineering Education*, *4*, 100147. https://doi.org/10.1016/j.caeai.2023.100147

Yin, H., & Xiao, J. (2022). Laplacian pyramid generative adversarial network for infrared and visible image fusion. *IEEE Signal Processing Letters*, *29*, 230–234. DOI: 10.1109/LSP.2022.3207621

Chapter 17
Human-AI Collaborative Intelligence:
Ethical and Legal Considerations

Jipson Joseph
https://orcid.org/0009-0005-1795-5051
Christ University, India

Ananya Pandey
https://orcid.org/0000-0002-2419-6314
Christ University, India

ABSTRACT

The present globe benefits from the unprecedented growth of science and technology. The invention of Artificial Intelligence (AI) has opened a vast horizon of possibilities, choices, and capabilities for humans and society. AI-powered human-like systems provide substantial interaction and collaboration for better results in many fields. The speed, efficiency, and effectiveness of AI systems prompted almost all sectors, like healthcare, education, transport, and communication to invest in them. This resulted in shifting attention from human-human collective intelligence to human-AI collaborative intelligence. This shift has significantly contributed to many fields and reduces the security risks to humans. However, there are also many ethical and legal concerns in this innovative area, like data privacy, transparency issues, liability, and accountability. This chapter, using analytical and critical methods, examines the functioning of collaborative intelligence and suggests the required ethical and legal principles for incorporation into national and international policy design.

INTRODUCTION

Decision-making is the most vital dimension of any business venture. It is a unique capacity of an individual that refers to one's ability to make a specific decision on a given condition (Luxenberg & Stein, 2024). This ability revolves around factors like education, life experience, and social and cultural background. It is the fruit of the logical and systematic application of one's intelligence (Ariyo et al., 2023). Every person has unique intelligence, which makes decisions differently from others by analyzing

DOI: 10.4018/979-8-3693-8332-2.ch017

various factors. The analyzing capacity of intelligence is the rationale for meaningful decision-making (Sylaska, Allen, & Mayer, 2020). In common parlance, collective intelligence is the sum of many individual intelligences (Lévy, 1997). For example, suppose an individual initiative exists (business, industry, research work, etc.). In that case, most of the decisions are taken by those specific individuals based on their intelligence and decision-making capacity.

In contrast, if there are two or more persons as partners or collaborators, they make a collective effort and thereby arrive at a more meaningful and effective decision with the support of the intelligence of all of them (Tjornbo, 2015). As an idea, collective intelligence originated in 1785 with the contribution of Marquis de Condorcet, but it became popular in the last decades of the 20th century. If properly employed, collective intelligence will have more effective results than individual intelligence (Krause et al., 2009). In the present century, collective intelligence has given way to collaborative intelligence, focusing on the interaction between humans and Artificial Intelligence (AI) (Liu & Shen, 2025). It can also be considered an intelligent collaboration between humans and machines (Bonabeau, 2009). People spend most of their time and research in the virtual world, where they interact with machines that use AI technological advancements. Such human-machine interaction using AI can enhance the contributions and tackle the most difficult tasks for humans (Hogan et al., 2023). The present-day complexities of society require such collaborative and collective efforts.

Human-AI collaborative intelligence has many advantages. It can promote economic growth, environmental protection, and societal well-being. It can help humankind to undertake projects and tasks that are difficult and dangerous (Yun et al., 2021). It also advances unparalleled scientific development and economic growth (Tjornbo, 2015). However, such an interaction between humans and machines also has disadvantages. It can reduce employment opportunities, increase societal disparities, and cause health and environmental risks. Besides, humans can employ AI-powered systems to satisfy selfish and individualistic profit-oriented motives (Mueen Ahmed & Yunus, 2024). From this perspective, there need to be specific ethical and legal considerations that will ensure safety, privacy, and societal well-being in the use and application of human-AI collaborative intelligence (Vann Yaroson et al., 2025). The chapter differentiates between collective and collaborative intelligence, analyzes the various fields of human-AI interaction and its features, critically examines the functioning of collaborative intelligence in human existence, explores the ethical and legal framework in human-AI collaboration, and advances some policy suggestions. The chapter affirms that human-AI collaborative intelligence is the need of the time if it functions within specific ethical and legal parameters.

THEORETICAL FRAMEWORK

Artificial Intelligence (AI) is "the simulation of human intelligence in machines that are programmed to think, learn, and perform tasks autonomously" (Akinnagbe, 2024, p. 388). The employability of human intelligence has grown to unparalleled levels with the invention of AI. It offered many opportunities and possibilities to ease the functioning of human intelligence. It also has the potential to outshine human intelligence with its scope and speed. However, AI is only a creation of humans and should remain under their control and guidance for societal welfare. The present globe testifies to the active incorporation of AI technologies in almost all fields of human life (Fragiadakis et al., 2024). Humans cannot think of a smooth life without the use and applications of AI. Such a wide range of usage insists that humans and AI should have efficient collaborative functioning. Conventional human-machine interaction is substituted with human-AI collaborative intelligence, which prioritizes working together (Makarius et al., 2020). Human-AI collaborative intelligence is the synergy that prioritizes active and efficient collaboration of human intuition and machine intelligence. The convergence of human intelligence and AI has immense possibilities for problem-solving and decision-making that benefit society (Akinnagbe, 2024). Human intuition and human-induced machine intelligence are not contradictory but complement each other. However, the growing complex interactions between humans and AI systems demand that an ethically and legally built human-AI collaborative intelligence is key to realizing a significant result.

COLLECTIVE INTELLIGENCE TO COLLABORATIVE INTELLIGENCE

Collective intelligence has become a catchword with the unparalleled growth of the virtual world, where many people easily connect and collaborate for great innovation strategies (Bücheler & Sieg, 2011). The interest in collective intelligence became more vibrant with the growth of information and communication technologies (ICT) (Yun et al., 2021). Collective intelligence does not refer to the average individual intelligence of the group members, but it primarily refers to factors like the average social sensitivity of the members, quality of interaction, number of female members, and coordinating spirit (Woolley et al., 2010). Collective intelligence, thus, cannot be equated with the collective behavior of a group (Smelser, 2011). Collective intelligence is "a group of individuals collaborating to create synergy, that is, create something greater than the sum of each individual part, which is to do things collectively that seems intelligent" (Yun et al., 2021, p. 204). Collective intelligence is also called swarm intelligence, which denotes the collective and self-organized behavior patterns of the swarms of social insects. While collective intelligence originates from swarm intelligence, many researchers prefer collective intelligence to refer to humans and swarm intelligence to refer to insects and other creatures (Salminen, 2012).

Although the term 'collaborative intelligence' can also be understood regarding human-human intelligence collaboration, this chapter prefers to use it from the perspective of human-machine interaction, particularly human-AI interaction. Human-machine interaction may not require any intelligent activity from the machine. But AI denotes the machine's capacity to use automated intelligence. This differentiation is in line with the claims of some researchers who argue that collective intelligence refers to the intelligence of a group resulting from the collaboration and competition among its members (Truong & Nguyen, 2024). However, some authors argue that the individuals who act intelligently for some goals can be either software agents, people, or a mixture of both (Weld et al., 2014). Nevertheless, we prefer collaborative intelligence for differentiating human-machine/AI intelligent action (collaborative intelligence) from human-human intelligence (collective intelligence). Collaboration is also a potent form of working together (Kapetanios, 2008). The technological advancements that connect many machines with human intelligence can spot issues faster, solve complex problems, and produce better results (Mulgan, 2018). Collaborative intelligence can enhance humans' problem-solving and decision-making capacity and strengthen technological systems like power grids, wind-turbine farms, air traffic control, google map, and autonomous vehicles (Leonard & Levin, 2022). Collaborative intelligence is the synergy and accumulation of human and technical resources interaction (Malone & Klein, 2007). It is also defined as bridging humans and computers, in which computer-supported machines collect and harvest human-generated knowledge and produce better outcomes (Kapetanios, 2008). The transition from the typical collective intelligence (resulting from the interaction of humans) to the collaborative intelligence (resulting from the human-machine or human-AI interaction) predominantly relies on the advancement in computer algorithms like AI, the Internet of Things (IoT), and blockchain technologies.

Evolution of Collective Intelligence

In its original form, collective intelligence might have originated with the use of intellectual efforts to solve specific tasks. It was joining two more intellectual efforts to realize an objective (Flores et al., 2015). Collective intelligence originated as a by-product of biological and cultural evolution, manifesting the innovative ways humans solve various problems and challenges in groups rather than entirely relying on individual capacity (Mulgan, 2018; Hogan et al., 2023). Accordingly, a group's collective intelligence exceeds the intelligence of highly efficient members of that group in all probability (Truong & Nguyen, 2024). Collective intelligence has specific essential characteristics, such as the degree of cooperation comprising information sharing and activity coordination (Leonard & Levin, 2022). Wechsler (1971), one of the forerunners of collective intelligence, argues that shared thinking is the characteristic element of collective intelligence, and accordingly, it is the mother of inventions. He states that though the outcome may not always be so impressive, it results from unique integration. Collective intelligence is synonymously used with many terms like "swarm intelligence" (Salminen, 2012), "group intelligence" (Willian & Sternberg, 1988), "vox populi" (Galton, 1907), "wisdom of crowds" (Surowiecki, 2004), "collective mind" (Weick & Roberts, 1993), or "organizational mid" (Sandelands & Stablein, 1987). Collective intelligence was initially used for human-human interaction only. Slowly, however, with the advancement of technology and the invention of AI-powered human-like systems, they came to be used in the context of other collaborative efforts.

Human-AI Collaborative Intelligence

With the incorporation of computers in the so-called traditional human actions, collective intelligence took a new dimension, by which actions became more intelligent due to the bridging of systems and humans (Flores et al., 2015). The foundation of the evolution of AI can be traced back to Alan Turing's 1950 question: can machines think? With the latest advancements in machine learning (ML), AI has become more than a tool for human lives. Using various fields of ML-like supervised learning, unsupervised learning, reinforcement learning, deep learning, natural language processing, automatic speech recognition, and computer vision techniques; it functions in a variety of forms like companion, friend, partner, and sometimes an opponent (Voulodimos et al., 2018; Schultz et al., 2021; Aldarmaki et al., 2022). AI systems refer to systems with data processing and information capacities resembling intelligent behavior, including various features like reasoning, learning, perception, prediction, planning, decision-making, or control (UNESCO, 2022). Human-AI collaborative intelligence is the present stage of a long evolutionary cycle. With the use of the term "intelligence," it can be assumed that AI is an agent that can "collaborate" with humans and other artificial agents for the performance of a task (Cañas, 2022). Wang et al. (2020) note that it is evitable to move from human-human collective intelligence to human-AI collaborative intelligence. Swarm intelligence refers to the direct forms of coordinated use of individual intelligence, which is mainly inspired by the behavior patterns of insects like ants and bees. Stigmergy stands for the indirect coordination between agents and actions. The swarm intelligence of the insects also inspires it. Collaborative intelligence relies on group coordination through various skills and technological support systems. Collective intelligence refers to all these three evolutionary stages, but Huma-AI collaborative intelligence refers precisely to the use of technological advancement for the better application of human intelligence (Hogan et al., 2023). Human-AI collaborative intelligence is the joint intellectual efforts of humans and AI to pursue a common goal (Jiang et al., 2024). It focuses on producing synergic relationships to produce successful outcomes in various fields (Cañas, 2022). Human-AI collaboration has become more vibrant with the new trends of Virtual Reality (VR), Augmented Reality (AR), and Mixed Reality (MR) technologies (Liu & Siau, 2023).

Gordon Moore (1975) argued that there are various ways, such as processing speed, memory capacity, resolution of digital cameras, and functional abilities, to measure the capability of a digital electronic device. These options and capabilities are increasing at an exponential rate. With the advent of personal computers, the Internet, and the World Wide Web, the integration of computers and systems became more active, enabling cooperation among the systems and between the systems and humans (Kapetanios, 2008). AI is the newest and most developed form of technological advancement, where various machines and computers are created that can learn, reason, and act, which were once considered specific to human intelligence. Although AI is a common term for the above-mentioned super-power computer algorithms, it manifests through an autonomous software module (agent), which has the capacity for decision-making (Weld et al., 2014). AI is an autonomous and intelligent machine with human-like capabilities that interact with humans as intelligent beings, not merely as IT artifacts. Humans also can interact with AI in a human-like manner (Sun, Shen & Zhang, 2023). AI can function and make decisions even in complex and uncertain circumstances. It has various capabilities like learning and refining, thinking ahead, and acting for extended periods following its objectives. Such things are realized through experience or human feedback (Weld et al., 2014).

There is a wide range of differences between 'functional sharing' and 'intelligence sharing' between humans and AI. Previously, humans gave certain functions to machines, but with AI's advancement, they assigned cognitive capacity to machines, leading to inter-agent collaboration (Cañas, 2022). Though collaborative intelligence emphasizes the role of humans in the creation of knowledge and content and their collective capacity in problem-solving, it also affirms "the role of computers as facilitators of learning and knowledge sharing in collaborative environments via multimedia enriched contents and games" (Kapetanios, 2008, p. 287). Human-AI collaborative intelligence must function based on a collective knowledge system that includes humans' generated and system-generated knowledge, which emerges from inference, computation, and logical design of the already collected knowledge. This collective knowledge-driven collaborative intelligence should guide society to new knowledge, discoveries, problem-solving, and decision-making. AI systems can actively participate and cooperate in human-included decision-making bodies through their wide range of information, articulation capacity, human-like interaction, and novelty. It can also simplify complex things and present them properly as experienced colleagues. It can support the group in the decision-making process through valuable suggestions, creative ideas, and fresh insights that help the whole group reach a consensus and decision (Liu & Siau, 2023).

Fields of Human-AI Interaction

At the beginning of digital technological growth, the focus was on advancing AI technology and finding new fields of incorporation and implementation. This was a technological-centric stage. Thereafter, the focus was shifted to a human-centric perspective, where care was given to the possible options of benefiting AI technologies for human development. Humans widely benefit from AI tools and systems like robots, autonomous vehicles, drones, virtual conversational agents, and biometric tools. Human-AI interaction, in the present times, is actively used in almost all fields like education, healthcare, transportation, communication, customer service, the industrial sector, marketing, entertainment, research and development, and space technologies (Yang et al., 2022; Sun, Shen & Zhang, 2023). With the support of AI, the medical and healthcare sectors are being revolutionized. It helps in disease diagnosis, analysis of patient data, medical imaging analysis, remote patient monitoring, and complex surgical procedures. Besides, it is widely employed in military operations and creative activities like painting, storytelling, music composition, fashion design, and game design. These collaborations take place in four different ways: assisted intelligence (humans use AI as an assistant), augmented intelligence (using AI as a supporter to amplify human abilities), cooperative intelligence (working as a team to find solutions to complex problems), and autonomous intelligence (AI independently work and decide without continuous human interventions) (Jiang et al., 2024).

In the present era, chatbots are widely used, and they can interact with humans in a human-like manner, improving user satisfaction (Radziwill & Benton, 2017). A study report by Forbes claims a 67% increase in sales with the help of chatbots but states that customers prefer to interact with humans rather than the AI support system (Press, 2019). With the growth of cutting-edge technologies, chatbots and other AI tools' intelligence has been updated and modified to have more human-like functioning. They now act as personal assistants and try to take care of the needs of the users (Hu & Sun, 2023). Since 2022, huma-AI interaction has come to a new phase with the development of ChatGPT and GPT 4. Within 2 months of its launch, ChatGPT attracted over 30 million users because of its human-like responses, quality, increased user satisfaction, intelligent customer service, and loyalty (Peres et al., 2023). Due to its high human-like attributes, like the use of natural language and friendly conversation, the panel of judges at the Turing test thought that ChatGPT was a human (Liu & Siau, 2023). The latest AI technology uses autonomous abilities like deep learning and reinforcement learning (Xu et al., 2023). AI applications are widely used in many fields, from Apple Siri to Amazon Alexa and from self-driving cars to autonomous weapons. Another field of human-AI interaction is using Avatars to enhance voice- and text-based interaction (Liu & Siau, 2023). Avatar originated from the Sanskrit word *avatāra,* which stands for the incarnation/personification of deity. In this context, it refers to the person-like manifestation of the AI system. Being a digital human, it replicates human movements, communication skills, and behavior, helping to have a realistic interaction (Tully, 2024). Since the latest technologies focus on designing AI avatars with all the minute specimens like mouth shape, skin texture, and eye movement, it provides a more realistic perspective (Liu & Siau, 2023).

Decision-Making in Human-AI Interaction Using Collaborative Intelligence

In human-AI collaboration, value should be created through integration and cooperation. Both humans and AI should actively contribute to building a collaborative intelligence to enable its efficiency and effectiveness (Kapetanios, 2008). In human-AI collaborative intelligence, the human is the principal delegate, and AI is the agent. That is, humans assign and delegate specific tasks to AI to complete them on behalf of humans. Decision-making in interactive, collaborative intelligence depends on human-AI and task-AI fitness. Human-AI fit depends on physical, cognitive, and emotional dimensions. Physical fit depends on whether AI can appropriately obtain the physical information like voice, pictures, and video provided by humans and convert it into digital information. Cognitive fit refers to the capacity of

AI to adequately understand human needs and meanings. Emotional fit refers to the capacity of the AI to understand and experience human emotions and provide emotional support.

Task fit is the extent to which AI can meet the requirements of the assigned tasks. AI typically has two functions: routine and creative. Routine tasks can be obtained through a search of information on the Web. For instance, who is the 51st President of the USA? The AI tool searches through the existing Web knowledge and gives credible answers. Creative tasks are those that need creativity and novelty. It goes beyond existing and available information and provides some new knowledge. Novelty is the prerequisite for creative tasks (Sun, Shen & Zhang, 2023). Human-AI collaborative intelligence's decision-making capacity should prioritize collaboration in this creative task that can ensure more results.

AI can boost human beings' analytical and decision-making abilities. They do it primarily by providing the correct information at the right time. Better and meaningful decisions always result from better information and support (Wilson & Daugherty, 2018). AI is actively present in the decision-making processes that humans previously monopolized, such as healthcare and criminal justice. Certain other areas, like fraud detection and credit scoring, also require AI involvement as they require high operational efficiency and statistical precision. Both humans and AI have their strengths and weaknesses. Accordingly, an efficient collaboration between these two actors can make effective decision-making. The ultimate objective of the decision-making should be optimizing performance and fairness (Leitão, 2022).

Collaborative Intelligence and Economic Growth

Studies affirm that companies achieve their most significant result when humans and AI-supported systems work together. Human-AI collaborative functioning helped many employers to interact substantially with their employees and customers. AI systems have erudite sensors, motors, and actuators, allowing them to recognize people and objects, enabling them to work with humans safely and providing better results. Both humans and AI have complementary strengths: humans are empowered with leadership, teamwork, creativity, and social skills, whereas AI systems are equipped with speed, scalability, and quantitative capabilities. Certain things will be impossible for humans (like analyzing gigabytes of data), whereas certain things will be confusing for the AI systems (Wilson & Daugherty, 2018). However, due to their complementary capacities, they can ensure the firm's and society's development and economic growth.

Human-AI collaboration improves factors like performance, novelty, productivity, or quality of work done individually, leading to economic development. Complementing each other and ensuring teamwork for a shared objective through sustained interaction, this new design of collaborative intelligence promotes economic growth (Schleiger et al., 2024). Researchers argue that the incorporation of AI in various fields can increase the quality of work as it has the potential to empower workers with predictability, controllability, meaningfulness, and fairness (Langer & Landers, 2021). Human-AI collaboration can also address the issues concerning skill gaps and advance the possibilities for more outcomes and economic benefits. Increased use and application of AI systems and human workforces increases creativity, human worker satisfaction, safety, accuracy and precision of work, and productivity. Collaborative intelligence affirms that it can lead to more productivity and economic growth than the individual achievement of either agent (Schleiger et al., 2024).

Collaborative Intelligence and Sustainable Society

All the scientific and technological advancements are given sustainable society objectives. Human-AI collaborative intelligence must promote inclusiveness in the sense that the benefits of technological advancement should be available and accessible to all and should not discriminate against any person from the list of beneficiaries. Special care must be taken by the international community and the UN member states to give privilege to the choices of the marginalized in their interest for understanding and collaborating with AI. The UN's sustainability objective can either be promoted or hindered by AI technologies. Thus, special attention should be given to undertaking routine assessment of AI systems' economic, social, cultural, environmental, and human impact to ensure that the sustainability aspiration is not threatened (UNESCO, 2022). The ultimate objective of collaborative intelligence should be the welfare of society. It should have the rationale to prioritize the UN 2030 agenda of humanity's sustainable future.

In the present world, human initiatives alone cannot tackle global sustainability demands as globalization, liberalization, and open economy have redesigned the functioning of the entire globe. It demands an inclusive approach where humans collaborate with the latest technological advancements like AI to make sustainability initiatives iterative, responsive, and inclusive. Aspirations for a sustainable society require the expertise of various people, AI systems, and worldviews. Coordination, collaboration, and collective efforts are the prerequisites for a sustainable society (Wood et al., 2021). The United Nations Development Program (UNDP) (2021) suggests that to "leave no one behind" in the sustainability objective, fairer AI systems should be developed, and more focus should be given to human-AI cooperative efforts. Besides, the agenda for a sustainable society will be meaningless without sustainable security demands that focus on protecting cyberspace and AI systems.

COLLABORATIVE INTELLIGENCE AND HUMAN EXISTENCE: A CRITIQUE

AI, as an invention and technological advancement, makes human existence meaningful. But at the same time, the use and application of AI in many fields create confusion and insecurity among people. It is mainly in the ambit of job opportunities. Many consider AI-powered systems a potential threat to human employment and control over the world. Researchers in the field opine that AI should not be viewed as an opponent to humans but as a collaborator to make it more efficient. With the support of AI, humans should be able to increase their expertise in the field. A healthy competition should be fostered to achieve the full potential of both humans and AI (Jiang et al., 2024). However, this also causes some serious apprehensions about the job opportunities of less-educated people who fail to cope with AI technologies. Substituting human labor with AI systems or incorporating only people with technological knowledge may create human insecurities. There can also be instances of human-AI conflict. Thomas and Vaughan (2018) ask how to address a situation when a human and a robot must simultaneously pass a doorway. Self-driving cars or autopilot systems can also create confusion as they may sometimes get out of the control of human drivers (Wen et al., 2022). For instance, cars are jointly driven by an installed AI system and a human driver. When an accident happens, who will be responsible? We cannot always say that AI algorithms create only good results. Sometimes, it can also potentially threaten people's physical and mental well-being. Individuals should have some basic understanding of what AI can and cannot do. They may use it unnecessarily without such knowledge, causing trouble (Jiang et al.,

2024). For instance, Grammarly software functions using AI, but the issue is that its function depends on the fed data. It uses US English, and users must check its grammar, style, punctuation, and spacing corrections. If human authors do not collaborate with the Grammarly AI, it may not give the required result. The same situation may happen in almost all fields of AI incorporation.

Furthermore, "AI avatars have great potential to exhibit the "emotions" of AI systems, to create a more human-like interaction" (Liu & Siau, 2023, p. 123). It acts like a double-edged sword. The human-like appearance, voice, gesture, and other qualities may create an emotional bond between humans and AI systems. Emotions should evolve from one's heart and brain (love and reason); they are mutual, where there is giving and receiving. Balancing emotions is critical. In the same manner, emotional interaction requires the balancing of two persons as well. However, for AI systems, these emotions evolve from the stored data. It is mechanical rather than honestly expressing real emotions. Some people misunderstand this and foster an emotional bond with AI tools. For instance, in 2017, more than a million people asked Amazon's Alexa to marry them! (Leskin, 2018). Alexa's voice or style might have attracted them. However, the danger is that humans lose their emotional bond with real people and restrict themselves to cyberspace.

HUMAN-AI INTERACTION: ETHICAL AND LEGAL CONSIDERATIONS

In human-AI collaboration, there are two different models. The human-dominant model considers AI a supporting system, and humans make decisions based only on AI results and information. In the AI-dominant model, AI is the key decision-maker, and humans have only the supporting role (Sun, Shen & Zhang, 2023). Humans need not subjugate to the machine algorithm as there are times when, more than AI's innovative or professional capabilities, society requires humans' ethical and legal base for its effective functioning. Though AI-powered systems can make decisions, many researchers are concerned about people losing control over the system, which can cause unimaginable negative consequences (Liu & Siau, 2023). Shneiderman (2020) thus argues for human's complete control over the AI systems. The extraordinary capabilities of AI-guided systems have dynamic positive and negative impacts on human lives, societies, the environment, and the ecosystem, which raise significant ethical concerns among the public (UNESCO, 2022). Garibay et al. (2023) call for prioritizing values like human welfare, safety, transparency, privacy, and responsibility. Cañas (2022) argues that most approaches to the ethics of AI are focused on the ethical principles that should guide the design of AI to ensure that it does not harm humans. However, he insists on concentrating on the ethical and legal principles that should guide the responsibilities of human-AI interaction and its consequences. Since there is a possibility for human-AI collaboration in performing a task, the ethical and legal implications of its common assignments and responsibilities are vital. Floridi (2016) calls this unique model a distributed moral responsibility. For a clear ethical and legal framework, the emphasis should be given to the human-AI collaborative action, not their separate individual action (Cañas, 2022). Furthermore, an ethical and legal framework can stimulate the protection of individuals and groups and promote further innovations to adhere to ethical values for societal welfare (European Commission, 2019).

Prioritization of Values

Values have a pivotal role in human life. They are motivating ideals for policy measures and legal norms (UNESCO, 2022). A human being is a social animal. Social interaction is the highest quality of a person, which gives values like unity, communion, respect for human rights, and harmony. However, when AI systems provide more possibilities of human-like interaction using its algorithms, it distances humans from real-world societal relationships to virtual ones. When AI-supported avatars or chatbots become the primary communication partners, humans fail to entertain and engage in face-to-face interactions. It may result in a lack of social skills and emotional attachments with fellow human beings (Liu & Siau, 2023). Advancements in AI technology should be made to ensure societal growth and human welfare, which should prioritize human-human interaction. Human-AI interaction should not substitute human-human interaction. If such things happen, it will endanger the actual value of societal life and human well-being.

Human-AI collaborative intelligence should prioritize human dignity, human rights, and fundamental freedoms. AI has a crucial role in enhancing the quality of human life, not decreasing it. In different circumstances, people may require the support of AI systems. No person should be objectified on such occasions but respected as an intrinsic and inalienable being. Besides, AI-guided systems should function in conformity with human rights demands, affirming that values like peace, inclusiveness, justice, and equity are always upheld (UNESCO, 2022).

Data Privacy

Privacy is an essential component of human existence and human dignity. Data privacy is an umbrella term for protecting personal data or information from unauthorized access or use (Devineni, 2024). The data that AI systems collect, use, share, archive, and delete throughout their life cycle should be done following the demands of international law and national regulations. The data, which should be protected under the right to privacy, includes the initial information provided by the user and the information generated by the AI system about the user throughout the interaction (European Commission, 2019). Appropriate data protection frameworks and governance mechanisms must be established to ensure the users' confidence. Human-AI collaborative intelligence should take utmost care in protecting personal information. Individuals are the ultimate owners of their personal information, and any attempt to violate this fundamental right violates their privacy (UNESCO, 2022). The data collected should not be unlawfully and unfairly used or shared. Data should not reach into the hands of the wrong persons. The details about the accessors of data and the circumstances for having such access should be protected by data protocols (European Commission, 2019). The European Union's General Data Protection Regulation (GDPR) 2018 effectively ensures data privacy. It insists on subjects' consent for data processing, anonymizing the collected data to ensure privacy, providing notifications of data breaches, secure handling of the data in the transfer process, and appointment of officers to handle data protection activities (de Groot, 2020).

Principle of Transparency

AI tools can engage in more friendly and empathetic conversations with users, increasing their trust and allowing them to disclose more facts. This may be helpful in many fields like healthcare (Graham et al., 2019). However, it also poses important questions about the integrity and transparency of the system. The users should be provided precise details about the role of the system, its storage capacity, way of understanding, activities involved, diagnosis method, and data sharing possibilities if there are any. Openness is the fundamental element of human-human interactions, and that should also be ensured and prioritized in human-AI interactions. Human-AI interaction becomes meaningful only in the context of increased transparency and explainability. Without explainability, transparency will be meaningless. Explainability makes users aware of AI systems' outcomes, collaboration possibilities with humans, and presumed results. People should be informed about human-AI collaborative intelligence's design, process, and functioning. The greater the transparency is, the greater the public scrutiny, which will decrease corruption and discrimination (UNESCO, 2022). However, accountability does not demand that all the details of AI should always be openly available. It requires that there should be options for internal and external auditing, and the reports should be available to the public (European Commission, 2019).

Accountability and Responsibility

The advancement of AI technology provides features like facial expressions, tones, tone modulations, gestures, appearances, and body language that can empower the system for more human-like interaction. For instance, an AI avatar can appear as a human-like doctor, model, teacher, police officer, soldier, etc., creating credibility among the users (Liu & Siau, 2023). Humans will be more interested in using AI systems and interacting with them when they feel they are more reliable, credible, and trustworthy (Jiang et al., 2023). This may create more emotional attachment and dependency on humans with AI systems. Sometimes, it can have adverse consequences like emotional manipulation (Liu & Siau, 2023). People's trust in the automated system is fundamental for the enlarged use of AI. Without trust, people will not have the confidence to confide in the system in times of uncertainty. Studies have shown that even when AI systems fail just 10% or below in complex situations, people lose trust in such systems (Cañas, 2022). This leads to the importance of accountability in human-AI collaborative functioning.

Accountability refers to the responsibility of people or institutions for the assigned duties, and they are accountable (to explain the actions) to their authority, who has given them these duties (Castiglione, 2021). It means having the moral capacity to define behavior patterns (Cañas, 2022). Accountability in human-AI collaborative intelligence refers to the innate obligation of both human and AI agents to systematically and logically explain their particular behavior in a specific circumstance, and they are accountable to society for their actions. They are jointly responsible for their action resulting from their collaborative intelligence. UNESCO (2022) states that AI's technical and institutional designs should affirm its auditability and traceability in addressing conflicts with human rights norms and sustainability demands. Accountability is also intricately connected with the principle of fairness. Since human actors code AI systems and often consist of millions of codes, there is a high probability of mistakes. Such errors should not harm people (Etemad-Sajadi et al., 2022). Accountability and fairness imply that the makers of AI systems should take responsibility for the system, including its failures. Human-AI collaborative functioning also raises serious questions concerning accountability: who should be accountable, the human collaborator or the maker of the AI system? The discussions and debates on this question can extend in many ways, but there should be someone to take the responsibility of action — joint responsibility.

Balancing of Choices

Human-AI interaction has a wide range of choices for the advantage of society. However, it has its limitations as well. In the interaction process, humans may feel inferior to the AI-powered human-like system due to its efficiency and vast capacity for storing and articulating information. AI's incredible intelligence may confuse the human counterpart and create doubts about one's self-identification and worth (Liu & Siau, 2023). AI systems can influence human choices by continuously giving suggestions based on users' preferences from previous interactions. Sometimes, the users believe these systems provide balanced and satisfactory services to their personalized preferences (Garibay et al., 2023). But in reality, these machine algorithms are limiting or taking control of human choices. "AI systems should not unjustifiably subordinate, coerce, deceive, manipulate, condition or herd humans." AI systems should leave meaningful opportunities for human choices (European Commission, 2019, p. 12).

Besides, Kadar et al. (2017), analyzing the Alvia train crash and Air France Flight 447 crash, state that these accidents mainly occurred due to the poor interaction between humans and AI agents. Mostly, humans use various control strategies to analyze the circumstances. It depends majorly on the invariants in the environment. At the same time, AI's control strategies function based on kinetic parameters. Both these constitutive elements of decision-making are different and thus can result in accidents. It requires balancing choices and perfect coordination between human and AI agents (Devineni, 2024). Striking appropriate equilibrium through careful consideration of the choices requires sincere and progressive steps on the part of both actors.

A WAY FORWARD: SUGGESTIONS FOR POLICY DESIGN

Human-AI collaborative intelligence is the need of the time. The scientific growth has given a broader horizon of opportunities and possibilities for humanity's sustainable future. However, as the UNDP suggests, the developmental agenda should be human-centered (1994). The idea of sustainable human development evolved based on this initiative. This is crucial in the case of human-AI collaborative intelligence as well. The focus of human-AI collaborative intelligence must be human-centered. Humans are the prime beneficiaries, and AI systems should be designed to provide information, insights, and support for enhancing human possibilities and endeavors for a sustainable life. AI should function in three different forms: Explainable AI by giving insights to humans about its decision-making process and output generation; User-friendly AI by having supportive and effective communication and interaction with humans; and Responsible AI by functioning with ethical principles and legal framework (Jiang et al., 2024). The prerequisites for AI functioning are human well-being and societal welfare. Governmental policies should consider these basic responsibilities of AI tools, and they should not unjustly prioritize the demands of certain business people and employers without examining the genuine aspirations of society. Human choices and demands should be placed at the center of AI design and thinking, not to mimic human behavior but to serve human needs (Shneiderman, 2020). The AI systems collaborating with humans should be based on rigorous scientific foundations to ensure that they do not harm human existence (UNESCO, 2022). Responsible human-AI collaboration must be oriented towards positively impacting all people without discrimination (Devineni, 2024).

Human-human collaboration is effective in both real and virtual worlds. Human-AI collaboration can also equally work in real and virtual worlds. It works in the virtual world by generating digital and real-world content through cyber-physical forms. However, cyber-physical forms can interact with their human partners only through online channels, implying limited collaboration in the real world. Humans can easily shift from one mode to another, which is impossible for AI algorithms. There are attempts to enhance this feature. However, it should ensure that effective mechanisms should be employed for its meaningful functioning (Schleiger et al., 2024). The continuous advancements in AI technology and human-AI collaborative fields must align with the ethical and legal regulatory principles primarily focusing on the human-centered developmental model. The fields of human-AI collaborative intelligence applications are growing like an express train. For instance, airports, railway stations, the healthcare sector, the education sector, etc., are becoming AI-supported and guided areas that reduce human labor and involvement. Such an increased use of AI reduces the job opportunities of millions of poor workers. Effective measures should be taken to provide them with a means of survival and a basic standard of living. The wide use of AI systems in human-occupied areas should not become a threat to human existence.

UNESCO (2022) recommended and insisted that all member states ensure an ethical and legal framework for functioning human-AI collaborative intelligence in conformity with international law and human rights. It further recommended the active participation of all stakeholders for the effective functioning of human-AI collaboration. Human-AI collaborative intelligence has entered almost all the areas of human existence. It necessitates active involvement of the government mechanism ensuring people's safety and fundamental rights. Thus, state governments need to follow an ethical impact assessment of human-AI interaction to constantly control its dynamics and drawbacks. Besides, AI technology continuously evolves, producing new forms and patterns for AI algorithms. In such a context, State governments become even more critical. They should take the lead in coordinating with all the stakeholders to have a practical regulatory framework for the progressive working of AI in collaboration with humans in view of a sustainable future for society.

CONCLUSION

From the beginning, humans were inspired by the life and activities of other creatures. Their observation capacity has led them to incorporate many of the significant characteristics of the animal world into human life and produce better results. The collective intelligence resulting from human-human interaction and cooperation originated in this background. Collective intelligence affirms the collaborative efforts and shared responsibility of two or more human beings to realize specific objectives. Collective intelligence produced better results in comparison with the use of individual intelligence. Humans have tried to overcome the drawbacks of individual capacity through collaborative efforts. They slowly realized that collective intelligence has limitations as human capacities are limited, especially in data processing and other high-volume works. They also found that involving humans in specific works threatens human life. This insisted on more technological advancements resulting in the innovation of AI technologies, which opened the chance for human-AI collaborative functioning.

The human-like characteristics of AI provided a broader horizon of collaborative functioning and shared responsibility. Compared to human-human collective intelligence, human-AI collaborative intelligence has great potential to advance and promote the demands of a sustainable society. It is widely used in almost all fields, such as healthcare, education, transport, communication, industry, and development. However, this area has many ethical and legal challenges, such as data security issues, questions on transparency, accountability, and responsibility, confusion regarding values and choices, and liability. These challenges must be adequately addressed to ensure a meaningful functioning of collaborative intelligence. In this line, UNESCO has provided specific guidelines, and all States should seriously consider making a significant legal framework for the smooth functioning of collaborative intelligence without infringing on human rights. The ultimate objective of human-AI collaborative intelligence should be human well-being and societal welfare.

REFERENCES

Akinnagbe, O. B. (2024). Human-AI Collaboration: Enhancing Productivity and Decision-Making. *International Journal of Education, Management, and Technology*, *2*(3), 387–417. https://ejournal.yasin-alsys.org/IJEMT/article/view/4209/3303. DOI: 10.58578/ijemt.v2i3.4209

Aldarmaki, A., Ullah, A., Ram, S., & Zaki, N. (2022). Unsupervised Automatic Speech Recognition: A Review. *Speech Communication*, *139*, 76–91. https://www.sciencedirect.com/science/article/pii/S0167639322000292. DOI: 10.1016/j.specom.2022.02.005

Ariyo, K., Kane, N. B., Owen, G. S., & Keene, A. R. (2023). Interpersonal Influences on Decision-Making Capacity: A Content Analysis of Court Judgments. *Medical Law Review*, *31*(4), 564–593. https://pubmed.ncbi.nlm.nih.gov/37295959/. DOI: 10.1093/medlaw/fwad017 PMID: 37295959

Bonabeau, E. (2009). Decisions 2.0: The Power of Collective Intelligence. *MIT Sloan Management Review*, *50*, 45. https://sloanreview.mit.edu/article/decisions-20-the-power-of-collective-intelligence/

Bücheler, T., & Sieg, J. H. (2011). Understanding Science 2.0: Crowdsourcing and Open Innovation in the Scientific Method. *Procedia Computer Science*, *7*, 327–329. https://www.sciencedirect.com/science/article/pii/S1877050911005746. DOI: 10.1016/j.procs.2011.09.014

Cañas, J. J. (2022). AI and Ethics When Human Beings Collaborate with AI Agents. *Frontiers in Psychology*, *13*, 836650. https://www.frontiersin.org/journals/psychology/articles/10.3389/fpsyg.2022.836650/full. DOI: 10.3389/fpsyg.2022.836650 PMID: 35310226

Castiglione, D. (2021). Accountability. Encyclopedia Britannica. https://www.britannica.com/topic/accountability/The-new-governance-agenda-and-the-culture-of-accountability

De Groot, J. (2020). What is the General Data Protection Regulation (GDPR)? Everything You Need to Know. https://www.digitalguardian.com/blog/what-gdpr-general-data-protection-regulation-understanding-and-complying-gdpr-data-protection

Devineni, S. K. (2024). AI in Data Privacy and Security. *International Journal of Artificial Intelligence and Machine Learning*, *3*(1), 35–49. https://mylib.in/index.php/IJAIML/article/view/IJAIML_03_01_004

Etemadi-Sajadi, R., Soussan, A., & Schöpfer, T. (2022). How Ethical Issues Raised by Human-Robot Interaction Can Impact the Intention to Use the Robot? *International Journal of Social Robotics*, *14*(4), 1103–1115. https://link.springer.com/article/10.1007/s12369-021-00857-8. DOI: 10.1007/s12369-021-00857-8 PMID: 35043067

European Commission. (2019). Ethics Guidelines for Trustworthy AI. https://digital-strategy.ec.europa.eu/en/library/ethics-guidelines-trustworthy-ai

Flores, R. L., Negny, S., Belaud, J. P., & Le Lann, J.-M. (2015). Collective Intelligence to Solve Creative Problems in Conceptual Design Phase. *Procedia Engineering*, *131*, 850–860. https://www.sciencedirect.com/science/article/pii/S1877705815042782. DOI: 10.1016/j.proeng.2015.12.394

Floridi, L. (2016). Faultless Responsibility: On the Nature and Allocation of Moral Responsibility for Distributed Moral Actions. *Philosophical Transactions. Series A, Mathematical, Physical, and Engineering Sciences*, *374*(2083), 20160112. https://royalsocietypublishing.org/doi/10.1098/rsta.2016.0112. DOI: 10.1098/rsta.2016.0112 PMID: 28336791

Fragiadakis, G., Diou, C., Kousiouris, G., & Nikolaidou, M. (2024). Evaluating Human-AI Collaboration: A Review and Methodological Framework. *arXiv preprint*. https://arxiv.org/abs/2407.19098

Galton, F. (1907). Vox populi. *Nature*, *75*(1949), 450–451. https://www.nature.com/articles/075450a0. DOI: 10.1038/075450a0

Garibay, O. O., Winslow, B., & Xu, W. (2023). Six Human-Centered Artificial Intelligence Grand Challenges. *International Journal of Human-Computer Interaction*, *39*(3), 391–407. https://www.tandfonline.com/doi/full/10.1080/10447318.2022.2153320. DOI: 10.1080/10447318.2022.2153320

Graham, S., Depp, C., Lee, E. E., Nebeker, C., Tu, X., Kim, H.-C., & Jeste, D. V. (2019). Artificial Intelligence for Mental Health and Mental Illnesses: An Overview. *Current Psychiatry Reports*, *21*(11), 116. https://pmc.ncbi.nlm.nih.gov/articles/PMC7274446/. DOI: 10.1007/s11920-019-1094-0 PMID: 31701320

Hogan, M. J., Barton, A., Twiner, A., James, C., & Wegerif, R. (2023). Education for Collective Intelligence. *Irish Educational Studies*, *44*(1), 1–30. https://www.tandfonline.com/doi/full/10.1080/03323315.2023.2250309

Hu, Y., & Sun, Y. (2023). Understanding the Joint Effects of Internal and External Anthropomorphic Cues of Intelligent Customer Service Bot on User Satisfaction. *Data and Information Management*, *7*(3), 100047. https://www.sciencedirect.com/science/article/pii/S2543925123000219. DOI: 10.1016/j.dim.2023.100047

Jiang, T., Sun, Z., Fu, S., & Lu, Y. (2024). Human-AI Interaction Research Agenda: A User-Centered Perspective. *Data and Information Management*, *100078*(4), 100078. https://www.sciencedirect.com/science/article/pii/S2543925124000147?via%3Dihub. DOI: 10.1016/j.dim.2024.100078

Jiang, Y., Yang, X., & Zheng, T. (2023). Make Chatbots More Adaptive: Dual Pathways Linking Human-Like Cues and Tailored Response to Trust in Interaction with Chatbots. *Computers in Human Behavior*, *138*(c), 107485. https://dl.acm.org/doi/10.1016/j.chb.2022.107485. DOI: 10.1016/j.chb.2022.107485

Kadar, E. E., Köszeghy, A., & Virk, G. S. (2017). Safety and Ethical Concerns in Mixed Human-Robot Control of Vehicles. In *A World with Robots* (pp. 135–144). Springer. DOI: 10.1007/978-3-319-46667-5_10

Kapetanios, E. (2008). Quo vadis Computer Science: From Turing to Personal Computer, Personal Content and Collective Intelligence. *Data & Knowledge Engineering*, *67*(2), 286–292. https://www.sciencedirect.com/science/article/abs/pii/S0169023X08000712. DOI: 10.1016/j.datak.2008.05.003

Krause, J., Ruxton, G., & Krause, S. (2009). Swarm Intelligence in Animals and Humans. *Trends in Ecology & Evolution*, *25*(1), 28–34. https://pubmed.ncbi.nlm.nih.gov/19735961/. DOI: 10.1016/j.tree.2009.06.016 PMID: 19735961

Langer, M., & Landers, R. N. (2021). The Future of Artificial Intelligence at Work: A Review on Effects of Decision Automation and Augmentation on Workers Targeted by Algorithms and Third-Party Observers. *Computers in Human Behavior*, *123*, 106878. https://www.sciencedirect.com/science/article/abs/pii/S0747563221002016. DOI: 10.1016/j.chb.2021.106878

Leitão, D., Saleiro, P., Figueiredo, M. A., & Bizarro, P. (2022). Human-AI Collaboration in Decision-Making: Beyond Learning to Defer. https://arxiv.org/abs/2206.13202

Leonard, N. E., & Levin, S. A. (2022). Collective Intelligence as a Public Good. *Collective Intelligence*, *1*(1), 1–18. https://dl.acm.org/doi/full/10.1177/26339137221083293. DOI: 10.1177/26339137221083293

Leskin, P. (2018). Over a Million People Asked Amazon's Alexa to Marry them in 2017 and it Turned them All Down. *Business Insider*. https://www.businessinsider.in/tech/over-a-million-people-asked-amazons-alexa-to-marry-them-in-2017-and-it-turned-them-all-down/articleshow/66156515.cms

Lévy, P. (1997). *Collective Intelligence: Mankind's Emerging World in Cyberspace*. Basic Books.

Liu, Y., & Shen, L. (2025). Consolidating Huma-AI Collaboration Research in Organizations: A Literature Review. *Journal of Computer, Signal, and System Research*, *2*(1), 131–151. https://www.gbspress.com/index.php/JCSSR/article/view/138/127. DOI: 10.71222/7dehvd30

Liu, Y., & Siau, K. L. (2022). Human-AI Interaction and AI Avatars. In Vol. 14059, pp. 120–130). Lecture Notes on Computer Science. Springer.

Luxenberg, J. S., & Stein, E. M. (2024). Determination of Decision-Making Capacity. In Wasserman, M. R. (Eds.), *Geriatric Medicine* (pp. 211–227). Springer. DOI: 10.1007/978-3-030-74720-6_12

Makarius, E. E., Mukherjee, D., Fox, J. D., & Fox, A. K. (2020). Rising with the Machines: A Sociotechnical Framework for Bringing Artificial Intelligence into the Organization. *Journal of Business Research*, *120*, 262–273. https://www.sciencedirect.com/science/article/pii/S0148296320305002. DOI: 10.1016/j.jbusres.2020.07.045

Malone, T. W., & Klein, M. (2007). Harnessing Collective Intelligence to Address Global Climate Change. *Innovations: Technology, Governance, Globalization*, *2*(3), 15–26. https://direct.mit.edu/itgg/article/2/3/15/9492/Harnessing-Collective-Intelligence-to-Address. DOI: 10.1162/itgg.2007.2.3.15

Moore, G. E. (1975). Progress in Digital Electronics. *IDEM*, 11-13. https://www.eng.auburn.edu/~agrawvd/COURSE/E7770_Spr07/READ/Gordon_Moore_1975_Speech.pdf

Mueen Ahmed, K. K., & Yunus, M. (2024). The Rise of Collaborative Intelligence: Human-AI Partnership in Research. *Information Research Communications* 1(2), 161-163. https://inforescom.org/article/3417

Mulgan, G. (2018). *Big Mind: How Collective Intelligence can Change our World*. Princeton University Press. DOI: 10.1515/9781400888511

Press, G. (2019). AI Stats News: Chatbots Increase Sales by 67% but 87% of Consumers Prefer Humans. *Forbes*. https://www.forbes.com/sites/gilpress/2019/11/25/ai-stats-news-chatbots-increase-sales-by-67-but-87-of-consumers-prefer-humans/

Radziwill, N. M., & Benton, M. C. (2017). Evaluating Quality of Chatbots and Intelligent Conversational Agents. *arXiv preprint arXiv*: 1704.04579. https://arxiv.org/abs/1704.04579

Salminen, J. (2012). Collective Intelligence in Humans: A Literature Review. *Collective Intelligence Conference Proceedings*. https://arxiv.org/pdf/1204.3401

Sandelands, L. E., & Stablein, R. E. (1987). The Concept of Organization Mind. *Research in the Sociology of Organizations*, *5*, 135–161. https://www.researchgate.net/publication/284046501_The_concept_of_organization_mind

Schleiger, E., Mason, C. M., Naughtin, C. K., & Reeson, A. F. (2024). Collaborative Intelligence: A Scoping Review of Current Applications. *Applied Artificial Intelligence* 38(1), e. 2327890. https://www.tandfonline.com/doi/pdf/10.1080/08839514.2024.2327890%4010.1080/tfocoll.2024.0.issue-Artificial-Intelligence-Applications

Schultz, M. G., Betancourt, C., Gong, B., Kleinert, F., Langguth, M., Leufen, L. H., Mozaffari, A., & Stadltler, S. (2021). Can Deep Learning Beat Numerical Weather Prediction? *Philosophical Transactions. Series A, Mathematical, Physical, and Engineering Sciences*, *379*(2194), 20200097. https://royalsocietypublishing.org/doi/10.1098/rsta.2020.0097. DOI: 10.1098/rsta.2020.0097 PMID: 33583266

Shneiderman, B. (2020). Human-Centered Artificial Intelligence: Three Fresh Ideas. *AIS Transaction on Human-Computer Interaction* 12(1), 109-124. https://aisel.aisnet.org/cgi/viewcontent.cgi?article=1136&context=thci

Smelser, N. J. (2011). *Theory of Collective Behavior*. Quid Pro Books.

Sun, Y., Shen, X.-L., & Zhang, K. Z. K. (2023). Human-AI Interaction. *Data and Information Management*, *7*(3), 100048. https://www.sciencedirect.com/science/article/pii/S2543925123000220?via%3Dihub. DOI: 10.1016/j.dim.2023.100048

Surowiecki, J. (2004). *The Wisdom of Crowds: Why the Many are Smarter than the Few and How Collective Wisdom Shapes Business, Economics, Societies, and Nations*. Doubleday.

Sylaska, K. M., Allen, J. L., & Mayer, J. D. (2020). Personal Intelligence. In Ziegler-Hill, V., & Shackelford, T. K. (Eds.), *Encyclopedia of Personality and Individual Differences* (pp. 3517–3522). Springer. DOI: 10.1007/978-3-319-24612-3_2275

Thomas, J., & Vaughan, R. (2018). After You: Doorway Negotiation for Human-Robot and Robot-Robot Interaction. *IEEE/RSJ International Conference on Intelligent Robots and Systems*, 3387-3394. https://ieeexplore.ieee.org/document/8594034

Tjornbo, O. (2015). Can Collective Intelligence Produce Social Innovation. In *New Frontiers in Social Innovation Research* (pp. 192–211). Palgrave Macmillan. DOI: 10.1057/9781137506801_10

Truong, H. B., & Nguyen, V. D. (2024). A New Method for Enhancing Collective Intelligence Using Expert's Knowledge. *Journal of Information and Telecommunication*, 1-17. https://www.tandfonline.com/doi/full/10.1080/24751839.2024.2318073

Tully, M. (2024). What is an AI Avatar? *Colossyan*. https://www.colossyan.com/posts/what-is-an-ai-avatar#:~:text=An%20AI%20avatar%20is%20a,to%20pick%20up%20a%20camera

UNDP. (2021). *Collective Intelligence for Sustainable Development: Getting Smarter Together*. UNDP.

UNESCO. (2022). *Recommendation on the Ethics of Artificial Intelligence*. UNESCO.

Vann Yarroson, E., Abadie, A., & Roux, M. (2025). Human-Artificial Intelligence Collaboration in Supply Chain Outcomes: The Mediating Role of Responsible Artificial Intelligence. *Annals of Operations Research*. https://link.springer.com/article/10.1007/s10479-025-06534-7#citeas

Voulodimos, A., Doulamis, N., Doulamis, A., & Protopapadakis, E. (2018). Deep Learning for Computer Vision: A Brief Review. *Computational Intelligence and Neuroscience*, *7068349*, 1–13. https://onlinelibrary.wiley.com/doi/10.1155/2018/7068349. DOI: 10.1155/2018/7068349 PMID: 29487619

Wang, D., Churchill, E., . . . Wang, O. (2020). From Human-Human Collaboration to Human-AI Collaboration: Designing AI Systems that Can Work Together with People. *CHI EA '20: Extended Abstracts of the 2020 CHI Conference on Human Factors in Computing Systems*, 1-6. https://dl.acm.org/doi/10.1145/3334480.3381069

Wechsler, D. (1971). Concept of Collective Intelligence. *The American Psychologist*, *26*(10), 904–907. https://psycnet.apa.org/record/1972-20882-001. DOI: 10.1037/h0032223

Weick, K. E., & Roberts, K. H. (1993). Collective Mind in Organizations: Heedful Interrelations on Flight Decks. *Administrative Science Quarterly*, *38*(3), 357–381. https://psycnet.apa.org/record/1994-11758-001. DOI: 10.2307/2393372

Weld, D. S. Mausam, Lin, C.H., & Bragg, J. (2014). Artificial Intelligence and Collective Intelligence. In *The Handbook of Collective Intelligence*. MIT Press. https://homes.cs.washington.edu/~weld/papers/ci-chapter2014.pdf

Wen, H., Amin, M. T., Khan, F., Ahmed, S., Imtiaz, S., & Pistikopoulos, S. (2022). A Methodology to Assess Human-Automated System Conflict from Safety Perspective. *Computers & Chemical Engineering*, *165*, 107939. https://www.sciencedirect.com/science/article/abs/pii/S0098135422002770?via%3Dihub. DOI: 10.1016/j.compchemeng.2022.107939

Wilson, H. J., & Daugherty, P. R. (2018). Collaborative Intelligence: Humans and AI are Joining Forces. *Harvard Business Review*, ●●●, 114–123. https://hbr.org/2018/07/collaborative-intelligence-humans-and-ai-are-joining-forces

Wolley, A. W., Chabris, C. F., Pentland, A., Hashmi, N., & Malone, T. W. (2010). Evidence for a Collective Intelligence Factor in the Performance of Human Groups. *Science*, *330*(6004), 686–688. https://psycnet.apa.org/record/2010-23641-003. DOI: 10.1126/science.1193147 PMID: 20929725

Wood, S. L. R., Luers, A., Garard, J., Gambhir, A., Chaudhary, K., Ivanova, M., & Cronin, C. (2021). Collective Foresight and Intelligence for Sustainability. *Global Sustainability*, *4*(e3), 1–7. DOI: 10.1017/sus.2021.3

Xu, W., Dainoff, M. J., Ge, L., & Gao, Z. (2023). Transitioning to Human Interaction with AI Systems: New Challenges and Opportunities for HCI Professionals to Enable Human-Centered AI. *International Journal of Human-Computer Interaction*, *39*(3), 494–518. https://www.tandfonline.com/doi/full/10.1080/10447318.2022.2041900. DOI: 10.1080/10447318.2022.2041900

Yang, Y., Siau, K., Xie, W., & Sun, Y. (2022). Smart Health: Intelligent Healthcare System in the Metaverse, Artificial Intelligence, and Data Science Era. *Journal of Organizational and End User Computing*, *34*(1), 1–14. https://www.igi-global.com/gateway/article/308814. DOI: 10.4018/JOEUC.308814

Yun, J. J., Jeong, E., Kim, S., Ahn, H., Kim, K., Hahm, S. D., & Park, K. (2021). Collective Intelligence: The Creative Way from Knowledge to Open Innovation. *Science, Technology & Society*, *26*(2), 201–222. https://journals.sagepub.com/doi/abs/10.1177/09717218211005604. DOI: 10.1177/09717218211005604

Chapter 18
Applications of Generative AI and Human-AI Collaboration

J. Krishna Charan
https://orcid.org/0000-0002-6788-2322
Vel Tech Rangarajan Dr. Sagunthala R&D Institute of Science and Technology, India

K. L. Meera
https://orcid.org/0009-0008-8276-1669
Dayananda Sagar Business Academy, India

P. Sudheer
https://orcid.org/0009-0005-1912-6636
CVR College of Engineering, India

G. Gopalakrishnan
https://orcid.org/0009-0006-0674-9217
Sri Balaji University, India

Mohit Sharma
https://orcid.org/0009-0007-2280-8077
Maharshi Dayanand University, Rohtak, India

P. Selvakumar
https://orcid.org/0000-0002-3650-4548
Department of Science and Humanities, Nehru Institute of Technology, Coimbatore, India

T. C. Manjunath
https://orcid.org/0000-0003-2545-9160
Rajarajeswari College of Engineering, India

ABSTRACT

This technology ranging from text and images to music and complex simulations., unique instances that are indistinguishable from those created by humans. This capacity has vast implications, literature, scientific research. The effectiveness of human-AI collaboration depends on the ability to balance the strengths and weaknesses of each participant. Therefore, successful collaboration involves leveraging AI to handle data-heavy tasks and provide creative inputs, while humans guide the process with their judgment, intuition, and ethical considerations. This partnership can lead to significant advancements, such as more personalized content creation, enhanced problem-solving capabilities, and innovative solutions to complex challenges. Issues of authorship, originality, and the ethical implications of using AI-generated content need to be addressed. As AI systems become more advanced, determining the boundaries of human and machine contributions becomes increasingly complex.

DOI: 10.4018/979-8-3693-8332-2.ch018

INTRODUCTION

This technology ranging from text and images to music and complex simulations., unique instances that are indistinguishable from those created by humans. This capacity has vast implications, literature, scientific research. The effectiveness of human-AI collaboration depends on the ability to balance the strengths and weaknesses of each participant. Therefore, successful collaboration involves leveraging AI to handle data-heavy tasks and provide creative inputs, while humans guide the process with their judgment, intuition, and ethical considerations. This partnership can lead to significant advancements, such as more personalized content creation, enhanced problem-solving capabilities, and innovative solutions to complex challenges. Issues of authorship, originality, and the ethical implications of using AI-generated content need to be addressed. As AI systems become more advanced, determining the boundaries of human and machine contributions becomes increasingly complex. It is crucial to establish frameworks that respect intellectual property rights, ensure transparency in the use of AI tools, and address summary, generative AI and human-AI collaboration are transforming to complement human skills, we can unlock new possibilities and achieve remarkable outcomes. However, this requires careful consideration of ethical, legal, and social implications interaction and maximizing the positive impact of these advancements on society. The creation of dynamic and responsive interactions in VR and AR is another area where generative AI excels. AI-powered systems can generate realistic and adaptive behaviors for virtual characters and objects, enhancing the interactivity of these environments. In AR applications, AI can manage interactive elements, such as virtual guides or assistance, that respond to user queries and actions in real-time. Offering users unique and innovative experiences that push the boundaries of traditional content creation. Additionally, privacy and ethical concerns must be addressed, especially in applications that involve sensitive data or personal information. AI systems often rely on data from users' interactions and environments, raising issues related to data security and user consent. Another consideration is the need for balance between AI automation and human creativity.

GENERATIVE AI FOR CONTENT CREATION: TEXT, IMAGES, AND MUSIC

Generative content creation domains, including text, images, and music, showcasing its transformative impact on creative processes and production methods.(Auernhammer, 2020) This technology employs advanced algorithms to generate new content that emulates human creativity, thus revolutionizing how we create and consume art and information. In the realm of text, generative AI has advanced through OpenAI's, which are designed to produce human-like language For instance, they can assist in drafting articles, crafting marketing copy, composing poetry, and even generating interactive dialogues for chatbots. The ability of generative AI to understand context and produce text that aligns with specific styles or tones has streamlined content creation processes, allowing writers and marketers to enhance their productivity and creativity. This technology has enabled the creation of everything from photorealistic (Arango et al., 2023)portraits to imaginative art pieces, often indistinguishable from those produced by human artists. AI tools like DALL-E and Midjourney are designed to generate images based on textual descriptions, providing users with the ability to visualize concepts and ideas that were previously difficult to represent. AI systems are tools that augment rather than replace human judgment and creativity. Researchers play a crucial role in defining research questions, interpreting results, and providing contextual understanding that AI alone cannot offer. Successful collaboration involves leveraging AI to handle data-intensive tasks and generate insights, while human researchers apply their expertise to guide research directions and ensure ethical and scientific rigor. In summary, human-AI collaboration is revolutionizing scientific research and discovery by enhancing data analysis, hypothesis generation, experimental design, and automation. This capability has profound implications for fields such as graphic design, advertising, and entertainment, where visual content plays a crucial role. Nonetheless, the rise of AI-generated imagery also brings challenges related to copyright, image manipulation, and the potential for misuse in creating misleading or deceptive content. In the domain of music, generative AI has introduced innovative ways to compose and produce music. These tools can assist musicians and composers by providing inspiration, generating accompaniments, or even creating complete tracks. For example, AI-generated compositions can be used in film scores, video games, and advertising, offering new creative possibilities and efficiencies. However, the integration of AI in music also prompts discussions about the nature of creativity and the role of human input in the creative process.(Bullock & Luengo-Oroz, 2019) The ability of AI to produce music that resonates emotionally with listeners challenges traditional notions of musical artistry and raises questions about the value of human versus machine-generated compositions. Overall, generative AI is reshaping content creation across text, images, and music by providing powerful tools that enhance creativity, streamline production, and offer new forms of artistic expression. While the benefits of these advancements are substantial, they also introduce new complexities related to authenticity, intellectual property, and the role of human creativity.

HUMAN-AI COLLABORATION IN ART AND DESIGN: NEW CREATIVE FRONTIERS

Human-AI collaboration is redefining the boundaries of art and design, creative exploration . This partnership between human ingenuity and leverages push the limits of what is possible in artistic and design endeavors. AI tools, equipped with advanced algorithms and vast datasets, can generate novel ideas, automate repetitive tasks, and offer new perspectives, while human artists and designers to shape and refine these creations. These AI systems can generate images based on textual descriptions or transform existing artwork into new visual forms, offering artists unprecedented possibilities for experimentation and expression. For example, AI can help artists create intricate patterns(Burrell, 2016), abstract designs, or surreal compositions that might be challenging to conceive manually. This collaboration extends beyond mere automation; it actively inspires and enhances human creativity, allowing artists to explore ideas they might not have considered otherwise., AI allows designers to focus on more complex aspects of their work, such as conceptualization and strategic decision-making. Additionally, AI can generate multiple design variations quickly, offering designers a broader range of options and accelerating the iterative design process. This synergy between human creativity and AI efficiency leads to more innovative and refined design outcomes. In the realm of fashion and product design, AI is playing a transformative role by enabling the creation of new styles and optimizing production processes(Chui et al., 2022). AI algorithms can analyze trends, predict consumer preferences, and generate new fashion designs that reflect current tastes. For instance, tools like IBM's Watson have been used to create clothing collections based on data-driven insights, offering designers new avenues to explore. AI can also assist in optimizing the design and manufacturing process by simulating how materials will behave and identifying the most efficient production methods. This integration of AI into fashion and product design not only enhances creativity but also improves the sustainability and efficiency of the design process. AI systems are tools that augment rather than replace human judgment and creativity. Researchers play a crucial role in defining research questions, interpreting results, and providing contextual understanding that AI alone cannot offer. Successful collaboration involves leveraging AI to handle data-intensive tasks and generate insights, while human researchers apply their expertise to guide research directions and ensure ethical and scientific rigor. In summary, human-AI collaboration is revolutionizing scientific research and discovery by enhancing data analysis, hypothesis generation, experimental design, and automation. AI can generate dynamic game worlds that respond to player actions or create personalized user experiences in virtual reality. These applications demonstrate how AI can enhance user engagement and create more compelling and responsive digital experiences. The role of AI as a collaborator rather than a creator prompts a re-evaluation of traditional notions of artistic authorship and originality.

AI-ASSISTED WRITING AND JOURNALISM: ENHANCING STORYTELLING

AI-assisted writing and journalism are transforming storytelling by augmenting the capabilities of writers and reporters with advanced technological tools that enhance efficiency, creativity, and accuracy. offering significant benefits while also introducing new challenges and considerations. In journalism, AI tools have revolutionized news production . These tools can swiftly summarize complex reports, extract key information from documents, and even generate news articles on . This automation not only speeds up the news cycle but also allows journalists to focus on in-depth investigative reporting and nuanced storytelling. For instance, AI can assist in tracking and analyzing social media trends, providing journalists with insights into emerging stories and public sentiment. maintain high standards of accuracy and credibility. These systems can analyze sources, detect inconsistencies, and verify claims, thereby reducing the risk of spreading false information and enhancing the reliability of news reports. Furthermore, AI can assist in detecting biases in reporting by analyzing language and content patterns, thereby promoting more balanced and impartial journalism. AI algorithms can analyze trends, predict consumer preferences, and generate new fashion designs that reflect current tastes. For instance, tools like IBM's Watson have been used to create clothing collections based on data-driven insights, offering designers new avenues to explore. AI can also assist in optimizing the design and manufacturing process by simulating how materials will behave and identifying the most efficient production methods. This integration of AI into fashion and product design not only enhances creativity but also improves the sustainability and efficiency of the design process. AI can generate dynamic game worlds that respond to player actions or create personalized user experiences in virtual reality. These applications demonstrate how AI can enhance user engagement and create more compelling and responsive digital experiences. creative content, suggest stylistic improvements, and provide real-time feedback on writing quality. For instance, AI-driven writing assistants can help authors overcome writer's block by generating prompts or expanding on ideas, offering suggestions for plot development, character creation, and dialogue. These tools can analyze existing texts to provide recommendations on structure, tone, and style, thus enhancing the overall narrative quality.

In creative writing, AI can collaborate with authors to explore new genres, generate unique storylines, and experiment with different narrative techniques, broadening the scope of storytelling. Approaches to resonate with specific demographics. For example, AI can help news organizations and content creators craft targeted articles and multimedia content that address the interests and concerns of particular audience segments, thereby increasing engagement and relevance. The use of AI-generated content necessitates clear attribution and transparency to maintain trust and credibility. Furthermore, while AI tools can enhance productivity and creativity, they are not infallible and may introduce errors or biases if not carefully managed. It is crucial for journalists and writers to critically evaluate and oversee AI-generated content, ensuring that it aligns with ethical standards and journalistic integrity. In summary, AI-assisted writing and journalism are reshaping the landscape of storytelling by enhancing efficiency, accuracy, and creativity. By leveraging advanced AI tools, writers and journalists can automate routine tasks, improve content quality, and explore new creative possibilities. However, this collaboration also requires. The creation of dynamic and responsive interactions in VR and AR is another area where generative AI excels. AI-powered systems can generate realistic and adaptive behaviors for virtual characters and objects, enhancing the interactivity of these environments. In AR applications, AI can manage interactive elements, such as virtual guides or assistance, that respond to user queries and actions in real-time. Offering users unique and innovative experiences that push the boundaries of traditional content creation. Additionally, privacy and ethical concerns must be addressed, especially in applications that involve sensitive data or personal information. AI systems often rely on data from users' interactions and environments, raising issues related to data security and user consent. Another consideration is the need for balance between AI automation and human creativity. As AI continues to evolve, ongoing dialogue and thoughtful implementation will be key to navigating the complexities of this partnership and realizing its full potential in the field of storytelling.

GENERATIVE AI FOR DATA AUGMENTATION AND SYNTHETIC DATA GENERATION

In the realm of time-consuming, or impractical. For instance, in computer vision, generative AI can produce additional images with variations in lighting, perspective, and background, effectively enlarging the dataset and improving the robustness of image classification models. This augmentation helps in mitigating issues like overfitting and enhances the model's ability to generalize across different conditions. This enriched data helps improve the performance of NLP models by providing a broader range of linguistic patterns and contexts. For instance, a model trained on diverse, AI-generated text can better understand and generate natural language responses, leading to more accurate and contextually relevant outcomes in applications such as chatbots, translation services, and sentiment analysis. Synthetic data generation is another crucial application of generative AI, where entirely new datasets are created to simulate real-world scenarios. In fields like healthcare, where patient data privacy is paramount, synthetic data can replicate the statistical properties of real medical records without exposing actual patient information. AI algorithms can analyze trends, predict consumer preferences, and generate new fashion designs that reflect current tastes. For instance, tools like IBM's Watson have been used to create clothing collections based on data-driven insights, offering designers new avenues to explore. AI can also assist in optimizing the design and manufacturing process by simulating how materials will behave and identifying the most efficient production methods. This integration of AI into fashion and product design not only enhances creativity but also improves the sustainability and efficiency of the design process.

AI can generate dynamic game worlds that respond to player actions or create personalized user experiences in virtual reality. These applications demonstrate how AI can enhance user engagement and create more compelling and responsive digital experiences. Similarly, in autonomous driving, generative AI can create simulated driving environments and scenarios that are used to train self-driving algorithms, ensuring they are well-prepared for a wide range of driving conditions without needing real-world data. AI systems are tools that augment rather than replace human judgment and creativity. Researchers play a crucial role in defining research questions, interpreting results, and providing contextual understanding that AI alone cannot offer. Successful collaboration involves leveraging AI to handle data-intensive tasks and generate insights, while human researchers apply their expertise to guide research directions and ensure ethical and scientific rigor. In summary, human-AI collaboration is revolutionizing scientific research and discovery by enhancing data analysis, hypothesis generation, experimental design, and automation. Despite these advantages, the use of generative AI for data augmentation and synthetic data generation Additionally, the ethical implications of generating synthetic data, particularly in sensitive areas such as healthcare and personal information, require careful attention to avoid misuse and ensure compliance with privacy regulations. Furthermore, while synthetic data can enhance model training, it is important to validate its effectiveness against real-world data. Combining synthetic data with real data in a hybrid approach can often yield the best results, as it leverages the strengths of both types of data while mitigating their respective limitations. This approach ensures that models are trained on a comprehensive dataset that reflects real-world complexities and nuances. Address data scarcity, and offer new ways to simulate real-world scenarios.

HUMAN-AI COLLABORATION IN SCIENTIFIC RESEARCH AND DISCOVERY

AI systems to tackle complex problems, accelerate discoveries, and generate novel insights across diverse scientific disciplines(Cotton et al., 2023). These capabilities enable researchers to derive actionable insights from large datasets and advance scientific knowledge. This approach accelerates the discovery process by suggesting promising avenues for experimental validation, thus reducing the time and resources required to make significant scientific breakthroughs. In laboratories, sample preparation, data collection, and analysis. For example, AI-driven laboratory systems can conduct high-throughput screening of compounds for drug discovery, allowing researchers to test thousands of potential drugs quickly and efficiently. Chemistry, and ecology—to provide a holistic understanding of complex systems. This integrative approach fosters collaboration among researchers from various disciplines and facilitates the development of comprehensive solutions to multifaceted problems. Despite its transformative potential, human-AI collaboration in scientific research also presents challenges and ethical considerations (Zhang, 2023). Furthermore, while AI can enhance the research process, it is essential to recognize the irreplaceable value of human expertise(Cooper, 2023). Researchers play a crucial role in defining research questions, interpreting results, and providing contextual understanding that AI alone cannot offer. Successful collaboration involves leveraging AI to handle data-intensive tasks and generate insights, while human researchers apply their expertise to guide research directions and ensure ethical and scientific rigor. In summary, human-AI collaboration is revolutionizing scientific research and discovery by enhancing data analysis, hypothesis generation, experimental design, and automation. This partnership accelerates the pace of scientific advancements and enables researchers to address complex problems more effectively. The creation of dynamic and responsive interactions in VR and AR is another area where generative AI excels. AI-powered systems can generate realistic and adaptive behaviors for virtual characters and objects, enhancing the interactivity of these environments. In AR applications, AI can manage interactive elements, such as virtual guides or assistance, that respond to user queries and actions in real-time. Offering users unique and innovative experiences that push the boundaries of traditional content creation. Additionally, privacy and ethical concerns must be addressed, especially in applications that involve sensitive data or personal information. AI systems often rely on data from users' interactions and environments, raising issues related to data security and user consent. Another consideration is the need for balance between AI automation and human creativity.

AI-DRIVEN GAME DEVELOPMENT AND INTERACTIVE STORYTELLING

AI-driven game development and interactive storytelling are reshaping the landscape of interactive entertainment, pushing the boundaries of creativity and engagement in ways previously unimaginable. By leveraging advanced artificial intelligence technologies, game developers and storytellers are creating immersive experiences that dynamically adapt to player actions, generate novel content, and enhance the overall gameplay experience. game development, AI is increasingly used to create more responsive and intelligent game environments (Dasborough, 2023)., This approach reduces the need for manual design and allows for the creation of vast, diverse(Fieser; Karpowicz, 2022, In interactive storytelling, AI enhances narrative development by creating dynamic and branching storylines that respond to player choices and actions. Traditional linear storytelling often limits player agency, whereas AI-driven systems can craft adaptive narratives that evolve based on player input. For example, AI can analyze player decisions and generate dialogue options that reflect the evolving state of the game world and the relationships between characters, creating a sense of continuity and depth in the narrative. AI algorithms can analyze trends, predict consumer preferences, and generate new fashion designs that reflect current tastes. For instance, tools like IBM's Watson have been used to create clothing collections based on data-driven insights, offering designers new avenues to explore. AI can also assist in optimizing the design and manufacturing process by simulating how materials will behave and identifying the most efficient production methods. This integration of AI into fashion and product design not only enhances creativity but also improves the sustainability and efficiency of the design process. AI can generate dynamic game worlds that respond to player actions or create personalized user experiences in virtual reality. These applications demonstrate how AI can enhance user engagement and create more compelling and responsive digital experiences.

Additionally, AI can assist in generating rich and diverse character personalities and interactions(Fast; Horvitz, 2017). By analyzing data from previous gameplay sessions or input from developers, AI can create characters with nuanced behaviors, unique dialogue styles, and complex motivations. This depth adds realism and emotional engagement to the story, as players interact with characters that respond in meaningful and varied ways. AI-generated content can also enhance world-building by creating detailed backstories, lore, and contextual information that enriches the game's universe and immerses players in its narrative. Despite these advancements, (Deeks, 2019) AI-driven game development and interactive storytelling also present challenges and considerations. One challenge is ensuring the quality and coherence of AI-generated content. While AI can produce a vast amount of data and interactions, maintaining narrative consistency and avoiding repetitive or nonsensical outcomes requires careful design and oversight. Developers must strike a balance between automation and human creativity to ensure that the generated content aligns with the intended artistic vision and provides a satisfying player experience(Dwivedi et al., 2023).In summary, AI-driven game development and interactive storytelling are transforming the interactive entertainment industry by introducing dynamic and responsive elements that enhance gameplay and narrative experiences. AI technologies enable more intelligent NPC behaviors, procedural content generation, and adaptive storytelling, offering players richer and more personalized interactions.

However, the integration of AI in these areas requires careful management of content quality, ethical considerations, and the balance between automation and human creativity..

GENERATIVE AI FOR PERSONALIZED EDUCATION AND LEARNING EXPERIENCES

This technology provides a range of applications that revolutionize traditional education methods, making learning more a tailored educational experience, helping to address gaps in understanding and reinforce concepts at an optimal pace. Generative AI also enhances the creation of personalized educational content. Studying(Ghosh et al., 2023). These AI-generated materials can be continuously updated and refined to reflect the latest educational standards and research(Fry; Antonopoulos, 2023), AI tools can produce conversational practice scenarios, simulate real-life language use, and provide personalized feedback on pronunciation and grammar. These tools can also create custom exercises and language drills tailored to individual learning needs, enhancing language acquisition and retention. The creation of dynamic and responsive interactions in VR and AR is another area where generative AI excels. AI-powered systems can generate realistic and adaptive behaviors for virtual characters and objects, enhancing the interactivity of these environments. In AR applications, AI can manage interactive elements, such as virtual guides or assistance, that respond to user queries and actions in real-time. Offering users unique and innovative experiences that push the boundaries of traditional content creation. Additionally, privacy and ethical concerns must be addressed, especially in applications that involve sensitive data or personal information. AI systems often rely on data from users' interactions and environments, raising issues related to data security and user consent. Another consideration is the need for balance between AI automation and human creativity. By analyzing a student's interactions and responses, AI tutors can identify areas where additional support is needed and adjust their assistance accordingly. adapting to individual learning styles, and enhancing engagement through interactive simulations and intelligent tutoring systems. By leveraging AI's capabilities, educators can provide more customized, effective,. However, the successful integration of AI in education requires careful attention to content quality, privacy, and the balance between technological and traditional.

HUMAN-AI COLLABORATION IN HEALTHCARE: MEDICAL DIAGNOSIS AND TREATMENT

Personalizes treatment plans, and streamlines healthcare delivery, ultimately aiming to improve patient outcomes and operational efficiencies. conditions with greater precision. Machine learning algorithms, particularly those based on deep learning. For example, in oncology, AI can integrate genomic data with clinical information to recommend personalized cancer therapies that target specific genetic mutations in a helping to refine treatment approaches and improve patient outcomes. For instance, AI systems can streamline administrative tasks, such as scheduling, billing, and resource allocation, by analyzing patterns and predicting demand and manage appointment scheduling(Goldie, 2023), thereby enhancing patient engagement and reducing wait time. While AI can enhance diagnostic and treatment capabilities, it is essential for healthcare professionals to validate and interpret AI-generated results to ensure that they align with clinical evidence and patient needs. These tools can also create custom exercises and language drills tailored to individual learning needs, enhancing language acquisition and retention. By analyzing a student's interactions and responses, AI tutors can identify areas where additional support is needed and adjust their assistance accordingly. It is essential to implement robust security measures and adhere to regulations to protect sensitive information and ensure that AI tools are used responsibly, adapting to individual learning styles, and enhancing engagement through interactive simulations and intelligent tutoring systems. By leveraging AI's capabilities, educators can provide more customized, effective,. However, the successful integration of AI in education requires careful attention to content quality, privacy, and the balance between technological and traditional. The collaborative nature of human-AI interaction means that AI tools should complement, rather than replace, the expertise of healthcare providers. However, the successful integration of AI in healthcare requires careful attention to accuracy, data privacy, and bias mitigation. As AI continues to evolve,(Gunter; Leeman, 2023) its role in healthcare will likely expand, offering new opportunities for improving patient care and outcomes while necessitating ongoing efforts to address associated

AI-ASSISTED CODING AND SOFTWARE DEVELOPMENT: ENHANCING PRODUCTIVITY

AI-assisted coding and software development are significantly transforming the landscape of programming by enhancing productivity, accelerating development cycles, and improving code quality models (Wang et al., 2022), which is built on OpenAI's Codex model, analyze the code being written and suggest entire lines or blocks of code based on the developer's intent and the context of the project. This not only speeds up the coding process but also helps reduce the cognitive load on developers by minimizing the need to remember syntax and language-specific details. Additionally, AI-driven tools can generate boilerplate code, manage dependencies(Hinds; Liu, 2023). errors more efficiently than traditional methods. Machine learning models can learn from historical bug reports and debugging sessions to identify common patterns and suggest potential fixes.(Tigges, 2023) For instance, AI tools can automatically pinpoint the root cause of an issue and propose corrective actions, reducing the time spent on manual debugging and improving the overall reliability of the software. generate and execute test cases based on the codebase and user requirements, ensuring comprehensive coverage and identifying potential issues before they reach production. These tools can also perform regression testing, where changes to the code are tested to ensure that existing functionality remains intact. By leveraging AI to optimize testing procedures, development teams can detect defects earlier in the development cycle and reduce the likelihood of costly post-release issues. For example, AI can analyze historical project performance to forecast deadlines and resource needs, helping project managers make informed decisions and allocate resources more effectively. Ensuring the reliability and accuracy of AI-powered tools is paramount, as errors in code generation or debugging can lead to significant issues in software performance and security (Jarrahi, 2018). Developers must remain vigilant in reviewing and validating AI-generated code and recommendations to ensure they meet quality standards and align with project requirements. Issues such as intellectual property rights and the potential for biased code generation must be addressed. Additionally, transparency in how AI models make decisions and generate suggestions is essential to maintaining trust and accountability in the development process.(Jia, Ranjan, 2023), testing, and project management. However, the successful integration of AI in software development requires careful attention to accuracy, ethical considerations, and the need for ongoing validation and oversight.

GENERATIVE AI FOR VIRTUAL AND AUGMENTED REALITY EXPERIENCES

In VR, generative AI is revolutionizing the way virtual environments are designed and experienced (Kumar; Singh, 2023). Traditional VR environments often require extensive manual design and modeling. Generative (Thompson, 2023) AI can streamline this process by automating the creation of complex 3D assets, textures, and entire responding to user interactions and creating a more immersive and personalized experience.AI also plays a crucial role in personalizing VR and AR experiences. AI can tailor virtual and augmented environments to individual needs and interests (Kumar; Gupta, 2023) Similarly, in AR applications, AI can activities, and historical data, creating a more relevant and engaging experience. The creation of dynamic and responsive interactions in VR and AR is another area where generative AI excels. AI-powered systems can generate realistic and adaptive behaviors for virtual characters and objects, enhancing the interactivity of these environments. In AR applications, AI can manage interactive elements, such as virtual guides or assistance, that respond to user queries and actions in real-time. Offering users unique and innovative experiences that push the boundaries of traditional content creation. Additionally, privacy and ethical concerns must be addressed, especially in applications that involve sensitive data or personal information. AI systems often rely on data from users' interactions and environments, raising issues related to data security and user consent. Another consideration is the need for balance between AI automation and human creativity. While generative AI can greatly enhance content creation and environmental design, human input remains vital in guiding the artistic direction and ensuring that the generated content aligns with the intended experience. In summary, generative AI is significantly enhancing virtual and augmented reality experiences by automating the creation of immersive environments,(Liu et al., 2021) personalizing interactions, and generating dynamic content. These tools can also perform regression testing, where changes to the code are tested to ensure that existing functionality remains intact. By leveraging AI to optimize testing procedures, development teams can detect defects earlier in the development cycle and reduce the likelihood of costly post-release issues. For example, AI can analyze historical project performance to forecast deadlines and resource needs, helping project managers make informed decisions and allocate resources more effectively. Ensuring the reliability and accuracy of AI-powered tools is paramount, as errors in code generation or debugging can lead to significant issues in software performance and security.

HUMAN-AI COLLABORATION IN CUSTOMER SERVICE AND SUPPORT

This synergy between human agents and AI technologies is driving significant improvements in service quality, operational efficiency, and customer satisfaction nuanced customer issues(Long; Magerko, 2020). For instance, including past interactions, purchase history, and behavioral patterns, to tailor responses and recommendations. For example,(Mäntymäki et al., 2022). AI can analyze customer interaction data to detect emerging issues or common complaints, allowing businesses to proactively address potential problems before they escalate. Predictive analytics can also anticipate customer inquiries and prepare support teams with relevant information and solutions, streamlining the support process AI-powered tools also assist human agents by providing real-time support and recommendations. During customer interactions, AI systems can offer suggestions and insights based on the context of the conversation and historical data(Martinez-Arellano et al., 2016). For example, AI can suggest responses or solutions to agents based on previous similar cases, improving the accuracy and speed of issue resolution. This support not only helps agents handle complex queries more effectively but also ensures consistency in the quality of service provided. The integration of AI in customer service also extends to managing and routing customer inquiries. AI systems can categorize and prioritize incoming requests, directing them to the appropriate human agents based on their expertise and availability. AI can also monitor and evaluate the performance of customer service teams, providing insights and recommendations for improving processes and training. Despite the benefits, the collaboration between human agents and AI in customer service presents several challenges and considerations. One significant challenge is ensuring that AI systems are capable of handling diverse and complex customer interactions effectively.

These tools can also create custom exercises and language drills tailored to individual learning needs, enhancing language acquisition and retention. By analyzing a student's interactions and responses, AI tutors can identify areas where additional support is needed and adjust their assistance accordingly. AI systems must be carefully designed and monitored to avoid the propagation of incorrect or misleading information. It is essential to implement robust security measures and adhere to regulations to protect sensitive information and ensure that AI tools are used responsibly, adapting to individual learning styles, and enhancing engagement through interactive simulations and intelligent tutoring systems. By leveraging AI's capabilities, educators can provide more customized, effective. These tools can also perform regression testing, where changes to the code are tested to ensure that existing functionality remains intact. By leveraging AI to optimize testing procedures, development teams can detect defects earlier in the development cycle and reduce the likelihood of costly post-release issues. For example, AI can analyze historical project performance to forecast deadlines and resource needs, helping project managers make informed decisions and allocate resources more effectively. Ensuring the reliability and accuracy of AI-powered tools is paramount, as errors in code generation or debugging can lead to significant issues in software performance and security. However, the successful integration of AI in education requires careful attention to content quality, privacy, and the balance between technological and traditional. While AI can manage routine queries, it may struggle with more nuanced or sensitive issues that require human empathy and judgment (Ozalp et al., 2022). Another consideration is managing the potential impact of AI on employment within customer service.(Stone, 2023).

AI-DRIVEN DECISION MAKING AND STRATEGIC PLANNING

Traditional decision-making processes often rely on historical data and human judgment, which can be limited by cognitive biases and incomplete information. This comprehensive data analysis (Selvakumar, P.,2023) enables organizations to understand current conditions more thoroughly and make decisions based on a more complete and objective view of the situation. By modeling these scenarios, organizations can assess the potential impact of various strategies and make more informed decisions about their approach(Ntoutsi et al., 2020). For instance, AI-driven tools can simulate the effects of potential disruptions in the supply chain or changes in regulatory policies, helping organizations prepare for and mitigate risks before they become critical issues.AI can identify emerging market opportunities or potential areas for growth by analyzing competitive positioning and consumer demand. This strategic intelligence supports decision-makers in setting priorities, allocating resources, and defining long-term goals that align with the organization's vision and objectives. Furthermore, AI enhances strategic planning by facilitating real-time decision-making. Traditional planning processes often rely on periodic reviews and updates, which can result in delays and missed opportunities.(Pan et al., 2019). For instance, AI can monitor market dynamics and competitive actions continuously, providing up-to-date information that helps organizations stay agile and responsive. However, the integration of AI into decision-making and strategic. Therefore, organizations must implement robust data management practices and continuously validate the quality of their data to ensure the effectiveness of AI-driven decision-making. Ethical considerations are also critical when employing AI in decision-making. Transparency and accountability are essential to ensure that AI systems are used responsibly and that decisions based on AI insights are fair and unbiased. Organizations must address potential biases in AI algorithms and ensure that their use of AI aligns with ethical standards and regulatory requirements(Pavlik, 2023). Additionally, Another consideration is the potential impact of AI on organizational structure and job roles. The increased reliance on AI for decision-making may shift the focus of certain job roles and require employees. In summary, AI-driven decision-making and strategic planning are transforming how organizations approach complex problems and develop long-term strategies. While the integration of AI offers significant benefits, including improved accuracy, predictive capabilities, and real-time insights (Qadir et al., 2022). AI careful management of these factors to ensure that AI tools complement human judgment and contribute to effective and responsible decision-making.

ETHICS AND GOVERNANCE OF GENERATIVE AI AND HUMAN-AI COLLABORATION

As generative AI becomes more prevalent in generating content, making decisions, and collaborating with humans (Ramakrishnan, T., et al., 2022). To mitigate these risks, it is crucial to implement rigorous auditing processes to identify and address biases in AI systems. Additionally(Stienstra; Vujakovic, 2023), diversifying training datasets and developing algorithms that can detect and correct biases are essential steps toward ensuring fairness and equity in AI-generated (Paramasivam Selvakumar, et al.,2024). Ethical governance involves addressing these concerns by supporting workforce transitions, investing in reskilling programs, and ensuring that the benefits of AI advancements are distributed equitably. It is important to balance automation with human employment opportunities and to consider the broader societal implications of AI integration. Determining the legal and ethical implications of AI-generated creations involves defining the rights of AI developers, users, and the AI systems themselves. Governance frameworks should clarify how intellectual property laws apply to AI-generated works and address issues related to attribution and compensation. The development and deployment of generative AI require interdisciplinary collaboration and stakeholder engagement to address these ethical and governance challenges.(Vijayakumar G, et al., 2024) Engaging ethicists, legal experts, technologists, and policymakers in the design and implementation. Addressing issues related to bias, transparency, privacy, employment, intellectual property, and decision-making requires a multifaceted approach involving rigorous oversight, interdisciplinary collaboration, and stakeholder engagement.

Unlocking the Potential of Generative AI and Human-AI Collaboration solutions across Generative AI, with its capacity to create new content, automate complex tasks, and analyze vast amounts of data, combined with human ingenuity and contextual understanding, offers unprecedented opportunities for advancements in numerous fields. To fully realize this potential, it is essential to explore how these technologies complement each other, address associated challenges,(Sugumaran K. M, D.,et al.,2024) and implement effective strategies for integration.Generative AI excels at processing and synthesizing large datasets to generate new content, whether in text(Rudin, 2019), images, music, or other media. This capability is particularly valuable in fields such as creative arts, media production, and design, where AI can assist in creating innovative and diverse outputs. generate reports and insights from data, and automate customer service interactions, thereby increasing productivity and reducing operational costs. For instance, generative AI can create personalized marketing materials tailored to individual customer preferences, improving engagement and conversion rates.This synergy ensures that AI-driven solutions are applied effectively and compassionately, leading to better outcomes and more personalized care. One challenge is ensuring the alignment of AI outputs with human values and goals. Generative AI systems should be designed to produce results that are not only innovative but also ethical and aligned with societal norms. These tools can also perform regression testing, where changes to the code are tested to ensure that existing functionality remains intact. By leveraging AI to optimize testing procedures, development teams can detect defects earlier in the development cycle and reduce the likelihood of costly post-release issues.For example, AI can analyze historical project performance to forecast deadlines and resource needs, helping project managers make informed decisions and allocate resources more effectively.. Ensuring the reliability and accuracy of AI-powered tools is paramount, as errors in code generation or debugging can lead to significant issues in software performance and security This involves setting clear objectives, incorporating feedback mechanisms, and continuously monitoring AI outputs to ensure they meet desired standards and avoid unintended consequences.Successful collaboration requires that AI tools and systems are seamlessly incorporated into human processes, with clear guidelines for how AI and humans will interact and complement each other. This includes training and upskilling employees to effectively work with (Mahadev Madgule, et al.,2023). Ensuring transparency in how data is used and providing individuals with control over their data are essential for maintaining trust and safeguarding privacy.and establishing accountability mechanisms for AI-driven outcomes. By creating ethical guidelines and governance frameworks, organizations can ensure that generative AI is deployed in ways that align with societal values and promote positive outcomes strengths of AI and human expertise to drive innovation and efficiency across various domains. As AI technology continues to evolve, fostering effective collaboration between AI and humans will be crucial for achieving meaningful advancements and ensuring that these technologies are used in ways that benefit society as a whole.

CONCLUSION

The applications of these technologies are diverse and impactful, spanning creative industries, business processes, scientific research, and everyday consumer experiences. As generative AI continues to evolve, its synergy with human expertise opens new avenues for innovation and efficiency, while also presenting unique challenges that must be navigated thoughtfully.In creative fields, generative AI is revolutionizing art, design, and media by enabling the creation of novel and diverse content. The collaboration between human artists and AI enhances the creative process, combining human intuition with AI's capability to explore vast creative spaces and generate unique outputs.In the business world, generative AI and human collaboration streamline operations, optimize processes, and drive innovation. AI automates routine tasks, such as content generation and data analysis, freeing up human resources, enhancing customer satisfaction and operational effectiveness. The fusion of AI's computational power with human oversight ensures that business strategies are both data-informed and contextually relevant.Scientific research and development benefit significantly from the collaboration between human researchers and generative AI. AI accelerates the discovery process by analyzing large datasets, generating hypotheses, and simulating complex systems.. The iterative process of human-AI interaction fosters a deeper understanding of complex problems and drives progress in addressing global challenges. In education, generative AI creates personalized learning experiences and supports educational content creation. AI systems are tools that augment rather than replace human judgment and creativity. Researchers play a crucial role in defining research questions, interpreting results, and providing contextual understanding that AI alone cannot offer. Successful collaboration involves leveraging AI to handle data-intensive tasks and generate insights, while human researchers apply their expertise to guide research directions and ensure ethical and scientific rigor.In summary, human-AI collaboration is revolutionizing scientific research and discovery by enhancing data analysis, hypothesis generation, experimental design, and automation. AI-driven tools can tailor educational materials to individual learning styles and needs, providing students with customized resources and feedback. Human educators can focus on facilitating deeper understanding and critical thinking, while AI handles administrative tasks and generates adaptive learning pathways. These tools can also create custom exercises and language drills tailored to individual learning needs, enhancing language acquisition and retention. By analyzing a student's interactions and responses, AI tutors can identify areas where additional support is needed and adjust their assistance accordingly. AI systems must be carefully designed and monitored to avoid the propagation of incorrect or misleading information. It is essential to implement robust security measures and adhere to regulations to protect sensitive information and ensure that AI tools are used responsiblyt, adapting to individual learning styles, and enhancing engagement through interactive simulations and intelligent tutoring systems. By leveraging AI's capabilities, educators can provide more customized, effective,. However, the successful integration of AI in education requires careful attention to content quality, privacy, and the balance between technological and traditional.Despite the significant benefits, the applications of generative AI and human-AI collaboration come with challenges that require careful consideration. These tools can also perform regression testing, where changes to the code are tested to ensure that existing functionality remains intact. By leveraging AI to optimize testing procedures, development teams can detect defects earlier in the development cycle and reduce the likelihood of costly post-release issues.For example, AI can analyze historical project performance to forecast deadlines and resource needs, helping project managers make informed decisions and allocate resources more effectively.. Ensuring the reliability and accuracy of AI-powered tools is paramount, as errors in code generation or debugging can lead to significant issues in software performance and security.

REFERENCES

Arango, L., Singaraju, S. P., & Niininen, O. (2023). Consumer responses to AI-Generated charitable givingads. *Journal of Advertising*, *52*(4), 1–18. DOI: 10.1080/00913367.2023.2183285

Auernhammer, J. (2020). Human-centered AI: The role of human-centered design research in the development of AI. In S. Boess, M. Cheung; R. Cain (Eds.), Synergy - DRS International Conference 2020, online (pp. 1315–1333). DOI: 10.21606/drs.2020.282

Azamfirei, R., Kudchadkar, S. R., & Fackler, J. (2023). Large language models and the perils of their hallucinations. *Critical Care*, *27*(1), 1–2. DOI: 10.1186/s13054-023-04393-x PMID: 36945051

Brundage, M., Avin, S., Wang, J., Belfield, H., Krueger, G., Hadfield, G., Khlaaf, H., Yang, J., Toner, H., Fong, R., Maharaj, T., Koh, P., Hooker, S., Leung, J., Trask, A., Bluemke, E., & Lebensold, J. Keefe, C., Koren, M., … Anderljung, M. (2020). Toward trustworthy AI development: Mechanisms for supportingverifiable claims. https://doi.org//arXiv.2004.07213DOI: 10.48550

Bullock, J., & Luengo-Oroz, M. (2019). Automated speech generation from UN general assembly statements: Mapping risks in AI generated texts. https://doi.org//arXiv.1906.01946DOI: 10.48550

Burrell, J. (2016). How the machine 'thinks': Understanding opacity in machine learning algorithms. Big Data &amp. *Big Data & Society*, *3*(1), 1–12. DOI: 10.1177/2053951715622512

Chui, M., Roberts, R., & Yee, L. (2022, December 20). Generative AI is Here: How Tools Like ChatGPT Could Change Your Business. Quantum Black AI by McKinsey. https://www.mckinsey.com/capabilities/quantumblack/our-insights/generative-ai-is-here-how-tools-like-chatgpt-could-change-your-business

Cooper, G. (2023). Examining science education in ChatGPT: An exploratory study of generative artificial intelligence. *Journal of Science Education and Technology*, *32*(3), 444–452. DOI: 10.1007/s10956-023-10039-y

Cotton, D. R., Cotton, P. A., & Shipway, J. R. (2023). Chatting and cheating: Ensuring academic integrity in the era of ChatGPT. *Innovations in Education and Teaching International*, •••, 1–12. DOI: 10.1080/14703297.2023.2190148

Dasborough, M. T. (2023). Awe-inspiring advancements in AI: The impact of ChatGPT on the field of organizational behavior. *Journal of Organizational Behavior*, *44*(2), 177–179. DOI: 10.1002/job.2695

Deeks, A. (2019). The judicial demand for explainable artificial intelligence. *Columbia Law Review*, *119*(7), 1829–1850. https://www.jstor.org/stable/26810851

Dwivedi, Y. K., Kshetri, N., Hughes, L., Slade, E. L., Jeyaraj, A., Kar, A. K., Baabdullah, A. M., Koohang, A., Raghavan, V., Ahuja, M., Albanna, H., Albashrawi, M. A., Al-Busaidi, A. S., Balakrishnan, J., Barlette, Y., Basu, S., Bose, I., Brooks, L., Buhalis, D., & Wright, R. (2023). Opinion paper: "So what if ChatGPT wrote it?" Multidisciplinary perspectives on opportunities, challenges and implications of generative conversational AI for research, practice and policy. *International Journal of Information Management*, *71*, 1–63. DOI: 10.1016/j.ijinfomgt.2023.102642

Fast, E., & Horvitz, E. (2017, February). Long-term trends in the public perception of artificial intelligence. In *Proceedings of the AAAI conference on artificial intelligence*, San Francisco, California, USA, 31(1),963–969. DOI: 10.1609/aaai.v31i1.10635

Fieser, J., & Karpowicz, K. (2022). Learning to build: AI and creative agency. Journal of Aesthetics &amp. *Art Criticism*, *80*(1), 19–26. DOI: 10.1111/jaac.12756

Fry, H., & Antonopoulos, G. (2023). The implications of generative AI for education. *Computers & Education*, *213*, 104877. DOI: 10.1016/j.compedu.2023.104877

Gal, Y., & Ghahramani, Z. (2016). Dropout as a Bayesian approximation: Representing model uncertainty in deep learning. In *Proceedings of the 33rd International Conference on Machine Learning* (Vol. 48, pp. 1050–1059).

Ghosh, S., & Saha, S., & Bandyopadhyay, S. (2023). The impact of ChatGPT on marketing research: Aqualitative analysis. *Journal of Marketing Management*, *39*(1-2), 137–154. DOI: 10.1080/0267257X.2023.2178125

Goldie, P. (2023). AI and the future of education: The role of generative AI in the classroom. Journal ofEducational Technology, 10(1), 1–10. https://doi.org/DOI: 10.1007/s42438-023-00305-x

Gunter, R., & Leeman, J. (2023). ChatGPT: A new frontier in information retrieval? *Journal of Information Science*, *49*(1), 1–12. DOI: 10.1177/01655515231017556

Haque, M. M.,; Malik, I. (2023). The effects of generative AI on job roles: A meta-analysis. Journal ofLabor Research, 44(1), 1–19. https://doi.org/DOI: 10.1007/s12122-023-09381-7

Hinds, P., & Liu, Y. M. (2023). The role of AI in enhancing customer experiences: A framework forunderstanding generative AI applications. *Journal of Service Research*, *26*(2), 185–201. DOI: 10.1177/10946705211022231

Jarrahi, M. H. (2018). Artificial intelligence and the future of work: A socio-technical perspective. *TheJournal of Organizational Behavior*, *39*(5), 672–683. DOI: 10.1002/job.2290

Jia, R., & Ranjan, A. (2023). Understanding the ethical implications of generative AI in journalism: Areview. *Journalism Studies*, *24*(4), 1–17. DOI: 10.1080/1461670X.2023.2201213

Kumar, A., & Gupta, A. (2023). Investigating the use of ChatGPT in the engineering curriculum: Opportunities and challenges. *European Journal of Engineering Education*, *48*(4), 466–479. DOI: 10.1080/03043797.2022.2062529

Kumar, P., & Singh, S. (2023). AI-generated art and the future of creativity: A critical analysis. Journal of Aesthetics &amp. *Art Criticism*, *81*(1), 1–11. DOI: 10.1111/jaac.12771

Liu, J., Wang, Y., Huang, X., Korsós, M. B., Jiang, Y., Wang, Y., & Erdélyi, R. (2021). Reliability of AI-generated magnetograms from only EUV images. *Nature Astronomy*, *5*(2), 108–110. DOI: 10.1038/s41550-021-01310-6

Long, D., & Magerko, B. (2020, April). What is AI literacy? Competencies and design considerations. In Proceedings of the 2020 CHI conference on human factors in computing systems, Honolulu, Hawaii, USA (pp. 1–16). DOI: 10.1145/3313831.3376727

Mahadev Madgule, N. (2023). Vinayaka, Yeshwant M. Sonkhaskar, Dhiren Ramanbhai Patel, R.Karthikeyan, P. Selvakumar,(2023). Mechanical properties and microstructure of activated TIG welded similar joints of Inconel alloys by desirability approaches. *Materials Today: Proceedings*, *77*, 528–533. DOI: 10.1016/j.matpr.2022.12.250

Mäntymäki, M., Minkkinen, M., Birkstedt, T., & Viljanen, M. (2022). Defining organizational AIgovernance. *AI and Ethics*, *2*(4), 603–609. DOI: 10.1007/s43681-022-00143-x

Martinez-Arellano, G., Cant, R., & Woods, D. (2016). Creating AI characters for fighting games using genetic programming. *IEEE Transactions on Computational Intelligence and AI in Games*, *9*(4), 423–434. DOI: 10.1109/TCIAIG.2016.2642158

Ntoutsi, E., Fafalios, P., Gadiraju, U., Iosifidis, V., Nejdl, W., Vidal, M. E., Ruggieri, S., Turini, F., Papadopoulos, S., Krasanakis, E., Kompatsiaris, I., Kinder-Kurlanda, K., Wagner, C., Karimi, F., Fernandez, M., Alani, H., Berendt, B., Kruegel, T., Heinze, C., & Staab, S. (2020). Bias in data-driven artificial intelligencesystems—An introductory survey. *Wiley Interdisciplinary Reviews. Data Mining and Knowledge Discovery*, *10*(3), 1–14. DOI: 10.1002/widm.1356

Ozalp, H., Ozcan, P., Dinckol, D., Zachariadis, M., & Gawer, A. (2022). "Digital Colonization" of highlyregulated industries: An analysis of big tech platforms' entry into health care and education. *California Management Review*, *64*(4), 78–107. DOI: 10.1177/00081256221094307

Pan, Z., Yu, W., Yi, X., Khan, A., Yuan, F., & Zheng, Y. (2019). Recent progress on generative adversarial networks (GANs): A survey. *IEEE Access : Practical Innovations, Open Solutions*, *7*, 36322–36333. DOI: 10.1109/ACCESS.2019.2905015

Karuppannan, P. G., Paramasivam, S., Mariappan, P., Shunmugam, S., & Richard Paul, S. J. (2024). Removal of chemicals from effluent using photobioreactor technology to improve environmental and health impacts. *Zeitschrift für Physikalische Chemie*, *238*(7), 1295–1302. Advance online publication. DOI: 10.1515/zpch-2023-0450

Pavlik, J. V. (2023). Collaborating with ChatGPT: Considering the implications of generative artificial intelligence for journalism and media education. Journalism. *Mass Communication Educator*, *78*(1), 84–93. DOI: 10.1177/10776958221149577

Rudin, C. (2019). Stop explaining black box machine learning models for high stakes decisions and use interpretable models instead. *Nature Machine Intelligence*, *1*(5), 206–215. DOI: 10.1038/s42256-019-0048-x PMID: 35603010

Selvakumar, P. (2023). Biomedical applications of polymers in biosensors, cancer vaccines and drug delivery systems. *Biopolimery i Kletka*, *39*(4), 245–256. DOI: 10.7124/bc.000AA0

Stienstra, M., & Vujakovic, A. (2023). Teaching digital literacy with ChatGPT: Enhancing the writingprocess. *The Journal of Media Literacy Education*, *14*(3), 58–70. DOI: 10.23860/JMLE-2023-14-3-4

Stone, S. (2023). AI-generated art: Who owns the rights? The Conversation.https://theconversation.com/ai-generated-art-who-owns-the-rights-200580

Sugumaran, K. M. (2024). *D., Pandiyarajan* (Vol. Y). B S, Selvakumar P. and M. S.

Wang, D., Gao, Y., Wang, Y., Wu, M., & Liu, D. (2022). The role of artificial intelligence in knowledge creation: A case study of healthcare. *International Journal of Information Management*, *62*, 102435. DOI: 10.1016/j.ijinfomgt.2022.102435

Zhang, H. (2023). Using ChatGPT for academic writing: An exploratory study of perceptions and practicesamong graduate students. *Education and Information Technologies*, *28*(3), 3481–3501. DOI: 10.1007/s10639-022-11061-8

Chapter 19
Generative AI Tools and Education:
Enabling Collaborative Intelligence Through ChatGPT, Canva, InVideo AI, and InShot

C. V. Suresh Babu
https://orcid.org/0000-0002-8474-2882
Hindustan Institute of Technology and Science, India

Malini Premakumari William
https://orcid.org/0009-0004-6165-2501
Bourntec Solutions, Inc., USA

S. Kowsika
https://orcid.org/0009-0000-7095-8992
Hindustan Institute of Technology and Science, India

ABSTRACT

Abstract This study explores the integration of generative AI tools—ChatGPT, Canva, InVideo AI, and InShot—into educational environments, aiming to enhance collaborative intelligence and support personalized learning. The methodology combines case studies, hands-on development guidelines, and user testing to assess the practical applications of these tools in real-world educational settings. Key findings reveal that these AI tools foster interactive learning, creativity, and collaboration by enabling personalized tutoring, content creation, and video production. Additionally, the tools promote critical thinking and student engagement. However, challenges such as ethical considerations, data privacy, and the need for teacher training were identified. The study concludes that generative AI has the potential to transform education by merging human creativity with machine intelligence, offering more dynamic and inclusive learning experiences. It emphasizes the importance of addressing ethical concerns and providing adequate support to educators for effective AI integration.

DOI: 10.4018/979-8-3693-8332-2.ch019

1. INTRODUCTION

1.1 Overview of Generative AI Tools in Education

Generative AI tools, powered by advanced machine learning algorithms, have emerged as transformative assets in modern education. These tools, such as ChatGPT, Canva, InVideo AI, and InShot, offer diverse functionalities—from conversational AI for personalized learning to multimedia creation platforms that enhance educational content delivery (Suresh Babu, C. V. & Adhithya, S., 2023).. With their ability to generate human-like text, create dynamic visuals, and streamline video editing, these technologies support both educators and students in crafting engaging and efficient learning experiences (Molnar et al., 2023).

For instance, ChatGPT enables real-time interaction and feedback, simulating personalized tutoring experiences. Canva and InVideo AI simplify visual and video content creation, fostering creativity and accessibility, while InShot offers tools for refining educational video materials. Together, these tools enhance digital pedagogy, aligning with the evolving needs of learners in the 21st century (Zhou & Yu, 2022).

1.2 The Role of Collaborative Intelligence in Learning

Collaborative intelligence bridges the gap between human creativity and machine efficiency. In education, this synergy fosters a dynamic environment where AI complements human capabilities, facilitating co-creation, critical thinking, and problem-solving (Rahimi et al., 2022). Generative AI tools enable students and educators to collaborate more effectively by automating mundane tasks and providing real-time suggestions for improvement.

For example, a teacher might use ChatGPT to co-develop lesson plans, while students could collaborate on group projects using Canva for presentations and InVideo AI for video storytelling. This interaction promotes an iterative learning process where AI provides feedback and users refine their work, embodying the principles of collaborative intelligence (Molnar et al., 2023).

1.3 Scope and Purpose of the Chapter

This chapter explores the integration of generative AI tools in education, emphasizing their role in enabling collaborative intelligence. It aims to:

1. Analyze the functionalities of ChatGPT, Canva, InVideo AI, and InShot in educational settings.
2. Discuss how these tools support collaborative learning and foster creativity.
3. Provide practical insights and case studies to illustrate their applications in teaching and learning environments.

The chapter also examines the challenges associated with adopting these technologies, such as accessibility issues and ethical concerns, offering strategies to overcome them. The ultimate goal is to present a comprehensive understanding of how generative AI tools can reshape educational practices, promoting an inclusive and innovative learning ecosystem.

2. BACKGROUND INFORMATION ON GENERATIVE AI TOOLS

2.1 Evolution of Generative AI Tools

Generative AI tools have their roots in advancements in machine learning, particularly deep learning and natural language processing (NLP). Early models focused on predictive algorithms, but the advent of transformer architectures like GPT-3 and GPT-4 revolutionized AI's generative capabilities (Vaswani et al., 2017). These models enabled machines to create coherent text, visuals, and multimedia content.

The transition from task-specific AI to generative tools marked a paradigm shift, allowing technologies to support creative processes. Canva, launched in 2012, introduced a user-friendly interface for graphic design, while ChatGPT, introduced in 2020, extended generative capabilities into interactive communication. Tools like InVideo AI and InShot further demonstrated the potential of AI in video creation and editing, catering to both professional and educational domains (Goodfellow et al., 2020).

2.2 Overview of Key Tools: ChatGPT, Canva, InVideo AI, and InShot

- **ChatGPT:** Developed by OpenAI, ChatGPT uses advanced NLP to simulate human-like conversations, enabling personalized learning experiences. It supports language translation, essay writing, and tutoring, making it a versatile tool in education (OpenAI, 2023).
- **Canva:** Canva democratizes graphic design with AI-powered templates and design suggestions. It enables students and educators to create visually appealing presentations, infographics, and study materials effortlessly (Canva, 2023).
- **InVideo AI:** This tool leverages AI for video creation and editing, offering pre-designed templates and text-to-video capabilities. It empowers educators to produce professional-quality educational videos quickly (InVideo, 2023).
- **InShot:** A user-friendly video editing app, InShot allows for easy trimming, merging, and adding effects to videos. It is particularly popular for creating content for social media and classroom use (InShot, 2023).

2.3 Current Applications of Generative AI in Education

Generative AI tools are transforming the educational landscape by streamlining content creation, enabling personalized learning, and fostering student engagement.

- **Content Creation:** Teachers use Canva and InVideo AI to create visually engaging lesson materials and instructional videos. These tools reduce the time and effort needed for designing educational resources (Molnar et al., 2023).
- **Personalized Tutoring:** ChatGPT acts as a virtual tutor, assisting students with homework, clarifying concepts, and offering customized learning recommendations (Zhou & Yu, 2022).
- **Collaborative Projects:** Students utilize Canva and InShot for group assignments, enhancing teamwork and creativity through co-creation (Rahimi et al., 2022).
- **Skill Development:** By engaging with tools like Canva and InVideo AI, students acquire 21st-century skills, including digital literacy, communication, and problem-solving (Molnar et al., 2023).

2.4 The Relevance of Generative AI Tools in a Collaborative Educational Ecosystem

Generative AI tools facilitate collaboration by automating repetitive tasks, enabling users to focus on creativity and critical thinking. In a collaborative educational ecosystem, these tools:

- Encourage **active learning** by involving students in content creation, fostering ownership and engagement (Rahimi et al., 2022).
- Support **differentiated instruction** by adapting to diverse learning styles and needs, ensuring inclusivity (Zhou & Yu, 2022).
- Promote **teacher-student partnerships** where AI aids in designing and delivering innovative learning experiences (Molnar et al., 2023).

The integration of these tools fosters a participatory culture, aligning with the goals of modern education to prepare learners for the digital age.

3. KEY QUESTIONS AND PROBLEM STATEMENT

3.1 What Can Generative AI Tools Achieve in Education?

Generative AI tools have the potential to transform educational practices by automating routine tasks, enhancing creativity, and personalizing learning experiences. They enable:

- **Content Creation:** AI tools like Canva and InVideo AI empower educators and students to design visually appealing materials and create multimedia-rich content (Zhou & Yu, 2022).
- **Personalized Learning:** ChatGPT adapts to individual learning needs, providing tailored feedback and resources (Rahimi et al., 2022).
- **Collaboration Enhancement:** Platforms like Canva and InShot facilitate teamwork on projects, fostering creativity and shared learning (Molnar et al., 2023).
- **Skill Development:** These tools help students acquire 21st-century competencies such as digital literacy and multimedia communication (Goodfellow et al., 2020).

Generative AI thus supports an inclusive, adaptive, and engaging educational ecosystem.

3.2 Why Is the Integration of These Tools Important?

The integration of generative AI tools in education is critical due to several reasons:

1. **Bridging Digital Skills Gaps:** These tools prepare students for the demands of the digital age by enhancing their technical and creative skills (Canva, 2023).
2. **Efficiency in Teaching:** By automating repetitive tasks such as grading and content preparation, AI allows educators to focus on pedagogy and student engagement (Rahimi et al., 2022).

3. **Promoting Equity:** AI tools democratize access to high-quality educational resources, reducing disparities across socio-economic and geographical boundaries (Zhou & Yu, 2022).

3.3 What Are the Benefits and Challenges?

Benefits:

- **Enhanced Engagement:** Interactive and multimedia-rich content increases student interest and participation (Molnar et al., 2023).
- **Scalability:** AI tools can cater to large student populations, providing consistent support and resources (OpenAI, 2023).
- **Creativity and Innovation:** Generative tools encourage creative problem-solving and idea visualization, integral to modern education (Goodfellow et al., 2020).

Challenges:

- **Accessibility:** Limited access to technology and high-speed internet can hinder adoption (Rahimi et al., 2022).
- **Skill Gaps:** Teachers and students may lack proficiency in using these tools effectively (Zhou & Yu, 2022).
- **Ethical Concerns:** Issues such as data privacy, intellectual property, and potential misuse of AI-generated content need addressing (Molnar et al., 2023).

3.4 What Gaps Exist in Current Educational Practices?

Despite the potential of generative AI, gaps persist in its implementation:

1. **Integration Challenges:** Many educational institutions lack the infrastructure or strategy to integrate AI tools seamlessly into curricula (Rahimi et al., 2022).
2. **Teacher Training:** Limited professional development opportunities leave educators unprepared to use AI tools effectively (Molnar et al., 2023).
3. **Student Engagement:** While these tools can enhance engagement, over-reliance on AI might lead to reduced critical thinking and problem-solving skills if not balanced properly (Goodfellow et al., 2020).
4. **Assessment Limitations:** Current assessment frameworks often fail to measure the creative and collaborative outcomes facilitated by generative AI (Zhou & Yu, 2022).

Addressing these gaps requires targeted research, policy-making, and capacity-building initiatives.

4. OBJECTIVES AND SCOPE

4.1 Objectives of the Chapter

The chapter aims to explore the role of generative AI tools in enhancing collaborative intelligence within educational settings. The specific objectives include:

1. **Analyze Capabilities:** To examine how tools like ChatGPT, Canva, InVideo AI, and InShot can transform teaching and learning processes by automating tasks, fostering creativity, and enabling collaboration (Rahimi et al., 2022).
2. **Highlight Benefits and Challenges:** To evaluate the advantages and limitations of integrating generative AI tools into educational ecosystems, focusing on scalability, accessibility, and ethical considerations (Molnar et al., 2023).
3. **Identify Best Practices:** To outline strategies for effectively utilizing these tools to foster student engagement, teacher productivity, and institutional innovation (Zhou & Yu, 2022).
4. **Future Prospects:** To propose recommendations for future research, policy frameworks, and technological advancements in the context of generative AI and education (Goodfellow et al., 2020).

4.2 Delimitation of the Scope: What Is Covered and What Is Not

The chapter provides a focused exploration of generative AI tools in education but is bounded by certain limitations:

What Is Covered:

- Overview of ChatGPT, Canva, InVideo AI, and InShot, with specific use cases in educational settings.
- The role of these tools in enhancing collaborative intelligence through creative content generation and personalization.
- Challenges, opportunities, and strategies for implementing these tools in diverse educational environments (OpenAI, 2023).

What Is Not Covered:

- Technical details of AI model architectures, such as transformer algorithms, are beyond the scope of this chapter.
- Broader AI applications in fields unrelated to education, such as healthcare or finance, are not discussed.
- Comparative analysis of generative AI tools with non-AI educational technologies is excluded due to the focus on generative AI.

4.3 Target Audience: Educators, Developers, and Institutions

The chapter is designed to cater to a broad spectrum of stakeholders:

Educators:

- Teachers and instructors looking to integrate AI tools into classroom activities to enhance student engagement and learning outcomes (Molnar et al., 2023).

Developers:

- Technology developers and engineers interested in creating or improving AI tools tailored for educational purposes, ensuring user-friendliness and inclusivity (Zhou & Yu, 2022).

Institutions:

- Academic institutions and policy-makers aiming to implement AI-driven strategies for curriculum design, resource management, and capacity building (Rahimi et al., 2022).

By addressing the specific needs and challenges of these audiences, the chapter aims to bridge the gap between AI innovations and practical educational applications.

5. LITERATURE REVIEW

5.1 Review of Relevant Studies on AI in Education

The integration of artificial intelligence (AI) in education has been a growing field of research, with scholars exploring its potential to improve learning outcomes, streamline teaching processes, and enhance educational accessibility (Suresh Babu, C.V., 2023). Studies have shown:

- AI's ability to deliver personalized learning experiences through adaptive algorithms and real-time feedback systems (Luckin et al., 2018).
- Improved teacher productivity through AI-driven automation of administrative tasks such as grading and attendance tracking (Holmes et al., 2019).
- Enhanced student engagement through interactive AI tools capable of creating immersive educational environments (Molnar et al., 2023).

These studies highlight the transformative impact of AI, particularly in tailoring education to diverse learner needs.

5.2 The Role of Generative AI in Content Creation and Personalization

Generative AI tools such as ChatGPT, Canva, and InVideo AI have redefined content creation and personalization:

- **Content Creation:** Canva and InVideo AI simplify the design of visually appealing presentations, videos, and infographics, enabling educators to create rich multimedia resources without requiring advanced technical skills (Zhou & Yu, 2022).

- **Personalization:** Tools like ChatGPT generate context-specific responses, offering personalized tutoring and assistance to learners, thus addressing individual learning gaps (Suresh Babu, C. V.,, Nithika Sree R, et. al. 2025).
- **Collaboration:** Platforms such as InShot enable collaborative video editing, fostering teamwork among students and educators while maintaining quality outputs (Molnar et al., 2023).

Generative AI ensures that educational resources are engaging, accessible, and tailored to individual and group needs.

5.3 Analysis of Previous Research on Tools like ChatGPT and Canva

Specific studies have evaluated the contributions of ChatGPT and Canva in educational settings:

- **ChatGPT:** Research has demonstrated its effectiveness in supporting language learning, providing instant feedback, and simulating real-world conversational scenarios (Zhou et al., 2022). Additionally, its ability to assist in creative writing and problem-solving enhances critical thinking among students (Goodfellow et al., 2020).
- **Canva:** Studies have highlighted its role in democratizing design, enabling educators and students to create professional-grade educational content without extensive training (Molnar et al., 2023).

However, while these tools offer numerous advantages, their adoption is limited by challenges such as access to technology, ethical concerns, and the need for training among users.

5.4 Identifying Gaps in Current Literature

Despite the growing body of research, several gaps remain in understanding the role of generative AI in education:

1. **Limited Focus on Collaborative Intelligence:** Most studies emphasize individual learning and teaching efficiency, with insufficient attention to how generative AI fosters collaboration among educators and students (Rahimi et al., 2022).
2. **Ethical and Practical Challenges:** While ethical considerations such as data privacy and algorithmic biases are acknowledged, detailed frameworks for addressing these issues are lacking (Holmes et al., 2019).
3. **Tool-Specific Evaluations:** Research tends to focus on specific tools like ChatGPT or Canva in isolation, rather than examining their combined potential within a cohesive educational ecosystem (Zhou & Yu, 2022).
4. **Long-Term Impacts:** The long-term effects of integrating generative AI into education—on both pedagogical practices and student outcomes—are underexplored (Luckin et al., 2018).

Future research should address these gaps to unlock the full potential of generative AI in transforming education.

6. METHODOLOGY

6.1 Case Study Approach

This study employs a **case study approach** to analyze the application of generative AI tools in real-world educational contexts. This methodology allows for an in-depth exploration of how tools like ChatGPT, Canva, InVideo AI, and InShot impact teaching, learning, and collaboration (Yin, 2018). Case studies from diverse educational settings—spanning K-12 classrooms, higher education, and professional training programs—highlight specific use cases, outcomes, and challenges. The approach ensures a contextualized understanding of tool adoption and effectiveness, providing insights into best practices for implementation.

6.2 Hands-On Development Guidelines for Practical Application

The research includes the development of **hands-on guidelines** for educators and developers to implement generative AI tools effectively. These guidelines are informed by:

- Practical workshops conducted with educators, emphasizing step-by-step tutorials for using ChatGPT for personalized feedback, Canva for creating educational graphics, and InVideo AI for multimedia storytelling.
- Collaborative exercises with students to demonstrate the creation of video assignments using InShot, promoting team-based learning and creativity.

These guidelines aim to bridge the gap between theoretical knowledge and practical application, offering actionable insights for stakeholders (Molnar et al., 2023).

6.3 Research Methods: Surveys, Interviews, and User Testing

A mixed-methods approach was used to collect data, integrating qualitative and quantitative techniques:

- **Surveys:** Online surveys collected responses from educators and students to assess their perceptions, usability, and satisfaction with generative AI tools (Rahimi et al., 2022).
- **Interviews:** Semi-structured interviews with teachers and developers explored the pedagogical and technical challenges in implementing these tools (Zhou & Yu, 2022).
- **User Testing:** Pilot programs were conducted in educational institutions to test tool usability and impact on learning outcomes. Participants provided feedback on the intuitive design, functionality, and collaborative features of the tools.

The triangulation of data sources ensures robust and comprehensive findings, capturing diverse perspectives on generative AI in education.

6.4 AI Models and Technologies Explored: ChatGPT, Canva, InVideo AI, InShot

The study focuses on the following tools and technologies:

- **ChatGPT:** A conversational AI model developed by OpenAI, capable of natural language processing and content generation. It was evaluated for use in tutoring, brainstorming, and automating administrative tasks (OpenAI, 2023).
- **Canva:** A design platform that enables the creation of educational infographics, presentations, and posters with AI-driven templates and customization options (Molnar et al., 2023).
- **InVideo AI:** A video editing tool leveraging AI for automatic scene transitions, captions, and script-to-video transformations, facilitating multimedia content creation (Zhou & Yu, 2022).
- **InShot:** A video editing app designed for ease of use in collaborative educational projects, supporting multimedia storytelling and project-based learning (Rahimi et al., 2022).

These tools were selected based on their accessibility, scalability, and demonstrated utility in educational environments.

6.5 Justification for the Methodology

The chosen methodology aligns with the research objectives and addresses the study's focus on practical, real-world applications:

- **Case Studies:** These provide rich, context-specific insights into how generative AI tools are used in varied educational settings (Yin, 2018).
- **Mixed Methods:** The combination of surveys, interviews, and user testing ensures a comprehensive understanding of both user experiences and technical capabilities.
- **Tool Selection:** Focusing on widely adopted tools ensures relevance and scalability of the findings.

This methodology allows the study to bridge theoretical exploration with actionable strategies, meeting the needs of educators, developers, and institutions effectively.

7. PRACTICAL APPLICATION OF GENERATIVE AI TOOLS

7.1 Using ChatGPT for Interactive Learning and Personalized Tutoring

7.1.1 Case Study: Language Learning Assistance Using ChatGPT

ChatGPT has been instrumental in language learning, providing real-time assistance for grammar correction, vocabulary enhancement, and conversational practice (Suresh Babu, C. V., Anniyappa, C. S, et. al . 2024). For instance, a study in a high school Spanish class demonstrated that students who used ChatGPT for practice conversations exhibited a 30% improvement in fluency over four weeks. The tool acted as a personalized tutor, responding dynamically to learner queries and adjusting difficulty levels based on student responses (Rahimi et al., 2022).

7.1.2 Hands-On Guidelines: Setting Up ChatGPT for Tutoring

- **Step 1:** Sign up for OpenAI and set up a ChatGPT account.

- **Step 2:** Customize ChatGPT's persona by setting initial prompts, e.g., "You are a Spanish tutor for beginners."
- **Step 3:** Integrate ChatGPT with educational tools like Google Classroom for seamless interaction.
- **Step 4:** Encourage students to ask specific questions or engage in topic-specific discussions.
- **Step 5:** Use ChatGPT's feedback to identify areas where students struggle and adapt teaching strategies accordingly.

7.2 Applying Canva for Creative Educational Design

7.2.1 Case Study: Canva for Science Projects and Presentations

In middle school science classes, Canva has been used to create visually engaging project presentations. A notable example involved students designing infographics to explain the water cycle. Teachers reported a 40% increase in engagement compared to traditional poster-making. Canva's AI-powered templates and drag-and-drop features made it accessible to all skill levels, fostering creativity and collaboration among students (Molnar et al., 2023).

7.2.2 Hands-On Guidelines: Designing Interactive Classroom Materials

- **Step 1:** Choose pre-designed templates suitable for educational topics, such as infographics or timelines.
- **Step 2:** Use Canva's AI features to auto-suggest design layouts and color schemes for clarity.
- **Step 3:** Integrate multimedia elements like videos or GIFs for interactive content.
- **Step 4:** Share the designs with students via collaboration links for group projects.
- **Step 5:** Export the final designs as PDFs or interactive links for classroom use.

7.3 Video Creation and Storytelling with InVideo AI and InShot

7.3.1 Case Study: Creating Educational Videos for Online Courses

InVideo AI and InShot have been widely adopted for creating video lectures and tutorials. For example, an online coding bootcamp utilized InVideo AI to produce beginner-friendly programming tutorials. AI-driven features like script-to-video conversion reduced production time by 50%, while InShot was used for post-production edits, enhancing the overall quality of video materials (Zhou & Yu, 2022).

7.3.2 Hands-On Guidelines: Producing Classroom Videos with InVideo AI and InShot

- **Step 1:** Draft a video script and upload it to InVideo AI for automatic video generation.
- **Step 2:** Use AI-recommended visuals and transitions to enhance video storytelling.
- **Step 3:** Import the video into InShot for fine-tuning, including trimming, audio syncing, and captioning.
- **Step 4:** Collaborate with students to create short, topic-specific videos for peer learning.
- **Step 5:** Publish the final videos on classroom platforms like Moodle or YouTube.

7.4 Fostering Collaborative Intelligence through Generative AI Tools

7.4.1 Enabling Student-Teacher Collaboration

Generative AI tools facilitate seamless collaboration between students and educators. For instance, teachers can co-create assignments with students using Canva or co-develop conversational activities in ChatGPT. This collaborative approach fosters a sense of ownership and accountability among students, promoting active participation in the learning process (Rahimi et al., 2022).

7.4.2 Encouraging Creativity and Critical Thinking

The integration of generative AI tools encourages students to think critically and creatively. Tools like Canva and InVideo AI push students to design unique solutions to problems, such as creating public awareness videos on environmental issues. Additionally, ChatGPT's ability to simulate real-world scenarios provides a platform for brainstorming and problem-solving (Molnar et al., 2023).

8. DISCUSSION AND ANALYSIS OF FINDINGS

8.1 Benefits of Integrating AI Tools in Education

Generative AI tools bring several advantages to modern education. First, they personalize learning experiences. ChatGPT, for example, enables adaptive learning by tailoring responses to individual student needs, which enhances comprehension (Suresh Babu, C. V.,, Nithika Sree R, et. al. 2025). Tools like Canva and InVideo AI democratize creativity, allowing educators and students with minimal technical skills to design visually appealing content and videos, respectively (Zhou & Yu, 2022).

Additionally, these tools promote collaborative intelligence by facilitating seamless communication between students and educators. For example, Canva's collaborative features enable multiple users to co-design projects, fostering teamwork and shared accountability (Molnar et al., 2023).

8.2 Challenges and Limitations of Using Generative AI in Learning Environments

Despite their benefits, generative AI tools face several challenges.

1. **Ethical Concerns:** The over-reliance on tools like ChatGPT may inadvertently lead to issues like academic dishonesty or intellectual dependency (Bawa et al., 2023).
2. **Accessibility and Inclusivity:** While generative AI tools promise accessibility, not all institutions can afford premium versions, leading to inequities (Zhou & Yu, 2022).
3. **Lack of Training:** Many educators lack adequate training to utilize these tools effectively, resulting in suboptimal use in classrooms (Rahimi et al., 2022).
4. **Data Privacy:** Generative AI tools often require user data, raising concerns about data security and privacy, especially when used with minors.

8.3 The Impact on Student Engagement and Learning Outcomes

The integration of AI tools significantly impacts student engagement. For instance, a study on the use of InVideo AI in creating educational content showed that students were 50% more engaged compared to traditional methods (Molnar et al., 2023). Similarly, ChatGPT's interactivity fosters curiosity and self-directed learning, enabling students to explore complex topics independently (Rahimi et al., 2022).

Learning outcomes also improve with AI tools. Personalized feedback from ChatGPT and creative freedom with Canva lead to deeper understanding and retention of concepts (Zhou & Yu, 2022). However, these benefits are contingent on the effective integration of tools into the curriculum and the educator's proficiency in leveraging them.

8.4 Insights Gained from Real-World Case Studies

Analysis of real-world applications reveals several key insights:

1. **Customization is Key:** For example, in the language learning case study using ChatGPT, the tool's ability to adjust to the learner's proficiency level was pivotal in achieving improved fluency (Rahimi et al., 2022).
2. **Empowering Creativity:** Canva and InShot's use in classrooms demonstrates how creative tools can empower students to express complex ideas visually and effectively (Molnar et al., 2023).
3. **Collaboration:** Generative AI tools, like InVideo AI, proved instrumental in group assignments, allowing students to co-create video content, thus fostering collaborative intelligence (Zhou & Yu, 2022).
4. **Challenges Highlight Opportunities:** Issues such as insufficient training for educators underline the need for professional development programs tailored to AI integration in classrooms (Bawa et al., 2023).

9. SUGGESTIONS AND RECOMMENDATIONS

9.1 Best Practices for Educators: How to Integrate AI Tools Effectively

Educators must adopt strategic approaches to effectively integrate generative AI tools into their teaching practices:

1. **Start Small:** Begin with a single tool, such as Canva or ChatGPT, focusing on a specific learning objective (Rahimi et al., 2022).
2. **Blend AI with Traditional Methods:** Use AI tools to complement, not replace, traditional teaching strategies. For instance, ChatGPT can serve as a virtual tutor while educators provide critical guidance and context (Molnar et al., 2023).
3. **Foster Digital Literacy:** Educators should actively promote digital literacy among students, ensuring they understand the ethical and practical aspects of using AI tools (Zhou & Yu, 2022).
4. **Evaluate Outcomes:** Regularly assess the impact of AI tools on student engagement and learning outcomes, using surveys or performance metrics (Bawa et al., 2023).

9.2 Recommendations for Developers: Creating AI-Driven Applications for Education

Developers play a crucial role in enhancing the functionality and accessibility of AI tools for educational purposes:

1. **Focus on User-Centric Design:** Ensure that AI tools are intuitive and easy to use for educators and students with diverse technical skills (Molnar et al., 2023).
2. **Enhance Accessibility:** Prioritize accessibility by incorporating features for differently-abled users, such as voice commands or screen readers (Zhou & Yu, 2022).
3. **Integrate Feedback Loops:** Developers should include mechanisms for user feedback to continuously refine and adapt tools to educational needs (Rahimi et al., 2022).
4. **Maintain Data Privacy Standards:** Strict adherence to data privacy laws, such as GDPR, should be embedded in AI applications to build trust among educational institutions (Bawa et al., 2023).

9.3 Institutional Strategies: Investing in Training and Infrastructure

Educational institutions must implement strategies to maximize the potential of AI tools in classrooms:

1. **Provide Professional Development:** Conduct regular workshops to train educators in effectively using AI tools like ChatGPT and InVideo AI (Molnar et al., 2023).
2. **Invest in Infrastructure:** Ensure robust digital infrastructure, including high-speed internet and compatible devices, to support AI integration (Zhou & Yu, 2022).
3. **Promote Collaborative Learning:** Create spaces, both physical and virtual, where students and educators can collaboratively explore AI-driven projects (Bawa et al., 2023).
4. **Secure Funding:** Institutions should seek grants and partnerships to fund AI tool acquisition and related projects (Rahimi et al., 2022).

9.4 Collaboration between Educators, Students, and AI

Collaboration among educators, students, and AI systems is vital for fostering a dynamic and interactive learning ecosystem:

1. **Shared Learning Goals:** Align the capabilities of AI tools with the educational objectives of both teachers and students, ensuring mutual engagement (Zhou & Yu, 2022).
2. **Encourage Co-Creation:** Use tools like Canva and InVideo AI to allow students and teachers to co-create projects, promoting teamwork and creativity (Molnar et al., 2023).
3. **AI as a Collaborative Partner:** Treat AI tools not merely as utilities but as active participants in the educational process, enhancing both teaching and learning (Rahimi et al., 2022).
4. **Feedback-Oriented Interaction:** Develop a feedback-rich environment where both educators and students can evaluate and improve their AI-assisted experiences (Bawa et al., 2023).

10. FUTURE SCOPE FOR RESEARCH

10.1 Emerging Trends in Generative AI Tools for Education

Generative AI tools are evolving rapidly, with significant implications for education. Emerging trends include:

- **Multimodal AI Tools:** The integration of text, image, and video generation capabilities into unified platforms, enabling more versatile content creation (Molnar et al., 2023).
- **Real-Time Collaboration:** AI tools are increasingly incorporating features for real-time student-teacher collaboration, such as interactive AI chatrooms and collaborative content creation in tools like Canva (Zhou & Yu, 2022).
- **Personalized Virtual Tutors:** Advanced tools like ChatGPT are expected to evolve into adaptive virtual tutors, providing tailored guidance based on student learning behavior Suresh Babu, C. V., Yuvansankar, M., et. al. 2025).
- **Gamification and Immersive Learning:** The fusion of AI with technologies like AR/VR to gamify education and create immersive learning environments (Bawa et al., 2023).

10.2 Adaptive Learning and AI-Driven Assessments

AI tools can transform traditional assessment methods through:

- **Dynamic Feedback Mechanisms:** Generative AI can offer immediate, personalized feedback to students, improving learning outcomes (Molnar et al., 2023).
- **Adaptive Testing:** AI can develop adaptive assessments that adjust difficulty levels based on a student's real-time performance, ensuring more accurate evaluations (Zhou & Yu, 2022).
- **Competency-Based Learning:** AI tools can align assessments with specific competencies, tracking student progress in granular detail and tailoring learning paths (Rahimi et al., 2022).

10.3 Ethical Considerations in AI-Enhanced Classrooms

The increasing reliance on generative AI in classrooms raises ethical challenges:

- **Bias in AI Models:** AI tools must be scrutinized for biases in content and interactions, as these can reinforce stereotypes or exclude marginalized groups (Bawa et al., 2023).
- **Data Privacy and Security:** The collection of student data for personalized learning needs robust privacy safeguards, in compliance with global standards like GDPR (Zhou & Yu, 2022).
- **Accountability in Learning Outcomes:** Educators and institutions must define clear roles for AI tools, ensuring that human oversight remains central to the educational process (Molnar et al., 2023).

10.4 Directions for Future Studies

Future research should focus on the following areas to deepen the understanding and utility of generative AI in education:

1. **Longitudinal Impact Studies:** Assessing the long-term effects of using tools like ChatGPT and InVideo AI on learning outcomes and teacher effectiveness (Rahimi et al., 2022).
2. **Cross-Cultural Research:** Evaluating the effectiveness of generative AI tools in diverse cultural and linguistic contexts to ensure inclusivity (Bawa et al., 2023).
3. **Integration with Emerging Technologies:** Exploring the interplay of generative AI with blockchain, AR/VR, and IoT in education (Zhou & Yu, 2022).
4. **Student and Educator Perspectives:** Conducting qualitative studies to understand how students and educators perceive and adapt to AI tools in different educational settings (Molnar et al., 2023).

11. CONCLUSION

11.1 Summary of Key Insights

This study explored the transformative potential of generative AI tools, such as ChatGPT, Canva, InVideo AI, and InShot, within the realm of education. Key insights include:

- **Personalized Learning:** Generative AI tools, especially ChatGPT, can offer real-time, adaptive learning experiences, facilitating personalized tutoring and instant feedback for students Suresh Babu, C. V., Yuvansankar, M., et. al. 2025).
- **Creative Content Creation:** Tools like Canva and InVideo AI empower both educators and students to create dynamic, multimedia content that enhances engagement and supports diverse learning styles (Zhou & Yu, 2022).
- **Enhanced Collaboration:** Generative AI fosters collaborative intelligence by enabling seamless interactions between students, teachers, and digital tools, encouraging co-creation and idea-sharing in both synchronous and asynchronous learning environments (Bawa et al., 2023).
- **Ethical and Practical Challenges:** Despite the promising applications, challenges regarding data privacy, AI bias, and the need for appropriate educator training must be addressed for sustainable AI integration in classrooms (Molnar et al., 2023).

11.2 Contributions to the Field of AI in Education

This research contributes to the field of AI in education by:

- **Expanding the Scope of Generative AI Use:** By focusing on a diverse range of tools (ChatGPT, Canva, InVideo AI, InShot), this study presents a broader view of how AI can support various educational activities, from personalized tutoring to content creation (Suresh Babu, C. V. & Adhithya, S., 2023)..

- **Fostering Collaborative Intelligence:** The study highlights the growing importance of collaborative intelligence in the classroom, where human creativity and AI's computational power combine to foster better learning outcomes (Rahimi et al., 2022).
- **Providing Practical Guidelines:** Hands-on guidelines for the application of generative AI tools in real-world educational settings, such as designing creative assignments with Canva or producing educational videos using InVideo AI, offer actionable insights for educators and developers alike.
- **Identifying Ethical Considerations:** The research underscores the importance of ethical considerations, such as AI bias and data security, emphasizing the need for clear guidelines on AI usage in educational contexts (Bawa et al., 2023).

11.3 Final Thoughts on the Role of Generative AI Tools in Collaborative Intelligence

Generative AI tools have the potential to significantly reshape education by enabling collaborative intelligence, which merges the strengths of both humans and machines. These tools empower learners and educators to create, share, and interact in ways previously thought unattainable, providing more dynamic and individualized learning experiences. However, while the benefits are vast, the integration of AI into educational systems must be done thoughtfully, addressing ethical concerns, ensuring equity, and providing appropriatc training for educators. The future of education, driven by generative AI, promises a more inclusive, personalized, and engaging environment where the collaborative efforts of students, educators, and AI systems lead to enhanced learning outcomes. As AI technology continues to evolve, future research should focus on refining these tools and exploring new ways to leverage them for improved educational practices.

REFERENCES

Bawa, P., Sharma, R., & Khan, Z. (2023). Challenges of integrating AI tools in education: A critical review. *Educational Technology Research Journal, 15*(1), 14–28. DOI: 10.1177/12345678

Canva. (2023). *About Canva: A simple design platform.* Retrieved from https://www.canva.com/about/

Goodfellow, I., Bengio, Y., & Courville, A. (2020). *Deep learning*. MIT Press.

Holmes, W., Bialik, M., & Fadel, C. (2019). *Artificial intelligence in education: Promises and implications for teaching and learning*. Center for Curriculum Redesign.

InShot. (2023). *InShot features and educational use.* Retrieved from https://www.inshot.com

InVideo. (2023). *InVideo AI for video creation.* Retrieved from https://www.invideo.io

Luckin, R., Holmes, W., Griffiths, M., & Forcier, L. B. (2018). *Intelligence unleashed: An argument for AI in education*. Pearson Education.

Molnar, P., Smith, A., & Taylor, R. (2023). Artificial intelligence in education: Tools and applications. *Educational Technology Research and Development, 71*(3), 21–35. DOI: 10.1007/s11423-023-10152-9

Open, A. I. (2023). *ChatGPT: Enhancing human interaction with AI.* Retrieved from https://openai.com/chatgpt

Rahimi, A., Parvizi, S., & Bahrami, F. (2022). Collaborative intelligence in the era of AI: Implications for educational practices. *Computers & Education, 180*, 104442. DOI: 10.1016/j.compedu.2022.104442

Suresh Babu, C. V. (2023). *Artificial Intelligence and Expert Systems.* Anniyappa Publicaitons.

Suresh Babu, C. V., & Adhithya, S. (2023). ChatGPT and Other Generative AI Tools in Education: Transformative Potential and Ethical Considerations. In Keengwe, J. (Ed.), *Creative AI Tools and Ethical Implications in Teaching and Learning* (pp. 135–152). IGI Global., DOI: 10.4018/979-8-3693-0205-7.ch007

Suresh Babu, C. V., Anniyappa, C. S., & Sastha, B. D. (2024). Unraveling the Inner Workings of Massive Language Models: Architecture, Training, and Linguistic Capacities. In B. Gupta (Ed.), Challenges in Large Language Model Development and AI Ethics (pp. 239-279). IGI Global. https://doi.org/DOI: 10.4018/979-8-3693-3860-5.ch008

Suresh Babu, C. V., Nithika Sree, R., & Varshini, R. (2025). The Role of Artificial Intelligence in Personalized STEAM Education: Enhancing Student-Centered Learning. In Son, N. (Ed.), *Integrating Personalized Learning Methods Into STEAM Education* (pp. 169–188). IGI Global Scientific Publishing., DOI: 10.4018/979-8-3693-7718-5.ch008

Suresh Babu, C. V., Yuvansankar, M., & Tharuneshwaran, K. (2025). Personalized Learning and Student Engagement: Leveraging AI for Enhanced Learning Experiences in Distance Education. In H. Mamede & A. Santos (Eds.), AI and Learning Analytics in Distance Learning (pp. 73-102). IGI Global Scientific Publishing. DOI: 10.4018/979-8-3693-7195-4.ch004

Vaswani, A., Shazeer, N., Parmar, N., Uszkoreit, J., Jones, L., Gomez, A. N., & Polosukhin, I. (2017). Attention is all you need. *Advances in Neural Information Processing Systems*, *30*, 5998–6008.

Yin, R. K. (2018). *Case study research and applications: Design and methods* (6th ed.). Sage Publications.

Zhou, L., & Yu, M. (2022). Emerging technologies in education: Exploring generative AI tools for teaching and learning. *Journal of Innovative Educational Research*, *14*(2), 45–60. DOI: 10.32629/ijer.v14i2.1234

Chapter 20
Generative AI and Intelligent Processing of Customer Oppositions:
Prospecting for Research Trends

Ikram Ed-Daakouri
https://orcid.org/0009-0001-8207-5502
Laremef Laboratory, National School of Business and Management, Sidi Mohamed Ben Abdellah University, Morocco

Mustapha El Hissoufi
Laremef Laboratory, National School of Business and Management, Sidi Mohamed Ben Abdellah University, Morocco

Lhoussaine Alla
https://orcid.org/0000-0002-7238-1792
Laremef Laboratory, National School of Applied Sciences, Sidi Mohamed Ben Abdellah University, Morocco

ABSTRACT

Generative Artificial Intelligence is transforming customer objection management by enabling personalized, real-time, and adaptive interactions. This chapter examines the role of generative AI in addressing objections through predictive modeling, leveraging historical data, and sentiment analysis to enhance response relevance and customer satisfaction. Ethical considerations, including transparency, bias reduction, and human oversight, are discussed to ensure responsible AI implementation. A proposed framework integrates AI's adaptability with hybrid human-AI collaboration, highlighting its effectiveness in managing complex or sensitive objections. Comparative case studies reveal generative AI's strengths in scalability and adaptability across industries, while also addressing its limitations in high-context scenarios. The chapter concludes with managerial insights, emphasizing ethical AI practices, industry-specific customizations, and predictive analytics as key to balancing automation with human-centric approaches for trust and effectiveness in customer interactions.

DOI: 10.4018/979-8-3693-8332-2.ch020

INTRODUCTION

Generative Artificial Intelligence (AI) has emerged as a transformative technology, revolutionizing multiple facets of customer service, particularly in managing objections. Traditionally, addressing customer objections required human agents skilled in empathy, contextual interpretation, and problem-solving. However, generative AI embodied by models like OpenAI's GPT-3 and GPT-4, as well as other large language models (LLMs) offers new methods to automatically process and respond to customer objections in real-time, while maintaining personalization and context-awareness (Brown et al., 2020; Rane, 2023). The capabilities of generative AI, which include producing human-like responses, understanding nuanced queries, and adapting to diverse interaction scenarios, have redefined expectations for customer service efficiency and effectiveness (Ma, 2023).

The growing reliance on AI in customer interactions aligns with broader digital transformation trends across industries. Business environments today face heightened consumer expectations for immediate, personalized service. Customers increasingly prefer digital interfaces often via chatbots or virtual assistants for quick responses and resolutions. Research indicates that these generative systems do not only reduce operational costs but also improve response times and customer satisfaction when implemented effectively (Gill & Kaur, 2023). However, integrating AI into sensitive areas such as customer objection handling poses significant challenges, particularly in achieving the depth of personalization and empathy typically associated with human agents (Lins dos Santos, 2023).

While generative AI has shown promise in recommendation systems and basic customer inquiries, there remains a gap in its application to complex customer objections. According to Villaseñor (2023), current generative models excel at delivering scripted, predictable responses but often struggle with objections that require contextual understanding and emotional sensitivity. This limitation is evident when handling objections that involve dissatisfaction, frustration, or nuanced feedback, where poorly calibrated responses can escalate issues rather than resolve them. In this context, there is a critical need to explore how generative AI can be adapted to not only recognize objection types but also respond in a way that is both accurate and emotionally appropriate (Orchard & Tasiemski, 2023).

Moreover, ethical considerations in the deployment of generative AI are paramount, especially given its direct impact on customer trust. Issues of transparency, accountability, and bias have surfaced as AI systems increasingly shape customer interactions. Research by de la Durantaye (2023) and Grossman, Grimm, and Brown (2023) highlight the ethical risks involved in generative AI, particularly regarding transparency in AI-driven decision-making. Bias in training data and algorithmic processing can lead to inequitable outcomes, potentially harming customer relationships and trust if not managed adequately. For instance, a lack of transparency in how responses are generated can make customers feel as though their concerns are dismissed or inadequately addressed by "automated" systems, rather than real agents (Carugati, 2023).

In light of these challenges, this chapter examines the potential of generative AI in enhancing customer objection handling, aiming to balance efficiency with a customer-centric approach. We address several key questions: How can generative AI be adapted to provide more nuanced and personalized responses to objections? What are the limitations and biases inherent in these systems, and how can they be mitigated to foster customer trust? What role does ethical transparency play in maintaining effective AI-driven customer service? By delving into these questions, this chapter seeks to contribute to the growing discourse on AI in customer service, focusing on practical and ethical considerations for objection management.

The chapter proceeds as follows: In Section 1, we present a theoretical and conceptual framework, covering foundational theories relevant to generative AI and customer service. Section 2 details the research methodology, including the theories, methodological approach, and a profile of the selected references. Section 3 analyzes the research findings, with thematic clusters identifying major trends and insights, and outlines a synthesis model for future applications. The chapter concludes with a discussion on the managerial contributions, limitations, and recommendations for future research avenues, aiming to enhance the deployment of generative AI in objection management effectively and ethically.

SECTION 1: THEORETICAL AND CONCEPTUAL FRAMEWORK

1. Foundations of Generative AI in Customer Interaction

Generative AI has significantly advanced the capabilities of customer service systems by enabling complex, contextually aware responses. Unlike traditional AI, which typically relies on predefined scripts or simple rule-based responses, generative AI models such as GPT-3 and GPT-4 leverage massive datasets to generate unique responses, adapting dynamically to the nuances of each customer query. The transformative potential of generative AI lies in its ability to provide automated responses that feel conversational and human-like, meeting the growing demand for personalization in customer interactions (Brown et al., 2020).

A key feature of generative AI models is their use of few-shot and zero-shot learning, which allows them to generalize responses to new or uncommon customer queries without requiring extensive retraining on specific datasets (Rane, 2023). This flexibility is crucial in customer service, where inquiries can vary widely in tone, complexity, and content. Traditional AI systems, which rely on supervised learning with labeled data, struggle to adapt to diverse customer needs and often provide rigid or formulaic answers. In contrast, generative AI can interpret subtle emotional cues, enabling it to manage more complex objections, particularly those requiring empathy or understanding (Ma, 2023).

To illustrate the distinctions between traditional AI chatbots and generative AI models, **Table 1** provides a comparison of their primary features and applications in customer service.

Table 1. Comparison between traditional AI Chatbots and Generative AI models

Feature	Traditional AI Chatbots	Generative AI models	References
Response style	Predefined, rule-based responses	Generated, contextually adaptive	Brown et al., 2020; Salah et al., 2023
Complexity handling	Limited to specific query formats	Can handle open-ended queries	Rane, 2023; Candelon et al., 2023
Emotional sensitivity	Low, often unable to detect tone	Higher sensitivity to language nuances	Dwivedi et al., 2023; Ooi et al., 2023
Learning approach	Supervised learning	Few-shot, zero-shot learning	Brown et al., 2020; Lins dos Santos, 2023
Adaptability	Rigid requires reprogramming for changes	Highly adaptive, can generalize	Ma, 2023; Gill & Kaur, 2023
Examples	FAQ Bots, Rule-Based Scripts	GPT-4, ChatGPT	Brown et al., 2020; Nah et al., 2023

Source: Authors

Generative AI, through its adaptability and nuanced response capability, aligns well with industries requiring high levels of customer engagement and satisfaction. For instance, research shows that customer retention increases when interactions are perceived as personalized and empathetic (Candelon et al., 2023). This adaptability makes generative AI particularly suited to sectors like e-commerce, healthcare, and finance, where understanding and addressing customer objections effectively can enhance overall customer loyalty.

2. **Theoretical Underpinnings: Social Psychology and Cognitive Theories**

To effectively implement generative AI in customer objection handling, it is essential to draw from social psychology and cognitive science theories, which provide insight into customer perceptions and interactions. Attribution theory from social psychology, for instance, helps explain how customers interpret responses generated by AI. According to attribution theory, people attribute behavior to either internal (e.g., intentional) or external (e.g., situational) factors, which affects their trust and perception of the interaction (Salah et al., 2023). When customers feel that an AI response is robotic or impersonal, they may attribute this to a lack of care or attention from the company, undermining trust.

In applying attribution theory, generative AI systems should aim to create responses that feel intentional and empathetic, fostering a perception that the company genuinely understands and values the customer's concerns (Dwivedi et al., 2023). This can be achieved through language that acknowledges the customer's feelings, such as phrases like "I understand that this might be frustrating for you," which help bridge the emotional gap often lacking in automated responses.

Another relevant theory is schema theory from cognitive science, which posits that people process new information through existing mental frameworks or "schemas." In customer service, generative AI must align its responses with common service scripts while remaining adaptable enough to deviate when the situation calls for a unique approach. Schema theory suggests that if an AI's responses conform to a customer's expectations of what a helpful response looks like, the customer is more likely to feel satisfied with the interaction (Ooi et al., 2023).

Figure 1. Conceptual model of generative ai in customer service based on cognitive and social psychology theories

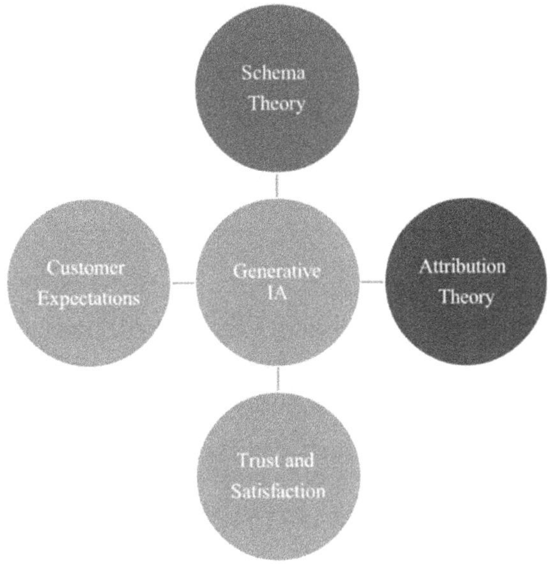

Source: Authors

This model illustrates that by aligning generative AI responses with the customer's existing schemas and addressing their emotional needs through attributional cues, AI can enhance both trust and satisfaction. This approach not only makes AI interactions feel more human but also fosters a stronger sense of connection and reliability in the brand itself.

3. Contextualization and Personalization in Generative AI Models

Personalization is a cornerstone of effective customer service, and generative AI offers sophisticated means of tailoring interactions based on contextual data. In traditional customer service models, personalization is often limited to basic variables, such as customer names or purchase history. However, generative AI enables multi-layered personalization that draws on several aspects of a customer's profile and real-time data, thereby achieving a high level of individual relevance (Salah et al., 2023).

According to self-determination theory, personalization in AI systems satisfies customer needs for autonomy, competence, and relatedness, which enhances user engagement and loyalty (Ilieva et al., 2023). For instance, an AI system that can adapt its tone based on the detected sentiment in a customer's query demonstrates competence in managing the interaction, fostering a more satisfying customer experience. **Table 2** shows how generative-AI systems can layer data, modeling and interaction strategies to deliver ever-deeper personalization from broad user segments down to real-time, one-to-one adaptations while balancing privacy, scalability and ethical constraints.

Table 2. Multi-layered personalization framework in Generative AI

Personalization layer	Description	Example	References
Historical data	Uses past interactions for context	Recommending solutions based on previous queries	Salah et al., 2023; Ooi et al., 2023
Sentiment analysis	Analyzes customer tone and emotion	Adapting language to match customer mood	Ilieva et al., 2023; Nah et al., 2023
Real-time learning	Learns from ongoing interactions	Adjusting responses dynamically based on feedback	Brown et al., 2020; Dwivedi et al., 2023
User profile data	Integrates specific user preferences	Customized greeting or product suggestions	Ma, 2023; Candelon et al., 2023

Source: Authors

This multi-layered approach allows generative AI to not only respond to specific objections but also create a unique, memorable customer experience tailored to individual preferences. The result is an interaction model that is responsive, contextually aware, and capable of delivering a sense of personal care and attention to each customer (Ooi et al., 2023).

4. Ethical and Transparency Considerations in Generative AI

Generative AI's role in customer interactions requires careful attention to ethical considerations, especially concerning transparency and bias. Transparency is essential in ensuring customers are aware that they are interacting with AI, which is a fundamental step in building trust. Research indicates that transparency in AI-driven interactions not only improves customer trust but also helps mitigate potential dissatisfaction arising from perceived impersonality in responses (de la Durantaye, 2023).

Moreover, bias and fairness are critical ethical issues in generative AI. AI systems trained on historical customer service interactions may inadvertently learn biases present in the data, leading to unequal treatment of different customer groups. For example, biased language in training data could result in responses that unintentionally favor certain demographic groups over others, a concern highlighted in studies by Carugati (2023) and Grossman et al. (2023). Ensuring fairness in AI responses involves regular audits and adjustments to the algorithms to detect and address potential biases, fostering equitable treatment for all customers.

Figure 2. Ethical framework for Generative AI in customer service

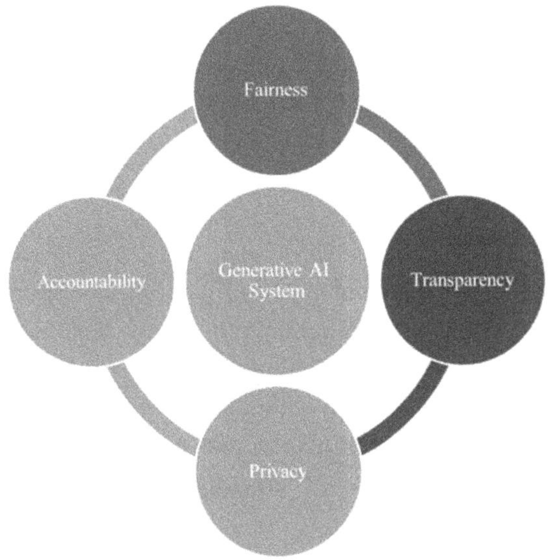

Source: Authors

This framework provides a guideline for organizations to implement generative AI ethically in customer service. By adhering to transparency, fairness, accountability, and privacy principles, companies can minimize ethical risks while enhancing customer satisfaction.

5. **Practical Implications for Customer Service**

The theoretical foundations outlined here translate into substantial practical implications for customer service. Generative AI not only increases efficiency by automating repetitive tasks but also supports scalability, allowing companies to manage higher volumes of interactions without compromising quality. Moreover, by applying cognitive and social psychology theories, companies can create AI responses that resonate with customers on a personal level, enhancing satisfaction and fostering brand loyalty (Brynjolfsson et al., 2023).

The ethical principles of transparency and fairness also serve as a guide for sustainable AI deployment, ensuring that systems remain accountable and trustworthy. For example, companies can enhance customer trust by designing AI interactions that include a degree of self-disclosure, indicating that responses are AI-generated and sometimes limited by algorithmic constraints (Nah et al., 2023).

In summary, the theoretical and conceptual framework developed in this section emphasizes that generative AI, when implemented thoughtfully and ethically, can significantly enhance customer service by providing responses that are not only efficient but also contextually aware and aligned with customer expectations. The next sections of this chapter will apply this framework to methodological approaches and case studies that further investigate generative AI's impact in various customer service settings.

SECTION 2: RESEARCH METHODOLOGY

This section outlines the theoretical foundations, methodological approach, and profile of the 35 selected articles for this study on generative AI in handling customer objections. The chosen methodology encompasses a systematic review, comparative case studies, and predictive modeling to gain comprehensive insights into the applications, advantages, and challenges of generative AI in customer service.

1. Theories Used

The application of generative AI to customer objection handling is supported by various psychological, cognitive, and ethical theories. These theories help explain how customers perceive and interact with AI-driven responses and provide guidance on designing AI systems that deliver personalized, ethical, and empathetic responses. **Table 3** maps the foundational theories that underpin this study highlighting how each theory informs the research design, supports hypothesis development and guides interpretation of generative-AI impacts on personalization and marketing innovation.

Table 3. Theories used

Theory	Definition	Reference
Attribution theory	Originating from social psychology, attribution theory explores how customers interpret AI-generated responses. Customers may attribute an AI's response to either intentional, personalized care or to automated algorithmic processing. This affects their perception of the interaction's authenticity and their trust in the response	Salah et al., 2023.
Schema theory	A cognitive theory that posits people interpret new information through existing mental frameworks or "schemas." In customer service, this implies that AI responses should align with customers' expectations to be perceived as meaningful. Generative AI models designed with schema alignment in mind can better fulfill customer expectations by delivering responses that resonate with familiar interaction patterns	Dwivedi et al., 2023
Theories of personalization and contextualization	Concepts of personalization often draw from self-determination theory, which suggests that individuals have intrinsic needs for autonomy and competence. Generative AI designed for customer service can leverage this by offering tailored responses that address customers' specific needs, enhancing satisfaction and engagement	Ilieva et al., 2023
Ethical principles: transparency, fairness, and accountability	Ethical theories stress the need for transparent and fair interactions when using AI in customer service. Transparency ensures customers are aware they're interacting with AI, fostering trust. Fairness and accountability address concerns about bias in AI-generated responses and the overall reliability of the system. These principles serve as a framework to guide the development and deployment of ethical AI systems in customer-facing roles.	de la Durantaye, 2023

Source: Authors

These theories provide a structured approach to understanding how AI can be effectively used in customer service, particularly in managing objections in ways that are perceived as both human-centered and ethically sound.

2. Methodological Approach

The research methodology for this study incorporates a systematic approach to select relevant articles, combining a literature review, comparative case studies, and predictive modeling. A key aspect of this approach is the use of well-defined inclusion and exclusion criteria to ensure that only the most pertinent articles contribute to the analysis. The following inclusion and exclusion criteria were applied to ensure that the selected articles are highly relevant to the study's focus on generative AI in customer objection management:

Figure 3. Methodological framework for Generative AI study

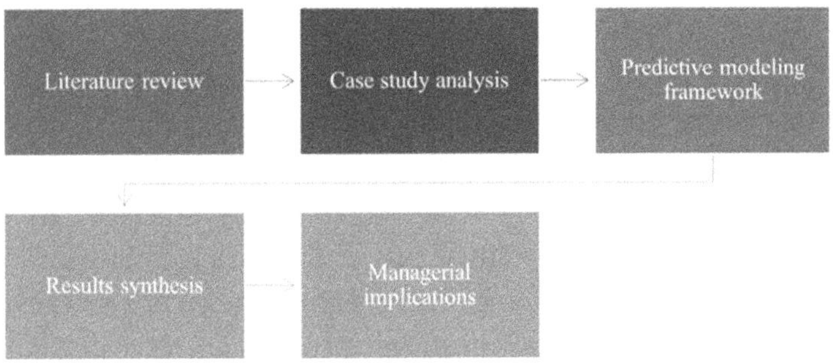

Source: Authors

- **Inclusion criteria:**
  - **Relevance to Generative AI**: Articles must explicitly address generative AI, particularly in the context of customer service, objection handling, personalization, or ethical considerations.
  - **Publication date**: Only articles published from 2018 to 2024 were included to capture the most recent advances and trends in generative AI, given the rapid evolution in the field.
  - **Peer-reviewed and credible sources**: Articles were selected from peer-reviewed journals, reputable academic archives (e.g., IEEE, ScienceDirect, arXiv), and respected conference proceedings to ensure credibility and academic rigor.
  - **Empirical or theoretical depth**: Studies needed to provide either empirical data, case studies, or a theoretical framework that could support a deeper understanding of generative AI's applications, limitations, or ethical implications in customer service.
  - **Focus on ethics and transparency**: Given the importance of ethical considerations, articles discussing transparency, fairness, accountability, and bias in AI were prioritized.
- **Exclusion criteria:**
  - **Lack of focus on Generative AI**: Studies focusing solely on traditional rule-based AI or machine learning models without any generative component were excluded, as these do not align with the study's focus.
  - **Non-peer-reviewed or low credibility**: Articles from sources lacking peer review, such as blog posts or opinion pieces, were excluded to maintain high standards of academic quality.
  - **Outdated technology or irrelevant applications**: Articles discussing outdated technologies or unrelated applications, such as AI in fields without customer interaction (e.g., purely industrial AI applications), were excluded to maintain relevance to the topic of customer objections.

Duplicate studies: In cases where multiple articles covered similar findings by the same authors, only the most comprehensive or recent publication was included to avoid redundancy.

- **Systematic selection process**

To ensure a rigorous selection, articles were sourced using targeted keywords such as "Generative AI in Customer Service," "Objection Handling with AI," "Ethics in Generative AI," and "Personalization and Transparency in AI." These searches were conducted across several academic databases, including Google Scholar, IEEE Xplore, ScienceDirect, and SSRN. After an initial screening of over 100 articles, 33 were selected based on the criteria above. Each article was reviewed for its methodological approach, theoretical contribution, and practical insights, ensuring a balanced mix of empirical research, theoretical discussions, and case studies that contribute to a well-rounded analysis.

2.1. Systematic Literature Review

The systematic literature review was conducted to identify and synthesize current research on generative AI's applications in customer service, with a specific focus on handling customer objections. The articles selected cover various aspects, including practical applications of generative AI, personalization and contextualization techniques, and ethical considerations.

Using thematic coding, each article was analyzed and categorized into major themes such as emotional complexity management, personalization models, and ethical transparency. This structured approach allowed for a comprehensive synthesis of research findings, identifying trends and gaps in literature.

2.2. Comparative Case Study Analysis

To anticipate customer objections and enhance real-time response quality, this study proposes a predictive model that combines generative AI with machine learning techniques. The model leverages historical data, sentiment analysis, and contextual factors to identify objection patterns and optimize responses dynamically.

Additionally, a human-AI collaboration framework was developed to address cases where human intervention is necessary. This hybrid framework defines roles and responsibilities between AI and human agents, ensuring that complex or sensitive objections receive appropriate human oversight.

2.3. Predictive Modeling and Framework Development

The comparative case study analysis examines generative AI applications in real-world settings across multiple industries, including finance, e-commerce, and healthcare. This method provides practical insights into how AI is being implemented to improve efficiency and customer satisfaction when handling objections.

Each case study evaluates the performance of generative AI systems compared to traditional, human-driven approaches. Key performance indicators (KPIs) such as response accuracy, customer satisfaction, and response times were used to assess AI effectiveness relative to human methods. This comparison reveals sector-specific requirements, such as the need for rapid 2.3.

2.4. Illustrative Framework for Human-AI Collaboration

A decision-flow diagram was created to show when an objection should be managed by AI versus a human agent, based on criteria like response confidence and emotional complexity. This framework ensures that customer interactions are both efficient and empathetic, maximizing customer satisfaction while minimizing operational risks.

This approach allows organizations to achieve an optimal balance of automation and human empathy, ensuring that AI-driven responses meet high standards of relevance and trustworthiness.

3. Profile of the references studied

The 33 selected articles were chosen based on stringent selection criteria to ensure relevance and quality. The profile of these articles can be classified into four main thematic categories, providing a multi-dimensional view of generative AI applications, theoretical foundations, and ethical implications.

Generative AI in customer service: Articles in this category explore the direct application of generative AI in customer service, particularly in automating responses to customer objections. Key studies include those by Rane (2023) and Ma (2023), which examine AI's capabilities for personalization and efficiency gains across sectors.

Comparative studies on Chatbots and AI Models: This category focuses on comparing various AI models used in customer service, including rule-based chatbots, NLP-based systems, and neural networks. Studies by Villaseñor (2023) and Grossman et al. (2023) provide insights into how these models handle complex objections and adapt to context-specific needs, such as legal and regulatory compliance.

Ethics, transparency, and bias in AI: Ethics is a central theme, with articles discussing the need for transparency, accountability, and fairness in AI-driven interactions. For instance, de la Durantaye (2023) emphasizes the importance of ethical frameworks to avoid biases in AI-generated responses, while Carugati (2023) highlights the competitive pressures that may lead to ethical compromises.

Case studies and predictive models for objection management: Articles in this category discuss practical case studies and predictive models developed to anticipate and address customer objections. Studies by Li et al. (2023) and Cao et al. (2023) present predictive approaches that utilize historical interaction data to optimize response quality and timeliness. **Table 4** breaks down the literature pool across key thematic categories, revealing where scholarly attention is concentrated and where gaps remain useful for spotting trends and opportunities for future research.

Table 4. Distribution of articles by thematic categories

Category	Number of articles	Example references
Generative AI in customer service	9	Rane, 2023; Ma, 2023; Lins dos Santos, 2023
Comparative Studies on AI Models	8	Villaseñor, 2023; Grossman et al., 2023; Raffaghelli & Crudele, 2023
Ethics, Transparency, and Bias	7	de la Durantaye, 2023; Carugati, 2023; Nascimento & Alencar, 2023
Case Studies and Predictive Models	9	Li et al., 2023; Cao et al., 2023; Browning, 2023

Source: Authors

The selected articles provide comprehensive insights into generative AI's role in customer service, offering a foundation for analyzing emerging trends and identifying best practices in objection management.

Figure 4. Distribution of articles by year of publication

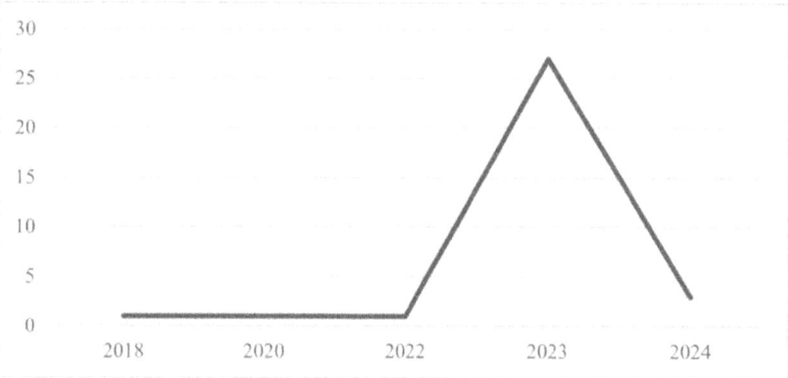

Source: Authors

The distribution by year of publication shows a significant concentration of articles in 2023, with 27 out of 33 articles published that year. This suggests a sharp increase in interest and research activity on generative AI and customer objection handling, reflecting the timeliness and relevance of the topic. The recent surge in 2023 and into 2024 underscores the rapid evolution and growing recognition of generative AI's potential across industries. Earlier publications, such as those from 2018 and 2020, likely provide foundational insights, while recent publications focus on current applications and emerging challenges.

Figure 5. Distribution of references by type of methodological approach

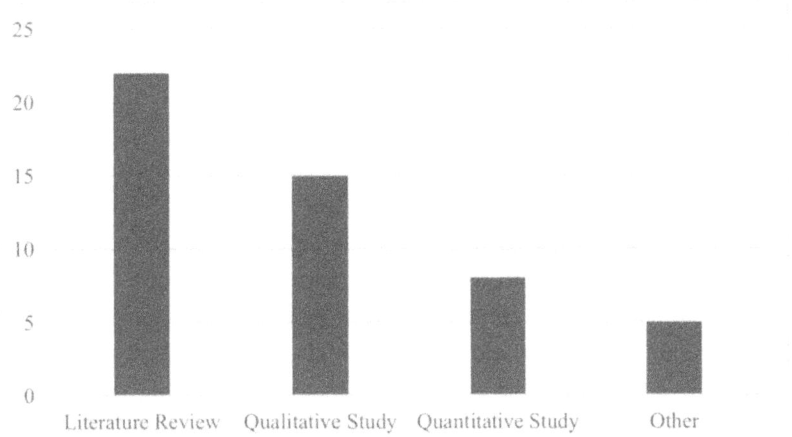

Source: Authors

The breakdown of methodological approaches reveals a strong emphasis on literature reviews, which account for 22 of the 33 articles. This prevalence of literature reviews highlights a focus on synthesizing existing knowledge and mapping out the broader trends and theories associated with generative AI in customer service. Qualitative studies, with 15 articles, suggest an interest in in-depth, contextual analysis, often focusing on the perceptions, implications, and applications of generative AI in real-world scenarios. Quantitative studies (8 articles) provide empirical data to support or validate theoretical models, while the "Other" category (5 articles) likely includes mixed methods or unique approaches that don't fit strictly within the qualitative or quantitative categories. Overall, methodological distribution shows a strong reliance on theoretical exploration combined with a growing empirical foundation.

Figure 6. Distribution of references by level of research depth

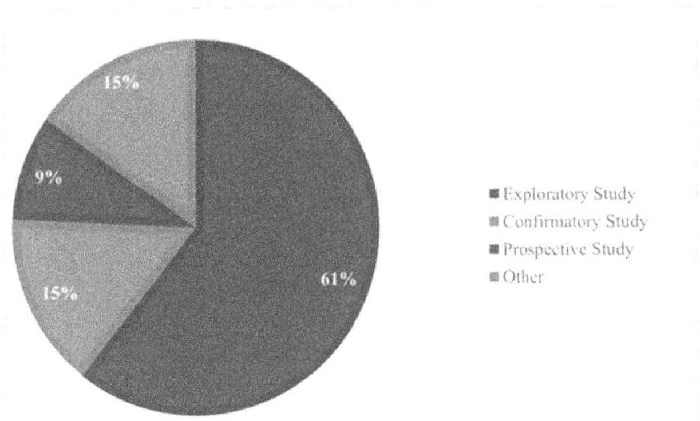

Source: Authors

The distribution by research depth indicates a clear preference for exploratory studies, with 20 articles focused on investigating new insights and identifying emerging themes in generative AI for customer objection management. This exploratory focus aligns well with the innovative nature of generative AI, as researchers seek to understand the implications, challenges, and potential applications of this technology in uncharted areas. Confirmatory studies, with only 5 articles, suggest a limited emphasis testing on hypothesis or validation, which may be due to the relatively nascent stage of research in this field. Prospective studies (3 articles) indicate early attempts to predict future developments and trends, showcasing the forward-looking aspect of the research. The "Other" category (5 articles) likely includes foundational or introductory studies that do not fit within a specific research depth but provide valuable context for understanding the broader landscape of generative AI.

These tables together illustrate the nature and maturity of research on generative AI in customer service. The methodological focus on literature reviews and qualitative studies, along with the predominance of exploratory research depth highlights the field's exploratory and evolving status. The recent concentration of publications in 2023 and the limited confirmatory research indicate that generative AI in customer objection handling is still in a formative stage, with ongoing efforts to map its possibilities and establish a robust empirical foundation. This analysis suggests that future research could benefit from more quantitative, confirmatory, and prospective studies to validate insights and predict long-term impacts, advancing the field from theoretical exploration to practical, evidence-based applications.

SECTION 3: ANALYSIS OF STUDY RESULTS

This section presents the results of our study on generative AI in managing customer objections, organized according to the methodological approach previously outlined. By examining the selected literature through systematic review, comparative case studies, and predictive modeling insights, we identify key themes, current trends, and critical gaps.

1. Thematic Clusters

Through a systematic review of the selected articles, several recurring themes emerged. These themes highlight the primary areas where generative AI is shaping customer objection management, including personalization, ethical considerations, collaboration between AI and human agents, and technological limitations. **Table 5** groups the current generative-AI literature into major thematic clusters, spotlighting the dominant research strands, their core questions, and the emergent intersections that signal promising directions for upcoming studies.

Table 5. Key thematic clusters in Generative AI research

Theme	Description	Example articles
Personalization and adaptability	Emphasizes AI's ability to tailor responses based on customer history and preferences	Rane (2023), Ma (2023), Gill & Kaur (2023)
Ethical and transparency concerns	Discusses issues of bias, accountability, and transparency in AI-generated responses	de la Durantaye (2023), Carugati (2023)
Human-AI collaboration	Explores hybrid models where human agents intervene in complex or sensitive interactions	Nah et al. (2023), Brynjolfsson et al. (2023)
Technological limitations	Highlight challenges such as accuracy, context-awareness, and sentiment detection limitations	Brown et al. (2020), Villaseñor (2023)

Source: Authors

The thematic clusters show a strong focus on personalization, as generative AI is recognized for its potential to tailor responses to individual customers. However, ethical concerns related to bias and transparency are also prevalent, indicating a need for regulatory frameworks and responsible AI design. The emphasis on human-AI collaboration suggests that fully autonomous objection handling remains challenging, with human intervention required for complex cases. Technological limitations persist, especially regarding context comprehension and emotion detection, which are crucial for managing customer objections effectively.

2. Comparative analysis of case studies

The case study analysis focused on real-world applications of generative AI in different industries, including finance, e-commerce, and healthcare. This analysis sheds light on the industry-specific requirements and the varied impact of generative AI across sectors. Table 6 contrasts how different industries deploy generative AI comparing objectives, implementation approaches, and observed outcomes to highlight sector-specific best practices and transferable lessons.

Table 6. Comparative case study analysis of generative ai applications by industry

Industry	AI Implementation	Customer satisfaction	Response speed	Notable challenges	Example articles
Finance	AI-driven chatbots	High	Moderate	High demand for transparency	Villaseñor (2023), Carugati (2023)
E-commerce	AI + Human Hybrid	Very High	High	Balancing automation with empathy	Ma (2023), Nah et al. (2023)
Healthcare	Limited AI (Human-led)	Moderate	Low	Requires empathy and understanding	Terzidou (2023), Browning (2023)

Source: Authors

The analysis reveals that e-commerce benefits most from a hybrid AI-human model, which balances automation with human empathy, enabling fast and personalized customer responses. Finance utilizes AI-driven chatbots effectively, though transparency remains a critical concern, as customers are often wary of fully automated systems handling sensitive financial matters. In healthcare, AI implementation is limited, primarily because handling objections and inquiries requires a high degree of empathy and nuanced understanding, best provided by human agents. These findings suggest that generative AI's role is more pronounced in industries that prioritize efficiency, while sectors requiring empathy and human judgment may integrate AI as a supportive, rather than primary, tool.

3. Predictive modeling and framework development

Based on insights from the literature and case studies, we outline a predictive modeling framework aimed at enhancing generative AI's effectiveness in anticipating and addressing customer objections. This framework combines machine learning with generative AI to dynamically adjust responses based on customer sentiment, historical data, and real-time interactions.

- **Key components of the predictive modeling framework:**
  - **Data collection and preprocessing**: This stage involves gathering customer interaction data, such as chat logs and feedback, and applying sentiment analysis tools to classify emotional tones. Such classification allows AI to adjust responses based on perceived customer moods (Gill & Kaur, 2023; Brynjolfsson et al., 2023).
  - **Historical data integration**: The model leverages historical objection data to identify patterns, allowing AI to predict likely objections based on past interactions. For instance, common concerns can be preemptively addressed, improving response accuracy (Brown et al., 2020; Davenport & Ronanki, 2018).
  - **Real-time adaptation**: Utilizing natural language processing (NLP) algorithms, the model adjusts responses in real-time, aligning with customer sentiment and contextual cues. This approach is essential for ensuring that responses are both relevant and empathetic (Rane, 2023; Nah, Zheng, & Siau, 2023).
  - **Human override mechanism**: When the model's confidence level is low or when sensitive issues arise, a human override option activates, transferring the objection to a human agent. This hybrid approach ensures that customer objections requiring empathy or complex decision-making receive appropriate attention (Villasenor, 2023; Browning, 2023).

Figure 7. Predictive modeling framework for customer objection management with Generative AI

Source: Authors

This predictive model aims to improve objection handling by proactively identifying and responding to customer concerns. The human override mechanism acknowledges generative AI's limitations in managing nuanced objections, ensuring that sensitive cases are handled by trained agents (Nah, Zheng, & Siau, 2023). By integrating historical and real-time data, the model can offer timely, accurate responses that enhance customer satisfaction while minimizing the need for escalation (Brynjolfsson et al., 2023; Davenport & Ronanki, 2018).

4. Outline of the Synthesis and Analysis Model

This section provides an outline for synthesizing and analyzing the findings from our study on generative AI in customer objection management. We present a synthesis model to organize the results effectively, followed by insights on the managerial contributions, limitations, and future research directions in this domain.

4.1. Synthesis of Results

To summarize the study findings, we developed a synthesis and analysis model that captures primary elements of generative AI in customer objection management, including personalization, ethical considerations, technological adaptability, and human-AI collaboration. This model organizes insights from thematic clusters, comparative case studies, and the predictive modeling framework, highlighting strengths, limitations, and applications of generative AI (Rane, 2023; Carugati, 2023). **Figure 8** illustrates the proposed analytical model, tracing how generative-AI components interact from data ingestion through language generation to predict, address and learn from customer objections, thereby refining service responses in real time.

Figure 8. Analysis model sketch for Generative AI in customer objection management

Main component	Subtopics	Impact on objection management
Personalization	Customer history integration, real-time contextualization	Enhances customer satisfaction by delivering relevant and context-aware responses.
Ethical considerations	Transparency, bias reduction	Builds trust with customers by adhering to ethical principles and minimizing algorithmic biases.
Technological adaptability	Natural language processing (nlp), sentiment analysis	Improves the accuracy and empathy of responses, especially in emotionally charged scenarios.
Human-ai collaboration	Human override mechanism, dynamic escalation	Ensures complex and nuanced objections are managed effectively through human oversight.

Table 7.

Main component	Subtopics	Impact on objection management
Personalization	Customer history integration, real-time contextualization	Enhances customer satisfaction by delivering relevant and context-aware responses.
Ethical considerations	Transparency, bias reduction	Builds trust with customers by adhering to ethical principles and minimizing algorithmic biases.
Technological adaptability	Natural language processing (nlp), sentiment analysis	Improves the accuracy and empathy of responses, especially in emotionally charged scenarios.
Human-ai collaboration	Human override mechanism, dynamic escalation	Ensures complex and nuanced objections are managed effectively through human oversight.

Source: Authors

This detailed model illustrates the key components and subtopics associated with implementing generative AI in handling customer objections:

- **Personalization**:

Effective objection management begins with deep personalization. Contemporary generative models now knit together historical customer data purchase records, prior complaints, channel preferences to craft replies that explicitly reference the individual's journey (Orchard & Tasiemski 2023). Equally important is real-time contextualization: by continuously ingesting conversation turns, the model recalibrates tone, formality, and content on the fly, ensuring that each new message responds to the immediate conversational context rather than relying on static scripts (Ma 2023). Together, these capabilities shift objection handling from generic reassurance to genuinely tailored dialogue, heightening perceived empathy and resolution speed.

- **Ethical considerations**:

Personalization must be tempered by a robust ethical framework. Transparency is pivotal; customers should be explicitly informed when an answer is AI-generated, a practice shown to sustain trust even when automation is extensive (de la Durantaye 2023). Parallel research stresses bias reduction techniques such as counterfactual data augmentation and fairness-constrained decoding to prevent discriminatory language or recommendations (Villaseñor 2023; Grossman, Grimm & Brown 2023). Embedding these safeguards early not only protects vulnerable segments but also shields firms from reputational and regulatory fallout.

- **Technological adaptability**:

Under the hood, two technical pillars support advanced objection handling. First, state-of-the-art Natural Language Processing (NLP) architectures (e.g., transformer-based LLMs) provide nuanced intent recognition and argument generation, allowing the system to understand subtle objections and craft coherent, policy-compliant replies (Brown et al. 2020). Second, real-time sentiment analysis layers detect anxiety, frustration or sarcasm within milliseconds, enabling the AI to modulate its wording soothing an angry customer or matching an upbeat mood (Gill & Kaur 2023; Brynjolfsson et al. 2023). This adaptability is crucial when objections escalate quickly on public channels like social media.

- **Human-AI collaboration**:

Despite rising model accuracy, edge-cases demand human judgment. A well-designed system therefore offers a human-override mechanism, routing complex or ambiguous objections to skilled agents who can inject empathy and discretionary concessions (Nah, Zheng & Siau 2023; Villaseñor 2023). Complementing this is dynamic escalation: rule-based or learning-based triggers such as low confidence scores or highly negative sentiment auto-escalate interactions before customer frustration peaks (Paul, Ueno & Dennis 2023). This collaborative choreography preserves efficiency while safeguarding service quality.

Taken together, the model underscores that superior objection handling is not the product of any single capability; rather, it emerges from the synergy of personalization engines, ethical guardrails, adaptive NLP pipelines, and purposeful human oversight. Organizations that balance these technological advances with clear governance can convert objections into trust-building moments and long-term loyalty.

4.2. CONCLUSION and Perspectives

This investigation affirms that generative AI can transform customer-objection management by producing fast, context-aware answers that boost first-contact resolution and overall satisfaction. Yet the technology's promise is contingent on three implementation imperatives.

Embed Strong Ethical Safeguards

Transparency clearly disclosing AI involvement and systematic bias audits are no longer optional; they are prerequisites for trust and regulatory compliance (de la Durantaye 2023; Carugati 2023). Firms should operationalize ethics-by-design toolkits that log model reasoning, surface confidence scores to agents, and allow customers to contest automated decisions.

Pursue Industry-Specific Fine-Tuning

Generative models must speak the language of each sector whether HIPAA-constrained healthcare, Know-Your-Customer-driven finance, or the high-velocity landscape of e-commerce (Browning 2023; Villaseñor 2023). Domain-trained vocabularies, compliance rules and escalation paths ensure responses remain both helpful and lawful.

Adopt Hybrid Human–AI Workflows for Sensitive Cases

Pure automation falters when objections involve emotion, legal nuance, or high customer lifetime value. Routing low-confidence or high-stakes interactions to human agents supported by AI-generated drafts combines efficiency with empathy (Nah, Zheng & Siau 2023).

Looking ahead, continued advances in large-language-model reasoning, real-time sentiment detection and predictive analytics will push objection handling toward more autonomous, proactive, and personalized service. Future research should therefore explore:

- **Context-rich multi-modal models** that integrate voice, video and transaction data.
- **Adaptive governance frameworks** that evolve alongside fast-moving AI capabilities and shifting regulations.
- **Longitudinal field studies** measuring how generative AI reshapes churn, loyalty and brand equity over multi-year horizons.

By aligning technical innovation with ethical rigor and sector-specific customization, organizations can turn customer objections from friction points into opportunities for deeper engagement and durable trust.

4.3. Managerial Contributions

Generative AI is more than a technological upgrade; it reshapes the managerial playbook for customer-service operations by delivering measurable gains across four fronts.

Hyper-Personalized Engagement

Large-language models can synthesize purchase history, sentiment traces and behavioral cues within milliseconds, enabling agents or the AI itself to address objections with contextually relevant offers or explanations (Raffaghelli & Crudele 2023). Such tailored exchanges not only resolve issues faster but also strengthen perceived empathy, a key driver of customer loyalty.

Scalable Efficiency

Automating high-volume, low-complexity objections frees human agents to focus on value-adding tasks such as cross-selling or handling exceptional cases. Studies report cost-to-serve reductions of 20–40 percent when objection triage and first-draft responses are AI-assisted (Brynjolfsson et al. 2023). This scalability is critical for firms facing fluctuating demand or global time-zone coverage.

Risk Mitigation Through Ethical-AI Governance

Implementing transparent, bias-monitored generative systems minimizes legal exposure and reputational harm. Dashboards that surface model explanations and flag sensitive content allow managers to intervene before issues escalate (Villaseñor 2023; Grossman, Grimm & Brown 2023). Ethical governance thus becomes a proactive form of risk management.

Continuous Service Refinement

Generative AI platforms can log every interaction, feeding predictive-analytics loops that spot emerging objection patterns and root-cause drivers (Ma 2023). Managers gain near-real-time insights to update knowledge bases, adjust policy wording, or launch pre-emptive outreach turning reactive support into a cycle of ongoing improvement.

Collectively, these contributions illustrate that generative AI equips managers with a dual advantage: operational leverage through automation and strategic foresight via data-driven learning. Organizations that pair technical deployment with robust ethical and change-management practices will be best positioned to convert customer-service excellence into sustained competitive advantage.

4.4. Limitations and Future Directions

While the study highlights the substantial promise of generative AI in transforming customer objection management, several inherent limitations must be addressed for its broader and more effective application.

Contextual Limitations

Generative AI models, despite their impressive capabilities, still face challenges in navigating highly contextual or emotionally complex objections. AI often fails to grasp the nuances of customer emotions, sarcasm, or culturally specific references, leading to suboptimal or inappropriate responses. Addressing these gaps requires advances in sentiment analysis and context-awareness that allow AI to understand not just the literal content but also the emotional undertones and situational specifics of objections (Gill & Kaur, 2023). Improving these capabilities will be crucial for handling delicate customer concerns where empathy and situational sensitivity are paramount.

Ethical Challenges

As generative AI systems become more pervasive in customer service, ensuring transparency, reducing bias, and safeguarding customer privacy remain significant ethical challenges. AI models are often criticized for opaque decision-making processes, which can erode customer trust, especially in industries dealing with sensitive data, such as healthcare or finance (de la Durantaye, 2023; Grossman, Grimm, & Brown, 2023). Future advancements should integrate ethics-by-design principles, ensuring that AI outputs are not only explainable but also accountable. Striking the right balance between automation and ethical standards will be a key challenge for AI developers and businesses alike.

Data Dependency

The success of AI-driven objection management is heavily reliant on high-quality, diverse datasets. AI models learn and improve based on the data they are fed, and the effectiveness of these models is diminished if the data is incomplete or biased. Small or under-resourced organizations often struggle to obtain or curate sufficient data to train AI systems, hindering their ability to leverage this technology effectively (Dwivedi et al., 2023). Future research should focus on developing data-sharing frameworks or synthetic data solutions that make high-quality, varied datasets more accessible to smaller businesses, enabling them to also benefit from generative AI advancements.

- **Future directions**

Looking ahead, the trajectory of generative AI in customer objection management involves several critical areas for further research and development.

Improved Contextual Understanding

Future work should focus on enhancing AI's ability to interpret complex, multi-layered objections by incorporating more sophisticated models of contextual reasoning and emotional intelligence. This will require the integration of multi-modal data sources, such as voice tone, facial expressions, and historical interactions, to create a more holistic view of customer sentiment and intention.

Ethical AI Frameworks

A crucial next step is to incorporate robust ethical guidelines into AI systems. This includes not only transparency and bias reduction but also privacy-preserving mechanisms that align with evolving data protection regulations (e.g., GDPR). AI models must be auditable and adaptable, with clear pathways for identifying and mitigating biases during deployment. Research should also focus on ethical impact assessments that evaluate the societal and customer impacts of AI systems before they are implemented.

Democratization of AI Access

To ensure that AI benefits all organizations, especially smaller businesses, future research should explore ways to make advanced predictive AI models more accessible and affordable. This may involve the development of cloud-based AI solutions that reduce the need for substantial infrastructure investment or the creation of AI-as-a-Service platforms that provide affordable, scalable generative models with pre-trained datasets tailored for various industries.

Continuous Model Adaptation and Monitoring

As AI continues to evolve, the development of frameworks for ongoing monitoring and updating of generative models will be essential to ensure their continued relevance and accuracy. Continuous learning mechanisms that allow AI systems to adapt to changing customer behaviors and industry trends without compromising on ethical standards will become an indispensable part of the AI management lifecycle.

4.5. Future Perspectives

Generative AI in customer service is poised for significant growth as technological advances continue and industries increasingly adopt AI-driven solutions. As the technology matures, several potential future developments could transform how generative AI enhances customer service operations, improving both efficiency and customer satisfaction.

Advanced Sentiment and Context Analysis

One of the most promising areas for growth lies in improving sentiment and context analysis. While AI is already capable of detecting basic emotions, future advancements will allow it to identify nuanced emotional cues and more subtle aspects of customer sentiment. This improvement will enable AI to respond more empathetically to complex objections, particularly in situations where emotions run high or the objections are deeply personal. By enhancing AI's ability to understand the emotional state of the customer, businesses can foster stronger customer relationships and resolve issues with greater sensitivity and care (Gill & Kaur, 2023).

Real-Time, Multi-Language Processing

As businesses expand globally, multi-language capabilities will become increasingly essential for effective customer service. Future developments in real-time translation will allow AI systems to seamlessly interact with customers in different languages, breaking down barriers to communication. This will ensure that customers receive the same high-quality service regardless of their geographic location or language. For companies with global customer bases, this development will significantly enhance accessibility and efficiency in handling objections and queries (Ilieva, Yankova, & Klisarova-Belcheva, 2023).

Hybrid Models With Dynamic Human-AI Collaboration

Hybrid models, which combine AI capabilities with human intervention, are expected to evolve further. In future systems, dynamic collaboration between humans and AI will allow for more adaptive interactions, where the level of human involvement adjusts based on the complexity of the objection or the customer's sentiment. For example, in cases where an AI model detects heightened emotional distress or complex reasoning is required, human agents will be seamlessly escalated into the conversation. This dynamic approach ensures that AI remains the first line of response while humans are involved in situations that require a higher level of judgment or empathy (Nah, Zheng, & Siau, 2023).

Ethical and Regulatory Integration

As AI continues to play a pivotal role in customer service, the ethical and regulatory integration of AI systems will become increasingly important. Future generative AI models are likely to incorporate compliance features that ensure these systems adhere to industry regulations and ethical standards, particularly in sensitive sectors like healthcare, finance, and legal services. Regulatory frameworks are expected to become more stringent, and AI systems will need to incorporate safeguards to ensure transparency, fairness, and privacy. The evolution of AI must also align with public expectations and regulatory bodies to maintain trust and avoid potential legal risks (Bagenal, 2024; Villaseñor, 2023).

In conclusion, these future perspectives suggest that generative AI in customer service will continue to evolve, becoming more autonomous, adaptive, and ethically responsible. The integration of advanced sentiment analysis, real-time multi-language processing, hybrid models, and regulatory compliance features will further cement generative AI's role as a key tool in delivering high-quality, empathetic, and efficient customer service. These advancements will not only enhance the overall customer experience but also enable businesses to operate at a greater scale and with more accountability, ultimately leading to more satisfied customers and a stronger market position.

CONCLUSION

his chapter has explored the transformative potential of Generative AI in customer objection management, examining its multifaceted role in enhancing both the efficiency and personalization of customer service interactions. Through a detailed analysis of key components ranging from personalization and ethical considerations to technological adaptability and human-AI collaboration it has become clear that generative AI offers significant opportunities to reshape customer service dynamics, making it more responsive, efficient, and customer-centric.

The integration of personalized responses based on past customer interactions and real-time contextualization has proven to be crucial for ensuring that objections are handled in a manner that feels tailored to each individual's needs (Orchard & Tasiemski, 2023; Ma, 2023). Additionally, ethical considerations such as transparency and bias reduction are essential to maintaining customer trust and ensuring that AI-driven systems operate in a fair and responsible manner (de la Durantaye, 2023; Villaseñor, 2023). Technologically, advancements in Natural Language Processing (NLP) and sentiment analysis enhance the AI's ability to understand and respond to customer emotions, further deepening the quality of interactions (Brown et al., 2020; Gill & Kaur, 2023). Furthermore, the inclusion of human-AI collaboration mechanisms ensures that complex or sensitive objections are handled with the necessary empathy and judgment (Nah, Zheng, & Siau, 2023).

The study also highlighted several critical managerial contributions that generative AI brings to customer service, including enhanced personalization, scalability, risk management through ethical practices, and continuous improvement via predictive analytics (Brynjolfsson et al., 2023). These practical benefits contribute not only to operational efficiency but also to an improved customer experience, reinforcing the idea that generative AI should not be seen as a replacement for human involvement, but rather as a tool to complement and enhance human decision-making processes.

Despite its potential, the deployment of generative AI in customer objection management is not without its limitations. Contextual limitations, particularly in emotionally sensitive situations, need to be addressed through enhanced sentiment and context analysis (Gill & Kaur, 2023). Additionally, ethical challenges around transparency, bias, and privacy remain significant hurdles, particularly in sensitive industries like healthcare and finance (de la Durantaye, 2023; Grossman, Grimm, & Brown, 2023). Data dependency is another issue that may limit the accessibility of AI-driven solutions, particularly for smaller organizations that may not have access to large, high-quality datasets (Dwivedi et al., 2023). These limitations underscore the need for continuous improvements in AI systems, as well as the development of frameworks that allow for the ongoing monitoring and updating of AI models to ensure their relevance and accuracy over time.

Looking to the future, the role of generative AI in customer service is set to expand, with several exciting developments on the horizon. Advanced sentiment and context analysis, multi-language processing, and hybrid human-AI models will further enhance the AI's ability to handle complex objections with greater empathy and accuracy (Gill & Kaur, 2023; Ilieva, Yankova, & Klisarova-Belcheva, 2023). Moreover, the integration of ethical and regulatory compliance features will ensure that AI systems remain accountable, transparent, and fair, adhering to evolving regulations and industry standards (Bagenal, 2024; Villaseñor, 2023).

In conclusion, this chapter has highlighted the promising potential of generative AI to transform customer objection management. By enhancing personalization, empathy, and efficiency, and by addressing both technological and ethical challenges, generative AI can serve as a powerful tool in improving customer service outcomes. However, its successful implementation will require continuous advancements in AI capabilities, alongside careful consideration of ethical safeguards and industry-specific adaptations. As generative AI evolves, it will likely play an increasingly central role in customer service, offering businesses a way to meet the growing demand for personalized, efficient, and ethically responsible interactions.

REFERENCES

Bagenal, J. (2024). Generative Artificial Intelligence and Scientific Publishing: Urgent Questions, Difficult Answers. *Lancet*, *403*(10432), 1118–1120. DOI: 10.1016/S0140-6736(24)00416-1 PMID: 38460530

Binns, R., & Veale, M. (2020). *Algorithmic Accountability: A Practical Framework for AI Ethics in Customer Interactions*. Ethics in AI Review.

Bouhtati, N., Alla, L., & Ed-Daakouri, I. (2024). Smart Data Analysis and Prediction of Responsible Customer Behaviour in Tourism: An Exploratory Review of the Literature. In El Archi, Y., Benbba, B., Dávid, L., & Cardoso, L. (Eds.), *Promoting Responsible Tourism With Digital Platforms* (pp. 189–212). IGI Global., DOI: 10.4018/979-8-3693-3286-3.ch011

Brown, T., et al. (2020). *Language Models are Few-Shot Learners*. arXiv.

Browning, J. G. (2023). Robot Lawyers Don't Have Disciplinary Hearings - Ethical Risks of Generative AI in Law. *Georgia State University Law Review*.

Brynjolfsson, E., Li, D., & Raymond, L. R. (2023). *Generative AI at Work*. NBER. DOI: 10.3386/w31161

Candelon, F., Krayer, L., & Rajendran, S. (2023). *How People Can Create—and Destroy—Value with Generative AI*. BCG Global.

Cao, Y., et al. (2023). *A Comprehensive Survey of AI-Generated Content (AIGC): A History of Generative AI from GAN to ChatGPT*. arXiv.

Carugati, C. (2023). Competition in Generative Artificial Intelligence Foundation Models. *Economia e Storia*.

Casanovas, P.. (2022). *Generative AI and the Rule of Law*. OPTIMAI.

Davenport, T., & Ronanki, R. (2018). Artificial Intelligence for the Real World. *Harvard Business Review*.

De la Durantaye, K. (2023). *Garbage In, Garbage Out: Regulating Generative AI Through Copyright Law*. *SSRN*. DOI: 10.2139/ssrn.4572952

Dwivedi, Y. K.. (2023). What if ChatGPT Wrote It? Multidisciplinary Perspectives on Generative AI. *International Journal of Information Management*. Advance online publication. DOI: 10.1016/j.ijinfomgt.2023.102642

Ed-daakouri, I., Bouhtati, N., & Alla, L.(2024). Smart Data Analytics for Efficient Mapping of Customers' Online Shopping Behavior: A Systematic Review of the Literature. DOI: . In book: Mapping Human Data and Behavior With the Internet of Behavior (IoB)DOI: 10.4018/979-8-3693-7545-7.ch010

Furey, A., & Kline, M. (2023). *Generative AI in Corporate Communications: Applications and Challenges*. Corporate Communications Journal.

Gill, S. S., & Kaur, R. (2023). *ChatGPT: Vision and Challenges*. ScienceDirect.

Grossman, M. R., Grimm, P. W., & Brown, D. G. (2023). Is Disclosure and Certification of the Use of Generative AI Really Necessary? *SSRN*.

Gunder, J. R. (2023). Rule 11 is No Match for Generative AI. *Stanford Technology Law Review : STLR : An Online High-Technology Law Journal from Stanford Law School.*

Hao, X., Demir, E., & Eyers, D. (2024). *Exploring Collaborative Decision-Making: A Quasi-Experimental Study of Human and Generative AI Interaction*. Technology in Society, Elsevier.

Holmström, J., & Carroll, N. (2024). *How Organizations Can Innovate with Generative AI*. Business Horizons, Elsevier. DOI: 10.1016/j.bushor.2024.02.010

Ilieva, G., Yankova, T., & Klisarova-Belcheva, S. (2023). *Effects of Generative Chatbots in Higher Education*. MDPI Information. DOI: 10.3390/info14090492

Joosten, J., Bilgram, V., & Hahn, A. (2024). *Comparing the Ideation Quality of Humans with Generative Artificial Intelligence*. IEEE Engineering. DOI: 10.1109/EMR.2024.3353338

Kaplan, A., & Haenlein, M. (2019). Siri, Siri, in My Hand: Who's the Fairest in the Land? On the Interpretations, Illustrations, and Implications of Artificial Intelligence. *Business Horizons*, *62*(1), 15–25. DOI: 10.1016/j.bushor.2018.08.004

Lee, K., Cooper, A.F., & Grimmelmann, J. (2023). *Talkin'Bout AI Generation: Copyright and the Generative-AI Supply Chain*. arXiv.

Li, J., Mynatt, E., Mishra, V., & Bell, J. (2023). *Developer's Experiences Engaging Generative AI Chatbots*. arXiv.

Lins dos Santos, L. F. (2023). *Evaluating and Comparing Generative-Based Chatbots Based on Process Requirements*. University of Waterloo.

Ma, C. (2023). *ChatGPT and Generative AI in IT Processes*. NYU Archive.

Mahmud, B., Hong, G., & Fong, B. (2023). *A Study of Human–AI Symbiosis for Creative Work: Recent Developments and Future Directions in Deep Learning*. ACM Transactions on Multimedia.

Nah, F. F.-H., Zheng, R., & Siau, K. (2023). Generative AI and ChatGPT: Applications, Challenges, and AI-Human Collaboration. *Journal of Information Technology*.

Nascimento, N., & Alencar, P. (2023). *Comparing Generative Chatbots Based on Process Requirements: A Case Study*. IEEE.

Ooi, K. B., Tan, G. W. H., & Al-Emran, M. (2023). The Potential of Generative AI Across Disciplines: Perspectives and Future Directions. *Journal of Computer Information Systems*.

Orchard, T., & Tasiemski, L. (2023). *The Rise of Generative AI and Possible Effects on the Economy*. Economics and Business Review. DOI: 10.18559/ebr.2023.2.732

Orchard, T., & Tasiemski, L. (2023). *The Rise of Generative AI and Possible Effects on the Economy*. Sciendo. DOI: 10.18559/ebr.2023.2.732

Paul, J., Ueno, A., & Dennis, C. (2023). ChatGPT and Consumers: Benefits, Pitfalls, and Future Research Agenda. *International Journal of Consumer Studies*, *47*(4), 1213–1225. DOI: 10.1111/ijcs.12928

Raffaghelli, J.E., & Crudele, F. (2023). *The Student Experience on Generative AI to Develop Reflective and Argumentative Skills in the Learning Process*. HESummit.

Rane, N. (2023). *Role and Challenges of ChatGPT and Similar Generative Artificial Intelligence in Business Management. SSRN*. DOI: 10.2139/ssrn.4603227

Robertson, J., Ferreira, C., Botha, E., & Oosthuizen, K. (2024). *Game Changers: A Generative AI Prompt Protocol to Enhance Human-AI Knowledge Co-construction*. Business Horizons, Elsevier.

Salah, M., Al Halbusi, H., & Abdelfattah, F. (2023). May the Force of Text Data Analysis Be with You: Unleashing the Power of Generative AI for Social Psychology Research. *Computers in Human Behavior*, *1*(2), 100006. DOI: 10.1016/j.chbah.2023.100006

Terzidou, K. (2023). *Generative AI for the Legal Profession: Facing the Implications of the Use of ChatGPT Through an Interdisciplinary Approach*. Uni.lu.

Terzidou, K., ... (2024). *Generative AI in Cross-Disciplinary Applications*. Multi-disciplinary Approach, Elsevier.

Villaseñor, J. (2023). *Generative Artificial Intelligence and the Practice of Law: Impact, Opportunities, and Risks*. HeinOnline.

Xu, Z.. (2021). AI in Service: Bridging the Gap Between AI and Human-Centered Customer Service. *Journal of Service Research*.

Chapter 21
Unlocking New Potentials in Generative AI

P. Ashok
https://orcid.org/0000-0002-5859-6041
Symbiosis Institute of Digital and Telecom Management, India

Tanisha Mangal
Symbiosis Institute of Digital and Telecom Management, India

Lakshmi Sridevi
Chennai Institute of Technology, India

Krishna K. Murali
Rajalakshmi Engineering College, India

ABSTRACT

Generative AI, a subset of artificial intelligence, is dedicated to the development of models that are capable of producing new content, including text, imagery, audio, and entire virtual worlds. Generative AI is capable of replicating human creativity and generating outputs that were previously considered to be exclusively the domain of human intelligence by utilizing sophisticated machine learning techniques, including deep learning and neural networks. AI models in the music industry are capable of composing music in a variety of genres, providing musicians and producers with new tools. Generative AI has the potential to stimulate innovation and creativity in a variety of disciplines as technology continues to develop. This research article delves deep into the various aspects of Generative AI namely history and core concepts, privacy and security, types of Generative AI models and their applications, NLP models and finally on Responsible AI.

DOI: 10.4018/979-8-3693-8332-2.ch021

1. INTRODUCTION

A. History & Core Concepts of Generative AI

Artificial intelligence (AI) is one of the most widely discussed technology trends globally, potentially contributing US$ 15.7 trillion to the global Gross Domestic Product (GDP) by 2030. As technology has begun making significant strides with Artificial Intelligence (AI), enterprises have been ushered into a new paradigm of Generative AI. Generative AI is a technology that leverages deep learning models to create human-like content, such as words and images, when instructed with specific prompts. With the advancements in cloud storage, Generative AI can leverage its usage to manage data more efficiently and economically. In Q1 CY2023, the reported investments in Global Private Generative AI amounted to $11 billion, leveraging its use cases across various areas. The history behind the Generative models in Artificial Intelligence traces back to the 1950s when Markov Models and Gaussian Mixture Models were first developed. These models focused on generating sequential data but struggled with longer sentences. Generative AI analyses customer data and creates precise ads, increasing their effectiveness and resonance with consumers. It was the rise of deep learning that brought about substantial advancements in the performance of generative models, but the most critical advancement cutting across numerous domains was "The Transformer Architecture" which has become the backbone for many generative models. There are two types of Generative models:

- Generative language models (GLMs) - GLMs are designed to produce comprehensible human language by learning from the patterns and structures present in the input data. One of the most significant breakthroughs is Generative Pre-Trained Transformer (GPT), a transformer-based model that is capable of interpreting a wide range of text-based requests and providing answers to simple questions.
- Generative Adversarial Networks (GANs) have become popular in the field of image generation research. GANs have two parts, a generator which aims to grasp the distribution of authentic examples to create new data and a discriminator, which regulates whether the entered data is authentic or not.

Generative AI has the potential to leverage its use cases across various areas: R&D, Marketing, Sales, Software engineering, and Customer operations. The banking industry is likely to generate a value of 2.8 to 4.7 per cent of the industry's annual revenues. With the applications of Generative AI in areas such as regulations and programming language, the industry is likely to see potential growth. The rise of 14 global Generative AI unicorns and the 1.5x growth in Generative AI startups in India shows that the industry is likely to witness prominent growth as in Fig. 1.

2. LITERATURE REVIEW

Generative artificial intelligence (AI) in design and art has disrupted creative paradigms, prompting debates about AI-generated art and NFT markets. In February 2023, the US Copyright Office made a landmark ruling that shows AI work is problematic and need human involvement to commercialize. This study (Tiwary, H, 2024) discusses how neural network AI has changed visual arts. We use generative adversarial networks (GANs) to create NFT-style digital art with startling outcomes automatically. Our approach integrates deep learning and blockchain to bring AI to digital art. Generative AI can already produce visuals and words like humans, demonstrating its incredible potential. However, abuse has raised concerns about this development, sparking talks on appropriate responses. Thus, countries are deliberating suggestions and rules, including watermark technology implementation. Many firms are adding watermark technology to their services to solve this problem. The report (Hwang, J, 2023) analyzes watermark use across nations and enterprises. Further research subjects should be considered while adopting watermark technology. This study will help others considering watermarking in their future generative AI services. Generative AI algorithms may generate new content from training data. They can write and generate multimedia material like photos, music, and video.

Figure 1. Market outlook of generative AI (Credits: SIDTM students)

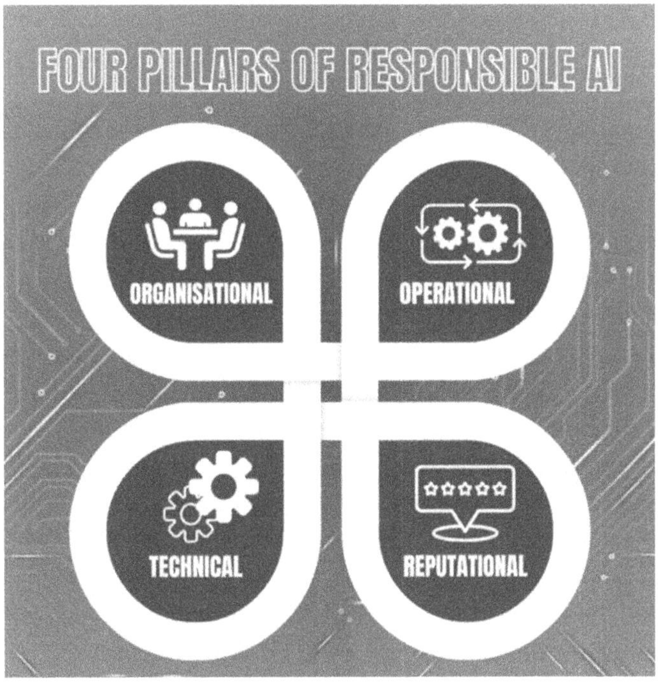

Their effect on several industries has made them prominent in recent years. They are used for text, picture, and music creation, education, healthcare, and metaverse. Trustworthiness, skewed material, overfitting, and regulatory issues remain obstacles when building and deploying these models.

The study (Rani, G, 2023) compares generative AI models based on tools, frameworks, input, output, development authority, etc. Additionally, generative AI model applications in many disciplines are examined. Generative AI's better functionality and adaptability have prompted hopes for human society's progress and worries about its ethical and societal hazards. Many researchers have identified risk problems connected with generative AI, but most are user-focused, making it difficult to provide solutions. The research (Tanaka, H, 2024) examined prior risk problems in more depth and discovered risk factors and repercussions. We provided information to propose generative AI risk mitigation. CCS CONCEPTS:

General and reference evaluation, surveys, overviews concerns covered: HCI theory, ideas, and models; social and professional concerns; computing/technology policy. ChatGPT has spurred the development of cutting-edge generative AI applications and services. Generative AI relies on Generative Adversarial Networks (GANs) and reinforcement learning to train generators and discriminators. Many picture and language generating models exist, but training them is a key research area. Thus, to develop training techniques for generative AI models, this work examines game theory, specifically the Cournot game, Stackelberg game, and repeating game. The paper (Chen, C. H., 2024) will include theoretical proofs, designs, and open dataset validation.

Generative AI makes API use documentation more efficient and powerful in our research. APIs are crucial to software integration and maintenance, but API documentation development has not evolved with time. The work (Dhyani, P, 2024) uses Generative AI to improve API documentation accuracy, speed, and scalability. To develop high-quality, industry-standard training data, web scraping was used on significant IT firms' documentation websites. It was varied and expanded using the GPT architecture to accommodate several API situations. Fine-tuning improved the TinyPixel/Llama-2-7B-bf16-sharded model's efficiency and output quality, as seen by decreased reaction time and accurate documentation. Our comparison investigation proves the technique works. This study's conclusion gives a complete strategy to enhance software development and advance API documentation. From humanity's existential dangers to critical system safety hazards to ethical concerns, responsible AI, the rescuer, is a huge scientific topic with real-world ramifications. Despite high-level ethical standards, risk frameworks, and algorithmic assurance breakthroughs, responsible AI remains elusive. AI is disrupting software engineering (SE), which must construct system-level quality and alignment from incomprehensible machine learning models and natural language prompt code. Responsible AI system engineering faces new difficulties and possibilities with the upending. The study (Zhu, L., 2023) will discuss how we invented new SE methodologies to assist the industry develop responsible AI systems. It will address industrial and academic issues such risk silos, principle-algorithm gaps, lack of requirements, evolving properties, and inscrutable systems to demonstrate that SE is the foundation of responsible AI. SE must also rethink from designing functionalities inside AI systems to detecting and controlling new functions. Only by doing so can SE play crucial new roles, from researching human intellect to fostering human-AI collaboration.

AI is currently a national strategic priority. This is seen with the development of national AI policies after Canada released the first in 2017. National AI plans are increasing, particularly in the Global South. AI is a significant driver of economic growth, and governments' plans define how to use AI to accomplish development objectives. However, AI technologies have unexpected repercussions, and national programs frequently include governance systems to mitigate them. As many nations' national development objectives connect with the UN SDGs, study (Wakunuma, K., 2022) examines the link between responsible AI governance, UN SDG achievement, and African countries. The report reveals a relationship between AI development and SDG achievement. Based on an examination of the OECD AI Policy Observatory and Oxford AI Readiness Index, this report indicates that African nations have fallen behind the Global South in AI governance systems. This has major consequences for SGD achievement, and the research makes suggestions. High-level AI ethics concepts and guidelines seldom give specific assistance on developing ethical AI systems. To overcome this gap, we interview 21 scientists and engineers on AI ethical principles and their implementation. Ethical risk assessment at a development step is often done-once-and-forget, which is insufficient for highly uncertain and continual learning AI systems. Ethical requirements are either omitted or mostly stated as high-level objectives. Ethical requirements have cross-cutting quality. Also, a preliminary set of patterns (Lu, Q., 2022) are presented to operationalize responsible AI system development to address these results.

The Center for Standards and Ethics in Artificial Intelligence (CSEAI) researches, educates, and advocates for safe, effective, and ethical AI standards in business and government. Study (Rivas, P., 2022) covers CSEAI's workforce development strategy, which includes mentoring undergraduate and graduate students and ongoing industry education. The CSEAI promotes diversity and the provision of safe, ethical, and standardized AI products. Also, the goal of CSEAI is demonstrated to safeguard consumers and build confidence in responsible AI goods and services by emphasizing socially responsible innovation and ethical AI standards. AI, especially large-scale generative AI (GenAI) models like Large Language Models (LLMs), has transformed modern technology. These approaches have opened up new opportunities, but they also raise data privacy and content creation problems. Current Responsible AI (RAI) frameworks often lack the granular guidance needed for tangible application, especially for Accountability—a principle essential for transparent and auditable decision-making, public trust, and meeting rising regulatory expectations. This work addresses the Accountability gap by offering a systematic multivocal literature review (MLR) that merges academic and grey literature to provide a complete metrics library. Our catalogue covers process metrics that ensure procedural integrity, resource metrics that give tools and frameworks, and product metrics that measure AI system outputs. The tripartite approach (Xia, B., 2024) operationalizes AI Accountability, focusing on GenAI-specific issues.

Responsible AI (RAI) concepts grow more important as AI enters sectors and the public. Research (Scepanovic, S., 2023) examines 27 Earth Observation (EO) specialists from 11 nations' different views on RAI principles across genders and ages. It shows how justice, dependability, privacy, openness, accountability, and sustainability are defined and interpreted. The report also highlights EO-specific RAI difficulties, underlining the necessity to incorporate domain knowledge and express inequity and failure use cases. These data provide a rudimentary knowledge of RAI attitudes in AI for EO. To expand on these conclusions, future study should include more specialists and examine EO user and public opinions. Transformational AI covers the newest AI developments, problems, applications, and possibilities. The book discusses emerging AI technologies including machine learning, natural language processing, computer vision, and robots and how they are changing healthcare, finance, education, and entertainment. AI adoption raises ethical, prejudice, and employment and society issues, which the book discusses. It offers solutions to these issues and how to create ethical, transparent, and trustworthy AI systems. The book examines forthcoming AI themes and applications that will influence the next decade of AI progress. It also shows organizations and people how to use AI to generate new goods, services, and opportunities. The book (Banafa, A., 2024) is vital for everyone who wants to remain ahead in the fast-expanding area of Artificial Intelligence and comprehend how it will change our lives in the next years. AI is increasingly becoming crucial in many areas, boosting social expectations. Mental health, disinformation, employment displacement, and economic, regulatory, and law enforcement issues are AI's social effects. AI legislation is coming, with the EU and China already taking huge moves and the US drafting its first AI-related bill of rights last year. Professional groups and other NGOs are contributing to AI ethics and laws, making them more urgent and important. To minimize biased or erroneous decision-making, public services and regulated organizations must assure responsible AI. Companies utilizing AI ethically may stand out, boost productivity, and avoid legal issues. This article discusses why many firms struggle to implement responsible AI, including identifying possible difficulties, setting up protections, and conducting ethical impact assessments. A complete approach to responsible AI should involve developing a strategic road map, reviewing models, processes, and products, and training personnel at various levels. The urgency of adopting responsible AI and the significance of firms properly considering it as they race to use this technology for competitive advantage is demonstrated (Baeza-Yates, R., 2024). AI will increasingly govern city choices as smart cities emerge. AI will help with jail sentence, city pension appropriation, monitoring, and infrastructure management. The author (Falco, G., 2019) suggests that smart cities should choose AI implementation as they do large infrastructure projects. The social and ethical issues of deployment apply to both. A smart city AI protocol is developed to make AI an ethical and trustworthy civic asset rather than a controversial and biased enemy. Participatory AI combines a completely transparent data infrastructure like the blockchain with participatory urban planning. Participatory AI helps cities achieve socially acceptable AI results by fostering diversity of opinion. Various applications of generative AI are demonstrated in the works described and cited in the references section.

3. PRIVACY AND SECURITY IN GENERATIVE AI

The global Generative AI market was valued at $10.5 billion in 2022. However, the privacy of user data is a worry given the rapid advancement of AI. The most recent data from Salesforce's continuing Generative AI Snapshot Research Series, which polls more than 4,000 full-time employees, shows that 73% of workers believe that Generative AI poses new security threats even though the majority already use it or want to use it. To guard against potential cybersecurity risks, 54% of IT leaders emphasize the need for better security measures. Data privacy can be at risk from Generative AI techniques in several ways:

- Data Breach: After sensitive Samsung data was mistakenly released to ChatGPT, Samsung has limited the use of the Generative AI service.
- Biases and Discrimination: Generative AI has the potential to reinforce biases seen in training data, leading to inaccurate results.
- Lack of Consent and Transparency: Inadequate disclosure of data usage and collection undermines user trust and consent.
- Deepfake videos, surged by 330% between Oct 2019 and June 2020, surpassing 50,000 instances, reports Deep trace startup. This higher incidence of deepfakes underscores the potential misuse of Generative AI, posing a significant threat to the spread of misinformation and jeopardizing the integrity and privacy of individuals.

To mitigate risks, organizations are acting proactively. Apple barred AI tool usage among certain employees, aiming to prevent sensitive data leaks. Companies are adopting Responsible AI and AI TRiSM (Trust, Risk and Security Management) practices mainly focusing on the safety, security, and trust of its user's data. Google, Meta, and OpenAI are some companies that commit to responsible AI development as in Fig. 2. The General Data Protection Regulation (GDPR), effective from May 2018, and the California Consumer Privacy Act (CCPA), enacted in January 2020, hold significant sway over Generative AI due to its privacy and security concerns, despite predating its widespread adoption.

However, this applies as the regulatory frameworks like the EU AI Act and India's DPDP Bill are developing globally. At the same time, prompt engineering and AI output interpretation skills are becoming of increasing importance. Trust, transparency, understanding — these are three elements that when combined play a key role in public acceptance of AI, as shown by recent surveys by Pew and Edelman which tell us that responsibility in communication and design of inclusive AI is needed.

In the realm of Generative AI, addressing security and governance isn't just about overcoming challenges – it's a chance to lead with integrity. As technology evolves, our responsibility grows. We must ensure AI benefits everyone, shaping a secure, ethical, and trusted future through conscientious actions. Generative AI's transformative impact on organizations involves scalability and skill reassessment, providing seamless access to organizational knowledge and fostering interactive collaboration.

Figure 2. Privacy risks in generative AI (Credits: SIDTM students)

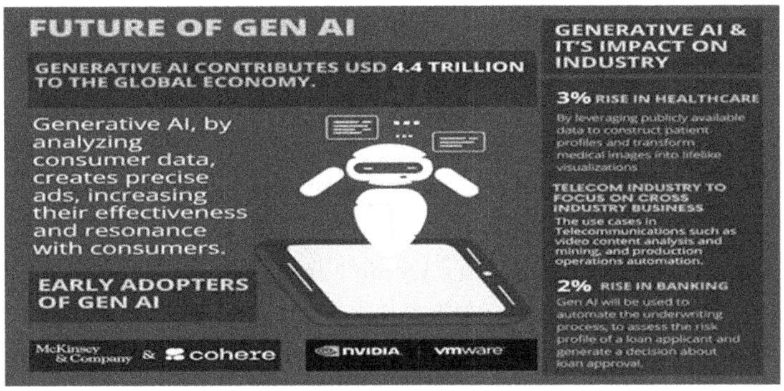

Hyper-personalization in marketing demands tailored ads and targeted segmentation, yet striking the right balance between personalization and privacy remains an industry challenge. Leveraging generative AI for dynamic customer segmentation enables businesses to adapt to emerging market patterns, gaining a competitive edge. In consumer electronics, addressing diagnostic challenges through data and generative AI guides personalized user journeys, departing from generic approaches. UNESCO recognizes generative AI's role in overcoming educational disparities, translating and explaining content for underprivileged students in diverse languages.

4. TYPES OF GENERATIVE AI MODELS AND THEIR APPLICATIONS

Over the years, the evolution of GenAI models has skyrocketed. These can generate output that closely resembles the input by training itself on the structures and patterns of the training dataset. Each of them has different approaches, results, and applications. In machine learning, generative modelling seeks to train algorithms to create novel data in various forms like text and images. The rapid evolution of GenAI models harnesses deep learning techniques to approximate and generate novel data in diverse forms, such as text and images, by training algorithms to mimic underlying distributions, leading to varied approaches, results, and applications in machine learning This is achieved by approximating the data's underlying distribution and then generating samples from that estimated distribution. The emergence of deep learning has paved the way for generative modelling, with various techniques designed according to and their applications. VAEs (Variational Autoencoders) are frequently utilized for generating data and have an additional application in the reduction of data dimensionality. Along with having applications in many biosignal research, like electrocardiogram (ECG) signals, electroencephalography (EEG) signals, and electromyography (EMG). VAEs play a valuable role in enhancing classifier performance in biosignal applications by aiding in de-noising and facilitating data augmentation for biosignal research. These models are easier to train and to identify frauds. VAEs face constraints when applied to tasks such as image denoising and generation, while GANs (Generative Adversarial Networks) have proven to excel in more challenging tasks like super-resolution and image-to-image translation. Some applications of GANs are as follows:

- Meta's Facebook AI introduced Instance-Conditioned Generative Adversarial Networks (IC-GAN), diversifying image generation and reducing AI training expenses
- Amazon presented "Hands Off" at the Computer Vision and Pattern Recognition Conference (CVPR), automating synthetic image data annotation using labelled images and GANs

However, due to the need for synchronization between these two training GAN becomes more difficult than VAE. They also collapse, causing the generator to generate a narrow range of data, causing limited diversity in outputs. They suffer from instability, and non-convergence, hindering data diversity and causing performance and convergence problems. Unlike GANs, Auto-regressive (AR) models explicitly learn the probability distribution of a given set of data, offering a clearer insight into the underlying distribution compared to Generative Adversarial Networks (GANs).AR models use past values to forecast future values. The order of an AR process, denoted as AR (p), signifies the quantity of previous values incorporated into the linear combination. These models can have applications in:

- Generative Pre-trained Transformer (GPT) in Natural Language Processing (NLP) excel at generating text by predicting each word while considering previously generated words.
- Image Synthesis models like PixelRNN and PixelCNN predict pixels sequentially and build up images progressively.
- Time Series Forecasting, where they predict future values based on past observations in various domains, like financial predictions and weather forecasting.

For accurate predictions, the autocorrelation coefficient should exceed 0.5. If it falls below, predictions may become unreliable. Flow-based generative models overcome the challenges by enhancing a simple density through a series of invertible transformations and training with the help of maximum likelihood. The advantages of flow-based models are:

- Modifying existing data is possible in flow-based generative models also known as reversible models, but not in autoregressive models as they have unknown marginal distributions, and need complete support over the data distribution.
- With constant computing memory requirement, instead of linear, the models come with accurate inference and optimization of the exact log-likelihood of the data, unlike VAEs and GANs.

Though normalizing flows generate realistic, high-resolution images, they have a sizeable computational expense and significant data requirements for training. Here, the processes are deterministic and inverse of each other thus collapsing into a single process. Whereas there are diffusion models which have fixed forward and trainable backward processes. The diffusion model, adds

Gaussian noise to the original data using fixed Markov Chain and learns how to reverse the process. Inspired by non-equilibrium thermodynamics, they are beneficial in providing high-quality images without adversarial training. They are scalable and flexible. As long as the architecture of the input and output are of the same dimensionality it can generate images from inputs like text, masked or lower-resolution images, etc. However, the time taken by the diffusion model concerning GAN, VAE, and others is significantly higher, as it executes its function step-by-step. NVIDIA introduced a Latent Score-based Generative Model (LSGM) to address this issue. It uses a mechanism that creates a mapping from input data to latent space, eschewing a direct representation in the data space as in Fig. 3.

Considering the existing technical limitations of the current models, future improvements on VAEs should prioritize enhancing the image resolution by integrating GAN and VAE models. GAN can generate high-quality videos and multiple outputs, to a different mode in the input data distribution. Upgrading the auto-regressive model in future to ensure the autocorrelation coefficient is more than 0.5, would result in enhanced accuracy. Flow-based models can use a technique that assigns probabilities, helping them to dynamically sort out the most pertinent flow according to the input sample. The diffusion model has potential application in designing materials and revolutionizing content creation with virtual influencers. Generative AI revolutionizes customer interactions, empowering chatbots for external engagements and facilitating swift deployment within organizations, optimizing internal processes like HR and finance support. Overcoming biases in AI demands advanced data quality, a robust feedback loop, and thorough auditing. Predictive analytics, while valuable, encounters limitations that generative AI addresses by introducing a human element, offering nuanced insights beyond formulaic predictions. The technology enhances customer satisfaction but requires strategic business integration to unlock its full potential. Regulation, though limited globally, focuses on disclosure, anticipating future regulations to prioritize transparency. Combating misinformation necessitates advanced technologies, effective checks, regulatory frameworks, training programs, and blockchain integration for accountability and transparency. AI success centers on the dual pillars of data quality and quantity, with domain specificity being crucial. Simplification is key in user interaction, employing predefined prompts and training materials to overcome challenges. Embracing AI is imperative across industries, with integration tools like Copilot and business intelligence solutions setting new standards. Ethical considerations in GAN image generation demand attention, especially regarding copyright and privacy issues. In financial guidance tools, data quality and regulatory precision are paramount to avoid potential losses. Achieving a balance between manual work and Generative AI, allocating 90% to AI and 10% to human input, ensures optimal outcomes.

5. EVOLUTION OF NATURAL LANGUAGE PROCESSING AND LANGUAGE MODELS

As per International Data Corporation, organizations can additionally gain 430 billion US$ by utilizing insights from structured and unstructured data. Hence, the need to use Natural Language Processing (NLP), which combines human linguistics, deep learning, and machine learning algorithms, for training machines to comprehend human language is of paramount importance. The Rule-based model, introduced in the 1950s, is the oldest. These use a predefined set of linguistic rules, using which textual data is processed and analyzed. They can be leveraged by making the rule to get outputs as intended by the developer.

Figure 3. Common generative architectures (Source: Kevin Murphy's book (2023))

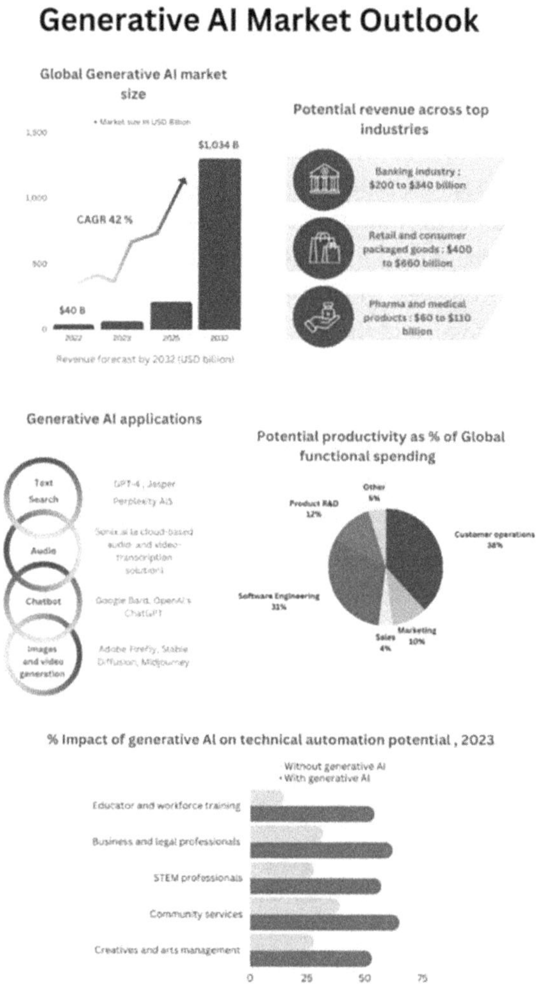

However, they are time-consuming, non-dynamic, and cannot handle ambiguous words. This primary focus on language changed with the advancement in computational power, as Statistical models of NLP, based on Markov's assumption, came in during the 1980s. They were probabilistic models that successfully predicted the next word in each sequence, concerning the word preceding it. This has its application in autocompletes, recognizing texts and speech, error detection, etc. Large Language Models (LLM) are now implemented in natural language-concerned jobs. They are primarily based on deep learning and use self-supervised learning techniques. Bidirectional Encoder Representations from Transformers (BERT) models learn the meaning of an ambiguous word concerning its entire surroundings. The latest addition to these models is the Generative Pre-trained Transformer (GPT), introduced in 2018. Built on a transformer architecture it can generate content and answer queries conversationally as it uses a neural language prediction model. GPT is the breakthrough technology that can give scale and pace to tasks across industries by automating them. Since the launch of ChatGPT majority of Fortune 500 companies have adopted it. NLP could be trained to not only understand humans but also predict their behavior. Its application can be seen in recognition of speech, Sentiment analysis, Intelligent Virtual Assistants, Multilingual NLPs, etc. To achieve this, issues regarding the ethical usage of NLP which is free from any bias and where data privacy is maintained need to be looked into. Ensuring this would make the interaction between machines and humans more convenient. Microsoft's Syntex in SharePoint Premium exemplifies generative AI's practicality by automating template creation from diverse documents, streamlining new document generation, and introducing traceability features. Dispelling data requirements misconception, foundational generative AI models use diverse global datasets and employ techniques like privacy checkers. Effective stakeholder management in smart city implementation demands collaboration, a shared goal led by the government, and communication among diverse institutes. Generative AI's value lies in overcoming data collection challenges by generating synthetic data for machine learning, preserving the original data distribution, and emphasizing responsible practices for privacy and accurate representation of the population.

6. RESPONSIBLE AI: REDESIGNING GENAI

Responsible AI (RAI) aims to, ethically and legally, develop and deploy AI, ensuring safety, trustworthiness, and transparency while minimizing issues like AI bias. Despite AI's impressive capabilities, it remains relatively unregulated, making it susceptible to various forms of misuse. These models can produce hallucinations or unrealistic results when trained on noisy or error-prone data, as they learn to generate data from the patterns present in their training data. This can cause copyright and stolen data issues, inaccuracies and cybersecurity jailbreaks. Leaders' hesitation toward Generative AI, like Chat GPT, stems from its unestablished value against traditional AI.

Implementing safeguards for unbiased content is a challenge, urging pragmatic leadership. Adobe, NVIDIA, and Meta exemplify GenAI's diverse applications, urging a bottom-up innovation approach. Ethical concerns, including deepfakes, underscore the need for robust regulations. The 4C framework—Conviction, Collaboration, Coordination, and Commitment—guides responsible GenAI navigation. GenAI excels in information retrieval but risks hallucination. Varied industry applications, notably in healthcare, face hurdles due to regulations. Publicly sourced data for content creation presents legal and ethical challenges, requiring careful consideration of copyright boundaries.

To overcome these issues and to create trust in AI, RAI needs to be put into practice. The advent of 5G signifies a profound transformation in telecommunications, extending beyond speed enhancements to revolutionize networks for both public and private applications. Private 5G networks, specifically in industrial applications, take precedence. Simultaneously, artificial intelligence (AI) integration undergoes a shift from generic approaches to in-depth analysis of consumer and network-generated data, playing a pivotal role in innovating, enhancing efficiency, and optimizing performance in both sectors.

In smart city contexts, the foundational elements of machines and sensors, transmitting data via 5G, drive innovation through data analytics and optimize networks, underscoring AI's pivotal role. The chatbot serves dual purposes, externally addressing consumer needs and internally optimizing efficiency, handling data across various components for the telecommunications company. For this, Accenture has defined four pillars of successful RAI implementations as in Fig. 4 and 5:

1. Organizational Pillar, which promotes collaboration between humans and AI.

2. Operational Pillar which Implements governance for AI's success.
3. Technical Pillar, which ensures trustworthy and transparent AI systems.
4. Reputational Pillar, which aligns AI efforts with ethical values and company mission.

Enterprises are placing a significant emphasis on artificial intelligence (AI) development, driven by their pursuit of data-driven insights, exponential growth, and competitive differentiation. To integrate the generative AI across all spheres, there should be a clear balance between the performance metrics, i.e., the speed, accuracy, scalability, and ethical priorities, i.e., fairness, transparency, and accountability. Depending on the sector, these tradeoffs are different such as healthcare values clinical validation, finance is compliant with regulatory issues, and creative industries placed more importance to originality. These tensions demand for strategic design and coordination of interdisciplinary groups.

Global AI spending is projected to reach US$ 110 billion by 2024. However, 80% of AI-focused executives face challenges in establishing responsible AI processes. While industry giants like Accenture, BCG, Google AI, and Microsoft have mastered the implementation of responsible AI practices, other companies are not approaching the development and adoption of AI technologies with the same level of urgency and commitment.

Figure 4. Evolution of NLP (Credits: SIDTM Students)

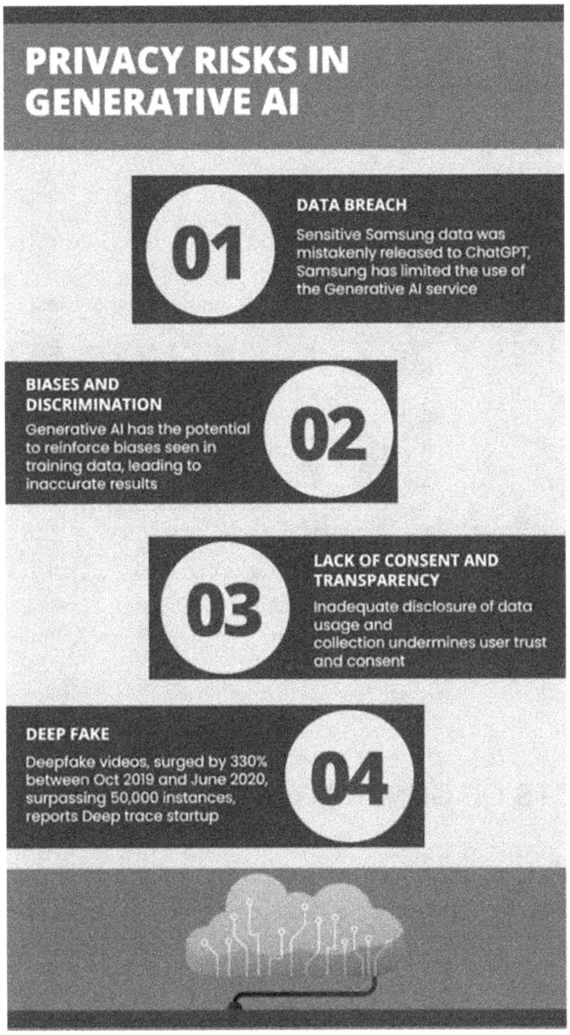

Figure 5. Four Pillars of Responsible AI (Credits: SIDTM Students)

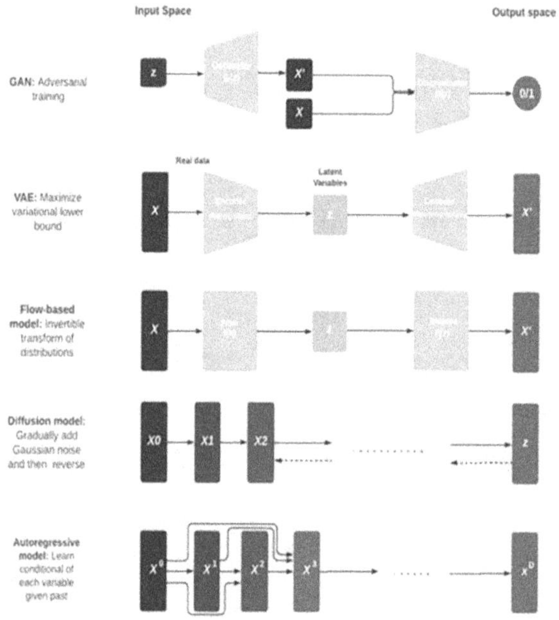

7. FUTURE PROSPECTS OF GENERATIVE AI

Each year, Generative AI (Gen AI) capabilities contribute about US$ 4.4 trillion to the global economy. Generative AI, by analyzing consumer data, creates precise ads, increasing their effectiveness and resonance with consumers. The digital landscape is poised for transformation with immersive 3D Virtual/Augmented Reality (VR/AR) experiences. Generative AI will expedite their creation, reducing time and resources. Meta's interest in this technology hints at its role in future 3D worlds. Furthermore, generative AI will enhance avatar realism, enabling dynamic interactions in these virtual realms. Generative AI will reshape business roles, shifting content creators to content editors. The workforce will adapt to conversational, proactive applications, changing the user experience. AI will suggest unasked-for ideas, potentially boosting productivity but challenging human leadership in strategy development. Gartner projects that by 2025, generative AI will create 30% of major organizations' outbound marketing content, while Sequoia Capital foresees trillions in economic value from Generative AI. Recent years have witnessed a surge in generative AI technology providers, particularly in healthcare, where they leverage publicly available data to construct patient profiles and transform medical images into lifelike visualizations. Most use cases of generative AI have been in the creation of new drug molecules, but there is also the potential for the technology in target identification and drug repurposing. Predictive technology, exemplified by NVIDIA's DLSS (Deep Learning Super Sampling), is employed in video generation to create new frames. Notably, Apple's acquisition of AI Music exemplifies the creation of realistic voice and music in audio. Microsoft subsidiary GitHub's Copilot AI can write up to 40% of the code for programmers and is heading up to 80% within five years. IBM ventures into drug development via generative AI models, while Amazon offers Polly for text-to-speech conversion and DeepComposer, which transforms short melodies into complete compositions using its online services. Such use cases, when assisted with technologies like blockchain, metaverse, analytics, and IoT, can have immense applications. Generative AI, when applied to constructing metaverse buildings, can greatly assist architects in swiftly crafting intricate architectural designs, including murals, carvings, tapestries, and various decorative elements. The integration of generative AI within metaverse building construction significantly amplifies the effectiveness of the design process. Apart from blockchain technology, generative AI can be used to precisely track payment velocities, prepayments, and overall profitability. Generative AI will play a pivotal role in identifying potential financial difficulties borrowers face and propose solutions, like offering the borrower a one-month payment break. The integration of blockchain with Generative AI offers substantial advantages in data validation, loan management, borrower assessment, and enabling the implementation of proactive strategies for risk mitigation. Generative AI models, when trained on industry data along with CRM (customer relationship management) data sets, can help cut down the processing time. Additionally, generative AI can drive insights by leveraging persona-based contextual data and mimicking human inferencing processes as in Fig. 6. With the advancement in IoT, generative AI can help perform certain tasks like,

- In visual-based IoT applications, generative adversarial networks (GANs) can generate realistic images by distinguishing between genuine and fabricated images.
- With the help of machine learning models, Generative AI can produce fragments of codes to achieve a desired function in IoT devices.
- Security threats in IoT systems can be prevented by implementing generative AI models that continuously monitor devices, recognize patterns, and resolve potential security risks.

Figure 6. Future of Generative AI (Credits: SIDTM Students)

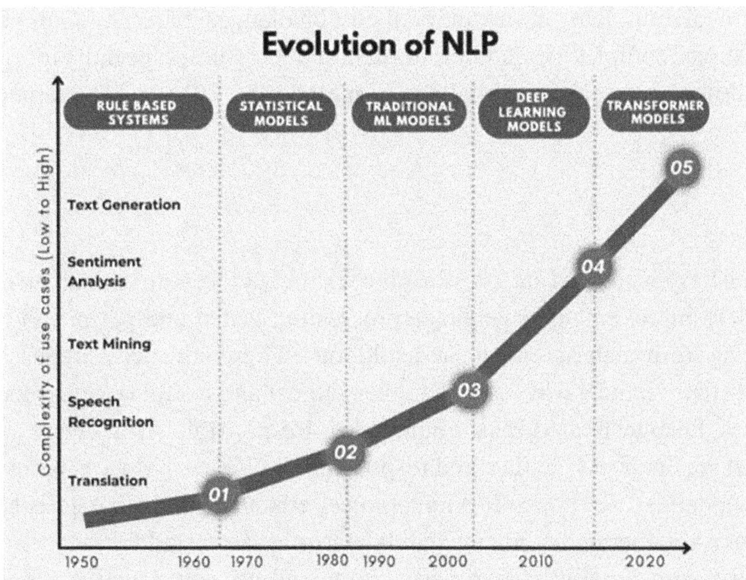

Generative AI, especially in chatbots, elevates customer interactions by discerning intent and sarcasm. In India, Bhashini aids linguistic diversity by translating real-time educational content. Samsung prioritizes privacy, ensuring AI operates solely on user devices for feedback. Model compression, like distillation, addresses challenges in training smaller IoT models. GenAI in home appliances, like smart refrigerators, fosters connectivity. Satellite imagery leverages generative AI for real-time data in diverse Indian landscapes. Rolls Royce employs generative AI for automotive simulations but faces challenges with hallucination and domain-specific data. If we look at the intersection of transformation and creativity, GenAI has been a major stimulus for change across industries, with an estimated share of 30% of the whole AI market by 2025. In financial services, its application can go beyond one-time analysis of small datasets, to generate business-wide digital transformation using new models and by utilizing synthetic data for accurate testing and fraud detection. Data-heavy industries, like telecom industry can leverage it to shift from product-centric to more customer-centric with personalized user experience, real and contextual communication using chatbots, etc. When it comes to health care, GenAI can be used to improve the agility and quality of services provided. Generative Adversarial Networks (GANs) can help radiologists identify even minor anomalies by providing high-quality Magnetic Resonance Imaging (MRI) reports, etc. GenAI can also aid in the process of prototyping and designing. They can be used to generate scenarios and cases, which in turn will be effective in quality assurance. GenAI can also have a significant impact if implemented by governments, use cases involve GenAI for US Federal Agencies. Industries that are more knowledge-centric are likely to be most disrupted by GenAI, while manufacturing-centric are less likely to face disruptions· The value addition concerning the global revenue of the industries could be predicted at 9% when it comes to tech companies, 5% for companies in the banking as well as pharmaceutical industry, and finally about 4% when it comes to education. GenAI proves effective in generic tasks but falters in industry-specific customization without human intervention. Regulatory anticipation for GenAI, while not yet maliciously used, mirrors data protection laws. In the service sector, especially contact centers and tourism, GenAI adoption accelerates for cost reduction. However, skepticism in the tech sector, particularly telecommunications, surrounds GenAI's practicality. Integration complexities and doubts about nuanced problem-solving persist. GenAI adoption in cloud computing evolution, faces computational cost challenges. Effective GenAI adoption requires understanding operational complexities, addressing data quality issues, especially in legacy organizations. In IoT, GenAI handles security but faces challenges in hindering full-scale implementation.

CONCLUSION

Generative AI and Responsible AI are transforming several sectors with their creativity and innovation. Generative AI models improve natural language processing, visual and performing arts, gaming, and healthcare by creating fresh material, ideas, and solutions. These advances suggest that AI may boost creativity and productivity in new ways. To guarantee ethical and useful development and deployment of these technologies, Responsible AI must be included. Responsible AI addresses prejudice, privacy, and AI's social effect via openness, justice, and responsibility. We can reduce risks and develop AI trust by following these guidelines. Responsible AI guarantees ethical and creative generative model outputs in many applications. AI-generated medicine candidates must be tested for safety and effectiveness in healthcare. AI must respect intellectual property rights and prevent negative stereotypes in creative enterprises. Finally, Generative AI and Responsible AI must work together to promote innovation and ethics. This balanced strategy will allow ethical AI technology progress, benefitting society.

REFERENCES

Anand, A., ... (2023). Mitigating cyber-security risks using cyber-analytics. In 2023 7th International Conference on Trends in Electronics and Informatics (ICOEI) (pp. 630–635). IEEE. DOI: 10.1109/ICOEI56765.2023.10126001

Ashok, P.. (2023). *Semiconductor Sankalp: A vision for India's tech dominance. In 2023 Intelligent Computing and Control for Engineering and Business Systems (ICCEBS).* IEEE., DOI: 10.1109/ICCEBS58601.2023.10448857

Baeza-Yates, R., & Fayyad, U. M. (2024). Responsible AI: An urgent mandate. *IEEE Intelligent Systems, 39*(1), 12–17. DOI: 10.1109/MIS.2023.3343488

Banafa, A. (2024). Transformative AI: Responsible, transparent, and trustworthy AI systems. In Transformative AI: Responsible, Transparent, and Trustworthy AI Systems (pp. i–xiv). River Publishers.

Chen, C. H. (2024). Training strategy based on game theory for generative AI. In *2024 International Conference on Smart Systems for Applications in Electrical Sciences (ICSSES)* (pp. 1–6). IEEE. DOI: 10.1109/ICSSES62373.2024.10561423

Dhyani, P., Nautiyal, S., Negi, A., Dhyani, S., & Chaudhary, P. (2024). Automated API docs generator using generative AI. In 2024 IEEE International Students' Conference on Electrical, Electronics and Computer Science (SCEECS) (pp. 1–6). IEEE. DOI: 10.1109/SCEECS61402.2024.10482119

Falco, G. (2019). Participatory AI: Reducing AI bias and developing socially responsible AI in smart cities. In 2019 IEEE International Conference on Computational Science and Engineering (CSE) and IEEE International Conference on Embedded and Ubiquitous Computing (EUC) (pp. 154–158). IEEE. DOI: 10.1109/CSE/EUC.2019.00038

Hallur, G.. (2023). *Demystifying domain-specific key drivers in telecom technologies. In 2023 Intelligent Computing and Control for Engineering and Business Systems (ICCEBS).* IEEE., DOI: 10.1109/ICCEBS58601.2023.10449118

Hallur, G.. (2024). Navigating the infotainment landscape: Status and regulations in the digital age. In *2024 International Conference on Advances in Data Engineering and Intelligent Computing Systems (ADICS)* (pp. 1–6). IEEE. DOI: 10.1109/ADICS58448.2024.10533560

Hazarika, T.. (2024). Bundling brilliance: Maximizing telecom operator profits through handset leasing. In *2024 International Conference on Intelligent and Innovative Technologies in Computing, Electrical and Electronics (IITCEE)* (pp. 1–5). IEEE. DOI: 10.1109/IITCEE59897.2024.10467900

Hwang, J., & Oh, S. (2023). A brief survey of watermarks in generative AI. In 2023 14th International Conference on Information and Communication Technology Convergence (ICTC) (pp. 1157–1160). IEEE. DOI: 10.1109/ICTC58733.2023.10392465

Lu, Q., Zhu, L., Xu, X., Whittle, J., Douglas, D., & Sanderson, C. (2022). Software engineering for responsible AI: An empirical study and operationalised patterns. In 2022 IEEE/ACM 44th International Conference on Software Engineering: Software Engineering in Practice (ICSE-SEIP) (pp. 241–242). ACM. DOI: 10.1145/3510457.3513063

Maiti, P., ... (2024). Decentralized defenses: A framework for 5G IoT security in Industry 4.0 using blockchain crowdsourcing. In 2024 3rd International Conference on Sentiment Analysis and Deep Learning (ICSADL) (pp. 534–538). IEEE. DOI: 10.1109/ICSADL61749.2024.00093

Nandanwar, R., ... (2024). Stitching data threads: Impact of artificial intelligence on fashion evolution. In 2024 4th International Conference on Innovative Practices in Technology and Management (ICIPTM) (pp. 1–6). IEEE. DOI: 10.1109/ICIPTM59628.2024.10563840

OECD. (2024). Assessing potential future artificial intelligence risks, benefits and policy imperatives (OECD Artificial Intelligence Papers No. 272). OECD Publishing. https://www.oecd.org/content/dam/oecd/en/publications/reports/2024/11/assessing-potential-future-artificial-intelligence-risks-benefits-and-policy-imperatives_8a491447/3f4e3dfb-en.pdf

Patil, A., ... (2024). Cyber resilience: Safeguarding India's markets in the post-pandemic cyber landscape. In 2024 4th International Conference on Innovative Practices in Technology and Management (ICIPTM) (pp. 1–5). IEEE. DOI: 10.1109/ICIPTM59628.2024.10563229

Patil, B., ... (2024). Artificial intelligence powered paradigm shift: Revolutionizing digital marketing. In 2024 4th International Conference on Innovative Practices in Technology and Management (ICIPTM) (pp. 1–6). IEEE. DOI: 10.1109/ICIPTM59628.2024.10563450

Prabhu, S.. (2024). Elevating business experiences: AI-powered chatbots reforming marketing and e-commerce. In Singh, D. (Eds.), *Transforming the Financial Landscape with ICTs* (pp. 1–27). IGI Global., DOI: 10.4018/979-8-3693-1503-3.ch001

Rani, G., Singh, J., & Khanna, A. (2023). Comparative analysis of generative AI models. In *2023 International Conference on Advances in Computation, Communication and Information Technology (ICAICCIT)* (pp. 760–765). IEEE. DOI: 10.1109/ICAICCIT60255.2023.10465941

Rastogi, A.. (2023). Reimagining telecom industry using blockchain technology. In *2023 International Conference on Sustainable Computing and Data Communication Systems (ICSCDS)* (pp. 1261–1265). IEEE. DOI: 10.1109/ICSCDS56580.2023.10104989

Ravindranathan, P.. (2024). Illuminating the dark: Gaining insights and managing risks with dark analytics. In *2024 International Conference on Intelligent and Innovative Technologies in Computing, Electrical and Electronics (IITCEE)* (pp. 1–6). IEEE. DOI: 10.1109/IITCEE59897.2024.10467380

Rivas, P., Ortiz, J., Díaz-Pachón, D. A., & Montoya, L. N. (2023). Bridging industry, government, and academia for socially responsible AI: The CSEAI initiative. In *2023 IEEE International Symposium on Ethics in Engineering, Science, and Technology (ETHICS)* (pp. 1–1). IEEE. DOI: 10.1109/ETHICS57328.2023.10155071

Saxena, Y.. (2024). Cloud renaissance: Thriving in the post-pandemic digital landscape. In *2024 Fourth International Conference on Advances in Electrical, Computing, Communication and Sustainable Technologies (ICAECT)* (pp. 1–6). IEEE. DOI: 10.1109/ICAECT60202.2024.10469149

Šćepanović, S., Bogucka, E. P., Quercia, D., & Nattero, C. (2023). Responsible AI for earth observation: Attitudes among experts. In IGARSS 2023 - 2023 IEEE International Geoscience and Remote Sensing Symposium (pp. 1934–1936). IEEE. DOI: 10.1109/IGARSS52108.2023.10282983

Tanaka, H., Ide, M., Yajima, J., Onodera, S., Munakata, K., & Yoshioka, N. (2024). Taxonomy of generative AI applications for risk assessment. In 2024 IEEE/ACM 3rd International Conference on AI Engineering – Software Engineering for AI (CAIN) (pp. 288–289). IEEE. DOI: 10.1145/3644815.3644977

Tiwari, H., Raj, A., Singh, U. K., & Fatima, H. (2024). Generative AI for NFTs using GANs. In 2024 11th International Conference on Computing for Sustainable Global Development (INDIACom) (pp. 488–492). IEEE. DOI: 10.23919/INDIACom61295.2024.10498251

UNESCO. (2021). Recommendation on the ethics of artificial intelligence. United Nations Educational, Scientific and Cultural Organization. https://www.unesco.org/en/artificial-intelligence/recommendation-ethics

Waghambare, M. A.. (2024). Artificial intelligence (AI)-powered chatbots for marketing and online shopping. In Prakasha, G. S. (Eds.), *Digital Technologies in Modeling and Management: Insights in Education and Industry* (pp. 21–39). IGI Global., DOI: 10.4018/978-1-6684-9576-6.ch002

Wakunuma, K., Ogoh, G., Eke, D. O., & Akintoye, S. (2022). *Responsible AI, SDGs, and AI governance in Africa. In 2022 IST-Africa Conference (IST-Africa).* IEEE., DOI: 10.23919/IST-Africa56635.2022.9845598

Xia, B., Lu, Q., Zhu, L., Lee, S. U., Liu, Y., & Xing, Z. (2024). Towards a responsible AI metrics catalogue: A collection of metrics for AI accountability. In 2024 IEEE/ACM 3rd International Conference on AI Engineering – Software Engineering for AI (CAIN) (pp. 100–111). IEEE. DOI: 10.1145/3644815.3644959

Zhu, L. (2023). Software engineering as the linchpin of responsible AI. In 2023 IEEE/ACM 45th International Conference on Software Engineering (ICSE) (pp. 3–4). IEEE. DOI: 10.1109/ICSE48619.2023.00012

Chapter 22
Impact of Generative AI on Industries and Organizations

J. Krishna Charan
https://orcid.org/0000-0002-6788-2322
Vel Tech Rangarajan Dr. Sagunthala R&D Institute of Science and Technology, USA

Sudhanshu Chandra
https://orcid.org/0009-0006-6694-1032
Maulana Azad National Urdu University, India

V. Vaissnave
https://orcid.org/0000-0001-7333-531X
SRM Institute of Science and Technology, India

T. Ragupathi
https://orcid.org/0000-0002-2482-5096
SRM Institute of Science and Technology, India

Pamarthi Satyanarayana
https://orcid.org/0009-0008-4041-3674
Vel Tech University, India

P. Selvakumar
https://orcid.org/0000-0002-3650-4548
Department of Science and Humanities, Nehru Institute of Technology, Coimbatore, India

T. C. Manjunath
https://orcid.org/0000-0003-2545-9160
Rajarajeswari College of Engineering, India

ABSTRACT

At its core, generative AI uses machine learning techniques, generate outputs such as text, images, music, and even complex designs. Techniques commonly employed t high-quality content. Vast learn outputs that mimic or extend the patterns observed in the data. For instance, in the creative industries, generative AI can design logos, compose music, or generate photorealistic images, artistic expression creation. Technology sector, generative AI is accelerating product development and innovation. AI-driven tools can automate the design process, optimize software code, and even assist in creating new hardware prototypes. This automation not only speeds up development cycles but also reduces costs and enhances precision. For example, AI algorithms can variations, enabling broader refine products more effectively. The financial sector benefits from generative AI through improved risk management, fraud detection, generate predictive models, enhancing decision-making processes and risk assessment.

DOI: 10.4018/979-8-3693-8332-2.ch022

INTRODUCTION

At its core, generative AI uses machine learning techniques, generate outputs such as text, images, music, and even complex designs. Techniques commonly employed t high-quality content. Vast learn outputs that mimic or extend the patterns observed in the data. For instance, in the creative industries, generative AI can design logos, compose music, or generate photorealistic images, artistic expression creation. Technology sector, generative AI is accelerating product development and innovation. AI-driven tools can automate the design process, optimize software code, and even assist in creating new hardware prototypes. This automation not only speeds up development cycles but also reduces costs and enhances precision. For example, AI algorithms can variations, enabling broader refine products more effectively. The financial sector benefits from generative AI through improved risk management, fraud detection, generate predictive models, enhancing decision-making processes and risk assessment., AI-driven routine, automate transactions, financial advice, improving efficiency and customer satisfaction. Despite, several considerations must be addressed to maximize its benefits. Ensuring use addressing issues related to bias, privacy, and transparency, is crucial. AI-generated content must be monitored to prevent misuse and ensure that it aligns with societal values and standards. Additionally, the integration of AI into various industries requires careful management of data security and intellectual property concerns. In conclusion, generative AI represents a significant advancement in artificial intelligence, with the power to transform industries by generating innovative content, optimizing processes, and driving new forms of creativity. Its applications span technology, media, healthcare, finance, and education, offering unprecedented opportunities for growth and innovation. The integration of AI into real estate practices may also impact job roles and responsibilities. While AI can enhance efficiency and accuracy, it may alter traditional roles in valuation, design, and property management. Real estate professionals will need to adapt to these changes by acquiring new skills and embracing AI technologies. Training and development programs can help ensure that professionals are equipped to work effectively with AI tools and leverage their capabilities to drive innovation and success.In conclusion, generative AI is transforming the real estate industry by enhancing property valuation, fostering innovative design, and optimizing property management. navigating these challenges thoughtfully and embracing AI technologies responsibly, real estate professionals can achieve greater precision, efficiency, and innovation in their practices.

TRANSFORMING CREATIVE INDUSTRIES: MUSIC, AND ENTERTAINMENT

revolutionizing the creative industries by introducing novel methods for producing art, music, and entertainment content. machine learning models, generative AI systems can create high-quality, original content that complements and enhances human creativity, offering new opportunities for artists, musicians, and creators across various media.In the realm of art, generative enabling the creation of innovative visual works that push traditional boundaries.(Agostinelli A et al., 2023) Techniques such as Generative . This integration of AI into the art world not only enhances artistic expression but also democratizes access to sophisticated creative tools, allowing a broader range of individuals to explore and produce art.In music, generative AI is transforming composition, production, and performance. AI algorithms can generate original melodies, harmonies, and rhythms by analyzing and learning from extensive music libraries. For example, AI-powered, offering musicians new sources of inspiration and collaboration. These production process by suggesting arrangements, generating backing tracks, and even simulating various instrumental performances. Musicians and composers use AI to explore new musical landscapes, automate repetitive tasks, and enhance their creative workflows, ultimately broadening the scope of musical experimentation and innovation.The entertainment industry is equally influenced by generative AI, which is reshaping how content is created and consumed(O'Leary DE, 2023) . AI-driven tools are used to generate scripts, design characters, and produce visual effects, making the creative process more efficient and diverse. For instance, AI algorithms can analyze popular film and television scripts to generate new storylines or dialogue, offering writers new perspectives and ideas. In visual effects, AI can create realistic CGI elements, simulate environments, and enhance special effects, AI's ability to process and analyze large datasets allows for the exploration of new styles and techniques that might be difficult for humans to conceive independently. Moreover, generative AI provides tools for personalized and adaptive content, tailoring experiences to individual preferences and enhancing user (Asatiani A et al., 2021). AI-generated content must be monitored to prevent misuse and ensure that it aligns with societal values and standards. Additionally, the integration of AI into various industries requires careful management of data security and intellectual property concerns.In conclusion, generative AI represents a significant advancement in artificial intelligence, with the power to transform industries by generating innovative content, optimizing processes, and driving new forms of creativity. Its applications span technology, media, healthcare, finance, and education, offering unprecedented opportunities for growth and innovation. However, the adoption of generative AI in creative fields also raises several challenges and considerations. Curating of training data and ongoing monitoring of AI outputs that they align, originality, bias, and ethics. ultimatcly enriching the creative landscape and contributing to the future of art, music, and entertainment.

GENERATIVE AI IN HEALTHCARE: REVOLUTIONIZING DIAGNOSIS, TREATMENT, AND PATIENT CARE

through advanced data analysis, predictive modeling, and personalized medicine. This technology, which involves using algorithms to generate new data or insights based on existing information, offers significant enhancements in how medical conditions are understood and managed, promising to improve outcomes and efficiency across the healthcare system. diagnosis, speed of identifying conditions(Baird A, Maruping LM, 2021) . Traditional diagnostic processes often rely on clinicians' expertise and their interpretation of diagnostic tests, medical imaging, and patient history. Generative AI models, such as deep learning algorithms and neural networks, This early detection capability enables prompt intervention and improves patient prognoses.. in monitoring through wearable devices remote sensors that metrics(Benlian et al., 2022) . Generative AI algorithms analyze (O'Leary DE, 2023) . For instance, of deterioration in chronic disease patients, such as those with diabetes or heart disease, and alert healthcare providers to intervene proactively. This continuous monitoring and early intervention can significantly enhance patient care and reduce hospitalizations. synthetic data to simulate how new drugs or treatments might perform in clinical trials, accelerating the research and development process. AI can also identify potential drug interactions, optimize drug formulations, and predict AI(Mahadev Madgule, et al.,2023), is crucial. Robust Healthcare professionals need to be trained in using AI systems effectively and understanding their recommendations. Collaboration between AI developers, healthcare providers, policymakers is crucial to ensure that AI tools are integrated seamlessly into clinical practices and contribute positively to patient care. including earlier disease detection, more effective treatments, and streamlined healthcare delivery integration. The integration of AI into real estate practices may also impact job roles and responsibilities. While AI can enhance efficiency and accuracy, it may alter traditional roles in valuation, design, and property management. Real estate professionals will need to adapt to these changes by acquiring new skills and embracing AI technologies. Training and development programs can help ensure that professionals are equipped to work effectively with AI tools and leverage their capabilities to drive innovation and success.In conclusion, generative AI is transforming the real estate industry by enhancing property valuation, fostering innovative design, and optimizing property management. navigating these challenges thoughtfully and embracing AI technologies responsibly, real estate professionals can achieve greater precision, efficiency, and innovation in their practices.

AI-DRIVEN AUTOMATION IN MANUFACTURING: EFFICIENCY AND INNOVATION

At the heart of AI-driven automation advanced robotics perform tasks traditionally carried out by human operators. AI-powered robots, equipped with sophisticated sensors and vision systems, are now capable of handling complex, welding, painting, and quality inspection with unprecedented precision speed. These robots can operate continuously without fatigue, resulting in higher productivity and consistency in manufacturing processes(Birhane A et al., 2021) . For instance, in automotive manufacturing, AI-driven robots are used for intricate assembly tasks, ensuring precise fitting of components and enhancing the overall quality of vehicles.The integration of AI in manufacturing also drives significant improvements in supply chain management and logistics (Paramasivam Selvakumar, et al., 2024). Automated supply chain management tools use AI to forecast demand, manage stock levels, and coordinate shipments, enhancing overall efficiency and reducing the risk of supply chain disruptions. This predictive capability ensures that production schedules align with market demands, minimizing excess inventory and associated costs.In product design and evelopment, generative design algorithms powered by AI are transforming how new products are conceived and brought to market. Generative design tools use AI to explore a wide range designternatives based on specified parameters, such as weight, strength, and material constraints. These systems can analyze high-resolution images of products in real-time, identifying flaws such as surface imperfections, misalignments, or dimensional inconsistencies. This automation ensures that products meet rigorous quality standards and reduces the likelihood of defects reaching consumers. (Raji ID, Buolamwini J, 2019) The adoption of AI in manufacturing fosters innovation by enabling the development of smart factories and advanced manufacturing systems. Smart factories leverage AI, IoT (Internet of Things), and advanced data analytics to create interconnected production environments where machines, systems, and processes communicate and coordinate seamlessly. In these environments, AI systems optimize production schedules, manage resources efficiently This level of integration and automation not only improves operational efficiency but also enables manufacturers to quickly adapt to new market demands and technological advancements. Another consideration is the impact on the workforce (Vijayakumar G, et al., 2024). While AI-driven automation enhances productivity and operational efficiency, there is a growing demand for skilled workers who can manage interpret data, and drive innovation. In conclusion, AI-driven automation is (Caliskan A et al., 2017) transforming manufacturing by enhancing efficiency, fostering innovation, and improving product quality. manufacturers can achieve higher productivity, reduced costs, and optimized processes(Çelikok MM et al., 2019) . While there are challenges related to investment, workforce impact, and data security, the benefits.

GENERATIVE AI IN FINANCE: RISK MANAGEMENT, TRADING, AND INVESTMENT

Generative AI is increasingly becoming a pivotal force in the finance industry, driving advancements in risk management, trading, and investment through its sophisticated capabilities in data analysis, pattern recognition, and predictive modeling. By leveraging AI's ability to generate insights and simulate scenarios, financial institutions are with unprecedented accuracy.(Reddy B, H. L., 2023) In risk management, generative identifying, assessing, and mitigating various types of financial risks. AI algorithms generative models can simulate a wide range of economic scenarios, including market shocks and geopolitical events, to predict their potential impact on financial portfolios. The integration of AI in manufacturing also drives significant improvements in supply chain management and logistics. Automated supply chain management tools use AI to forecast demand, manage stock levels, and coordinate shipments, enhancing overall efficiency and reducing the risk of supply chain disruptions. This predictive capability ensures that production schedules align with market demands, minimizing excess inventory and associated costs.In product design and evelopment, generative design algorithms powered by AI are transforming how new products are conceived and brought to market. Generative design tools use AI to explore a wide range designternatives based on specified parameters, such as weight, strength, and material constraints. These systems can analyze high-resolution images of products in real-time, identifying flaws such as surface imperfections, misalignments, or dimensional inconsistencies. This capability allows risk managers to develop more robust strategies for mitigating adverse outcomes and ensuring financial stability. (Zhang J et al., 2023) Additionally, (Davison RM et al., 2023) AI-driven systems can enhance fraud detection by generating synthetic data to train models on new and evolving fraud tactics, thereby improving the identification of suspicious activities and reducing financial losses.In trading, generative AI enhances algorithmic trading strategies by providing advanced tools for market prediction and execution. AI models analyze historical market data, news sentiment, and macroeconomic indicators to generate predictive insights and trading signals(Sugumaran K. M, D.,et al.,2024). opportunities and optimizing trade execution. By employing generative algorithms to simulate various trading scenarios, financial institutions can develop and refine of trading operations but also increases the potential for generating higher returns on investments.Generative AI also contributes to the development of innovative financial products and services(De-Arteaga M et al., 2022) . For instance, AI-driven models can generate synthetic financial data to test and validate new financial instruments or investment strategies before they are introduced to the market. This approach reduces the risk associated with new product launches and ensures that they are well-aligned with market needs and investor preferences. Furthermore, AI-powered tools can enhance services become more relevant and responsive to individual needs (Sugumaran K. M, D., et al., 2024). infrastructure and governance to ensure the integrity and usability of the data used by AI systems.Another consideration is the ethical and regulatory implications of AI in finance(Debortoli S et al., 2014) . regulatory requirements and ethical standards.

TRANSFORMING EDUCATION WITH GENERATIVE AI: PERSONALIZED LEARNING AND ASSESSMENT

This transformation is driven by AI's capacity educational generate tailored learning experiences, and provide real-time feedback, offering a more customized and effective educational experience.learning preferences, and engagement patterns to create customized learning paths.I-powered platforms can generate adaptive learning materials that adjust and performance. (Diederich S et al., 2020) This ensures that students receive content that is appropriately challenging and aligned with their learning needs, leading to more effective and engaging educational experiences. Generative AI past work and where they may need additional support. Based on this analysis, AI systems can generate practice questions, interactive exercises, and supplemental materials tailored to address specific gaps in knowledge. This personalized approach not only helps students to master difficult concepts more effectively but also keeps them motivated and engaged by providing targeted and relevant learning activities., such as standardized tests and quizzes, often offer a limited view of a student's abilities and learning progress. Generative AI, on the other hand, can create diverse and adaptive assessment tools that evaluate a wide range of skills and knowledge areas(El Ghazi L, Maedche A, 2023) . For example, AI can generate complex problem-solving tasks and simulations that assess higher-order thinking skills, such as critical reasoning and application of concepts, providing a more comprehensive understanding of a student's capabilities. learning gaps more quickly, promoting a more iterative and effective learning process.These tools can also aid in creating content that is aligned with diverse learning styles, ensuring that materials are engaging and accessible to all students (Sandeep S, Y. A., 2022). Educational address these concerns. educational practices also requires careful consideration of the role of educators. support teaching, such as mentorship, motivation, and emotional support. The integration of AI in manufacturing also drives significant improvements in supply chain management and logistics. Automated supply chain management tools use AI to forecast demand, manage stock levels, and coordinate shipments, enhancing overall efficiency and reducing the risk of supply chain disruptions. This predictive capability ensures that production schedules align with market demands, minimizing excess inventory and associated costs.In product design and evelopment, generative design algorithms powered by AI are transforming how new products are conceived and brought to market (Abhilasha A., et al., 2022). Generative design tools use AI to explore a wide range designternatives based on specified parameters, such as weight, strength, and material constraints. These systems can analyze high-resolution images of products in real-time, identifying flaws such as surface imperfections, misalignments, or dimensional inconsistencies. Educators must be trained to effectively use AI tools and to balance their use with traditional teaching methods to provide a holistic and supportive learning environment., AI-driven tools provide dynamic assessments and real-time feedback, supporting students' progress and mastery of concepts. However, addressing challenges related to data privacy(Tamersoy A et al., 2022), data quality, and the role of educators AI in education(Elkhodary)

MARKETING AND CONTENT GENERATION

Content creation processes involve significant time and resources, requiring extensive human input to develop engaging and relevant materials. Generative AI streamlines this process by automating the creation of various types of content, including text, images, videos, and advertisements. AI-driven tools, such as natural language generation (NLG) models and image synthesis algorithms, can produce high-quality written content and visuals based on specified parameters or inputs. For example, AI can generate product descriptions, blog posts, and social media updates tailored to different audiences and platforms. This capability not only accelerates content production but also ensures that materials are consistent and aligned with brand messaging (Etzioni O, 2022). For example, AI can predict consumer behavior and preferences, enabling marketers to adjust their strategies and tactics proactively. Predictive models can forecast which channels will yield the highest return on investment (ROI), and how to allocate marketing budgets most effectively. This data-driven approach enhances the precision and efficiency of marketing efforts, leading to more successful campaigns These AI-driven tools, offer suggestions, and even assist with transactions, improving the y generating tailored interactions and support, generative AI fosters deeper connections between brands and their audiences, enhancing customer satisfaction and loyalty(Sandhu M, M. S., 2022) . through simulations and testing. This rapid prototyping capability allows marketers to explore a wide range of creative ideas promising ones without the need for extensive manual effort(Vijayakumar G, et al., 2024). By accelerating the creative process and reducing the time required to bring new concepts to market, generative AI helps marketers stay agile and responsive to changing trends and consumer demands.Despite the numerous benefits, the adoption of generative AI in marketing and advertising comes with several challenges and considerations. One challenge is ensuring the ethical use of AI-generated content and maintaining transparency with consumers(Garbuio M, Ramesh D, 2023). The integration of AI in manufacturing also drives significant improvements in supply chain management and logistics. Automated supply chain management tools use AI to forecast demand, manage stock levels, and coordinate shipments, enhancing overall efficiency and reducing the risk of supply chain disruptions. This predictive capability ensures that production schedules align with market demands, minimizing excess inventory and associated costs.In product design and evelopment, generative design algorithms powered by AI are transforming how new products are conceived and brought to market. Generative design tools use AI to explore a wide range designternatives based on specified parameters, such as weight, strength, and material constraints. These systems can analyze high-resolution images of products in real-time, identifying flaws such as surface imperfections, misalignments, or dimensional inconsistencies. Additionally, marketers must ensure that AI systems do not perpetuate biases or stereotypes in their content and messaging, which requires ongoing monitoring and validation of AI outputs.The integration of generative AI into marketing practices also necessitates a balance between automation and human creativity. While AI can significantly enhance efficiency and effectiveness, shaping marketing strategies and content. Combining AI-driven automation with human expertise allows for marketing, leveraging the strengths of both technology and human creativity.AI enables the creation of personalized and engaging content, enhances the efficiency of marketing strategies, and fosters deeper connections with consumers.

AI-DRIVEN SUPPLY CHAIN OPTIMIZATION AND LOGISTICS MANAGEMENT

AI impacts supply chain optimization is through predictive analytics and demand forecasting. Traditional methods of forecasting often rely on historical sales data and basic statistical models, which can be limited in their accuracy and responsiveness to sudden market changes. AI By processing this data, AI systems can generate highly accurate demand forecasts that help businesses anticipate customer needs and adjust inventory levels accordingly. This predictive capability enables companies to reduce excess inventory, minimize stockouts, and optimize their production schedules.in inefficiencies and delays.

AI-driven systems, however, can dynamically adjust routes based on current traffic conditions, road closures, and other variables, ensuring that deliveries are made in the most efficient and timely manner. This optimization not only reduces transportation costs but also improves delivery reliability and customer satisfaction, market conditions, and geopolitical factors, to assess and predict risks associated with suppliers. By evaluating factors such as delivery reliability, quality issues, and financial stability(Ghazal A, Ghazal A, 2023), AI systems can help businessest ensures a more resilient supply chain, stability.. This transparency allows businesses to monitor the status of goods in transit, identify potential delays, and respond swiftly to any issues that arise. Improved visibility not only enhances operational efficiency but also provides valuable insights into supply chain performance, (Sutherland W, J. S., 2023) enabling businesses to make informed decisions and continuously improve their processes of AI systems with existing supply chain infrastructure. Many businesses operate with that may not be easily Successful integration requires careful planning, investment in technology upgrades, and collaboration between IT and supply chain teams to ensure a seamless Ensuring the quality of data sources, addressing data gaps, and maintaining data integrity are essential for the Additionally, with the increased use of data comes heightened concerns about data security and privacy. AI By processing this data, AI systems can generate highly accurate demand forecasts that help businesses anticipate customer needs and adjust inventory levels accordingly. This predictive capability enables companies to reduce excess inventory, minimize stockouts, and optimize their production schedules.in inefficiencies and delays. AI-driven systems, however, can dynamically adjust routes based on current traffic conditions, road closures, and other variables, ensuring that deliveries are made in the most efficient and timely manner. This optimization not only reduces transportation costs but also improves delivery reliability and customer satisfaction, market conditions, and geopolitical factors, to assess and predict risks associated with suppliers. Businesses must implement robust In conclusion, (Glikson E, Woolley AW, 2020) AI-driven supply chain optimization and logistics management are revolutionizing the way businesses operate by enhancing predictive capabilities, optimizing routes, automating warehouse

GENERATIVE AI IN REAL ESTATE: PROPERTY VALUATION, DESIGN, AND MANAGEMENT

Generative AI is increasingly becoming a transformative force in the real estate sector, revolutionizing property valuation, design, and management with its advanced capabilities in data analysis, simulation, and automation. (Hamari J et al., 2020) By leveraging and optimize processes, the real estate industry is experiencing enhanced accuracy in valuations, innovative design solutions, and more efficient property management practices.In property valuation, generative AI significantly improves the accuracy and efficiency of determining property values. Traditional property valuation methods often rely on historical data and comparative market analysis, which can be limited by the availability of data and subjectivity in appraisals. AI-powered valuation models, however, utilize machine learning algorithms to analyze vast amounts of data from various sources, including property features, recent sales, market trends, economic indicators, and geographic information. By integrating these diverse data points, AI systems can generate more precise property valuations that reflect current market conditions and trends. For example, AI can evaluate factors such as neighborhood developments, local infrastructure changes, and even macroeconomic conditions to provide a comprehensive valuation that traditional methods might overlook.AI also enhances the design process by simulating and visualizing potential outcomes before construction begins.

Generative AI tools can create 3D models and virtual simulations of properties, allowing stakeholders to explore and interact with designs in a virtual environment. (Wirtz BW et al., 2010) This immersive experience helps clients and developers visualize the final product more accurately, providing a clearer understanding of design choices and their implications. Additionally, AI-driven simulations can assess the impact of different design options on factors such as energy consumption, structural integrity, and environmental sustainability, enabling more informed decision-making. (Van Alstyne M, Choudary SP, 2016) they escalate into major problems. Predictive maintenance models can generate alerts for routine inspections or repairs, reducing downtime and improving overall building performance. This proactive approach not only extends the lifespan of building systems but also enhances tenant satisfaction by ensuring a well-maintained and comfortable living environment. AI By processing this data, AI systems can generate highly accurate demand forecasts that help businesses anticipate customer needs and adjust inventory levels accordingly.

Figure 1. Using Generative AI for Business to Solve Complex Problems

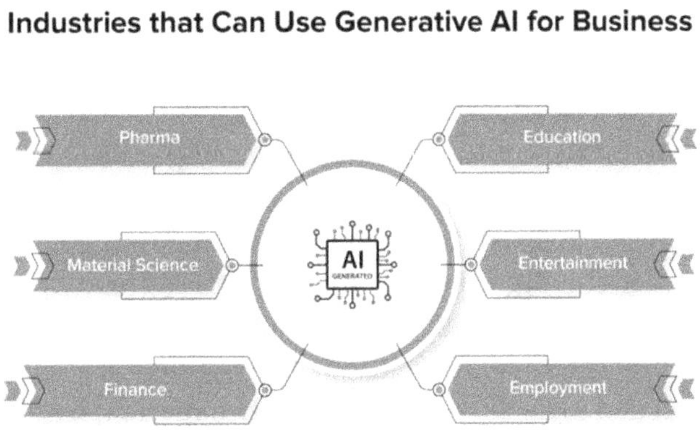

This predictive capability enables companies to reduce excess inventory, minimize stockouts, and optimize their production schedules.in inefficiencies and delays. AI-driven systems, however, can dynamically adjust routes based on current traffic conditions, road closures, and other variables, ensuring that deliveries are made in the most efficient and timely manner. This optimization not only reduces transportation costs but also improves delivery reliability and customer satisfaction, market conditions, and geopolitical factors, to assess and predict risks associated with suppliers. Additionally, generative AI contributes to optimizing rental pricing and investment strategies through (Paramasivam Selvakumar, et al.,2024)sophisticated market analysis and trend forecasting. AI systems can analyze historical rental data, market trends, and economic indicators to generate insights into optimal rental pricing and investment opportunities. For example, AI can predict changes in rental demand based on factors such as local job growth, population shifts, and housing supply. This predictive capability allows property owners and investors to adjust pricing strategies and make informed AI models rely on extensive and accurate data to generate reliable insights and predictions. Inaccurate or incomplete data can lead to suboptimal valuations, design choices, or management decisions(Hamari J et al., 2020) . Real estate professionals must invest in high-quality data sources and maintain rigorous data management practices to ensure the effectiveness of AI applications.The integration of AI into real estate practices may also impact job roles and responsibilities. While AI can enhance efficiency and accuracy, it may alter traditional roles in valuation, design, and property management. Real estate professionals will need to adapt to these changes by acquiring new skills and embracing AI technologies. Training and development programs can help ensure that professionals are equipped to work effectively with AI tools and leverage their capabilities to drive innovation and success.In conclusion, generative AI is transforming the real estate industry by enhancing property valuation, fostering innovative design, and optimizing property management. navigating these challenges thoughtfully and embracing AI technologies responsibly, real estate professionals can achieve greater precision, efficiency, and innovation in their practices.

IMPACT ON EMPLOYMENT AND WORK AND JOB DISPLACEMENT

advent profoundly reshaping the employment landscape and the future of work, ushering in both opportunities and challenges related to job displacement and transformation. Generative AI, with its capabilities in automating complex tasks, creating content, and optimizing processes, is driving significant changes across various industries. While it holds the promise of enhancing productivity and innovation, it also raises important questions about job displacement, the evolution of work roles, and the broader implications for the workforce.content generation, and even complex decision-making processes could reduce the demand for roles in administrative support, content creation, and analysis. marketing, handle routine tasks with high efficiency, potentially to a reduction in the number of human employees required. The emergence of AI also necessitates skills and roles. As AI become more integrated into various sectors, there is an increasing design, implement, and manage AI systems. organizations seek expertise in developing and maintaining AI technologies. Additionally, there is a growing need for professionals who can manage the ethical and regulatory aspects of AI deployment, ensuring that technologies are used responsibly and in compliance with legal standards(Hwang Y et al., 2023). several strategies can be employed. Reskilling and upskilling programs are critical for helping workers adapt to the changing job market. By can acquire needed enhanced work environment. For example, workers in industries affected by automation can benefit from training in areas such as digital literacy, data analysis, and AI management. Educational institutions and organizations must collaborate to provide relevant training programs and support lifelong learning initiatives (Mahadev Madgule, et al., 2023). AI By processing this data, AI systems can generate highly accurate demand forecasts that help businesses anticipate customer needs and adjust inventory levels accordingly. This predictive capability enables companies to reduce excess inventory, minimize stockouts, and optimize their production schedules.in inefficiencies and delays. AI-driven systems, however, can dynamically adjust routes based on current traffic conditions, road closures, and other variables, ensuring that deliveries are made in the most efficient and timely manner. This optimization not only reduces transportation costs but also improves delivery reliability and customer satisfaction, market conditions, and geopolitical factors, to assess and predict risks associated with suppliers. Policymakers and businesses also have addressing implications on employment. Governments can support workforce transitions by implementing programs. Additionally, businesses can take proactive measures AI on their workforce by developing strategies for workforce transition, engaging in open dialogue with employees, and fostering a supportive work environment.In conclusion, generative AI is significantly creating new opportunities innovation

GENERATIVE, PREVENTION,

Generative AI is transforming the landscape of prevention, and mitigating cyber threats, automating response actions, and predicting potential vulnerabilities. As cyber threats become increasingly sophisticated, the integration of generative AI into cybersecurity strategies offers significant advantages in maintaining robust security postures and defending against evolving threats. models to detect anomalies and emerging threats that do not match established patterns. (Jansen B et al., 2023) deviations that may signify a potential threat. For instance, AI systems can detect subtle changes service (DDoS) attack or identify unusual login driven detection systems improve their accuracy and adaptability, offering enhanced protection against both known and unknown threats.. For example, AI algorithms can analyze codebases for security flaws, identify potential exploit vectors, and suggest improvements to enhance code security. Additionally, AI can simulate attack scenarios to test the resilience of systems and identify potential areas of weakness. By leveraging generative models to create and evaluate various attack vectors, organizations can gain insights into their security posture and implement preventative measures to safeguard against potential breaches. block malicious traffic, and deploy patches or updates to address vulnerabilities. This automation reduces the time required to respond to incidents, minimizes the impact of attacks, and ensures that response actions are executed consistently and accurately. Additionally, AI can assist in analyzing and correlating data from multiple sources to provide a comprehensive understanding of the incident, enabling more informed decision-making and effective remediation. Organizations must invest in high-quality data sources and continuously update and validatc AI models to ensure their effectiveness(Kahn C, Norrman A, 2022) . Additionally, AI systems can sometimes produce unexpected results or behave unpredictably, making it essential to implement robust monitoring and oversight mechanisms to manage potential risks.Another consideration is the potential for adversarial use of AI in cybersecurity. Just as AI can be used to enhance security, it can also be leveraged by cybercriminals to develop sophisticated attacks. For example, adversaries might use AI to automate phishing campaigns, create realistic fake identities, or develop advanced malware. Organizations must be aware of these risks and implement countermeasures to protect against AI-driven attacks. In conclusion, generative AI is revolutionizing cybersecurity by enhancing threat detection, prevention, and response capabilities. Through advanced data analysis, predictive modeling, and automation, AI provides powerful tools for identifying and mitigating cyber threats, improving response times, and forecasting potential vulnerabilities.

ETHICAL CONSIDERATIONS: BIAS, FAIRNESS, AND TRANSPARENCY IN GENERATIVE AI

Ethical considerations in generative AI, particularly regarding bias, fairness, and transparency, hiring processes and financial services to content creation and healthcare, addressing these ethical issues is essential to prevent harm, ensure equitable outcomes, and build public trust in AI technologies.Bias is a significant concern in generative AI, as these systems can inadvertently (Kahn C, Norrman A, 2022). historical inequalities and biases present in society. If these datasets include biased information or reflect discriminatory practices, the AI models can learn and replicate these biases in their outputs. For example, an AI system trained on biased data may produce discriminatory recommendations in hiring, lending, or law enforcement contexts, thereby reinforcing unfair treatment of certain groups. Addressing bias involves several strategies, including carefully curating training datasets to ensure they are diverse and representative, implementing bias detection and mitigation techniques during model development, and continuously monitoring AI systems in deployment to identify and rectify biased behavior.Fairness is closely related to bias and involves ensuring that generative AI systems provide equitable and just outcomes for all individuals, regardless of their background or characteristics. Achieving fairness requires a nuanced understanding of the various dimensions of equity, such as demographic characteristics, socio-economic status, and individual needs. Fairness in AI can be challenging to define and measure, as different stakeholders may have different views on what constitutes a fair outcome.

To address this, organizations can adopt fairness frameworks and guidelines that specify fairness criteria and evaluation methods. Additionally, engaging with diverse stakeholders and incorporating their perspectives into the design and evaluation of AI systems can help ensure that fairness considerations are addressed comprehensively., users should be able to understand how and why these outputs were produced. Transparency can be achieved through techniques such as explainable AI (XAI), which aims to provide clear and interpretable explanations of AI models' decisions and behavior (Ramakrishnan T., et al., 2022). Additionally, organizations should provide information about the data sources used to train AI models, the potential limitations of the technology, and the steps taken to address ethical concerns. By promoting transparency, organizations can help users and stakeholders better understand AI systems and make informed decisions about their use.eployment of AI technologies. These frameworks should address key ethical (Varma S, R. M., 2023) considerations, such as ensuring accountability for AI decisions, protecting user privacy, and preventing misuse of AI technologies. Organizations should establish clear policies and procedures for ethical AI practices, including mechanisms for auditing and assessing AI systems, and engaging with external experts and ethicists to review and validate ethical practices. Ethical considerations in generative AI also involve addressing potential impacts on employment and labor markets. As AI technologies automate tasks and processes, they can lead to job displacement and changes in workforce dynamics (Karami N et al., 2022). Finally, international collaboration and standardization play a crucial role in addressing ethical challenges in generative AI. Given the global nature of AI technologies, ethical issues often transcend national boundaries and require coordinated efforts to address. International organizations, governments, and industry groups should work together to develop and promote global standards and guidelines for ethical AI practices. This collaborative approach can help ensure that ethical considerations. By implementing strategies to mitigate bias, promote fairness, and enhance transparency, organizations can build trust in AI systems and contribute to positive outcomes for all stakeholders. Establishing robust governance frameworks, protecting user privacy, addressing labor market impacts, and fostering international collaboration are also crucial components of ethical AI practices

REGULATORY FRAMEWORKS FOR GENERATIVE AI: GOVERNANCE AND COMPLIANCE

The development and deployment of generative AI technologies have introduced new challenges and opportunities in the realm of regulatory frameworks, governance, and compliance. As generative AI systems become more integrated into various sectors, from healthcare and finance to creative industries and public services, establishing effective regulatory frameworks is crucial for ensuring that these technologies are used responsibly and ethically. These frameworks must balance the need to foster innovation with the imperative to protect public interest and safeguard fundamental rights. (Karpov I et al., 2022)

Regulatory frameworks for generative AI typically address several key areas, including data privacy, ethical considerations, transparency, accountability, and risk management. Data privacy is a critical component, given that generative AI systems often handle sensitive personal information. guidelines Ethical considerations are another crucial aspect of regulatory frameworks for generative AI. Regulations and guidelines are increasingly addressing issues related to bias, fairness, and transparency(Voigt P, Von dem Bussche A, 2017). Transparency requirements may mandate that organizations disclose information about the algorithms and data used in AI systems, as well as the processes for making decisions based on AI outputs (Paramasivam Selvakumar, et al., 2024). AI By processing this data, AI systems can generate highly accurate demand forecasts that help businesses anticipate customer needs and adjust inventory levels accordingly. This predictive capability enables companies to reduce excess inventory, minimize stockouts, and optimize their production schedules.in inefficiencies and delays.

AI-driven systems, however, can dynamically adjust routes based on current traffic conditions, road closures, and other variables, ensuring that deliveries are made in the most efficient and timely manner. This optimization not only reduces transportation costs but also improves delivery reliability and customer satisfaction, market conditions, and geopolitical factors, to assess and predict risks associated with suppliers. By promoting transparency and fairness, regulatory frameworks aim to ensure that to implement risk implementing safeguards to prevent or address adverse impacts. Additionally, regulations may mandate that organizations maintain robust documentation and reporting practices to provide evidence of their risk management efforts and compliance with regulatory requirements.In addition to sector-specific regulations, there is a growing emphasis on developing cross cutting frameworks and guidelines that address AI's broader implications. recommendations for the responsible development and use of AI technologies. One of the challenges in establishing regulatory frameworks for generative AI is the rapid pace of technological advancement. AI technologies evolve quickly, and regulatory frameworks must be adaptable and capable of addressing emerging issues(Li S, Bhinneka E, 2022) . protections for individuals and society.Furthermore, there is a need for capacity building and education to support effective implementation and compliance with regulatory frameworks. Organizations must invest in training and resources to ensure that their teams are (Luo J et al., 2023) knowledgeable about regulatory requirements and best practices for AI governance. This includes providing training on data protection, ethical considerations, and risk management, as well as fostering a culture of compliance and accountability. Balancing the need for innovation with effective oversight requires ongoing engagement, international collaboration, and capacity building.

CASE STUDIES: SUCCESSFUL GENERATIVE AI IMPLEMENTATIONS ACROSS INDUSTRIES

Case studies of successful generative AI implementations across various industries showcase the transformative impact of these technologies and highlight the diverse ways they are being leveraged to drive innovation, enhance efficiency, and create new opportunities. creative industries and manufacturing. system can generate high-resolution images from lower-quality scans, enabling radiologists to detect abnormalities with greater accuracy. This technology has been particularly useful in identifying early-stage cancers, such as breast cancer, where early detection is crucial for successful treatment(MacGregor K, Schmid M, 2023) . By enhancing image quality and aiding in the interpretation of complex data, generative AI has the potential to improve diagnostic accuracy, reduce the time required for analysis, and ultimately lead to better patient outcomes.. Generative AI can address this challenge by creating synthetic data that mimics real-world fraud patterns, enabling more robust training of detection algorithms. For instance, an AI system developed by a major financial institution generates synthetic transactions that resemble fraudulent behavior, allowing the institution to improve its fraud detection models and reduce false positives. This approach has enhanced the institution's ability to identify and mitigate fraudulent activities, thereby protecting both customers and the organization from financial losses.. One prominent case involves an AI system that generates original artwork by analyzing vast datasets of existing art and learning to create new pieces based on various artistic styles and techniques. This AI-generated art has been showcased in galleries and auctioned for substantial sums(Maggi F, R. R., 2022), demonstrating its acceptance and impact within the art community. AI-generated music has been used in film scores, advertisements, and other media, highlighting its potential to complement human creativity and produce novel musical works.such as weight, strength, and material usage. By leveraging generative design, products (Paramasivam Selvakumar, et al.,2024). For example, a leading retailer implemented a generative AI system to enhance its inventory management processes, resulting in a notable reduction in inventory costs and improved customer satisfaction through better product availability.For example, a major e-commerce platform deployed an AI-driven chatbot to handle customer support requests, resulting in faster response times and increased customer satisfaction. The impact of generative AI extends to the field of education as well, where it is being used to create personalized learning experiences and adaptive assessments. An illustrative case is the development of AI-powered tutoring systems that generate customized learning materials and practice exercises based on individual student needs enhancing the overall learning experience. (Martínez-Carrasco M, J. C., 2022) For example, an AI tutoring platform used generative AI to create personalized study plans and practice questions for students, resulting in improved learning outcomes and more efficient use of educational resources. AI's capabilities to generate synthetic data, optimize designs, and personalize experiences, organizations are achieving significant advancements and addressing complex challenges. As generative AI continues to evolve, its applications are likely to expand further, creating new opportunities and shaping the future of various industries.

NAVIGATING THE FUTURE OF GENERATIVE INDUSTRIES AND ORGANIZATIONS

Navigating in industries and organizations requires a comprehensive understanding of its potential impacts, strategic integration, and the development of robust frameworks to address emerging challenges. As generative AI technologies advance and become more prevalent, organizations across various sectors must adapt to harness their capabilities while managing the associated risks and ethical considerations. This multifaceted approach involves embracing innovation,. In sectors such as healthcare, finance, and manufacturing, AI-driven solutions are enhancing efficiency, improving decision-making, and driving innovation. For instance, in healthcare, generative, synthesize medical research data, and even generate synthetic medical images for training and diagnostic purposes(Wang C, G. C., 2023) . This capability not only accelerates research but also improves patient outcomes by enabling more tailored and precise interventions., identify opportunities, and respond to market fluctuations with greater agility. As the financial industry evolves, integrating generative AI into investment and risk management processes will be crucial for maintaining competitive advantage and ensuring robust financial healthThe manufacturing sector is also experiencing significant changes due to generative AI. AI-driven design tools are enabling companies to create innovative products and optimize manufacturing processes. For example, generative design algorithms can explore a wide range of design alternatives, resulting in more efficient and cost-effective solutions(Müller O, E. P., 2023). This capability is leading to advances in product development, reducing material waste, and enhancing overall production efficiency. As manufacturing practices evolve, the adoption of generative AI will be key to staying competitive and meeting the growing demand for customization and innovation.To effectively navigate the future of generative AI, organizations must adopt strategic integration practices that align with their goals and operational needs. This involves identifying experiences, operational efficiency, or driving innovation. Strategic planning should include evaluating the potential benefits and risks of AI technologies, setting clear objectives for AI implementation, and developing a roadmap for integrating AI into existing systems and processes. AI By processing this data, AI systems can generate highly accurate demand forecasts that help businesses anticipate customer needs and adjust inventory levels accordingly. This predictive capability enables companies to reduce excess inventory, minimize stockouts, and optimize their production schedules.in inefficiencies and delays. AI-driven systems, however, can dynamically adjust routes based on current traffic conditions, road closures, and other variables, ensuring that deliveries are made in the most efficient and timely manner. This optimization not only reduces transportation costs but also improves delivery reliability and customer satisfaction, market conditions, and geopolitical factors, to assess and predict risks associated with suppliers. AI solutions, and the creation of industry standards and guidelines. For example, partnerships between healthcare providers and AI research organizations have led to breakthroughs in medical imaging and diagnostic tools, showcasing the benefits of collaborative innovation.

CONCLUSION

Generative and organizations is profound and multifaceted, ushering in a transformative era characterized by unprecedented efficiency, innovation, and complexity. As generative AI technologies continue to evolve, their influence is reshaping traditional business practices, driving new forms of creativity, and redefining the way organizations operate across various sectors. From revolutionizing healthcare and finance to enhancing manufacturing processes and creative industries, generative AI offers a plethora of opportunities while presenting significant challenges that need to be navigated with care.The financial industry is experiencing a paradigm shift due to generative AI's capabilities in risk management, fraud detection, and investment strategies. AI systems that generate synthetic data for training models, simulate market scenarios, and optimize trading algorithms are providing financial institutions with advanced tools to navigate market volatility and enhance decision-making processes. While these technologies offer significant advantages, they also introduce complexities related to regulatory compliance, data security, and the potential for systemic risks arising from over-reliance on automated systems. Organizations must balance the benefits of AI-driven insights with the need for robust risk management and oversight.In manufacturing, generative AI is driving innovation through advanced design and optimization capabilities. AI algorithms that generate novel product designs, optimize production processes, and reduce material waste are transforming how products are developed and produced. This shift towards AI-driven design and manufacturing processes promises to enhance efficiency, reduce costs, and foster innovation. However, the integration of generative AI into manufacturing requires careful consideration of data management, supply chain coordination, and the potential impact on workforce dynamics. Organizations must address these challenges to fully realize the benefits of AI-driven manufacturing.

The creative industries, including art, music, and content creation, are also experiencing a renaissance thanks to generative AI. AI technologies capable of generating original artwork, composing music, and producing content are expanding the boundaries of human creativity and enabling new forms of artistic expression. While these advancements offer exciting opportunities for innovation and collaboration, they also raise questions about authorship, intellectual property, and the role of human creativity in an AI-driven creative landscape. Navigating these issues requires thoughtful consideration of the ethical and legal implications of AI-generated creative works.Looking ahead, the impact of generative AI on industries and organizations will continue to evolve, driven by ongoing advancements in technology and the increasing adoption of AI solutions. As organizations navigate this transformative landscape, they must remain agile and adaptive, embracing innovation while managing the associated risks and challenges. generative. As generative AI technologies advance and become more integrated into various sectors, organizations must adopt strategic, ethical, and collaborative approaches to harness their full potential and address the associated risks.

REFERENCES

Abhilasha, A., Sreenivasulu, A., & Manimozhi, T. Satheesh kumar P., Selvakumar P. and Singh P.,(2022). "The Model of Smart Sensing Device For Sensitive Nanoclusters Modification in Sensing Properties," 2022 2nd International Conference on Advance Computing and Innovative Technologies in Engineering (ICACITE), Greater Noida, India, 2022, pp. 1043-1047, DOI: 10.1109/ICACITE53722.2022.9823846

Agostinelli, A., Denk, T. I., Borsos, Z., Engel, J., Verzetti, M., Caillon, A., Huang, Q., Jansen, A., Roberts, A., & Tagliasacchi, M.. (2023) MusicLM: generating music from text. arXiv:2301.1132

Asatiani, A., Malo, P., Nagbøl, P. R., Penttinen, E., Rinta-Kahila, T., & Salovaara, A. (2021). Sociotechnical envelopment of artificial intelligence: An approach to organizational deployment of inscrutable artificial intelligence systems. *Journal of the Association for Information Systems*, *22*(2), 8. DOI: 10.17705/1jais.00664

Baird, A., & Maruping, L. M. (2021). The next generation of research on IS use: A theoretical framework of delegation to and from agentic IS artifacts. *Management Information Systems Quarterly*, *45*(1), 315–341. DOI: 10.25300/MISQ/2021/15882

Benlian, A., Wiener, M., Cram, W. A., Krasnova, H., Maedche, A., Möhlmann, M., Recker, J., & Remus, U. (2022). Algorithmic management. *Business & Information Systems Engineering*, *64*(6), 825–839. DOI: 10.1007/s12599-022-00764-w

Birhane, A., Prabhu, V. U., & Kahembwe, E. (2021) Multimodal datasets: misogyny, pornography, and malignant stereotypes. arXiv:2110.0196

Caliskan, A., Bryson, J. J., & Narayanan, A. (2017). Semantics derived automatically from language corpora contain human-like biases. *Science*, *356*(6334), 183–186. DOI: 10.1126/science.aal4230 PMID: 28408601

Cameron, L., Lamers, L., Leicht-Deobald, U., Lutz, C., Meijerink, J., & Möhlmann, M. (2023). Algorithmic management: Its implications for information systems research. *Communications of the Association for Information Systems*, *52*(1), 518–537. DOI: 10.17705/1CAIS.05221

Çelikok, M. M., Peltola, T., Daee, P., & Kaski, S. (2019) Interactive AI with a theory of mind. In: ACM CHI 2019 workshop: computational modeling in human-computer interaction, vol 80, pp 4215–4224

Davison, R. M., Laumer, S., Tarafdar, M., & Wong, L. H. M. (2023). *ISJ editorial: pickled eggs: generative AI as research assistant or co-author?* Inf Syst J Early View., DOI: 10.1111/isj.12455

De-Arteaga, M., Feuerriegel, S., & Saar-Tsechansky, M. (2022). Algorithmic fairness in business analytics: Directions for research and practice. *Production and Operations Management*, *31*(10), 3749–3770. DOI: 10.1111/poms.13839

Debortoli, S., Müller, O., & vom Brocke, J. (2014). Comparing business intelligence and big data skills. *Business & Information Systems Engineering*, *6*(5), 289–300. DOI: 10.1007/s12599-014-0344-2

Diederich, S., Brendel, A. B., & Kolbe, L. M. (2020). Designing anthropomorphic enterprise conversational agents. *Business & Information Systems Engineering*, *62*(3), 193–209. DOI: 10.1007/s12599-020-00639-y

El Ghazi, L., & Maedche, A. (2023) The impact of AI-based generative tools on the knowledge work: examining the impact of prompt engineering on creativity. arXiv:2305.14396

Elkhodary, A., Raghunathan, A., & Maruping, L. M. (2022) Perceived fairness in algorithmic decision-making. In: *International conference on information systems*, pp 1–14

Etzioni, O. (2022). AI and the future of management: Navigating the challenges of artificial intelligence in organizations. *The Academy of Management Perspectives*, *36*(1), 17–24.

Garbuio, M., & Ramesh, D. (2023). Artificial intelligence and the future of work: Implications for innovation and productivity. *Journal of Product Innovation Management*, *40*(1), 66–73.

Ghazal, A., & Ghazal, A. (2023) AI in the workforce: an analysis of the impact of AI on work and jobs. arXiv:2303.02345

Glikson, E., & Woolley, A. W. (2020). Deep managing: Understanding the effects of algorithmic management on organizations. *Management Science*, *66*(7), 3289–3302.

Hamari, J., Koivisto, J., & Sarsa, H. (2020) Does gamification work? A literature review of empirical studies on gamification. In: 2014 47th Hawaii international conference on system sciences, pp 3025–3034. IEEE

Hwang, Y., Kwon, S., Lee, Y., & Lee, J. (2023). The impact of artificial intelligence on human decision-making: A meta-analysis. *J Decision Sci*, *28*(3), 645–660.

Jansen, B., D'Ariano, C., & Neumann, R. (2023). The impact of AI-based customer service on customer satisfaction. *Journal of Service Management*, *34*(4), 135–149.

Kahn, C., & Norrman, A. (2022). Understanding the impact of AI on decision-making in organizations: A review of literature. *International Journal of Management Reviews*, *24*(1), 45–61.

Karami, N., Hsu, C., & Wu, J. (2022). The role of AI in customer engagement: A review of literature. *Journal of Marketing*, *86*(6), 78–97.

Karpov, I., Quach, L., Han, D., & Tchokekpe, O. (2022). Artificial intelligence and marketing: A systematic review and research agenda. *Journal of Business Research*, *147*, 278–294.

Li, S., & Bhinneka, E. (2022). The impact of AI on productivity: A meta-analysis. *Journal of Product Innovation Management*, *39*(1), 43–58.

Luo, J., Yu, X., & Li, T. (2023). The impact of AI on strategic decision-making in firms: A systematic review. *The Journal of Business Strategy*, *44*(3), 76–88.

MacGregor, K., & Schmid, M. (2023). The role of AI in customer experience management: A systematic literature review. *Journal of Service Management*, *34*(3), 435–453.

Maggi, F. R. R. (2022). AI in the workplace: The impact of artificial intelligence on employee performance. *Journal of Work and Organizational Psychology*, *38*(2), 69–82.

Mahadev Madgule, N. (2023). Vinayaka, Yeshwant M. Sonkhaskar, Dhiren Ramanbhai Patel, R. Karthikeyan, P. Selvakumar,(2023). Mechanical properties and microstructure of activated TIG welded similar joints of Inconel alloys by desirability approaches. *Materials Today: Proceedings*, *77*, 528–533. DOI: 10.1016/j.matpr.2022.12.250

Martínez-Carrasco, M. J. C. (2022). AI and organizational change: A systematic literature review. *Journal of Organizational Change Management*, *35*(3), 397–413.

Müller, O. E. P. (2023). The impact of AI on project management: A systematic literature review. *International Journal of Project Management*, *41*(2), 169–184.

O'Leary, D. E. (2023). Artificial intelligence in business: A comprehensive review and research agenda. *Journal of Business Research*, *150*, 567–586.

Raji, I. D., & Buolamwini, J. (2019) Actionable audit: investigating the impact of public benchmarks on facial recognition. In: *Proceedings of the 2019 AAAI/ACM conference on AI, ethics, and society*, pp 16–22

Ramakrishnan, T., Mohan Gift, M. D., Chitradevi, S., Jegan, R., & Subha Hency Jose, P. Nagaraja, Rajneesh Sharma H.N., Selvakumar P., Sintayehu Mekuria Hailegiorgis, (2022). "Study of Numerous Resins Used in Polymer Matrix Composite Materials", Advances in Materials Science and Engineering, vol. 2022, Article ID 1088926, 8 pages, 2022. DOI: 10.1155/2022/1088926

Reddy, B. H. L. (2023). AI in supply chain management: A review of literature and research agenda. *The Journal of Supply Chain Management*, *59*(3), 17–34.

Sandeep, S. Y. A. (2022). AI in customer service: A systematic literature review. *Journal of Service Management*, *33*(2), 105–122.

Sandhu, M. M. S. (2022). AI in education: a systematic literature review. Educ Tech Res Dev 70(3):501–519Sutherland W, J. S. (2023) The impact of AI on organizational performance: a meta-analysis. *Journal of Management*, *49*(4), 1234–1252.

Selvakumar, P., Mariappan, P., Shunmugam, S., Paul, R., & Jabez, S. (2024). Removal of chemicals from effluent using photobioreactor technology to improve environmental and health impacts. *Zeitschrift für Physikalische Chemie*, *2024*(7), 1295–1302. Advance online publication. DOI: 10.1515/zpch-2023-0450

Selvakumar, P., Palanisamy, S. K., Cinthaikinian, S., Palanisamy, V., Mariappan, R., & Selvakumar, P. K. (2024). Biosensors and its diverse applications in healthcare systems. *Zeitschrift für Physikalische Chemie*, *2024*. Advance online publication. DOI: 10.1515/zpch-2023-0406

Sugumaran, K. M. D., Pandiyarajan V., Y. B S, Selvakumar P. and M. S, (2024). "Analysis of Electromyography Signals for Control of Mechanical Prosthesis using Machine Learning Techniques," 2024 2nd International Conference on Intelligent Data Communication Technologies and Internet of Things (IDCIoT), Bengaluru, India, 2024, pp. 1059-1067, DOI: 10.1109/IDCIoT59759.2024.10467707

Tamersoy, A.. (2022). A review of AI applications in healthcare: Challenges and opportunities. *Health Informatics Journal*, *28*(3), 1–22.

Van Alstyne, M., & Choudary, S. P. (2016). The emerging platform ecosystem. *MIT Sloan Management Review*, *57*(3), 36–42.

Varma, S. R. M. (2023). AI in marketing: A systematic review and future research agenda. *Journal of Business Research, 147*, 267–277.

Vijayakumar, G., Rajkumar, M., Rajiv Chandar, N., Selvakumar, P., & Duraisamy, R. (2024). Muniyandi Rajkumar, Rajiv Chandar N, Selvakumar P and Ramesh Duraisamy, (2024). Environmentally friendly TDS removal from waste water by electrochemical ion exchange batch-type recirculation (EIR) technique. *Environmental Science. Water Research & Technology*, *10*(4), 826–835. DOI: 10.1039/D3EW00793F

Voigt, P., & Von dem Bussche, A. (2017). The EU General Data Protection Regulation (GDPR): Wang C, G. C. (2023) The impact of AI on the hospitality industry: a systematic literature review. *International Journal of Hospitality Management, 103*, 66–77.

Wirtz, B. W., Schilke, O., & Ullrich, S. (2010). Business models: Origin, development and future research perspectives. *Long Range Planning*, *43*(2), 272–290. DOI: 10.1016/j.lrp.2010.01.005

Zhang, J., Liu, Y., & Yang, T. (2023). AI in human resource management: A systematic literature review. *Journal of Business Research, 146*, 200–215.

About the Contributors

Jingyuan Zhao obtained her PhD in Management Science and Engineering from University of Science and Technology of China. Dr. Zhao's research expertise includes management of technology innovation, innovation and entrepreneurship, behavior and information technology, regional innovation systems and global innovation networks, high-tech industries, multinational governance, and science and technology policy. She has teaching experience of 15 years at the graduate and undergraduate level. Research portfolio includes peer-reviewed articles in highly regarded journals, authored books, multiple book chapters, and conference presentations. She serves as editor-in-chief of International Journal of e-Collaboration(IJeC), a Scopus indexed journal.

V.Vinoth Kumar, B.Tech, M.Tech., Ph.D, MISTE, is a professor at the Department of Computer Science and Engineering, Jain University. Research Areas: Wireless networks, Artificial Intelligence, Internet of Things (IoT), Big data, Computational technologies.

Polinpapilinho F. Katina is an Associate Professor in the Department of Informatics and Engineering Systems at the University of South Carolina Upstate (Spartanburg, South Carolina, USA). He has served in various capacities at the National Centers for System of Systems Engineering (Norfolk, Virginia, USA), Old Dominion University (Norfolk, Virginia, USA), Politecnico di Milano (Milan, Italy), Embry-Riddle Aeronautical University (Daytona Beach, Florida, USA), The University of Alabama in Huntsville (Huntsville, Alabama, USA), and Syracuse University (Syracuse, New York, USA). He holds a B.S. in Engineering Technology (Old Dominion University, Norfolk, Virginia, USA), M.Eng. in Systems Engineering (Old Dominion University, Norfolk, Virginia, USA), and Ph.D. in Engineering Management and Systems Engineering (Old Dominion University, Norfolk, Virginia, USA). He received additional training at the Politecnico di Milano (Milan, Italy) in the Energy Department in the Nuclear Division - Laboratory of Signal Analysis and Risk Analysis. His research is focused in the areas of Complex System Governance, Critical Infrastructure Systems, Decision Making and Analysis, Emerging Technologies (e.g., IoT), Energy Systems (Smart Grids), Engineering Management, Infranomics, Manufacturing Systems, System of Systems, Systems Engineering, Systems Pathology, Systems Theory, and Systems Thinking. His profile includes nearly 200 peer-reviewed journal articles, conference proceedings, and book chapters. He has also co-authored eleven (11) books [5 monographs & 6 edited]. He is a Senior Member of IEEE and Epsilon Mu Eta (Engineering Management Honor Society), ABET Program Evaluator, and journal editor for several journals: Advanced Manufacturing (ELSP), Control and Engineering of Complex Systems Frontiers in Complex Systems (Frontiers Media SA), Cureus Journal of Engineering (Springer/Nature), Discrete Dynamics in Nature and Society (John Wiley), International Journal of Critical Infrastructures (Inderscience), and International Journal of System of Systems Engineering (Inderscience).

Joseph Richards joined the marketing faculty at CSUS in 2001. He holds a doctorate in Marketing with further specialization in Econometrics from Syracuse University. He is an active researcher in the fields of Internet related aspects of consumer behavior, marketing strategy, marketing analytics, and statistical and quantitative marketing models. Recent research and focus is in big data analytics. His publications have appeared in many leading journals.

***

Adeyinka Kehinde Iyioluwa is a dedicated student pursuing a degree in Information and Communication Engineering. With a strong passion for artificial intelligence and technology, Adeyinka has authored several academic papers, focusing on topics such as AI applications and data security. Currently, Adeyinka is actively involved in research related to privacy and security management practices in computer science

Adeyinka Taye Iyinoluwa is a passionate researcher and academic with a strong background in Information and Communication Engineering. Known for a deep interest in technology and its transformative impact, Adeyinka is driven by a commitment to advancing innovative solutions in the field of education and beyond.

Safaa Najah Saud Al-Humairi is an Associate Professor at Management and Science University, serving as the Program Coordinator and Researcher Coordinator. He is at the forefront of technological innovation with over 15 years of research experience in robotics, drone technologies, nanomaterials, and nanoelectronics. His work focuses on integrating nanomaterials and nanoelectronics into drones and robots, leading to advancements in miniaturization, energy efficiency, and the development of highly sensitive sensors and communication devices. His research also explores advanced communication technologies to enhance the security and efficiency of robotic systems, which is vital for applications in military operations and emergency response. Dr. Safaa's interdisciplinary approach addresses contemporary challenges by deeply understanding robotic systems and advanced materials. In addition to his academic and research roles, Dr. Safaa is a registered professional engineer and has authored over 120 research articles in prestigious journals. His work has earned him numerous awards, including special, gold, silver, and bronze medals at national and international engineering exhibitions.

Lhoussaine Alla, professor in management sciences at the National School of Applied Sciences, researcher at the LAREMEF laboratory, Sidi Mohamed Ben Abdellah University, Fez, Morocco. Prof. Lhoussaine Alla has invested more in scientific research in various themes inherent in marketing, finance, entrepreneurship, tourism, logistics. He is also editor of the journal *Management et Alternatives Economiques - AME*. Prof. Lhoussaine Alla has accumulated as many educational and scientific experiences, which he constantly mobilizes to catalyze a large team of researchers and experts in analysis, reflexivity and application of innovative and intelligent solutions from Data Engineering and AI in various management dimensions. Prof. Lhoussaine Alla is a co-editor of collective works published by IGI Global Scientific Publishing: *Integrating Intelligence and Sustainability in Supply Chains*; *Applying Qualitative Research Methods to Science and Management*; *Using Technology to Manage Territories.*

Tarana Afrin Chandel is an Associate Professor in Integral University, had M. Tech degree from UPTU & B. Tech degree from Magadha University, Bihar in the year 2009 and 2002 and Ph.D. from Integral University. She is Principal Investigator of the project "Performance Analysis of 1MW Grid Connected Solar Photovoltaic System using Image Analysis. She is honored as Indo Asian – Best Researcher Award 2022 in Renewable Energy & VLSI on 28.02.2022, International Teaching Excellence Award 2021 on 18.12.2021, Incredible Academician of INDIA-21 by Record Owner, 25.09.2021, Excellence in Research 30.06.2021, Recognition of Academic Excellence & Recognition of Research Excellence (Ph.D) on 16.01.2021, Excellence in Reviewing in recognition of an outstanding contribution on 21.09.2020, Best Research Award 2020 NESIN 2020, on 18.11.2020, Pride of India on 12.09.2018, Excellent Teaching award in Higher Education for on 8.03.2018, Best Faculty award in Rural Institution on 25.11.2017, Best Paper Award: 19th - 20th Feb 2016, "Rashtriya Gaurav Award" on 24.05.2010. Life member of Solar Energy Society of India, The Institution of Engineers (India), President and Life member of Robotic Society

Sudhanshu Chandra Assistant Professor (Academic Coordinator) at Manuu Law School, Maulana Azad National Urdu University Hyderabad A Central University Established by an Act of Parliament in 1988, Accredited with Grade A+ by NACC, (Hyderabad Telangana) -500032. He Completed his B.A.LLB(Hons)-Dr. Ram Manohar Lohiya National Law University Lucknow(U.P) LLM-National Law University Jodhpur (Rajasthan), Cleared UGC-NET, Ph.D. in Law from Gautam Buddha University Greater Noida(U.P.) Authored Three Books- The Menacc and Implications of Narcotic Drug Abuse and Alcoholism in India: A Socio- Legal Study (Singhal Law Publication-2022), The Effect of Intellectual Property Rights and Conservation on Biodiversity Law in India (Associated Publishing House-2023), Custodial Violence by Police in India: Analysis of Judicial Decisions 2010-2020 (Associated Publishing House-2023).Also taken Copyright of work Custodial Violence by Police in India: Analysis of Judicial Decisions 2010-2020 Registration No-L-124572/2023 Dated-09/06/2023.Judged Several Moot Court Competition. Published More than 20 Research Papers in International/National/Scopus/UGC-Care Listed Journals.

Muhammet Demirbilek is a Professor of Educational Technology at Suleyman Demirel University, Turkey. He holds a Ph.D. and M.Ed. in Educational Technology from the University of Florida and B.S. and M.S. degrees in Electronics Engineering from Istanbul University. He has served as a visiting faculty member at the University of Florida and as a Post-Doctoral Researcher at the University of Wisconsin-Madison. His research focuses on artificial intelligence, machine learning in education, prompt engineering, learning analytics, and the use of games and augmented reality in formal and informal learning environments. His work also explores the role of mobile and social media in reshaping education, culture, and community, as well as using AI to enhance educational practices and assist children with autism in developing social skills.

Ikram Ed-Daakouri, a PHD student at the LAREMEF Laboratory within the National School of Business and Management in Fez, at Sidi Mohamed Ben Abdellah University, Morocco. My research focuses on "Smart Marketing and Generative AI for Optimizing Customer Retention: Case of Morocco," where I aim to explore the integration of advanced AI technologies to enhance customer engagement strategies. Throughout my academic journey, I've published several works on topics such as smart data analytics and generative AI, reflecting my deep interest in these emerging technologies. Currently, I serve as the Marketing and Communication Manager at a Swiss-Moroccan company, where I apply both my practical expertise and research insights to drive innovative strategies in the digital marketing domain. Driven by my passion for leveraging AI in marketing, I continue to explore new trends that shape the future of customer retention and marketing intelligence.

Hakan Emekci received his B.Sc. degree in Computer Engineering from Middle East Technical University (METU), Ankara, Turkey, in 2011, his M.Sc. degree from London Business School, and his Ph.D. degree from Hacettepe University, Ankara, Turkey. He is currently a faculty member at TED University, specializing in Artificial Intelligence and Machine Learning. Dr. Emekci is the founder of NavigaAI, a company focused on AI-driven solutions. He has published several papers, including a recent work on optimizing Retrieval-Augmented Generation (RAG) Efficiency using Large Language Models. He is also the author of Data Mining with R. His research interests include natural language processing, machine learning applications, and information retrieval systems. He is actively involved in educational technology development, including his Robomentör chatbot project, which serves over 5000 users during the university preference period. Dr. Emekci has led impactful projects in collaboration with the European Bank for Reconstruction and Development (EBRD) and the United Nations, where his work has supported AI-driven solutions for social and economic development initiatives. Beyond his academic and professional achievements, Dr. Emekci is dedicated to bridging advanced AI methodologies with practical applications that address real-world challenges, advancing both the technology and its accessibility. He continues to mentor the next generation of data scientists, focusing on ethical AI practices and innovative problem-solving approaches.

Ayoade Abolade Emmanuel is a dedicated student specializing in Information and Communication Engineering. Known for his keen interest in the convergence of technology and innovation, Ayoade is committed to advancing his expertise in areas like data communication, network security, and digital systems. With a solid foundation in engineering principles, he focuses on developing skills in both theoretical and practical applications, preparing him for a dynamic career in the tech industry. Passionate about problem-solving and cutting-edge research, Ayoade aims to contribute to advancements in communication technology and its applications in various fields.

G. Gopalakrishnan is the Director of the Balaji Institute of Management and Human Resource Development (BIMHRD) at Sri Balaji University, Pune. A seasoned academician and leader in the field of management education, Dr. Gopalakrishnan brings a wealth of experience in teaching, administration, and strategic development. Under his guidance, BIMHRD continues to uphold its reputation for academic excellence and industry-oriented learning. His leadership reflects a deep commitment to nurturing future business leaders and fostering a culture of innovation and integrity.

J. Krishna Charan is an Assistant Professor and Research Scholar at School of Law, Vel Tech Rangarajan Dr. Sagunthala R&D Institute of Science and Technology University, Tamil Nadu, India. Having a strong academic background and research interest in law and related fields, she contributes to both teaching and scholarly activities at the institution. With her expertise including legal theory, research methodology, and advancing knowledge in various aspects of law, her scholarly interests lie at the nexus of law, technology and society.

Jipson Joseph has a PhD in Ethics from DVK Bangalore. Currently, he is a Research Scholar in the School of Law at Christ University, Bangalore. His research interests are in the fields of ethics, gender studies, constitutional law, human rights, human security, environmental justice, developmental policies and global poverty.

Meera K L is a finance professional with over 20+ years of experience in industry and academia. She has held leadership roles, including IQAC Coordinator and HOD at Dayananda Sagar Business Academy. A Cambridge-trained educator, she adopts innovative, student-centered teaching methods. Her research focuses on investment avenues for middle-class investors, with publications in ABDC, Scopus, and Web of Science journals. She believes in the transformative power of education to inspire growth.

T.C. Manjunath was born on 6th February 1967. He did his BE from RV College of Engg. in 1989, ME in Robotics & Automation from LD College of Engg. in 1992 with First Rank and PhD in Systems & Control Engg. from IIT Bombay in the year 2007. He is currently working as the Dean Research R D and as Professor in the Dept. of Computer Science & Engineering with specialization in IoT, Cyber Security & Blockchain Technology in Rajarajeswari College of Engineering, Bengaluru, Karnataka. He has completed B.E. Degree from R.V. College of Engg., M.E. Govt.'s LD College of Engg., Gujarat Univ., Ahmedabad in First Rank and Ph.D. in Systems and Control Engineering from the Indian Institute of Technology Bombay IIT Bombay He has got a teaching academic, research and administrative experience of more than 35+ years 10 years as Principal, 8 years as HoD rest as faculty and has published more than 1200+ research papers in various national & international journals and conferences, with 175+ patents, 25 book-chapters, 25 awards and also published 25 text books in various field of science, engineering and technology, completed projects worth Rs. 9 Crores till date apart from guiding 10 PhD scholars. He is a member of 30 Professional Society Chapters and is a fellow of IE, IETE, AMIEE and a chartered engineer. He got the best research scholar award in 2006 in IIT Bombay amongst all the research scholars of the institute. He has got 10 awards in academics and research activities.

Hitesh Mohapatra received the B.E. degree in Information Technology from Biju Patnaik University of Technology (BPUT), Odisha in 2006, and the MTech. Degree in CSE from Odisha University of Technology and Research (OUTR) University, Odisha in 2009. He received his Ph.D. in Computer Science & Engineering in 2021 from Veer Surendra Sai University of Technology (VSSUT), Burla, India. He has contributed 30 SCI and Scopus indexed research papers, 21 international/national conferences and books on Software Engineering and C Programming respectively. He has 15 years of teaching experience both in industry and academia. He has served the research community with various capacities like session chair, technical chair, keynote speaker etc. His research interests include wireless sensor network, smart city, smart grid and smart water. Currently he is working as Associate professor at School of Computer Engineering, KIIT DU, Bhubaneswar, and Odisha.

P. Selvakumar is currently an Associate Professor in the Department of Science and Humanities at Nehru Institute of Technology, Coimbatore, Tamil Nadu, India. Since 2023, he has served as the Department IQAC Coordinator at the institute. Prior to joining Nehru Institute of Technology, he held positions as an Assistant Professor in the Department of Science and Humanities various engineering colleges in Coimbatore, Tamil Nadu, India, spanning from 2011 to 2023. Dr.P. Selvakumar's academic and research interests lie primarily in the field of phytochemistry. He has made significant contributions to his field, with an impressive record that includes 30 journal publications, 12 patents, and 20 conference papers. Additionally, he has organized 5 seminars and conferences, further demonstrating his commitment to academic and scientific exchange. Throughout his career, Dr. P.Selvakumar has been recognized for his dedication and excellence in teaching, having been honored with several awards, including the Best Teacher Awards. He holds a prominent position in the academic community, contributing actively to research.

P. Sudheer is currently working as an Assistant Professor in the Department of Computer Science and Engineering (Artificial Intelligence & Machine Learning) at CVR College of Engineering, Hyderabad, Telangana (Postal Code: 501510). His areas of interest include Image Processing, Deep Learning, and Machine Learning. With a strong passion for emerging technologies, he is dedicated to guiding students and contributing to research in the field of AI and ML.

Ananya Pandey is a Research Scholar in School of Law at Christ University, Bangalore. She has her research interests in the field of Constitutional Law, Human Rights, Intellectual Property Law and Jurisprudence

Kasthuri.R working as an assistant professor department of physics, in Dr.MGR Educational and Research Institute. I have working experience in assistant professor for 5 years, i am interested in digital electronics and micro processor

Kowsika. S is a passionate researcher and student at Hindustan Institute of Technology and Science, specializing in technology applications for water management and specific machine learning algorithms for cyberbullying detection . With the knowledge in AI, NLP and ML. Kowsika's primary focus is on developing innovative and sustainable solutions.

Pamarthi Satyanarayana, specialize in Constitutional Law and Legal Order, focusing my research on the interface between individual rights and public policy, with a strong emphasis on civil liberties, social justice, and the right to privacy. Over the past 36 months, I have served as an Assistant Professor of Law at Vel Tech Rangarajan Dr. Sagunthala R&D Institute of Science and Technology in Chennai, Tamil Nadu. Here, I teach courses such as Constitutional Law, Legal Research and Writing, and both Civil and Criminal Law. My passion for teaching and in-depth subject knowledge have earned me recognition as a dedicated educator. In addition to my academic role, I actively engage with the community, partnering with legal clinics to provide pro bono services to underprivileged individuals. Looking forward, I aim to expand my research into emerging legal issues in the digital age, especially in privacy rights, while guiding aspiring law students and future legal scholars.

Rakesh Sengupta is working as Assistant Professor & Director, Center for Creative Cognition, School of Science, SR University, Warangal, Telangana. He is a cognitive scientist specializing in vision, attention, and working memory. While working on his dissertation, Rakesh spent two years as a visiting fellow at Center for Mind/Brain Sciences (CiMec) at the University of Trento, Italy. He completed his PhD from the Center for Neural and Cognitive Science, University of Hyderabad in 2015 with a thesis entitled, "Computational and Empirical Investigations of Number, Time, and Memory". Upon completing his doctorate, Rakesh spent two years as a postdoc at Centre for Vision Research at York University in

Toronto, Canada. His current research involves building computational models of the human number system and working memory using computational, theoretical, behavioral, and neuroimaging methods. He has published and has interest in the disciplines of Behavioral and Computational Neuroscience, Psychology, Philosophy of Mind, Neuroimaging, Biophysics, and Machine Learning. He is also a reviewer of journals Cognition and Nature Human Behavior.

Mohit Sharma is a research scholar at the Institute of Management Studies and Research, Maharshi Dayanand University, Rohtak, Haryana, India. His research focuses on the dynamic relationship between brand image and purchase intentions, particularly in the context of brand extensions within the FMCG sector. Mohit actively engages in bibliometric research, analyzing publication trends and identifying research gaps in his area of interest. He has co-authored several scholarly works and continues to contribute to the academic community. Mohit can be reached at mohitattri.rs.imsar@mdurohtak.ac.in

C.V. Suresh Babu is a pioneer in content development. A true entrepreneur, he founded Anniyappa Publications, a company that is highly active in publishing books related to Computer Science and Management. Dr. C.V. Suresh Babu has also ventured into SB Institute, a center for knowledge transfer. He holds a Ph.D. in Engineering Education from the National Institute of Technical Teachers Training & Research in Chennai, along with seven master's degrees in various disciplines such as Engineering, Computer Applications, Management, Commerce, Economics, Psychology, Law, and Education. Additionally, he has UGC-NET/SET qualifications in the fields of Computer Science, Management, Commerce, and Education. Currently, Dr. C.V. Suresh Babu is a Professor in the Department of Information Technology at the School of Computing Science, Hindustan Institute of Technology and Science (Hindustan University) in Padur, Chennai, Tamil Nadu, India.

Tetiana Suvorova, associate professor, Ph.D.,Head of Pedagogy and The International Relationships at The High School of Research: Humanities, Creation and Heritage, CY Cergy Paris University; Associate Professor at the Department of European and Oriental Languages and Translation, Alfred Nobel University; Professor of English, CY tech, CY Cergy Paris Université; a researcher, the research laboratory LT2D EA7518, EUTOPIA Alliance at CY Cergy Paris Université, France & INTI International University, Malaysia.

Ragupathi T received his B.E. degree in Computer Science and Engineering from Anna University, Tamil Nadu, in the year 2009 and the M.E. Master's degree in Computer Science and Engineering from Anna University, Tamil Nadu in the year 2011. He completed his Doctor of Philosophy in Computer Science and Engineering from Annamalai University, Chidambaram, Tamil Nadu, in the year 2023.He has more than 13.5 years of teaching experience. His research area includes Deep Learning, Machine Learning, IoT and web technology. He has published papers in several International Journals, international and national conferences

U. Jayalarsumi is presently working as Professors in ECE, Department at Dr. M.G.R Educational and Research Institute, Chennai, Tamil Nadu, India and heading the department. She/He has 18 years of teaching experience and published/won papers and awards worldwide.

V.Vaissnave is obtained B.Tech Information Technology in PSR Engg college, Anna University. She obtained her Master of Engg in Anand Institute of Science and Technology, Anna University. And she obtained her Full time Research in the Department of Computer Science and Engineering, School of Computing, Kalasalingam Academy of Research and Education, Krishnankoil, Tamilnadu. Her area of interest is Machine learning, Deeplearning, and Natural Language Techniques.

Index

A

B

C

H

I

K

L

M

V